Contents

1

17

19

26

Italian Beef And Green Beans Mix

Servings: 6
Cooking Time: 30 Minutes
Ingredients:
- 2 spring onions chopped
- 1 red bell pepper, chopped
- 1 pound beef, ground
- ½ cup veggie stock
- A pinch of salt and black pepper
- 1 tablespoon Italian seasoning
- 1 tablespoon cilantro, chopped
- 1 teaspoon olive oil
- ½ pound green beans, trimmed and halved

Directions:
1. Set your instant pot on sauté mode, add the oil, heat it up, add the meat Italian seasoning, salt and pepper and brown for 5 minutes. Add the rest of the ingredients, toss, put the lid on and cook on High for 25 minutes. Release the pressure naturally for minutes, divide everything between plates and serve for breakfast.

Nutrition Info: calories 259, fat 9.4, fiber 2.4, carbs 6.7, protein 8

Egg And Carrot Spread

Servings: 3
Cooking Time: 25 Mins
Ingredients:
- 4 Eggs, whisked
- 3 Carrots, shredded, boiled
- Salt and black pepper to taste
- 3 tbsp Butter

Directions:
1. In a blender, pulse the carrots to a puree. Add them to the Instant Pot and let simmer for 2 minutes on Sauté. Add eggs, butter, salt, and pepper. Stir continually for minutes. Serve chilled.

Nutrition Info: Calories 129, Protein 6.2g, Net Carbs 2.1g, Fat 10g

Bacon Avocado Bomb

Servings: 4
Cooking Time: 25 Minutes
Ingredients:
- 1 avocado, pilled, pitted, halved
- 4 bacon slices
- ½ teaspoon ground cinnamon
- 1 teaspoon coconut cream

- ½ teaspoon chili flakes

Directions:
1. Sprinkle the avocado with ground cinnamon and chili flakes.
2. Then fill it with coconut cream and wrap in the bacon slices.
3. Secure the avocado bomb with toothpicks, if needed and wrap in the foil.
4. Place it in the instant pot and close the lid.
5. Cook the bomb on saute mode for 2minutes.
6. Then remove the foil and slice the avocado bomb into the servings.

Nutrition Info:
Per Serving: calories 209, fat 18, fiber 3.6, carbs 4.9, protein 8

Avocado Boats With Omelet

Servings: 2
Cooking Time: 10 Minutes
Ingredients:
- 1 avocado, halved, pitted
- 2 eggs, beaten
- 1 tablespoon cream
- 1 teaspoon fresh dill
- 1 oz Parmesan, grated
- 1 cup water, for cooking

Directions:
1. Remove ½ part of avocado meat with the help of the scooper. You will get avocado boats. In the mixing bowl combine together eggs, cream, dill, and Parmesan. Pour the egg mixture in the prepared avocado boats. Pour water and insert the steamer rack in the instant pot. Carefully arrange the avocado boats in the instant pot. You can cover the surface of every avocado boat with foil if desired. Cook the meal for minutes on Steam mode.

Nutrition Info: calories 319, fat 4, fiber 6.8, carbs 10, protein 10

Cheesy Spinach Casserole

Servings: 6
Cooking Time: 30 Mins
Ingredients:
- 1 cup Spinach, chopped
- ½ lb Cheddar cheese
- ½ lb Mozzarella cheese
- 1 Onion, chopped
- 4 Eggs, whisked
- 1 yellow Bell Pepper, chopped
- Salt and black pepper to taste
- 2 tbsp Olive oil

Directions:

1. In a bowl add the eggs, spinach, mozzarella cheese, cheddar cheese, bell pepper, and onion, mix well. Season with salt and pepper. Grease a baking dish with olive oil. Pour in the mixture.
2. Pour 1 cup water in the pot and insert a trivet. Put the dish on the trivet. Seal the lid and cook for 15 minutes on High. Once ready, let the pressure release naturally for 10 minutes.

Nutrition Info: Calories 531, Protein 31g, Net Carbs 6.1g, Fat 4g

Cups With Greens

Servings: 2
Cooking Time: 3 Minutes
Ingredients:
- 3 eggs, beaten
- ¼ cup cauliflower stalks, chopped
- 2 oz broccoli raab, chopped
- 1 tablespoon heavy cream
- ½ teaspoon ground black pepper
- ¾ teaspoon butter

Directions:
1. Blend the cauliflower stalk and broccoli raab in the blender until smooth.
2. Mix up together the blended greens and beaten eggs.
3. Add heavy cream, ground black pepper, and butter.
4. Pour the water in the instant pot.
5. After this, pour the egg mixture into the small cups and transfer them in the instant pot.
6. Close the lid and cook on the "Manual" program (High Pressure). Cook the meal for 3 minutes. Make a quick release.

Nutrition Info:
Per Serving: calories 143, fat 8, fiber 0.4, carbs 2.6, protein 9.4

Stuffed Lettuce Boats

Servings: 2
Cooking Time: 5 Minutes
Ingredients:
- 4 oz shrimps
- 1 tablespoon heavy cream
- ¾ teaspoon salt
- ¼ teaspoon dried oregano
- 4 lettuce leaves
- ½ teaspoon butter

Directions:
1. Peel the shrimps sprinkle with the salt, heavy cream, and dried oregano.
2. Chop the garlic clove and add in shrimps.
3. Set the "Stew" mode and put the shrimp mixture inside. Cook the meal for 5 minutes.
4. Fill the lettuce leaves with cooked shrimps.

Nutrition Info:
Per Serving: calories 104, fat 4.7, fiber 0.1, carbs 1.5, protein 1

Meat Cups

Servings: 4
Cooking Time: 15 Minutes
Ingredients:

- 4 quill eggs
- 10 oz ground pork
- 1 jalapeno pepper, chopped
- ½ teaspoon salt
- 1 teaspoon dried dill
- 1 tablespoon butter, softened
- 1 cup water, for cooking

Directions:

1. In the mixing bowl, mix up ground pork, chopped jalapeno pepper, salt, dill, and butter.
2. When the meat mixture is homogenous, transfer it in the silicone muffin molds and press the surface gently.
3. Then pour water in the instant pot and insert the trivet.
4. Place the meat cups on the trivet.
5. Then crack the eggs over the meat mixture and close the lid.
6. Cook the meal on manual mode (high pressure) for 15 minutes.
7. Then make a quick pressure release.

Nutrition Info:
Per Serving: calories 143, fat 6.4, fiber 0.1, carbs 0.4, protein 9

Salmon And Eggs Mix

Servings: 4
Cooking Time: 12 Minutes
Ingredients:

- 4 ounces smoked salmon, skinless, boneless and cut into strips
- 4 eggs
- A pinch of salt and black pepper
- ½ cup coconut cream
- 1 tablespoon chives, chopped
- 1 tablespoon cilantro, chopped
- Cooking spray

Directions:

1. In a bowl, mix the salmon with the eggs and the rest of the ingredients except the cooking spray and whisk well. Grease the instant pot with the cooking spray, pour the salmon mix, spread, put the lid on and cook on High for minutes. Release the pressure naturally for 10 minutes, divide the mix between plates and serve.

Nutrition Info: calories 167, fat 9, fiber 0.7, carbs 2.1, protein 4

Sausage Casserole

Servings: 5
Cooking Time: 50 Minutes
Ingredients:
- 10 ground Italian sausages
- 1 teaspoon Italian seasonings
- 4 eggs, beaten
- ½ teaspoon salt
- 1 teaspoon sesame oil
- ¼ cup Cheddar cheese, shredded
- 1 cup water, for cooking

Directions:
1. Preheat the instant pot on Sauté mode for 5 minutes. Then pour sesame oil inside, add Italian sausages. Cook them for minutes on sauté mode. Stir the sausages every 2 minutes. Meanwhile, mix up together eggs, salt, Italian seasonings, and Cheddar cheese. When the ground sausages are cooked, add them in the egg mixture and stir. Transfer the mixture in the baking pan and flatten it. Then clean the instant pot bowl and pour water inside. Insert the steamer rack. Place the baking pan with casserole in the instant pot. Cook it for 35 minutes on Sauté mode.

Nutrition Info: calories 424, fat 6, fiber 0, carbs 2.4, protein 8

Basil And Parsley Scramble

Servings: 4
Cooking Time: 15 Mins
Ingredients:
- 8 Eggs
- 3 tbsp chopped Basil
- ¼ tsp Garlic Powder
- Salt and black pepper to taste
- ¼ cup Milk
- 1 tbsp Butter

Directions:
1. Melt butter on Sauté. Beat the eggs in a bowl and stir in the remaining ingredients. Pour the egg mixture into the IP and stir for about 5 minutes with a spatula, until the eggs are set. When set, divide the eggs among 4 plates. Serve and enjoy!

Nutrition Info: Calories 295, Protein 12g, Net Carbs 4.2g, Fat 15g

Bacon Tacos

Servings: 4
Cooking Time: 5 Minutes
Ingredients:
- 10 bacon slices

- ½ cup Cheddar cheese, shredded
- ½ cup white cabbage, shredded
- 1 tablespoon taco seasonings
- 1 teaspoon coconut oil
- 8 oz chicken breast, skinless, boneless
- 1 tomato, chopped

Directions:

1. Rub the chicken breast with Taco seasonings well and place it in the instant pot. Add coconut oil and cook the chicken for 20 minutes on Saute mode. Flip the chicken breast after minutes of cooking. Then remove the cooked chicken from the instant pot and chop it. Line the table with paper foil. Put the bacon crosswise on it to get the shape of the net. Then with the help of the round cutter make 4 rounds (tortillas). Preheat the instant pot on Saute mode well. Then place the first bacon round. Cook it for 3 minutes from each side. Repeat the same steps with all bacon rounds. After this, place the cooked bacon "net" on the plate. Top every bacon "net" with chopped chicken, cheese, and tomato. Fold it in the shape of tacos.

Nutrition Info: calories 401, fat 1, fiber 0.4, carbs 3.5, protein 4

Cinnamon Pancakes

Servings: 3
Cooking Time: 45 Minutes
Ingredients:

- 2 eggs, beaten
- 1 teaspoon matcha green tea powder
- 1 teaspoon vanilla extract
- 1 teaspoon ground cinnamon
- 1 teaspoon baking powder
- 1 tablespoon apple cider vinegar
- 1 tablespoon Erythritol
- 1 tablespoon sesame oil
- 1 cup almond flour
- ¼ cup cream
- 2 eggs, beaten
- 1 teaspoon matcha green tea powder
- 1 teaspoon vanilla extract
- 1 teaspoon ground cinnamon
- 1 teaspoon baking powder
- 1 tablespoon apple cider vinegar
- 1 tablespoon Erythritol
- 1 tablespoon sesame oil
- 1 cup almond flour
- ¼ cup cream

Directions:

1. In the big bowl mix up together eggs, vanilla extract, apple cider vinegar, baking powder, and cream. Then add matcha green tea powder, ground cinnamon, Erythritol, and almond flour. Whisk the liquid until smooth. Brush the instant pot bowl with ½ tablespoon of sesame oil and pour the 3 part of all liquid inside. Cook it for 15 minutes on Manual mode (low pressure). Cook the pancake for an additional 5 minutes for the golden-brown crust. Repeat the same steps with the remaining batter. In the end, you should get 3 pancakes.
2. In the big bowl mix up together eggs, vanilla extract, apple cider vinegar, baking powder, and cream. Then add matcha green tea powder, ground cinnamon, Erythritol, and almond flour. Whisk the liquid until smooth. Brush the instant pot bowl with ½ tablespoon of sesame oil and pour the 3 part of all liquid inside. Cook it for 15 minutes on Manual mode (low pressure). Cook the pancake for an additional 5 minutes for the golden-brown crust. Repeat the same steps with the remaining batter. In the end, you should get 3 pancakes.

Nutrition Info: calories 157, fat 3, fiber 1.5, carbs 9.5, protein 5.9

Sage Chicken And Turkey Stew

Servings: 4
Cooking Time: 25 Minutes
Ingredients:
- ½ pound turkey breast, skinless, boneless and cubed
- ½ pound chicken breast, skinless, boneless and cubed
- 1 tablespoon sage, chopped
- 1 teaspoon olive oil
- ¼ pound tomatoes, cubed
- 1 shallot, chopped
- A pinch of salt and black pepper
- 2 tablespoons tomato paste
- 2 and ½ cups chicken stock
- 1 tablespoon cilantro, chopped

Directions:
1. Set your instant pot on Sauté mode, add oil, heat it up, add the turkey, chicken and the shallots, and brown for 5 minutes. Add the rest of the ingredients except the cilantro, put the lid on and cook on High for 20 minutes. Release the pressure naturally for minutes, divide the stew into bowls, sprinkle the cilantro on top and serve.

Nutrition Info: calories 147, fat 3.7, fiber 1.2, carbs 2.5, protein 4

Curry Tomato Cream

Servings: 4
Cooking Time: 20 Minutes
Ingredients:
- 1 pound tomatoes, peeled and chopped
- A pinch of salt and black pepper
- 3 garlic cloves, minced
- 1 tablespoon cilantro, chopped

- 2 cups coconut cream
- 2 cups chicken stock
- 1 tablespoon red curry paste
- 2 tablespoons chives, chopped

Directions:
1. In your instant pot, combine the tomatoes with salt, pepper, garlic and the stock, put the lid on and cook on High for 20 minutes. Release the pressure naturally for minutes, transfer the soup to a blender, add the cream and curry paste, pulse well, divide into bowls and serve with the chives and cilantro sprinkled on top.

Nutrition Info: calories 320, fat 2, fiber 4.1, carbs 8.1, protein 4.2

Cod And Tomato Passata

Servings: 4
Cooking Time: 12 Minutes
Ingredients:
- 4 cod fillets, boneless and skinless
- A pinch of salt and black pepper
- 2 tablespoons chives, chopped
- 2 tablespoons olive oil
- 2 teaspoons lime juice
- 1 cup tomato passata
- 1 tablespoon basil, chopped

Directions:
1. Set your instant pot on sauté mode, add the oil, heat it up, add the cod and cook for minute on each side. Add the rest of the ingredients, put the lid on and cook on High for 10 minutes. Release the pressure naturally for 10 minutes, divide everything between plates and serve.

Nutrition Info: calories 75, fat 7.1, fiber 1, carbs 3.4, protein 0.9

Garlic Beef Mix

Servings: 6
Cooking Time: 20 Minutes
Ingredients:
- 2 pounds beef, cubed
- 1 tablespoon olive oil
- ½ cup okra
- 3 spring onions, chopped
- A pinch of salt and black pepper
- 1 cup chicken stock
- 1 cup tomato passata
- 2 tablespoons mustard
- 1 cup cheddar cheese, shredded

Directions:

1. Set the instant pot on Sauté mode, add the oil, heat it up, add the meat and brown for 5 minutes. Add the rest of the ingredients except the cheese, put the lid on and cook on High for minutes. Release the pressure naturally for 10 minutes, sprinkle the cheese on top, leave the mix aside for 10 minutes, divide it into bowls and serve.

Nutrition Info: calories 411, fat 3, fiber 1.6, carbs 5, protein 4

Beef Soup

Servings: 4
Cooking Time: 25 Minutes
Ingredients:
- 1 and ½ pound beef meat, cubed
- 2 tablespoons olive oil
- A pinch of salt and black pepper
- 1 cup scallions, chopped
- 1 tablespoon sweet paprika
- 6 cups veggie stock
- 1 tablespoon parsley, chopped

Directions:
1. Set your instant pot on sauté mode, add the oil, heat it up, add the meat and the scallions and brown for 5 minutes. Add the rest of the ingredients, put the lid on and cook on High for 20 minutes. Release the pressure naturally for minutes, ladle the soup into bowls and serve.

Nutrition Info: calories 73, fat 7.3, fiber 1.3, carbs 2.9, protein 0.8

Hot Sausages Soup

Servings: 3
Cooking Time: 23 Minutes
Ingredients:
- 2 cups spinach, chopped
- 2 cups beef broth
- 7 oz sausages, chopped
- 1 teaspoon ghee
- ½ teaspoon salt
- ½ teaspoon ground cumin
- ½ teaspoon ground coriander
- ½ teaspoon dried celery
- ½ teaspoon onion powder
- 2 bell peppers, chopped

Directions:
1. Preheat the instant pot on sauté mode and place ghee inside. Melt it and add sausages. Cook the sausages for minutes. Stir them from time to time with the help of the spatula. After this, sprinkle the sausages with salt, ground cumin, coriander, dried celery, and onion powder. Add beef broth and bell peppers. Close and seal the lid. Cook the soup on manual mode

(high pressure) for 5 minutes. Then make a quick pressure release and open the lid. Stir the soup and add spinach. Cook the soup for 5 minutes more on sauté mode.

Nutrition Info: calories 295, fat 4, fiber 1.6, carbs 7.8, protein 6

Egg & Cheese Salad With Dill

Servings: 3
Cooking Time: 4 Minutes
Ingredients:

- 3 eggs
- 2 tablespoons cream cheese
- 1 tablespoon dried dill
- ½ cup Cheddar cheese, shredded
- ¼ teaspoon minced garlic
- 1 cup water, for cooking

Directions:

1. Pour water and insert rack in the instant pot. Place the eggs in the instant pot, close the lid and cook them for 4 minutes on Manual mode (high pressure) Then make a quick pressure release. Cool the eggs in cold water for minutes. After this, peel the eggs and grate them. In the mixing bowl combine together grated eggs, shredded cheese, minced garlic, dill, and cream cheese. Mix up the salad well.

Nutrition Info: calories 165, fat 13, fiber 0.1, carbs 1.4, protein 11

Hot Cod Stew

Servings: 4
Cooking Time: 12 Minutes
Ingredients:

- 1 pound cod fillets, boneless, skinless and cubed
- 1 cup chicken stock
- 1 tablespoon hot sauce
- 1 tablespoon hot paprika
- A pinch of salt and black pepper
- 1 tablespoon cilantro, chopped

Directions:

1. In your instant pot, combine the cod with the rest of the ingredients, put the lid on and cook on High for minutes. Release the pressure fast for 5 minutes, divide the stew into bowls and serve.

Nutrition Info: calories 100, fat 4.3, fiber 1, carbs 3.2, protein 1.4

Creamy Broccoli Stew

Servings: 4
Cooking Time: 50 Mins
Ingredients:

- 1 cup Heavy Cream
- 3 oz Parmesan cheese
- 1 cup Broccoli florets
- 2 Carrots, sliced
- ½ tbsp Garlic paste
- ¼ tbsp Turmeric powder
- Salt and black pepper to taste
- ½ cup Vegetable broth
- 2 tbsp Butter

Directions:
1. Melt butter on Sauté mode. Add garlic and sauté for 30 seconds. Add broccoli and carrots, and cook until soft, for 2-3 minutes. Season with salt and pepper. Stir in the vegetable broth and seal the lid. Cook on Meat/Stew for 40 minutes. When ready, do a quick pressure release. Stir in the heavy cream.

Nutrition Info: Calories 239, Protein 8g, Net Carbs 5.1g, Fat 4g

Zucchini Cranberry Muffins

Servings: 4
Cooking Time: 18 Minutes
Ingredients:
- 2 tbsp flaxseed meal + 6 tbsp water
- 2/3 cup olive oil
- 1 tsp vanilla extract
- 1 cup swerve sugar
- 1 ½ cups almond flour
- 1 tsp baking soda
- 1 tsp cinnamon powder
- ¼ tsp salt
- 2 tsp baking powder
- 1 cup dried cranberries
- 1 cup grated zucchinis

Directions:
1. In a small bowl, whisk the flaxseed meal with water and allow sitting for minutes to thicken. After, whisk in the olive oil and vanilla.
2. In a medium bowl, combine the swerve sugar, almond flour, baking soda, cinnamon powder, salt, and baking powder. Mix in the flax egg mixture well and fold in the cranberries and zucchinis.
3. Spoon the mixture into a 12-holed silicon egg mold and cover with foil.
4. Pour 2 cups of water into the inner pot, fit in a trivet and place the egg mold on top.
5. Lock the lid in place; select Manual mode on High Pressure, and set the timer for 8 minutes.
6. After baking, perform a natural pressure release for 10 minutes, then a quick pressure release to let out the remaining steam and open the lid.
7. Remove the egg mold and foil.

8. Pop out each muffin from the tray and place on a wire rack to cool.
9. Serve the muffins after slightly cooled.

Nutrition Info:
Per Serving: : Calories 377 Fats 45g Carbs 3.89g Net Carbs 2.29g Protein 6.29g

Spiced Hard-boiled Eggs

Servings: 4
Cooking Time: 10 Minutes
Ingredients:
- 4 eggs
- ½ teaspoon dried sage
- ¼ teaspoon chili flakes
- 1 teaspoon butter, softened
- ¼ teaspoon dried parsley
- ¼ teaspoon dried thyme
- 1 cup water, for cooking

Directions:
1. Pour water in the instant pot and insert the steamer rack. Place the eggs on the rack and close the lid. Cook the eggs on Manual (high pressure) for 5 minutes. Then make a quick pressure release. Cool the eggs in ice water for minutes. Meanwhile, churn together sage, butter, chili flakes, parsley, and thyme. Then peel the eggs and cut them into halves. Spread every egg half with a spiced butter mixture.

Nutrition Info: calories 72 fat 5.3, fiber 0.1, carbs 0.5, protein 5.6

Chicken Strips

Servings: 5
Cooking Time: 15 Minutes
Ingredients:
- 1-pound chicken fillet
- ½ teaspoon ground turmeric
- ½ teaspoon salt
- ½ teaspoon ground black pepper
- 2 tablespoons heavy cream
- 1 cup of coconut milk
- 1 teaspoon olive oil

Directions:
1. Cut the chicken fillet into the strips and sprinkle with ground turmeric, salt, ground black pepper, and heavy cream.
2. Preheat the olive oil on saute mode for 3 minutes,
3. Then place the chicken strips in hot oil in one layer. Cook them for 1 minute from each side and add coconut cream.
4. Close and seal the lid.

5. Cook the chicken strips on Manual (high pressure) for 10 minutes. Make a quick pressure release.

Nutrition Info:

Per Serving: calories 313, fat 3, fiber 1.2, carbs 3.1, protein 5

Bell Peppers And Cauliflower Salad

Servings: 4

Cooking Time: 20 Minutes

Ingredients:

- 1 cauliflower head, florets separated
- 1 tablespoon avocado oil
- 2 spring onions, chopped
- ¼ red bell pepper, sliced
- ¼ yellow bell pepper, sliced
- ¼ green bell pepper, sliced
- A pinch of salt and black pepper
- 2 eggs

Directions:

1. Set the instant pot on Sauté mode, add the oil, heat it up, add the bell peppers and sauté them for 4 minutes. Add the rest of the ingredients, toss a bit, put the lid on and cook on High for minutes. Release the pressure naturally for 10 minutes, divide the mix into bowls and serve for breakfast.

Nutrition Info: calories 63, fat 3, fiber 2.3, carbs 6, protein 4.5

Cinnamon Strawberry Oatmeal

Servings: 6

Cooking Time: 10 Minutes

Ingredients:

- 2 cups almond milk
- ½ cup coconut cream
- 1 tablespoon cinnamon powder
- 1 cup coconut flakes
- 1 cup strawberries, halved

Directions:

1. In your instant pot, mix the almond milk with the rest of the ingredients, toss a bit, put the lid on and cook on High for minutes. Release the pressure fast for 5 minutes, divide the mix into bowls and serve.

Nutrition Info: calories 285, fat 4, fiber 3.9, carbs 7.5, protein 2.9

Spicy Eggs

Servings: 2

Cooking Time: 3 Minutes

Ingredients:
- 4 eggs
- ¾ teaspoon chili powder
- ¼ teaspoon jalapeno pepper
- 1 teaspoon cream cheese

Directions:
1. Pour cup of water in the instant pot bowl and add eggs.
2. Close the lid of the instant pot and seal it.
3. Chose the "Steam" program + High Pressure. Cook the eggs for minutes. Make QPR.
4. Place the eggs in the icy water.
5. Peel the eggs and cut them into the halves.
6. Sprinkle the egg halves with the chili powder.
7. In the shallow bowl mix up cream cheese and chopped jalapeno pepper.
8. Top the eggs with jalapeno mixture.

Nutrition Info:
Per Serving: calories 135, fat 9.5, fiber 0.4, carbs 1.3, protein 3

Bacon And Eggs

Servings: 4
Cooking Time: 15 Minutes
Ingredients:
- 1 shallot, chopped
- 1 and ½ cups bacon, chopped
- 2 cups cheddar cheese, shredded
- 4 eggs, whisked
- 1 cup almond milk
- 1 tablespoon avocado oil
- A pinch of salt and black pepper

Directions:
1. Set the instant pot on Sauté mode, add the oil, heat it up, add the bacon and the shallot and cook for 2-3 minutes. Add the rest of the ingredients, toss, put the lid on and cook on High for minutes. Release the pressure naturally for 10 minutes, divide the mix between plates and serve.

Nutrition Info: calories 392, fat 37, fiber 1.4, carbs 4.6, protein 21

Hot Jalapeno Poppers Mix

Servings: 2
Cooking Time: 11 Minutes
Ingredients:
- 5 oz chicken fillet
- 2 jalapeno peppers, sliced
- ½ teaspoon ranch seasonings
- 2 teaspoons cream cheese

- ½ teaspoon sesame oil
- ¼ cup heavy cream
- 1 oz Parmesan, grated

Directions:

1. Chop the chicken fillet and sprinkle it with ranch seasonings. Then preheat the instant pot on sauté mode for 2 minutes and add sesame oil. Then add chicken and sauté it for 3 minutes from each side. After this, place the cooked chicken in the bowl and shred it with the help of the fork. Return the chicken back in the instant pot and add cream cheese, heavy cream, sliced jalapeno, and Parmesan. Mix up well. Sauté the meal for 3 minutes more or until the cheese is melted.

Nutrition Info: calories 262, fat 3, fiber 0.6, carbs 2.1, protein 8

Mushroom & Goat Cheese Keto Broccoli And Almonds Mix

Servings: 4
Cooking Time: 15 Minutes
Ingredients:

- 1 cup broccoli florets
- ½ cup coconut flakes
- 1 cup heavy cream
- ½ cup almonds, toasted and chopped
- 2 eggs, whisked
- Cooking spray

Directions:

1. Grease the instant pot with the cooking spray, add the broccoli and almonds and the pour the eggs mixed with the heavy cream on top. Sprinkle the coconut on top, put the lid on and cook on High for minutes. Release the pressure fast for 5 minutes, divide the mix between plates and serve.

Nutrition Info: calories 248, fat 8, fiber 3, carbs 6.6, protein 6.9

Ham Muffins

Servings: 2
Cooking Time: 6 Minutes
Ingredients:

- 2 eggs, beaten
- 4 oz ham, chopped
- ½ teaspoon avocado oil
- 1 cup water, for cooking

Directions:

1. Pour water in the instant pot.
2. Then brush the muffin molds with avocado oil from inside.
3. In the mixing bowl, mix up ham and beaten eggs.

4. After this, pour the mixture into the muffin molds.
5. Place the muffins in the instant pot. Close and seal the lid.
6. Cook the meal on manual mode (high pressure) for minutes. Then make a quick pressure release and remove the muffins.

Nutrition Info:
Per Serving: calories 192, fat 6, fiber 2.4, carbs 6, protein 8

Steamed Egg Custard

Servings: 4
Cooking Time: 8 Minutes
Ingredients:
- 4 large eggs
- 4 tbsp water
- ¾ tsp fish sauce
- 2 tbsp freshly chopped scallions

Directions:
1. Beat the eggs in a large ramekin until very smooth. Mix in water and fish sauce until well combined.
2. Pour 1 cup of water into the inner pot and sit in the ramekin making sure the water is halfway up the dish.
3. Lock the lid in place; select Manual mode on High Pressure and set the timer to 2 minutes.
4. After cooking, perform a natural pressure release for 5 minutes, then a quick pressure release to let out the remaining steam, and open the lid.
5. Carefully remove the ramekin, stir the eggs and top with the scallions.
6. Return the ramekin to the inner pot; lock the lid in place and steam again for 1 minute in Manual mode on High pressure.
7. Perform a quick pressure release until all the steam is out and open the lid.
8. Carefully remove the ramekin, allow cooling for 2 minutes and serve the custard with low-carb bread.

Nutrition Info:
Per Serving: : Calories 18 Fats 76g Carbs 0.4g Net Carbs 0.4g Protein 6.34g

Quick And Easy Breakfast Porridge

Servings: 1
Cooking Time: 10 Mins
Ingredients:
- 2 tbsp Ground Almonds
- 1 tbsp Chia Seeds
- 1 tbsp Flaxseed Meal
- 2 tbsp Hemp Seeds
- 2 tbsp Shredded Coconut
- ¼ tsp Granulated Stevia
- ½ tsp Vanilla Extract

- Fresh raspberries for topping

Directions:

1. Place all ingredients inside your IP. Add in ½ cup water, stir and seal the lid. Press Manual and cook on High for 4 minutes. When done, do a quick pressure release Top with raspberries and serve.

Nutrition Info: Calories 335, Protein 15g, Net Carbs 1.5g, Fat 29g

Sweet Porridge

Servings: 2
Cooking Time: 10 Minutes
Ingredients:

- ¾ cup of coconut milk
- ¼ cup of organic almond milk
- ¾ cup of water
- 1 tablespoon almond butter
- 2 teaspoons chia seeds
- 1 teaspoon hemp seeds
- 1 tablespoon toasted coconut
- 2 tablespoons walnuts, chopped
- 1 teaspoon vanilla extract
- 1 teaspoon liquid stevia

Directions:

1. Preheat the instant pot on sauté mode for 5 minutes. Then pour coconut milk, organic almond milk, and water inside. On sauté mode bring the liquid to boil and switch off the instant pot. Stirring constantly add chia seeds, hemp seeds, toasted coconut, and walnuts. Then add almond butter, vanilla extract, and liquid stevia. Stir the mixture for minute or until it will be thick. Then transfer it in the serving bowls. The porridge is recommended to serve warm/hot.

Nutrition Info: calories 380, fat 3, fiber 6.1, carbs 4, protein 8.3

Egg, Sausage & Cheese Bundt

Servings: 4
Cooking Time: 25 Mins
Ingredients:

- 8 Eggs, cracked into a bowl
- 8 oz Breakfast Sausage, chopped
- 3 Bacon Slices, chopped
- 1 large Green Bell pepper, chopped
- 1 large Red Bell pepper, chopped
- 1 cup chopped Green Onion
- 1 cup grated Cheddar Cheese
- 1 tsp Red Chili Flakes
- Salt and black pepper to taste

- ½ cup Milk, full fat
- 4 slices zero Carb Bread, cubed
- 2 cups Water

Directions:
1. Add sausage, bacon, bell peppers, onion, chili, cheddar, salt, pepper, and milk to a bowl and beat well. Grease a bundt pan with cooking spray and pour in the egg mixture. Drop bread slices in the egg mixture all around while using a spoon to push them into the mixture. Pour the water inside the IP, and fit in a trivet. Place the bundt pan on top, seal the lid, select Manual for 8 minutes on High.
2. Once ready, press Cancel and do a quick pressure release. Use a napkin to gently remove the bundt pan onto a flat surface. Run a knife around the egg in the bundt pan, place a serving plate on the bundt pan, and turn over. Slice and serve.

Nutrition Info: Calories 267, Protein 20g, Net Carbs 2g, Fat 9g

Stuffed Hard-boiled Eggs

Servings: 6
Cooking Time: 5 Minutes
Ingredients:
- 6 eggs
- 3 oz Provolone cheese, grated
- 1 teaspoon chili pepper, chopped
- 1 tablespoon coconut cream
- ½ teaspoon ground paprika
- 1 cup of water

Directions:
1. Pour water in the instant pot.
2. Add eggs and close the lid.
3. Cook the on manual mode (high pressure) for 5 minutes. Then allow the natural pressure release and open the lid.
4. Cool and peel the eggs.
5. After this, cut the eggs into halves and remove the egg yolks.
6. Mash the egg yolks and mix them up with grated cheese, coconut cream, chili pepper, and ground paprika.
7. Then fill the egg white halves with egg yolk mixture.

Nutrition Info:
Per Serving: calories 119, fat 8.8, fiber 0.2, carbs 1, protein 9.3

Layered Casserole

Servings: 4
Cooking Time: 15 Minutes
Ingredients:
- 1 cup ground chicken
- 1 cup Cheddar cheese, shredded

- 2 tablespoons cream cheese
- 1 teaspoon butter, melted
- ½ teaspoon taco seasonings
- ½ teaspoon salt
- 1 cup leek, chopped
- ¼ cup of water

Directions:

1. Grease the instant pot bowl with butter. In the mixing bowl combine together ground chicken and taco seasonings. Then place the ground chicken in the instant pot and flatten it to make the chicken layer. After this, top the chicken with leek and salt. Then top the leek with cheese. Mix up together cream cheese and water. Pour the liquid over the casserole and close the lid. Cook the casserole on Saute mode for minutes.

Nutrition Info: calories 222, fat 7, fiber 0.4, carbs 4.1, protein 9

Cheddar Muffins

Servings: 3
Cooking Time: 12 Minutes
Ingredients:

- 2 oz Cheddar cheese, shredded
- 2 tablespoons almond flour
- 2 tablespoon butter, softened
- 1 tablespoon heavy cream
- ¼ teaspoon baking powder
- ½ teaspoon lemon juice
- 1 cup water, for cooking

Directions:

1. Pour water in the instant pot.
2. Then mix up together all remaining ingredients and stir until homogenous.
3. Put the muffin batter in the muffin molds and insert them in the instant pot.
4. Close and seal the lid.
5. Cook the Cheddar muffins for 12 minutes on high pressure (manual mode).
6. When the time is finished, make a quick pressure release.

Nutrition Info:
Per Serving: calories 269, fat 1, fiber 2, carbs 4.6, protein 8.9

Breakfast Muffins

Servings: 2
Cooking Time: 15 Minutes
Ingredients:

- 2 eggs, beaten
- ¼ cup organic almond milk
- 2 tablespoons almond flour
- ¾ teaspoon butter

Directions:

1. Pour cup of water in the instant pot bowl.
2. Beat the eggs in the bowl and combine together with the almond milk and almond flour.
3. Whisk the mixture.
4. Put the egg mixture in the muffin molds. Add butter.
5. Place the trivet in the instant pot and transfer the muffins in it.
6. Close the instant pot lid and set the "Steam".
7. Cook the muffins for 10 minutes.
8. After this, make the quick release (QPR) for 5 minutes.

Nutrition Info:

Per Serving: calories 256, fat 3, fiber 3, carbs 6.3, protein 1

Spinach And Artichokes Muffins

Servings: 12
Cooking Time: 20 Minutes
Ingredients:

- 1 cup baby spinach, chopped
- 1 cup canned artichoke hearts, drained and chopped
- A pinch of salt and black pepper
- 1 and ½ cups water
- Cooking spray
- 3 cups almond flour
- 1 teaspoon baking soda
- 4 eggs

Directions:

1. In a bowl, mix the spinach with the artichokes and the rest of the ingredients except the water and the cooking spray and stir well. Grease a muffin tray with the cooking spray and pour the muffin mix inside. Add the water to your instant pot, add the trivet, add the muffin tray inside, put the lid on and cook on High for 20 minutes. Release the pressure naturally for minutes, cool the muffins down and serve for breakfast.

Nutrition Info: calories 66, fat 4.5, fiber 0.2, carbs 0.6, protein 5.8

Wontons

Servings: 2
Cooking Time: 12 Minutes
Ingredients:

- 5 oz ground pork
- 1 tablespoon chives, chopped
- 1 tablespoon dried cilantro
- ¼ teaspoon oyster sauce
- ½ teaspoon soy sauce
- ½ teaspoon garlic powder
- 1 egg, beaten

- 1 cup water, for cooking

Directions:

1. In the mixing bowl combine together ground pork, chives, cilantro, oyster sauce, soy sauce, and garlic powder. Then add egg and mix up the mixture until homogenous. Pour water in the instant pot and insert the steamer rack. Then transfer the ground pork mixture in the silicone egg molds and transfer the mold in the instant pot. Cook the wontons on Manual mode (high pressure) for minutes. Then allow the natural pressure release for 10 minutes more.

Nutrition Info: calories 136, fat 4.7, fiber 0.1, carbs 0.9, protein 6

Raspberry Toast Casserole

Servings: 4
Cooking Time: 15 Minutes
Ingredients:

- 1 loaf low carb bread
- ¼ cup raspberries
- 1 cup almond milk
- 1 tbsp swerve brown sugar
- 2 tbsp arrowroot starch
- 1 tsp vanilla extract
- 2 tbsp melted butter
- A pinch salt
- ¼ tsp cinnamon powder
- Sugar-free maple syrup for topping

Directions:

1. Cut the bread into inch slices, spread in the bottom of a medium heatproof bowl, and top with the raspberries
2. In a medium bowl, whisk the almond milk, swerve sugar, arrowroot starch, vanilla extract, butter, salt, and cinnamon powder. Pour the mixture all over the bread mixture and cover the bowl with foil.
3. Pour 2 cups of water into the inner pot, fit in a trivet with handles, and place the bowl on the trivet.
4. Lock the lid in place; select Manual mode on High Pressure and set the timer for 15 minutes.
5. When the timer beeps, perform a natural pressure release for 10 minutes, then a quick pressure release to let out the remaining steam and open the lid.
6. With napkins on your hands, remove the bowl from the pot and allow slight cooling.
7. Dish the casserole onto plates and drizzle with some maple syrup.
8. Serve warm.

Nutrition Info:
Per Serving: Calories 287 Fats 85g Carbs 49g Net Carbs 7.19g Protein 7.93g

Soft Eggs

Servings: 2

Cooking Time: 4 Minutes
Ingredients:
- ¼ teaspoon ground black pepper
- ¼ teaspoon salt
- ½ teaspoon butter, melted
- 2 eggs
- 1 cup water, for cooking

Directions:
1. Pour water in the instant pot and insert the steamer rack. Place the eggs on the rack and close the instant pot lid. Cook the eggs on Manual mode (Low pressure) for 4 minutes. Then cool the eggs in the ice water and peel them. Cut the eggs into halves and sprinkle with salt, ground black pepper, and melted butter.

Nutrition Info: calories 72, fat 5.3, fiber 0.1, carbs 0.5, protein 5.6

Egg Muffins

Servings: 4
Cooking Time: 5 Minutes
Ingredients:
- 4 eggs, beaten
- 1 bell pepper, chopped
- ¼ cup fresh parsley, chopped
- ¼ teaspoon ground paprika
- ¼ teaspoon salt
- ¼ cup cream cheese
- 1 cup water, for cooking

Directions:
1. In the mixing bowl combine together eggs, bell pepper, parsley, ground paprika, salt, and cream cheese. When the mixture is homogenous, pour it in the silicone muffin molds. Pour water in the instant pot and insert trivet. Place the muffin molds on the trivet and close the lid. Cook the egg muffins on Manual mode (high pressure) for 5 minutes. Then make a quick pressure release and remove the muffins from the instant pot.

Nutrition Info: calories 125, fat 9.6, fiber 0.6, carbs 3.3, protein 7.1

Strawberries And Nuts Salad

Servings: 4
Cooking Time: 10 Minutes
Ingredients:
- ½ cup almonds, chopped
- ½ cup walnuts, chopped
- 2 cups strawberries, halved
- 1 tablespoon stevia
- ½ teaspoon nutmeg, ground
- 1 cup coconut cream

Directions:

1. In your instant pot, mix the strawberries with the cream and the rest of the ingredients, put the lid on and cook on Low for minutes. Release the pressure naturally for 10 minutes, divide the mix into bowls and serve.

Nutrition Info: calories 328, fat 8, fiber 5.4, carbs 7.6, protein 8.1

Breakfast Sandwich

Servings: 4
Cooking Time: 15 Minutes
Ingredients:

- 1 cup lettuce
- 2 cups ground chicken
- 1 tablespoon coconut flour
- 1 teaspoon salt
- 1 tablespoon butter
- ½ teaspoon ground nutmeg
- 3 oz scallions, chopped

Directions:

1. Preheat the instant pot on saute mode for 5 minutes.
2. Then add butter and melt it.
3. Add chopped scallions
4. After this, add ground chicken and ground nutmeg. Stir the mixture well and cook for minutes.
5. Then add coconut flour and salt. Saute the meal for 10 minutes.
6. Fill the lettuce with the ground chicken and transfer it on the plate. The sandwiches are cooked.

Nutrition Info:
Per Serving: calories 177, fat 8.6, fiber 1.5, carbs 3.2, protein 1

Pecan-pumpkin Spice Porridge

Servings: 4
Cooking Time: 16 Minutes
Ingredients:

- ½ cup grated dried coconut, unsweetened
- ⅙ cup coconut flour
- ⅙ cup psyllium husk powder
- 1 cup coconut milk + more for topping
- 1 ½ cups water
- A pinch of salt
- 1 tbsp sugar-free maple syrup
- ¼ cup pumpkin puree
- 1 tsp cinnamon powder
- ½ tsp vanilla extract

54

- 2 tbsp pumpkin seeds
- ¼ cup chopped pecans

Directions:

1. Mix all the ingredients in the inner pot except for the pumpkin seeds and pecans. Make sure that the pumpkin puree is well combined.
2. Lock the lid in place; select Manual mode on High Pressure and set the timer to 6 minutes.
3. When done cooking, perform a natural pressure release for 10 minutes, and then a quick pressure release to let out the remaining steam.
4. Open the lid, stir and spoon porridge into serving bowls.
5. Top with more coconut milk as desired and then the pumpkin seeds and pecans.
6. Serve warm.

Nutrition Info:

Per Serving: Calories 263 Fats 77g Carbs 02g Net Carbs 5.52g Protein 6.22g

Spanish Zucchini Tortilla

Servings: 3

Cooking Time: 15 Mins

Ingredients:

- 3 Eggs
- 1 large Zucchini, cut into strips
- 1 Onion, chopped
- ½ tbsp Thyme, chopped
- Salt and white Pepper to taste
- 2 tbsp Olive oil
- Chopped Parsley, for garnish

Directions:

1. Crack the eggs in a bowl and whisk for minute. Add zucchini strips, onion, thyme, salt, and pepper, and mix well. Add 2 cups of water into the Instant Pot and place a trivet inside.
2. Spray a medium-sized baking dish with olive oil, transfer the eggs mixture into a pan and place on the trivet. Seal the lid and cook on Manual mode for 10 minutes on High. Once ready, do a quick release. Garnish the tortilla with parsley.

Nutrition Info: Calories 233, Protein 3g, Net Carbs 4.1g, Fat 4g

Bell Peppers With Omelet

Servings: 2

Cooking Time: 14 Minutes

Ingredients:

- 1 large bell pepper
- 2 eggs, beaten
- 1 tablespoon coconut cream
- ¼ teaspoon salt
- ¼ teaspoon dried oregano
- 1 cup of water

Directions:
1. Cut the bell peppers into halves and remove the seeds.
2. After this, in the mixing bowl mix up eggs, coconut cream, salt, and oregano.
3. Pour water in the instant pot and insert the rack.
4. Then pour the egg mixture in the pepper halves.
5. Transfer the peppers on the rack and close the lid.
6. Cook the meal on Manual mode (high pressure) for 14 minutes. Then make a quick pressure release.

Nutrition Info:
Per Serving: calories 100, fat 6.3, fiber 1.1, carbs 5.4, protein 6.3

Cocoa Oatmeal

Servings: 6
Cooking Time: 10 Minutes
Ingredients:
- 1 cup almond milk
- 1 cup coconut cream
- 1 cup coconut flakes, unsweetened
- 2 tablespoons stevia
- 1 teaspoon cocoa powder
- 2 teaspoons vanilla extract

Directions:
1. In your instant pot, mix the almond milk with the rest of the ingredients, put the lid on and cook on High for minutes. Release the pressure naturally for 10 minutes, divide the mix into bowls and serve.

Nutrition Info: calories 236, fat 6, fiber 3.1, carbs 6.5, protein 2.3

Breakfast Kale Bread

Servings: 6
Cooking Time: 60 Minutes
Ingredients:
- 1 egg, beaten
- 1 teaspoon baking powder
- 1 teaspoon lemon juice
- 1 cup kale, grinded
- 1 tablespoon flaxseeds meal
- ½ cup coconut flour
- ¼ cup almond meal
- ¼ teaspoon salt
- 2 tablespoons sesame oil
- ½ teaspoon dried sage
- 1/3 cup water
- 1 teaspoon pumpkin seeds, chopped

- 1 cup water, for cooking

Directions:

1. Mix up together beaten egg, baking powder, lemon juice, 3 cup of water, dried sage, sesame oil, salt, almond meal, and coconut flour. Then add flaxseeds meal and grinded kale. Knead the soft and non-sticky dough. After this, line the round baking pan with paper foil and put the kneaded dough inside. Press it little. Sprinkle the surface of dough with pumpkin seeds. Pour water in the instant pot and insert the trivet. Arrange the baking pan with dough on the trivet and close the lid. Cook the kale bread 45 minutes on manual (high pressure). Then allow the natural pressure release for 15 minutes more. Open the instant pot lid and remove the baking pan with bread from it. Cool the bread for 10-15 minutes.

Nutrition Info: calories 129, fat 8.9, fiber 5.1, carbs 9.7, protein 3.8

Swiss Cheese Egg Scramble

Servings: 4
Cooking Time: 5 Minutes
Ingredients:

- 1 tbsp butter
- 1 large yellow onion, sliced
- ½ tsp freshly chopped rosemary
- 1 tsp Worcestershire sauce
- 4 large eggs
- 3 tbsp almond milk
- ¼ cup shredded Gruyère cheese + extra for garnishing
- Salt and black pepper to taste

Directions:

1. Set the IP in Sauté mode and adjust to medium heat.
2. Melt the butter in the inner pot and sauté the onion until softened, 3 minutes. Mix in the rosemary and Worcestershire sauce.
3. In a medium bowl, whisk the eggs with the almond milk and pour into the pot
4. Lock the lid in place; select Manual mode on High Pressure and set the timer to 2 minutes.
5. When the timer stops, perform a quick pressure release to let out all the steam and open the lid.
6. Stir in the Gruyere cheese until melted and season with salt and black pepper.
7. Dish the food, garnish with more cheese and serve warm.

Nutrition Info:
Per Serving: Calories 176 Fats 08g Carbs 5.66g Net Carbs 4.36g Protein 9.57g

Herby Eggs In Avocados

Servings: 4
Cooking Time: 4 Minutes
Ingredients:

- 2 large ripe avocados, halved and pitted
- 4 large eggs, cracked into a bowl

- Salt and black pepper to taste
- 1 ½ tsp dried herb mix
- ½ cup Mexican four-cheese blend

Directions:
1. Pour cup of water into the inner pot.
2. Spoon out half of the flesh out of each avocado and arrange (open side up) in a steamer basket.
3. Fill the avocados with an egg each, season with salt, black pepper, herb mix, and the cheese blend.
4. Carefully put the steamer basket into the inner pot, lock the lid in place and set the pot in manual mode on High Pressure for minutes.
5. After cooking, do a quick pressure release to release all the steam and open the lid.
6. Carefully remove the avocados onto serving plates and serve immediately.

Nutrition Info:
Per Serving: Calories 124 Fats 98g Carbs 2.54g Net Carbs 1.64g Protein 8.42g

Lemon Ricotta Cheesecake

Servings: 5
Cooking Time: 35 Mins
Ingredients:
- 10 oz Cream Cheese
- ¼ cup Swerve Sweetener + 1 tsp Swerve Sweetener
- ½ cup Ricotta Cheese
- One Lemon, zested and juiced
- 2 Eggs, cracked into a bowl
- 1 tsp Lemon Extract
- 3 tbsp Sour Cream
- 1 ½ cups Water

Directions:
1. In an electric mixer, add cream cheese, quarter cup of swerve, ricotta cheese, lemon zest, lemon juice, and lemon extract. Mix the ingredients until a smooth consistency is formed. Adjust the sweet taste to your liking with more swerve sweetener. Reduce the speed and add the eggs. Fold in at low speed until fully incorporated. Make sure not to fold the eggs on high speed to prevent a cracked crust.
2. Grease a springform pan with cooking spray and use a spatula to spoon the mixture into the pan. Level the top with the spatula and cover with foil.
3. In the IP, fit in a trivet and pour in the water. Place the cake pan on top of the trivet. Seal the lid, select Steam mode on High pressure for 15 minutes.
4. Mix the sour cream and one tablespoon of swerve sweetener; set aside. Once ready, do a natural pressure release for 10 minutes. Place the springform pan on a flat surface, and open it. Use a spatula to spread the sour cream mixture on the warm cake and refrigerate for 8 hours. Slice and serve.

Nutrition Info: Calories 181, Protein 5g, Net Carbs 2g, Fat 25g

Egg&cheese

Servings: 1
Cooking Time: 6 Minutes
Ingredients:

- 2 eggs, beaten
- 1 oz Parmesan, grated
- 1 oz Swiss cheese, grated
- ¼ cup heavy cream
- ½ teaspoon dried cilantro
- ½ teaspoon almond butter

Directions:

1. Toss the almond butter in the instant pot and melt it on saute mode.
2. Then add eggs and cream cheese. Sprinkle the ingredients with dried cilantro and cook on saute mode for 4 minutes.
3. When the egg mixture is solid, stir it gently to get the small egg pieces.
4. After this, add grated cheese and close the lid. Cook the meal for 2 minutes more.

Nutrition Info:
Per Serving: calories 192, fat 6, fiber 2.4, carbs 6, protein 8

Mushroom Frittata

Servings: 4
Cooking Time: 35 Minutes
Ingredients:

- 2 tbsp butter
- 1 cup sliced cremini mushrooms
- Salt and black pepper to taste
- 2 cups water
- 8 large eggs
- ½ cup heavy cream
- 1 tsp dried thyme
- 1 cup shredded asiago cheese

Directions:

1. Set the IP in Sauté mode and adjust to medium heat.
2. Melt the butter in the inner pot and cook the mushrooms until softened, 5 minutes. Season with salt and black pepper; transfer to a plate and set aside.
3. Clean the inner pot, return to the base, pour in 2 cups of water, and fit in a trivet. Grease a 7-inch springform pan with cooking spray and set aside.
4. In a medium bowl, beat eggs, heavy cream, thyme, salt, and black pepper. Pour the mixture into springform pan, sprinkle with the cheese, cover with foil, and place on the trivet.
5. Lock the lid in place; select Manual mode on High Pressure and set the timer to 20 minutes.
6. After cooking, do a natural pressure release for 10 minutes, then a quick pressure to release remaining steam and open the lid.
7. Carefully remove the pan, uncover, and release the frittata onto a wide plate.

8. Slice and serve warm.

Nutrition Info:

Per Serving: : Calories 391 Fats 98g Carbs 2.62g Net Carbs 2.42g Protein 8g

Omelet "3-cheese"

Servings: 2

Cooking Time: 3 Minutes

Ingredients:

- 2 eggs, beaten
- 1 oz Mozzarella, shredded
- ¾ teaspoon dried oregano
- ½ teaspoon coconut oil
- 1 oz Cheddar cheese, shredded
- 1 oz Provolone cheese, grated
- ½ cup water, for cooking

Directions:

1. Mix up eggs, all cheese, and dried oregano.
2. After this, grease the pan with the coconut and pour the egg mixture inside.
3. Pour ½ cup of water in the instant pot bowl and place the pan with eggs inside.
4. Cook omelet on "Manual" mode for minutes (natural pressure release).

Nutrition Info:

Per Serving: calories 221, fat 5, fiber 0.2, carbs 1.7, protein 8

Keto Oatmeal

Servings: 2

Cooking Time: 1.5 Hours

Ingredients:

- 2 tablespoons coconut flakes
- 1 tablespoon flax seeds
- 2 tablespoons hemp seeds
- ½ cup of coconut milk
- 1 tablespoon almond meal
- 1 teaspoon Erythritol
- 1 teaspoon vanilla extract
- ¼ cup of water

Directions:

1. Combine together all ingredients in the instant pot and stir well with the spoon. Close the lid and cook Keto oatmeal for 5 hours on Low pressure (Manual mode). Stir the cooked meal well before serving.

Nutrition Info: calories 239, fat 22, fiber 3.3, carbs 9, protein 5.3

Eggs, Leeks And Turkey Mix

Servings: 4
Cooking Time: 15 Minutes
Ingredients:

- 2 leeks, chopped
- ½ cup chicken stock
- 2 tablespoons olive oil
- 2 garlic cloves, minced
- 8 eggs, whisked
- 1 turkey breast, skinless, boneless and cut into strips

Directions:

1. Set your instant pot on Sauté mode, add the oil, heat it up, add the leeks, garlic and the meat and brown for 5 minutes. Add the rest of the ingredients, toss, put the lid on and cook on High for minutes. Release the pressure naturally for 10 minutes, divide the mix between plates and serve.

Nutrition Info: calories 216, fat 16, fiber 0.8, carbs 7.6, protein 9

Spinach And Tomato Cheesy Braise

Servings: 3
Cooking Time: 20 Mins
Ingredients:

- 1 cup baby Spinach, sliced
- 2 Tomatoes, chopped
- 1 cup Mushrooms, sliced
- 1 tbsp Ginger powder
- 1 tbsp Garlic paste
- ¼ lb Parmesan cheese, shredded
- ½ lb Mozzarella cheese, shredded
- 2 Eggs, whisked
- Salt and black pepper to taste
- ¼ tbsp Thyme
- 2 tbsp Butter, melted

Directions:

1. In the Instant Pot, add the butter and garlic; cook for 30 seconds on Sauté mode.
2. Then, add spinach, tomatoes, thyme, salt, black pepper, eggs, ginger, mozzarella and mushrooms; mix well. Seal the lid and cook on High for 15 minutes. Once ready, do a quick release. Sprinkle with the grated Parmesan and serve.

Nutrition Info: Calories 424, Protein 51g, Net Carbs 8.9g, Fat 21g

Noatmeal

Servings: 4
Cooking Time: 5 Hours

Ingredients:
- ½ cup coconut shred
- 1 teaspoon ground cinnamon
- 1 teaspoon Erythritol
- 3 tablespoons flaxseeds
- 3 tablespoons sunflower seeds
- ½ cup coconut cream
- ½ cup of water
- ½ teaspoon butter

Directions:
1. In the mixing bowl, mix up coconut shred, ground cinnamon, Erythritol, flaxseeds, sunflower seeds, coconut cream, water, and butter.
2. Transfer the mixture in the instant pot bowl.
3. Set the slow cook mode and cook the meal for 5 hours.
4. Then stir it well and transfer in the serving ramekins.

Nutrition Info:
Per Serving: calories 215, fat 4, fiber 4.6, carbs 8.1, protein 2.1

Egg Pate

Servings: 6
Cooking Time: 5 Minutes
Ingredients:
- 8 eggs
- 1 oz avocado, mashed
- 2 tablespoons cream cheese
- ½ teaspoon salt
- 1 cup water, for cooking

Directions:
1. Pour cup of water in the instant pot bowl and add eggs.
2. Set the "Steam" mode on your instant pot and cook the eggs for 5 minutes (QR).
3. Meanwhile, mix up cream cheese and mashed avocado.
4. Peel the cooked eggs and put them in the blender. Blend the eggs until smooth.
5. Churn together eggs and avocado mash mixture.
6. The egg pate is cooked.

Nutrition Info:
Per Serving: calories 105, fat 7.9, fiber 0.3, carbs 1, protein 7.7

Spinach Frittata

Servings: 4
Cooking Time: 10 Minutes
Ingredients:
- 6 eggs, whisked
- 1 cup baby spinach

- 1 spring onion, minced
- ½ teaspoon garlic powder
- A pinch of salt and black pepper
- 1 cup water
- Cooking spray

Directions:

1. In a bowl, combine the eggs with the spinach and the rest of the ingredients except the water and the cooking spray and whisk well. Grease a pan with the cooking spray and pour the frittata mix inside. Put the water in the instant pot, add the trivet, put the pan inside, put the lid on and cook on High for minutes. Release the pressure naturally for 10 minutes, divide the frittata between plates and serve.

Nutrition Info: calories 103, fat 6.4, fiber 1.1, carbs 2.5, protein 8.4

Asparagus And Eggs Mix

Servings: 6
Cooking Time: 20 Minutes
Ingredients:

- 1 asparagus stalk, halved
- 6 eggs, whisked
- ¼ cup scallions, chopped
- 1 red chili pepper, chopped
- A pinch of salt and black pepper
- ¼ teaspoon chili powder
- 1 tablespoon olive oil

Directions:

1. Set the instant pot on Sauté mode, add the oil, heat it up, add the asparagus and the scallions and cook for 2-3 minutes. Add the eggs and the rest of the ingredients, toss, put the lid on and cook on High for minutes. Release the pressure fast for 5 minutes, divide the mix between plates and serve.

Nutrition Info: calories 85, fat 6.7, fiber 0.2, carbs 0.8, protein 5.6

Leek Frittata

Servings: 4
Cooking Time: 15 Minutes
Ingredients:

- 4 eggs, whisked
- 2 leeks, sliced
- 1 shallot, chopped
- 1 tablespoon sweet paprika
- A pinch of salt and black pepper
- 1 red bell pepper, chopped
- Cooking spray

Directions:

1. Grease your instant pot with the cooking spray, add leeks, shallot and the rest of the ingredients, toss, spread well into the pot, put the lid on and cooking o High for minutes. Release the pressure naturally for 10 minutes, divide the frittata between plates and serve.

Nutrition Info: calories 106, fat 9.4, fiber 1.9, carbs 6.6, protein 6.8

Cranberry Cauliflower Pudding

Servings: 4
Cooking Time: 3 Minutes
Ingredients:
- 2 cups cauliflower rice
- 1 ½ cups coconut milk
- ½ tsp nutmeg powder
- 1 tsp vanilla extract
- ¼ cup sugar-free maple syrup
- ½ cup dried cranberries
- ¼ cup almonds

Directions:
1. Mix all the ingredients except for the almonds in the inner pot.
2. Lock the lid in place; select Manual mode on High Pressure and set the timer for 3 minutes.
3. When done cooking, perform a natural pressure release for 10 minutes, then a quick pressure release to let out the remaining steam and open the lid.
4. Stir the pudding and dish into serving bowls.
5. Top with the almonds and serve warm.

Nutrition Info:
Per Serving: Calories 231 Fats 76g Carbs 9.45g Net Carbs 5.75g Protein 7.17g

Delicious Scallions And Eggs

Servings: 2
Cooking Time: 10 Mins
Ingredients:
- 2 Eggs
- 1 cup Water
- ½ lb Scallions, chopped
- ½ cup Sesame seeds
- ½ tbsp Garlic powder
- Salt and black pepper to taste

Directions:
1. Mix water and eggs in a bowl. Add scallions, sesame seeds, garlic powder, salt and pepper in the IP. Pour in the egg mixture. Set on Manual mode for 5 minutes on High. Do a quick release and serve.

Nutrition Info: Calories 348, Protein 7g, Net Carbs 6.2g, Fat 27g

Salmon Veggie Cakes

Servings: 4
Cooking Time: 40 Mins
Ingredients:

- 2 (5 oz) packs Steamed Salmon Flakes
- 1 Red Onion, chopped
- Salt and black pepper to taste
- 1 tsp Garlic Powder
- 2 tbsp Olive oil
- 1 Red Bell pepper, seeded and chopped
- 4 tbsp Butter, divided
- 3 Eggs, cracked into a bowl
- 1 cup Low Carb Breadcrumbs
- 4 tbsp Mayonnaise
- 2 tsp Sugar-free Worcestershire Sauce
- ¼ cup chopped Parsley

Directions:

1. Heat half of the butter and the oil on Sauté. Add onions and bell peppers. Cook for minutes, stirring occasionally. Set aside. In a bowl, mix salmon flakes, bell pepper, onion, breadcrumbs, eggs, mayo, Worcestershire sauce, garlic, salt, pepper, and parsley. Mix well while breaking the salmon into the smallest possible pieces. Use your hands to mold 4 patties out of the mixture and set them on a plate.
2. Press Sauté and melt the remaining butter. Fry the patties until golden brown. Remove onto a wire rack to rest for minutes. Serve with lettuce and radish salad with a mild drizzle of herb vinaigrette.

Nutrition Info: Calories 264, Protein 4g, Net Carbs 2g, Fat 5g

Vegetable Frittata

Servings: 4
Cooking Time: 10 Minutes
Ingredients:

- 4 eggs, beaten
- 2 oz Pecorino cheese, grated
- 3 oz okra, chopped
- 2 oz radish, chopped
- 1 tablespoon cream cheese
- 1 teaspoon sesame oil

Directions:

1. Heat up sesame oil in the instant pot on saute mode.
2. Add chopped okra and radish and saute the vegetables for 4 minutes.
3. Then stir them well and add cream cheese and beaten eggs.
4. Stir the mixture well and top with cheese.

5. Close the lid and cook the frittata on saute mode for 6 minutes more.

Nutrition Info:

Per Serving: calories 163, fat 1, fiber 0.9, carbs 2.5, protein 9

Mexican Chili Eggs

Servings: 4

Cooking Time: 30 Mins

Ingredients:

- 1 cup shredded Cheddar Cheese
- 1 cup Heavy Cream
- 4 Eggs
- 1/3 cup chopped canned Chilies
- 2 tbsp chopped Cilantro
- 1 tbsp chopped Parsley
- ¼ tsp Garlic Powder
- ¼ tsp Onion Powder
- ¼ tsp Cumin
- Salt and black pepper to taste

Directions:

1. Pour cup of water in and lower the trivet. In a bowl, beat eggs and stir in the remaining ingredients. Grease a baking dish with cooking spray and pour the egg mixture inside. Place the baking dish on top of the trivet. Seal the lid, and cook on High for 20 minutes. After the beep, release the pressure naturally for 10 minutes. Remove the dish. Cut into 4 pieces and serve.

Nutrition Info: Calories 270, Protein 14g, Net Carbs 4.5g, Fat 19g

Bacon Egg Cups

Servings: 2

Cooking Time: 15 Minutes

Ingredients:

- 2 eggs
- 4 bacon slices
- ¼ teaspoon dried parsley
- 1 teaspoon butter, soften
- ¼ teaspoon salt

Directions:

1. Brush the muffin molds with butter. Then place the bacon slices in the muffin molds to cover the muffin molds sides. Crack the eggs in the muffin molds and sprinkle them with parsley and salt. Cover the molds with foil and arrange it in the instant pot. Cook the meal for minutes on Saute mode.

Nutrition Info: calories 240, fat 3, fiber 0, carbs 0.4, protein 6

Tomato And Peppers Salad

Servings: 4
Cooking Time: 10 Minutes
Ingredients:

- A pinch of salt and black pepper
- 3 cups baby spinach, chopped
- 1 pound cherry tomatoes, cubed
- 3 green onions, chopped
- 1 tablespoon olive oil
- 1 tablespoon balsamic vinegar
- ½ pound mixed bell peppers, cut into strips

Directions:

1. Set the instant pot on Sauté mode, add the oil, heat it up, add the onions and sauté for 2 minutes. Add the tomatoes and the rest of the ingredients, put the lid on and cook on High for 8 minutes. Release the pressure naturally for minutes, divide the mix into bowls and serve for breakfast.

Nutrition Info: calories 60, fat 8.1, fiber 2, carbs 6.1, protein 1.9

Zucchini Roll

Servings: 2
Cooking Time: 12 Minutes
Ingredients:

- ½ zucchini, grated
- 9 oz chicken breast, skinless, boneless
- 1 tablespoon butter
- ½ teaspoon white pepper
- ¼ teaspoon thyme

Directions:

1. Beat the chicken breast well with the help of the kitchen hammer to get the tender piece.
2. Then sprinkle the chicken breast with the white pepper and thyme.
3. Put the grated zucchini over the chicken breast and flatten it well.
4. Roll up the chicken breast.
5. Wrap the zucchini roll in the foil.
6. Set the instant pot mode "Poultry" and place the zucchini roll in the instant pot bowl.
7. Cook the zucchini roll for 12 minutes. Then make naturally pressure release.
8. Slice the cooked zucchini roll.

Nutrition Info:
Per Serving: calories 206, fat 9.1, fiber 0.7, carbs 2.1, protein 8

Zucchini Meat Cups

Servings: 4
Cooking Time: 15 Minutes

Ingredients:
- 1 cup zucchini, grated
- ½ cup ground beef
- 1.4 cup carrot, grated
- 1 teaspoon onion powder
- ½ teaspoon salt
- ¼ cup Cheddar cheese, shredded
- 1 tablespoon sesame oil
- ½ teaspoon ground black pepper
- 1 cup water, for cooking

Directions:
1. Squeeze the grated zucchini, if needed and place it in the big mixing bowl. Add ground beef, carrot, onion powder, salt, cheese, and ground black pepper. Then brush the muffin molds (cups) with sesame oil. Place the zucchini-meat mixture in the muffin molds. Pour water in the instant pot. Insert the steamer rack. Place the muffin molds with the meat-zucchini mixture in the instant pot. Cook the meal for minutes on Manual (High pressure). Then allow the natural pressure release for 10 minutes.

Nutrition Info: calories 121, fat 7.1, fiber 1.4, carbs 5.5, protein 9

Pork Pie

Servings: 4
Cooking Time: 30 Minutes
Ingredients:
- ½ cup heavy cream
- A pinch of salt and black pepper
- 4 eggs, whisked
- 2 cups pork meat, ground and browned
- 2 green onions, chopped
- 1 cup cheddar cheese, shredded
- 1 cup water

Directions:
1. In a bowl, mix the eggs with the rest of the ingredients except the water, whisk well and spread into a pie pan. Add the water to your instant pot, add the trivet, add the pan inside, put the lid on and cook on High for 30 minutes. Release the pressure naturally for minutes, divide the mix between plates and serve hot for breakfast.

Nutrition Info: calories 231, fat 3, fiber 0.2, carbs 1.7, protein 13

Eggs Benedict

Servings: 3
Cooking Time: 1 Minute
Ingredients:
- 3 eggs
- 3 turkey bacon slices, fried

- 1 teaspoon butter
- ½ teaspoon ground black pepper
- 1 cup of water
- ¼ teaspoon salt

Directions:
1. Grease the eggs molds with butter and crack eggs inside.
2. Sprinkle them with ground black pepper and salt.
3. Pour water in the instant pot and insert the rack.
4. Then place the eggs in the molds in the rack and close the lid.
5. Cook the eggs for 1 minute on Manual mode (high pressure).
6. Then make a quick pressure release and transfer the eggs on the plate.
7. Top the eggs with bacon slices.

Nutrition Info:
Per Serving: calories 95, fat 6.2, fiber 0.1, carbs 0.6, protein 8.6

Egg Caprese Cups

Servings: 2
Cooking Time: 3 Minutes
Ingredients:
- 2 thin slices ham
- 2 eggs
- 2 tbsp shredded mozzarella cheese
- 1 tsp dried basil
- 2 cherry tomatoes, halved
- Salt and black pepper to taste

Directions:
1. Pour ½ cups of water into the inner pot and fit in a trivet.
2. Line medium ramekins with one ham each, crack an egg into each cup and top with the mozzarella, basil, and tomatoes. Season with salt, black pepper, and cover with foil. Place the ramekins on the trivet.
3. Lock the lid in place; select Manual mode on High Pressure and set the timer to minutes.
4. After cooking, perform a quick pressure release to let out the steam and open the lid.
5. Use tongs to remove the pliers, take off the foil and serve immediately.

Nutrition Info:
Per Serving: Calories 67 Fats 9.13g Carbs 1.35g Net Carbs 1.15g Protein 6.07g

Bacon, Cheese, And Veggie Egg Bake

Servings: 4
Cooking Time: 30 Minutes
Ingredients:
- 6 slices bacon, chopped
- 1 cup chopped cauliflower
- ½ cup diced mushrooms

- 6 large eggs
- ½ cup shredded cheddar cheese
- Salt and pepper
- ¼ cup heavy cream
- 1 ½ cups water

Directions:

1. Turn the Instant Pot on to the Sauté setting and let it heat up.
2. Add the bacon and cook until crisp.
3. Stir in the vegetables and cook for minutes, often stirring, until tender.
4. Grease a heatproof bowl with cooking spray.
5. Whisk together the eggs, cheese, and cream then season with salt and pepper.
6. Pour the egg mixture into the greased bowl then stir in the bacon and veggies.
7. Place the bowl in the pot on top of a trivet and pour in 1 ½ cups water.
8. Close and lock the lid then press the Manual button and adjust the timer to 20 minutes.
9. When the timer goes off, do a Quick Release by pressing Cancel and switching the steam valve to "venting."
10. When the pot has depressurized, open the lid.
11. Remove the bowl and turn the egg bake out and slice to serve.

Nutrition Info: calories 275 fat 21g ,protein 19g ,carbs 3g ,fiber 1g ,net carbs 2g

Spinach Oatmeal Bowl

Servings: 4
Cooking Time: 9 Minutes
Ingredients:

- 1 tbsp olive oil
- ¼ cup finely chopped red onion
- ½ cup chicken broth
- ½ cup almond flour
- ½ cup coconut flour
- 2 tbsp unsweetened shredded coconut
- 1 tbsp chia seeds
- 1 tbsp golden flaxseed meal
- Salt and black pepper to taste
- 4 oz ham, chopped
- 4 oz baby spinach, chopped
- 2 scallions, chopped for garnishing
- ¼ tsp red chili flakes

Directions:

1. Set the IP in Sauté mode and adjust to medium heat.
2. Heat the olive oil in the inner pot and sauté the onion until softened, 3 minutes.
3. Stir in chicken broth, almond flour, coconut flour, shredded coconut, chia seeds, flaxseed meal, salt, and black pepper.
4. Lock the lid in place; select Manual mode on High Pressure and set the timer to minutes.

5. After cooking, perform a quick pressure to let out the steam, open the lid and set the IP in Sauté mode.
6. Stir in the ham, spinach, and allow the spinach to wilt. Adjust the taste with salt and black pepper.
7. Dish the food into serving bowls, garnish with the scallions and chili flakes, and serve warm with hard-boiled eggs.

Nutrition Info:

Per Serving: : Calories 268 Fats 97g Carbs 6.04g Net Carbs 3.34g Protein 1g

Classic Shakshuka

Servings: 4
Cooking Time: 9 Minutes
Ingredients:
- 3 tbsp ghee
- 1 small red onion, chopped
- 1 medium green chili, deseeded and minced
- ½ medium red bell pepper, deseeded and chopped
- 2 garlic cloves, minced
- Salt and black pepper to taste
- 2 cups diced tomatoes with their juice
- ½ tsp smoked paprika
- ½ tsp coriander powder
- ½ tsp red chili flakes
- ½ tsp cumin powder
- 4 large eggs
- ⅓ cup crumbled goat cheese
- 2 tbsp freshly chopped cilantro

Directions:
1. Set the IP in Sauté mode and adjust to Medium heat.
2. Melt the ghee in the inner pot and sauté the onion, green chili, bell pepper, and garlic. Season with salt, black pepper, and cook until fragrant and softened 4 minutes.
3. Mix in the tomatoes, paprika, coriander, red chili flakes, and cumin.
4. Lock the lid in place; select Manual mode on High Pressure and set the timer to 3 minutes.
5. After cooking, perform a quick pressure to let out all the steam and open the lid.
6. Create four holes in the sauce and crack an egg into each hole.
7. Lock the lid in place again; select Manual mode on High Pressure and set the timer for 2 minutes.
8. After cooking, perform a quick pressure to let out the steam and unlock the lid.
9. Top the shakshuka with the goat cheese and cilantro.
10. Dish and serve warm.

Nutrition Info:

Per Serving: Calories 357 Fats 28g Carbs 9.67g Net Carbs 8.37g Protein 6g

Strawberry Keto Bread Pudding

Servings: 4
Cooking Time: 16 Minutes
Ingredients:

- 3 tbsp flaxseed meal + 9 tbsp water
- 1 ½ cup unsweetened almond milk
- 1 cup coconut cream
- 6 cups cubed low-carb bread
- 2 tbsp melted butter
- ¼ cup strawberries, chopped
- ½ cup goji berries
- 2 tbsp swerve sugar
- 1 tsp vanilla extract
- Sugar-free maple syrup for topping

Directions:

1. In a small bowl, mix the flaxseed meal with water and set aside to thicken for minutes. After, whisk in the almond milk and coconut cream.
2. In a heatproof bowl, combine the bread, butter, strawberries, goji berries, swerve sugar, and vanilla extract. Pour the coconut cream mixture on top and mix well. Cover the bowl with foil.
3. Pour 1 ½ cups of water into the inner pot, fit in a trivet and place the bowl on top.
4. Lock the lid in place; select Manual mode on High Pressure, and set the timer for 15 minutes.
5. When ready, perform a natural pressure release for 10 minutes, then a quick pressure release, and open the lid.
6. Carefully remove the bowl and foil; allow cooling for 1 minute, and spoon the pudding onto serving plates.
7. Drizzle with some maple syrup and serve immediately.

Nutrition Info:
Per Serving: : Calories 595 Fats 15g Carbs 96g Net Carbs 8.06g Protein 94g

Margherita Egg Cups

Servings: 2
Cooking Time: 5 Minutes
Ingredients:

- 2 eggs
- 4 oz Mozzarella, shredded
- ½ tomato, chopped
- 1 teaspoon butter, softened
- ½ teaspoon fresh basil, chopped
- 1 cup water, for cooking

Directions:

1. Grease the small ramekins with softened butter and crack the eggs inside.

2. Then top the eggs with chopped tomato, basil, and Mozzarella.
3. Pour water and insert the steamer rack in the instant pot.
4. Place the ramekins with eggs on the rack. Close and seal the lid.
5. Cook the meal on manual (high pressure) for minutes. Allow the natural pressure release for 5 minutes.

Nutrition Info:
Per Serving: calories 243, fat 3, fiber 0.2, carbs 3, protein 7

Mediterranean-style Frittata

Servings: 4
Cooking Time: 10 Minutes
Ingredients:
- 6 large eggs
- 1 cup fresh chopped spinach
- ½ cup diced tomatoes
- ½ cup feta cheese, crumbled
- ¼ cup sliced black olives
- Salt and pepper
- ½ teaspoon dried Italian seasoning

Directions:
1. Whisk together all of the ingredients.
2. Pour the mixture into a greased pan that fits in the pot.
3. Place the pan in the Instant Pot on top of a trivet.
4. Pour in 1 cup of water then close and lock the lid.
5. Press the Manual button and adjust the timer to minutes.
6. When the timer goes off, let the pressure vent for 10 minutes then do a Quick Release by pressing Cancel and switching the steam valve to "venting."
7. When the pot has depressurized, open the lid.
8. Remove the pan from the pot and let the frittata rest for 5 minutes before serving.

Nutrition Info: calories 175 fat 5g ,protein 5g ,carbs 3g ,fiber 1g ,net carbs 2g

Oatmeal

Servings: 4
Cooking Time: 21 Minutes
Ingredients:
- 1 tbsp butter
- 1 cup sliced cremini mushrooms
- 1 tsp thyme leaves
- 1 garlic clove, minced
- Salt and black pepper to taste
- 1 cup chopped baby spinach
- 1 ½ cup cauliflower rice
- 2 tbsp flaxseed meal

- ½ cup vegetable broth
- ¼ tsp red pepper flakes
- ¼ cup crumbled goat cheese

Directions:

1. Set the IP in Sauté mode and adjust to Medium heat.
2. Melt the butter in the inner pot and sauté the mushrooms until slightly softened, 4 to 5 minutes. Mix in the thyme, garlic, salt, and black pepper and cook until fragrant, 3 minutes.
3. Add the spinach to wilt and then the cauliflower rice, flaxseed meal, vegetable broth, and red pepper flakes.
4. Lock the lid in place; select Manual mode on High Pressure and set the timer to 3 minutes.
5. After cooking, perform a natural pressure release for 10 minutes, then a quick pressure release to let out the remaining steam and open the lid.
6. Stir and adjust the taste with salt and black pepper.
7. Dish the food into serving bowls and top with the goat cheese.
8. Serve warm.

Nutrition Info:

Per Serving: : Calories 94 Fats 7.64g Carbs 3.88g Net Carbs 2.08g Protein 5.52g

Egg Breakfast Burritos

Servings: 4

Cooking Time: 15 Minutes

Ingredients:

- 8 eggs
- ½ cup heavy cream
- ½ tsp garlic powder
- Salt and black pepper to taste
- 1 medium yellow onion, diced
- 1 medium red bell pepper, deseeded and diced
- 2 tbsp freshly chopped chives
- ¾ cup chopped turkey ham
- 4 low-carb tortilla wraps
- ¾ cup grated cheddar cheese

Directions:

1. In a medium bowl, whisk the eggs, heavy cream, garlic powder, salt, and black pepper. Mix in onion, bell pepper, chives, and ham. Pour the mixture into a large ramekin and cover with foil.
2. Pour cups of water into the inner pot, fit in a trivet, and place the ramekin on top.
3. Lock the lid in place; select Manual mode on High Pressure and set the timer to 10 minutes.
4. After cooking, perform a natural pressure release for 5 minutes, and then a quick pressure release to let out the remaining steam.
5. Open the lid, remove the ramekin and scramble the eggs.
6. Lay the tortilla wraps on a clean, flat surface and divide the eggs on top. Sprinkle with the cheddar cheese and roll.
7. Cut the burritos into halves and serve immediately.

Nutrition Info:
Per Serving: Calories 322 Fats 23g Carbs 7.88g Net Carbs 6.58g Protein 47g

Creamy Blueberries And Nuts

Servings: 6
Cooking Time: 8 Minutes
Ingredients:
- ½ cup walnuts, chopped
- ½ cups almonds, chopped
- 2 teaspoons swerve
- 1 cup blueberries
- 1 teaspoon vanilla extract
- 1 cup coconut cream

Directions:
1. In your instant pot, combine the walnuts with the almonds and the rest of the ingredients, toss, put the lid on and cook on High for 8 minutes. Release the pressure fast for 5 minutes, divide the mix into bowls and serve for breakfast.

Nutrition Info: calories 218, fat 7, fiber 3.2, carbs 5.8, protein 5.3

Leeks And Pork Mix

Servings: 4
Cooking Time: 30 Minutes
Ingredients:
- 1 pound pork meat, ground
- ¼ cup coconut cream
- 2 leeks, chopped
- 4 eggs, whisked
- 1 tablespoon sweet paprika
- 1 tablespoon chives, chopped
- A pinch of salt and black pepper
- ¼ teaspoon garlic powder
- 1 tablespoon olive oil

Directions:
1. Set your instant pot on sauté mode, add the oil, heat it up, add the leeks and sauté for 5 minutes. Add the meat and brown for 4-5 minutes more. Add the eggs and the rest of the ingredients, toss, put the lid on and cook on High for 20 minutes. Release the pressure naturally for minutes, divide the mix between plates and serve for breakfast.

Nutrition Info: calories 160, fat 8, fiber 1.8, carbs 7.1, protein 6.9

Giant Pancake

Servings: 6
Cooking Time: 30 Mins

Ingredients:
- 3 cups Almond flour
- ¾ cup Stevia Sugar
- 5 Eggs
- 1/3 cup Olive oil
- 1/3 cup Sparkling Water
- 1/3 tsp Salt
- 1 ½ tsp Baking Soda
- 2 tbsp Monk Fruit Syrup
- A dollop of Whipped Cream

Directions:
1. Fit in a trivet and add 2 cup of water. Pour the almond flour, stevia sugar, eggs, olive oil, sparkling water, salt, and baking soda into a food processor to blend until smooth. Pour the resulting batter into a greased pan and place on top of the trivet. Let sit for 15 minutes. Seal the lid, select Multigrain on Low pressure for 15 minutes.
2. Once ready, press Cancel, release the pressure quickly. Stick in a toothpick and once it comes out clean, the pancake is done. Gently run a spatula around the pancake to let loose any sticking. Then, slide the pancakes into a serving plate. Top with whipped cream and drizzle with monk syrup. Serve.

Nutrition Info: Calories 271, Protein 13g, Net Carbs 3.1g, Fat 16g

Zucchini Spread

Servings: 4
Cooking Time: 12 Minutes
Ingredients:
- 4 zucchinis, sliced
- A pinch of salt and black pepper
- ½ cup heavy cream
- ½ cup cream cheese, soft
- 2 garlic cloves, minced
- ½ cup veggie stock
- 1 tablespoon avocado oil
- 1 tablespoon dill, chopped

Directions:
1. In your instant pot, mix the zucchinis with the stock, salt and pepper, put the lid on and cook on High for minutes. Release the pressure naturally for 10 minutes, drain the zucchinis, transfer them to a blender, add the rest of the ingredients, pulse, divide into bowls and serve as a morning spread.

Nutrition Info: calories 193, fat 5, fiber 2.5, carbs 7.8, protein 5.2

Cheese Egg Balls

Servings: 4
Cooking Time: 14 Minutes

Ingredients:
- 4 eggs, beaten
- ½ cup Mozzarella, shredded
- 1 teaspoon dried basil
- 1 tablespoon heavy cream
- 1 cup water, for cooking

Directions:
1. Mix up together eggs, dried basil, and heavy cream. Then pour the liquid in the silicone egg molds. Top every mold with Mozzarella. Then pour water in the instant pot and insert the trivet. Place the silicone egg molds on the trivet. Cook the egg balls for 7 minutes on Manual mode (High pressure). Then allow the natural pressure release for 7 minutes more. Cool the egg balls to the room temperature and remove from the silicone molds.

Nutrition Info: calories 86, fat 6.4, fiber 0, carbs 0.6, protein 6.6

Mini Casserole In Jars

Servings: 4
Cooking Time: 15 Minutes
Ingredients:
- 1 cup ground pork
- ¼ onion, diced
- 1 garlic clove, diced
- ½ cup Cheddar cheese, shredded
- ½ cup kale, chopped
- 1 teaspoon coconut oil, melted
- ½ teaspoon salt
- 1 cup water, for cooking

Directions:
1. Mix up together ground pork, diced onion, garlic, and salt. Then brush the mason jars with coconut oil. After this, fill every jar with ground pork mixture. Top the ground pork with kale and Cheddar cheese and place the jars on the trivet. Cover every jar with foil. Pour water in the instant pot and insert the trivet. Cook the casseroles on Manual (High pressure) for minutes. Then allow the natural pressure release for 10 minutes and remove the casserole from the instant pot.

Nutrition Info: calories 307, fat 1, fiber 0.3, carbs 0.2, protein 24

Pulled Pork Hash With Eggs

Servings: 4
Cooking Time: 15 Minutes
Ingredients:
- 4 eggs
- 10 oz pulled pork, shredded
- 1 teaspoon coconut oil
- 1 teaspoon red pepper

- 1 teaspoon fresh cilantro, chopped
- 1 tomato, chopped
- ¼ cup of water

Directions:
1. Melt the coconut oil in the instant pot on saute mode.
2. Then add pulled pork, red pepper, cilantro, water, and chopped tomato.
3. Cook the ingredients for 5 minutes.
4. Then stir it well with the help of the spatula and crack the eggs over it.
5. Close the lid.
6. Cook the meal on manual mode (high pressure) for 7 minutes. Then make a quick pressure release.

Nutrition Info:
Per Serving: calories 275, fat 3, fiber 0.6, carbs 5.7, protein 4

Classic Breakfast Casserole

Servings: 4
Cooking Time: 20 Minutes
Ingredients:
- 7 oz breakfast sausages, chopped
- 4 oz Monterey Jack cheese, shredded
- ½ red onion, sliced
- 1 bell pepper, diced
- 2 oz avocado, chopped
- 4 eggs, beaten
- ¼ cup heavy cream
- ½ teaspoon salt
- ½ teaspoon cayenne pepper
- 1 teaspoon coconut oil

Directions:
1. Toss the coconut oil in the instant pot and melt it on sauté mode. Then add onion and chopped breakfast sausages. Cook them on sauté mode for 5 minutes. Stir them from time to time. Then add bell pepper and cook the ingredients for 3 minutes more. Meanwhile, mix up together cheese, eggs, avocado, cayenne pepper, salt, and heavy cream. Pour the liquid over the breakfast sausages and close the lid. Cook the casserole on sauté mode for minutes or until the egg mixture is solid.

Nutrition Info: calories 417, fat 8, fiber 1.7, carbs 5.6, protein 23

Cheddar, Ham, And Chive Egg Cups

Servings: 4
Cooking Time: 10 Minutes
Ingredients:
- 4 large eggs
- ½ cup diced yellow onion

- ½ cup diced ham
- 2 tablespoons chopped chives
- ½ cup shredded cheddar cheese
- Salt and pepper
- ¼ cup heavy cream

Directions:

1. Whisk together the eggs, onions, ham, cheese, chives, and heavy cream in a bowl.
2. Season with salt and pepper then pour into four ½-pint jars.
3. Place the lids loosely on top of the jars and place them in the Instant Pot on a trivet.
4. Pour in 2 cups of water then close and lock the lid.
5. Press the Manual button and adjust the timer to minutes on High Pressure.
6. When the timer goes off, do a Quick Release by pressing Cancel and switching the steam valve to "venting."
7. When the pot has depressurized, open the lid.
8. Remove the jars from the Instant Pot and serve the eggs immediately.

Nutrition Info: calories 190 fat 14g ,protein 13g ,carbs 3g ,fiber 0.5g ,net carbs 2.5g

Egg Soup

Servings: 2
Cooking Time: 15 Minutes
Ingredients:

- 2 eggs, beaten
- 2 cups chicken broth
- 1 tablespoon chives, chopped
- ½ teaspoon salt
- ½ teaspoon chili flakes

Directions:

1. Pour chicken broth in the instant pot. Add chives, salt, and chili flakes. Saute the liquid for minutes. Then add beaten eggs and stir the soup well. Cook the soup for 5 minutes more.

Nutrition Info: calories 102, fat 5.8, fiber 0.1, carbs 1.3, protein 5

Keto "potato" Soup

Servings: 2
Cooking Time: 4 Minutes
Ingredients:

- 1 cup cauliflower, chopped
- 1 oz bacon, chopped, cooked
- 2 oz Cheddar cheese, shredded
- 2 tablespoons cream cheese
- 1 oz leek, chopped
- 1 cup of water
- ½ teaspoon salt
- ½ teaspoon cayenne pepper

Directions:

1. Pour water in the instant pot. Add cauliflower, cream cheese, leek, salt, and cayenne pepper. Close the lid and cook soup mixture for 4 minutes on Manual mode (high pressure). Allow the natural pressure release for minutes. Then add cheese and stir the soup until it is melted. With the help of the immersion blender, blend the soup until you get the creamy texture. Then ladle the soup in the serving bowls and top with bacon.

Nutrition Info: calories 248, fat 19, fiber 1.6, carbs 5.7, protein 3

Cheesy Coconut Cream

Servings: 4
Cooking Time: 20 Minutes
Ingredients:

- 2 tablespoons olive oil
- ½ cup spring onions, chopped
- 6 cups chicken stock
- A pinch of salt and black pepper
- 2 tablespoons parsley, chopped
- 2 cups coconut cream
- 1 cup cheddar cheese, grated

Directions:

1. Set your instant pot on Sauté mode, add the oil, heat it up, add the spring onions and sauté for 2-3 minutes. Add the rest of the ingredients, whisk, put the lid on and cook on High for minutes. Release the pressure naturally for 10 minutes, divide the soup into bowls and serve.

Nutrition Info: calories 313, fat 5, fiber 2, carbs 6.1, protein 7.4

Spinach Tomatoes Mix

Servings: 2
Cooking Time: 14 Mins
Ingredients:

- 2 tbsp Butter
- 1 Onion, chopped
- 2 cloves Garlic, minced
- 1 tbsp Cumin powder
- 1 tbsp Paprika
- 2 Tomatoes, chopped
- 2 cups Vegetable broth
- 1 small bunch of Spinach, chopped
- Cilantro for garnishing

Directions:

1. Melt the butter on Sauté mode. Add onion, garlic, and cumin powder, paprika, and vegetable broth; stir well. Add in tomatoes and spinach. Seal the lid, press Manual and cook on High pressure for minutes. When ready, do a quick pressure release.

Nutrition Info: Calories 125, Protein 7.7g, Net Carbs 8.3g, Fat 5.5g

Feta & Cauliflower Rice Stuffed Bell Peppers

Servings: 3
Cooking Time: 30 Mins
Ingredients:

- 1 green Bell Pepper
- 1 red Bell Pepper
- 1 yellow Bell Pepper
- ½ cup Cauliflower rice
- 1 cup Feta cheese
- 1 Onion, sliced
- 2 Tomatoes, chopped
- Salt and black pepper to taste
- 2-3 Garlic clove, minced
- 3 tbsp Lemon juice
- 3-4 green Olives, chopped
- 3-4 tbsp Olive oil
- Yogurt Sauce:
- 1 clove Garlic, pressed
- 1 cup Greek Yogurt
- Salt, to taste
- juice from 1 Lemon
- 1 tbsp fresh Dill

Directions:

1. Grease the Instant Pot with olive oil. Make a cut at the top of the bell peppers near the stem. Place feta cheese, onion, olives, tomatoes, cauliflower rice, salt, black pepper, garlic powder, and lemon juice into a bowl; mix well.
2. Fill up the bell peppers with the feta mixture and insert in the Instant Pot. Set on Manual and cook on High pressure for minutes. When the timer beeps, allow the pressure to release naturally for 5 minutes, then do a quick pressure release.
3. To prepare the yogurt sauce, combine garlic, yogurt, lemon juice, salt, and fresh dill.

Nutrition Info: Calories 388, Protein 5g, Net Carbs 7.9g, Fat 4g

Spinach Soup

Servings: 4
Cooking Time: 20 Minutes
Ingredients:

- 2 teaspoons olive oil
- 1 scallion, chopped
- 1 celery stalk, chopped
- 4 cups baby spinach

- 4 garlic cloves, minced
- 2 teaspoons cumin, ground
- 6 cups veggie stock
- 1 teaspoon basil, dried

Directions:
1. Set your instant pot on sauté mode, add the oil, heat it up, add the scallion and garlic and sauté for 5 minutes. Add the celery, cumin and the basil and sauté for 4 minutes more. Add the spinach and the stock, put the lid on and cook on High for minutes. Release the pressure naturally for 10 minutes, ladle the soup into bowls and serve.

Nutrition Info: calories 37, fat 3.1, fiber 1, carbs 3, protein 1.4

Artichokes Cream

Servings: 4
Cooking Time: 15 Minutes
Ingredients:
- 2 cups artichoke hearts, chopped
- 3 tablespoons ghee
- 6 cups chicken stock
- 1 shallot, chopped
- ¼ teaspoon lime juice
- 1 teaspoon rosemary, dried
- ½ cup coconut cream
- A pinch of salt and black pepper

Directions:
1. Set your instant pot on Sauté mode, add the ghee, heat it up, add the shallot and cook for 2 minutes. Add the rest of the ingredients, put the lid on and cook on High for minutes. Release the pressure naturally for 10 minutes, blend the soup using an immersion blender, ladle into bowls and serve.

Nutrition Info: calories 169, fat 6, fiber 0.3, carbs 3, protein 1.8

Kalua Chicken

Servings: 3
Cooking Time: 15 Minutes
Ingredients:
- 3 bacon slices
- ¼ teaspoon salt
- ¼ teaspoon of liquid smoked
- 6 chicken thighs, skinless, boneless
- 1/3 cup water

Directions:
1. Place the bacon at the bottom of the instant pot bowl. Sprinkle the chicken thighs with salt and liquid smoker and place over the bacon. Then add water, close and seal the lid. Cook the chicken on manual mode (high pressure) for minutes. When the time is over, allow the

natural pressure release and transfer the chicken tights on the chopping board. Shred the chicken and transfer it in the serving plates. Chop the cooked bacon. Sprinkle the cooked chicken with instant pot liquid and cooked bacon.

Nutrition Info: calories 363, fat 9, fiber 0, carbs 0.3, protein 45

Keto Coconut Almond Cake

Servings: 6
Cooking Time: 65 Mins
Ingredients:

- 1 ½ cups Almond flour
- 1 cup Shredded Coconut, unsweetened
- ½ cup Truvia
- 1 ½ tsp Baking Powder
- 1 ½ tsp Apple Pie Spice
- 4 Eggs
- ½ cup Melted Butter
- 1 cup Heavy Cream

Directions:

1. Pour all the dry ingredients into a bowl and mix well. Add the wet ingredients one after the other, mixing until fully incorporated. Grease an 8-inch cake tin and pour the batter into it.
2. Cover the tin with foil and A pinch the edges of the tin to tighten the foil. Pour cups of water into the Instant Pot and fit in a trivet with handles. Place the cake tin on the trivet.
3. Seal the lid, select Cake mode for 40 minutes on High. Once ready, do a natural pressure release for 10 minutes; then release the remaining pressure. Cool the cake, slice and serve.

Nutrition Info: Calories 235, Protein 2.9g, Net Carbs 2g, Fat 6.5g

Easy Shrimp

Servings: 2
Cooking Time: 9 Mins
Ingredients:

- 1 lb Shrimp, peeled and deveined
- 2 Garlic cloves, crushed
- 1 tbsp Butter.
- A pinch of red Pepper
- Salt and black pepper to taste
- 1 cup Parsley, chopped

Directions:

1. Melt butter on Sauté mode. Add shrimp, garlic, red pepper, salt and pepper. Cook for 5 minutes, stirring occasionally the shrimp until pink. Serve topped with parsley.

Nutrition Info: Calories 245, Protein 45g, Net Carbs 4.8g, Fat 4g

Asparagus Gremolata

Servings: 2
Cooking Time: 20 Mins
Ingredients:

- 1 lb Asparagus, hard ends cut off
- 1 cup Water
- Gremolata:
- 2 Lemons, zested
- 2 Oranges, zested
- 4 cloves Garlic, minced
- ½ cup Chopped Parsley
- Salt to taste
- Pepper to taste

Directions:

1. Mix all gremolata ingredients in a bowl; set aside. Pour water in the pot and fit a steamer basket. Add asparagus to the basket, seal the lid and cook on Steam for 4 minutes on High. Once ready, quickly release the pressure. Remove asparagus and serve with gremolata.

Nutrition Info: Calories 125, Protein 3g, Net Carbs 2g, Fat 3.4g

Cheddar Soup

Servings: 3
Cooking Time: 5 Minutes
Ingredients:

- 1 cup chicken broth
- 1 cup heavy cream
- 1 teaspoon xanthan gum
- 2 cups broccoli, chopped
- ½ cup cheddar cheese, shredded
- ½ teaspoon salt
- 1 teaspoon ground black pepper
- ½ teaspoon chili flakes
- 1 teaspoon ground cumin

Directions:

1. Pour chicken broth and heavy cream in the instant pot. Add broccoli, salt, ground black pepper, chili flakes, and ground cumin. Close and seal the lid. Cook the mixture on manual mode (high pressure) for 5 minutes. Then allow the natural pressure release for minutes and open the lid. Add xanthan gum and blend the soup with the help of the immersion blender. Ladle the soup in the bowls and top with cheddar cheese.

Nutrition Info: calories 252, fat 9, fiber 1.8, carbs 6.5, protein 9

Keto Carrot Cake

Servings: 6 To 8

Cooking Time: 70 Mins
Ingredients:
- 5 Eggs
- 1 ¼ cup Almond flour
- ½ cup Swerve Sweetener
- 1 tsp Baking Powder
- 1 ½ tsp Apple Pie Spice
- ½ cup Coconut Oil
- ½ cup Heavy Cream
- 1 ½ cup Carrots, shredded
- ½ cup Walnuts, chopped
- 2 cups Water

Directions:
1. Grease an 8-inch cake tin; set aside. Place all ingredients in a bowl, and mix evenly with a cake mixer. Pour the batter into the cake tin and cover the tin with foil. A pinch the edges of the pan to tighten the foil. Pour the water into the Instant Pot and fit in a trivet with handles.
2. Place the tin on top. Seal the lid, select Cake mode for 40 minutes on High. Once ready, do a natural release for 10 minutes; then quickly release the pressure. Let cool before slicing.

Nutrition Info: Calories 301, Protein 9g, Net Carbs 2g, Fat 29g

Coconut Soup

Servings: 4
Cooking Time: 13 Minutes
Ingredients:
- 2 cups of coconut milk
- 2 cups of water
- 1 teaspoon dried lemongrass
- 1 tablespoon lemon juice
- 1 teaspoon curry paste
- ½ cup white mushrooms, chopped
- 1 teaspoon butter

Directions:
1. Melt the butter in sauté mode. Add mushrooms and sauté them for 3 minutes. Then stir the vegetables and add lemongrass, lemon juice, and curry paste. Add water and coconut milk. Stir the mixture until the curry paste is dissolved. Close the lid and cook the soup on soup mode for minutes.

Nutrition Info: calories 296, fat 4, fiber 2.8, carbs 7.5, protein 3.1

Coconut Broccoli Soup

Servings: 4
Cooking Time: 15 Minutes
Ingredients:
- 1 broccoli head, florets separated

- 4 cups chicken stock
- A pinch of salt and white pepper
- ¼ teaspoon garlic powder
- 1 tablespoon chives, chopped
- 2 cups cheddar cheese, shredded
- 1 cup coconut cream

Directions:
1. In your instant pot, combine the broccoli with the stock and the rest of the ingredients except the cheese and the cream, stir, put the lid on and cook o High for minutes. Release the pressure naturally for 10 minutes, set the pot on Sauté mode again, add the cheese and the cream, stir, blend using an immersion blender, cook for 5 minutes more, divide into bowls and serve.

Nutrition Info: calories 376, fat 5, fiber 1.4, carbs 4.9, protein 2

Italian Style Salad

Servings: 2
Cooking Time: 5 Minutes
Ingredients:
- 8 oz shrimps, peeled
- 1 teaspoon Italian seasonings
- 1 teaspoon olive oil
- ½ cup cherry tomatoes, halved
- ¼ teaspoon chili flakes
- ½ teaspoon coconut oil

Directions:
1. Toss coconut oil in the instant pot. Melt it on sauté mode and add peeled shrimps. Cook the shrimps for minute from each side. Then place the shrimps in the bowl. Add chili flakes, Italian seasonings, halved cherry tomatoes, and olive oil. Shake the salad before serving.

Nutrition Info: calories 173, fat 5.5, fiber 0.5, carbs 3.5, protein 2

Crab Salad

Servings: 2
Cooking Time: 2 Minutes
Ingredients:
- 10 oz crab meat
- 1 tablespoon sour cream
- 1 tablespoon cream
- ¼ teaspoon minced garlic
- 1 tablespoon cream cheese
- ½ teaspoon lime juice
- ½ red onion, diced
- ¼ cup fresh cilantro, chopped
- ¼ cup fresh spinach, chopped

- ¼ teaspoon salt
- ¼ teaspoon ground cumin
- 1 cup water, for cooking

Directions:

1. Pour water in the instant pot. Line the trivet with the paper foil and insert the instant pot. Place the crab meat on the trivet and cook it on Manual mode (high pressure) for 2 minutes. Then make a quick pressure release and remove the crab meat from the instant pot. Chop it and place it in the salad bowl. Add diced onion, spinach, and cilantro. In the shallow bowl make the salad dressing: whisk together sour cream, cream, minced garlic, cream cheese, and lime juice. Then add salt and ground cumin. Add the dressing in the salad and stir it well.

Nutrition Info: calories 175, fat 6, fiber 0.8, carbs 6.4, protein 9

Zucchini And Lamb Stew

Servings: 4
Cooking Time: 30 Minutes
Ingredients:

- 2 tablespoons olive oil
- 2 zucchinis, sliced
- A pinch of salt and black pepper
- 1 pound lamb shoulder, cubed
- 2 tablespoons tomato passata
- ¼ cup veggie stock
- 1 teaspoon sweet paprika
- 1 tablespoon dill, chopped

Directions:

1. Set your instant pot on Sauté mode, add the oil, heat it up, the meat and brown for 5 minutes. Add the rest of the ingredients, put the lid on and cook on High for 25 minutes. Release the pressure naturally for minutes, divide the stew into bowls and serve.

Nutrition Info: calories 292, fat 6, fiber 1.5, carbs 4.5, protein 4

Mexican Cod Fillets

Servings: 3
Cooking Time: 20 Mins
Ingredients:

- 3 Cod fillets
- 1 Onion, sliced
- 2 cups Cabbage
- Juice from 1 Lemon
- 1 Jalapeno Pepper
- ½ tsp Oregano
- ½ tsp Cumin powder
- ½ tsp Cayenne Pepper

- 2 tbsp Olive oil
- Salt and black pepper to taste

Directions:
1. Heat the oil on Sauté, and add onion, cabbage, lemon juice, jalapeño pepper, cayenne pepper, cumin powder and oregano, and stir to combine. Cook for 8- minutes.
2. Season with salt and pepper. Arrange the cod in the sauce. Seal the lid and press Manual. Cook for 5 minutes on High pressure. When ready, do a quick release and serve.

Nutrition Info: Calories 306, Protein 21g, Net Carbs 6.8g, Fat 4g

Beef And Cauliflower Stew

Servings: 4
Cooking Time: 25 Minutes
Ingredients:
- 1 tablespoon olive oil
- 2 shallots, chopped
- A pinch of salt and black pepper
- 1 pound beef stew meat, cubed
- 15 ounces canned tomatoes, chopped
- 5 cups chicken stock
- 1 tablespoon cilantro, chopped

Directions:
1. Set your instant pot on Sauté mode, add the oil, heat it up, add the shallot and the meat and brown for 5 minutes. Add the rest of the ingredients, put the lid on and cook on High for 20 minutes.. Release the pressure naturally for minutes, divide the stew into bowls and serve.

Nutrition Info: calories 272, fat 5, fiber 1.3, carbs 5.1, protein 6

Eggplant Soup

Servings: 4
Cooking Time: 15 Minutes
Ingredients:
- 1 tablespoon avocado oil
- 1 celery stalk, chopped
- 1 shallot chopped
- 3 eggplants, cubed
- 2 tomatoes, chopped
- 8 cups chicken stock
- A pinch of salt and black pepper
- 2 tablespoons rosemary, chopped

Directions:
1. Set your instant pot on Sauté mode, add the oil, heat it up, add the shallot and celery, stir and sauté for 3 minutes. Add the eggplants and the rest of the ingredients, put the lid on and cook on High for minutes. Release the pressure naturally for 10 minutes, ladle the soup into bowls and serve.

Nutrition Info: calories 144, fat 5.7, fiber 0.2, carbs 5.3, protein 6.1

Fajita Soup

Servings: 4
Cooking Time: 20 Minutes
Ingredients:

- ¼ cup cream cheese
- 12 oz chicken fillet
- ½ teaspoon taco seasonings
- 2 bell peppers, chopped
- ½ cup canned tomatoes
- 3 cups beef broth
- ½ teaspoon salt
- ¼ cup heavy cream
- 1 jalapeno pepper, sliced
- 1 chili pepper, sliced
- 1 tablespoon butter
- ½ teaspoon minced garlic

Directions:

1. Melt the butter in sauté mode and add chicken fillet. Sprinkle it with taco seasonings, salt, and minced garlic. Cook it for 4 minutes from each side. After this, add cream cheese, canned tomatoes, cream, and bell peppers. Close the lid and cook the soup on manual mode (high pressure) for minutes. Then make a quick pressure release and open the lid. Shred the chicken with the help of the fork. Add sliced chili pepper and jalapeno pepper in the soup and cook it on sauté mode for 5 minutes more.

Nutrition Info: calories 320, fat 3, fiber 1.2, carbs 7.6, protein 4

Broccoli Rice With Mushrooms

Servings: 3
Cooking Time: 30 Mins
Ingredients:

- 2 tbsp Olive oil
- 1 small Red Onion, chopped
- 1 Carrot, chopped
- 2 cups Button Mushrooms, chopped
- ½ Lemon, zested and juiced
- Salt to taste
- Pepper to taste
- 2 cloves Garlic, minced
- ½ cup Broccoli rice
- ½ cup Chicken Stock
- 5 Cherry Tomatoes
- Parsley Leaves, chopped for garnishing

Directions:
1. Set on Sauté. Heat oil, and cook the carrots and onions for 2 minutes. Stir in mushrooms, and cook for 3 minutes. Stir in pepper, salt, lemon juice, garlic, and lemon zest.
2. Stir in broccoli and chicken stock. Drop the tomatoes over the top, but don't stir. Seal the lid, and cook on High pressure for 10 minutes. Once ready, do a natural pressure release for 4 minutes, then quickly release the remaining pressure. Sprinkle with parsley and stir evenly.

Nutrition Info: Calories 160, Protein 6g, Net Carbs 10g, Fat 2g

Pork Chops And Thyme Mushrooms

Servings: 4
Cooking Time: 25 Minutes
Ingredients:
- 3 garlic cloves, minced
- 1 tablespoon olive oil
- 1 spring onion, chopped
- 10 white mushrooms, sliced
- 4 pork chops, bone-in
- 1 cup beef stock
- 1 tablespoon thyme, chopped
- 1 cup coconut cream

Directions:
1. Set your instant pot on sauté mode, add oil, heat it up, add the garlic and the mushrooms and sauté for 2 minutes. Add the meat and brown it for 2-3 minutes more. Add the rest of the ingredients, put the lid on and cook on High for 20 minutes. Release the pressure naturally for minutes, divide everything between plates and serve.

Nutrition Info: calories 444, fat 38, fiber 2.2, carbs 6.3, protein 6

Salsa Chicken

Servings: 2
Cooking Time: 17 Minutes
Ingredients:
- ¼ cup hot salsa
- 10 oz chicken breast, skinless, boneless
- 1 teaspoon taco seasoning
- ¼ teaspoon salt
- ¼ teaspoon chili flakes
- 1 tablespoon cream cheese
- ¼ cup chicken broth

Directions:
1. Place the chicken breast in the instant pot. Sprinkle the poultry with taco seasoning, salt, and chili flakes. Then add cream cheese, salsa, and chicken broth. Close and seal the lid. Cook the meal on manual mode (high pressure) for minutes. Then allow the natural pressure

release for 10 minutes and shred the chicken. Serve the shredded chicken with hot sauce from the instant pot.

Nutrition Info: calories 198, fat 5.5, fiber 0.5, carbs 3.3, protein 5

Cayenne Pork And Artichokes Stew

Servings: 4
Cooking Time: 25 Minutes
Ingredients:

- 1 spring onion, chopped
- 2 and ½ pounds pork stew meat, cubed
- 15 ounces canned tomatoes, chopped
- 2 red chilies, chopped
- 1 and ½ cups canned artichoke hearts, chopped
- 2 garlic cloves, minced
- 2 tablespoons avocado oil
- 1 tablespoon cayenne pepper
- A pinch of salt and black pepper
- 1 teaspoon basil, dried

Directions:

1. Set your instant pot on sauté mode, add the oil, heat it up add the onion and the meat and brown for 5 minutes. Add the rest of the ingredients, put the lid on and cook on High for 20 minutes. Release the pressure naturally for minutes, divide the stew into bowls and serve.

Nutrition Info: calories 36, fat 6.4, fiber 2.1, carbs 3.5, protein 1.4

Stuffed Cabbages

Servings: 4
Cooking Time: 1 Hour 40 Min
Ingredients:

- 1 medium Cabbage, cut into halves
- 1 ½ cups Cauliflower, riced
- ½ lb Ground Beef
- ¼ Chopped Parsley
- 2 cloves Garlic, minced
- 1 Egg, beaten
- Salt and black pepper to taste
- 1 tsp Oregano
- ½ cup Tomato Sauce
- ¼ cup Sour Cream
- 1 tbsp Swerve Sweetener

Directions:

1. Pour cup of water in the pot and lower a steamer basket. Place the halves of the cabbage on the basket. Seal the lid, select Manual mode and cook on High pressure for 5 minutes.

2. Once ready, quickly release the pressure. Remove the cabbage, let it cool and remove as many large leaves off it as possible. Set aside.
3. In a bowl, add garlic, salt, beef, egg, and cauli rice; mix well. In another bowl, mix the sour cream, tomato sauce, swerve and ¼ cup of water. Pour half of the tomato sauce in a casserole. Set aside.
4. Lay each cabbage leaf on a flat surface, scoop 2 tbsp of the beef mixture onto each leaf and roll. Arrange the rolls in the casserole dish and pour the remaining tomato sauce over the rolls. Bake it in the oven at 350 F for 1 hour. Flip the cabbages 30 minutes into baking.

Nutrition Info: Calories 290, Protein 2g, Net Carbs 1g, Fat 13g

Spinach Almond Tortilla

Servings: 3
Cooking Time: 15 Mins
Ingredients:
- 1 cup Almond flour + extra for dusting
- 1 cup Spinach, chopped
- ¼ tbsp Chili flakes
- ¼ cup Mushrooms, sliced
- Salt and black pepper to taste
- 2 tbsp Olive oil

Directions:
1. In a bowl, combine flour, mushrooms, spinach, salt, and flakes; mix well. Add ¼ cup of water and make a thick batter. Roll out the batter until is thin. Heat oil on Sauté mode.
2. Cook the tortilla for 5 minutes until golden brown. Serve with cilantro sauce and enjoy.

Nutrition Info: Calories 165, Protein 5g, Net Carbs 2.1g, Fat 9g

Faux Beet Risotto

Servings: 2
Cooking Time: 20 Mins
Ingredients:
- 4 Beets, tails and leafs removed
- 2 tbsp Olive oil
- 1 big head Cauliflower, cut into florets
- 4 tbsp cup Full Milk
- 2 tsp Red Chili Flakes
- Salt and black pepper to taste
- ½ cup Water

Directions:
1. Pour the water in the Instant Pot and fit a steamer basket. Place the beets and cauliflower in the basket. Seal the lid, and cook on High Pressure mode for 4 minutes.
2. Once ready, do a natural pressure release for 10 minutes, then quickly release the pressure. Remove the steamer basket with the vegetables and discard water. Remove the beets' peels.

3. Place veggies back to the pot, add salt, pepper, and flakes. Mash with a potato masher. Hit Sauté, and cook the milk for 2 minutes. Stir frequently. Dish onto plates and drizzle with oil.

Nutrition Info: Calories 153, Protein 3.6g, Net Carbs 2.5g, Fat 9g

Chicken Paprika

Servings: 2
Cooking Time: 25 Minutes
Ingredients:
- 2 chicken thighs, skinless, boneless
- 2 tablespoons ground paprika
- 1 tablespoon almond meal
- 1 teaspoon tomato paste
- ½ teaspoon dried celery root
- ½ cup heavy cream
- 1 tablespoon butter
- ½ teaspoon salt
- ½ teaspoon white pepper
- ¼ teaspoon ground nutmeg
- 1 tablespoon lemon juice

Directions:
1. Melt butter in sauté mode. Meanwhile, rub the chicken thighs with salt and white pepper. Cook the chicken thighs on sauté mode for 4 minutes from each side. Meanwhile, in the mixing bowl combine together almond meal, dried celery root, and ground nutmeg. In the separated bowl combine together heavy cream, tomato paste, and lemon juice. Pour the heavy cream liquid in the chicken. Then add almond meal mixture and stir gently. Cook the meal on meat mode for minutes.

Nutrition Info: calories 476, fat 3, fiber 3.3, carbs 6.5, protein 8

Clean Salmon With Soy Sauce

Servings: 2
Cooking Time: 35 Mins
Ingredients:
- 2 Salmon fillets
- 2 tbsp Avocado oil
- 2 tbsp Soy sauce
- 1 tbsp Garlic powder
- 1 tbsp fresh Dill to garnish
- Salt and black pepper to taste

Directions:
1. To make the marinade, thoroughly mix the soy sauce, avocado oil, salt, pepper and garlic powder into a bowl. Dip salmon in the mixture and place in the refrigerator for 20 minutes.
2. Transfer the contents to the Instant pot. Seal, set on Manual and cook for 10 minutes on high pressure. When ready, do a quick release. Serve topped with the fresh dill.

Nutrition Info: Calories 512, Protein 65g, Net Carbs 3.2g, Fat 21g

Scallops With Mushroom Special

Servings: 2
Cooking Time: 25 Mins
Ingredients:

- 1 lb Scallops
- 2 Onions, chopped
- 1 tbsp Butter
- 2 tbsp Olive oil
- 1 cup Mushrooms
- Salt and black pepper to taste
- 1 tbsp Lemon juice
- ½ cup Whipping Cream
- 1 tbsp chopped fresh Parsley

Directions:

1. Heat the oil on Sauté. Add onions, butter, mushrooms, salt and pepper. Cook for 3 to 5 minutes. Add the lemon juice and scallops. Lock the lid and set to Manual mode.
2. Cook for 15 minutes on High pressure. When ready, do a quick pressure release and carefully open the lid. Top with a drizzle of cream and fresh parsley.

Nutrition Info: Calories 312, Protein 31g, Net Carbs 7.3g, Fat 4g

Shredded Chicken Salad

Servings: 4
Cooking Time: 12 Minutes
Ingredients:

- 9 oz Chinese cabbage, shredded
- 10 oz chicken fillet
- ½ teaspoon lemon juice
- ¼ cup heavy cream
- 1 teaspoon white pepper
- ½ cup of water
- ½ teaspoon salt
- ½ teaspoon ground turmeric
- ¼ teaspoon dried sage
- 1 tablespoon cream cheese
- 1 tablespoon sour cream
- ½ teaspoon dried dill

Directions:

1. Rub the chicken fillet with white pepper, salt, ground turmeric, and dried sage. Place it in the instant pot. Add water and heavy cream. Close and seal the lid Cook the chicken on manual mode (high pressure) for minutes. Then make a quick pressure release. Remove the chicken fillet from the instant pot and shred it. Put the shredded chicken in the salad bowl.

Add sour cream and cream cheese in the instant pot (to the cream mixture). Then add dill and stir it. Sprinkle the salad with lemon juice and ½ of the cream mixture from the instant pot. Mix up the salad well.

Nutrition Info: calories 187, fat 9.7, fiber 0.9, carbs 2.4, protein 22

Bone Broth Soup

Servings: 2
Cooking Time: 10 Minutes
Ingredients:
- 1 eggplant, trimmed, chopped
- 2 cups bone broth
- ¼ cup carrot, grated
- 1 tablespoon butter
- ½ teaspoon salt
- 1 teaspoon dried dill

Directions:
1. In the mixing bowl combine together eggplants and salt. Leave the vegetables for 5 minutes. Meanwhile, toss the butter in the instant pot and melt it on sauté mode. Add grated carrot and cook it for 2 minutes. Meanwhile, dry the eggplants. Add them in the carrot and stir. Sprinkle the vegetables with dried dill. Then add bone broth and close the lid. Cook the soup for 5 minutes on Manual mode (high pressure). Then make a quick pressure release.

Nutrition Info: calories 200, fat 6.2, fiber 8.5, carbs 1, protein 5

Provolone Chicken Soup

Servings: 4
Cooking Time: 18 Minutes
Ingredients:
- 3 oz bacon, chopped
- 10 oz chicken fillet, chopped
- 3 oz Provolone cheese, grated
- 1 tablespoon cream cheese
- 1 white onion, diced
- ½ teaspoon salt
- ½ teaspoon ground black pepper
- 1 teaspoon dried parsley
- 1 garlic clove, diced
- 4 cups of water

Directions:
1. Place the chopped bacon in the instant pot and cook it for 5 minutes on sauté mode. Stir it from time to time to avoid burning. After this, transfer the cooked bacon in the plate and dry little with the paper towel. Then add onion and diced garlic in the instant pot. Sauté the vegetables for 2 minutes and add chicken and cream cheese. Stir well and sauté the ingredients for 5 minutes. After this, add salt, ground black pepper, dried parsley, water, and

95

Provolone cheese. Stir the soup mixture well. Close the lid and cook the soup for 5 minutes on manual mode (high pressure). Then make a quick pressure release. Add the cooked bacon in the soup. Stir the cooked soup well before serving.

Nutrition Info: calories 346, fat 7, fiber 0.7, carbs 3.8, protein 4

No Crust Tomato And Spinach Quiche

Servings: 3
Cooking Time: 40 Mins
Ingredients:

- 14 large Eggs
- 1 cup Full Milk
- Salt and black pepper to taste
- 4 cups fresh Baby Spinach, chopped
- 3 Tomatoes, diced
- 3 Scallions, sliced
- 2 Tomato, sliced into firm rings
- ½ cup Parmesan Cheese, shredded
- Water for boiling

Directions:

1. Place the trivet in the pot and pour in ½ cups of water. Break the eggs into a bowl, add salt, pepper, and milk and whisk it. Share the diced tomatoes, spinach and scallions into 3 ramekins, gently stir, and arrange 3 slices of tomatoes on top in each ramekin.
2. Sprinkle with Parmesan cheese. Gently place the ramekins in the pot, and seal the lid. Select Manual and cook on High Pressure for minutes. Once ready, quickly release the pressure.
3. Carefully remove the ramekins and use a paper towel to tap soak any water from the steam that sits on the quiche. Brown the top of the quiche with a fire torch.

Nutrition Info: Calories 310, Protein 12g, Net Carbs 0g, Fat 27g

Lime Pork Bowls

Servings: 6
Cooking Time: 20 Minutes
Ingredients:

- 2 pounds pork stew meat, cubed
- 1 teaspoon garlic, minced
- 1 shallot, chopped
- 1 tablespoon beef stock
- 2 teaspoon lime juice
- ½ teaspoon chili powder
- 1 teaspoon sweet paprika
- ½ cup tomato passata
- 1 tablespoon olive oil
- A pinch of salt and black pepper

Directions:

1. Set your instant pot on sauté mode, add the oil, heat it up, add the shallot, garlic and the meat and brown for 5 minutes. Add the rest of the ingredients, put the lid on and cook on High for minutes. Release the pressure naturally for 10 minutes, divide the mix between plates and serve.

Nutrition Info: calories 351, fat 1, fiber 0.6, carbs 2.4, protein 20

Simple Salmon With Eggs

Servings: 3
Cooking Time: 10 Mins
Ingredients:

- 1 lb Salmon, cooked, mashed
- 2 Eggs, whisked
- 2 Onions, chopped
- 2 stalks celery, chopped
- 1 cup Parsley, chopped
- 1 tbsp Olive oil
- Salt and black pepper to taste

Directions:

1. Mix salmon, onion, celery, parsley, and salt and pepper, in a bowl. Form into 6 patties about inch thick and dip them in the whisked eggs. Heat oil in the Instant pot on Sauté mode.
2. Add the patties to the pot and cook on both sides, for about 5 minutes and transfer to the plate. Allow to cool and serve.

Nutrition Info: Calories 331, Protein 38g, Net Carbs 5.3g, Fat 16g

Pork And Baby Spinach

Servings: 4
Cooking Time: 20 Minutes
Ingredients:

- 1 pound pork stew meat, cubed
- 1 tablespoon olive oil
- ½ cup shallots, chopped
- 1 cup red bell peppers, chopped
- 2 garlic cloves, minced
- 1 cup beef stock
- 1 teaspoon chili powder
- 4 cups baby spinach

Directions:

1. Set your instant pot on sauté mode, add the oil, heat it up, add the meat and shallots and brown for 5 minutes. Add the rest of the ingredients except the spinach, put the lid on and cook on High for minutes. Release the pressure naturally for 10 minutes, set the pot on Sauté mode again, add the spinach, toss, cook everything for 5 minutes more, divide between plates and serve.

Nutrition Info: calories 310, fat 9, fiber 1.3, carbs 7.6, protein 3

Chicken And Avocado Mix

Servings: 8
Cooking Time: 17 Minutes
Ingredients:

- 2 chicken breasts, skinless, boneless and halved
- 2 cups tomato passata
- A pinch of salt and black pepper
- 2 avocados, peeled, pitted and cubed
- 1 cup cheddar cheese, shredded
- 1 tablespoon olive oil

Directions:

1. Set your instant pot on sauté mode, add the oil, heat it up, add the chicken and brown for 5 minutes. Add the rest of the ingredients except the cheese and toss. Sprinkle the cheese on top, put the lid on and cook on High for minutes. Release the pressure naturally for 10 minutes, divide everything between plates and serve.

Nutrition Info: calories 198, fat 4, fiber 4.6, carbs 6.6, protein 5.4

Spiral Ham

Servings: 5
Cooking Time: 12 Minutes
Ingredients:

- 1-pound spiral ham, sliced
- 1 tablespoon Erythritol
- 2 tablespoons butter, melted
- ½ teaspoon minced ginger
- 1 teaspoon mustard
- 1 cup water, for cooking

Directions:

1. In the shallow bowl combine together Erythritol, butter, minced ginger, and mustard. Then pour water and insert the trivet in the instant pot. Line the trivet with foil. Brush the spiral ham with butter mixture generously and transfer the ham in the instant pot. Cook the ham on manual mode (high pressure) for minutes. When the time is over, make a quick pressure release and open the lid. Place the cooked spiral ham in the serving plate.

Nutrition Info: calories 237, fat 6, fiber 0.1, carbs 7.6, protein 3

Butternut Squash Soup

Servings: 6
Cooking Time: 25 Minutes
Ingredients:

- 2 cups butternut squash, chopped
- 2 garlic cloves, peeled, diced
- 1 teaspoon curry powder

- ½ teaspoon ginger, minced
- 1 white onion, diced
- 1 teaspoon salt
- 1 teaspoon ground paprika
- 1 tablespoon butter
- 5 cups chicken broth
- 2 tablespoons Ricotta cheese

Directions:
1. Melt butter in sauté mode. Then add garlic and onion. Saute the vegetables until they are golden brown. Then add butternut squash, ginger, salt, ground paprika, and ricotta cheese. Then add curry powder and chicken broth. Close the lid and cook the soup on manual mode (high pressure) for minutes. Then make a quick pressure release. Blend the soup with the help of the immersion blender.

Nutrition Info: calories 87, fat 3.6, fiber 1.4, carbs 8.7, protein 5.5

Aromatic Lasagna With Basil

Servings: 6
Cooking Time: 10 Minutes
Ingredients:
- 2 eggplants, peeled, sliced
- 1 cup ground pork
- 3 tablespoons marinara sauce
- 1 white onion, diced
- 1 oz fresh basil, chopped
- ½ cup Ricotta cheese
- ½ cup Mozzarella, shredded
- ½ teaspoon dried oregano
- ¼ teaspoon salt
- 1 cup water, for cooking

Directions:
1. In the mixing bowl combine together ground pork, diced onion, basil, and dried oregano. Add salt and stir the meat mixture well with the help of the spoon. Line the baking pan with paper foil. Then place the sliced eggplants in the baking pan to make the layer. Sprinkle the eggplants with marinara sauce. Top the marinara sauce with ground pork mixture. Then spread the mixture with Ricotta cheese and shredded Mozzarella. Cover the lasagna with foil. Pour water in the instant pot and insert the trivet. Place the lasagna on the trivet and close the lid. Cook the lasagna for minutes on manual mode (high pressure). Then make a quick pressure release. Cool the cooked lasagna little before serving.

Nutrition Info: calories 251, fat 5, fiber 7.2, carbs 9, protein 7

Chicken And Mustard Sauce

Servings: 4
Cooking Time: 15 Minutes

...ss, boneless and halved

... taste

...stard
...il, chopped

...ur instant pot on sauté mode, add the oil, heat it up, add the chicken and brown for 2-3 ...inutes. Add the rest of the ingredients, put the lid on and cook on High for minutes. Release the pressure naturally for 10 minutes, divide everything between plates and serve.
Nutrition Info: calories 34, fat 3.6, fiber 0.1, carbs 0.7, protein 0.3

Spinach Saag

Servings: 3
Cooking Time: 10 Minutes
Ingredients:
- 1-pound spinach, chopped
- 2 tablespoons ghee
- 1 teaspoon garam masala
- ½ teaspoon ground coriander
- 1 teaspoon salt
- ½ teaspoon ground thyme
- ½ teaspoon cayenne pepper
- ½ teaspoon ground turmeric
- 1 teaspoon minced garlic
- ¼ cup of water

Directions:
1. Place ghee in the instant pot and melt it on sauté mode. After this, add garam masala, ground coriander, salt, thyme, cayenne pepper, turmeric, and minced garlic. Stir the mixture and cook it for minute. Then add spinach and water. Mix up the greens well with the help of the spatula. Close the lid and cook the meal on sauté mode for 5 minutes. Switch off the instant pot. Open the lid and blend the spinach until you get a smooth puree. Place the spinach saag in the serving plates.

Nutrition Info: calories 114, fat 9.2, fiber 3.6, carbs 6.3, protein 4.5

Tilapia Delight

Servings: 4
Cooking Time: 16 Mins
Ingredients:
- 4 Tilapia fillets

- 4 tbsp Lemon juice
- 2 tbsp Butter
- 2 Garlic cloves
- ½ cup Parsley
- Salt and black pepper to taste

Directions:
1. Melt butter on Sauté and add garlic cloves, parsley, salt, and pepper. Cook for 2 to 3 minutes. Then, add tilapia and lemon juice and stir well. Seal the lid and set on Manual mode. Cook for minutes on High pressure. When the timer beeps, allow the pressure to release naturally, for 5 minutes.

Nutrition Info: Calories 135, Protein 7g, Net Carbs 1.3g, Fat 4.4g

Creamed Savoy Cabbage

Servings: 3
Cooking Time: 20 Mins
Ingredients:
- 2 medium Savoy Cabbages, finely chopped
- 2 small Onions, chopped
- 2 cups Bacon, chopped
- 2 ½ cups Mixed Bone Broth, see recipe above
- ¼ tsp Mace
- 2 cups Coconut Milk
- 1 Bay Leaf
- Salt to taste
- 3 tbsp Chopped Parsley

Directions:
1. Set on Sauté. Add the bacon crumbles and onions; cook until crispy. Add bone broth and scrape the bottom of the pot. Stir in bay leaf and cabbage. Cut out some parchment paper and cover the cabbage with it.
2. Seal the lid, select Manual mode and cook on High Pressure for 4 minutes. Once ready, press Cancel and quickly release the pressure. Select Sauteé, stir in the milk and nutmeg. Simmer for 5 minutes, add the parsley.

Nutrition Info: Calories 27, Protein 4g, Net Carbs 3.1g, Fat 3g

Kale Soup

Servings: 4
Cooking Time: 17 Minutes
Ingredients:
- 3 cups of water
- 9 oz sausages, chopped
- 2 oz Parmesan
- ½ cup heavy cream
- 2 cups kale, chopped

- ½ teaspoon ground black pepper
- ¼ onion, diced
- 1 teaspoon dried basil
- 1 tablespoon olive oil

Directions:

1. Pour olive oil in the instant pot and add the onion. Saute the onion for 3 minutes. Then stir well and add sausages. Mix up well and cook them for 3 minutes. After this, add water, kale, basil, and ground black pepper. Saute the mixture for 8 minutes. Then add heavy cream and Parmesan. Close the lid and cook the soup on manual mode (high pressure) for 3 minutes. Then make a quick pressure release. Let the cooked kale soup cool for -15 minutes before serving.

Nutrition Info: calories 364, fat 2, fiber 0.7, carbs 5.3, protein 4

Chicken & Dumplings Soup

Servings: 4
Cooking Time: 25 Minutes
Ingredients:

- 4 cups chicken broth
- 4 chicken wings
- ½ onion, diced
- 1 tablespoon dried dill
- ½ teaspoon salt
- ¼ cup coconut flour
- 2 tablespoons water
- 1 teaspoon ghee

Directions:

1. In the mixing bowl combine together water and coconut flour. Knead the non-sticky dough. Add more coconut flour if the dough is sticky. Then make the log from the dough and cut it into pieces. After this, place the ghee in the instant pot and preheat it on sauté mode. When the ghee is melted, add diced onion and cook it until light brown. After this, add chicken wings, dried ill, and salt. Add chicken broth and close the lid. Cook the soup on manual mode (high pressure) for minutes. Then make a quick pressure release. Open the lid and add prepared dough pieces (dumplings). Sauté the soup for 5 minutes more.

Nutrition Info: calories 179, fat 9.5, fiber 3.5, carbs 8, protein 9

Beef Cabbage Soup

Servings: 6
Cooking Time: 15 Minutes
Ingredients:

- 1 cup white cabbage, shredded
- ½ cup kale, chopped
- 11 oz beef sirloin, chopped
- ½ teaspoon salt

102

- 1 teaspoon dried basil
- ½ teaspoon fennel seeds
- ½ teaspoon ground black pepper
- 1 garlic clove, diced
- 1 teaspoon almond butter
- 5 cups of water

Directions:

1. Put almond butter in the instant pot and melt it on sauté mode. Add white cabbage and diced garlic. Cook the vegetables for 5 minutes. Stir them occasionally. Then add chopped beef sirloin, fennel seeds, ground black pepper, salt, and stir well. Add basil and water. Then add kale and close the lid. Cook the soup on Manual mode (high pressure) for 5 minutes. Then make a quick pressure release.

Nutrition Info: calories 120, fat 4.8, fiber 0.8, carbs 2.1, protein 7

Lazy Meat Mix

Servings: 2
Cooking Time: 45 Minutes
Ingredients:

- 3 oz chicken fillet, chopped
- 4 oz pork chops, chopped
- 4 oz beef sirloin, chopped
- 1 onion, chopped
- 1 teaspoon tomato paste
- 1 teaspoon dried rosemary
- 1 cup of water
- ½ teaspoon salt
- 1 teaspoon olive oil

Directions:

1. Preheat the olive oil on sauté mode. Then add chicken, pork chops, and beef sirloin. Add onion and cook the ingredients for 3 minutes. Then stir them well and add tomato paste, dried rosemary, water, and salt. Stir it well until tomato paste is dissolved. Then close the lid and cook the meat mix on meat mode for 40 minutes.

Nutrition Info: calories 414, fat 3, fiber 1.6, carbs 6, protein 43

Chili Mushrooms Stew

Servings: 4
Cooking Time: 15 Minutes
Ingredients:

- 2 spring onions, chopped
- 2 teaspoons avocado oil
- 2 garlic cloves, minced
- 1 teaspoon chili powder
- A pinch of salt and black pepper

- 6 cups mushrooms, sliced
- 2 cups veggie stock
- 1 cup tomato passata
- 1 tablespoon chives, chopped

Directions:

1. Set your instant pot on Sauté mode, add the oil, heat it up, add the onions and the garlic and sauté for 2 minutes. Add the mushrooms and sauté for 2 minutes more. Add the rest of the ingredients except the cilantro, put the lid on and cook on High for minutes. Release the pressure naturally for 10 minutes, divide the stew into bowls and serve with the chives sprinkled on top.

Nutrition Info: calories 56, fat 4.5, fiber 2.2, carbs 3.7, protein 4.7

Shrimp With Linguine

Servings: 4
Cooking Time: 20 Mins
Ingredients:

- 1 lb Shrimp, cleaned
- 1 lb Linguine
- 1 tbsp Butter
- ½ cup white Wine
- ½ cup Parmesan cheese, shredded
- 2 Garlic cloves, minced
- 1 cup Parsley, chopped
- Salt and black pepper to taste
- ½ cup Coconut Cream, for garnish
- ½ Avocado, diced, for garnish
- 2 tbsp fresh Dill, for garnish

Directions:

1. Melt the butter on Sauté. Stir in linguine, garlic cloves and parsley. Cook for 4 minutes until aromatic. Add shrimp and white wine; season with salt and pepper, seal the lid.
2. Select Manual and cook for 5 minutes on High pressure. When ready, quick release the pressure. Unseal and remove the lid. Press Sauté, add the cheese and stir well until combined, for 30-40 seconds. Serve topped with the coconut cream, avocado, and dill.

Nutrition Info: Calories 412, Protein 48g, Net Carbs 5.6g, Fat 21g

Chili Verde

Servings: 2
Cooking Time: 3 Hours 5 Minutes
Ingredients:

- 9 oz pork shoulder, chopped
- ½ cup salsa Verde
- 1 teaspoon sesame oil
- ½ cup chicken broth

- ¼ teaspoon cayenne pepper
- ¼ teaspoon salt

Directions:
1. Pour sesame oil in the instant pot and preheat it on sauté mode for 3 minutes. Meanwhile, mix up together pork shoulder, cayenne pepper, and salt. Add the pork shoulder in the hot oil and sauté the meat for 2 minutes. Then stir it with the help of the spatula and add chicken broth and salsa Verde. Close the lid. Cook the meal on manual (low pressure) for 3 hours. When the time is over, shred the meat.

Nutrition Info: calories 418, fat 1, fiber 0.3, carbs 2.9, protein 7

Keto Taco Soup

Servings: 5
Cooking Time: 25 Minutes
Ingredients:
- 2 cups ground beef
- 1 teaspoon onion powder
- 1 teaspoon taco seasonings
- 1 garlic clove, diced
- 1 teaspoon chili flakes
- 1 teaspoon ground cumin
- 1 tablespoon tomato paste
- ½ cup heavy cream
- 5 cups of water
- 1 teaspoon coconut oil
- 1 tablespoon cream cheese
- 1 jalapeno pepper, sliced

Directions:
1. Toss the coconut oil in the instant pot and melt it on sauté mode. Add ground beef and onion powder. After this, add taco seasonings and diced garlic. Mix up the ingredients well. Then sprinkle the meat mixture with chili flakes and ground cumin. Saute the ground beef for minutes. Mix it up with the help of the spatula every 3 minutes. Then add tomato paste, heavy cream, and water. Add sliced jalapeno pepper and close the lid. Cook the soup on Manual (high pressure) for 10 minutes. Then allow the natural pressure release for 10 minutes and ladle the soup into the bowls.

Nutrition Info: calories 170, fat 7, fiber 0.3, carbs 2.4, protein 2

Asian Style Zucchini Soup

Servings: 4
Cooking Time: 25 Minutes
Ingredients:
- ½ teaspoon minced ginger
- ¼ teaspoon minced garlic
- 1 teaspoon coconut oil

- 10 oz beef sirloin steak, chopped
- ½ cup cremini mushrooms, sliced
- 4 cups chicken broth
- ½ teaspoon salt
- 1 zucchini, trimmed
- 1 teaspoon chives, chopped

Directions:
1. Heat up instant pot on sauté mode. Toss coconut oil and melt it. Then add minced ginger and minced garlic. Stir well and add chopped steak. Sauté the mixture for 5 minutes. Meanwhile, with the help of the spiralizer make the zucchini noodles. Add mushrooms in the beef mixture. Then sprinkle it with salt. Add chicken broth and cook the soup on Manual mode (high pressure) for minutes. Then make a quick pressure release and open the lid. Add spiralized noodles and stir the soup. Let it rest for 5 minutes. Top the cooked soup with chives.

Nutrition Info: calories 191, fat 7, fiber 0.6, carbs 3.2, protein 2

Tortilla Soup

Servings: 2
Cooking Time: 30 Minutes
Ingredients:
- ½ Poblano pepper, chopped
- ¼ teaspoon minced garlic
- ¼ teaspoon ground coriander
- ½ cup tomatoes, canned
- 1 tablespoon dried cilantro
- ¼ teaspoon salt
- 2 cups chicken broth
- 8 oz chicken breast, skinless, boneless
- 1 tablespoon lemon juice
- 1 teaspoon butter
- ¼ cup Cheddar cheese, shredded
- 2 low carb tortillas, chopped

Directions:
1. Melt butter in sauté mode. When the butter is melted, add chopped Poblano pepper, minced garlic, ground coriander, and dried cilantro. Add chicken breast and cook the ingredients for minutes. Stir them from time to time. After this, add canned tomatoes, salt, and chicken broth. Close the lid and cook the soup on manual mode (high pressure) for 15 minutes. Then make a quick pressure release and open the lid. Add lemon juice and sauté the soup for 5 minutes more. Ladle the soup into the bowls and top with Cheddar cheese and chopped low carb tortillas.

Nutrition Info: calories 336, fat 13, fiber 8.3, carbs 1, protein 2

Squash Spaghetti With Bolognese Sauce

Servings: 3
Cooking Time: 15 Mins
Ingredients:
- 1 large Squash, cut into 2 and seed pulp removed
- 2 cups Water
- Bolognese Sauce to serve

Directions:
1. Place the trivet and add the water. Add in the squash, seal the lid, select Manual and cook on High Pressure for 8 minutes. Once ready, quickly release the pressure. Carefully remove the squash; use two forks to shred the inner skin. Serve with bolognese sauce.

Nutrition Info: Calories 37, Protein 0.9g, Net Carbs 7.8g, Fat 0.4g

Smoky Pulled Pork

Servings: 4
Cooking Time: 20 Minutes
Ingredients:
- 1-pound pork loin
- 1 teaspoon smoked paprika
- ½ teaspoon liquid smoke
- ½ teaspoon ground coriander
- ½ teaspoon salt
- 1 teaspoon onion powder
- 1 teaspoon tomato paste
- 1 cup chicken broth

Directions:
1. Put the pork loin in the instant pot. Add smoked paprika, liquid smoke, ground coriander, salt, onion powder, tomato paste, and chicken broth. Close the lid and cook the pork on manual mode (high pressure) for 20 minutes. When the time is over, make a quick pressure release and open the lid. Remove the pork loin from the instant pot and shred it. Place the cooked pulled pork in the bowl and sprinkle it with ½ part of liquid from the instant pot.

Nutrition Info: calories 233, fat 8, fiber 0.3, carbs 1.3, protein 7

Lemon Carnitas

Servings: 4
Cooking Time: 30 Minutes
Ingredients:
- 13 oz pork butt, chopped
- ¼ cup white onion, diced
- 1 teaspoon ghee
- ½ teaspoon garlic powder
- 1 tablespoon lemon juice

- ¼ teaspoon grated lemon zest
- ½ teaspoon chipotle powder
- 1 cup of water
- ½ teaspoon salt
- 1 cup lettuce leaves

Directions:

1. Put pork butt, white onion, ghee, garlic powder, lemon juice, grated lemon zest, and chipotle powder in the instant pot. Saute the ingredients for 5 minutes. Then mix up the meat mixture with the help of the spatula and add salt and water. Close and seal the lid and cook ingredients on manual mode (high pressure) for 25 minutes. When the time is over, make a quick pressure release and open the lid. Shred the cooked pork with the help of the fork. Then fill the lettuce leaves with shredded pork.

Nutrition Info: calories 194 fat 7.3, fiber 0.3, carbs 1.4, protein 9

Green Beans With Ham

Servings: 3
Cooking Time: 6 Minutes
Ingredients:

- 2 cups green beans, chopped
- 7 oz ham, chopped
- ½ white onion, chopped
- 1 teaspoon olive oil
- ½ teaspoon salt
- ½ teaspoon ground nutmeg
- 1 cup water, for cooking

Directions:

1. Pour water and insert the steamer rack in the instant pot. Place the green bean, ham, and onion in the rack and close the lid. Cook the ingredients on steam mode for 6 minutes. Then make a quick pressure release and transfer the ingredients in the big bowl. Sprinkle them with ground nutmeg, salt, and olive oil. Stir well.

Nutrition Info: calories 153, fat 7.5, fiber 3.8, carbs 9.7, protein 5

Chicken And Brussels Sprouts Stew

Servings: 4
Cooking Time: 25 Minutes
Ingredients:

- 1 tablespoon avocado oil
- 2 scallions, chopped
- 1 pound chicken breasts, skinless, boneless and cubed
- ½ pound Brussels sprouts, halved
- 1 teaspoon basil, chopped
- 1 and ½ cups chicken stock
- A pinch of salt and black pepper

- 1 tablespoon tomato paste

Directions:
1. Set your instant pot on Sauté mode, add the oil, heat it up, add the scallions and the chicken and brown for 5 minutes. Add the remaining ingredients, put the lid on and cook on High for 20 minutes. Release the pressure naturally for minutes, divide the stew into bowls and serve.

Nutrition Info: calories 250, fat 9.1, fiber 2.7, carbs 6.7, protein 1

Egg Fried Cauli Rice

Servings: 3
Cooking Time: 20 Mins
Ingredients:
- 2 heads Cauliflower, cut in big chunks
- 8 Eggs, beaten
- 3 tbsp Butter
- 5 cloves Garlic, minced
- 1 large White Onion, chopped
- 2 tsp Olive oil
- 2 tsp Soy Sauce
- Salt to taste
- ½ cup Water

Directions:
1. Pour water in the Instant Pot and fit in a steamer basket. Place the cauli chunks in the basket. Seal the lid and cook on High Pressure for minute. Once ready, quickly release the pressure.
2. Remove the cauli chunks onto a plate. Discard the water in the pot and clean dry. Select Sauté, and melt olive oil and butter. Add the eggs and stir frequently to break as they cook.
3. Add onions and garlic, stir and cook for 2 minutes. Add cauli chunks, and use a masher to break the chunks into a rice-like consistency. Stir in soy sauce and salt, and cook for more minutes. Serve cauli rice as a side dish.

Nutrition Info: Calories 47, Protein 4g, Net Carbs 2g, Fat 2.8g

Zucchini Noodles In Parmesan Toss

Servings: 4
Cooking Time: 20 Mins
Ingredients:
- 3 large Zucchinis, spiralized
- 2 tbsp Olive oil
- 3 cloves Garlic, minced
- 1 Lemon, zested and juiced
- Salt and black pepper to taste
- 5 Mint Leaves, chopped
- 6 tbsp Parmesan Cheese, grated

Directions:

1. Set on Sauté. Heat the oil, and add lemon zest, garlic, and salt. Stir and cook for 30 seconds. Add zucchini and pour lemon juice over. Coat the noodles quickly but gently with the oil. Cook for seconds, press Cancel. Sprinkle the mint leaves and cheese over and toss gently.

Nutrition Info: Calories 15, Protein 10g, Net Carbs 2g, Fat 2g

Basil Shrimp And Eggplants

Servings: 4
Cooking Time: 10 Minutes
Ingredients:

- 2 eggplants, cubed
- 2 tablespoons veggie stock
- 2 tablespoons olive oil
- A pinch of salt and black pepper
- 4 garlic cloves, minced
- 1 pound shrimp, peeled and deveined
- Juice of 1 lime
- ½ teaspoon sweet paprika
- 2 tablespoons basil, chopped

Directions:

1. Set your instant pot on sauté mode, add the oil, heat it up, add the garlic and the eggplants and sauté for 2 minutes. Add the shrimp and the rest of the ingredients, put the lid on and cook on Low for 8 minutes. Release the pressure naturally for minutes, divide everything into bowls and serve for lunch.

Nutrition Info: calories 269, fat 9.5, fiber 5.4, carbs 6.7, protein 8

Cod And Shrimp Stew

Servings: 4
Cooking Time: 14 Minutes
Ingredients:

- 1 and ½ pounds shrimp, peeled and deveined
- 1 and ½ pounds cod fillets, boneless, skinless and cubed
- 20 ounces canned tomatoes, chopped
- 3 garlic cloves, minced
- 2 tablespoons parsley, chopped
- 2 cups veggie stock
- 1 tablespoon basil, dried
- A pinch of salt and black pepper

Directions:

1. In your instant pot, mix the shrimp with the cod and the rest of the ingredients, put the lid on and cook on High for minutes. Release the pressure fast for 5 minutes, divide the stew into bowls and serve.

Nutrition Info: calories 130, fat 7.5, fiber 1.8, carbs 6.4, protein 1.5

Green Beans Soup

Servings: 4
Cooking Time: 15 Minutes
Ingredients:
- 2 tablespoons olive oil
- 1 shallot, chopped
- 1 teaspoon garlic, minced
- 1 red bell pepper, chopped
- 8 cups chicken stock
- 1 and ½ pounds green beans, trimmed and halved
- 1 cup tomatoes, chopped
- 1 tablespoon chili powder
- 1 cup coconut cream

Directions:
1. Set your instant pot on sauté mode, add the oil, heat it up, add the shallot and the garlic and sauté for 2 minutes. Add the rest of the ingredients, put the lid on and cook on High for minutes. Release the pressure naturally for 10 minutes, divide the soup into bowls and serve.

Nutrition Info: calories 242, fat 9, fiber 2.8, carbs 8.9, protein 3.7

Simple Mushroom Chicken Mix

Servings: 2
Cooking Time: 18 Mins
Ingredients:
- 2 Tomatoes, chopped
- ½ lb Chicken, cooked and mashed
- 1 cup Broccoli, chopped
- 1 tbsp Butter
- 2 tbsp Mayonnaise
- ½ cup Mushroom soup
- Salt and black pepper to taste
- 1 Onion, sliced

Directions:
1. Once cooked, put the chicken into a bowl. In a separate bowl, mix the mayo, mushroom soup, tomatoes, onion, broccoli, and salt and pepper. Add the chicken.
2. Grease a round baking tray with butter. Put the mixture in a tray. Add cups of water into the Instant Pot and place the trivet inside. Place the tray on top. Seal the lid, press Manual and cook for 14 minutes on High pressure. When ready, do a quick release.

Nutrition Info: Calories 561, Protein 5g, Net Carbs 6.3g, Fat 5g

Creamy Brussels Sprouts Stew

Servings: 4
Cooking Time: 25 Minutes

Ingredients:
- 1 tablespoon olive oil
- 2 shallots, chopped
- 1 pound Brussels sprouts, halved
- A pinch of salt and black pepper
- 1 cup chicken stock
- 1 cup coconut cream
- 1 tablespoon chives, chopped

Directions:
1. Set your instant pot on Sauté mode, add the oil, heat it up, add the shallots and sauté for 5 minutes. Add the rest of the ingredients except the chives, put the lid on and cook on High for 20 minutes. Release the pressure fast for 5 minutes, add the chives, stir the stew, divide it into bowls and serve.

Nutrition Info: calories 220, fat 7, fiber 5.6, carbs 6.8, protein 5.4

Turkey Stew

Servings: 4
Cooking Time: 20 Minutes
Ingredients:
- 1 turkey breast, skinless, boneless and cubed
- 1 teaspoon olive oil
- A pinch of salt and black pepper
- 1 tablespoon avocado oil
- 1 celery stalk, chopped
- 2 cups chicken stock
- 2 cups tomatoes, chopped
- 1 tablespoons cilantro, chopped

Directions:
1. Set your instant pot on Sauté mode, add the oil, heat it up, add the meat and cook for 5 minutes. Add the rest of the ingredients, put the lid on and cook on High for minutes. Release the pressure naturally for 10 minutes, divide the stew into bowls and serve.

Nutrition Info: calories 81, fat 4.3, fiber 1.5, carbs 6, protein 8.6

Mushroom And Chicken Soup

Servings: 4
Cooking Time: 20 Minutes
Ingredients:
- 1 shallot, chopped
- 1 quart chicken stock
- 1 pound mushrooms, sliced
- 1 tablespoon olive oil
- A pinch of salt and black pepper
- 2 tablespoons ginger, minced

- 1 pound chicken breast, skinless, boneless and cubed

Directions:
1. Set your instant pot on sauté mode, add the oil, heat it up, add the shallot and the mushrooms and cook for 4 minutes. Add the rest of the ingredients, put the lid on and cook on High for minutes. Release the pressure naturally for 10 minutes, divide everything into bowls and serve.

Nutrition Info: calories 203, fat 7.4, fiber 1.5, carbs 6.4, protein 5

Lemoned Broccoli

Servings: 3
Cooking Time: 15 Mins
Ingredients:
- 1 lb Broccoli, cut in biteable sizes
- 3 Lemon Slices
- Salt to taste
- Pepper to taste

Directions:
1. Pour the ¼ cup Water into the Instant Pot. Add the broccoli and sprinkle with lemon juice, pepper, and salt. Seal the lid, secure the pressure valve, and Manual in Low Pressure mode for 3 minutes. Once ready, quickly release the pressure. Drain the broccoli and serve as a side dish.

Nutrition Info: Calories 34, Protein 2.8g, Net Carbs 5.6g, Fat 0.4g

Cobb Salad

Servings: 4
Cooking Time: 21 Minutes
Ingredients:
- 1-pound chicken breast, skinless, boneless
- 1 avocado, pitted, peeled
- 4 eggs
- 1 cup lettuce, chopped
- 1 tablespoon lemon juice
- ¼ teaspoon salt
- ½ teaspoon white pepper
- ½ cup white cabbage, shredded
- 4 oz Feta cheese, crumbled
- 1 tablespoon coconut oil
- ½ teaspoon chili flakes
- 1 tablespoon heavy cream
- 1 tablespoon apple cider vinegar
- ½ teaspoon garlic powder
- 1 cup water, for cooking

Directions:

1. Pour water and insert the trivet in the instant pot. Place the eggs on the trivet and close the lid. Cook them in manual mode (high pressure) for 5 minutes. Then make a quick pressure release. Cool the eggs in ice water. Then peel the eggs. Cut the eggs and avocado into the wedges. After this, rub the chicken breast with lemon juice, salt, and coconut oil. Place the chicken breast in the instant pot and cook it on sauté mode for 7 minutes from each side. The cooked chicken should be light brown. Make the sauce: whisk together chili flakes, olive oil, heavy cream, apple cider vinegar, and garlic powder. In the big salad bowl combine together lettuce, eggs, avocado, white pepper, white cabbage, and crumbled feta. Chop the cooked chicken roughly and add in the salad. Shake the salad well. Then sprinkle the cooked cobb salad with sauce.

Nutrition Info: calories 417, fat 9, fiber 3.8, carbs 7.4, protein 9

Kale Stew

Servings: 4
Cooking Time: 20 Minutes
Ingredients:
- 1 shallot, chopped
- 2 garlic cloves, minced
- 1 pound kale, torn
- 20 ounces canned tomatoes, chopped
- 2 tablespoons olive oil
- A pinch of salt and black pepper
- ½ teaspoon cayenne pepper
- 1 tablespoon parsley, chopped

Directions:
1. Set the instant pot on Sauté mode, add the oil, heat it up, add the shallot and garlic and cook for 2 minutes. Add the other ingredients, put the lid on and cook on High for minutes. Release the pressure naturally for 10 minutes, divide the stew into bowls and serve.

Nutrition Info: calories 145, fat 7.3, fiber 3.5, carbs 5.2, protein 4.8

Vegetable En Papillote

Servings: 3
Cooking Time: 20 Mins
Ingredients:
- 1 cup Green Beans
- 4 small Carrots, widely julienned
- Salt and black pepper to taste
- 1 clove Garlic, crushed
- 2 tbsp Butter
- 2 slices Lemon
- 1 tbsp Chopped Thyme
- 1 tbsp Oregano
- 1 tbsp Chopped Parsley

- 17 inch Parchment Paper

Directions:
1. Add all ingredients, except lemon slices and butter, in a bowl and toss. Place the paper on a flat surface and add the mixed ingredients at the center of the paper. Put the lemon slices on top and drop the butter over. Wrap it up well.
2. Pour 1 cup of water in and lower the trivet with handle. Put the veggie pack on the trivet, seal the lid, and cook on High Pressure for minutes. Once ready, do a quick release. Carefully remove the packet and serve veggies in a wrap on a plate.

Nutrition Info: Calories 60, Protein 3g, Net Carbs 1g, Fat 3g

Delicious Creamy Crab Meat

Servings: 3
Cooking Time: 15 Mins
Ingredients:
- 1 lb Crab meat
- ½ cup Cream cheese
- 2 tbsp Mayonnaise
- Salt and black pepper to taste
- 1 tbsp Lemon juice
- 1 cup Cheddar cheese, shredded

Directions:
1. Mix mayo, cream cheese, salt and pepper, and lemon juice in a bowl. Add in crab meat and make small balls. Place the balls inside the pot. Seal the lid and press Manual.
2. Cook for 10 minutes on High pressure. When done, allow the pressure to release naturally for 10 minutes. Sprinkle the cheese over and serve!

Nutrition Info: Calories 443, Protein 41g, Net Carbs 2.5g, Fat 4g

Lobster Salad

Servings: 4
Cooking Time: 4 Minutes
Ingredients:
- 4 lobster tails, peeled
- 1 teaspoon avocado oil
- ¼ teaspoon salt
- 2 cucumbers, chopped
- ¼ cup whipped cream
- 1 tablespoon apple cider vinegar
- 1 teaspoon dried dill
- ½ cup celery stalk, chopped
- 1 cup water, for cooking

Directions:
1. Pour water and insert the trivet in the instant pot. Arrange the lobster tails on the trivet and cook them on Manual mode (high pressure) for 4 minutes. Then make a quick pressure

release. Cool the cooked lobster tails little and chop them roughly. Place the chopped lobster tails in the salad bowl. Add cucumbers, dried ill, and celery stalk. After this, make the salad sauce: in the shallow bowl combine together salt, avocado oil, whipped cream, dill, and apple cider vinegar. Sprinkle the salad with sauce and mix up it well with the help of 2 spoons.

Nutrition Info: calories 139, fat 3.7, fiber 1, carbs 6.3, protein 1.3

Shrimp And Olives Stew

Servings: 4
Cooking Time: 10 Minutes
Ingredients:

- 1 and ½ pounds shrimp, peeled and deveined
- 1 cup black olives, pitted and halved
- 2 tablespoons olive oil
- 2 scallions, chopped
- 2 tomatoes, cubed
- 1 tablespoon sweet paprika
- ½ cup chicken stock

Directions:

1. Set your instant pot on Sauté mode, add the oil, heat it up, add the scallions and cook for 2 minutes. Add the rest of the ingredients, put the lid on and cook on Low for 8 minutes. Release the pressure naturally for minutes, divide the stew into bowls and serve.

Nutrition Info: calories 118, fat 11, fiber 2.7, carbs 6.1, protein 1.3

Healthy Halibut Fillets

Servings: 2
Cooking Time: 15 Mins
Ingredients:

- 2 Halibut fillets
- 1 tbsp Dill
- 1 tbsp Onion powder
- 1 cup Parsley, chopped
- 2 tbsp Paprika
- 1 tbsp Garlic powder
- 1 tbsp Lemon Pepper
- 2 tbsp Lemon juice

Directions:

1. Mix lemon juice, lemon pepper, garlic powder, and paprika, parsley, dill and onion powder in a bowl. Pour the mixture in the Instant pot and place the halibut fish over it.
2. Seal the lid, press Manual mode and cook for 10 minutes on High pressure. When ready, do a quick pressure release by setting the valve to venting.

Nutrition Info: Calories 283, Protein 5g, Net Carbs 6.2g, Fat 4g

Parsley Meatloaf

Servings: 7
Cooking Time: 30 Minutes
Ingredients:

- 2 cups ground beef
- 1 tablespoon parsley, chopped
- 1 teaspoon minced garlic
- 1 egg, beaten
- 1 teaspoon chili powder
- 2 oz Parmesan, grated
- 1 teaspoon butter, melted
- 1 tablespoon pork rinds
- 1 cup water, for cooking

Directions:

1. In the big bowl combine together ground beef, parsley, minced garlic, egg, chili powder, Parmesan, and pork rinds. Mix up the mixture until smooth. After this, pour water and insert the rack in the instant pot. Line the rack with foil and place the ground beef mixture on it. Make the shape of the meatloaf with the help of the fingertips. Then brush the surface of meatloaf with butter and close the lid. Cook the meatloaf for 30 minutes on Manual mode (high pressure). Then make a quick pressure release. Cool the meatloaf well.

Nutrition Info: calories 127, fat 8.4, fiber 0.2, carbs 0.7, protein 2

Chicken & Mushroom Bowl

Servings: 2
Cooking Time: 20 Minutes
Ingredients:

- 1 cup cremini mushrooms, sliced
- 10 oz chicken breast, skinless, boneless, chopped
- ½ cup heavy cream
- 1 teaspoon salt
- ½ teaspoon ground paprika
- ½ teaspoon cayenne pepper
- 1 tablespoon coconut oil

Directions:

1. Melt coconut oil in the instant pot on sauté mode. Add cremini mushrooms and sauté them for 5 minutes. After this, add chopped chicken breast. Sprinkle the ingredients with salt, ground paprika, and cayenne pepper. Cook them for 5 minutes more. Then add heavy cream and close the lid. Cook the meal on poultry mode for minutes.

Nutrition Info: calories 336, fat 6, fiber 0.5, carbs 2.9, protein 7

Meat & Collard Greens Bowl

Servings: 4

Cooking Time: 18 Minutes

Ingredients:
- 1 cup ground pork
- 2 cups collard greens, chopped
- 1 tablespoon butter
- ½ teaspoon salt
- 1 teaspoon minced garlic
- 1 teaspoon ground paprika
- 1 teaspoon ground turmeric
- ¼ cup chicken broth

Directions:
1. Melt the butter in sauté mode and add ground pork. Sprinkle it with salt, minced garlic, ground paprika, and ground turmeric. Cook the ground pork on sauté mode for minutes. Stir it from time to time to avoid burning. After this, add collard greens and chicken broth. Cook the meal on manual mode (high pressure) for 5 minutes. When the time is finished, make a quick pressure release. Mix up the cooked meal well before serving.

Nutrition Info: calories 271, fat 5, fiber 1.1, carbs 2.2, protein 1

Southwestern Chili

Servings: 2

Cooking Time: 25 Minutes

Ingredients:
- 1 cup ground beef
- ¼ cup celery stalk, chopped
- ¼ onion, chopped
- 1 teaspoon chili powder
- ¼ teaspoon salt
- 1 tablespoon tomato paste
- 1 cup chicken stock
- 1 teaspoon butter
- ½ teaspoon smoked paprika
- 1 tablespoon salsa

Directions:
1. Put the butter in the instant pot bowl. Add ground beef and cook it on sauté mode for 5 minutes. Then stir the ground beef and sprinkle it with chili powder, salt, smoked paprika, and salsa. Add tomato paste, onion, and celery stalk. Add chicken stock. Close the lid and cook chili on stew mode for 20 minutes.

Nutrition Info: calories 173, fat 7, fiber 1.6, carbs 5.1, protein 3

Bell Peppers And Kale Soup

Servings: 4

Cooking Time: 15 Minutes

Ingredients:

- 4 red bell peppers, deseeded and roughly chopped
- ½ pound kale, torn
- A pinch of salt and black pepper
- 1 cup tomato passata
- 4 cups chicken stock
- 1 tablespoon cilantro, chopped

Directions:

1. In your instant pot, mix the bell peppers with the kale and the rest of the ingredients, put the lid on and cook on High for minutes. Release the pressure naturally for 10 minutes, ladle the soup into bowls and serve.

Nutrition Info: calories 100, fat 6.3, fiber 2.2, carbs 3.7, protein 2

Greek Turkey And Sauce

Servings: 4
Cooking Time: 25 Minutes
Ingredients:

- 1 turkey breast, skinless, boneless and cubed
- 1 tablespoon lime juice
- 1 cup Greek yogurt
- 1 cup tomato passata
- 1 tablespoon avocado oil
- 1 tablespoon garam masala
- ¼ teaspoon ginger, grated
- A pinch of salt and black pepper

Directions:

1. Set the instant pot on Sauté mode, add the oil, heat it up, add the turkey, ginger and garam masala, stir and brown for 5 minutes. Add the rest of the ingredients, toss, put the lid on and cook on High for 20 minutes. Release the pressure naturally for minutes, divide the mix between plates and serve.

Nutrition Info: calories 20, fat 4.6, fiber 1.1, carbs 3.6, protein 0.9

Warm Radish Salad

Servings: 4
Cooking Time: 11 Minutes
Ingredients:

- 3 cups radish, sliced
- 7 oz chicken fillet, chopped
- 1 tablespoon lemon juice
- 1 teaspoon olive oil
- ¼ teaspoon salt
- 1 teaspoon butter
- 1 tablespoon dried parsley
- ½ teaspoon sesame oil

Directions:

1. Mix up together chopped chicken fillet with lemon juice, olive oil, and salt. Place the chicken in the instant pot and cook it on sauté mode for 3 minutes from each side. Then add radish and butter, and sauté the ingredients for 5 minutes. Transfer the cooked salad in the bowl. Add dried parsley and sesame oil. Mix up the salad.

Nutrition Info: calories 133, fat 6.5, fiber 1.4, carbs 3.1, protein 15

Lunch Pot Roast

Servings: 4
Cooking Time: 60 Minutes
Ingredients:

- 1-pound beef chuck pot roast, chopped
- 1 cup turnip, chopped
- 1 cup zucchini, chopped
- 1 garlic clove, diced
- 1 teaspoon salt
- 1 teaspoon coconut aminos
- 1 teaspoon ground black pepper
- 1 teaspoon butter
- 2 cups of water

Directions:

1. Put all ingredients in the instant pot and close the lid. Set meat mode and cook the meal for 60 minutes. When the time is over, open the lid and stir the ingredients carefully with the help of the spoon.

Nutrition Info: calories 269, fat 5, fiber 1.1, carbs 3.6, protein 2

Garlic Buttered Sprouts

Servings: 2
Cooking Time: 15 Mins
Ingredients:

- ½ lb Brussels Sprouts, trimmed and washed
- ½ cup Water
- 3 tbsp Butter
- 4 clove Garlic, minced
- ½ cup Parmesan Cheese, grated

Directions:

1. Pour the water in the Instant Pot and fit a steamer basket. Add the brussels sprouts to the basket. Seal the lid and cook on High Pressure mode for 3 minutes.
2. Once ready, quickly release the pressure, open the lid and remove the basket. Discard the water and clean dry. Select Sauté, melt the butter and cook the garlic for 1 minute. Add the brussel sprouts; toss evenly. Press Cancel. Serve sprouts and garnish with Parmesan.

Nutrition Info: Calories 38, Protein 3g, Net Carbs 0g, Fat 2g

Parsley Beef Bowls

Servings: 6
Cooking Time: 20 Minutes
Ingredients:

- 2 pounds beef roast, thinly sliced
- 1 tablespoon parsley, chopped
- 3 garlic cloves, minced
- A pinch of salt and black pepper
- ½ cup veggie stock
- 1 tablespoon lemon juice
- 2 tablespoons olive oil
- 1 teaspoon balsamic vinegar
- 1 cup feta cheese, crumbled

Directions:

1. Set the instant pot on Sauté mode, add the oil, heat it up, add the meat and garlic and brown for 5 minutes. Add salt, pepper and the rest of the ingredients except the cheese, put the lid on and cook on High for minutes. Release the pressure naturally for 10 minutes, divide the mix into bowls, sprinkle the cheese on top and serve for lunch.

Nutrition Info: calories 390, fat 4, fiber 0.1, carbs 1.6, protein 9.5

Tomato And Pork Soup

Servings: 4
Cooking Time: 25 Minutes
Ingredients:

- 1 and ½ pounds pork stew meat, cubed
- 8 cups chicken stock
- 15 ounces tomatoes, chopped
- A pinch of salt and black pepper
- 1 tablespoon chives, chopped

Directions:

1. In your instant pot, mix all the ingredients except the chives, put the lid on and cook on High for 25 minutes. Release the pressure naturally for minutes, divide the soup into bowls and serve.

Nutrition Info: calories 39, fat 4.3, fiber 1.2, carbs 3.4, protein 2.4

Bell Pepper Cream

Servings: 4
Cooking Time: 20 Minutes
Ingredients:

- 1 shallot, chopped
- 2 tablespoons olive oil
- 4 red bell peppers, roughly chopped

- 2 tomatoes, cubed
- 3 tablespoons tomato paste
- 6 cups chicken stock
- ½ teaspoon red pepper flakes
- 1 teaspoon chives, chopped

Directions:

1. Set the instant pot on Sauté mode, add the oil, heat it up, add the shallot and cook for 2 minutes Add the rest of the ingredients except the chives, put the lid on and cook on High for minutes. Release the pressure naturally for 10 minutes, blend the soup using an immersion blender, divide it into bowls and serve.

Nutrition Info: calories 134, fat 8.4, fiber 2.8, carbs 5.4, protein 3.3

Turkey Breasts With Chicken Sausage

Servings: 8
Cooking Time: 25 Minutes
Ingredients:

- 1 (3-pound turkey breast, skinless, boneless and butterflied
- Salt, to taste
- 1/4 teaspoon freshly ground black pepper, or more to taste
- 1/2 teaspoon cayenne pepper
- 6 ounces chicken sausage, removed from casing
- 3 ounces bacon, finely diced
- 1 cup button mushrooms, thinly sliced
- 1 teaspoon garlic, pressed
- 1 tablespoon fresh basil, roughly chopped
- 1 tablespoon fresh parsley, roughly chopped
- 1 tablespoon olive oil

Directions:

1. Pat dry the turkey breast with kitchen towels. Lay the turkey breast flat on a cutting board. Sprinkle it with salt, black pepper, and cayenne pepper.
2. Press the "Sauté" button to heat up your Instant Pot. Cook chicken sausage, bacon, and mushrooms for 3 to 4 minutes.
3. Stir in the garlic, basil, and parsley, and cook an additional minute. Spread this stuffing mixture on the turkey breast; roll the turkey around the stuffing and wrap kitchen twine around the breast.
4. Press the "Sauté" button again. Heat olive oil and sear turkey breasts for 2 minutes per side.
5. Clean the Instant Pot and add 1 ½ cups of water and trivet to the inner pot. Lower the stuffed turkey breast onto the trivet.
6. Secure the lid. Choose "Manual" mode and High pressure; cook for 20 minutes. Once cooking is complete, use a natural pressure release; carefully remove the lid. Bon appétit!

Nutrition Info:

Per Serving: 517 Calories; 3g Fat; 0.9g Total Carbs; 4g Protein; 0g Sugars

Two-cheese Chicken Drumsticks

Servings: 5
Cooking Time: 25 Minutes
Ingredients:

- 1 tablespoon olive oil
- 5 chicken drumsticks
- 1/2 teaspoon marjoram
- 1/2 teaspoon thyme
- 1 teaspoon shallot powder
- 2 garlic cloves, minced
- 1/2 cup chicken stock
- 1/4 cup dry white wine
- 1/4 cup full-fat milk
- 6 ounces ricotta cheese
- 4 ounces cheddar cheese
- 1/4 teaspoon ground black pepper
- 1/2 teaspoon cayenne pepper
- Sea salt, to taste

Directions:

1. Press the "Sauté" button and heat the oil. Once hot, brown chicken drumsticks for 3 minutes; turn the chicken over and cook an additional 3 minutes,
2. Now, add marjoram, thyme, shallot powder, garlic, chicken stock, wine, and milk.
3. Secure the lid. Choose the "Manual" setting and cook for 15 minutes. Once cooking is complete, use a natural pressure release; carefully remove the lid.
4. Shred the chicken meat and return to the Instant Pot. Press the "Sauté" button and stir in ricotta cheese, cheddar cheese, black pepper, and cayenne pepper.
5. Cook for a couple of minutes longer or until the cheese melts and everything is heated through.
6. Season with sea salt, taste and adjust the seasonings. Bon appétit!

Nutrition Info:
Per Serving: 409 Calories; 8g Fat; 4.8g Carbs; 7g Protein; 2.4g Sugars

Two-cheese Turkey Bake

Servings: 8
Cooking Time: 30 Minutes
Ingredients:

- 2 pounds turkey breasts
- 2 garlic cloves, halved
- Sea salt and ground black pepper, to taste
- 1 teaspoon paprika
- 1 tablespoon butter
- 10 slices Colby cheese, shredded

- 2/3 cup mayonnaise
- 1/3 cup sour cream
- 1 cup Romano cheese, preferably freshly grated

Directions:
1. Rub the turkey breast with garlic halves; now, sprinkle with salt, black pepper, and paprika.
2. Press the "Sauté" button to heat up the Instant Pot. Melt the butter and sear the turkey breast for to 3 minutes per side.
3. In a mixing bowl, combine shredded Colby cheese, mayonnaise, sour cream, 1/2 cup of grated Romano.
4. Spread this mixture over turkey breast; top with the remaining Romano cheese.
5. Secure the lid. Choose "Manual" mode and High pressure; cook for 20 minutes. Once cooking is complete, use a quick pressure release; carefully remove the lid. Bon appétit!

Nutrition Info:
Per Serving: 472 Calories; 33g Fat; 3.2g Carbs; 9g Protein; 0.7g Sugars

Basil Balsamic Chicken

Servings: 4
Cooking Time: 35 Minutes
Ingredients:
- 1 tbsp dried basil
- 6 garlic cloves, minced
- Salt and black pepper to taste
- ½ tsp smoked paprika
- 4 chicken thighs, skinless and boneless
- 2 tbsp olive oil
- 4 tbsp balsamic vinegar
- 1 lemon, zested and juiced
- 1 cup chicken broth
- 1 large white onion, diced

Directions:
1. In a medium bowl, combine the basil, garlic, salt, black pepper, and paprika. Season the chicken on both sides with the spice mixture.
2. Set the IP in Sauté mode and adjust to Medium heat.
3. Heat the olive oil in the inner pot and sear the chicken in the oil on both sides until golden brown, 7 minutes. Transfer to a plate and set aside.
4. Pour the balsamic vinegar, lemon zest, lemon juice, and chicken broth into the inner pot. Stir and scrape the bottom of the pot to release any stuck bits. Mix in the chicken broth, onion, and add the chicken.
5. Lock the lid in place; select Manual mode on High Pressure and set the timer to 18 minutes.
6. After cooking, perform a natural pressure release for 10 minutes, then a quick pressure release to let out the remaining steam and open the lid.
7. Dish the food and serve warm.

Nutrition Info:
Per Serving: Calories 148 Fats 07g Carbs 6.05g Net Carbs 5.85g Protein 26g

Indian Chicken Korma

Servings: 3
Cooking Time: 15 Minutes
Ingredients:

- 9 oz chicken fillet, chopped
- ½ teaspoon minced ginger
- ¼ teaspoon minced garlic
- ¼ teaspoon Serrano pepper, chopped
- ½ tomato, chopped
- 1 tablespoon peanuts, chopped
- 1 teaspoon ghee
- 1 cup of water
- ¼ teaspoon fennel seeds
- ¼ teaspoon cumin seeds
- ½ teaspoon ground coriander
- ½ teaspoon ground cumin
- ½ teaspoon smoked paprika
- ½ teaspoon salt
- ½ teaspoon ground turmeric
- ¼ teaspoon ground cinnamon
- ¼ teaspoon ground cardamom
- 1 teaspoon garam masala

Directions:

1. Blend the minced ginger, garlic, Serrano pepper, and tomato until smooth. Then mix up together the blended mixture with chicken. After this, blend peanuts with ¼ cup of water. Place the chicken mixture and ghee in the instant pot. Add fennel seeds, cumin seeds, ground coriander, cumin, paprika, salt, turmeric, cinnamon, cardamom, and garam masala. Carefully stir the chicken with the help of the spatula. Add remaining water and close the lid. Cook the meal on manual (high pressure) for minutes. Then make the quick pressure release and open the lid. Add the blended peanut mixture and close the lid. Cook the chicken korma for 5 minutes on stew mode.

Nutrition Info: calories 199, fat 9.4, fiber 0.9, carbs 2.1, protein 7

Duck And Hot Eggplant Mix

Servings: 4
Cooking Time: 30 Minutes
Ingredients:

- 2 duck legs, skinless, boneless and cubed
- 1 tablespoon olive oil
- 2 eggplants, sliced
- A pinch of salt and black pepper
- 1 tablespoon hot paprika

- 2 tablespoons tomato paste
- 2 cups chicken stock
- 1 and ½ teaspoons chili powder
- 1 tablespoon cilantro, chopped

Directions:

1. Set your instant pot on Sauté mode, add the oil, heat it up, add the meat and the rest of the ingredients except the eggplants, stock and cilantro, toss and cook for 5 minutes. Add the eggplant and stock, put the lid on and cook on High for 25 minutes. Release the pressure naturally for minutes, divide the mix between plates and serve with the cilantro sprinkled on top.

Nutrition Info: calories 338, fat 17, fiber 2.6, carbs 6.6, protein 30

Bacon-wrapped Tenders

Servings: 2
Cooking Time: 15 Minutes
Ingredients:

- 4 oz chicken fillet
- 2 bacon slices
- ½ teaspoon ground paprika
- ¼ teaspoon salt
- 1 teaspoon olive oil
- 1 cup water, for cooking

Directions:

1. Cut the chicken fillet on 2 tenders and sprinkle them with salt, ground paprika, and olive oil.
2. Wrap the chicken tenders in the bacon and transfer in the steamer rack,
3. Pour water and insert the steamer rack with the chicken tenders in the instant pot.
4. Close and seal the lid and cook the meal on manual mode (high pressure) for 15 minutes.
5. When the time is finished, allow the natural pressure release for 10 minutes.

Nutrition Info:
Per Serving: calories 232, fat 5, fiber 0.2, carbs 0.6, protein 5

Turkey Green Beans Chili

Servings: 4
Cooking Time: 39 Minutes
Ingredients:

- 1 lb. ground turkey
- 1 medium yellow onion, diced
- 2 garlic cloves, minced
- 2 tbsp tomato paste
- Salt and black pepper to taste
- 1 cup chopped green beans
- 2 cups chicken broth
- 1 (8 oz) can tomato sauce

- 1 cup chopped tomatoes
- 2 green chilies, chopped
- 1 tsp cumin powder
- 2 tsp chili powder
- ¼ cup grated cheddar cheese

Directions:

1. Set the IP in Sauté mode and adjust to Medium heat.
2. Add the turkey to the inner pot and cook until brown while occasionally stirring, 6 minutes. Mix in the onion, garlic, tomato paste, salt, and black pepper, and cook until the onion softens, 3 minutes.
3. Mix the remaining ingredients except for the cheddar cheese.
4. Lock the lid in place; select Manual mode on High Pressure and set the timer to 13 minutes.
5. Allow the IP to sit uncovered for 10 minutes, perform a natural pressure release for 10 minutes, and then a quick pressure release, and open the lid.
6. Stir and adjust the taste with salt and black pepper.
7. Dish the chili into serving bowls, top with the cheddar cheese and serve warm.

Nutrition Info:
Per Serving: Calories 766 Fats 84g Carbs 66g Net Carbs 9.46g Protein 153g

Chicken Tonnato

Servings: 4
Cooking Time: 15 Minutes
Ingredients:

- 1 teaspoon capers
- 2 oz tuna, canned
- ½ teaspoon minced garlic
- 1 teaspoon dried oregano
- 1 teaspoon lemon juice
- 1 tablespoon fresh basil, chopped
- 4 tablespoons ricotta cheese
- 2 tablespoons avocado oil
- ¼ teaspoon salt
- ½ teaspoon ground black pepper
- 1-pound chicken breast, skinless, boneless
- 1 cup water, for cooking

Directions:

1. Pour water in the instant pot and add chicken breast. Close and seal the lid and cook the chicken on manual (high pressure) for minutes. When the time is over, allow the natural pressure release for 10 minutes. Meanwhile, place all remaining ingredients from the list above in the food processor. Blend the mixture until smooth. When the chicken is cooked, remove it from the instant pot and slice into servings. Then arrange the chicken in the plate and top with blended sauce.

Nutrition Info: calories 189, fat 6.2, fiber 0.6, carbs 1.8, protein 8

French-style Chicken Liver Pâté

Servings: 8
Cooking Time: 15 Minutes
Ingredients:

- 1 pound chicken livers
- 1/2 cup leeks, chopped
- 2 garlic cloves, crushed
- 2 tablespoons olive oil
- 1 tablespoon poultry seasonings
- 1 teaspoon dried rosemary
- 1/2 teaspoon dried marjoram
- 1/4 teaspoon dried dill weed
- 1/2 teaspoon paprika
- 1/2 teaspoon red pepper flakes
- Salt, to taste
- 1/2 teaspoon ground black pepper
- 1 cup water
- 1 tablespoon stone ground mustard

Directions:

1. Press the "Sauté" button to heat up the Instant Pot. Now, heat the oil.
2. Once hot, sauté the chicken livers until no longer pink.
3. Add the remaining ingredients, except for the mustard, to your Instant Pot.
4. Secure the lid. Choose the "Manual" setting and cook for 10 minutes at High pressure. Once cooking is complete, use a quick pressure release; carefully remove the lid.
5. Transfer the cooked mixture to a food processor; add stone ground mustard. Process until smooth and uniform. Bon appétit!

Nutrition Info:
Per Serving: 109 Calories; 6.5g Fat; 2.3g Total Carbs; 10g Protein; 0.3g Sugars

Thyme Chicken Gizzards

Servings: 4
Cooking Time: 25 Minutes
Ingredients:

- 1-pound chicken gizzards, chopped
- 1 cup of water
- 1 teaspoon dried thyme
- 1 tablespoon butter
- 1 teaspoon salt
- ½ teaspoon peppercorns

Directions:

1. Put all ingredients in the instant pot.
2. Close and seal the lid.

3. Cook the chicken gizzards on manual mode (high pressure) for 25 minutes.
4. Allow the natural pressure release for 15 minutes before opening the lid.

Nutrition Info:

Per Serving: calories 50, fat 3.4, fiber 0.2, carbs 0.3, protein 4.5

Turkey Legs Delight

Servings: 6

Cooking Time: 40 Minutes

Ingredients:

- 3 tablespoons sesame oil
- 2 pounds turkey legs
- Sea salt and ground black pepper, to your liking
- A bunch of scallions, roughly chopped
- 1 ½ cups turkey broth

Directions:

1. Press the "Sauté" button and heat the sesame oil. Now, brown turkey legs on all sides; season with salt and black pepper.
2. Add the scallions and broth.
3. Secure the lid. Choose the "Manual" setting and cook for minutes. Once cooking is complete, use a natural pressure release; carefully remove the lid.
4. You can thicken the cooking liquid on the "Sauté" setting if desired. Serve warm.

Nutrition Info:

Per Serving: 339 Calories; 3g Fat; 1.3g Total Carbs; 7g Protein; 0.4g Sugars

Ranch And Lemon Whole Chicken

Servings: 6

Cooking Time: 40 Mins

Ingredients:

- 1 Chicken (medium size)
- 1 ½ cups Chicken Broth
- 1 Onion, quartered
- 1 ½ tsp Ranch Seasoning
- ½ tsp Lemon Pepper
- 1 Lemon, halved
- 1 Thyme Sprig
- 1 Rosemary Sprig
- 2 Garlic Cloves
- 1 tbsp Butter

Directions:

1. In a bowl combine the Ranch seasoning and lemon pepper, and rub the seasoning onto the chicken. Melt butter on Sauté. add the chicken and sear on all sides, until golden. Set aside.

2. Stuff the chicken's cavity with lemon, onion, garlic, thyme, and rosemary. Place the chicken back in the Instant Pot and pour the broth in. Seal the lid and cook on POULTRY for 30 minutes on High.
3. When ready, do a quick pressure release. Let chicken sit for 10 minutes before serving.

Nutrition Info: Calories 243, Protein 25g, Net Carbs 2.5g, Fat 28g

Simple Chicken Wings

Servings: 4
Cooking Time: 20 Mins
Ingredients:
- 2 lb Chicken wings
- 1 cup BBQ sauce

Directions:
1. Put the chicken wings in the Instant pot and cover them with the BBQ sauce. Seal the lid and cook on High for 20 minutes. When ready, do a quick release.

Nutrition Info: Calories 305, Protein 51g, Net Carbs 3.3g, Fat 9g

Thyme Duck And Coconut

Servings: 6
Cooking Time: 30 Minutes
Ingredients:
- 2 big duck legs, boneless, skinless and cubed
- 1 tablespoon olive oil
- 1 tablespoon thyme, chopped
- ½ cup coconut, unsweetened and shredded
- 1 cup coconut cream
- A pinch of salt and black pepper
- 1 cup chicken stock

Directions:
1. Set your instant pot on sauté mode, add the oil, heat it up, add the meat and brown for 5 minutes. Add the rest of the ingredients, put the lid on and cook on High for 25 minutes. Release the pressure naturally for minutes, divide everything between plates and serve.

Nutrition Info: calories 273, fat 6, fiber 1.7, carbs 3.7, protein 3

Holiday Chicken Wrapped In Prosciutto

Servings: 5
Cooking Time: 20 Minutes
Ingredients:
- 5 chicken breast halves, butterflied
- 2 garlic cloves, halved
- Sea salt, to taste
- 1/4 teaspoon ground black pepper, or more to taste

- 1/2 teaspoon red pepper flakes
- 1 teaspoon marjoram
- 10 strips prosciutto

Directions:
1. Prepare the Instant Pot by adding ½ cups of water and metal trivet to the bottom.
2. Rub chicken breast halves with garlic. Then, season the chicken with salt, black pepper, red pepper, and marjoram.
3. Then, wrap each chicken breast into 2 prosciutto strips; secure with toothpicks. Arrange wrapped chicken on the metal trivet.
4. Secure the lid. Choose the "Poultry" setting and cook for 15 minutes under High pressure. Once cooking is complete, use a natural pressure release; carefully remove the lid. Bon appétit!

Nutrition Info:
Per Serving: 548 Calories; 4g Fat; 1.1g Carbs; 3g Protein; 0g Sugars

Keto Chicken Burger

Servings: 2
Cooking Time: 10 Minutes
Ingredients:
- ½ cup ground chicken
- 1 tomato, sliced
- 4 lettuce leaves
- ¼ teaspoon cayenne pepper
- 1 teaspoon dried dill
- ½ teaspoon onion powder
- ¼ teaspoon garlic powder
- 1 tablespoon almond meal
- ¼ teaspoon salt
- 1 cup water, for cooking

Directions:
1. Pour water and insert the trivet in the instant pot. In the mixing bowl combine together ground chicken with cayenne pepper, dried dill, onion powder, garlic powder, salt, and almond meal. Stir the ground mixture until smooth. Then make 2 balls from the ground chicken mixture, press them gently in the shape of a burger and place them in the trivet. Close the lid and cook the chicken balls for minutes on manual mode (high pressure). When the time is over, make the quick pressure release. Place the chicken balls on 2 lettuce leaves. Top them with sliced tomato and remaining lettuce leaves.

Nutrition Info: calories 96, fat 4.2, fiber 1, carbs 3.3, protein 3

Traditional Hungarian Paprikash

Servings: 6
Cooking Time: 25 Minutes
Ingredients:

- 1 tablespoon lard, at room temperature
- 1 ½ pounds chicken thighs
- 1/2 cup tomato puree
- 1 ½ cups water
- 1 yellow onion, chopped
- 1 large-sized carrot, sliced
- 1 celery stalk, diced
- 2 garlic cloves, minced
- 2 bell peppers, seeded and chopped
- 1 Hungarian wax pepper, seeded and minced
- 1 teaspoon cayenne pepper
- 1 tablespoon Hungarian paprika
- 1 teaspoon coarse salt
- 1/2 teaspoon ground black pepper
- 1/2 teaspoon poultry seasoning
- 6 ounces sour cream
- 1 tablespoon arrowroot powder
- 1 cup water

Directions:

1. Press the "Sauté" button to heat up the Instant Pot. Now, melt the lard until hot; sear the chicken thighs for 2 to 3 minutes per side.
2. Add the tomato puree, 1 ½ cups of water, onion, carrot, celery, garlic, peppers, and seasonings.
3. Secure the lid. Choose the "Manual" setting and cook for 20 minutes at High pressure. Once cooking is complete, use a quick pressure release; carefully remove the lid.
4. In the meantime, thoroughly combine sour cream, arrowroot powder and 1 cup of water; whisk to combine well.
5. Add the sour cream mixture to the Instant Pot to thicken the cooking liquid. Cook for a couple of minutes on the residual heat.
6. Ladle into individual bowls and serve immediately.

Nutrition Info:
Per Serving: 402 Calories; 7g Fat; 8.1g Carbs; 21g Protein; 3.4g Sugars

Oregano Chicken With Sautéed Kale

Servings: 4
Cooking Time: 20 Mins
Ingredients:

- 2 pounds chicken breast
- 3 tablespoons olive oil
- 1 cup chicken broth
- 1 teaspoon dried oregano
- ¼ teaspoon onion powder
- ¼ teaspoon garlic powder

- Pinch of salt & pepper
- ½ cup breadcrumbs
- 4 cups kale, chopped
- 2 tablespoons butter
- 2 red onions, chopped

Directions:
1. Mix dry spices with crumbs; dip chicken in olive oil and dust with bread crumb mix.
2. Add broth to the instant pot and then insert a metal trivet. Place the chicken over the trivet and lock lid; cook on manual high for Mins.
3. Add butter to a skillet over medium heat and sauté red onion until fragrant; stir in kale and cook for about Mins or until just wilted; season with salt and pepper. Serve the chicken over the fried kale.

Nutrition Info:
Per Serving: Calories: 133; Total Fat: 13 g; Carbs: 2.3 g; Dietary Fiber: 0.8 g; Sugars: 0.6 g; Protein: 8 g; Cholesterol: 64 mg; Sodium: 243 mg

Tso Chicken Drumsticks

Servings: 6
Cooking Time: 20 Minutes
Ingredients:
- 6 chicken thighs
- 1 tablespoon apple cider vinegar
- 1 tablespoon coconut aminos
- ½ teaspoon ginger, grated
- 1 teaspoon Splenda
- ½ teaspoon chili flakes
- ¼ cup avocado oil
- 1/3 cup water

Directions:
1. Heat up avocado oil on saute mode for 3 minutes and add chicken thighs.
2. Saute the chicken for 6 minutes.
3. Then add the rest of the ingredients and stir them gently.
4. Close and seal the lid and cook the meal on Poultry mode for 10 minutes.
5. Carefully stir the cooked chicken.

Nutrition Info:
Per Serving: calories 179, fat 2, fiber 0.4, carbs 1.8, protein 1

Chicken Moussaka

Servings: 6
Cooking Time: 55 Minutes
Ingredients:
- 1 teaspoon avocado oil
- 1 cup ground turkey

- 1 cup eggplants, peeled, chopped
- 1 green bell pepper, chopped
- ¼ cup onion, diced
- ¼ teaspoon garlic, diced
- ½ cup green beans, boiled
- 1 tomato, chopped
- ½ cup heavy cream
- ½ teaspoon salt
- ½ teaspoon white pepper
- 1 cup water, for cooking

Directions:
1. Brush the instant pot casserole mold with avocado oil. Then add ground turkey inside and sprinkle it with salt and white pepper. Stir the turkey gently with the help of the fork. After this, top the turkey with eggplants, bell pepper, and onion. Sprinkle the ingredients with garlic, green beans, and chopped tomato. After this, pour the heavy cream over the mixture and cover it with foil. Secure the edges of the casserole mold. Pour water and insert the trivet in the instant pot. Place the casserole mold on the trivet and close the lid. Cook moussaka for 55 minutes on stew/meat mode.

Nutrition Info: calories 94, fat 4.6, fiber 1.4, carbs 4.3, protein 9.7

Chicken And Balsamic Mushrooms

Servings: 4
Cooking Time: 20 Minutes
Ingredients:
- 2 chicken breasts, skinless, boneless and cubed
- 1 tablespoon balsamic vinegar
- 1 pound white mushrooms, sliced
- 1 tablespoon rosemary, chopped
- 1 cup chicken stock
- A pinch of salt and black pepper
- 1 tablespoon avocado oil
- 2 tablespoons tomato passata

Directions:
1. Set your instant pot on Sauté mode, add the oil, heat it up, add the chicken and the mushrooms and brown for 5 minutes. Add the rest of the ingredients, put the lid on and cook on High for 20 minutes. Release the pressure naturally for minutes, divide everything between plates and serve.

Nutrition Info: calories 252, fat 9.4, fiber 1.8, carbs 5.1, protein 4

Indian-style Chicken Legs

Servings: 5
Cooking Time: 25 Minutes
Ingredients:

- 5 chicken legs, boneless, skin-on
- 2 garlic cloves, halved
- Sea salt, to taste
- 1/4 teaspoon black pepper, preferably freshly ground
- 1/2 teaspoon smoked paprika
- 2 teaspoons olive oil
- 1 tablespoon yellow mustard
- 1 teaspoon curry paste
- 4 strips pancetta, chopped
- 1 shallot, peeled and chopped
- 1 cup roasted vegetable broth, preferably homemade

Directions:

1. Rub the chicken legs with garlic halves; then, season with salt, black pepper, and smoked paprika.
2. Press the "Sauté" button to heat up your Instant Pot.
3. Once hot, heat the oil and sauté chicken legs for 4 to 5 minutes, turning once during cooking. Add a splash of chicken broth to deglaze the bottom of the pan.
4. Spread the legs with mustard and curry paste. Add pancetta, shallot and remaining vegetable broth.
5. Secure the lid. Choose "Manual" mode and High pressure; cook for 14 minutes. Once cooking is complete, use a natural pressure release; carefully remove the lid. Bon appétit!

Nutrition Info:
Per Serving: 477 Calories; 1g Fat; 4.5g Total Carbs; 8g Protein; 1.4g Sugars

Easy Turkey Salad

Servings: 6
Cooking Time: 25 Minutes
Ingredients:

- 2 pounds turkey breast, boneless and skinless
- 1/2 teaspoon black pepper, preferably freshly ground
- 1/2 teaspoon red pepper flakes, crushed
- Seasoned salt, to taste
- 2 sprigs thyme
- 1 sprig sage
- 2 garlic cloves, pressed
- 1 leek, sliced
- 1/2 cup mayonnaise
- 1 ½ tablespoons Dijon mustard
- 1/2 cup celery, finely diced
- 1 cucumber, chopped

Directions:

1. Prepare your Instant Pot by adding ½ cups of water and a metal trivet to the bottom of the inner pot.

2. Now, sprinkle turkey breast with black pepper, red pepper, and salt. Lower the seasoned turkey breast onto the trivet. Top with thyme, sage, and garlic.
3. Now, secure the lid. Choose the "Poultry" setting and cook for 20 minutes under High pressure. Once cooking is complete, use a natural pressure release; carefully remove the lid.
4. Allow the turkey to cool completely. Slice the turkey into strips.
5. Add the remaining ingredients and transfer the mixture to a salad bowl. Serve well-chilled. Bon appétit!

Nutrition Info:
Per Serving: 321 Calories; 2g Fat; 4.4g Total Carbs; 35g Protein; 1.4g Sugars

Hot Chicken Wingettes With Cilantro Dip

Servings: 6
Cooking Time: 1 Hour 15 Minutes
Ingredients:
- 10 fresh cayenne peppers, trimmed and chopped
- 3 garlic cloves, minced
- 1 ½ cups white vinegar
- 1/2 teaspoon black pepper
- 1 teaspoon sea salt
- 1 teaspoon onion powder
- 12 chicken wingettes
- 2 tablespoons olive oil
- Dipping Sauce:
- 1/2 cup mayonnaise
- 1/2 cup sour cream
- 1/2 cup cilantro, chopped
- 2 cloves garlic, minced
- 1 teaspoon smoked paprika

Directions:
1. Place cayenne peppers, 3 garlic cloves, white vinegar, black pepper, salt, and onion powder in a container. Add chicken wingettes, and let them marinate, covered, for hour in the refrigerator.
2. Add the chicken wingettes, along with the marinade and olive oil to the Instant Pot.
3. Secure the lid. Choose the "Manual" setting and cook for 6 minutes. Once cooking is complete, use a quick pressure release; carefully remove the lid.
4. In a mixing bowl, thoroughly combine mayonnaise, sour cream, cilantro, garlic, and smoked paprika.
5. Serve warm chicken with the dipping sauce on the side. Bon appétit!

Nutrition Info:
Per Serving: 296 Calories; 5g Fat; 3g Carbs; 8g Protein; 4.3g Sugars

Balsamic Chicken

Servings: 4

Cooking Time: 50 Mins

Ingredients:

- 2 lb Chicken Thighs, Bone in and skin on
- 2 tbsp Olive oil
- Salt and Pepper to taste
- 1 ½ cups diced Tomatoes
- ¾ cup Yellow Onion
- 2 tsp minced Garlic
- ½ cup Balsamic Vinegar
- 3 tsp chopped fresh Thyme
- 1 cup Chicken Broth
- 2 tbsp chopped Parsley

Directions:

1. Put the chicken thighs on a cutting board and use paper towels to pat dry. Season with salt and pepper. Heat oil on Sauté, and put the chicken with skin side down.
2. Cook until golden brown on each side for 9 minutes. Remove on a clean plate. Add the onions and tomatoes, and sauté for 3 minutes stirring occasionally. Top the onions with the garlic too and cook for 30 seconds, then, stir in the broth, salt, thyme, and balsamic vinegar.
3. Add the chicken back to the pot. Seal the lid, select Poultry and cook on High for 20 minutes. Meanwhile, preheat an oven to 0 F.
4. Once ready, do a quick pressure release. Select Sauté mode. Remove the chicken onto a baking tray using tongs and leave the sauce in the pot to thicken for about 10 minutes.
5. Tuck the baking tray in the oven and let the chicken broil on each side to golden brown for about minutes. Remove and set aside to cool slightly. Adjust the salt and pepper and when cooked to your desired thickness, press Cancel.
6. Place the chicken in a serving bowl and spoon the sauce all over it. Garnish with parsley and serve with thyme roasted tomatoes, carrots, and radishes.

Nutrition Info: Calories 277, Protein 34g, Net Carbs 2g, Fat 10g

Instant Pot Chicken Curry

Servings: 1 Serving

Cooking Time: 25 Mins

Ingredients:

- 4 tbsp. coconut oil
- 100 grams chicken, diced
- ¼ cup chicken broth
- Pinch of turmeric
- Dash of onion powder
- 1 tablespoon minced red onion
- Pinch of garlic powder
- ¼ teaspoon curry powder
- Pinch of sea salt
- Pinch of pepper

- Stevia
- Pinch of cayenne

Directions:
1. Set your instant pot to manual high, melt coconut oil and then stir in garlic and onion. Cook until fragrant and stir in chicken. In a small bowl, stir together spices, Stevia, and chicken broth until dissolved, stir into the chicken and lock lid. Cook for 20 Mins and then naturally release the pressure. Serve hot.

Nutrition Info:
Per Serving: Calories: 170; Total Fat: 5 g; Carbs: 5.3 g; Dietary Fiber: 0.6 g; Sugars: 0.8 g; Protein: 5 g; Cholesterol: 77 mg; Sodium: 255 mg

Chicken Rosemary Soup

Servings: 4
Cooking Time: 25 Minutes
Ingredients:
- 2 tbsp olive oil
- 1 large white onion, chopped
- 1 celery stalk, chopped
- 6 garlic cloves, minced
- 2 tbsp fresh rosemary leaves
- 1 cup green beans, cut into three pieces each
- 2 chicken breasts, cut into 1-inch cubes
- 4 cups chicken stock
- Salt and black pepper to taste
- 1 lemon, juiced
- 2 tbsp freshly chopped parsley to garnish

Directions:
1. Set the IP in Sauté mode and adjust to Medium heat.
2. Heat the olive oil in the inner pot and sauté the onion, celery, and garlic until softened, 3 minutes.
3. Mix in rosemary, green beans, chicken, chicken stock, salt, and black pepper.
4. Lock the lid in place; select Manual mode on High Pressure and set the timer to 12 minutes.
5. After cooking, perform a natural pressure release for 10 minutes, a quick pressure release to let out the remaining steam, and open the lid.
6. Stir in the lemon juice and adjust taste with salt and black pepper.
7. Dish the soup into serving bowls and garnish with the parsley.

Nutrition Info:
Per Serving: Calories 269 Fats 68g Carbs 6.09g Net Carbs 3.69g Protein 8.13g

Southern Chicken Stew

Servings: 6
Cooking Time: 25 Minutes
Ingredients:

- 2 slices bacon
- 6 chicken legs, skinless and boneless
- 3 cups water
- 2 chicken bouillon cubes
- 1 leek, chopped
- 1 carrot, trimmed and chopped
- 4 garlic cloves, minced
- 1/2 teaspoon dried thyme
- 1/2 teaspoon dried basil
- 1 teaspoon Hungarian paprika
- 1 bay leaf
- 1 cup double cream
- 1/2 teaspoon ground black pepper

Directions:
1. Press the "Sauté" button to heat up your Instant Pot. Now, cook the bacon, crumbling it with a spatula; cook until the bacon is crisp and reserve.
2. Now, add the chicken legs and cook until browned on all sides.
3. Add the water, bouillon cubes, leeks, carrot, garlic, thyme, basil, paprika, and bay leaf; stir to combine.
4. Secure the lid. Choose the "Poultry" setting and cook for 15 minutes at High pressure. Once cooking is complete, use a natural pressure release; carefully remove the lid.
5. Fold in the cream and allow it to cook in the residual heat, stirring continuously. Ladle into individual bowls, sprinkle each serving with freshly grated black pepper and serve warm. Bon appétit!

Nutrition Info:
Per Serving: 453 Calories; 6g Fat; 5.9g Total Carbs; 6g Protein; 2.6g Sugars

Cajun Chicken Salad

Servings: 2
Cooking Time: 25 Minutes
Ingredients:
- 8 oz chicken fillet
- 1 teaspoon Cajun seasonings
- 1 teaspoon tomato paste
- ¼ teaspoon salt
- ½ cup chicken broth
- 1 cup radish, chopped
- 1 tablespoon fresh parsley, chopped
- 1 cup lettuce, chopped
- 1 tablespoon olive oil
- ½ teaspoon chili flakes
- 1 teaspoon apple cider vinegar

Directions:

1. Rub the chicken with Cajun seasonings and place it in the instant pot. Add tomato paste and chicken broth. Stir the mixture gently. Close the lid and cook the chicken on stew mode for 25 minutes. Meanwhile, in the salad bowl combine together chopped radish and lettuce. Sprinkle the vegetables with salt, olive oil, and chili flakes. Add apple cider vinegar and mix up well. When the chicken is cooked, remove it from the instant pot, cool little and chop. Add chopped chicken in the salad bowl. Mix up the salad well with the help of the spoon.

Nutrition Info: calories 302, fat 9, fiber 1.3, carbs 3.7, protein 8

Chicken With Almond Gravy

Servings: 2
Cooking Time: 15 Minutes
Ingredients:
- 12 oz chicken breast, skinless, boneless
- ½ teaspoon salt
- ½ teaspoon white pepper
- ½ teaspoon ground black pepper
- ½ cup organic almond milk
- ½ teaspoon paprika

Directions:
1. Mix up together salt, white pepper, ground black pepper, and paprika.
2. Rub the chicken breast with the spice mixture generously.
3. After this, place the chicken breast in the instant pot bowl.
4. Add almond milk and close the lid.
5. Set the "Poultry" program and cook the chicken for 8 minutes. NPR -minutes.
6. Slice the chicken breast and sprinkle with the remaining gravy.

Nutrition Info:
Per Serving: calories 112, fat 5, fiber 0.3, carbs 2.6, protein 5

Italian-style Turkey Meatloaf

Servings: 6
Cooking Time: 35 Minutes
Ingredients:
- 2 pounds ground turkey
- 2/3 cup pork rind crumbs
- 1/2 cup Parmigiano-Reggiano, grated
- 1 tablespoon coconut aminos
- 2 eggs, chopped
- Sea salt, to taste
- 1/4 teaspoon ground black pepper
- 1 yellow onion, peeled and chopped
- 2 garlic cloves, minced
- 4 ounces tomato paste
- 1 tablespoon Italian seasoning

- 1/2 cup tomato sauce
- 1 cup water
- 1 teaspoon mustard powder
- 1/2 teaspoon chili powder

Directions:
1. Prepare your Instant Pot by adding a metal rack and ½ cups of water to the bottom of the inner pot.
2. In a large mixing bowl, thoroughly combine ground turkey with pork rind crumbs, Parmigiano-Reggiano, coconut aminos, eggs, salt, black pepper, onion, garlic, tomato paste, Italian seasoning.
3. Shape this mixture into a meatloaf; lower your meatloaf onto the metal rack.
4. Then, in a mixing bowl, thoroughly combine tomato sauce with water, mustard and chili powder. Spread this mixture over the top of your meatloaf.
5. Secure the lid. Choose the "Meat/Stew" setting and cook for 20 minutes at High pressure. Once cooking is complete, use a natural pressure release; carefully remove the lid.
6. Afterwards, place your meatloaf under the preheated broiler for 5 minutes. Allow the meatloaf to rest for to 8 minutes before slicing and serving. Bon appétit!

Nutrition Info:
Per Serving: 449 Calories; 7g Fat; 8.1g Carbs; 2g Protein; 3.7g Sugars

Thanksgiving Turkey With Mushroom Gravy

Servings: 6
Cooking Time: 30 Minutes
Ingredients:
- 2 pounds turkey breast, boneless and skinless
- Seasoned salt and ground black pepper, to taste
- 1/2 teaspoon smoked paprika
- 1/4 teaspoon mustard powder
- 1 head cauliflower, broken into small florets
- 1 cup scallions, chopped
- 2 cloves garlic, crushed
- 1 celery with leaves, chopped
- 1 bay leaf
- 1 ½ cups water
- 1 tablespoon butter
- 6 ounces Cremini mushrooms, chopped

Directions:
1. Spritz your Instant Pot with a nonstick cooking spray.
2. Place turkey breasts on the bottom of the Instant Pot. Season them with salt, black pepper, paprika, and mustard powder.
3. Top with cauliflower, scallions, garlic, and celery. Afterwards, add bay leaf and water.

4. Secure the lid. Choose the "Poultry" setting and cook for 20 minutes under High pressure. Once cooking is complete, use a natural pressure release; carefully remove the lid.
5. Remove the turkey from the Instant Pot. Transfer the cooking liquid along with vegetables to your food processor; puree until silky and smooth.
6. Press the "Sauté" button and melt the butter. Sauté the mushrooms until fragrant, approximately 4 minutes.
7. Stir in pureed vegetables and continue to cook until the sauce is thickened. Spoon mushroom gravy over turkey breasts. Bon appétit!

Nutrition Info:
Per Serving: 280 Calories; 8g Fat; 4.9g Carbs; 2g Protein; 1.9g Sugars

Traditional Hungarian Goulash

Servings: 4
Cooking Time: 25 Mins
Ingredients:
- 1 tbsp ghee
- 1 pound chicken thighs
- ½ cup tomato paste
- 1 onion, chopped
- 1 carrot, sliced
- 1 celery stalk, diced
- 2 garlic cloves, minced
- 2 red bell peppers, chopped
- 1 tsp cayenne pepper
- 1 tbsp Hungarian paprika
- Salt and black pepper to taste
- ½ tsp poultry seasoning
- 1 cup buttermilk
- 1 tbsp arrowroot powder

Directions:
1. Set your IP to Sauté and melt the ghee. Brown the chicken thighs for 2-3 minutes on each side. Put in the tomato paste, cups of water, onion, carrot, celery, garlic, red bell peppers, and seasonings.
2. Seal the lid, select Manual on High, and cook for 15 minutes. When done, perform a quick pressure release. Whisk the buttermilk, arrowroot powder, and 1 cup water. Pour the mixture into the pot and cook for a few minutes until thickens. Share into serving bowls and serve right away.

Nutrition Info: Calories 370, Protein 24g, Net Carbs 5.1g, Fat 23g

Crack Chicken

Servings: 4
Cooking Time: 20 Minutes
Ingredients:

- 1 cup chicken broth
- 1 teaspoon dried dill
- 1 teaspoon dried oregano
- ½ teaspoon onion powder
- 1-pound chicken breast, skinless, boneless
- ½ teaspoon salt
- 2 tablespoons mascarpone cheese
- 2 oz Cheddar cheese, shredded

Directions:
1. Pour the chicken broth in the instant pot.
2. Add dried ill, oregano, onion powder, chicken breast, and salt.
3. Close and seal the lid.
4. Cook the chicken breast on manual mode (high pressure) for 15 minutes.
5. Then make a quick pressure release and transfer the cooked chicken in the bowl.
6. Blend the chicken broth mixture with the help of the immersion blender.
7. Add mascarpone cheese and Cheddar cheese. Saute the liquid for 2 minutes on saute mode.
8. Meanwhile, shred the chicken.
9. Add it in the mascarpone mixture and mix it up. Saute the meal for 3 minutes more.

Nutrition Info:
Per Serving: calories 212, fat 8.9, fiber 0.2, carbs 1.3, protein 8

Dijon Chicken Legs

Servings: 4
Cooking Time: 15 Mins
Ingredients:
- 2 tbsp olive oil
- 1 ½ pounds chicken legs
- 1 tomato, chopped
- 2 garlic cloves, sliced
- 1 tablespoon chicken seasoning
- Salt black pepper to taste
- ½ tsp paprika
- 1 cup mayonnaise
- 2 tbsp horseradish sauce
- ½ lemon, cut into slices

Directions:
1. Set your IP to Sauté and heat the oil. Cook the chicken for 2-3 minutes per side until browned. Add in tomatoes, garlic, chicken seasoning, salt, black pepper, paprika, and cup water. Seal the lid, select Manual on High, and cook for 10 minutes. When done, perform a natural pressure release. Mix the mayonnaise and horseradish sauce in a bowl. Serve with the chicken and decorate with lemon slices.

Nutrition Info: Calories 321, Protein 22g, Net Carbs 4.3g, Fat 20g

Chicken Meatballs In Pasta Sauce

Servings: 4
Cooking Time: 9 Minutes
Ingredients:

- 2 cups chicken broth
- 4 tbsp tomato paste
- 1/3 cup freshly chopped basil
- 1 tsp mixed dried herbs
- 1 tsp onion powder
- ¼ tsp red chili flakes
- 5 garlic cloves, minced
- 24 frozen chicken meatballs
- 1 (25 oz) jar tomato sauce
- Salt and black pepper to taste
- ¼ cup grated Parmesan cheese

Directions:

1. In the inner pot, mix the chicken broth and tomato paste well, and stir in the remaining ingredients making sure not to break the meatballs.
2. Lock the lid in place; select Manual mode and set the timer to 4 minutes.
3. After cooking, perform a natural pressure release for 5 minutes, then a quick pressure release to let out the remaining steam and open the lid.
4. Carefully stir and adjust the taste with salt and black pepper.
5. Dish the food into serving bowls and top with the Parmesan cheese.
6. Serve warm.

Nutrition Info:
Per Serving: Calories 225 Fats 45g Carbs 6.35g Net Carbs 3.85g Protein 93g

Garlic Chicken In Cream Sauce

Servings: 4
Cooking Time: 24 Minutes
Ingredients:

- 2 tbsp olive oil
- 4 chicken breasts, skinless and boneless
- Salt and black pepper to taste
- 3 tbsp butter
- 1 small yellow onion, finely chopped
- 5 garlic cloves, minced
- 1 cup almond milk
- ½ cup chicken broth
- ½ lemon, juiced + 1 lemon, sliced
- 2 tbsp freshly chopped parsley

Directions:

1. Set the IP in Sauté mode and adjust to Medium heat.
2. Heat the olive oil in the inner pot, season the chicken with salt, black pepper, and cook in the oil until golden brown on both sides, 4 minutes. Transfer to a paper towel-lined plate and set aside.
3. Melt the butter in the inner pot and sauté the onion until softened, minutes. Stir in the garlic and cook until fragrant, 30 seconds.
4. Mix in the almond milk, chicken broth, and lay the chicken in the sauce.
5. Lock the lid in place; select Manual mode on High Pressure and set the timer to 4 minutes.
6. After cooking, perform a natural pressure release for 10 minutes, then a quick pressure release to let out the remaining steam and open the lid.
7. Stir in the lemon juice, stick in the lemon slices, and simmer in Sauté mode for 1 to 2 minutes. Adjust the taste with salt and black pepper.
8. Dish the food into serving bowls, garnish with the parsley, and serve warm.

Nutrition Info:
Per Serving: Calories 903 Fats 77g Carbs 4.54g Net Carbs 3.84g Protein 74g

Zucchini Eggs

Servings: 2
Cooking Time: 15 Mins
Ingredients:

- 2 Eggs, whisked
- 1 large Zucchini, sliced
- 1 tsp Garlic powder
- Salt and black pepper to taste
- 3 tbsp Butter

Directions:
1. Melt butter on Sauté. Add zucchini and cook for 3-4 minutes. Pour the eggs mixture and spread evenly. Cook for 2-3 minutes; then flip and cook for 3 more. Season with salt and pepper, and serve.

Nutrition Info: Calories 177, Protein 7.1g, Net Carbs 1.5g, Fat 8g

Creamy Strawberry Glazed-chicken

Servings: 4
Cooking Time: 17 Minutes
Ingredients:

- 1 tbsp olive oil
- 1 lb. chicken breasts, halved
- Salt and black pepper to taste
- 1 cup fresh strawberries, chopped
- 1 small red chili, minced
- ½ cup chicken broth
- 2 green onions, thinly sliced
- 2 tbsp scallions

Directions:

1. Set the IP in Sauté mode and adjust to Medium heat.
2. Heat the olive oil in the inner pot, season the chicken with salt, black pepper, and cook on both sides in the oil until golden brown and cooked within, 10 minutes. Place the chicken and set aside for serving.
3. Mix the remaining ingredients in the fat except for the green onions.
4. Lock the lid in place; select Manual mode on High Pressure and set the timer to 2 minutes.
5. After cooking, perform a natural pressure release for minutes, then quick a pressure release to let out the remaining steam, and open the lid.
6. Stir the sauce while mashing the strawberries with the back of the spoon.
7. Spoon the glaze all over the chicken, garnish with the scallions and serve warm.

Nutrition Info:

Per Serving: Calories 288 Fats 07g Carbs 4.09g Net Carbs 3.19g Protein 6g

Spicy Chicken Wingettes

Servings: 6

Cooking Time: 1 Hour 15 Minutes

Ingredients:

- 10 fresh cayenne peppers, trimmed and chopped
- 3 garlic cloves, minced
- 1 ½ cups white vinegar
- 1/2 teaspoon black pepper
- 1 teaspoon sea salt
- 1 teaspoon onion powder
- 12 chicken wingettes
- 2 tablespoons olive oil
- Dipping Sauce:
- 1/2 cup mayonnaise
- 1/2 cup sour cream
- 1/2 cup cilantro, chopped
- 2 cloves garlic, minced
- 1 teaspoon smoked paprika

Directions:

1. Place cayenne peppers, 3 garlic cloves, white vinegar, black pepper, salt, and onion powder in a container. Add chicken wingettes, and let them marinate, covered, for hour in the refrigerator.
2. Add the chicken wingettes, along with the marinade and olive oil to the Instant Pot.
3. Secure the lid. Choose the "Manual" setting and cook for 6 minutes. Once cooking is complete, use a quick pressure release; carefully remove the lid.
4. In a mixing bowl, thoroughly combine mayonnaise, sour cream, cilantro, garlic, and smoked paprika.
5. Serve warm chicken with the dipping sauce on the side. Bon appétit!

Nutrition Info:

Per Serving: 296 Calories; 5g Fat; 6.9g Total Carbs; 8g Protein; 3.3g Sugars

Chicken Meatballs With Parmesan

Servings: 4
Cooking Time: 25 Mins
Ingredients:

- 1 pound ground Chicken
- ½ Onion, grated
- ½ cup Almond flour
- ¼ cup grated Parmesan Cheese
- ¼ cup Tomato Sauce
- 1 Egg
- Salt and black pepper to taste

Directions:

1. Pour cup water in the pot and lower a trivet. Place all ingredients in a large bowl and mix until well combined. Shape into meatballs, and arrange on a previously greased baking dish.
2. Place the dish on top of the trivet and seal the lid, Cook on High for 15 minutes. After the beep, do a quick pressure release and open the lid carefully. Serve immediately.

Nutrition Info: Calories 223, Protein 22g, Net Carbs 2g, Fat 12g

Chicken, Cabbage And Leeks

Servings: 4
Cooking Time: 30 Minutes
Ingredients:

- 2 chicken breasts, skinless, boneless and cubed
- A pinch of salt and black pepper
- 1 tablespoon ghee, melted
- 1 red cabbage, shredded
- 2 leeks, sliced
- 1 cup chicken stock
- 1 tablespoon tomato passata
- 1 tablespoon basil, chopped
- 1 tablespoon balsamic vinegar

Directions:

1. Set the instant pot on Sauté mode, add the ghee, heat it up, add the meat and the leeks and brown for 5 minutes. Add the rest of the ingredients except the basil, toss, put the lid on and cook on High for 25 minutes Release the pressure naturally for minutes, divide the mix between plates, sprinkle the basil on top and serve.

Nutrition Info: calories 275, fat 9, fiber 0.6, carbs 6.7, protein 7

Turkey Bolognese Sauce

Servings: 4
Cooking Time: 17 Minutes
Ingredients:

- ¼ cup carrot, grated
- ½ white onion, minced
- 1 garlic clove, diced
- ¼ teaspoon salt
- 10 oz ground turkey
- 1/3 teaspoon chili flakes
- ½ teaspoon dried thyme
- 1 teaspoon tomato paste
- 1 oz Swiss cheese, grated
- ½ scoop stevia powder
- 1 tablespoon coconut oil
- 1/3 cup water

Directions:
1. Toss coconut oil in the instant pot and melt it on sauté mode. Then add carrot, garlic, and onion. Cook the ingredients for 5 minutes. Stir them with the help of the spatula after 3 minutes of cooking. Then add salt and ground turkey, Sprinkle the ingredients with chili flakes, dried thyme, and stevia powder. Mix up well and sauté for 3 minutes. After this, mix up water with tomato paste. Pour the liquid over the ground turkey. Stir the sauce well and close the lid. Cook it on manual mode (high pressure) for 4 minutes. When the time is over, make the quick pressure release and open the lid. Top the sauce with Swiss cheese and mix up until the cheese is melted. The sauce is cooked.

Nutrition Info: calories 205, fat 2, fiber 0.6, carbs 2.9, protein 6

Instant Pot Asian Chicken Lettuce Wraps

Servings: 2
Cooking Time: 1 Hour
Ingredients:
- 1-pound ground chicken
- 2 minced cloves garlic
- 2 large carrots, grated
- 1 medium red bell pepper, diced
- 1 teaspoon Stevia
- 1/4 cup low-sodium soy sauce
- 1/4 tsp. crushed red pepper flakes
- 1/4 cup ketchup

Directions:
1. Combine all ingredients in your instant pot and cook on high setting for hour. Shred the chicken and return to the pot. Stir to mix well and divide among lettuce leaves. Roll to form wraps and serve.

Nutrition Info:
Per Serving: Calories: 262; Total Fat: 8.6 g; Carbs: 1g; Dietary Fiber: 1.4 g; Sugars: 7.7 g; Protein: 8 g; Cholesterol: 101 mg; Sodium: 1170 mg

Quick Chicken Fajitas

Servings: 4
Cooking Time: 30 Mins
Ingredients:

- 2 lb Chicken Breasts, skinless and cut in 1-inch slices
- ¼ cup Chicken Broth
- 1 Yellow Onion, sliced
- 1 Green Bell peppers, seeded and sliced
- 1 Yellow Bell pepper, seeded and sliced
- 1 Red Bell pepper, seeded and sliced
- 2 tbsp Cumin Powder
- 2 tbsp Chili Powder
- Salt to taste
- Half a Lime
- Cooking Spray
- Fresh cilantro, to garnish
- Assembling:
- Low Carb Tacos
- Guacamole
- Salsa
- Cheese

Directions:

1. Grease the pot with cooking spray and line the bottom with the bell peppers and onion. Lay the chicken on the bed of peppers and sprinkle with salt, chili powder, and cumin powder.
2. Squeeze some lime juice and pour in the broth. Seal the lid, select Poultry and cook on High for minutes. Once ready, do a quick pressure release. Dish the chicken with the vegetables and juice. Add the cheese, guacamole, salsa, and tacos in one layer on the side of the chicken.

Nutrition Info: Calories 352, Protein 7g, Net Carbs 0g, Fat 1g

Bacon Chicken

Servings: 3
Cooking Time: 15 Minutes
Ingredients:

- 12 oz chicken breast, boneless, skinless
- 5 oz bacon, sliced
- ½ teaspoon cayenne pepper
- ½ teaspoon ground white pepper
- ½ teaspoon minced garlic
- 1 teaspoon salt
- 1 tablespoon butter
- ¾ cup of water

Directions:

1. Stir together cayenne pepper, ground white pepper, minced garlic, and salt.
2. Then beat the chicken breast with the help of the kitchen hammer gently. It will make the final taste of meat tender and juicy.
3. Pu the butter and bacon on it.
4. Roll up the chicken breast to make the roll.
5. Secure the chicken roll with the help of the kitchen twine.
6. Wrap the roll into the foil.
7. Pour 1 cup of water in the instant pot bowl and place the trivet.
8. Place the chicken roll on the trivet and close the lid.
9. Set the "Steam" mode and High pressure.
10. Cook the chicken roll for 15 minutes. Then use the natural pressure release method.

Nutrition Info:
Per Serving: calories 421, fat 5, fiber 0.2, carbs 1.2, protein 7

Asiago Chicken Drumsticks

Servings: 4
Cooking Time: 5 Hours
Ingredients:

- 4 chicken drumsticks, boneless
- 1/3 teaspoon salt
- ¼ teaspoon white pepper
- ½ teaspoon onion powder
- 1 teaspoon minced onion
- 1 teaspoon dried dill
- 1/3 cup chicken broth
- ¼ cup apple cider vinegar
- 2 tablespoons cream cheese
- 5 oz Asiago cheese, grated
- 1 teaspoon arrowroot powder

Directions:

1. In the big bowl combine together salt, white pepper, onion powder, minced onion, dried dill, chicken broth, and apple cider vinegar. Add cream cheese and 3 oz of Asiago cheese. Whisk the mixture until salt is dissolved. Then add chicken drumsticks and let the ingredients marinate for minutes. Then transfer the chicken drumsticks and ½ part of chicken broth liquid in the instant pot. Close and seal the lid. Cook the meal on Low pressure (manual mode) for 4 hours. When the time is over, open the lid. Combine together the remaining chicken liquid and remaining Asiago cheese. Add arrowroot and stir it. Pour the liquid over the chicken and close the lid. Cook the meal o Low pressure for 1 hour more.

Nutrition Info: calories 233, fat 6, fiber 0.1, carbs 1.6, protein 4

Italian Chicken Stew

Servings: 4

Cooking Time: 20 Minutes

Ingredients:

- 1 small yellow onion, chopped
- 1 (14-ounce) can diced tomatoes
- 1 ½ cups chicken broth
- 12 ounces boneless chicken thighs
- 1 tablespoon olive oil
- 1 teaspoon dried Italian seasoning
- 1 tablespoon tomato paste

Directions:

1. Turn the Instant Pot on to the Sauté setting and let it heat up.
2. Add the olive oil then sauté the onion for 5 minutes until softened.
3. Add the tomatoes, chicken broth, tomato paste, and seasoning.
4. Stir well then add the chicken and close and lock the lid.
5. Press the Manual button and adjust the timer to 10 minutes on High Pressure.
6. When the timer goes off, let the pressure vent for 10 minutes then do a Quick Release by pressing Cancel and switching the steam valve to "venting."
7. When the pot has depressurized, open the lid.
8. Remove the chicken with a slotted spoon and shred it with two forks.
9. Simmer the cooking liquid on the Sauté setting until it thickens then stir the chicken back in to serve.

Nutrition Info: calories 255 fat 5g ,protein 18g ,carbs 6.5g ,fiber 1.5g ,net carbs 5g

Blt Chicken Wrap

Servings: 4

Cooking Time: 10 Minutes

Ingredients:

- 4 low carb tortillas
- 4 bacon slices
- 1 cup lettuce, chopped
- 10 oz chicken fillet
- ½ teaspoon salt
- ¼ teaspoon cayenne pepper
- 2 oz Parmesan, grated
- 1 tablespoon heavy cream
- 1 tablespoon lemon juice
- 1 cup water, for cooking

Directions:

1. Place the bacon in the instant pot and cook it on sauté mode for 3 minutes. Then flip it on another side and cook for 2 minutes more. Place the cooked bacon on the tortillas. Then clean the instant pot and pour water inside. Insert the trivet. Rub the chicken with salt and cayenne pepper and put it in the instant pot. Close the lid. Cook it on steam mode for minutes. Then make a quick pressure release and open the lid. Chop the chicken and put it

over the bacon. Add lettuce and Parmesan. In the mixing bowl, mix up together lemon juice and heavy cream. Pour the mixture over Parmesan. Roll the tortillas into the wraps.

Nutrition Info: calories 379, fat 7, fiber 7.1, carbs 4, protein 3

Chicken, Peppers And Mushrooms

Servings: 4
Cooking Time: 25 Minutes
Ingredients:

- 2 chicken breasts, skinless, boneless and cubed
- 1 shallot, chopped
- 2 red bell peppers, cubed
- 2 green bell peppers, cubed
- 2 garlic cloves, minced
- 1 pound white mushrooms, halved
- A pinch of salt and black pepper
- 1 cup chicken stock

Directions:

1. In your instant pot, mix the chicken with the rest of the ingredients, put the lid on and cook on High for 25 minutes. Release the pressure naturally for minutes, divide everything between plates and serve.

Nutrition Info: calories 283, fat 9.2, fiber 2.8, carbs 4.4, protein 5

Sesame Chicken

Servings: 4
Cooking Time: 20 Minutes
Ingredients:

- 2 chicken breasts, skinless, boneless and cubed
- A pinch of salt and black pepper
- 1 teaspoon sesame seeds
- 4 garlic cloves, minced
- 1 cup tomato passata
- 1 tablespoon parsley, chopped
- 1 tablespoon oregano, chopped

Directions:

1. In your instant pot, mix all the ingredients except the sesame seeds, put the lid on and cook on High for 20 minutes. Release the pressure naturally for minutes, divide everything between plates and serve with the sesame seeds sprinkled on top.

Nutrition Info: calories 243, fat 9, fiber 1.6, carbs 5.4, protein 1

Saucy Chicken Drumettes With Squashsta

Servings: 8
Cooking Time: 55 Minutes

Ingredients:

- 2 tablespoons grapeseed oil
- 8 chicken drumettes
- 2 cloves garlic, minced
- Sea salt and ground black pepper, to taste
- 2 ripe tomatoes, pureed
- 2 tablespoons capers, rinsed and drained
- 1 cup broth, preferably homemade
- 1 tablespoon flaxseed meal
- 1 (3-pound spaghetti squash, halved
- 1 tablespoon olive oil
- Coarse sea salt, to taste

Directions:

1. Press the "Sauté" button to heat up the Instant Pot. Heat the grapeseed oil.
2. Brown the chicken drumettes for to 3 minutes per side.
3. Add the garlic, salt, black pepper, tomatoes, capers, and broth.
4. Secure the lid. Choose "Manual" mode and High pressure; cook for 10 minutes. Once cooking is complete, use a natural pressure release; carefully remove the lid.
5. Reserve the chicken drumettes. Press the "Sauté" button again and add the flaxseed meal to the Instant Pot.
6. Thicken the tomato sauce for a couple of minutes or until your desired thickness is achieved.
7. Preheat your oven to 380 degrees F. Place squash halves, cut-side down on a lightly greased baking pan. Drizzle olive oil over them and sprinkle with sea salt.
8. Roast for 40 minutes. Afterwards, scrape the flesh to create "spaghetti". Serve with warm chicken drumettes and tomato sauce. Enjoy!

Nutrition Info:
Per Serving: 224 Calories; 9.4g Fat; 7g Carbs; 4g Protein; 1.1g Sugars

Garlic Soy-glazed Chicken

Servings: 6
Cooking Time: 35 Minutes
Ingredients:

- 2 pounds boneless chicken thighs
- Salt and pepper
- 1 tablespoon minced garlic
- ¼ cup soy sauce
- ¾ cup apple cider vinegar

Directions:

1. Season the chicken with salt and pepper, then add it to the Instant Pot, skin-side down.
2. Whisk together the apple cider vinegar, soy sauce, and garlic then add to the pot.
3. Close and lock the lid, then press the Manual button and adjust the timer to 15 minutes.
4. When the timer goes off, let the pressure vent naturally.
5. When the pot has depressurized, open the lid.

6. Remove the chicken to a baking sheet and place under the broiler for 3 to 5 minutes until the skin is crisp.
7. Meanwhile, turn the Instant Pot on to Sauté and cook until the sauce thickens, stirring as needed.
8. Serve the chicken with the sauce spooned over it.

Nutrition Info: calories 335 fat 23g ,protein 5g ,carbs 1.5g ,fiber 0g ,net carbs 1.5g

Tropical Turkey Salad

Servings: 6
Cooking Time: 30 Mins
Ingredients:
- 2 cups chopped cooked turkey
- 1/2 cup chopped green onion
- 1 cup chopped orange segments
- 1 cup diced red bell pepper
- 1 cup pineapple chunks
- 1 cup diced celery
- 1 tablespoon fresh lemon juice
- 1 teaspoon liquid Stevia
- 2 tablespoons mango chutney
- 1/3 cup sour cream
- 1/4 teaspoon curry powder

Directions:
1. Add water to an instant pot and insert a trivet; season turkey with salt and pepper and place over the trivet. Lock lid and cook for 30 Mins. Let pressure come down naturally.
2. In a small bowl, whisk together lemon juice, sour cream, Stevia, and curry powder until well blended; refrigerate until ready to use.
3. In a bowl, mix the turkey with the remaining ingredients; drizzle with dressing and toss until well coated. Refrigerate for at least 1 hour before serving.

Nutrition Info:
Per Serving: Calories: 126; Total Fat: 3.2 g; Carbs: 9.6 g; Protein: 4 g; Cholesterol: 38 mg; Sodium: 46 mg

Picante Chicken Soup With Mushrooms

Servings: 5
Cooking Time: 20 Mins
Ingredients:
- 2 tbsp olive oil
- 1 leek, chopped
- 4 cloves garlic, minced
- 1 cup mushrooms, sliced
- 2 cups snow peas
- 1 serrano pepper, seeded and sliced

- 1 celery stick, chopped
- 2 tomatoes, chopped
- 1 tbsp dry white wine
- Salt and black pepper to taste
- 1 tsp dried basil
- 5 cups chicken broth
- ½ pound chicken breasts, cubed

Directions:
1. Set your IP to Sauté and heat the oil. Add in the leek, celery, garlic, and mushrooms and cook until tender, about 5 minutes. Stir in tomatoes, snow peas, white wine, salt, and black pepper. Mix in the remaining ingredients.
2. Seal the lid, select Manual on High, and cook for 15 minutes. Once ready, perform a quick pressure release. Remove the chicken to a plate and let it cool for 5 minutes. Discard the bones and return it in the Pot. Share into serving bowls and serve warm.

Nutrition Info: Calories 181, Protein 13g, Net Carbs 8.3g, Fat 10g

Chicken Lazore

Servings: 4
Cooking Time: 20 Minutes
Ingredients:
- 3 tsp garlic powder
- 2 tsp cayenne powder
- 2 tsp onion powder
- 2 tsp paprika
- Salt and black pepper to taste
- 4 chicken breasts, cut into strips
- 1 tbsp butter
- 1 tbsp olive oil
- 2/3 cup chicken broth
- 2 cups heavy cream
- 3 tbsp chopped fresh parsley

Directions:
1. In a small bowl, mix the garlic powder, cayenne powder, onion powder, paprika, salt, black pepper and season the chicken with the spice mixture.
2. Set the IP in Sauté mode and adjust to Medium heat.
3. Heat the butter and olive oil in the inner pot and cook the chicken in batches on all sides until brown, 5 minutes. Pour in the chicken broth and stir.
4. Lock the lid in place; select Manual mode on High Pressure and set the timer to 10 minutes.
5. After cooking, perform a quick pressure release and open the lid.
6. Set the IP in Sauté mode and mix in the heavy cream. Cook until the sauce thickens, 4 to 5 minutes. Adjust the taste with salt and black pepper.
7. Dish the food into serving bowls, garnish with parsley and serve warm.

Nutrition Info:

Per Serving: Calories 963 Fats 83g Carbs 7.13g Net Carbs 5.93g Protein 32g

Anniversary Chicken

Servings: 2
Cooking Time: 21 Minutes
Ingredients:

- 8 oz chicken breast, skinless, boneless
- ½ teaspoon chili flakes
- ½ teaspoon salt
- ½ teaspoon chili powder
- ¼ teaspoon ground turmeric
- ¼ teaspoon garlic powder
- 1 teaspoon coconut oil
- 1 cup water, for cooking

Directions:

1. Rub the chicken breast with chili flakes, salt, chili powder, turmeric, and garlic powder. Heat up the coconut oil in the instant pot on sauté mode for 3 minutes. Then place the chicken breast in the coconut oil and cook it for 4 minutes from each side; remove the chicken from the instant pot. Clean the instant pot and pour water inside. Insert the trivet in the instant pot. Then place the chicken breast on the trivet and close the lid. Cook the poultry on manual mode (high pressure) for minutes. When the time is over, make the quick pressure release. Slice the chicken breast into servings.

Nutrition Info: calories 153, fat 5.3, fiber 0.3, carbs 0.8, protein 2

Southern Turkey Soup

Servings: 4
Cooking Time: 20 Minutes
Ingredients:

- 2 teaspoons coconut oil
- 2 onions, chopped
- 2 garlic cloves, finely chopped
- 1/2 teaspoon freshly grated ginger
- 2 tomatoes, chopped
- 1 celery stalk with leaves, chopped
- 1 teaspoon dried basil
- 1/2 teaspoon dried rosemary
- 1 bay leaf
- 1/4 teaspoon freshly ground black pepper
- 1/2 teaspoon red pepper flakes, crushed
- Sea salt, to taste
- 3 turkey thighs
- 4 cups roasted vegetable broth
- 1/4 cup fresh parsley, finely minced

Directions:
1. Press the "Sauté" button to heat up the Instant Pot. Now, heat the oil. Cook the onion and garlic until softened and aromatic.
2. Add grated ginger, tomatoes, celery, basil, rosemary, bay leaf, black pepper, red pepper, salt, turkey thighs and vegetable broth.
3. Secure the lid. Choose the "Manual" setting and cook for 15 minutes at High pressure. Once cooking is complete, use a quick pressure release; carefully remove the lid.
4. Remove turkey thighs from the soup; discard the bones, shred the meat and return it to the Instant Pot.
5. Add fresh parsley and stir well. Serve in individual bowls. Bon appétit!

Nutrition Info:
Per Serving: 429 Calories; 2g Fat; 6.7g Total Carbs; 2g Protein; 3.1g Sugars

Chicken Tenders With Garlic

Servings: 2
Cooking Time: 15 Mins
Ingredients:
- 1 lb Chicken tenders
- 2 Garlic cloves, minced
- 2 tsp Paprika
- 2 tsp Oregano powder
- 2 tsp Olive oil
- 1 Onion, chopped
- 2 cups green Beans, frozen
- 1 cup Almond flour
- 1 cup Chicken stock
- 1 Egg, raw
- Salt and black pepper to taste

Directions:
1. Mix chicken tenders, garlic, paprika, oregano, onion, green beans, flour and chicken stock, in a bowl. Add egg, and stir well. Season with salt and pepper. Seal the lid, press Manual and cook for minutes on High. When ready, release the pressure quickly and serve hot.

Nutrition Info: Calories 436, Protein 53g, Net Carbs 9.1g, Fat 18g

Basil Chicken Mix

Servings: 4
Cooking Time: 25 Minutes
Ingredients:
- 2 chicken breasts, skinless, boneless and halved
- 1 cup chicken stock
- 1 and ½ tablespoons basil, chopped
- ¼ cup red bell peppers, cut into strips
- 4 garlic cloves, minced

- 1 tablespoon chili powder

Directions:

1. In your instant pot, combine the chicken with the rest of the ingredients, put the lid on and cook on High for 25 minutes. Release the pressure fast for 5 minutes, divide everything between plates and serve.

Nutrition Info: calories 230, fat 4, fiber 0.8, carbs 2.7, protein 2

Sweet Mustard Chicken

Servings: 4

Cooking Time: 21 Minutes

Ingredients:

- 2 tbsp butter
- 4 chicken thighs, bone-in
- Salt and black pepper to taste
- 3 tbsp Dijon mustard
- 1 tbsp coconut aminos
- 1 tbsp sugar-free maple syrup
- ½ cup chicken broth
- 3 garlic cloves, minced
- 1 tbsp freshly chopped parsley

Directions:

1. Set the IP in Sauté mode and adjust to Medium heat.
2. Melt the butter in the inner pot, season the chicken with salt, black pepper, and sear in the butter until golden brown on both sides, 6 minutes.
3. Meanwhile, in a medium bowl, mix the mustard, coconut aminos, maple syrup, chicken broth, and garlic. Pour the mixture over the chicken.
4. Lock the lid in place; select Manual mode on High Pressure and set the timer to 5 minutes.
5. After cooking, do a natural pressure release for 10 minutes, then a quick pressure release to let out the remaining steam and open the lid.
6. Stir in the parsley and adjust the taste with salt and black pepper.
7. Dish the chicken with sauce onto serving plates and serve warm.

Nutrition Info:

Per Serving: Calories 741 Fats 57g Carbs 3.17g Net Carbs 2.37g Protein 19g

Zoodle In Chicken Sauce

Servings: 4

Cooking Time: 10 Minutes

Ingredients:

- 1 tbsp olive oil
- 1 lb. ground chicken
- Salt and black pepper to taste
- 1 large yellow onion, chopped
- 1 garlic clove, minced

- 1 celery stalk, chopped
- 1 (25 oz) jar unsweetened tomato sauce
- 2 cups chicken broth
- 4 large zucchinis
- ½ cup grated Swiss cheese for topping

Directions:
1. Set the IP in Sauté mode and adjust to Medium heat.
2. Heat the olive oil in the inner pot and cook the chicken until no longer pink, 5 minutes. Season with salt, black pepper, and mix in the onion, garlic, and celery. Cook until vegetables soften, 3 minutes.
3. Add the tomato sauce, chicken broth, salt, black pepper, and zucchini.
4. Lock the lid in place; select Manual mode and set the timer to 2 minutes.
5. After cooking, perform a quick pressure release to let out the steam and open the lid.
6. Stir, dish the food, top with the cheese and serve warm.

Nutrition Info:
Per Serving: Calories 772 Fats 32g Carbs 03g Net Carbs 63g Protein 43g

Veggie Turkey Soup

Servings: 4
Cooking Time: 35 Mins
Ingredients:
- 1 tbsp olive oil
- ½ pound turkey breast, chopped
- 1 carrot, chopped
- 1 leek, chopped
- 1 parsnip, chopped
- 2 garlic cloves, minced
- 4 cups vegetable broth
- Salt and black pepper to taste
- 1 bunch fresh Thai basil
- ¼ tsp dried dill
- ½ tsp turmeric powder
- 2 cups Collard greens, torn into pieces

Directions:
1. Set your IP to Sauté and warm the olive oil. Cook the turkey for 2-3 minutes per side. Set aside. Put in the carrot, leek, parsnip, and garlic and cook until soft, about 5 minutes. Pour in vegetable broth, salt, black pepper, Thai basil, dill, and turmeric powder. Seal the lid, select Manual, and cook for minutes. Once ready, do a natural pressure release. Stir in the Collard greens until they wilt. Serve.

Nutrition Info: Calories 190, Protein 14g, Net Carbs 7.2g, Fat 8g

Family Chicken Wrapped In Prosciutto

Servings: 5

Cooking Time: 20 Minutes
Ingredients:

- 5 chicken breast halves, butterflied
- 2 garlic cloves, halved
- Sea salt, to taste
- 1/4 teaspoon ground black pepper, or more to taste
- 1/2 teaspoon red pepper flakes
- 1 teaspoon marjoram
- 10 strips prosciutto

Directions:

1. Prepare the Instant Pot by adding ½ cups of water and metal trivet to the bottom.
2. Rub chicken breast halves with garlic. Then, season the chicken with salt, black pepper, red pepper, and marjoram.
3. Then, wrap each chicken breast into 2 prosciutto strips; secure with toothpicks. Arrange wrapped chicken on the metal trivet.
4. Secure the lid. Choose the "Poultry" setting and cook for 15 minutes under High pressure. Once cooking is complete, use a natural pressure release; carefully remove the lid. Bon appétit!

Nutrition Info:
Per Serving: 548 Calories; 4g Fat; 1.1g Total Carbs; 3g Protein; 0g Sugars

Butter Chicken Stew

Servings: 4
Cooking Time: 25 Minutes
Ingredients:

- 4 tablespoons butter
- ½ cup asparagus, chopped
- 1 garlic clove, peeled, diced
- ½ teaspoon minced ginger
- 1 teaspoon tomato paste
- ½ teaspoon garam masala
- ½ teaspoon smoked paprika
- ½ teaspoon ground cumin
- ½ cup whipped cream
- 1 teaspoon dried parsley
- 10 oz chicken thighs, skinless, boneless
- ¼ cup chicken broth
- ¼ teaspoon salt
- ¼ teaspoon chili flakes

Directions:

1. Place butter in the instant pot. Add diced garlic, minced ginger, and garam masala. Cook the ingredients on sauté mode for 4 minutes. Stir the mixture from time to time. Then add ground cumin, parsley, and chicken thighs/ Sprinkle the chicken with salt and chili flakes.

Cook it for 3 minutes from each side on sauté mode. Add chicken broth and whipped cream. Close the lid. Cook the chicken for minutes on steam mode (high pressure). Then make quick pressure release and open the lid. Add asparagus and close the lid. Cook the stew for 5 minutes more on stew mode.

Nutrition Info: calories 291, fat 6, fiber 0.6, carbs 2.1, protein 9

Lemon & Pepper Turkey Meatloaf

Servings: 4
Cooking Time: 35 Mins
Ingredients:
- 1 pound ground turkey
- 1 cup pork rind crumbs
- ½ cup Grana Padano cheese, grated
- 1 tbsp coconut aminos
- 2 eggs
- Salt and black pepper, to taste
- 1 onion, chopped
- 2 garlic cloves, minced
- 4 oz tomato paste
- 1 tbsp lemon & pepper seasoning
- ½ cup tomato sauce
- 1 cup water
- 1 tsp mustard powder
- ½ tsp chili powder

Directions:
1. In a bowl, mix the ground turkey with pork rinds, Grana Padano cheese, coconut aminos, eggs, salt, black pepper, onion, garlic, tomato paste, and lemon & pepper seasoning. Place the mixture into a meatloaf.
2. Pour 1 cup of water in your IP and fit in a rack. Place the meatloaf on the rack. In another bowl, combine the tomato sauce with water, mustard, and chili powder. Top the meatloaf with the mixture.
3. Seal the lid, select Manual on High, and cook for 20 minutes. Once ready, perform a natural pressure release. Let rest for 6-8 minutes before slicing. Serve warm.

Nutrition Info: Calories 384, Protein 33g, Net Carbs 5.4g, Fat 16g

Easy One-pot Mexican Chili

Servings: 6
Cooking Time: 35 Minutes
Ingredients:
- 1 tablespoon olive oil
- 1 pound turkey, ground
- 1/2 pound pork, ground
- 1 onion, finely chopped

- 2 garlic cloves, minced
- 2 ripe tomatoes, pureed
- 1 Mexican chili pepper, minced
- 1/2 teaspoon ground cumin
- 1 teaspoon red pepper flakes
- Salt and ground black pepper, to taste
- 1 cup chicken stock
- 1 ½ cups Mexican cheese blend

Directions:
1. Press the "Sauté" button to heat up the Instant Pot. Heat the olive oil and brown the turkey and pork until no longer pink or about 3 minutes.
2. Add the remaining ingredients, except for Mexican cheese blend, to your Instant Pot.
3. Secure the lid. Choose "Poultry" mode and High pressure; cook for 15 minutes. Once cooking is complete, use a natural pressure release; carefully remove the lid.
4. Ladle into soup bowls; top each bowl with Mexican cheese blend and serve hot.

Nutrition Info:
Per Serving: 391 Calories; 27g Fat; 8.1g Carbs; 4g Protein; 4.9g Sugars

Ground Chicken And Zucchini Casserole

Servings: 4
Cooking Time: 15 Minutes
Ingredients:
- 3 teaspoons olive oil
- 1 pound ground chicken
- 1/2 cup parmesan cheese, grated
- 2 tablespoons pork rind crumbs
- Coarse sea salt and freshly ground black pepper, to taste
- 2 garlic cloves, minced
- 1 teaspoon dried basil
- 1/2 teaspoon dried oregano
- 1/2 teaspoon dried sage
- 1/2 pound zucchini, thinly sliced
- 2 ripe tomatoes, pureed
- 1/2 cup water
- 1 teaspoon mustard powder
- 1 teaspoon minced jalapeño
- 4 ounces Monterey-Jack cheese, shredded

Directions:
1. Press the "Sauté" button to heat up the Instant Pot. Now, heat teaspoon of olive oil until sizzling.
2. Brown ground chicken for minutes, crumbling it with a wide spatula or fork. Now, add parmesan cheese, pork rind crumbs, salt, black pepper, garlic, basil, oregano, and sage.
3. Cook an additional minute and reserve.

4. Wipe down the Instant Pot with a damp cloth; spritz the inner pot with a nonstick cooking spray. Arrange 1/3 of zucchini slices on the bottom.
5. Spread 1/3 of meat mixture over zucchini. Repeat the layering two more times.
6. In a mixing bowl, whisk tomatoes with the remaining 2 teaspoons of olive oil, water, mustard powder, and jalapeno.
7. Pour this tomato sauce over the casserole.
8. Secure the lid. Choose "Manual" mode and High pressure; cook for 10 minutes. Once cooking is complete, use a quick pressure release; carefully remove the lid.
9. Then, top the casserole with shredded cheese; allow it to melt on the residual heat. Bon appétit!

Nutrition Info:
Per Serving: 459 Calories; 9g Fat; 6.8g Carbs; 8g Protein; 1.8g Sugars

Chicken Thighs In Gravy

Servings: 4
Cooking Time: 31 Minutes
Ingredients:
- 1 tbsp coconut oil
- 1 ½ lbs. chicken thighs
- Salt and black pepper to taste
- 2 medium yellow onions, thinly sliced
- 3 garlic cloves, minced
- 2 tbsp grainy mustard
- ½ cup white wine
- ½ cup chicken broth
- 1 tsp dried rosemary
- 1 tbsp almond flour
- 1 tbsp chopped fresh parsley for garnishing

Directions:
1. Set the IP in Sauté mode and adjust to Medium heat.
2. Heat the coconut oil in the inner pot, season the chicken with salt, black pepper, and sear in the oil on both sides until golden brown, 6 minutes. Plate and set aside.
3. Sauté the onion and garlic until softened, minutes. Mix in the mustard, white wine, chicken broth, and rosemary. Simmer for 1 minute and lay in the chicken.
4. Lock the lid in place; select Manual mode on High Pressure and set the timer to 10 minutes.
5. After cooking, perform a natural pressure release for 10 minutes, then a quick pressure release to let out all the steam, and open the lid.
6. Remove the chicken onto serving plates and set the IP in Sauté mode.
7. Stir the flour into the sauce and allow thickening for 1 minute. Adjust the taste with salt and black pepper.
8. Stir in the parsley and spoon the sauce all over the chicken.
9. Serve warm.

Nutrition Info:
Per Serving: Calories 675 Fats 44g Carbs 3.35g Net Carbs 2.65g Protein 31g

Curried Chicken Patties

Servings: 4
Cooking Time: 23 Mins
Ingredients:

- 1 Egg
- ¼ cup grated Parmesan Cheese
- 1 pound Ground Chicken
- 1 tbsp chopped Parsley
- ¼ cup Cauliflower Rice
- 1 tsp Curry Powder
- Salt and black pepper to taste
- 2 tbsp Olive oil
- 1 ½ cups Water

Directions:

1. Pour in water t and lower the trivet. Grease a baking dish that fits in the pot with cooking spray.Place the chicken, egg, curry powder, parsley, cauliflower, and parmesan in a large bowl.
2. Season with salt and pepper, and mix the mixture with hands. Shape the mixture into 4 patties and arrange them in the baking dish. Place the dish on top of the trivet and seal the lid.
3. Cook for 10 minutes on High. When ready, do a quick pressure release. Set the baking dish aside and discard the water. Wipe the pot clean. Set on Sauté and heat half of the oil. Place 2 patties inside and cook for 2 minutes per side, until golden. Repeat with the remaining oil and patties. Serve with tomato or yogurt dip.

Nutrition Info: Calories 223, Protein 25g, Net Carbs 2g, Fat 19g

Creamy Chicken Drumsticks

Servings: 6
Cooking Time: 20 Minutes
Ingredients:

- 2 ripe tomatoes, chopped
- 1/2 cup roasted vegetable broth, preferably homemade
- 1 red onion, chopped
- 1 red bell pepper, seeded and chopped
- 1 green bell pepper, seeded and chopped
- 4 cloves garlic
- 1 teaspoon curry powder
- 1/2 teaspoon paprika
- 1/4 teaspoon ground black pepper
- Sea salt, to taste
- A pinch of grated nutmeg
- 1/2 teaspoon ground cumin

- 2 pounds chicken drumsticks, boneless, skinless
- 2 tablespoons butter
- 1/3 cup double cream
- 1 tablespoon flaxseed meal

Directions:

1. Add tomatoes, vegetable broth, onion, peppers, garlic, curry powder, paprika, black pepper, salt, grated nutmeg, and ground cumin to the bottom of your Instant Pot.
2. Add chicken drumsticks. Secure the lid. Choose "Manual" mode and High pressure; cook for 1minutes. Once cooking is complete, use a natural pressure release.
3. Allow it to cool completely and reserve the chicken.
4. In a mixing dish, whisk the remaining ingredients and add this mixture to the Instant Pot; press the "Sauté" button and bring it to a boil.
5. Now, add the chicken back to the cooking liquid. Press the "Cancel" button and serve immediately. Bon appétit!

Nutrition Info:
Per Serving: 351 Calories; 7g Fat; 7g Total Carbs; 5g Protein; 3.3g Sugars

Hot Butter Chicken

Servings: 4
Cooking Time: 40 Mins
Ingredients:

- ¼ lb Chicken, Boneless, pieces
- 1 cup Tomato puree
- 1-inch Ginger slice
- 1-2 red Chilies, diced
- ½ tsp Garlic paste
- Salt and black pepper to taste
- 4 tbsp Butter

Directions:

1. In a blender, add tomato puree, chilies, ginger, garlic, salt, and pepper and blend well. Melt butter on Sauté mode and fry the chicken for 5- minute. Transfer the tomato mixture and combine. Simmer for 10-15 minutes until the chicken tenders.

Nutrition Info: Calories 154, Protein 10g, Net Carbs 4.3g, Fat 9.4g

Spinach Stuffed Chicken

Servings: 2
Cooking Time: 18 Minutes
Ingredients:

- 10 oz chicken breast, skinless, boneless
- 3 oz Goat cheese, crumbled
- 1 cup spinach, chopped
- ½ teaspoon salt
- ½ teaspoon onion powder

- ¼ teaspoon ground turmeric
- ¼ teaspoon dried thyme
- 1 teaspoon apple cider vinegar
- 1 tablespoon olive oil
- 1 cup water, for cooking

Directions:

1. Pour olive oil in the instant pot and heat it up on sauté mode for 2-3 minutes. Add spinach. Sprinkle it with salt, onion powder, ground turmeric, and dried thyme. Stir the ingredients well and sauté for 5 minutes. Stir with the help of the spatula from time to time. When the time is over, add crumbled Goat cheese and apple cider vinegar and mix up. Transfer the mixture in the bowl and clean the instant pot. Cut the chicken breast into 2 servings. Cut the chicken breast in the shape of Hasselback. Fill every Hasselback cut with spinach mixture. Wrap the chicken in the foil. Pour water and insert the steamer rack in the instant pot. Place the wrapped chicken on the rack and close the lid. Cook the meal on steam mode (high pressure) for minutes. When the time is over, allow the natural pressure release and open the lid. Remove the chicken from the foil.

Nutrition Info: calories 421, fat 8, fiber 0.5, carbs 2.2, protein 6

Creamy Garlic Tuscan Chicken Thighs

Servings: 4
Cooking Time: 41 Mins
Ingredients:

- 6 Chicken Thighs, fat removed
- 6 oz Cream Cheese
- 3 cups Spinach
- ½ cup Sundried Tomatoes
- 2 tbsp Chicken Stock Seasoning
- ½ cup Parmesan Cheese, grated
- 4 cloves Garlic, minced
- 2 tsp Olive oil
- 2 cups Chicken Broth
- 1 ½ cups Unsweetened Almond Milk
- 3 tbsp Heavy Cream
- 3 tsp Italian Seasoning
- 2 tsp Water
- Salt and black pepper to taste
- Chopped Parsley to garnish

Directions:

1. Season chicken with pepper, salt, and Italian seasoning. Heat oil on Sauté, and brown the chicken for 6 minutes in total. Add milk, broth, stock seasoning and Italian seasoning. Seal the lid, and cook on High for minutes. Once ready, quickly release the pressure. Remove the chicken on a plate.

2. To the pot, add tomatoes, heavy cream, cheese cream, Parmesan, spinach and garlic. Select Sauté and cook for 5 minutes. Add the chicken to the sauce, and coat well. Top with parsley.

Nutrition Info: Calories 211, Protein 17g, Net Carbs 6g, Fat 9g

Budget-friendly Turkey Salad

Servings: 6
Cooking Time: 25 Minutes
Ingredients:

- 2 pounds turkey breast, boneless and skinless
- 1/2 teaspoon black pepper, preferably freshly ground
- 1/2 teaspoon red pepper flakes, crushed
- Seasoned salt, to taste
- 2 sprigs thyme
- 1 sprig sage
- 2 garlic cloves, pressed
- 1 leek, sliced
- 1/2 cup mayonnaise
- 1 ½ tablespoons Dijon mustard
- 1/2 cup celery, finely diced
- 1 cucumber, chopped

Directions:

1. Prepare your Instant Pot by adding ½ cups of water and a metal trivet to the bottom of the inner pot.
2. Now, sprinkle turkey breast with black pepper, red pepper, and salt. Lower the seasoned turkey breast onto the trivet. Top with thyme, sage, and garlic.
3. Now, secure the lid. Choose the "Poultry" setting and cook for 20 minutes under High pressure. Once cooking is complete, use a natural pressure release; carefully remove the lid.
4. Allow the turkey to cool completely. Slice the turkey into strips.
5. Add the remaining ingredients and transfer the mixture to a salad bowl. Serve well-chilled. Bon appétit!

Nutrition Info:
Per Serving: 321 Calories; 2g Fat; 4.4g Carbs; 35g Protein; 1.4g Sugars

Chicken Zucchini Rings

Servings: 2
Cooking Time: 20 Minutes
Ingredients:

- 1 zucchini, trimmed
- 6 oz ground chicken
- ½ teaspoon chili flakes
- ½ teaspoon salt
- ½ teaspoon ginger paste
- 1 cup keto marinara sauce

Directions:
1. Slice the zucchini into the thick rings and remove the zucchini meat from the ring.
2. In the mixing bowl, mix up ground chicken, chili flakes, salt, and ginger paste.
3. Then fill the zucchini rings with chicken mixture and place them in the instant pot.
4. Add marinara sauce, close and seal the lid.
5. Cook the meal on manual mode (high pressure) for 20 minutes. Make a quick pressure release.

Nutrition Info:
Per Serving: calories 203, fat 7.5, fiber 1.7, carbs 7.1, protein 3

Chicken Drumsticks De Provance

Servings: 2
Cooking Time: 15 Minutes
Ingredients:
- 1 tablespoon herbs de Provance
- 4 chicken drumstick
- ¼ cup full-fat cream
- 1 teaspoon butter

Directions:
1. Rub the chicken drumstick with the herbs de Provance.
2. Melt the butter and mix it up with the full-fat cream.
3. Place the chicken drumstick on the foil and sprinkle with the creamy liquid.
4. Pour 1 cup of water in the instant pot and place the trivet there.
5. Transfer the chicken on the instant pot trivet.
6. Lock the instant pot lid and seal it.
7. Set the "Poultry" mode and timer for 15 minutes (High pressure).
8. When the poultry is cooked – use the quick pressure release method.

Nutrition Info:
Per Serving: calories 192, fat 8.8, fiber 0, carbs 0.9, protein 6

Chicken Pasta

Servings: 4
Cooking Time: 20 Minutes
Ingredients:
- ¼ cup Monterey Jack cheese, shredded
- 1 tablespoon mascarpone cheese
- ½ cup coconut cream
- 1 teaspoon ground black pepper
- ½ teaspoon salt
- 1-pound chicken fillet, sliced
- 1 teaspoon olive oil

Directions:
1. Sprinkle the chicken fillet with ground black pepper and salt.

2. Then put it in the instant pot, add olive oil and cook on saute mode for 10 minutes.
3. Stir the chicken and add coconut cream and mascarpone cheese. Mix up well.
4. Add shredded cheese and close the lid.
5. Saute the chicken pasta for 10 minutes on saute mode.
6. Stir the cooked chicken pasta well before serving.

Nutrition Info:
Per Serving: calories 329, fat 4, fiber 0.8, carbs 2.2, protein 7

South American Garden Chicken

Servings: 4
Cooking Time: 17 Minutes
Ingredients:
- 1 cup cauliflower, chopped
- 1 celery stalk, chopped
- 1 tablespoon lemon juice
- 4 chicken thighs, skinless, boneless
- 1 teaspoon pumpkin puree
- ½ teaspoon salt
- 1 teaspoon ground black pepper
- ½ cup chicken broth
- 1 teaspoon ghee
- 1 bay leaf
- ½ onion, diced

Directions:
1. Sprinkle the chicken thighs with salt and ground black pepper. Place them in the instant pot. Add ghee. Cook the chicken on sauté mode for 4 minutes. Then flip it on another side and cook for 5 minutes more. After this, add celery stalk and cauliflower. Add diced onion. Then add pumpkin puree, lemon juice, and chicken broth. Close and seal the lid. Cook the meal on manual mode (high pressure) for 8 minutes. Then allow the natural pressure release for 5 minutes.

Nutrition Info: calories 170, fat 7.4, fiber 1.3, carbs 3.6, protein 4

Shredded Chicken Pizza Casserole

Servings: 6
Cooking Time: 30 Mins
Ingredients:
- 1 pound Chicken Breast
- 1 ¾ cups Marinara Sauce
- 1 tbsp Butter
- ½ tsp Italian Seasoning
- 4 ounces Pepperoni, sliced
- 6 ounces shredded Mozzarella Cheese
- ¼ cup Chicken Broth

- Salt and black pepper to taste

Directions:
1. Combine everything, except the cheese, in your Instant Pot. Give it a good stir and seal the lid. Select Manual and set the cooking time to minutes. Cook on High. Release the pressure quickly. Shred the chicken. Stir in the mozzarella cheese and set to Sauté. Cook for 5 minutes, until the cheese melts.

Nutrition Info: Calories 335, Protein 27g, Net Carbs 3g, Fat 11g

Turkey And Hot Lemon Sauce

Servings: 4
Cooking Time: 30 Minutes
Ingredients:
- 2 turkey breasts, skinless, boneless and cubed
- 1 shallot, minced
- 1 tablespoon ghee, melted
- 1 tablespoon lemon juice
- 1 tablespoon lemon zest, grated
- A pinch of salt and black pepper
- 1 teaspoon red pepper flakes
- 1 cup chicken stock

Directions:
1. Set your instant pot on Sauté mode, add the ghee, heat it up, add the shallot and the meat and brown for 5 minutes. Add the rest of the ingredients, put the lid on and cook on High for 25 minutes. Release the pressure naturally for minutes, divide everything between plates and serve.

Nutrition Info: calories 227, fat 9.1, fiber 0.2, carbs 0.8, protein 5

Chicken Fillets With Keto Sauce

Servings: 4
Cooking Time: 15 Minutes
Ingredients:
- 1 tablespoon peanut oil
- 1 pound chicken fillets
- Salt and freshly ground black pepper, to taste
- 1/2 teaspoon dried basil
- 1 cup broth, preferably homemade
- Cheese Sauce:
- 3 teaspoons butter, at room temperature
- 1/3 cup double cream
- 1/3 cup Neufchâtel cheese, at room temperature
- 1/3 cup Gruyère cheese, preferably freshly grated
- 3 tablespoons milk
- 1/2 teaspoon granulated garlic

- 1 teaspoon shallot powder

Directions:

1. Press the "Sauté" button and add peanut oil. Once hot, sear the chicken fillets for 3 minutes per side.
2. Season the chicken fillets with salt, black pepper, and basil; pour in the broth.
3. Secure the lid. Choose the "Manual" setting and cook for 6 minutes. Once cooking is complete, use a natural pressure release; carefully remove the lid.
4. Clean the Instant Pot and press the "Sauté" button. Now, melt the butter and add double cream, Neufchâtel cheese, Gruyère cheese and milk; add granulated garlic and shallot powder.
5. Cook until everything is heated through. Bon appétit!

Nutrition Info:

Per Serving: 314 Calories; 3g Fat; 1.7g Carbs; 9g Protein; 1.5g Sugars

Whole Rotisserie Chicken

Servings: 4

Cooking Time: 52 Minutes

Ingredients:

- 1 white onion, peeled
- 1 lemon, halved
- 1 whole chicken, cleaned (to fit into the instant pot)
- Salt and black pepper to taste
- 1 tsp garlic powder
- 1 tsp paprika
- 2 tbsp olive oil
- 1 cup chicken broth
- 3 fresh thyme sprigs

Directions:

1. Put the onion and lemon inside the chicken.
2. In a small bowl, combine salt, black pepper, garlic powder, and paprika. Rub the chicken thoroughly with the spice, within the cavity and on the body.
3. Set the IP in Sauté mode and adjust to Medium heat.
4. Heat the olive oil in the inner pot, place the chicken (with breast side down first) in the inner pot and cook for 5 minutes. Turn the chicken and turn the opposite side for minutes. Pour in the chicken broth and drop in the thyme.
5. Lock the lid in place; select Manual mode on High Pressure and set the timer for 2minutes.
6. Once ready, do a natural pressure release for 15 minutes, then a quick pressure release, and open the lid.
7. Take out the chicken, allow sitting for 3 minutes, and brush with the sauce.
8. Slice and serve warm.

Nutrition Info:

Per Serving: Calories 405 Fats 77g Carbs 5.52g Net Carbs 4.52g Protein 93g

Perfected Butter Chicken

Servings: 3
Cooking Time: 20 Mins
Ingredients:

- 4 Chicken Breasts, skinless and cubed
- 1 tbsp Olive oil
- 1 Onion, chopped
- Salt and black pepper to taste
- 1 tsp Garlic Powder
- 1 tsp Ginger Powder
- 1 tsp Turmeric
- 1 tsp Paprika
- 1 tsp Cayenne Powder
- 2 cups Diced Tomato
- 2 tbsp Tomato Puree
- 1 cup Coconut Milk
- 1 cup Coconut Cream
- ¼ cup Almonds, sliced
- ¼ cup Chopped Cilantro

Directions:

1. Heat oil on Sauté, and cook the onions and salt for 3 minutes. Add the remaining listed spices, salt, and pepper. Stir and cook for 2 minutes. Add the tomatoes and coconut milk and stir.
2. Add chicken, stir, and seal the lid. Cook on High for 10 minutes. Once ready, quickly release the pressure. Add tomato puree, coconut cream and cilantro. Serve stew with almond slices.

Nutrition Info: Calories 243, Protein 24g, Net Carbs 4g, Fat 13g

Easy Roasted Chicken Drumettes

Servings: 4
Cooking Time: 2 Hours 25 Minutes
Ingredients:

- 2 tablespoons olive oil
- 1 tablespoon tamari sauce
- 2 teaspoons champagne vinegar
- 2 garlic cloves, smashed
- 1/2 teaspoon turmeric powder
- 1 teaspoon freshly grated ginger
- 1/2 teaspoon sea salt
- 1/4 teaspoon ground black pepper
- 1 teaspoon paprika
- 1 ½ pounds chicken drumettes

- 1/2 cup fresh chives, roughly chopped
- 2 tablespoons black sesame seeds, toasted

Directions:
1. Place all of the above ingredients, except for fresh chives and black sesame seeds, in a mixing dish; cover and let it marinate for 2 hours in your refrigerator.
2. Add 1 ½ cups of water and metal trivet to the Instant Pot.
3. Then, place the chicken on the trivet.
4. Now, secure the lid. Choose the "Poultry" setting and cook for 20 minutes under High pressure. Once cooking is complete, use a quick pressure release; carefully remove the lid.
5. Preheat your oven to broil. Place the chicken drumettes on a parchment-lined baking sheet; spoon the reserved marinade over them.
6. Now, broil the chicken drumettes for 3 minutes on each side or until they are crisp and browned.
7. Serve garnished with fresh chives and toasted sesame seeds. Enjoy!

Nutrition Info:
Per Serving: 283 Calories; 9g Fat; 2.3g Carbs; 7g Protein; 0.3g Sugars

Thai Sweet And Spicy Chicken

Servings: 4
Cooking Time: 25 Minutes
Ingredients:
- 4 chicken breasts, cut into 1-inch cubes
- 1/3 cup coconut aminos
- 2 tbsp teriyaki sauce
- 1/3 cup unsweetened tomato ketchup
- 2 tbsp chili sauce
- 2 ½ tbsp sugar-free maple syrup
- 3 garlic cloves, minced
- 1 tbsp freshly grated ginger
- ½ tsp onion powder
- ¼ cup chicken broth
- Salt and black pepper to taste
- 1 ½ tbsp arrowroot starch

Directions:
1. Mix all the ingredients in the inner pot except for the arrowroot starch.
2. Lock the lid in place; select Manual mode on High Pressure and set the timer to 1minutes.
3. After cooking, perform a natural pressure release for 10 minutes, then a quick pressure release to let out the remaining steam, and open the lid.
4. Set the IP in Sauté mode and stir in the arrowroot starch. Cook until the sauce is syrupy, 2 to 3 minutes.
5. Dish the food into serving bowls and serve warm.

Nutrition Info:
Per Serving: Calories 688 Fats 17g Carbs 9.56g Net Carbs 7.36g Protein 92g

Creole Chicken Cauliflower Bowl

Servings: 4
Cooking Time: 6 Minutes
Ingredients:

- 2 tbsp olive oil
- 4 chicken breasts, thinly sliced
- 1 tsp Creole seasoning
- 2 green bell peppers, deseeded and sliced
- 1 cup cauliflower rice
- ½ cup chicken broth
- Salt to taste
- 2 chives, chopped
- 2 tbsp freshly chopped parsley
- 2 tbsp sesame seeds to garnish

Directions:

1. Set the IP in Sauté mode and adjust to Medium heat.
2. Heat the olive oil in the inner pot, season the chicken with the Creole seasoning, and cook with the bell peppers in the oil until the chicken is golden brown on both sides, 5 minutes and the peppers soften.
3. Stir in cauliflower, chicken broth, and salt.
4. Lock the lid in place; select Manual mode on High Pressure and set the timer to 1 minute.
5. After cooking, perform a quick pressure to let out all the steam, and open the lid.
6. Mix in the chives, parsley and dish the food onto serving plates.
7. Garnish with the sesame seeds and serve warm.

Nutrition Info:
Per Serving: Calories 852 Fats 51g Carbs 5.32g Net Carbs 3.82g Protein 78g

Hot Spicy Chicken Soup

Servings: 5
Cooking Time: 20 Minutes
Ingredients:

- 2 tablespoons grapeseed oil
- 2 banana shallots, chopped
- 4 cloves garlic, minced
- 1 cup Cremini mushrooms, sliced
- 2 bell peppers, seeded and sliced
- 1 serrano pepper, seeded and sliced
- 2 ripe tomatoes, pureed
- 1 teaspoon porcini powder
- 2 tablespoons dry white wine
- Sea salt and ground black pepper, to your liking
- 1 teaspoon dried basil

- 1/2 teaspoon dried dill weed
- 5 cups broth, preferably homemade
- 4 chicken wings

Directions:

1. Press the "Sauté" button and heat the oil. Once hot, sauté the shallots until just tender and aromatic.
2. Add the garlic, mushrooms, and peppers; cook an additional 3 minutes or until softened.
3. Now, stir in tomatoes, porcini powder, white wine, salt, and black pepper. Add the remaining ingredients and stir to combine.
4. Secure the lid. Choose "Manual" mode and High pressure; cook for 18 minutes. Once cooking is complete, use a quick pressure release.
5. Make sure to release any remaining steam and carefully remove the lid. Remove the chicken wings from the Instant Pot. Discard the bones and chop the meat.
6. Add the chicken meat back to the Instant Pot. Ladle into individual bowls and serve warm. Bon appétit!

Nutrition Info:
Per Serving: 238 Calories; 17g Fat; 5.4g Carbs; 4g Protein; 2.6g Sugars

Tabasco Chicken And Kale

Servings: 4
Cooking Time: 25 Minutes
Ingredients:

- 2 chicken breasts, skinless, boneless and cubed
- 2 tablespoons ghee, melted
- 1 tablespoon Tabasco sauce
- 2 cups kale, chopped
- A pinch of salt and black pepper
- 1 tablespoon basil, chopped
- 1 cup chicken stock

Directions:

1. Set your instant pot on sauté mode, add the ghee, heat it up, add the meat and brown for 5 minutes Add the rest of the ingredients, put the lid on and cook on High for 20 minutes. Release the pressure naturally for minutes, divide everything between plates and serve.

Nutrition Info: calories 291, fat 9, fiber 0.5, carbs 3.8, protein 2

Mexican-style Chicken Tacos

Servings: 6
Cooking Time: 30 Minutes
Ingredients:

- Low Carb Tortillas:
- 2 ounces pork rinds, crushed into a powder
- A pinch of baking soda
- A pinch of salt

175

- 2 ounces ricotta cheese
- 3 eggs
- 1/4 cup water
- Nonstick cooking spray
- Chicken:
- 1 ½ pounds chicken legs, skinless
- 4 cloves garlic, pressed or chopped
- 1/2 cup scallions, chopped
- 1 teaspoon dried basil
- 1/2 teaspoon dried thyme
- 1/2 teaspoon dried rosemary
- 1 teaspoon dried oregano
- Sea salt, to your liking
- 1/3 teaspoon ground black pepper
- 1/4 cup freshly squeezed lemon juice
- 1 cup water
- 1/4 cup dry white wine
- 1/2 cup salsa, preferably homemade

Directions:

1. To make low carb tortillas, add pork rinds, baking soda, and salt to your food processor; pulse a few times.
2. Now, fold in the cheese and eggs; mix until well combined. Add the water and process until smooth and uniform.
3. Spritz a pancake pan with a nonstick cooking spray. Preheat the pancake pan over moderate heat.
4. Now, pour the batter into the pan and prepare like you would a tortilla. Reserve keeping the tortillas warm.
5. Then, press the "Sauté" button and cook chicken legs for 2 to 4 minutes per side; reserve. Add the garlic and scallions and cook until aromatic.
6. Add the remaining ingredients, except for salsa. Return the chicken legs back to the Instant Pot.
7. Secure the lid. Choose the "Poultry" setting and cook for 15 minutes. Once cooking is complete, use a quick pressure release; carefully remove the lid.
8. Shred the chicken with two forks and discard the bones; serve with prepared tortillas and salsa. Enjoy!

Nutrition Info:
Per Serving: 443 Calories; 3g Fat; 4.6g Total Carbs; 7g Protein; 1.7g Sugars

Chicken Legs With Salsa Sauce

Servings: 5
Cooking Time: 15 Minutes
Ingredients:
- 5 chicken legs, skinless and boneless

- 1/2 teaspoon sea salt
- Salsa Sauce:
- 1 cup pureed tomatoes
- 1 teaspoon granulated garlic
- 2 bell peppers, deveined and chopped
- 1 minced jalapeño, chopped
- 1 cup onion, chopped
- 2 tablespoons fresh cilantro, minced
- 3 teaspoons lime juice

Directions:
1. Press the "Sauté" button to heat up your Instant Pot. Sear the chicken legs for 2 to 3 minutes on each side or until delicately browned. Season with sea salt.
2. In a mixing bowl, thoroughly combine the remaining ingredients to make your salsa. Spoon the salsa mixture over the browned chicken legs.
3. Secure the lid. Choose "Manual" mode and High pressure; cook for 10 minutes. Once cooking is complete, use a natural pressure release; carefully remove the lid. Bon appétit!

Nutrition Info:
Per Serving: 355 Calories; 3g Fat; 6.8g Total Carbs; 2g Protein; 3.7g Sugars

Teriyaki-style Chicken Pot

Servings: 4
Cooking Time: 15 Mins
Ingredients:
- ½ cup coconut aminos
- ½ cup rice wine vinegar
- 2 tbsp sugar-free soy sauce
- 6 drops liquid stevia
- 1 tbsp cornstarch
- 1/3 cup water
- 2 tbsp olive oil
- 1 pound chicken legs, boneless and skinless
- 1 tsp garlic powder
- 1 tsp minced fresh ginger
- Salt and black pepper, to taste
- ½ tsp sweet paprika
- 1 cup chicken stock

Directions:
1. Set your IP to Sauté and stir in the coconut aminos, vinegar, soy sauce, liquid stevia, and cornstarch. Pour in the water and bring to a boil. Cook until thickens. Reserve the sauce.
2. Wipe clean the pot and heat the olive oil. Brown the chicken. Put in the garlic powder and minced fresh ginger. Season with salt, black pepper, and paprika. Stir in the chicken stock and half of teriyaki sauce. Seal the lid, select Manual, and cook for 15 minutes. Once ready,

perform a natural pressure release for 10 minutes. Top with the remaining teriyaki sauce to serve.

Nutrition Info: Calories 231, Protein 23g, Net Carbs 4.8g, Fat 12g

Turkey And Creamy Garlic Mix

Servings: 4
Cooking Time: 25 Minutes
Ingredients:

- 1 big turkey breast, skinless, boneless and cubed
- 1 tablespoon ghee, melted
- 1 and ½ cups coconut cream
- A pinch of salt and black pepper
- 2 tablespoons tomato passata
- 2 tablespoons garlic, minced
- 1 teaspoon basil, dried

Directions:

1. Set your instant pot on Sauté mode, add the ghee, heat it up, add the meat and the garlic and brown for 5 minutes Add the rest of the ingredients, put the lid on and cook on High for 20 minutes. Release the pressure naturally for minutes, divide between plates and serve.

Nutrition Info: calories 229, fat 8.9, fiber 0.2, carbs 1.8, protein 6

Gruyère And Turkey Au Gratin

Servings: 4
Cooking Time: 40 Minutes
Ingredients:

- 1 tablespoon canola oil
- 1 pound turkey legs, boneless and skinless
- 6 ounces smoked deli ham
- 8 ounces Cottage cheese
- 1/2 teaspoon mustard powder
- 1/3 teaspoon cayenne pepper, or more to taste
- 1 cup water
- 2 cups Gruyère cheese, shredded
- Salt and ground black pepper, to taste

Directions:

1. Press the "Sauté" button to heat up the Instant Pot. Now, heat the oil and cook the turkey legs until no longer pink.
2. Add ham, Cottage cheese, mustard powder, cayenne pepper, and water; gently stir to combine.
3. Secure the lid. Choose the "Meat/Stew" setting and cook for minutes under High pressure. Once cooking is complete, use a natural pressure release; carefully remove the lid.
4. Add shredded Gruyère cheese and continue to cook in the residual heat until the cheese has melted completely.

5. Season with salt and black pepper; taste, adjust the seasonings and serve. Bon appétit!

Nutrition Info:

Per Serving: 540 Calories; 35g Fat; 2.9g Carbs; 8g Protein; 1.8g Sugars

Mustard Chicken Breast

Servings: 2

Cooking Time: 15 Minutes

Ingredients:

- 10 oz chicken breast, boneless
- 1 tablespoon sunflower oil
- 2 teaspoons mustard
- 1 cup of water

Directions:

1. Pour water in the instant pot and insert the steamer rack.
2. In the shallow bowl, mix up sunflower oil and mustard.
3. Rub the chicken breast with mustard mixture and wrap in the foil.
4. Put the wrapped chicken on the steamer rack and close the lid.
5. Cook the meal in manual mode for 1minutes. Make a quick pressure release.

Nutrition Info:

Per Serving: calories 239, fat 5, fiber 0.5, carbs 1.2, protein 9

Basic Chicken Thighs

Servings: 4

Cooking Time: 20 Minutes

Ingredients:

- 4 chicken thighs
- 2 tablespoons avocado oil
- 1/2 teaspoon dried basil
- 1 teaspoon dried oregano
- 1/2 cup chicken broth
- 1/3 cup white wine
- Salt and pepper, to taste
- 4 garlic cloves, minced
- 1 teaspoon paprika
- 1/2 teaspoon dried marjoram

Directions:

1. Press the "Sauté" button and heat the avocado oil. Saute the chicken thighs for 2-3 minutes.
2. Then stir in the paprika, white wine, garlic, salt, pepper, dried basil, dried oregano, chicken broth and dried marjoram.
3. Secure the lid. Choose the "Manual" setting and cook for 1minutes. When cooking is complete, use a natural pressure release and carefully remove the lid.
4. Serve with your favorite keto salad. Bon appétit!

Nutrition Info:

Per Serving: 496 Calories; 1g Fat; 4.7g Carbs; 7g Protein; 2.2g Sugars

Cream Of Chicken & Cauliflower

Servings: 4
Cooking Time: 15 Mins
Ingredients:
- 3 tbsp butter
- 2 chicken breasts
- 1 onion, chopped
- ½ fennel bulb, chopped
- 1 garlic clove, minced
- 1 head cauliflower, broken into florets
- 1 tbsp fresh thyme, chopped
- ½ cup sour cream

Directions:
1. Set your IP to Sauté and melt the butter. Brown the chicken for 3 minutes on all sides. Add in the onion, fennel, and garlic, cook for 3 minutes until tender. Pour in broth.
2. Seal the lid, select Manual on High, and cook for 10 minutes. Once ready, perform a natural pressure release. Shred the chicken using two forks and return it in the pot. Stir in the cauliflower and seal the lid again. Cook for another 5 minutes on Manual. Do a quick pressure release.
3. Transfer the soup to a food processor and pulse until smooth. Stir in sour cream and divide between bowls. Sprinkle with thyme to serve.

Nutrition Info: Calories 403, Protein 33g, Net Carbs 3.9g, Fat 25g

Asian-style Turkey Meatballs

Servings: 6
Cooking Time: 15 Minutes
Ingredients:
- 1 pound ground turkey
- 1/2 pound ground pork
- 1/2 cup Parmesan cheese, grated
- 2 eggs, whisked
- 1/2 cup green onions
- 2 cloves garlic, minced
- 1/2 teaspoon grated ginger
- 2 tablespoons Shaoxing wine
- 2 tablespoons dark soy sauce
- Sea salt and ground black pepper, to taste
- 2 tablespoons sesame oil
- 1 cup tomato sauce

Directions:

1. In a mixing dish, thoroughly combine ground turkey, pork, Parmesan cheese, eggs, green onions, garlic, ginger, Shaoxing wine, dark soy sauce, salt, and black pepper; mix until everything is well incorporated.
2. Press the "Sauté" button and heat the sesame oil. Sear the meatballs for a couple of minutes or until browned on all sides. Add tomato sauce.
3. Secure the lid. Choose the "Manual" setting and cook for 10 minutes under High pressure. Once cooking is complete, use a quick pressure release; carefully remove the lid.
4. Serve your meatballs with the sauce. Bon appétit!

Nutrition Info:
Per Serving: 590 Calories; 7g Fat; 5g Carbs; 2g Protein; 2.4g Sugars

Creamy Ranch Chicken

Servings: 4
Cooking Time: 27 Minutes
Ingredients:
- 2 bacon slices, chopped
- 1 oz pack ranch seasoning
- 1 cup chicken broth
- 4 chicken breasts
- 4 oz cream cheese, softened
- 2 tbsp chopped fresh green onions

Directions:
1. Set the IP in Sauté mode and adjust to Medium heat.
2. Cook the bacon in the inner pot until crispy and brown, 5 minutes.
3. Stir in ranch seasoning, chicken broth, and chicken.
4. Lock the lid in place; select Manual mode on High Pressure and set the timer to 12 minutes.
5. After cooking, perform a natural pressure release for 10 minutes, then a quick pressure release to let out the remaining steam, and open the lid.
6. Place the chicken and set the pot in Sauté mode.
7. Use two forks to shred the chicken into strands and stir into the sauce along with the cream cheese. Allow melting and mix in the green onions.
8. Serve the food warm.

Nutrition Info:
Per Serving: Calories 818 Fats 26g Carbs 5.74g Net Carbs 4.74g Protein 52g

Cajun Chicken

Servings: 4
Cooking Time: 18 Minutes
Ingredients:
- 1 tbsp olive oil
- 4 chicken breasts, cut into 1-inch cubes
- 1 tbsp Cajun seasoning
- 1 small white onion, chopped

- 3 garlic cloves, minced
- 1 tbsp tomato paste
- 1 cup chicken broth
- ½ cup chopped green beans
- ½ cup chopped mixed bell peppers
- Salt to taste

Directions:

1. Set the IP in Sauté mode and adjust to Medium heat.
2. Heat the olive oil in the inner pot and season the chicken with Cajun seasoning and sear in the oil until golden on the outside, 5 minutes.
3. Mix in onion, garlic, and cook until fragrant, minutes. Add the tomato paste, chicken broth, green beans, and bell peppers.
4. Lock the lid in place; select Manual mode on High Pressure and set the timer to 10 minutes.
5. Allow cooking, perform a quick pressure release to let out the steam and open the lid.
6. Stir and adjust the taste with salt and black pepper.
7. Dish and serve warm.

Nutrition Info:

Per Serving: Calories 820 Fats 73g Carbs 5.79g Net Carbs 2.93g Protein 19g

Sunday Funday Chicken Drumettes

Servings: 8

Cooking Time: 55 Minutes

Ingredients:

- 2 tablespoons grapeseed oil
- 8 chicken drumettes
- 2 cloves garlic, minced
- Sea salt and ground black pepper, to taste
- 2 ripe tomatoes, pureed
- 2 tablespoons capers, rinsed and drained
- 1 cup broth, preferably homemade
- 1 tablespoon flaxseed meal
- 1 (3-pound spaghetti squash, halved
- 1 tablespoon olive oil
- Coarse sea salt, to taste

Directions:

1. Press the "Sauté" button to heat up the Instant Pot. Heat the grapeseed oil.
2. Brown the chicken drumettes for to 3 minutes per side.
3. Add the garlic, salt, black pepper, tomatoes, capers, and broth.
4. Secure the lid. Choose "Manual" mode and High pressure; cook for 10 minutes. Once cooking is complete, use a natural pressure release; carefully remove the lid.
5. Reserve the chicken drumettes. Press the "Sauté" button again and add the flaxseed meal to the Instant Pot.
6. Thicken the tomato sauce for a couple of minutes or until your desired thickness is achieved.

7. Preheat your oven to 380 degrees F. Place squash halves, cut-side down on a lightly greased baking pan. Drizzle olive oil over them and sprinkle with sea salt.
8. Roast for 40 minutes. Afterwards, scrape the flesh to create "spaghetti". Serve with warm chicken drumettes and tomato sauce. Enjoy!

Nutrition Info:
Per Serving: 224 Calories; 9.4g Fat; 7g Total Carbs; 4g Protein; 1.1g Sugars

Indian Style Chicken

Servings: 2
Cooking Time: 4 Minutes
Ingredients:
- ¼ teaspoon cumin seeds
- ½ teaspoon turmeric
- 1 teaspoon ground paprika
- ¾ teaspoon chili paste
- ½ teaspoon ground coriander
- ½ cup of coconut milk
- 14 oz chicken breast, skinless, boneless
- 1 tablespoon coconut oil

Directions:
1. Blend together the cumin seeds, turmeric, ground paprika, chili paste, coriander, coconut milk, and coconut oil.
2. When the mixture is smooth – pour it in the instant pot bowl.
3. Chop the chicken breast roughly and transfer it in the spice mixture. Stir gently with the help of the spatula.
4. Lock the lid and seal it.
5. Set the "Manual" mode for 4 minutes (High pressure).
6. After this, make quick-release pressure.
7. Enjoy!

Nutrition Info:
Per Serving: calories 435, fat 6, fiber 1.9, carbs 5.1, protein 8

Celery Salad With Chicken

Servings: 2
Cooking Time: 6 Minutes
Ingredients:
- 1 cup celery, raw, diced
- 5 oz chicken breast, chopped
- 1 tablespoon butter
- 1 tablespoon lemon juice
- ½ teaspoon chili flakes
- 1 tablespoon fresh dill, chopped
- ½ tomato, chopped

- ¾ cup of water

Directions:

1. Toss the butter in the instant pot and preheat it on the "Saute" mode.
2. Add chopped chicken breast. Sprinkle it with the chili flakes and cook for 4 minutes.
3. Add water and close the lid. Seal the lid and set the "Manual" mode + press timer for minutes (High Pressure). Make the quick pressure release then.
4. Add tomato and celery in the salad bowl.
5. Add fresh dill and lemon juice.
6. After this, add chicken breast (don't use the chicken water).
7. Stir the salad directly before serving and enjoy!

Nutrition Info:

Per Serving: calories 148, fat 7.8, fiber 1.3, carbs 3.2, protein 16

Garlicky Chicken With Parsnip & Mushrooms

Servings: 4
Cooking Time: 20 Mins
Ingredients:

- 2 tsp olive oil
- 1 pound chicken breast halves, cubed
- 1 tsp cayenne pepper
- 1 onion, chopped
- Salt black pepper to taste
- 1 cup mushrooms, sliced
- 1 parsnip, chopped
- 1 carrot, chopped
- 4 garlic cloves, minced
- 2 cups vegetable broth
- 2 bay leaves
- ½ cup butter
- 2 tbsp fresh cilantro, chopped

Directions:

1. Set your IP to Sauté and heat the oil. Cook the chicken for 7-8 minutes on all sides. Put in the cayenne pepper, onion, salt, black pepper, and mushrooms and cook until tender, about 5 minutes. Stir in the parsnip, carrot, garlic, broth, and bay leaves.
2. Seal the lid, select Manual on High, and cook for 1minutes. Once ready, perform a quick pressure release. Stir in the butter, cook until the liquid is thicken. Garnish with cilantro to serve.

Nutrition Info: Calories 468, Protein 25g, Net Carbs 5.9g, Fat 25g

Vinegar Chicken Fillets

Servings: 4

Cooking Time: 25 Minutes

Ingredients:

- 1 teaspoon Cajun seasonings
- ¼ cup apple cider vinegar
- 1-pound chicken fillet
- 1 tablespoon sesame oil
- ¼ cup of water

Directions:

1. Put all ingredients in the instant pot. Close and seal the lid.
2. Cook the chicken fillets on manual mode (high pressure) for minutes.
3. Allow the natural pressure release for 10 minutes.

Nutrition Info:

Per Serving: calories 249, fat 8, fiber 0, carbs 0.1, protein 8

Drumsticks In Asiago-parsley Sauce

Servings: 4

Cooking Time: 23 Minutes

Ingredients:

- 1 tbsp olive oil
- 4 large drumsticks
- Salt and black pepper to taste
- 4 garlic cloves, minced
- 2 limes, juiced
- 1 tsp chili powder
- 1 tsp red chili flakes
- ½ chopped fresh parsley
- 1 cup chicken broth
- 1 cup grated Asiago cheese
- 8 oz cream cheese, softened

Directions:

1. Set the IP in Sauté mode and adjust to Medium heat.
2. Heat the olive oil in the inner pot, season the drumsticks with salt, black pepper, and sear in oil until golden brown on the outside, 5 minutes.
3. Stir in the garlic, lime juice, chili powder, red chili flakes, parsley, and chicken broth.
4. Lock the lid in place; select Manual mode on High Pressure and set the timer to 10 minutes.
5. After cooking, perform a natural pressure release for minutes, then a quick pressure release to let out the remaining steam, and open the lid.
6. Set the IP in Sauté mode and mix in the Asiago and cream cheeses until melted, 2 to 3 minutes.
7. Dish the food and serve warm.

Nutrition Info:

Per Serving: Calories 633 Fats 19g Carbs 6.61g Net Carbs 5.81g Protein 7g

Chicken, Kale And Artichokes

Servings: 4
Cooking Time: 25 Minutes
Ingredients:

- 1 pound chicken breast, skinless, boneless and cubed
- 1 shallot, minced
- 4 garlic cloves, minced
- 1 pound kale, torn
- A pinch of salt and black pepper
- 1 cup canned artichoke hearts, drained
- 1 cup chicken stock
- 2 tablespoons avocado oil

Directions:

1. Set your instant pot on Sauté mode, add the oil, heat it up, add the shallot, garlic and the chicken and sauté for 5 minutes. Add the rest of the ingredients, toss, put the lid on and cook on High for 20 minutes. Release the pressure naturally for minutes, divide the mix between plates and serve.

Nutrition Info: calories 288, fat 9.5, fiber 2.1, carbs 5.6, protein 6

Bell Pepper And Egg Tortilla

Servings: 3
Cooking Time: 25 Mins
Ingredients:

- 4 Eggs, whisked
- 1 red Bell Pepper, chopped
- 1 Onion, chopped
- Salt and black pepper to taste
- 3 tbsp Butter

Directions:

1. In a bowl, add eggs, onion, bell peppers, salt, and pepper, mix well. Melt butter on Sauté mode. Pour the eggs mixture and spread all over and seal the lid. Cook for minutes, flipping once halfway through cooking. Serve hot and enjoy.

Nutrition Info: Calories 133, Protein 6.5g, Net Carbs 3.2g, Fat 10g

Chicken&cheddar Biscuits

Servings: 4
Cooking Time: 10 Minutes
Ingredients:

- 3 oz chicken fillet, cooked, shredded
- 2 tablespoons almond flour
- 1 egg, beaten
- ½ teaspoon minced garlic

- ¼ cup coconut cream
- 3 oz Cheddar cheese, shredded
- 1 cup water, for cooking

Directions:
1. In the mixing bowl, mix up shredded chicken, almond flour, egg, minced garlic, coconut cream, and shredded cheese.
2. Then transfer the homogenous mixture in the muffin molds and flatten them gently with the help of the spoon.
3. Pour water and insert the steamer rack in the instant pot.
4. Place the muffin molds on the rack. Close and seal the lid.
5. Cook the meal on manual mode (high pressure) for 10 minutes. Allow the natural pressure release for 10 minutes.

Nutrition Info:
Per Serving: calories 257, fat 3, fiber 1.8, carbs 4.3, protein 2

Pulled Chicken

Servings: 2
Cooking Time: 12 Minutes
Ingredients:
- ¼ teaspoon smoked paprika
- ½ teaspoon ground cumin
- 3 tablespoons sugar-free ketchup
- 1 cup of water
- 1 teaspoon Erythritol
- 10 oz chicken fillet

Directions:
1. Put all the ingredients in the instant pot. Close and seal the lid.
2. Cook the meal on Manual (high pressure) for 1minutes.
3. Then make a quick pressure release and open the lid.
4. Shred the chicken with the help of 2 forks and transfer in the serving bowls.
5. Add ½ part of the remaining liquid from the instant pot.

Nutrition Info:
Per Serving: calories 280, fat 7, fiber 0.2, carbs 7.4, protein 1

Chicken And Herbs Sauce

Servings: 4
Cooking Time: 25 Minutes
Ingredients:
- 2 chicken breasts, skinless, boneless and halved
- 2 tablespoons ghee, melted
- 1 cup chicken stock
- 2 bay leaves
- A pinch of salt and black pepper

- 1 tablespoon chervil, chopped
- 1 tablespoon chives, chopped
- 1 tablespoon cilantro, chopped
- 1 tablespoon thyme, chopped

Directions:

1. Set your instant pot on Sauté mode, add the ghee, heat it up, add the chervil, chives, cilantro, bay leaves and thyme and cook for 2 minutes. Add the meat and brown for 3 minutes more. Add the rest of the ingredients, put the lid on and cook on High for 20 minutes. Release the pressure naturally for minutes, divide the mix between plates and serve.

Nutrition Info: calories 277, fat 15, fiber 0.3, carbs 0.9, protein 2

Grilled Herb Marinade Chicken With Sautéed Mushrooms

Servings: 4
Cooking Time: 30 Mins
Ingredients:

- 1 cup chopped mixed fresh herb leaves (basil, parsley, cilantro)
- 2 large garlic cloves, chopped
- 1/4 cup apple cider vinegar
- 1/4 cup extra-virgin olive oil
- 3 teaspoons sea salt
- 1/4 teaspoon pepper
- 2 lbs. chicken breasts, boneless, skinless, sliced in half lengthwise
- 4 cups button mushrooms
- 1 1/2 tablespoons butter
- 2 red onions, chopped

Directions:

1. In a food processor, process together herbs, garlic, vinegar, oil, salt and pepper until smooth; transfer to a Ziploc bag and add chicken. Shake to coat chicken well and refrigerate for about 30 Mins.
2. Set your instant pot on manual high and heat in oil; add chicken and cook for 5 Mins per side or until browned. Remove chicken and add water to the pot; insert a trivet and place the chicken over the trivet. Lock lid and cook for 30 Mins. Let pressure come down naturally.
3. Add butter to a skillet over medium heat and sauté red onion until fragrant; stir in mushrooms and cook for about 6 Mins or until tender; season with salt and pepper. Serve grilled chicken over the sautéed mushrooms.

Nutrition Info:
Per Serving: Calories: 504; Fat: 34g; Carbs: 9.9g; Protein: 6g

Italian-style Turkey Breasts

Servings: 6
Cooking Time: 25 Minutes

Ingredients:
- 2 pounds turkey breast
- Sea salt and ground black pepper, to taste
- 1 teaspoon paprika
- 1 tablespoon olive oil
- 1 cup water
- Pesto Sauce:
- 2 tablespoons pine nuts, toasted
- 1/2 cup fresh basil leaves
- 1/3 cup Parmesan cheese, grated
- 1/3 cup olive oil
- 1 garlic clove, halved
- Salt and ground black pepper, to taste

Directions:
1. Season turkey breast with salt, black pepper, and paprika.
2. Press the "Sauté" button to heat up the Instant Pot. Heat 1 tablespoon of olive oil and sear the turkey breast for to 3 minutes per side.
3. Pour in the water and secure the lid. Choose "Poultry" mode and High pressure; cook for 20 minutes. Once cooking is complete, use a quick pressure release; carefully remove the lid.
4. To make the pesto sauce, add the pine nuts and fresh basil leaves to your food processor.
5. Add the remaining ingredients and process until everything is well incorporated. Serve the prepared turkey breast with pesto sauce. Bon appétit!

Nutrition Info:
Per Serving: 391 Calories; 3g Fat; 1.8g Total Carbs; 9g Protein; 0.4g Sugars

Cheesy Baked Turkey

Servings: 4
Cooking Time: 40 Mins
Ingredients:
- 1 tbsp canola oil
- 1 pound turkey breast, boneless and skinless
- 6 oz Parma ham
- 8 oz Cottage cheese
- ½ tsp mustard powder
- 1/3 tsp cayenne pepper
- 2 cups emmental cheese, shredded
- Salt and black pepper, to taste

Directions:
1. Set your IP to Sauté and heat the oil. Place the turkey and cook until no longer pink, about 5-6 minutes. Stir in the Parma ham, Cottage cheese, mustard powder, cayenne pepper, and cup water.Seal the lid, select Manual on High, and cook for 15 minutes. When done, d a quick pressure release. Add in emmental cheese; stir until the cheese has melted. Season with salt and pepper. Serve.

Nutrition Info: Calories 524, Protein 53g, Net Carbs 7.8g, Fat 29g

Healthy Chicken Curry

Servings: 1 Serving
Cooking Time: 20 Mins
Ingredients:

- 1 tablespoon olive oil
- 100 grams chicken, diced
- ¼ cup chicken broth
- Pinch of turmeric
- Dash of onion powder
- 1 tablespoon minced red onion
- Pinch of garlic powder
- ¼ teaspoon curry powder
- Pinch of sea salt
- Pinch of pepper
- Stevia
- Pinch of cayenne
- 1 cup riced cauliflower
- 1 tablespoon butter
- 1 red onion

Directions:

1. Prepare cauliflower by melting butter in a skillet and then sautéing red onion. Stir in cauliflower and cook for about 4 Mins or until tender. Set aside until ready to serve.
2. Set an instant pot on sauté mode, heat oil and sauté onion and garlic; stir in chicken and cook until browned. Stir spices in chicken broth and Stevia and add to the pot. Lock lid and cook on high for 15 Mins. Release the pressure naturally and serve hot over sautéed cauliflower.

Nutrition Info:
Per Serving: Calories: 213; Fat: 4g; Carbs: 2.3g; Protein: 5g

Green Sandwich

Servings: 2
Cooking Time: 10 Minutes
Ingredients:

- 4 oz kale leaves
- 8 oz chicken fillet
- 1 tablespoon butter
- 1 oz lemon
- ¼ cup of water

Directions:

1. Dice the chicken fillet.
2. Squeeze the lemon juice over the poultry.

3. Transfer the poultry into the instant pot; add water and butter.
4. Close the lid and cook the chicken on the "Poultry" mode for 10 minutes.
5. When the chicken is cooked – place it on the kale leaves to make the medium sandwiches.

Nutrition Info:
Per Serving: calories 298, fat 2, fiber 1.3, carbs.7.2, protein 7

Chicken Parmigiana

Servings: 4
Cooking Time: 22 Minutes
Ingredients:
- 4 chicken thighs, boneless and skinless
- 6 cups unsweetened marinara sauce
- Salt and black pepper to taste
- ¼ tsp red chili flakes
- 1 tsp dried oregano
- 1 tsp dried basil
- 1 tsp garlic powder
- 1 cup grated Parmigiano-Reggiano cheese
- 2 cups grated mozzarella cheese
- 1 tsp dried parsley for garnishing

Directions:
1. Cut chicken into inch cubes and add to the inner pot. Mix in the marinara sauce, salt, black pepper, red chili flakes, oregano, basil, and garlic powder.
2. Lock the lid in place; select Manual mode on High Pressure and set the timer to 1minutes.
3. After cooking, perform a natural pressure release for 10 minutes, then a quick pressure release to let out the remaining steam, and open the lid.
4. Set the IP in Sauté mode and sprinkle the cheeses on top. Continue cooking until the cheeses melt.
5. Sprinkle the dried parsley on top and dish the food.
6. Serve warm.

Nutrition Info:
Per Serving: Calories 142 Fats 7.07g Carbs 8.05g Net Carbs 5.85g Protein 26g

Thai Coconut Chicken

Servings: 4
Cooking Time: 15 Minutes
Ingredients:
- 1 tablespoon coconut oil
- 1 pound chicken, cubed
- 1 shallot, peeled and chopped
- 2 cloves garlic, minced
- 1 teaspoon fresh ginger root, julienned
- 1/3 teaspoon cumin powder

- 1 teaspoon Thai chili, minced
- 1 cup vegetable broth, preferably homemade
- 1 tomato, peeled and chopped
- 1/3 cup coconut milk, unsweetened
- 1 teaspoon Thai curry paste
- 2 tablespoons tamari sauce
- 1/2 cup sprouts
- Salt and freshly ground black pepper, to taste

Directions:
1. Press the "Sauté" button to heat up the Instant Pot. Now, heat the coconut oil. Cook the chicken for 2 to 3 minutes, stirring frequently; reserve.
2. Then, in pan drippings, cook the shallot and garlic until softened; add a splash of vegetable broth, if needed.
3. Add ginger, cumin powder and Thai chili and cook until aromatic or 1 minute more.
4. Now, stir in vegetable broth, tomato, coconut milk, Thai curry paste, and tamari sauce.
5. Secure the lid. Choose the "Manual" setting and cook for 10 minutes under High pressure. Once cooking is complete, use a quick pressure release; carefully remove the lid.
6. Afterwards, add sprouts, salt, and black pepper and serve immediately. Bon appétit!

Nutrition Info:
Per Serving: 192 Calories; 7.5g Fat; 5.4g Carbs; 2g Protein; 2.2g Sugars

Chicken Provencal

Servings: 4
Cooking Time: 17 Minutes
Ingredients:
- 1 tablespoon coconut oil
- 2 oz pancetta, chopped
- 3 oz leek, chopped
- 1-pound chicken fillet, chopped
- ½ teaspoon ground thyme
- ½ teaspoon salt
- ½ teaspoon ground black pepper
- 2 tablespoons apple cider vinegar
- ½ cup mushrooms, sliced
- 1 cup chicken broth

Directions:
1. Place the coconut oil in the instant pot and melt it on sauté mode. Add pancetta and cook it for 5 minutes. Stir it from time to time. After this, add leek and mix up well. Cook the ingredients for 3 minutes. Then add chicken. Sprinkle the mixture with ground thyme, salt, and ground black pepper. Mix up the ingredients well and cook for 2 minutes. After this, add mushrooms and apple cider vinegar. Add chicken broth and close the lid. Cook the meal on manual mode (high pressure) for 7 minutes. When the time is over, make a quick pressure release and transfer the meal in the serving bowls.

Nutrition Info: calories 348, fat 2, fiber 0.6, carbs 4.1, protein 9

Asian Meatball Soup

Servings: 6
Cooking Time: 20 Minutes
Ingredients:

- Meatballs:
- 1 pound ground chicken
- 1/2 pound ground pork
- 1/4 cup fresh cilantro, chopped
- 2 tablespoons scallions, finely chopped
- 1 teaspoon garlic powder
- 1/2 Chinese Five-spice powder
- 1/2 teaspoon grated ginger
- 1 tablespoon soy sauce
- Sea salt, to taste
- 1/2 teaspoon ground black pepper
- 1/2 teaspoon red pepper flakes, crushed
- 1 egg, well-beaten
- Soup:
- 1 tablespoon olive oil
- 1 teaspoon dried rosemary
- 1 teaspoon dried thyme
- 1 tablespoon fresh dill, chopped
- 1/2 teaspoon cumin
- 1/2 cup tomato puree, sugar-free
- 2 celery stalks, chopped
- 1 ½ cups Chinese cabbage, chopped
- 6 cups chicken bone broth, preferably homemade

Directions:

1. In a mixing bowl, combine all ingredients for the meatballs. Shape the meat mixture into balls; set aside.
2. Press the "Sauté" button to heat up the Instant Pot. Heat the olive oil and sear the meatballs on all sides until crisp and browned.
3. Stir in the remaining ingredients.
4. Secure the lid. Choose the "Poultry" setting and cook for 15 minutes under High pressure. Once cooking is complete, use a quick pressure release; carefully remove the lid. Bon appétit!

Nutrition Info:
Per Serving: 375 Calories; 1g Fat; 5.8g Total Carbs; 1g Protein; 2.5g Sugars

Chicken Legs In Hot Red Sauce

Servings: 4

Cooking Time: 15 Mins

Ingredients:

- 1 pound chicken legs, skinless and boneless
- Salt and black pepper to taste
- 2 tbsp olive oil
- 1 cup canned tomatoes, chopped
- 2 garlic cloves, minced
- 1 cup roasted red bell pepper, chopped
- 1 tsp smoked paprika
- 1 habanero pepper, minced
- 1 onion, chopped
- 2 tbsp fresh cilantro, minced

Directions:

1. Set your IP to Sauté and brown the chicken for 6 minutes. Season with salt. Add in cup water. Seal the lid, select Manual on High, and cook for 15 minutes. Perform a natural pressure release.
2. In your food processor, combine tomatoes, garlic, roasted bell pepper, smoked paprika, habanero pepper, onion, and olive oil. Pulse until smooth. Pour the mixture over the chicken. Stir and cook for 3 minutes on Sauté. Serve sprinkled with cilantro.

Nutrition Info: Calories 236, Protein 23g, Net Carbs 7.3g, Fat 12g

Chicken Fillets In Creamy Cheese Sauce

Servings: 4

Cooking Time: 25 Mins

Ingredients:

- 3 pancetta slices, chopped
- 10 oz Ricotta cheese, crumbled
- 1 pound chicken breasts, cubed
- Salt to taste
- ½ tsp cayenne pepper
- 4 oz gouda cheese, shredded

Directions:

1. Select Sauté on IP and cook pancetta for 5 minutes until crispy. Set aside. Add in chicken and cook for 5 minutes. Pour in ¼ cups water and ricotta cheese and sprinkle with salt and cayenne pepper.
2. Seal the lid, select Manual on High, and cook for 15 minutes. When done, perform a quick pressure release. Stir in gouda cheese until melts. Ladle into serving bowls and serve topped with bacon.

Nutrition Info: Calories 440, Protein 41g, Net Carbs 3.3g, Fat 29g

Low Carb Turkey Ratatouille

Servings: 4

Cooking Time: 25 Mins

Ingredients:

- 4 tablespoons extra-virgin olive oil
- 2 pounds boneless turkey cutlet
- 1 cup mushrooms
- 1 sweet red pepper
- 1 medium zucchini
- 1 eggplant
- 1/2 cup tomato puree
- 1 tsp garlic
- 1 tsp leaf basil
- 1/8 tsp salt
- 1/2 teaspoon sweetener
- 1/8 tsp black pepper

Directions:

1. Set your instant pot to manual high and heat oil; sprinkle the meat with salt and pepper and sauté for about 3 Mins per side; transfer to a plate and add the remaining oil to the pot. Sauté red pepper, zucchini and eggplant for about 5 Mins. Stir in garlic, mushrooms, basil, tomato puree. Cook for 5 Mins and then stir in turkey, salt and pepper. Lock lid and cook on high for Mins. Let pressure come down on its own. Serve hot.

Nutrition Info:

Per Serving: Calories: 568; Total Fat: 8 g; Carbs: 4g; Dietary Fiber: 5.8 g; Sugars: 7.6 g; Protein: 6 g; Cholesterol: 172 mg; Sodium: 250 mg

Chicken Cashew Stew

Servings: 4
Cooking Time: 34 Minutes
Ingredients:

- For the cooking base:
- 1 tbsp coconut oil
- ½ cup coconut aminos
- 3 tbsp unsweetened tomato ketchup
- 3 tbsp balsamic vinegar
- 1 tbsp swerve brown sugar
- 1 tbsp sugar-free maple syrup
- 1 tbsp minced garlic
- 1 tbsp minced ginger
- ½ tsp red chili flakes, or to taste
- For the stew:
- 1 tbsp coconut oil
- 4 chicken breasts, cut into 2-inch cubes
- Salt and black pepper to taste
- 1 medium red onion, quartered
- 2 cups chopped green beans

- 2 tbsp chicken broth
- 2 tbsp arrowroot starch
- 1 cup cashews

Directions:
1. For the cooking base:
2. In a medium bowl, mix all the ingredients and set aside.
3. For the stew:
4. Set the IP in Sauté mode and adjust to Medium heat.
5. Melt the coconut oil in the inner pot, season the chicken with salt, black pepper, and sear the in the oil until golden brown, 6 minutes. Plate and set aside.
6. Stir in onions, green beans, and cook until softened, 3 minutes.
7. Mix in the cooking base and chicken broth, and return the chicken to the pot.
8. Lock the lid in place, select Manual mode on High Pressure and set the timer to 3 minutes.
9. After cooking, allow sitting for 10 minutes, perform a natural pressure release for 10 minutes, then a quick pressure release, and open the lid.
10. Adjust the taste with salt, black pepper, and mix in the arrowroot starch and cashews.
11. Set the IP in Sauté mode and allow the sauce to thicken, 1 to 2 minutes.
12. Dish the stew and serve warm.

Nutrition Info:
Per Serving: Calories 624 Fats 33g Carbs 15g Net Carbs 9.65g Protein 91g

Chicken Cordon Bleu Casserole

Servings: 4
Cooking Time: 15 Minutes
Ingredients:
- 2 cups chicken broth
- 4 chicken breasts, cut into strips
- 2/3 lb. ham, cubed
- Salt and black pepper to taste
- 1 tbsp Dijon mustard
- 1 tsp garlic powder
- ¼ cup shredded Parmesan cheese
- ¼ cup shredded Gouda cheese
- ½ cup heavy cream
- 2 tbsp unsalted butter, melted
- 1 cup crushed pork rinds

Directions:
1. Pour the chicken broth in the inner pot and lay in the chicken and ham. Season with salt, black pepper, mustard, and garlic powder.
2. Lock the lid in place; select Manual mode on High Pressure and set the timer to 10 minutes.
3. After cooking, perform a quick pressure release to let out the steam, and open the lid.
4. Mix in heavy cream and cheese, and melt in Sauté mode, 5 minutes.
5. Spoon cordon bleu onto serving plates and set aside.

6. Mix the butter and pork rinds in a bowl, spoon the mixture on the food and serve immediately.

Nutrition Info:

Per Serving: Calories 637 Fats 29g Carbs 3.88g Net Carbs 3.48g Protein 56g

No Beans Chicken Chili

Servings: 4
Cooking Time: 27 Minutes
Ingredients:

- 1 tbsp olive oil
- 1 lb. ground chicken
- ¼ tsp cumin powder
- ½ tsp cayenne powder
- Salt and black pepper to taste
- 1 cup chicken broth
- 1 cup diced tomatoes
- 1 cup grated American cheese for topping
- 1 cup sour cream for topping

Directions:

1. Set the IP in Sauté mode and adjust to Medium heat.
2. Heat the olive oil in the inner pot and cook the chicken until brown while frequently stirring, 5 minutes.
3. Season with the cumin powder, cayenne powder, salt, black pepper, and cook for 2 minutes.
4. Mix in the chicken broth and tomatoes.
5. Lock the lid in place; select Manual mode on High Pressure and set the timer for 10 minutes.
6. Once ready, do a natural pressure release for 10 minutes, then a quick pressure release to let out the remaining steam and open the lid.
7. Stir and adjust the taste with salt and black pepper.
8. Dish the chili into serving bowls and top with the cheese and sour cream.
9. Serve warm.

Nutrition Info:

Per Serving: Calories 721 Fats 16g Carbs 7.06g Net Carbs 6.36g Protein 21g

Chicken With Avocado Cream

Servings: 6
Cooking Time: 20 Mins
Ingredients:

- 4 lb organic Chicken breasts
- 1 tsp Coconut oil
- 1 tsp Paprika
- 1 ½ cups Pacific Chicken Bone Broth
- 1 tsp dried Thyme
- Salt and black pepper to taste

- 1 tsp Ginger
- 2 tsp Lemon juice
- 6 cloves peeled Garlic
- 1 Avocado

Directions:

1. In a bowl, mix paprika, thyme, salt, dried ginger, and pepper. Then rub the seasoning onto chicken. Heat oil on Sauté mode. Add the breasts side down and cook for 3 minutes. Flip the chicken and pour in broth, lemon juice, and garlic cloves. Lock the lid and cook for minutes on High on Manual.
2. Prepare the avocado cream by whisking the contents of the avocado with tsp of coconut oil and ½ tsp. of salt. Once the timer beeps, quickly release the pressure. Remove the chicken from the pot and pour the sauce over, to serve.

Nutrition Info: Calories 455, Protein 61g, Net Carbs 1.5g, Fat 5g

Chicken And Spinach Bowl

Servings: 4
Cooking Time: 15 Minutes
Ingredients:

- 10 oz chicken fillet, chopped
- ½ teaspoon paprika
- ¼ teaspoon salt
- ¼ teaspoon ground black pepper
- ½ teaspoon cayenne pepper
- 1 tablespoon sesame oil
- 1 red onion, sliced
- 1 cup fresh spinach, chopped
- ¼ cup of water

Directions:

1. Heat up instant pot on sauté mode for 3 minutes.
2. In the mixing bowl combine together paprika, salt, chicken fillet, ground black pepper, ½ tablespoon of sesame oil, and cayenne pepper. Shake the ingredients gently and place them in the instant pot. Close the lid and sauté them for 5 minutes. Then stir the chicken well and add water. Close the lid and sauté it for 10 minutes more. Meanwhile, mix up together spinach and red onion. Add remaining sesame oil. Place the spinach mixture in the serving bowls and top them with cooked chicken.

Nutrition Info: calories 179, fat 8.8, fiber 1, carbs 3.2, protein 1

Chicken And Almonds Mix

Servings: 4
Cooking Time: 25 Minutes
Ingredients:

- 1 cup chicken stock
- 2 tablespoons avocado oil

- 2 chicken breasts, skinless, boneless and halved
- 1 tablespoon balsamic vinegar
- tablespoons almonds, chopped
- A pinch of salt and black pepper
- 1 tablespoon chives, chopped

Directions:
1. Set your instant pot on sauté mode, add the oil, heat it up, add the chicken and brown for 5 minutes. Add the rest of the ingredients, put the lid on and cook on High for 20 minutes. Release the pressure fast for 5 minutes, divide between plates and serve.

Nutrition Info: calories 254, fat 7, fiber 0.9, carbs 1.6, protein 34

Chicken Drumsticks In Creamy Butter Sauce

Servings: 6
Cooking Time: 20 Minutes
Ingredients:
- 2 ripe tomatoes, chopped
- 1/2 cup roasted vegetable broth, preferably homemade
- 1 red onion, chopped
- 1 red bell pepper, seeded and chopped
- 1 green bell pepper, seeded and chopped
- 4 cloves garlic
- 1 teaspoon curry powder
- 1/2 teaspoon paprika
- 1/4 teaspoon ground black pepper
- Sea salt, to taste
- A pinch of grated nutmeg
- 1/2 teaspoon ground cumin
- 2 pounds chicken drumsticks, boneless, skinless
- 2 tablespoons butter
- 1/3 cup double cream
- 1 tablespoon flaxseed meal

Directions:
1. Add tomatoes, vegetable broth, onion, peppers, garlic, curry powder, paprika, black pepper, salt, grated nutmeg, and ground cumin to the bottom of your Instant Pot.
2. Add chicken drumsticks. Secure the lid. Choose "Manual" mode and High pressure; cook for 1minutes. Once cooking is complete, use a natural pressure release.
3. Allow it to cool completely and reserve the chicken.
4. In a mixing dish, whisk the remaining ingredients and add this mixture to the Instant Pot; press the "Sauté" button and bring it to a boil.
5. Now, add the chicken back to the cooking liquid. Press the "Cancel" button and serve immediately. Bon appétit!

Spicy Chicken Manchurian

Servings: 4
Cooking Time: 17 Minutes
Ingredients:

- ½ cup olive oil
- 4 tbsp arrowroot starch divided
- 2 eggs, beaten
- 2 tbsp coconut aminos, divided
- Salt and black pepper to taste
- 4 chicken breasts, cut into 1-inch cubes
- 2 tbsp coconut oil
- 1 red chili, sliced
- 1 tbsp fresh garlic paste
- 1 tbsp fresh ginger paste
- 2 tbsp hot sauce
- ½ tsp sugar-free maple syrup
- 2 tbsp chicken broth
- 2 scallions, sliced for garnishing

Directions:

1. Set the IP in Sauté mode and adjust to Medium heat.
2. Heat the olive oil in the inner pot.
3. Meanwhile, in a medium bowl, whisk the arrowroot starch, eggs, coconut aminos, and black pepper. Add the chicken to the mixture and mix to coat properly.
4. Fry the chicken in the oil until golden brown on all sides, 8 minutes. Transfer to a paper towel-lined plate to drain grease.
5. Empty the inner pot, clean and return to the base.
6. Heat the coconut oil in the inner pot and sauté the red chili, garlic, and ginger until fragrant, 1 minute.
7. Stir in the hot sauce, maple syrup, chicken broth, and arrange the chicken in sauce.
8. Lock the lid in place; select Manual mode on High Pressure and set the timer to 3 minutes.
9. After cooking, perform a natural pressure release for 5 minutes, then a quick pressure release to let out the remaining steam and open the lid.
10. Stir and adjust the taste with salt and black pepper.
11. Dish the food and garnish with the scallions.
12. Serve warm.

Nutrition Info:
Per Serving: Calories 783 Fats 69g Carbs 68g Net Carbs 9.68g Protein 94g

Baked Turkey Breast Tenderloins

Servings: 6

Cooking Time: 40 Minutes

Ingredients:

- 6 turkey breast tenderloins
- 4 cloves garlic, halved
- 2 tablespoons grapeseed oil
- 1/2 teaspoon paprika
- 1/2 teaspoon dried basil
- 1/2 teaspoon dried oregano
- 1/2 teaspoon dried marjoram
- 1 cup water
- Sea salt, to taste
- 1/4 teaspoon ground black pepper, or more to taste

Directions:

1. Rub turkey fillets with garlic halves. Now, massage tablespoon of oil into your turkey and season it with paprika, basil, oregano, marjoram, water, salt, and black pepper.
2. Press the "Sauté" button and add another tablespoon of oil. Brown the turkey fillets for 3 to 4 minutes per side.
3. Add the rack to the Instant Pot; lower the turkey onto the rack.
4. Secure the lid. Choose the "Manual" setting and cook for 30 minutes. Once cooking is complete, use a natural pressure release; carefully remove the lid.
5. Serve right away. Bon appétit!

Nutrition Info:

Per Serving: 255 Calories; 7.1g Fat; 0.7g Total Carbs; 7g Protein; 0g Sugars

Chicken Zucchini Enchiladas

Servings: 6

Cooking Time: 13 Minutes

Ingredients:

- 1 tablespoon avocado oil
- ½ white onion, diced
- 1 green bell pepper, chopped
- 1 chili pepper, chopped
- ½ teaspoon ground cumin
- ½ teaspoon ground coriander
- 1 garlic clove, diced
- 1-pound chicken breast, cooked, shredded
- 1 cup Cheddar cheese, shredded
- 2 zucchini, trimmed
- ½ cup heavy cream
- 1 tablespoon Enchilada sauce

Directions:

1. Put onion and bell pepper in the instant pot. Add avocado oil, ground cumin, coriander, and diced garlic. Cook the ingredients on sauté mode for 5 minutes. Stir them from time to time.

Then add shredded chicken and Enchilada sauce. Mix up the mixture well and cook it for 3 minutes more. Transfer the cooked mixture into the mixing bowl. After this, clean the instant pot. Slice the zucchini lengthwise. You should get slices. Place the layer of 3 zucchini slices on the chopping board and spread it with chicken mixture. Roll it and transfer in the instant pot. Repeat the same step with all remaining zucchini and chicken mixture. Then top the zucchini rolls with Cheddar cheese and heavy cream. Close and seal the lid. Cook enchiladas for 5 minutes on manual mode (high pressure). When the time is over, make a quick pressure release.

Nutrition Info: calories 225, fat 4, fiber 1.6, carbs 6.2, protein 2

Greek Burger

Servings: 2
Cooking Time: 20 Minutes
Ingredients:

- 1 cup ground chicken
- 1 tablespoon lemon juice
- 2 tablespoons coconut flour
- ½ teaspoon minced garlic
- ½ teaspoon dried parsley
- 1 cup water, for cooking

Directions:

1. In the mixing bowl, mix up ground chicken, lemon juice, coconut flour, minced garlic, and dried parsley.
2. Make burgers and place them in the baking pan.
3. Pour water and insert the steamer rack in the instant pot.
4. Then place the pan with burgers on the steamer. Close and seal the lid.
5. Cook the meal on manual mode (high pressure) for 20 minutes. Allow the natural pressure release for 10 minutes.

Nutrition Info:
Per Serving: calories 173, fat 6.5, fiber 3.1, carbs 5.1, protein 9

Hot Chicken Pot

Servings: 4
Cooking Time: 25 Mins
Ingredients:

- 2 tbsp olive oil
- 4 chicken breast halves, boneless and skinless
- 1 onion, chopped
- 1 tsp garlic paste
- 1 cup almond milk
- 2 Roma tomatoes, chopped
- 1 tsp curry powder
- 1 tbsp tamari sauce

- 1 tbsp balsamic vinegar
- Salt and black pepper, to taste
- ½ tsp cayenne pepper
- ½ tsp ginger powder
- 1 celery stalk, chopped
- 1 bell pepper, chopped
- 1 bay leaf
- 1 tbsp flaxseed meal

Directions:
1. Set your IP to Sauté and heat the olive oil. Brown the breast for 3-4 minutes on each side. Stir in the onion, garlic, almond milk, tomatoes, curry powder, tamari sauce, vinegar, vermouth, salt, cayenne pepper, black pepper, ginger powder, celery, bay leaf, and bell pepper.
2. Seal the lid, select Manual on High, and cook for minutes. When done, perform a quick pressure release. Add in the flaxseed meal. Cook in the residual heat. Share into serving bowls and serve.

Nutrition Info: Calories 651, Protein 64g, Net Carbs 9.9g, Fat 37g

Instant Pot Grilled Chicken & Green Onion

Servings: 1 Serving
Cooking Time: 40 Mins
Ingredients:
- 3 ounces chicken breast
- 1 tablespoon olive oil
- 1 green onion, chopped
- Pinch of garlic powder
- Pinch of sea salt
- Pinch of pepper
- 1 cup steamed green beans

Directions:
1. Set your instant pot on manual high and heat in oil; add chicken and cook for 5 Mins per side or until browned. Remove chicken and add water to the pot; insert a trivet. Place the chicken in aluminum foil and top with onion slices. Sprinkle with garlic powder, salt and pepper and wrap the foil; place over the trivet. Lock lid and cook for 30 Mins. Let pressure come down naturally.
2. Serve chicken over steamed green beans.

Nutrition Info:
Per Serving: Calories: 176; Total Fat: 6.3 g; Carbs: 3.4 g; Dietary Fiber: 0.8 g; Sugars: 1.5 g; Protein: 5 g; Cholesterol: 76 mg; Sodium: 61 mg

Jalapeno And Cheddar Chicken

Servings: 4
Cooking Time: 22 Mins
Ingredients:

- 1 pound Chicken Breasts
- 8 ounces Cream Cheese
- 8 ounces shredded Cheddar Cheese
- 3 Jalapenos, seeded and diced
- ½ cup Water
- 7 ounces Sour Cream
- Salt and black pepper to taste

Directions:

1. Add water, cream cheese, and sour cream, to the Instant Pot. Whisk until well-combined. Stir in the jalapenos and cheddar. Add in the chicken and seal the lid.
2. Set the cooking time to 1minutes and cook on High. When the timer goes off, do a quick pressure release. Shred the chicken with forks and stir. Serve hot.

Nutrition Info: Calories 305, Protein 23g, Net Carbs 4g, Fat 25g

Peanut Chicken Bowls

Servings: 4
Cooking Time: 17 Minutes
Ingredients:

- ¾ cup chicken broth
- 1 cup peanut sauce
- Salt to taste
- 4 chicken breasts, cut into 1-inch cubes
- 2 large red bell peppers, spiralized with Blade A
- 1 cup asparagus, trimmed and cut into 3 pieces each
- 1 tbsp chopped peanuts to garnish
- 1 tsp freshly chopped cilantro to garnish

Directions:

1. Mix the chicken broth, peanut sauce, and salt in the inner pot until well combined and add the chicken.
2. Lock the lid in place; select Manual mode on High Pressure and set the timer to 1minutes.
3. After cooking, perform a quick pressure release to let out the steam, and open the lid.
4. Stir in the bell peppers and asparagus.
5. Lock the lid in place; select Manual mode on High Pressure and set the timer to minutes.
6. After cooking, perform a quick pressure release to let out the steam, and open the lid.
7. Stir; adjust taste with salt, black pepper, and dish the food into serving bowls.
8. Garnish with peanuts and cilantro.
9. Serve warm.

Nutrition Info:
Per Serving: Calories 709 Fats 08g Carbs 93g Net Carbs 2.93g Protein 24g

Sage Chicken And Broccoli

Servings: 4
Cooking Time: 30 Minutes
Ingredients:
- 1 pound chicken breast, skinless, boneless and cubed
- 1 cup broccoli florets
- 3 garlic cloves, minced
- 1 cup tomato passata
- A pinch of salt and black pepper
- 2 tablespoons olive oil
- 1 tablespoon sage, chopped

Directions:
1. Set pot on Sauté mode, add the oil, heat it up, add the garlic and the chicken and sauté for 5 minutes. Add the rest of the ingredients, put the lid on and cook on High for 25 minutes. Release the pressure naturally for minutes, divide the mix between plates and serve.

Nutrition Info: calories 217, fat 1, fiber 1.8, carbs 5.9, protein 4

Simple Chicken Soup

Servings: 2
Cooking Time: 46 Mins
Ingredients:
- 2 tbsp Olive oil
- 1 large Carrot, chopped
- 1 large Celery Stalk, chopped
- 1 large White Onion, chopped
- 6 cloves Garlic, minced
- 1 Green Chili Pepper, sliced
- Salt and black pepper to taste
- 1 inch Ginger, grated
- 2 cups Chicken Broth
- 1 cup Water
- 2 tbsp Palin Vinegar
- 1 lb Chicken Breasts

Directions:
1. Heat oil on Sauté, and add all vegetables. Stir and cook for 3 minutes. Stir in broth, chicken, vinegar and water. Seal the lid and cook on Soup for minutes on High.
2. Once ready, release pressure naturally for 10 minutes, then quickly release the pressure. Remove the chicken, shred and return to the pot. Select Sauté and cook for 3 minutes.

Nutrition Info: Calories 146, Protein 14g, Net Carbs 4g, Fat 4g

Chicken Cacciatore

Servings: 5

Cooking Time: 25 Minutes
Ingredients:
- 5 chicken thighs, boneless
- ½ teaspoon salt
- ½ teaspoon ground black pepper
- 2 garlic cloves, diced
- ¼ onion, diced
- ¼ cup bell pepper, chopped
- ½ cup cremini mushrooms, chopped
- ¼ cup tomatoes, canned
- ½ teaspoon dried rosemary
- ½ teaspoon dried cumin
- ½ teaspoon dried thyme
- ¼ teaspoon ground coriander
- ½ cup kale, chopped
- 1 tablespoon coconut oil
- ½ cup chicken broth

Directions:
1. Toss the coconut oil in the instant pot and melt it on sauté mode. Then place the chicken thighs in the hot oil and cook them for 3 minutes from each side or until the chicken is light brown. After this, sprinkle the chicken with salt and ground black pepper. Add garlic, onion, and bell pepper. Add mushrooms and stir the ingredients. Then add canned tomatoes, rosemary, cumin, thyme, and ground coriander. Stir the ingredients with the help of the spatula well and add chicken broth. Close and seal the lid. Cook the meal on manual mode (high pressure) for minutes. When the time is over, make a quick pressure release and open the lid. Add kale and close the lid. Cook the meal for 2 minutes more on manual mode (high pressure). Then make a quick pressure release and open the lid. Stir the meal well before serving.

Nutrition Info: calories 319, fat 8, fiber 0.7, carbs 3.2, protein 5

Lamb Soup

Servings: 4
Cooking Time: 25 Minutes
Ingredients:
- ½ cup broccoli, roughly chopped
- 7 oz lamb fillet, chopped
- ¼ teaspoon ground cumin
- ¼ daikon, chopped
- 2 bell peppers, chopped
- 1 tablespoon avocado oil
- 5 cups beef broth

Directions:
1. Saute the lamb fillet with avocado oil in the instant pot for 5 minutes.

2. Then add broccoli, ground cumin, daikon, bell peppers, and beef broth.
3. Close and seal the lid.
4. Cook the soup on manual mode (high pressure) for 20 minutes.
5. Allow the natural pressure release.

Nutrition Info:

Per Serving: calories 169, fat 6, fiber 1.3, carbs 6.8, protein 21

Easy Taco Chicken Soup

Servings: 4

Cooking Time: 23 Minutes

Ingredients:

- 1 pound boneless chicken thighs, chopped
- ½ cup diced yellow onion
- 2 cups chicken broth
- 1 tablespoon chipotle chilis in adobo, chopped
- Salt and pepper
- 1 (8-ounce) package cream cheese, chopped
- 1 tablespoon ground cumin

Directions:

1. Turn the Instant Pot on to the Sauté setting and let it heat up.
2. Add the chicken and sauté for 3 minutes, stirring, until browned.
3. Stir in the rest of the ingredients aside from the cream cheese.
4. Close and lock the lid, then press the Manual button and adjust the timer to 18 minutes on High Pressure.
5. When the timer goes off, let the pressure vent for 10 minutes then press Cancel to do a Quick Release by switching the steam valve to "venting."
6. When the pot has depressurized, open the lid.
7. Stir in the cream cheese until it is melted and fully incorporated.
8. Season with salt and pepper, then serve with fresh cilantro, if desired.

Nutrition Info: calories 470 fat 38g ,protein 27g ,carbs 4.5g ,fiber 1g ,net carbs 3.5g

Chicken Curry Stew

Servings: 4

Cooking Time: 30 Minutes

Ingredients:

- 1 lb. chicken thighs, skinless and boneless
- 1/3 cup coconut oil
- Salt and black pepper to taste
- 2 tbsp curry powder
- 2 tbsp ginger garlic paste
- 1 lb. broccoli, chopped into small florets
- 1 large red bell pepper, deseeded and chopped
- ¼ cup chicken broth

- 1 ½ cups unsweetened coconut milk
- ¼ cup chopped fresh cilantro

Directions:
1. Set the IP in Sauté mode and adjust to Medium heat.
2. Cut the chicken into cubes.
3. Heat 2 tablespoons of the coconut oil in the inner pot, season the chicken with salt and black pepper, and cook in the oil until golden brown on the outside, 5 minutes. Spoon onto a plate and set aside.
4. Stir the curry powder, ginger-garlic paste, broccoli, and bell pepper into the oil, and cook until softened and fragrant, 5 minutes.
5. Return the chicken to the pot and stir in the chicken broth and coconut milk.
6. Lock the lid in place; select Manual mode on High Pressure and set the timer to 10 minutes.
7. After cooking, perform a natural pressure release for 10 minutes, then a quick pressure release to let out the remaining steam and open the lid.
8. Stir in the cilantro and adjust the taste with salt and black pepper.
9. Serve.

Nutrition Info:
Per Serving: Calories 678 Fats 73g Carbs 26g Net Carbs 26g Protein 97g

Spiced Turnip Soup

Servings: 4
Cooking Time: 29 Minutes
Ingredients:
- 3 tbsp butter
- 1 large white onion, chopped
- 2 garlic cloves, minced
- 1 tsp cumin powder
- 1 tsp coriander powder
- 1 tbsp turmeric powder
- 3 large turnips, peeled and diced
- 3 cups vegetable stock
- 1 cup almond milk
- 2 tbsp toasted pine nuts for topping
- 2 tsp chopped fresh cilantro to garnish

Directions:
1. Set the IP in Sauté mode and adjust to medium heat.
2. Melt the butter in the inner pot and sauté the onion until softened, 3 minutes. Stir in the garlic, cumin, coriander, turmeric, and cook until fragrant, 1 minute.
3. Add the turnips and vegetable stock.
4. Lock the lid in place; select Manual mode on High Pressure and set the timer to 15 minutes.
5. After cooking, perform a natural pressure release for 10 minutes, then a quick pressure release to let out the remaining steam and open the lid.
6. Using an immersion blender, puree ingredients until smooth and adjust the taste with salt, black pepper, and mix in the almond milk.

7. Dish the soup into serving bowls, top with the pine nuts, and garnish with the cilantro.

Nutrition Info:

Per Serving: Calories 360 Fats 43g Carbs 53g Net Carbs 9.93g Protein 35g

Cream Of Mushrooms Soup

Servings: 6

Cooking Time: 35 Minutes

Ingredients:

- 3 cups cremini mushrooms, sliced
- 1 cup of coconut milk
- 1 tablespoon almond flour
- 1 teaspoon salt
- 1 teaspoon ground black pepper
- 4 cups chicken broth
- 3 tablespoons butter

Directions:

1. Melt the butter on saute mode.
2. Add cremini mushrooms and saute them for 10 minutes. Stir them with the help of the spatula from time to time.
3. After this, in the bowl mix up salt, almond flour, and ground black pepper. Add coconut milk and stir the liquid.
4. Pour the liquid over the mushrooms.
5. Add chicken broth. Close and seal the lid.
6. Cook the soup on saute mode for 25 minutes.

Nutrition Info:

Per Serving: calories 206, fat 6, fiber 1.7, carbs 5.5, protein 6.2

Steak Soup

Servings: 5

Cooking Time: 40 Minutes

Ingredients:

- 5 oz scallions, diced
- 1 tablespoon coconut oil
- 1 oz daikon, diced
- 1-pound beef round steak, chopped
- 1 teaspoon dried thyme
- 5 cups of water
- ½ teaspoon ground black pepper

Directions:

1. Heat up coconut oil on saute mode for 2 minutes.
2. Add daikon and scallions.
3. After this, stir them well and add chopped beef steak, thyme, and ground black pepper.
4. Saute the ingredients for 5 minutes more and then add water.

5. Close and seal the lid.
6. Cook the soup on manual mode (high pressure) for 35 minutes. Make a quick pressure release.

Nutrition Info:

Per Serving: calories 232, fat 11, fiber 0.9, carbs 2.5, protein 5

Green Bean & Spinach Soup

Servings: 4
Cooking Time: 15 Mins
Ingredients:

- 1 cup baby Spinach
- 1 cup Green Beans
- 2 cups Vegetable broth
- ½ cup Almond Milk
- 4-5 Garlic cloves, minced
- 1 cup Heavy cream
- ½ cup Tofu
- ½ tbsp Chili flakes
- Salt and black pepper to taste
- 2 tbsp Olive oil
- Fresh Dill, to garnish

Directions:

1. Heat oil and cook garlic cloves for minute on Sauté. Add broth, spinach, beans, tofu, cream, chili and salt, mix well. Seal the lid and cook on High pressure for 10 minutes.
2. When done, do a quick pressure release. Carefully open the lid. Pour in the milk and cook for 5 minutes on Sauté mode without the lid. Serve in bowls topped with fresh dill.

Nutrition Info: Calories 239, Protein 4g, Net Carbs 7.3g, Fat 21g

Chorizo Soup

Servings: 3
Cooking Time: 17 Minutes
Ingredients:

- 8 oz chorizo, chopped
- 1 teaspoon tomato paste
- 4 oz scallions, diced
- 1 tablespoon dried cilantro
- ½ teaspoon chili powder
- 1 teaspoon avocado oil
- 2 cups beef broth

Directions:

1. Heat up avocado oil on saute mode for minute.
2. Add chorizo and cook it for 6 minutes, stir it from time to time.
3. Then add scallions, tomato paste, cilantro, and chili powder. Stir well.

4. Add beef broth.
5. Close and seal the lid.
6. Cook the soup on manual mode (high pressure) for 10 minutes. Make a quick pressure release.

Nutrition Info:

Per Serving: calories 387, fat 2, fiber 1.3, carbs 5.5, protein 3

Hearty Lamb & Cabbage Stew

Servings: 4
Cooking Time: 2 Hours 30 Mins
Ingredients:

- 2 tbsp. coconut oil
- 200g lamb chops, bone in
- 1 lamb or beef stock cube
- 2 cups water
- 1 cup shredded cabbage
- 1 onion, sliced
- 2 carrots, chopped
- 2 sticks celery, chopped
- 1 tsp. dried thyme
- 1 tbsp. balsamic vinegar
- 1 tbsp. almond flour

Directions:

1. Set your instant pot to manual high and heat in oil; brown in the lamb chops and then add in the remaining ingredients. Cook on high for 2 hours and then let pressure come down naturally. Remove bones from the meat.
2. To thicken your sauce, ladle ¼ cup of sauce into a bowl and whisk in almond flour. Return to the pot and stir well; lock lid and cook for 30 Mins on manual high.

Nutrition Info:

Per Serving: Calories: 384; Total Fat: 4 g; Carbs: 6.8 g; Dietary Fiber: 4.8 g; Sugars: 1.5 g; Protein: 4 g; Cholesterol: 223 mg; Sodium: 822 mg

Hot Instant Pot Vegetable Soup

Servings: 4-6
Cooking Time: 30 Mins
Ingredients:

- 1 pound curly kale, torn
- 12 ounces baby spinach
- ¼ cup brown Arborio rice, rinsed
- 2 yellow onions, chopped
- 4 tablespoons olive oil
- 3 cups plus 2 tablespoons water
- 4 cups homemade vegetable broth

- 1 tablespoon fresh lemon juice
- 1 large pinch of cayenne pepper
- Salt, to taste

Directions:

1. Add the two tablespoons of olive oil in a large pan and cook the onions over medium heat. Sprinkle with salt and cook for 5 Mins until they start browning.
2. Lower the heat and pour in two tablespoons of water. Cover and lower the heat and cook for Mins until the onions caramelize, stirring frequently.
3. Meanwhile, add the remaining water, broth, and some salt to an instant pot and stir in the rice. Lock the lid and cook on high pressure for 5 Mins. Naturally release the pressure and then stir in kale, onions, spinach and cayenne and lock the lid. Let sit for about 5 Mins.
4. Use an immersion blender to puree the rice mixture until smooth then stir in the lemon juice. Serve in soup bowls and drizzle each with some olive oil.

Nutrition Info:
Per Serving: Calories: 202; Total Fat: 4 g; Carbs: 8.3g; Dietary Fiber: 3.1g; Sugars: 2.8 g; Protein: 3.1 g; Cholesterol: 0 mg; Sodium: 109 mg

Cordon Blue Soup

Servings: 4
Cooking Time: 6 Minutes
Ingredients:

- 4 cups chicken broth
- 7 oz ham, chopped
- 3 oz Mozzarella cheese, shredded
- 1 teaspoon ground black pepper
- ½ teaspoon salt
- 2 tablespoons ricotta cheese
- 2 oz scallions, chopped

Directions:

1. Put all ingredients in the instant pot bowl and stir gently.
2. Close and seal the lid; cook the soup on manual mode (high pressure) for 6 minutes.
3. Then allow the natural pressure release for 10 minutes and ladle the soup into the bowls.

Nutrition Info:
Per Serving: calories 196, fat 1, fiber 1.2, carbs 5.3, protein 3

Caribbean Cod Soup

Servings: 4
Cooking Time: 16 Minutes
Ingredients:

- 4 tbsp butter
- 3 stalks celery, chopped
- 2 medium onions, chopped
- Salt and black pepper to taste

- 3 cups chicken broth
- 4 rutabagas, peeled and chopped
- 4 bay leaves
- 1 habanero pepper, minced
- 4 cod fillets, cut into 1-inch cubes
- 3 scallions, thinly sliced
- 1 tbsp freshly chopped parsley to garnish

Directions:
1. Set the IP in Sauté mode and adjust to medium heat.
2. Melt the butter in the inner pot and sauté the celery and onion until softened, 3 minutes. Season with salt and black pepper.
3. Stir in the chicken broth, rutabagas, bay leaves, habanero pepper, and cod.
4. Lock the lid in place; select Manual mode on High Pressure and set the timer to 3 minutes.
5. After cooking, perform a natural pressure release for 10 minutes, then a quick pressure release to let out the remaining steam, and open the lid.
6. Adjust the taste with salt, black pepper, and stir in the scallions.
7. Dish the soup, garnish with the parsley, and serve warm.

Nutrition Info:
Per Serving: Calories 520 Fats 54g Carbs 57g Net Carbs 17g Protein 79g

Pork Stew

Servings: 6
Cooking Time: 3 Minutes
Ingredients:
- ½ cup daikon, chopped
- 1 oz green onions, chopped
- 1-pound pork tenderloin, chopped
- 1 lemon slice
- 1 teaspoon ground black pepper
- 1 tablespoon butter
- 1 tablespoon heavy cream
- 3 cups of water

Directions:
1. Put all ingredients in the instant pot and mix up them with the help of the spatula.
2. Then close and seal the lid. Set manual mode (high pressure) and cook the stew for minutes.
3. Allow the natural pressure release for 15 minutes.

Nutrition Info:
Per Serving: calories 137, fat 5.5, fiber 0.3, carbs 0.9, protein 1

Zucchini Leek Soup With Cottage Cheese

Servings: 4
Cooking Time: 17 Minutes
Ingredients:

- 1 tbsp olive oil
- 1 leek stalk, chopped
- 3 large zucchinis, chopped
- 1 medium white onion, chopped
- 2 garlic cloves, minced
- 1 tbsp mixed dried herbs
- 4 cups vegetable stock
- Salt and black pepper to taste
- 1 cup heavy cream
- 1 cup cottage cheese

Directions:
1. Set the IP in Sauté mode and adjust to medium heat.
2. Heat the olive oil in the inner pot and sauté the leek, zucchinis and onion until softened, 5 minutes. Stir in the garlic and mixed herbs; cook until fragrant, 30 seconds.
3. Mix in the vegetable stock and season with the salt and black pepper.
4. Lock the lid in place; select Manual mode on High Pressure and set the timer to 1 minute.
5. After cooking, perform a natural pressure release for 10 minutes, then a quick pressure release to let out the remaining steam and open the lid.
6. Using an immersion blender, puree the soup and season with salt and black pepper.
7. Dish the soup into serving bowls and top with the cottage cheese.
8. Serve warm.

Nutrition Info:
Per Serving: Calories 219 Fats 9g Carbs 27g Net Carbs 9.07g Protein 7.73g

Garden Soup

Servings: 5
Cooking Time: 29 Minutes
Ingredients:
- ½ cup cauliflower florets
- 1 cup kale, chopped
- 1 garlic clove, diced
- 1 tablespoon olive oil
- 1 1 teaspoon sea salt
- 6 cups beef broth
- 2 tablespoons chives, chopped

Directions:
1. Heat up olive oil in the instant pot on saute mode for 2 minutes and add clove.
2. Cook the vegetables for minutes and stir well.
3. Add kale, cauliflower, sea salt, chives, and beef broth.
4. Close and seal the lid.
5. Cook the soup on manual mode (high pressure) for minutes.
6. Then make a quick pressure release and open the lid.
7. Ladle the soup into the bowls.

Nutrition Info:

Per Serving: calories 80, fat 4.5, fiber 0.5, carbs 2.3, protein 6.5

Healthy Keto Hot & Sour Soup

Servings: 6
Cooking Time: 60 Mins
Ingredients:

- 1 pound curly kale, torn
- 12 ounces baby spinach
- 1 pound ground turkey
- 2 yellow onions, chopped
- 2 tablespoons olive oil
- 3 cups plus 2 tablespoons water
- 4 cups homemade vegetable broth
- 1 tablespoon fresh lemon juice
- 1 large pinch of cayenne pepper
- Salt, to taste
- 2 avocados, diced, to serve
- 1 cup chopped toasted almonds to serve

Directions:

1. Add the two tablespoons of olive oil in a large pan and cook the onions over medium heat. Sprinkle with salt and cook for 5 Mins until they start browning.
2. Lower the heat and pour in two tablespoons of water. Cover and lower the heat and cook for Mins until the onions caramelize, stirring frequently.
3. Meanwhile, add the remaining water, broth, and some salt to an instant pot and stir in the turkey. Lock the lid and cook on high pressure for 5 Mins. Naturally release the pressure and the stir in kale, onions, spinach and cayenne and lock the lid. Let sit for about 5 Mins.
4. Serve in soup bowls and topped with avocado and toasted almonds. Enjoy!

Nutrition Info:
Per Serving: Calories: 489; Total Fat: 7g; Protein: 8g; Carbs: 59g

Italian Meatball Zoodle Soup

Servings: 4
Cooking Time: 1 Hour 40 Mins
Ingredients:

- 8 cups beef stock
- 1 medium zucchini – spiralled
- 2 ribs celery – chopped
- 1 small onion – dice
- 1 carrot – chopped
- 1 medium tomato – diced
- 1 ½ tsp. garlic salt
- 1 ½ lb. ground beef
- ½ cup parmesan cheese – shredded

- 6 cloves garlic – minced
- 1 egg
- 4 tbs. fresh parsley – chopped
- 1 ½ tsp. sea salt
- 1 ½ tsp. onion powder
- 1 tsp. Italian seasoning
- 1 tsp. dried oregano
- ½ tsp. black pepper

Directions:
1. Set your instant pot on manual high; mix in beef stock, zucchini, celery, onion, carrot, tomato, and garlic salt. Cook until veggies are tender.
2. In a large mixing bowl, combine ground beef, Parmesan, garlic, egg, parsley, sea salt, onion powder, oregano, Italian seasoning, and pepper. Mix until all ingredients are well incorporated. Form into approximately 30 meatballs. Heat olive oil in a large skillet over medium-high heat. Once the pan is hot, add meatballs and brown on all sides. No need to worry about cooking them all the way through as they will be going into the instant pot. Add meatballs to the pot and lock lid. Cook on high for 1 ½ hours. Let pressure come down on its own.

Nutrition Info:
Per Serving: Calories: 352: Fat: 19g; Carbs: 4.5g; Protein: 40g

Instant Pot Detox Veggie Soup

Servings: 1 Serving
Cooking Time: 10 Mins
Ingredients:
- 1 medium cauliflower
- 8 cups water
- 1 tsp. lemon juice
- 3 tsp. ground flax seeds
- 3 cups spinach
- 1 tsp. cayenne pepper
- 1 tsp. black pepper
- 1 tsp. soy sauce

Directions:
1. Core cauliflower and cut the florets into large pieces; reserve stems for juicing.
2. Add cauliflower to an instant pot and add water; lock lid and cook on high pressure for 10 Mins. Release pressure naturally and then transfer the cauliflower to a blender along with cups of cooking liquid; blend until very smooth. Add the remaining ingredients and continue blending until very smooth. Serve hot or warm.

Nutrition Info:
Per Serving: Calories: 198; Total Fat: 2 g; Carbs: 1 g; Dietary Fiber: 6.3 g; Sugars: 2.9 g; Protein: 1.8 g; Cholesterol: 0 mg; Sodium: 213 mg

Pressure Cooked Lamb-bacon Stew

Servings: 2
Cooking Time: 2 Hours
Ingredients:

- 2 cloves garlic, minced
- 1 leek, sliced
- 2 celery ribs, diced
- 1 cup sliced button mushrooms
- 2 Vidalia onions, thinly sliced
- 2 tbsp. butter
- 2 cups chicken stock
- 200g lamb, cut in cubes
- 4 oz. cream cheese
- 1 cup heavy cream
- 1 packet bacon – cooked crisp, and crumbled
- 1 tsp. salt
- 1 tsp. pepper
- 1 tsp. garlic powder
- 1 tsp. thyme

Directions:

1. Set your instant pot on manual high setting and melt in butter; sear lamb meat until browned. Add in garlic, leeks, celery, mushrooms, onions, and cook for about 5 Mins; stir in the remaining ingredients and lock lid. Cook on high for 2 hours and then let pressure come down on its own.

Nutrition Info:
Per Serving: Calories: 365; Total Fat: 2 g; Carbs: 9 g; Dietary Fiber: 6.6 g; Sugars: 4.3 g; Protein: 1 g; Cholesterol: 91 mg; Sodium: 843 mg

Hearty Beef And Bacon Chili

Servings: 4
Cooking Time: 40 Minutes
Ingredients:

- 6 slices bacon, chopped
- 2 small red peppers, chopped
- 1 pound ground beef (80% lean)
- 1 cup diced tomatoes
- Salt and pepper
- 1 teaspoon garlic powder
- 2 tablespoons chili powder
- 1 cup low-carb tomato sauce

Directions:

1. Turn on the Instant Pot to the Sauté setting and add the chopped bacon.

2. Let the bacon cook until it is crisp then remove it with a slotted spoon.
3. Add the red peppers to the pot.
4. Cook for 5 minutes, stirring, then add the rest of the ingredients.
5. Close and lock the lid, then press the Bean/Chili button to cook for 30 minutes.
6. When the timer goes off, let the pressure vent for 10 minutes then press Cancel to do a Quick Release by switching the steam valve to "venting."
7. Open the lid when the pot has depressurized and stir in the bacon.
8. Season with salt and pepper to taste then serve hot.

Nutrition Info: calories 470 fat 30g ,protein 38g ,carbs 12g ,fiber 3.5g ,net carbs 8.5g

Instant Pot Spiced Coconut Fish Stew

Servings: 4
Cooking Time: 30 Mins
Ingredients:
- 1 1/2 lb. fish fillets
- 1 cup coconut milk
- 2 tbsp. coconut oil
- 1 cup onion chopped
- 1 tbsp. garlic
- 1 tbsp. ginger
- 1/2 serrano or jalapeno
- 1 cup tomato chopped
- 1 tsp ground coriander
- 1/4 tsp ground cumin
- 1/2 tsp turmeric
- 1 tsp lime juice
- 1/2 tsp black pepper and salt

Directions:
1. Set your instant pot on sauté mode; heat in oil and cook onion, garlic and ginger until fragrant. Add in fish and cook for 5 Mins per side or until browned and then stir in the remaining ingredients. Lock lid. Cook on meat/stew setting for 20 Mins and then let pressure come down on its own.

Nutrition Info:
Per Serving: Calories: 190; Total Fat: 5 g; Carbs: 6 g; Dietary Fiber: 2 g; Sugars: 3 g; Protein: 16g; Cholesterol: 33 mg; Sodium: 458 mg

White Chicken Chili

Servings: 4
Cooking Time: 50 Mins
Ingredients:
- 3 Chicken Breasts, cubed
- 3 cups Chicken Broth
- 1 tbsp Butter

- 1 White Onion, chopped
- Salt and black pepper to taste
- 1 Cauliflower, cut in small florets
- 1 tsp Cumin Powder
- 1 tsp dried Oregano
- ½ cup Heavy Whipping Cream
- 1 cup Sour Cream

Directions:
1. Melt the butter on Sauté, and add the onion and chicken. Stir and cook for 6 minutes. Stir in the florets, cumin powder, oregano, salt, and pepper. Pour in the broth, stir, and seal the lid.
2. Select Meat/Stew and cook on High pressure for minutes. Once ready, do a quick pressure release. Add the whipping and sour creams. Stir well and dish the sauce into serving bowls. Serve warm with a mix of steamed bell peppers, broccoli, and green beans.

Nutrition Info: Calories 102, Protein 7g, Net Carbs 0g, Fat 33g

Jalapeno Soup

Servings: 4
Cooking Time: 10 Minutes
Ingredients:
- 2 jalapeno peppers, sliced
- 3 oz pancetta, chopped
- ½ cup heavy cream
- 2 cups of water
- ½ cup Monterey jack cheese, shredded
- ½ teaspoon garlic powder
- 1 teaspoon coconut oil
- ½ teaspoon smoked paprika

Directions:
1. Toss pancetta in the instant pot, add coconut oil and cook it for 4 minutes on saute mode. Stir it from time to time.
2. After this, add sliced jalapenos, garlic powder, and smoked paprika.
3. Stir the ingredients for 1 minute.
4. Add heavy cream and water.
5. Then add Monterey Jack cheese and stir the soup well.
6. Close and seal the lid; cook the soup for 5 minutes on manual mode (high pressure); make a quick pressure release.

Nutrition Info:
Per Serving: calories 234, fat 20, fiber 0.4, carbs 1.7, protein 8

Veggie Walnut Chili

Servings: 4
Cooking Time: 30 Mins
Ingredients:

- 4 Celery Stalks, chopped
- 2 (15 oz) cans Diced Tomatoes
- 1 tbsp Olive oil
- 3 Carrots, chopped
- 2 cloves Garlic, minced
- 2 tsp Smoked Paprika
- 2 Green Bell peppers, diced
- 1 tbsp Cinnamon Powder
- 1 tbsp Cumin Powder
- 1 Sweet Onion, chopped
- 2 cups Tomato Sauce
- 1.5 oz sugar-free Dark Chocolate, chopped
- 1 small Chipotle, minced
- 1 ½ cups Walnuts, chopped + extra to garnish
- Salt and black pepper to taste
- Chopped Cilantro to garnish

Directions:

1. Heat the oil on Sauté, and add the onion, celery, and carrots. Sauté for 4 minutes. Add the garlic, cumin, cinnamon, and paprika. Stir and let the sauce cook for 2 minutes.
2. Then, stir in the bell peppers, tomatoes, tomato sauce, chipotle, and walnuts. Seal the lid, select Meat/Stew and cook on High pressure for 15 minutes. Once ready, do a quick pressure release. Pour in the chopped chocolate and stir until well-incorporated. Season with salt and pepper. Dish the chili into a serving bowl, garnish with the remaining walnuts and cilantro. Serve with zoodles.

Nutrition Info: Calories 260, Protein 15g, Net Carbs 0g, Fat 5.7g

Baby Spinach Green Soup With Asparagus

Servings: 5
Cooking Time: 30 Mins
Ingredients:

- 2 Zucchinis
- A handful Kale
- 2 celery sticks
- 4 Asparagus spears
- ¼ lb baby Spinach
- 1 small Onion
- A ¼ quarter of deseeded Chili
- 2 Garlic cloves, minced
- 2 tbsp Coconut oil
- Salt and black pepper to taste
- 1 cub Vegetable stock
- 2 tsp spirulina
- ½ cup fresh Parsley, chopped

Directions:

1. Start by peeling and chopping the onion. Mix with garlic, and chili; and set aside for minutes. Finely chop the parsley and the vegetables.
2. Heat tsp of oil on Sauté, then add the onion and cook until soft for 3 minutes. Add the garlic, chili., chopped vegetables, leaves, stock, salt, and pepper; then lock the lid
3. Cook on High pressure for 10 minutes. Once ready, release the pressure quickly and blend the ingredients. Add spirulina and zoodles, and cook for 5 more minutes, on Sauté. Garnish with parsley.

Nutrition Info: Calories 110, Protein 4g, Net Carbs 3.1g, Fat 4g

Sweet And Sour Tomato Soup

Servings: 3
Cooking Time: 35 Mins
Ingredients:

- 1 cup Tomato sauce
- ½ cup Tomato Ketchup
- 2 cups Vegetable broth
- ¼ cup Water
- 3 tbsp Almond flour
- 2 tbsp Vinegar
- 2 Garlic cloves, minced
- Salt and black pepper to taste
- 1 tbsp Olive oil

Directions:

1. Set the Instant Pot on Sauté mode. Heat the oil and add garlic cloves; cook for minute.
2. Add tomato puree, tomato ketchup, and vinegar and cook for another minutes. Stir in vegetable broth, and season with salt and pepper. Let simmer for 20-25 minutes on
3. Combine water with almond flour and mix well. Gradually add this mixture into the soup and stir continuously for 1-2 minutes. Pour into serving bowls and enjoy.

Nutrition Info: Calories 176, Protein 5g, Net Carbs 4.3g, Fat 7.3g

Tasty Instant Pot Greek Fish Stew

Servings: 5
Cooking Time: 20 Mins
Ingredients:

- 5 large white fish fillets
- 1 large red onion, chopped
- 4 cloves of garlic
- 1 leek, sliced
- 1 carrot, chopped
- 3 sticks celery, chopped
- 1 can tomatoes
- 1/2 tsp. saffron threads

- 8 cups fish stock
- 2 tbsp. fresh lemon juice
- 1 tbsp. lemon zest
- handful parsley leaves chopped
- handful mint leaves chopped

Directions:
1. Combine all ingredients in your instant pot and lock lid; cook on high for 20 Mins and then release pressure naturally. Serve with gluten-free bread.

Nutrition Info:
Per Serving: Calories: 443; Total Fat: 4 g; Carbs: 9.7 g; Dietary Fiber: 1.8 g; Sugars: 3.5 g; Protein: 8 g; Cholesterol: 153 mg; Sodium: 871 mg

Instant Pot Tomato Basil Soup

Servings: 6
Cooking Time: 20 Mins
Ingredients:
- 2 cloves fresh garlic
- 4 cups tomato puree
- 2 cups vegetable broth
- ¼ cup coconut oil
- ¼ cup coconut cream
- ½ cup fresh basil leaves
- pinch of Stevia, if desired
- 1 teaspoon sea salt

Directions:
1. Blend together garlic and tomatoes in a blender until very smooth; pour into your instant pot and add broth, coconut oil and salt. Lock lid and cook on high pressure for 20 Mins. When done, release pressure naturally and then stir in chopped basil and coconut cream. Blend the mixture with an immersion blender until smooth and then serve. Enjoy!

Nutrition Info:
Per Serving: Calories: 327; Total Fat: 3 g; Carbs: 7 g; Dietary Fiber: 5.5 g; Sugars: 1 g; Protein: 15 g; Cholesterol: 0 mg; Sodium: 618 mg

Italian Shrimp Soup

Servings: 4
Cooking Time: 7 Minutes
Ingredients:
- 1 tbsp olive oil
- 1 medium red onion, chopped
- 1 celery stick, chopped
- 1 red chili, minced
- 6 garlic cloves, minced
- ¾ cup white wine

- 4 cups chicken stock
- 2 cups chopped tomatoes
- 1 tsp Italian seasoning
- 1 lb. jumbo shrimp, peeled and tails intact
- Salt and black pepper to taste
- ¼ cup heavy cream
- 1 lemon, zested and juiced
- ¼ cup freshly chopped parsley

Directions:
1. Set the IP in Sauté mode and adjust to Medium heat.
2. Heat the olive oil the inner pot and sauté the onion, celery, and red chili until softened, 3 minutes. Stir in the garlic and cook until fragrant, 30 seconds.
3. Mix in the white wine, chicken stock, tomatoes, Italian seasoning, shrimp, salt, and black pepper.
4. Lock the lid in place; select Manual mode on High Pressure and set the timer to 3 minutes.
5. After cooking, perform a quick pressure release to let out the steam, and open the lid.
6. Remove the shrimp into a bowl and set aside.
7. Using an immersion blender, puree the soup until smooth and mix in the heavy cream. Adjust the taste with salt, black pepper, and return the shrimp to the soup.
8. Stir in the lemon zest, lemon juice, and dish the soup
9. Garnish with the parsley and serve warm.

Nutrition Info:
Per Serving: Calories 215 Fats 8.02g Carbs 46g Net Carbs 8.16g Protein 14g

Instant Pot Beef And Sweet Potato Stew

Servings: 6
Cooking Time: 25 Mins
Ingredients:
- 4 tablespoons olive oil
- 2 pounds ground beef
- 3 cups beef stock
- 2 sweet potatoes, peeled and diced
- 1 clove garlic, minced
- 1 onion, diced
- 1 (14-oz) can petite minced tomatoes
- 1 (14-oz) can tomato sauce
- 3-4 tbsp. chili powder
- ¼ tsp. oregano
- 2 tsp. salt
- ½ tsp. black pepper
- Cilantro, optional, for garnish

Directions:

1. Brown the beef in a pan over medium heat; drain excess fat and then transfer it to an instant pot. Stir in the remaining ingredients and lock lid; cook on high for 25 Mins and then release pressure naturally. Garnish with cilantro and serve warm.

Nutrition Info:
Per Serving: Calories: 240; Total Fat: 6 g; Carbs: 12 g; Dietary Fiber: 3.5 g; Sugars: 4.2 g; Protein: 3 g; Cholesterol: 81 mg; Sodium: 1201 mg

Taco Soup

Servings: 6
Cooking Time: 20 Minutes
Ingredients:
- 1 cup ground beef
- 1 bell pepper, chopped
- 1 garlic clove, diced
- ½ cup crushed tomatoes
- 2 tablespoons cream cheese
- 4 cups beef broth
- 1 tablespoon coconut oil
- 1 teaspoon taco seasonings

Directions:
1. Heat up coconut oil in the instant pot on saute mode.
2. Then add ground beef and sprinkle it with taco seasonings. Stir well and cook the meat on saute mode for 5 minutes.
3. After this, add bell pepper, garlic clove, crushed tomatoes, cream cheese, and beef broth.
4. Close the lid and cook the soup on manual mode (high pressure) for 15 minutes.
5. Then allow the natural pressure release for 10 minutes and open the lid.
6. Ladle the soup.

Nutrition Info:
Per Serving: calories 117, fat 7.1, fiber 1, carbs 4.4, protein 8.6

Buffalo Style Soup

Servings: 2
Cooking Time: 10 Minutes
Ingredients:
- 6 oz chicken, cooked
- 2 oz Mozzarella, shredded
- 4 tablespoons coconut milk
- ¼ teaspoon white pepper
- ¾ teaspoon salt
- 2 tablespoons keto Buffalo sauce
- 1 oz celery stalk, chopped
- 1 cup of water

Directions:

1. Place the chopped celery stalk, water, salt, white pepper, coconut milk, and Mozzarella in the instant pot. Stir it gently.
2. Set the "Manual" mode (High pressure) and turn on the timer for 7 minutes.
3. Shred the cooked chicken and combine it together with Buffalo Sauce.
4. Make quick pressure release and transfer the soup on the bowls.
5. Add shredded chicken and stir it.

Nutrition Info:
Per Serving: calories 287, fat 8, fiber 1.5, carbs 4.3, protein 5

Asparagus Soup

Servings: 4
Cooking Time: 17 Minutes
Ingredients:
- 1 cup asparagus, chopped
- 2 cups of coconut milk
- 1 teaspoon salt
- ½ teaspoon cayenne pepper
- 3 oz scallions, diced
- 1 teaspoon olive oil

Directions:
1. Saute the chopped asparagus, scallions, and olive oil in the instant pot for 7 minutes.
2. Then stir the vegetables well and add cayenne pepper, salt, and coconut milk
3. Cook the soup on manual mode (high pressure) for 10 minutes.
4. After this, make a quick pressure release and open the lid.
5. Blend the soup until you get the creamy texture.

Nutrition Info:
Per Serving: calories 300, fat 9, fiber 4, carbs 9.6, protein 3.9

Chicken & Green Onion Soup

Servings: 3
Cooking Time: 20 Mins
Ingredients:
- 1 lb Chicken breast, shredded
- 2 cups Chicken stock
- 1 tbsp Ginger
- 2 tbsp Sesame oil
- Salt to taste
- 2 green Onions, chopped

Directions:
1. Heat sesame oil on Sauté. Mix in stock, chicken breast, ginger, salt and green onions. Seal the lid and cook on High pressure for minutes. When done, do a quick pressure release.

Nutrition Info: Calories 294, Protein 32g, Net Carbs 0.9g, Fat 18g

Instant Pot Keto Bolognese Mince Soup

Servings: 6
Cooking Time: 1 Hour 5 Mins
Ingredients:

- 1kg beef mince
- 2 brown onions, diced
- 4 cloves garlic, crushed
- 1 cup tomato paste
- 2 tbsp. chicken stock powder or 2 Knorr Jelly pots
- 1 tin tomato soup
- 1 thin diced tomato
- 1/4 cup sweet chili sauce
- 1 tbsp. oregano
- 2 bay leaves
- 2 cups water
- 1 cup finely grated carrot
- 3-4 finely chopped sticks of celery
- 2 cups finely chopped mushrooms

Directions:

1. In an instant pot, add the olive oil and set on manual high. Brown the beef and add the onions and garlic. Cook for 2 Mins more. Mix the tomato paste into the pot and cook for another 2 Mins. Mix in the remaining ingredients and lock lid. Cook on high for hour and then release the pressure naturally.

Nutrition Info:
Per Serving: Calories: 187: Fat: 5.2g; Carbs: 8g; Protein: 27g

Flu Soup

Servings: 4
Cooking Time: 15 Minutes
Ingredients:

- 1 cup mushrooms, chopped
- 1 cup spinach, chopped
- 3 oz scallions, diced
- 2 oz Cheddar cheese, shredded
- 1 teaspoon cayenne pepper
- 1 cup organic almond milk
- 2 cups chicken broth
- ½ teaspoon salt

Directions:

1. Put all ingredients in the instant pot and close the lid.
2. Set the manual mode (high pressure) and cook the soup for 15 minutes.
3. Make a quick pressure release.

4. Blend the soup with the help of the immersion blender.
5. When the soup will get smooth texture – it is cooked.

Nutrition Info:
Per Serving: calories 228, fat 9, fiber 2.3, carbs 6.6, protein 8.5

Seafood Stew

Servings: 4
Cooking Time: 20 Minutes
Ingredients:

- ½ teaspoon ground cumin
- ½ teaspoon ground paprika
- ½ teaspoon ground turmeric
- 8 oz cod, chopped
- ½ cup crushed tomatoes
- 1 teaspoon coconut oil
- ½ teaspoon sesame seeds

Directions:
1. Sprinkle the chopped cod with cumin, paprika, turmeric, and sesame seeds.
2. Then heat up coconut oil in the instant pot on saute mode.
3. Add cod and cook it for 2 minutes from each side.
4. Then add crushed tomatoes and close the lid.
5. Saute the stew for 1minutes.

Nutrition Info:
Per Serving: calories 87, fat 1.9, fiber 1.2, carbs 3, protein 9

Instant Pot Coconut Fish Stew

Servings: 1 Serving
Cooking Time: 42 Mins
Ingredients:

- 1 tablespoon olive oil
- 1 red onion
- 1 tablespoon onion powder
- 150g tilapia filet
- ¼ cup coarsely chopped celery
- 2 cloves garlic
- 1 ½ cups vegetable broth
- ½ teaspoon parsley
- ½ teaspoon basil
- White pepper
- Sea salt

Directions:
1. Heat oil in your instant pot set over manual high heat; sauté onion until fragrant and then add in the fish. Cook for about 6 Mins per side or until browned. Add in the remaining

ingredients and lock lid; cook on high for 30 Mins and then let pressure come down on its own.

Nutrition Info:
Per Serving: Calories: 237; Fat: 4g; Carbs: 5.4g; Protein: 6g

Delicious Seafood Stew

Servings: 6
Cooking Time: 20 Mins
Ingredients:
- 3 tablespoons olive oil
- 2 pounds seafood (1 pound large shrimp & 1 pound scallops)
- 1/2 cup chopped white onion
- 3 garlic cloves, minced
- 1 tbsp. tomato paste
- 1 can (28 oz.) crushed tomatoes
- 4 cups vegetable broth
- 1 pound yellow potatoes, diced
- 1 tsp. dried basil
- 1 tsp. dried thyme
- 1 tsp. dried oregano
- 1/8 tsp. cayenne pepper
- 1/4 tsp. crush red pepper flakes
- 1/2 tsp. celery salt
- salt and pepper
- handful of chopped parsley

Directions:
1. Mix all ingredients, except seafood, in your instant pot and lock lid; cook on high for about Mins. Quick release the pressure and then stir in seafood and continue; lock lid and cook on high for five Mins and then let pressure come down on its own. Serve hot with crusty gluten-free bread and garnished with parsley.

Nutrition Info:
Per Serving: Calories: 323; Total Fat: 3 g; Carbs: 7.7 g; Dietary Fiber: 0.8 g; Sugars: 1.9 g; Protein: 1 g; Cholesterol: 478 mg; Sodium: 1323 mg

Creamy Instant Pot Chicken & Tomato Soup

Servings: 4
Cooking Time: 1 Hour
Ingredients:
- 8 frozen skinless boneless chicken breasts
- 2 tbsp. Italian Seasoning
- 1 tbsp. dried basil

- 2 cloves garlic, minced
- 1 large onion, chopped
- 2 cups coconut milk (full fat) to avoid separation
- 2 cans diced tomatoes and juice
- 2 cups chicken stock
- 1 small can of tomato paste
- sea salt & pepper

Directions:
1. Put all the above ingredients into the instant pot and cook on high setting for hour. Let pressure come down on its own.
2. Shred the chicken, cover the pot until ready to serve.

Nutrition Info:
Per Serving: Calories: 227; Total Fat: 3.8g; Carbs: 6.4g; Protein: 30g

Three- Ingredient Instant Pot Veggie Beef Soup

Servings: 2
Cooking Time: 30 Mins
Ingredients:
- 500g ground beef mince
- 500ml tomato-vegetable juice cocktail
- 2 packages frozen mixed vegetables

Directions:
1. Place ground beef mince in your instant pot; cook on manual high until browned. Stir in juice cocktail and mixed vegetables. Lock lid and cook on high for 30 Mins and then let pressure come down on its own.

Nutrition Info:
Per Serving: Calories: 251: Fat: 12g; Carbs: 5g; Protein: 3g

Thyme Chicken Soup

Servings: 4
Cooking Time: 24 Minutes
Ingredients:
- 2 tbsp olive oil
- 1 large white onion, chopped
- 1 celery stalk, chopped
- 6 garlic cloves, minced
- 2 tbsp fresh thyme leaves
- 2 chicken breasts, cut into 1-inch cubes
- 4 cups chicken stock
- Salt and black pepper to taste
- 1 lemon, juiced

- 2 tbsp freshly chopped parsley to garnish

Directions:

1. Set the IP in Sauté mode and adjust to medium heat.
2. Heat the olive oil in the inner pot and sauté the onion and celery until softened, 3 minutes. Mix in the garlic, thyme, and cook until fragrant, 1 minute.
3. Add the chicken, chicken stock, salt, and black pepper.
4. Lock the lid in place; select Manual mode on High Pressure and set the timer to 10 minutes.
5. After cooking, perform a natural pressure release for 10 minutes, then a quick pressure release to let out the remaining steam and open the lid.
6. Stir the soup, adjust the taste with salt and black pepper, and mix in the lemon juice.
7. Dish the soup, garnish with parsley, and serve warm.

Nutrition Info:
Per Serving: Calories 325 Fats 28g Carbs 3.92g Net Carbs 3.32g Protein 94g

Easy Cheesy Turkey Stew

Servings: 5
Cooking Time: 25 Mins
Ingredients:

- 2 tbsp. coconut oil
- 1/2 red onion
- 1 lb. ground turkey
- 2 cups coconut milk
- 2 garlic cloves
- 1 tbsp. mustard
- 2 cups riced cauliflower
- 1 tsp salt
- 1 tsp. black pepper
- 1 tsp. thyme
- 1 tsp. celery salt
- 1 tsp. garlic powder

Directions:

1. Melt coconut oil in an instant pot, add garlic and onion and cook until fragrant. Stir in ground turkey until crumbled.
2. Stir in cauliflower and spices until well mixed. Cook until meat is browned. Stir in coconut milk and lock lid. Cook on high for Mins and then let pressure come down on its own. Stir in shredded cheese and serve.

Nutrition Info:
Per Serving: Calories: 475; Total Fat: 39 g; Carbs: 5g; Protein: 7g

Chili Chicken Asparagus Soup

Servings: 4
Cooking Time: 24 Minutes
Ingredients:

- 2 tbsp olive oil
- 1 large yellow onion, chopped
- 2 celery stalks, chopped
- 1 lb. asparagus, chopped
- 5 garlic cloves, minced
- 2 chicken breasts, cut into ½-inch cubes
- 4 cups chicken stock
- 1 tsp dried mixed herbs
- 2 bay leaves
- Salt and black pepper to taste
- ½ tsp cayenne powder
- ½ lemon, juiced

Directions:

1. Set the IP in Sauté mode and adjust to medium heat.
2. Heat the olive oil in the inner pot and sauté the onion, celery, and asparagus until softened, 3 minutes. Mix in the garlic and cook until fragrant, 1 minute.
3. Stir in the chicken, chicken stock, mixed herbs, bay leaves, salt, black pepper, and cayenne powder.
4. Lock the lid in place; select Manual mode on High Pressure and set the timer to 10 minutes.
5. After cooking, perform a natural pressure release for 10 minutes, then a quick pressure release to let out the remaining steam and open the lid.
6. Stir the soup, adjust the taste with salt and black pepper, and mix in the lemon juice.
7. Dish the soup, garnish with parsley, and serve warm.

Nutrition Info:
Per Serving: Calories 374 Fats 76g Carbs 9.21g Net Carbs 6.01g Protein 5g

Mustard Baby Spinach Soup

Servings: 3
Cooking Time: 19 Mins
Ingredients:

- 2 tbsp Ginger, minced
- 4 Garlic cloves, minced
- 1 tbsp Mustard seeds
- 1 tbsp Olive oil
- 1 cup Heavy cream
- 3 cups Vegetable broth
- 1 tbsp Coriander powder
- 4 cups baby Spinach

Directions:

1. Heat oil on Sauté mode. Stir in the mustard seeds, garlic, coriander powder and broth. Add spinach and heavy cream. Seal the lid and set to Manual. Cook on High pressure for minutes. When done, release the pressure quickly.

Nutrition Info: Calories 215, Protein 5g, Net Carbs 2.1g, Fat 5g

Tomatillos Fish Stew

Servings: 2
Cooking Time: 12 Minutes
Ingredients:

- 2 tomatillos, chopped
- 10 oz salmon fillet, chopped
- 1 teaspoon ground paprika
- ½ teaspoon ground turmeric
- 1 cup coconut cream
- ½ teaspoon salt

Directions:

1. Put all ingredients in the instant pot.
2. Close and seal the lid.
3. Cook the fish stew on manual mode (high pressure) for 12 minutes.
4. Then allow the natural pressure release for 10 minutes.

Nutrition Info:
Per Serving: calories 479, fat 9, fiber 3.8, carbs 9.6, protein 8

Mushroom Beef Soup

Servings: 4
Cooking Time: 30 Minutes
Ingredients:

- 1 tbsp olive oil
- 1 lb. ground beef
- 1 lb. chopped mixed mushrooms
- 1 medium onion, quartered
- 5 celery ribs, halved
- 2 tbsp coconut aminos
- 5 cups chicken broth
- 2 bay leaves
- 2 tsp dried thyme
- 1 tbsp lemon juice
- 1/8 tsp chili pepper
- Salt and black pepper
- 4 scallions, chopped

Directions:

1. Set the IP in Sauté mode and adjust to medium heat.
2. Heat the olive oil in the inner pot, and cook the beef until brown, 5 minutes. Mix in the mushrooms, celery, and onion. Stir and cook until softened, 5 minutes.
3. Add the coconut aminos, chicken broth, bay leaves, thyme, lemon juice, chili pepper, salt, and black pepper.
4. Lock the lid in place; select Manual mode on High Pressure and set the timer to 10 minutes.

5. After cooking, perform a natural pressure release for 10 minutes, then a quick pressure release to let out the remaining steam and open the lid.
6. Stir the soup, adjust the taste with salt and black pepper, and mix in the scallions.
7. Serve the soup warm.

Nutrition Info:

Per Serving: Calories 329 Fats 56g Carbs 75g Net Carbs 7.45g Protein 9g

Instant Pot Loaded Protein Stew

Servings: 2
Cooking Time: 1 Hour
Ingredients:

- 1-pound ground chicken
- 2 minced cloves garlic
- 2 large carrots, grated
- 1 medium red bell pepper, diced
- 1 teaspoon Stevia
- 1/4 cup low-sodium soy sauce
- 1/4 tsp. crushed red pepper flakes
- 1/4 cup ketchup

Directions:

1. Combine all ingredients in your instant pot and cook on high setting for hour. Shred the chicken and return to the pot.

Nutrition Info:

Per Serving: Calories: 262; Total Fat: 8.6 g; Carbs: 1g; Dietary Fiber: 1.4 g; Sugars: 7.7 g; Protein: 8 g; Cholesterol: 101 mg; Sodium: 1170 mg

Sausage And Cauliflower Stew

Servings: 4
Cooking Time: 28 Minutes
Ingredients:

- 1 tbsp olive oil
- 1 lb. sweet Italian sausage, casing removed and chopped
- 1 lb. hot Italian sausage, casing removed and chopped
- 1 medium onion, chopped
- 1 leek, chopped
- 3 garlic cloves, minced
- 1 cup beef broth
- 1 large heard cauliflower, coarsely chopped
- 1 cup chopped tomatoes
- ½ tsp dried thyme
- 4 oz cream cheese
- Salt and black pepper to taste

Directions:

1. Set the IP in Sauté mode and adjust to Medium heat.
2. Heat the olive oil in the inner pot and cook the sausages until brown, 5 to 7 minutes. Spoon onto a plate and set aside.
3. Stir the onion, leek, and garlic into the oil, and cook until softened and fragrant, minutes.
4. Mix in the beef broth, cauliflower, tomatoes, thyme, and sausages.
5. Lock the lid in place; select Manual mode on High Pressure and set the timer to 8 minutes.
6. After cooking, perform a natural pressure release for 10 minutes, then a quick pressure release to let out the remaining steam and open the lid.
7. Set the IP in Sauté mode and mix in the cream cheese. Cook until melted and adjust the taste with salt and black pepper.
8. Serve.

Nutrition Info:
Per Serving: Calories 762 Fats 33g Carbs 48g Net Carbs 88g Protein 61g

Instant Pot Spicy Green Soup

Servings: 2
Cooking Time: 15 Mins
Ingredients:
- 2 tablespoons olive oil
- 5 cups water
- 1 cup chickpeas
- 1 green bell pepper, chopped
- 1 red onion, chopped
- 4 celery stalks, chopped
- 2 cups chopped spinach
- 1 tsp. dried mint
- 1/2 tsp. ground cumin
- 1/2 tsp. ground ginger
- 1/2 tsp. cardamom
- 2 cloves of garlic
- 1 tbsp. coconut milk
- Pinch of sea salt
- pinch of pepper

Directions:
1. Combine all ingredients, except spinach and coconut milk, in your instant pot and lock lid; cook on high pressure for Mins and then release the pressure naturally. Stir in spinach; let sit for about 5 Mins and then blend the mixture until very smooth.
2. Serve the soup in soup bowls and add coconut milk. Season with salt and more pepper and enjoy!

Nutrition Info:
Per Serving: Calories: 317; Total Fat:1 2.8 g; Carbs: 2 g; Dietary Fiber: 6.3 g; Sugars: 4 g; Protein: 3 g; Cholesterol: 0 mg; Sodium: 356 mg

Best Beef Stew For A King!

Servings: 2
Cooking Time: 2 Hours 10 Mins
Ingredients:

- 200g beef meat, cubed
- 1 tsp. Salt
- 1 tsp. pepper
- 1 medium onion, finely chopped
- 2 celery ribs, sliced
- 2 cloves of garlic, minced
- 1 can tomato paste
- 3 cups beef stock
- 2 tbsp. Worcestershire sauce
- 1 cup frozen mixed veggies
- 1 tablespoon almond flour
- 1 tablespoon water

Directions:

1. Combine all ingredients except flour, frozen veggies, and water in your instant pot.
2. Cook on high setting for hours. Let pressure come down on its own.
3. Stir together water and flour; stir into the pot and then add in veggies; lock lid and cook for 10 Mins.

Nutrition Info:

Per Serving: Calories: 368; Total Fat: 3 g; Carbs: 6 g; Dietary Fiber: 5.8 g; Sugars: 6.9 g; Protein: 6 g; Cholesterol: 89 mg; Sodium: 2691 mg

Creamy Turkey Stew

Servings: 4
Cooking Time: 46 Minutes
Ingredients:

- 5 bacon slices, chopped
- 2 tbsp olive oil
- 1 lb. turkey thigh and leg meat, cut into cubes
- Salt and black pepper to taste
- 1 garlic clove, minced
- 1 leek, halved and sliced
- 1 cup chopped white button mushrooms
- 2 tbsp fresh rosemary leaves
- 2 tbsp whole grain mustard
- 2/3 cup chicken broth
- 1 cup coconut cream
- 1 tsp xanthan gum
- ½ cup chopped fresh parsley

Directions:
1. Set the IP in Sauté mode and adjust to medium heat.
2. Cook the bacon in the inner pot until brown and crispy, 5 minutes. Transfer to a plate and set aside.
3. Heat the olive oil in the inner pot, season the turkey with salt, black pepper, and sear in the oil until golden brown on the outside, 8 to 10 minutes. Transfer the meat to the side of the bacon.
4. Stir the garlic, leek, and mushrooms into the oil, and cook until softened and fragrant, 5 minutes.
5. Season with the thyme, salt, black pepper, mustard, and return the bacon and turkey to the pot. Mix in the chicken broth.
6. Lock the lid in place; select Manual mode on High Pressure and set the timer to 12 minutes.
7. After cooking, perform a natural pressure release for 10 minutes, then a quick pressure release to let out the remaining steam and open the lid.
8. Set the IP in Sauté mode and mix in the coconut cream, xanthan gum, and adjust the taste with salt and black pepper. Cook until thickened, 3 to 4 minutes.
9. Stir in the parsley and spoon the stew into serving bowls. Enjoy!

Nutrition Info:
Per Serving: Calories 582 Fats 22g Carbs 15g Net Carbs 7.65g Protein 01g

Chicken Soup

Servings: 2
Cooking Time: 20 Minutes
Ingredients:
- 8 oz chicken breast, skinless, boneless
- 2 cups of water
- 1 tablespoon scallions, diced
- 1 teaspoon salt
- 1 tablespoon fresh dill, chopped

Directions:
1. Pour water in the instant pot.
2. Chop the chicken breast and add it in the water.
3. Then add scallions, salt, and close the lid.
4. Cook the soup on manual mode (high pressure) for 20 minutes.
5. Then make a quick pressure release and ladle the soup in the bowls.
6. Top the soup with fresh dill.

Nutrition Info:
Per Serving: calories 134, fat 2.9, fiber 0.3, carbs 1.1, protein 4

Pizza Soup

Servings: 3
Cooking Time: 22 Minutes
Ingredients:

- ¼ cup cremini mushrooms, sliced
- 1 teaspoon tomato paste
- 4 oz Mozzarella, shredded
- ½ jalapeno pepper, sliced
- ½ teaspoon Italian seasoning
- 1 teaspoon coconut oil
- 5 oz Italian sausages, chopped
- 1 cup of water

Directions:
1. Melt the coconut oil in the instant pot on saute mode.
2. Add mushrooms and cook them for 10 minutes.
3. After this, add chopped sausages, Italian seasoning, sliced jalapeno, and tomato paste.
4. Mix up the ingredients well and add water.
5. Close and seal the lid and cook the soup on manual mode (high pressure) for 12 minutes.
6. Then make a quick pressure release and ladle the soup in the bowls. Top it with Mozzarella.

Nutrition Info:
Per Serving: calories 289, fat 2, fiber 0.2, carbs 2.5, protein 7

Instant Pot Easy Everyday Chicken Soup

Servings: 3
Cooking Time: 1 Hour
Ingredients:
- 3 skinned, bone-in chicken breasts
- 6 skinned and boned chicken thighs
- 1 tsp salt
- ½ tsp freshly ground pepper
- ½ tsp chicken spice seasoning
- 3-4 carrots sliced
- 4 celery ribs, sliced
- 1 sweet onion, chopped
- 2 cans evaporated milk
- 2 cups chicken stock

Directions:
1. Prepare Chicken: Rub chicken pieces with salt, pepper, and chicken spice seasoning. Place breasts in an instant pot, top with thighs.
2. Add carrots and next 3 ingredients. Whisk evaporated milk and stock until smooth. Pour soup mixture over vegetables. Lock lid and cook on high for 1 hour. Let pressure come down on its own. Remove chicken; cool 10 Mins. Debone and shred chicken. Stir chicken into soup-and-vegetable mixture. Cook on manual high for 1 hour before serving.

Nutrition Info:
Per Serving: Calories: 282; Total Fat: 18g; Carbs: 5.6g; Protein: 24g

Tomato Chicken Soup

Servings: 4
Cooking Time: 18 Minutes
Ingredients:

- 1 tbsp olive oil
- 1 cup chopped chives
- 2 green chilies, minced
- 2 garlic cloves, minced
- 2 chicken breasts, cut into 1-inch cubes
- 4 cups chicken broth
- ½ tsp cumin powder
- 2 tomatoes, chopped
- Salt and black pepper to taste
- 1/3 cup chopped fresh parsley
- 2 limes, juiced
- 3 medium avocados, halved, pitted, and sliced
- 1 cup coconut cream for topping

Directions:

1. Set the IP in Sauté mode and adjust to medium heat.
2. Heat the olive oil in the inner pot and sauté the chives, green chilies, and garlic until fragrant, 1 minute.
3. Mix in the chicken, chicken broth, cumin powder, tomatoes, salt, and black pepper.
4. Lock the lid in place; select Manual mode on High Pressure and set the timer to 7 minutes.
5. After cooking, perform a natural pressure release for 10 minutes, then a quick pressure release to let out the remaining steam and open the lid.
6. Stir in the cilantro and lime juice. Adjust the taste with salt and black pepper.
7. Dish the soup and top with avocados, and coconut cream.
8. Serve warm.

Nutrition Info:
Per Serving: Calories 747 Fats 99g Carbs 6g Net Carbs 8g Protein 75g

Avocado Broccoli Soup With Pecans

Servings: 4
Cooking Time: 5 Minutes
Ingredients:

- 1 tbsp avocado oil
- 3 garlic cloves, minced
- 1 tbsp fresh ginger paste
- 1 tsp turmeric powder
- 1 tsp cumin powder
- 1 medium head broccoli, cut into florets
- 4 cups vegetable broth

- Salt and black pepper to taste
- 1 large avocado, pitted and peeled
- 1 cup coconut milk
- ¼ cup pecans

Directions:
1. Set the IP in Sauté mode and adjust to medium heat.
2. Heat the avocado oil in the inner pot and stir-fry the garlic, ginger, turmeric, and cumin powder until fragrant, 30 seconds.
3. Mix in the broccoli, vegetable broth, salt, and black pepper.
4. Lock the lid in place; select Manual mode on High Pressure and set the timer to minutes.
5. After cooking, perform a quick pressure release to let out the steam and open the lid.
6. Stir the avocado and coconut milk into the soup and using an immersion blender, puree the soup until smooth. Adjust the taste with salt and black pepper.
7. Dish into serving bowls, top with the pecans, and serve warm.

Nutrition Info:
Per Serving: Calories 313 Fats 9g Carbs 79g Net Carbs 6.49g Protein 4.15g

Instant Pot Broccoli & Blue Cheese Soup

Servings: 3
Cooking Time: 2 Hours
Ingredients:
- 2 red onions, diced
- 4 stick celery, sliced
- 4 leeks, sliced (white part only)
- 2 tbsp. butter
- 1 liter chicken stock
- 2 large heads of broccoli, cut into florets
- 140g (1 1/4 cups) crumbled blue cheese
- 125ml cream

Directions:
1. Combine all ingredients in an instant pot; lock lid and cook on stew setting for 2 hours. Let pressure come down on its own. Using a hand blender, blitz the soup until smooth. Ladle into bowls and top with extra crumbles of blue cheese (if desired).

Nutrition Info:
Per Serving: Calories: 174: Fat: 10g; Carbs: 8g; Protein: 7.5g

Chicken Enchilada Soup

Servings: 6
Cooking Time: 20 Mins
Ingredients:
- 1 ½ pounds chicken thighs, boneless, skinless
- 3 cloves garlic, minced
- 1 bell pepper, thinly sliced

- 1 onion, thinly sliced
- 1 can roasted crushed tomatoes
- 1/2 cup water
- 2 cups bone broth
- 1/2 tsp smoked paprika
- 1 tsp oregano
- 1 tbsp. chili powder
- 1 tbsp. cumin
- 1/2 tsp sea salt
- 1/2 tsp pepper
- For garnish:
- fresh cilantro
- 1 avocado

Directions:

1. Combine all ingredients in your instant pot, except garnishes; lock lid and cook on high pressure for 20 Mins. Release pressure naturally and shred the chicken with fork. Serve in soup bowls garnished with cilantro and avocado.

Nutrition Info:

Per Serving: Calories: 313; Total Fat: 5 g; Carbs: 8.9 g; Dietary Fiber: 3.9 g; Sugars: 2.6 g; Protein: 4 g; Cholesterol: 101 mg; Sodium: 290 mg

Leek Soup

Servings: 4
Cooking Time: 15 Minutes
Ingredients:

- 7 oz leek, chopped
- 2 oz Monterey Jack cheese, shredded
- 1 teaspoon Italian seasonings
- ½ teaspoon salt
- 4 tablespoons butter
- 2 cups chicken broth

Directions:

1. Heat up butter in the instant pot for 4 minutes.
2. Then add chopped leek, salt, and Italian seasonings.
3. Cook the leek on saute mode for 5 minutes. Stir the vegetables from time to time.
4. After this, add chicken broth and close the lid.
5. Cook the soup on saute mode for 10 minutes.
6. Then add shredded cheese and stir it till the cheese is melted.
7. The soup is cooked.

Nutrition Info:

Per Serving: calories 208, fat 17, fiber 0.9, carbs 7.7, protein 6.8

Onion-mushroom Soup

Servings: 4
Cooking Time: 9 Minutes
Ingredients:

- 3 tbsp butter
- 2 medium brown onions, chopped
- 2 cups sliced white button mushrooms
- 2 tbsp almond flour
- 4 cups chicken broth
- 1 cup cauliflower rice
- 1 bay leaf
- Salt and black pepper to taste
- 2 tbsp chopped fresh parsley

Directions:

1. Set the IP in Sauté mode and adjust to medium heat.
2. Melt the butter in the inner pot and sauté the onions and mushrooms until softened, 5 minutes.
3. Stir in the almond flour until roux forms and then gradually mix in the chicken broth a few tablespoons at a time until smooth. Stir in cauliflower rice, bay leaf, salt and black pepper.
4. Lock the lid in place; select Manual mode on High Pressure and the timer to minutes.
5. After cooking, perform a quick pressure release to let out the steam and open the lid.
6. Stir the soup, adjust taste with salt and black pepper, and dish the soup.
7. Garnish with the parsley and serve warm.

Nutrition Info:
Per Serving: Calories 114 Fats 9.12g Carbs 7.88g Net Carbs 6.08g Protein 26g

Instant Pot Chicken And Vegetable Stew

Servings: 4-6
Cooking Time: 30 Mins
Ingredients:

- 4 tablespoons olive oil
- 2 red onions, chopped
- 1 pound diced chicken
- 1 pound curly kale, torn
- 12 ounces baby spinach
- 3 cups plus 2 tablespoons water
- 4 cups homemade vegetable broth
- 1 tablespoon fresh lemon juice
- 1 large pinch of cayenne pepper
- Salt, to taste

Directions:

1. In an instant pot, heat oil on sauté setting and then sauté onion and salt until fragrant. Add in diced chicken and cook for 5 Mins or until browned. Stir in the remaining ingredients; lock lid and cook on high pressure for 20 Mins. Release pressure naturally.

Nutrition Info:
Per Serving: Calories: 202; Total Fat: 4 g; Carbs: 8.3g; Dietary Fiber: 3.1g; Sugars: 2.8 g; Protein: 3.1 g; Cholesterol: 0 mg; Sodium: 109 mg

Lemony Veggie Soup Cayenne

Servings: 4
Cooking Time: 25 Mins
Ingredients:
- 1-pound curly kale, torn
- 12 ounces baby spinach
- ¼ cup brown Arborio rice, rinsed
- 2 yellow onions, chopped
- 4 tablespoons olive oil
- 3 cups plus 2 tablespoons water
- 4 cups homemade vegetable broth
- 1 tablespoon fresh lemon juice
- 1 large pinch of cayenne pepper
- Salt, to taste

Directions:
1. Add the two tablespoons of olive oil in a large pan and cook the onions over medium heat. Sprinkle with salt and cook for 5 Mins until they start browning.
2. Lower the heat and pour in two tablespoons of water. Cover and lower the heat and cook for Mins until the onions caramelize, stirring frequently.
3. Meanwhile, add the remaining water, broth, and some salt to an instant pot and stir in the rice. Lock the lid and cook on high pressure for 5 Mins. Naturally release the pressure and then stir in kale, onions, spinach and cayenne and lock the lid. Let sit for about 5 Mins.
4. Use an immersion blender to puree the rice mixture until smooth then stir in the lemon juice. Serve in soup bowls and drizzle each with some olive oil.

Nutrition Info:
Per Serving: Calories: 102; Total Fat: 4 g; Carbs: 8.3g; Dietary Fiber: 3.1g; Sugars: 2.8 g; Protein: 3.1 g; Cholesterol: 0 mg; Sodium: 109 mg

Chili Spinach Soup

Servings: 3
Cooking Time: 40 Mins
Ingredients:
- 1 cup baby Spinach
- 2 cups Vegetable broth
- ½ cup Almond Milk
- 2 Garlic cloves, minced

- ½ tbsp Chili flakes
- ¼ cup sour Cream
- 2 tbsp Olive oil

Directions:

1. In the pot, add all ingredients except sour cream, and seal the lid. Set on Manual, and cook for 25 minutes on High. When done, allow for a natural pressure release, for minutes. Transfer to a food processor and blend until creamy. Top with sour cream and serve.

Nutrition Info: Calories 134, Protein 2g, Net Carbs 4.2g, Fat 4g

Tasty Mushroom Coconut Milk Soup

Servings: 4
Cooking Time: 10 Mins
Ingredients:

- 1 ½ pounds mushrooms, trimmed
- 2 tablespoons olive oil
- 1 clove garlic, minced
- 2 red onions, chopped
- 4 cups vegetable stock
- 1 cup coconut milk
- 1 tablespoon fresh thyme
- 1/8 teaspoon sea salt
- Thyme sprigs
- 1/8 teaspoon pepper

Directions:

1. Grill the mushrooms, turning frequently, for about 5 Mins or until charred and tender; set aside.
2. In an instant pot, sauté red onion in oil. Stir in vegetable stock and cook for a few Mins. Add the remaining ingredients and lock the lid; cook on high pressure for 3 Mins and then release the pressure naturally. Transfer the mixture to a blender and blend until very smooth. Serve garnished with thyme sprigs.

Nutrition Info:
Per Serving: Calories: 338; Total Fat: 2 g; Carbs: 1 g; Dietary Fiber: 5.8 g; Sugars: 9.3 g; Protein: 8.8 g; Cholesterol: 0 mg; Sodium: 89 mg

Beef Bourguignon Stew

Servings: 4
Cooking Time: 56 Minutes
Ingredients:

- 4 bacon slices, chopped
- 1 lb. beef stew meat, cut into 1-inch cubes
- Salt and black pepper to taste
- 1 small brown onion
- 2 celery stalks, chopped

- 1 garlic clove, minced
- 1 cup dry red wine
- 1 cup beef stock
- 2 tbsp unsweetened tomato paste
- 1 bay leaf
- ½ tsp dried thyme
- ½ tsp arrowroot starch
- 1 tbsp chopped fresh parsley

Directions:
1. Set the IP in Sauté mode and adjust to medium heat.
2. Cook the bacon in the inner pot until brown and crispy, 5 minutes. Transfer to a plate and set aside.
3. Heat the olive oil in the inner pot, season the meat with salt, black pepper, and sear in the oil until golden brown on the outside, 8 to 10 minutes. Transfer the meat to the side of the bacon.
4. Stir the onion, celery, and garlic into the oil, and cook until softened and fragrant, 5 minutes.
5. Mix in the red wine and cook until reduced by one-third, 2 minutes. Add the remaining ingredients except for the arrowroot starch; stir.
6. Lock the lid in place; select Manual mode on High Pressure and set the timer to 20 minutes.
7. After cooking, perform a natural pressure release for 10 minutes, then a quick pressure release to let out the remaining steam and open the lid.
8. Set the IP in Sauté mode and mix in the arrowroot starch, and adjust the taste with salt and black pepper. Cook until thickened, 3 to 4 minutes.
9. Stir in the parsley and spoon the stew into serving bowls. Enjoy!

Nutrition Info:
Per Serving: Calories 280 Fats 84g Carbs 5.7g Net Carbs 4.7g Protein 02g

Cilantro & Spinach Soup

Servings: 4
Cooking Time: 20 Mins
Ingredients:
- 1 cup baby Spinach
- 1 bunch cilantro, chopped
- 2 cups Vegetable broth
- 1 cup Heavy Cream
- ½ cup Almond Milk
- 4-5 Garlic cloves, minced
- ½ tbsp Chili flakes
- Salt and black pepper to taste
- 2 tbsp Olive oil

Directions:
1. Heat oil and add garlic cloves, cook for minute on Sauté mode. Add broth, spinach, cilantro, cream, chili flake, and salt, mix well. Seal the lid and cook on High pressure for 10 minutes.

Allow the pressure to release naturally for 10 minutes. Pour in milk and cook for 5 minutes on Sauté.

Nutrition Info: Calories 187, Protein 2g, Net Carbs 3.1g, Fat 3g

Mexican Sweet Pepper Soup

Servings: 4
Cooking Time: 14 Minutes
Ingredients:

- 3 tbsp olive oil
- 1 cup chopped mixed bell peppers
- 1 small turnip, peeled and chopped
- 1 garlic clove, minced
- Salt and black pepper to taste
- 1 tsp Mexican seasoning
- 4 cups vegetable broth
- ¼ tsp dried oregano
- 1 cup heavy cream
- 2 tbsp freshly chopped parsley

Directions:

1. Set the IP in Sauté mode and adjust to medium heat.
2. Heat the olive oil in the inner pot and sauté the peppers and turnip until softened, 5 minutes. Mix in the garlic and cook until fragrant, 1 minute. Season with salt, black pepper and the Mexican seasoning until fragrant, 1 minute.
3. Mix in the vegetable broth and oregano.
4. Lock the lid in place; select Manual mode on High Pressure and set the timer to 5 minutes.
5. After cooking, perform a quick pressure release to let out the steam and open the lid.
6. Set the IP in Sauté mode and mix in the heavy cream; cook for 1 to 2 minutes
7. Adjust the taste with salt and black pepper, and dish the soup.
8. Garnish with parsley and serve warm.

Nutrition Info:
Per Serving: Calories 221 Fats 45g Carbs 5.78g Net Carbs 3.98g Protein 2.43g

Cauliflower Soup

Servings: 4
Cooking Time: 6 Minutes
Ingredients:

- 2 cups cauliflower, chopped
- 1 cup coconut cream
- 2 cups beef broth
- 2 tablespoons fresh cilantro
- 3 oz Provolone cheese, chopped

Directions:

1. Put cauliflower, coconut cream, beef broth, cilantro, and cheese in the instant pot.

2. Cook the soup on manual (high pressure) for 6 minutes. Then allow the natural pressure release for 4 minutes.
3. Blend the soup with the help of the immersion blender.

Nutrition Info:
Per Serving: calories 244, fat 7, fiber 2.6, carbs 6.9, protein 2

Paprika Zucchini Soup

Servings: 2
Cooking Time: 1 Minute
Ingredients:
- 1 zucchini, grated
- 1 teaspoon ground paprika
- ½ teaspoon cayenne pepper
- ½ cup of coconut milk
- 1 cup beef broth
- 1 tablespoon dried cilantro
- 1 oz Parmesan, grated

Directions:
1. Put the grated zucchini, paprika, cayenne pepper, coconut milk, beef broth, and dried cilantro in the instant pot.
2. Close and seal the lid.
3. Cook the soup on manual (high pressure) for 1 minute. Make a quick pressure release.
4. Ladle the soup in the serving bowls and top with parmesan.

Nutrition Info:
Per Serving: calories 223, fat 4, fiber 2.9, carbs 8.4, protein 9.7

Butter Squash Soup

Servings: 6
Cooking Time: 25 Mins
Ingredients:
- 1 peeled and diced Butternut Squash.
- 1 peeled and diced Green Smith apple
- 1 tbsp Ginger powder or pureed Ginger
- 4 cups Chicken broth
- 1 cup Heavy cream
- 2 tbsp Coconut oil
- Salt and black pepper to taste

Directions:
1. Add the coconut oil and add some of the butternut squash cubes in. Brown lightly for 5 minutes on Sauté. Add the remaining squash and the rest of the ingredients. Seal the lid and cook for minutes on High pressure. When done, do a quick release. Puree the mixture in a blender. Serve and enjoy.

Nutrition Info: Calories 235, Protein 7g, Net Carbs 6.2g, Fat 13g

Instant Pot Lemon Chicken Stew

Servings: 2
Cooking Time: 1 Hour 30 Mins
Ingredients:

- 2 carrots, chopped
- 2 ribs celery, chopped
- 1 onion, chopped
- 10 large green olives
- 4 cloves garlic, crushed
- 2 bay leaves
- ½ tsp. dried oregano
- ¼ tsp. salt
- ¼ tsp. pepper
- 6 boneless skinless chicken thighs
- ¾ cup chicken stock
- ¼ cup almond flour
- 2 tbsp. lemon juice
- ½ cup chopped fresh parsley
- grated zest of 1 lemon

Directions:

1. In your instant pot, combine carrots, celery, onion, olives, garlic, bay leaves, oregano, salt and pepper. Arrange chicken pieces on top of vegetables. Add broth and ¾ cup water. Lock lid and cook on high setting for ½ hours. Let pressure come down naturally. Discard bay leaves.
2. In a small bowl, whisk together a cup of cooking liquid and flour until very smooth; whisk in lemon juice and pour the mixture into your pot. Cook on manual high for about 15 Mins or until thickened.
3. In a small bowl, mix together lemon zest and chopped parsley; sprinkled over the chicken mixture and serve. Enjoy!

Nutrition Info:
Per Serving: Calories: 392; Total Fat: 4 g; Carbs: 2 g; Dietary Fiber: 6.7 g; Sugars: 2.4 g; Protein: 2 g; Cholesterol: 103 mg; Sodium: 1213 mg

Pumpkin Soup

Servings: 3
Cooking Time: 16 Mins
Ingredients:

- 2 tbsp Olive oil
- 1 Onion, chopped
- 1 Carrot, chopped
- 2 cloves Garlic, minced
- 2 tsp Curry powder

- 4 cups Vegetable broth
- 2 tbsp Pumpkin seeds
- Salt and black pepper to taste

Directions:

1. Heat oil on Sauté. Cook onion and garlic for 3 minutes. Add broth, pumpkin seeds, curry powder, garlic, and carrots. Season with salt and pepper. Seal the lid and press the Manual button. Cook on High pressure for minutes. When done, allow the pressure to release naturally for 10 minutes.

Nutrition Info: Calories 356, Protein 27g, Net Carbs 5.1g, Fat 23g

Instant Pot Spiced And Creamy Vegetable Stew With Cashews

Servings: 4
Cooking Time: 19 Mins
Ingredients:

- 2 tablespoons olive oil
- 1 cup diced red onion
- ⅔ cups diced carrot
- 2 cups diced cauliflower
- ⅛ teaspoons dried thyme
- 1 ⅓ tablespoons curry powder
- 2 ⅔ cups vegetable broth
- ½ cup coconut cream
- ⅛ teaspoons salt
- ⅛ teaspoons pepper
- Toasted cashews for serving

Directions:

1. Heat oil in your instant pot and sauté red onion, cauliflower and carrots for 4 Mins; stir in spices and stock and lock lid. Cook on manual for Mins and then let pressure come down naturally. Stir in coconut cream and cook on manual high for 5 Mins. Serve the stew topped with toasted cashews.

Nutrition Info:

Per Serving: Calories: 318; Total Fat: 27 g; Carbs: 15 g; Dietary Fiber: 4 g; Sugars: 5 g; Protein: 5 g; Cholesterol: 0 mg; Sodium: 182 mg

Bacon Soup

Servings: 4
Cooking Time: 20 Minutes
Ingredients:

- 3 oz bacon, chopped
- 1 cup cheddar cheese, shredded
- 1 tablespoon scallions, chopped

- 3 cups beef broth
- 1 cup of coconut milk
- 1 teaspoon curry powder

Directions:
1. Heat up the instant pot on saute mode for 3 minutes and add bacon.
2. Cook it for 5 minutes. Stir it from time to time.
3. Then add scallions and curry powder. Cook the ingredients for 5 minutes more. Stir them from time to time.
4. After this, add coconut milk and beef broth.
5. Add cheddar cheese and stir the soup well.
6. Cook it on manual mode (high pressure) for 10 minutes. Make a quick pressure release.
7. Mix up the soup well before serving.

Nutrition Info:
Per Serving: calories 398, fat 6, fiber 1.5, carbs 5.1, protein 20

Thai Green Soup

Servings: 4
Cooking Time: 5 Minutes
Ingredients:
- 1 tbsp coconut oil
- 1 large green squash, deseeded and julienned
- 1 small yellow onion, thinly sliced
- 1 tsp unsweetened fish sauce
- 6 cups vegetable stock
- Salt and black pepper to taste
- ½ cup chopped green beans
- ¼ cup freshly chopped cilantro

Directions:
1. Set the IP in Sauté mode and adjust to medium heat.
2. Heat the coconut oil in the inner pot and sauté the squash and onion until softened, 3 minutes.
3. Stir in the fish sauce, vegetable stock, salt, black pepper, and green beans.
4. Lock the lid in place; select Manual mode on High Pressure and set the timer to 2 minutes.
5. After cooking, perform a quick pressure release to let out the steam and open the lid.
6. Stir in the cilantro, dish the soup, and serve warm.

Nutrition Info:
Per Serving: Calories 71 Fats 3.93g Carbs 9.13g Net Carbs 6.43g Protein 1.89g

Low Carb Curried Vegetable Soup

Servings: 2
Cooking Time: 10 Mins
Ingredients:
- 1 tablespoon olive oil

- 1 medium spring onion
- 1 cup cauliflower, steamed
- 1 cup beef stock
- 125ml coconut milk
- 10 cashew nuts
- ½ teaspoon coriander
- ½ teaspoon turmeric
- ½ teaspoon cumin
- 2 tablespoons fresh parsley, finely chopped
- salt and pepper, to taste

Directions:
1. Place the cauliflower and onion in an instant pot and add chicken stock. Stir in coriander, turmeric, cumin and a pinch of salt. Lock lid and cook high for Mins. Quick release the pressure. Using a hand blender, puree the ingredients in the pot until smooth. Stir in the
2. coconut milk. Serve with roasted cashew nuts and top with parsley.

Nutrition Info:
Per Serving: Calories: 258: Fat: 6g; Carbs: 8g; Protein: 27g

Egg Drop Soup

Servings: 4
Cooking Time: 10 Minutes
Ingredients:
- 4 cups chicken broth
- 2 tablespoons fresh dill, chopped
- 2 eggs, beaten
- 1 teaspoon salt

Directions:
1. Pour chicken broth in the instant pot.
2. Add salt and bring it to boil on Saute mode.
3. Then add beaten eggs and stir the liquid well.
4. Add dill and saute it for 5 minutes.
5. The soup is cooked.

Nutrition Info:
Per Serving: calories 74, fat 3.6, fiber 0.2, carbs 2, protein 7.9

Cabbage Soup

Servings: 3
Cooking Time: 12 Minutes
Ingredients:
- ½ cup ground pork
- ½ cup white cabbage, shredded
- 2 cups chicken broth
- ½ teaspoon ground coriander

- ½ teaspoon salt
- 1 teaspoon butter
- ½ teaspoon chili flakes

Directions:
1. Melt the butter in the instant pot on saute mode.
2. Add cabbage and sprinkle it with ground coriander, salt, and chili flakes.
3. Add chicken broth and ground pork.
4. Close and seal the lid and cook the soup on manual mode (high pressure) for 12 minutes.

Nutrition Info:
Per Serving: calories 350, fat 9, fiber 0.3, carbs 1.3, protein 2

Zucchini Yogurt Soup

Servings: 4
Cooking Time: 15 Minutes
Ingredients:
- 1 tbsp olive oil
- 2 garlic cloves, minced
- 1 medium white onion, chopped
- 1 large zucchini, chopped
- 1 cup vegetable stock
- 1 small avocado, pitted, and peeled
- 2 cups Greek yogurt
- ½ tsp chopped fresh dill
- 1 lemon, juiced
- ¼ cup freshly chopped parsley + more for garnishing
- Salt and white pepper to taste

Directions:
1. Set the IP in Sauté mode and adjust to medium heat.
2. Heat the olive oil in the inner pot and sauté the garlic and onion until softened, 5 minutes. Stir in zucchini and vegetable stock.
3. Lock the lid in place; select Manual mode on High Pressure and set timer to 10 minutes.
4. After cooking, perform a quick pressure release to let out the steam and open the lid.
5. Stir in avocado, Greek yogurt, dill, lemon juice, parsley, salt, and white pepper. Using an immersion blender, puree the soup until smooth.
6. Dish the soup, garnish with more parsley, and serve warm.

Nutrition Info:
Per Serving: Calories 208 Fats 89g Carbs 46g Net Carbs 16g Protein 6.18g

Creamy Cauli & Beef Soup

Servings: 4
Cooking Time: 26 Mins
Ingredients:
- 1 pound ground Beef

- 3 ½ cups Cauliflower Rice
- 1 cup Sour Cream
- 4 cups Beef Broth
- ¼ cup grated Parmesan Cheese
- Salt and black pepper to taste
- ¼ Onion, diced
- 2 tbsp Butter

Directions:

1. Melt butter on Sauté. Stir-fry the onion for 2 minutes and add in the beef. Season with salt and pepper, and cook for 4 minutes. Pour in broth and cauliflower. Seal the lid, select Manual and cook on High for minutes. When ready, do a quick pressure release. Stir in sour cream and Parmesan.

Nutrition Info: Calories 322, Protein 27g, Net Carbs 3.8g, Fat 21g

Creamy Chicken Mushroom Stew

Servings: 4
Cooking Time: 55 Mins
Ingredients:

- 4 Chicken Breasts, diced
- 1 ¼ lb White Button Mushrooms, halved
- 3 tbsp Olive oil
- 1 large Onion, sliced
- 5 cloves Garlic, minced
- Salt and black pepper to taste
- 1 ¼ tsp Arrowroot Starch
- ½ cup Spinach, chopped
- 1 Bay Leaf
- 1 ½ cup Chicken Stock
- 1 tsp Dijon Mustard
- 1 ½ cup Sour Cream
- 3 tbsp Chopped Parsley

Directions:

1. Heat the oil and stir-fry the onion for 3 minutes, on Sauté. Stir in mushrooms, chicken, garlic, bay leaf, salt, pepper, Dijon mustard, and chicken broth.
2. Seal the lid, press Meat/Stew and cook on High pressure for 15 minutes. Once ready, do a natural pressure release for 5 minutes, then a quick pressure release.
3. On Sauté, stir the stew, remove the bay leaf, and scoop some of the liquid into a bowl. Add the arrowroot starch to the liquid and mix until completely lump-free. Pour the liquid into the sauce, stir, and let the sauce thicken.
4. Top with the sour cream, stir, and pree Keep Warm. After minutes, dish the sauce into serving bowls and garnish with parsley. Serve with squash mash and steamed green peas.

Nutrition Info: Calories 170, Protein 1g, Net Carbs 0g, Fat 6.3g

Beef Chuck & Green Cabbage Stew

Servings: 2
Cooking Time: 3 Hours
Ingredients:

- 1 packet frozen baby carrots
- 2 onions, roughly chopped
- 1 cup chopped cabbage
- 4 garlic cloves, smashed
- 2 bay leaves
- 4 pieces of beef chuck with marrow
- Salt & pepper
- 1 thin diced tomato, drained
- 1 cup chicken stock

Directions:

1. Place the baby carrots and chopped onions into the bottom of your instant pot. Layer the cabbage wedges on top and add the crushed garlic cloves and bay leaves.
2. Season the beef shanks generously with salt and pepper then add them on top of the veggies.
3. Pour in the diced tomatoes and broth before putting on the lid. Set the pot on high for hours. Let pressure come down naturally.
4. Once ready, allow to cool then pack in freezer friendly bags or jars and freeze until when you are ready to eat.

Nutrition Info:
Per Serving: Calories: 394; Total Fat: 4 g; Carbs: 1 g; Dietary Fiber: 4.1 g; Sugars: 6.8 g; Protein: 6 g; Cholesterol: 152 mg; Sodium: 509 mg

"ramen" Soup

Servings: 2
Cooking Time: 15 Minutes
Ingredients:

- 1 zucchini, trimmed
- 2 cups chicken broth
- 2 eggs, boiled, peeled
- 1 tablespoon coconut aminos
- 5 oz beef loin, strips
- 1 teaspoon chili flakes
- 1 tablespoon chives, chopped
- ½ teaspoon salt

Directions:

1. Put the beef loin strips in the instant pot.
2. Add chili flakes, salt, and chicken broth.
3. Close and seal the lid. Cook the ingredients on manual mode (high pressure) for 15 minutes. Make a quick pressure release and open the lid.
4. Then make the s from zucchini with the help of the spiralizer and add them in the soup.

5. Add chives and coconut aminos.
6. Then ladle the soup in the bowls and top with halved eggs.

Nutrition Info:

Per Serving: calories 254, fat 8, fiber 1.1, carbs 6.2, protein 6

Pressure Cooker Vegetable And Fish Stew

Servings: 4
Cooking Time: 19 Mins
Ingredients:

- 2 tbsp. extra-virgin olive oil
- 1 red onion, sliced
- 2 jalapeño peppers, seeds removed and diced
- 4 cups sliced green cabbage
- 1 carrot, peeled and chopped
- 4 cups crushed tomatoes
- 2 cup diced white fish filet
- 4 cup vegetable broth
- 3 tbsp. apple cider vinegar
- 2 tsp. Stevia
- ½ tsp. salt
- ¼ tsp. black pepper

Directions:

1. Heat extra virgin olive oil in an instant pot set on sauté mode and stir in red onion, jalapenos, cabbage, and carrot; sauté for about 7 Mins or until almost tender.
2. Stir in tomatoes, fish, broth, apple cider vinegar, and Stevia, salt and pepper until well combined. Lock lid and cook on high pressure for 1Mins. Let pressure come down naturally. Serve hot.

Nutrition Info:

Per Serving: Calories: 222; Total Fat: 7 g; Carbs: 7 g; Dietary Fiber: 5.9 g; Sugars: 6.3 g; Protein: 9 g; Cholesterol: 0 mg; Sodium: 112 mg

Gumbo

Servings: 4
Cooking Time: 15 Minutes
Ingredients:

- 2 chicken thighs, boneless, chopped
- 4 oz shrimps, peeled
- ½ bell pepper, chopped
- 3 oz sausages, chopped
- 1 celery stalk, chopped
- 1 cup beef broth
- 1 teaspoon tomato paste
- ½ teaspoon Cajun seasonings

Directions:
1. Heat up the instant pot on saute mode for 3 minutes.
2. Then add chicken thighs, shrimps, bell pepper, sausages, celery stalk, beef broth, tomato paste, and Cajun seasonings.
3. Gently mix up the ingredients and close the lid.
4. Cook the gumbo for 15 minutes on manual mode (high pressure).
5. Then make a quick pressure release and stir the meal well.

Nutrition Info:
Per Serving: calories 261, fat 3, fiber 0.3, carbs 2.2, protein 2

Instant Pot Spicy Coconut Cauliflower Soup

Servings: 4
Cooking Time: 14 Mins
Ingredients:
- 1 ⅓ tablespoons olive oil
- 2 cups diced cauliflower
- ⅔ cups diced carrot
- 1 cup diced red onion
- ⅛ teaspoons dried thyme
- 1 ⅓ tablespoons curry powder
- 2 ⅔ cups vegetable broth
- ⅛ teaspoons salt
- ⅛ teaspoons pepper

Directions:
1. Heat oil in your instant pot and sauté red onion, cauliflower and carrots for 4 Mins; stir in spices and stock and lock lid. Cook on manual for Mins and then let pressure come down naturally. Stir in coconut milk and then blend with an immersion blender until smooth. Serve topped with toasted cashews.

Nutrition Info:
Per Serving: Calories: 318; Total Fat: 27 g; Carbs: 15 g; Dietary Fiber: 4 g; Sugars: 5 g; Protein: 5 g; Cholesterol: 0 mg; Sodium: 182 mg

Curried Chicken Stew

Servings: 2
Cooking Time: 1 Hour 40 Mins
Ingredients:
- 2 bone-in chicken thighs
- 2 tbsp. olive oil
- 3 carrots, diced
- 1 sweet onion, chopped
- 1 cup coconut milk

- 1/4 cup hot curry paste
- Toasted almonds
- Coriander
- Sour cream to serve

Directions:

1. Set your instant pot to manual high setting; heat oil and cook chicken for 8 Mins or until browned. Stir in carrots and onion and cook for about 3 Mins.
2. In a bowl, combine curry paste and coconut milk; whisk until well blended and pour over chicken mixture.
3. Lock lid and cook on high for 1 ½ hours and then let pressure come down naturally.
4. Serve the stew topped with toasted almonds, coriander, fresh chili and a dollop of sour cream.

Nutrition Info:
Per Serving: Calories: 409; Total Fat: 5 g; Carbs: 7 g; Dietary Fiber: 1.9 g; Sugars: 3.4 g; Protein: 3 g; Cholesterol: 231 mg; Sodium: 609 mg

Instant Pot Seafood Soup

Servings: 3
Cooking Time: 1 Hour 30 Mins
Ingredients:

- 12 slices bacon, chopped
- 2 cloves garlic, minced
- 6 cups chicken stock
- 3 stalks celery, diced
- 2 large carrots, diced
- ground black pepper to taste
- ½ teaspoon red pepper flakes
- 2 cups onions
- 2 cup uncooked prawns, peeled and deveined
- 500g white fish fillet, cut into bite-size pieces
- 1 can evaporated milk

Directions:

1. Set your instant pot to manual high; fry bacon in coconut oil or olive oil, add onion and garlic.
2. Pour chicken stock into the pot and stir celery, and carrots into the stock. Season with black pepper and red pepper flakes. Lock lid and cook on high for 1 hour. Let pressure come down naturally. Stir prawns and fish into the soup and cook 30 Mins on manual high. Stir evaporated milk into chowder, heat thoroughly, and serve.

Nutrition Info:
Per Serving: Calories: 281; Total Fat: 9.5g; Carbs: 7.8g; Protein: 39g

Instant Pot French Onion Soup

Servings: 2

Cooking Time: 1 Hour 10 Mins
Ingredients:
- 4 cups organic beef broth
- 1 large red onion, thinly sliced
- 1/2 tsp. garlic powder
- 2 tbsp. Worcestershire Sauce
- 4 tbsp. grated Parmesan cheese
- 2 packets Stevia
- 1/2 tsp. dried thyme
- sea salt & pepper
- 4 slices thin Swiss cheese

Directions:
1. Set your instant pot to manual high and heat oil; cook in onion until caramelized and then stir in cup beef broth and garlic powder. Stir in the remaining ingredients; cook on high for 1 hour. Let pressure come down naturally. Ladle the soup into an ovenproof bowl and stir in Swiss cheese; place in a preheated oven at 150°F and cook for about 5 Mins or until cheese is melted.

Nutrition Info:
Per Serving: Calories: 210; Total Fat: 2 g; Carbs: 7.3 g; Dietary Fiber: 0.8 g; Sugars: 3.5 g; Protein: 4 g; Cholesterol: 36 mg; Sodium: 991 mg

Bok Choy Soup

Servings: 1
Cooking Time: 2 Minutes
Ingredients:
- 1 bok choy stalk, chopped
- ¼ teaspoon nutritional yeast
- ½ teaspoon onion powder
- ¼ teaspoon chili flakes
- 1 cup chicken broth

Directions:
1. Put all ingredients from the list above in the instant pot.
2. Close and seal the lid and cook the soup on manual (high pressure) for minutes.
3. Make a quick pressure release.

Nutrition Info:
Per Serving: calories 58 fat 1.7, fiber 1.3, carbs 4.5, protein 6.9

Chili Pork Cubes

Servings: 2
Cooking Time: 20 Minutes
Ingredients:
- 10 oz pork loin
- ¼ cup of water

- 1 teaspoon chili paste
- ½ teaspoon ground black pepper
- ½ teaspoon salt

Directions:
1. Chop the pork loin into the medium pieces.
2. Sprinkle the meat with the salt and ground black pepper.
3. add chili paste in the meat.
4. Mix up the meat mixture with the help of the hands.
5. Pour water in the instant pot bowl and add meat mixture.
6. Close the lid and set the "Meat/Stew" mode. Cook the meal for 25 minutes.
7. Then chill the meat until warm.

Nutrition Info:
Per Serving: calories 353, fat 2, fiber 0.1, carbs 1.3, protein 39

Buffalo Thick Pork Soup

Servings: 4
Cooking Time: 20 Minutes
Ingredients:
- 2 tablespoons butter
- 1 pound pork loin, boneless and cubed
- 1/2 cup celery, diced
- 1 tablespoon hot sauce
- 1/3 cup blue cheese powder
- Seasoned salt and ground black pepper, to taste
- 1/2 teaspoon onion powder
- 1/2 teaspoon garlic powder
- 1 teaspoon paprika
- 1/4 teaspoon dried dill weed
- 4 cups beef bone stock
- 1 cup heavy cream

Directions:
1. Press the "Sauté" button to heat up the Instant Pot. Now, melt the butter and cook pork loin for 2 to 4 minutes, stirring frequently.
2. Add the celery, hot sauce, blue cheese powder, salt, pepper, onion powder, garlic powder, paprika, dill, and beef bone stock.
3. Secure the lid. Choose "Manual" mode and High pressure; cook for 12 minutes. Once cooking is complete, use a quick pressure release; carefully remove the lid.
4. Add heavy cream and press the "Sauté" button one more time. Let the soup simmer until thickened. Serve hot and enjoy!

Nutrition Info:
Per Serving: 443 Calories; 7g Fat; 3.7g Carbs; 6g Protein; 1.9g Sugars

Southern-style Beef Brisket

Servings: 6
Cooking Time: 1 Hour 15 Minutes
Ingredients:

- 1 tablespoon ghee, at room temperature
- 2 pounds beef brisket
- 1 yellow onion, sliced
- 1/2 teaspoon black peppercorns
- 1/2 teaspoon salt
- 1/2 cup roasted tomato salsa
- 1 cup chicken bone broth
- 1 teaspoon dried sage, crushed
- 1 teaspoon dried rosemary
- 1 teaspoon chili powder
- 1/2 teaspoon dried Mexican oregano
- 1 teaspoon fish sauce
- 1/4 cup vodka

Directions:

1. Press the "Sauté" button to heat up the Instant Pot. Then, melt the ghee until hot. Cook the beef brisket for 3 minutes per side; reserve.
2. Add yellow onion and cook until tender and aromatic. Now, add the remaining ingredients, except for vodka, to your Instant Pot. Return the beef back to the Instant Pot.
3. Secure the lid. Choose "Manual" mode and High pressure; cook for 60 minutes. Once cooking is complete, use a natural pressure release; carefully remove the lid.
4. Now, remove brisket from the Instant Pot; allow it to sit for 10 minutes before slicing. Skim the fat from the top of the cooking liquid.
5. Press the Sauté" button. Now, add vodka and let it simmer until the cooking liquid is reduced.
6. Lastly, slice the brisket across the grain. Spoon the vodka sauce over beef brisket and serve. Enjoy!

Nutrition Info:
Per Serving: 371 Calories; 5g Fat; 6.4g Total Carbs; 2g Protein; 3.1g Sugars

Beef And Savoy Cabbage Mix

Servings: 4
Cooking Time: 25 Minutes
Ingredients:

- 1 pound beef stew meat, cubed
- 1 Savoy cabbage, shredded
- 2 garlic cloves, minced
- 1 tablespoon olive oil
- A pinch of salt and black pepper

- 1 and ½ cups tomato passata
- 1 tablespoon parsley, chopped

Directions:
1. Set the instant pot on Sauté mode, add the oil, heat it up, add the meat and the garlic and brown for 5 minutes. Add the rest of the ingredients, put the lid on and cook on High for 20 minutes. Release the pressure naturally for minutes, divide the mix between plates and serve.

Nutrition Info: calories 243, fat 6, fiber 0.1, carbs 0.6, protein 5

Caramelized Onion Pork Chops With Steamed Green Beans And Avocado

Servings: 6
Cooking Time: 40 Mins
Ingredients:
- 4 tablespoon vegetable oil
- 2 cups sliced onions
- 2 lb. pork loin chops
- 3 teaspoons seasoning salt
- 2 teaspoons ground black pepper
- 1 onion, cut into strips
- 1 cup water
- 2 cups chopped green beans, steamed
- 3 avocados, diced

Directions:
1. Season the chops with salt and pepper; heat oil in an instant pot set on manual high and brown the chops for about 5 Mins per side. Stir in onions and water and lock lid. Cook on high for 20 Mins and then quick release the pressure.
2. Meanwhile, add the remaining oil to a skillet set over medium-low heat; add in onions and cook, stirring, for about 10 Mins or until caramelized.
3. Serve the chops with caramelized onions and steamed green beans topped with avocado slices. Enjoy!

Nutrition Info:
Per Serving: Calories: 595; Fat: 41g; Carbs: 8g; Protein: 1g

Spanish Style Pork Shoulder

Servings: 3
Cooking Time: 40 Minutes
Ingredients:
- 12 oz pork shoulder
- ½ cup chili Verde
- 1 tablespoon butter
- ¼ cup beef broth

- ¾ teaspoon ground black pepper
- ½ teaspoon salt

Directions:
1. Chop the pork shoulder and sprinkle the meat with the ground black pepper and salt.
2. Toss the butter in the instant pot and saute it for 1 minute or until it is melted.
3. After this, add pork shoulder and saute it for 10 minutes.
4. After this, add beef broth and chili Verde.
5. Lock the instant pot lid and seal it.
6. Set the "Bean/Chili" mode and set the timer on 30 minutes (High Pressure).
7. When the time is over – make a natural pressure release.
8. Serve it!

Nutrition Info:
Per Serving: calories 370, fat 2, fiber 0.1, carbs 0.4, protein 9

Chili Spare Ribs

Servings: 3
Cooking Time: 25 Minutes
Ingredients:
- 9 oz pork spare ribs
- 1 teaspoon tomato paste
- 2 tablespoons avocado oil
- 1 teaspoon chili powder
- ½ teaspoon chili flakes
- 1 teaspoon apple cider vinegar
- ¼ teaspoon salt
- 1 cup water, for cooking

Directions:
1. In the shallow bowl whisk together tomato paste, avocado oil, chili powder, chili flakes, salt, and apple cider vinegar. Generously brush the spare ribs with tomato paste mixture and leave for minutes to marinate. Meanwhile, pour water and insert the steamer rack in the instant pot. Place the ribs in the instant pot baking pan. Then place the pan on the rack and close the lid. Cook the spare ribs for 25 minutes on Manual mode (high pressure). When the time is finished, make the quick pressure release and transfer the meal on the plate.

Nutrition Info: calories 176, fat 12, fiber 0.8, carbs 1.4, protein 5

Garlic Lamb And Chard

Servings: 6
Cooking Time: 35 Minutes
Ingredients:
- 2 pounds lamb shoulder, cubed
- 1 cup chard, chopped
- 3 garlic cloves, crushed
- A pinch of salt and black pepper

- 1 cup beef stock
- 2 tablespoons olive oil
- 1 tablespoon rosemary, chopped
- 1 tablespoon chives, chopped

Directions:
1. Set your instant pot on Sauté mode, add the oil, heat it up, add the garlic and the lamb and brown for 5 minutes. Add the rest of the ingredients except the chives, put the lid on and cook on High for 30 minutes. Release the pressure naturally for minutes, divide the mix between plates and serve with the chives sprinkled on top.

Nutrition Info: calories 329, fat 16, fiber 0.4, carbs 1.1, protein 2

Lamb And Mushroom Stew

Servings: 4
Cooking Time: 47 Minutes
Ingredients:
- 1 tbsp olive oil
- 1 lb. lamb shoulder, cut into 1-inch cubes
- Salt and black pepper to taste
- 1 small onion, chopped
- ½ lb. baby white button mushrooms
- 1 garlic clove minced
- ½ tbsp tomato paste
- 1 cup cherry tomatoes, halved
- ½ cup chicken broth
- ½ cup fresh chopped parsley

Directions:
1. Set the IP in Sauté mode and adjust to Medium heat.
2. Heat the olive oil in the inner pot, season the lamb with salt and black pepper, and sear in the oil until brown outside, 6 to 7 minutes.
3. Stir in onion and mushrooms, and cook until softened, 5 minutes. Stir in the garlic and cook until fragrant, seconds.
4. Mix in the tomato paste, tomatoes, chicken broth, and season with salt and black pepper.
5. Lock the lid in place; select Manual mode on High Pressure and set the timer to 2minutes.
6. After cooking, perform natural pressure release for 10 minutes, then a quick pressure release to let out the remaining steam.
7. Open the lid, stir in the parsley, and adjust the taste with salt and black pepper.
8. Dish food into serving bowls and serve.

Nutrition Info:
Per Serving: : Calories 359 Fats 23g Carbs 25g Net Carbs 9.55g Protein 84g

Fresh Spicy Meatloaf

Servings: 4
Cooking Time: 45 Minutes

Ingredients:
- 1 pound ground sirloin
- 1/2 cup pork rinds, crushed
- 2 eggs, beaten
- 1/4 cup milk
- 1/2 cup green onions
- 1 tablespoon green garlic
- 1 bell pepper, chopped
- Sea salt freshly ground black pepper, to taste
- 1 teaspoon dried basil
- 1/2 teaspoon dried rosemary
- 1 cup tomato purée
- 1/2 teaspoon mustard seeds
- 1 teaspoon dried ancho chili pepper, minced
- 1 ½ cups water

Directions:
1. Mix the ground meat, pork rinds, eggs, milk, green onions, green garlic, bell pepper, salt, pepper, basil, and rosemary.
2. Press the mixture into a loaf pan. Mix the tomato purée with mustard seeds and dried ancho chili pepper. Top the meatloaf with this tomato mixture.
3. Add the water and a metal rack to the Instant Pot. Now, cover the meatloaf with a sheet of aluminum foil and make a foil sling.
4. Secure the lid. Choose "Meat/Stew" mode and High pressure; cook for 35 minutes. Once cooking is complete, use a quick pressure release; carefully remove the lid.
5. Allow the meatloaf to sit for to 10 minutes before slicing and serving. Bon appétit!

Nutrition Info:
Per Serving: 353 Calories; 20g Fat; 4.7g Total Carbs; 9g Protein; 2.8g Sugars

Icelandic Lamb

Servings: 4
Cooking Time: 45 Minutes
Ingredients:
- 3 oz celery ribs, chopped
- ¼ cup scallions, chopped
- 4 oz turnip, chopped
- 1 teaspoon tomato paste
- ½ teaspoon ground black pepper
- ½ teaspoon salt
- 4 cups of water
- 12 oz lamb fillet, chopped

Directions:
1. Put all ingredients in the instant pot and stir well until the tomato paste is dissolved.
2. Then close and seal the lid.

3. Cook the lamb on manual (high pressure) for 45 minutes.
4. Then make the quick pressure release, open the lid, and mix up the lamb well.

Nutrition Info:

Per Serving: calories 173, fat 6.3, fiber 1.1, carbs 3.3, protein 5

Brown Gravy Pork Roast

Servings: 4
Cooking Time: 25 Mins
Ingredients:

- 2 lb Pork Roast, cut into slabs
- 1 tbsp Italian Seasoning
- 1 tbsp Ranch Dressing
- 1 tsp Red Wine Vinegar
- 2 cloves Garlic, minced
- Salt and black pepper to taste
- 1 small Onion, chopped
- 1 tbsp Olive oil
- 2 tsp Onion Powder
- ½ tsp Paprika
- 4 tbsp Brewed Coffee
- 1 ½ cups Beef Broth
- 2 tbsp Xanthan Gum
- 2 tbsp Water
- Chopped Parsley to garnish

Directions:

1. Season the pork roast with salt and pepper and set aside. In a bowl, add the Italian seasoning, ranch dressing, red wine vinegar, garlic, onion powder, paprika, and coffee. Set on Sauté.
2. Add the oil to the pot and sauté the onion until translucent. Pour the gravy coffee mixture and broth in; add the pork roast. Seal the lid, select Meat/Stew and cook on High for 1minutes. Once ready, do a quick pressure release. Remove the pork roast with a slotted spoon onto a serving plate.
3. Mix the xanthan gum with the water in a small bowl and add to the sauce. Select Sauté mode. Stir and cook the sauce to thicken which is about 4 minutes. Once the gravy is ready, turn off the pot and spoon the gravy over the pork. Garnish with parsley and serve with a turnip mash.

Nutrition Info: Calories 190, Protein 19g, Net Carbs 2g, Fat 10g

Blackberry Pork Chops

Servings: 2
Cooking Time: 15 Minutes
Ingredients:

- ¼ cup blackberries

- 1 teaspoon Erythritol
- 1 teaspoon butter, melted
- 1 teaspoon cream
- 2 pork chops
- ½ teaspoon ground paprika
- ¼ teaspoon salt
- ½ teaspoon dried cilantro
- 1 cup water, for cooking

Directions:
1. Pour water and insert the trivet in the instant pot. Then rub the pork chops with cilantro, salt, and ground paprika. Put the pork chops on the trivet and close the lid. Cook the meat on manual mode (high pressure) for 8 minutes Then make the quick pressure release and open the lid. Place the blackberries, Erythritol, and cream in the blender and blend the mixture until smooth. Clean the instant pot and remove the trivet. Pour the blended blackberry mixture in the instant pot. Add butter and bring the liquid to boil on sauté mode. Then add the cooked pork chops. Coat the meat well in the blackberry sauce and cook for minute from each side on sauté mode. Serve the pork chops with remaining blackberry sauce.

Nutrition Info: calories 283, fat 1, fiber 1.2, carbs 2.1, protein 4

Oxtail Ragout

Servings: 4
Cooking Time: 55 Mins
Ingredients:
- 1 tbsp Butter
- 1 medium Onion, chopped
- 1 Celery Stalk, chopped
- 1 Carrot, chopped
- ¾ cup Beef Broth
- ½ cup Diced Tomatoes
- 1 Bay Leaf
- 1 tsp dried Thyme
- 1 tsp dried Rosemary
- Salt and black pepper to taste
- 2 Oxtail Joints, separated
- 1 tsp Plain Vinegar

Directions:
1. Melt butter on Sauté, and cook the onion, celery and carrots for 3 minutes. Add the remaining ingredients, except the meat. Cook for 2 minutes and add the oxtail.
2. Seal the lid. Select Manual and cook on High Pressure for 30 minutes. Once ready, do a natural pressure release for 10 minutes. Remove any excess fat, stir and serve.

Nutrition Info: Calories 168, Protein 7g, Net Carbs 6.1g, Fat 13g

Thai Basil Beef Stir-fry

Servings: 4
Cooking Time: 11 Minutes
Ingredients:

- ¼ cup coconut aminos
- 1 tsp sugar-free maple syrup
- 1 tbsp unsweetened fish sauce
- 1 tsp chili paste
- 1 tbsp unsweetened oyster sauce
- 1 tsp fresh garlic puree
- 1 tsp arrowroot starch
- 1 tbsp olive oil
- 4 steaks, thinly sliced
- 1 yellow onion, thinly sliced
- 1 cup thinly sliced mixed bell peppers
- 3 garlic cloves, minced
- 1 tsp freshly grated ginger
- 1 cup Thai basil
- 1 tsp sesame seeds for garnishing
- Salt and black pepper to taste

Directions:

1. In a medium bowl, whisk the coconut aminos, maple syrup, fish sauce, chili paste, oyster sauce, garlic paste, and arrowroot starch. Set aside.
2. Set the IP in Sauté mode and adjust to Medium heat.
3. Heat the olive oil and cook the beef until brown on both sides, 5 to 6 minutes.
4. Top with the onions, bell peppers and cook until softened, 3 minutes. Add the garlic and ginger; cook until fragrant, 1 minute.
5. Pour in the sauce, stir and cook until syrupy, 1 minute.
6. Stir in the Thai basil and adjust the taste with salt and black pepper as needed.
7. Dish the food, garnish with the sesame seeds and serve warm.

Nutrition Info:
Per Serving: : Calories 301 Fats 41g Carbs 3.44g Net Carbs 2.74g Protein 14g

Vegetable Lasagna With Meat

Servings: 2
Cooking Time: 20 Minutes
Ingredients:

- 1 large zucchini, grated
- 8 oz ground beef
- 1 tablespoon coconut milk
- 1 oz provolone cheese, shredded
- ½ tomato, sliced

- 1 teaspoon butter, softened
- 1 cup water, for cooking

Directions:
1. Grease the lasagna mold with butter.
2. Put ½ part of zucchini in the mold and flatten it.
3. Then add ground beef, coconut milk, and sliced tomato.
4. Then top the ingredients with remaining zucchini and flatten well.
5. Pour water and insert the lasagna mold in the into the instant pot.
6. Close and seal the lid.
7. Cook the meal on manual (high pressure) for 20 minutes. Then make a quick pressure release.

Nutrition Info:
Per Serving: calories 323, fat 9, fiber 2.1, carbs 6.7, protein 3

Beef & Sweet Potato Enchilada Casserole

Servings: 6
Cooking Time: 20 Mins
Ingredients:
- 2 small sweet potatoes
- 2 tablespoons olive oil
- 1-pound ground beef
- 1 can black beans, drained
- 1 cup frozen corn
- 1 can red enchilada sauce
- 4 tablespoon chopped fresh cilantro
- 2 teaspoon ground cumin
- 1 teaspoon garlic powder
- 1 teaspoon onion powder
- 1 small can diced olives
- 1 cup shredded parmesan cheese

Directions:
1. Peel and cook the sweet potatoes; mash and mix with 2 tablespoons of cilantro.
2. In an instant pot set on manual high, cook the ground beef until browned. Stir in beans, corn, sauce and spices until well combined; sprinkle with half of the cheese and top with sweet potatoes, olives and cilantro. Cover with the remaining cheese and lock lid. Cook on high for Mins and then let pressure come down on its own.

Nutrition Info:
Per Serving: Calories: 315; Total Fat: 2 g; Carbs: 9 g; Dietary Fiber: 5 g; Sugars: 3.2 g; Protein: 6 g; Cholesterol: 54 mg; Sodium: 172 mg

Non-traditional Beef Bowl

Servings: 4
Cooking Time: 20 Minutes

Ingredients:
- 1 yellow onion chopped
- 1 teaspoon chili powder
- 2 teaspoons smoked paprika
- ½ teaspoon dried cumin
- ½ teaspoon dried oregano
- 1 cup vegetable broth
- 1 red bell pepper, deseeded and sliced
- 1 can diced tomatoes
- 1 lb. ground beef
- 1 cup cheddar cheese, shredded
- 1 tablespoon olive oil
- Salt and pepper, to taste
- 1 tablespoon soy sauce
- 1/3 cup fresh cilantro leaves, chopped

Directions:
1. Press the "Sauté" button to preheat your Instant Pot. Heat the olive oil and cook the ground beef for 3 minutes.
2. Then stir in the red bell pepper, vegetable broth, onion, tomatoes, soy sauce. chili powder, smoked paprika, salt, pepper, cumin, and oregano.
3. Secure the lid. Choose the "Manual" mode and cook for 8 minutes at High pressure. When cooking is complete, use a natural pressure release and carefully remove the lid.
4. Serve into bowls and top with the shredded cheddar cheese and fresh cilantro. Bon appetite!

Nutrition Info:
Per Serving: 344 Calories; 6g Fat; 7g Carbs; 4g Protein; 3.4g Sugars

Noodle-less Classic Lasagna

Servings: 6
Cooking Time: 20 Minutes
Ingredients:
- 1 tablespoon olive oil
- 1 1/3 pounds ground pork
- 1 teaspoon garlic, finely minced
- 2 tablespoons scallions, finely chopped
- 1 teaspoon dried oregano
- 1 teaspoon dried basil
- 1/2 teaspoon dried rosemary
- 20 ounces pasta sauce, sugar-free
- 1 cup cream cheese
- 1 cup Romano cheese
- 2 eggs
- 6 ounces Swiss cheese, sliced

Directions:

1. Press the "Sauté" button to heat up the Instant Pot. Heat the olive oil and cook the ground meat with the garlic and scallions for 2 to 4 minutes, stirring continuously.
2. Add oregano, basil, rosemary, and pasta sauce. Now, add 1/of this meat sauce to a lightly greased baking dish.
3. Then, in a mixing bowl, thoroughly combine the cream cheese, Romano cheese, and eggs. Place this cheese mixture over the meat layer.
4. Add the remaining 1/2 of the meat mixture. Top with Swiss cheese. Cover with a sheet of aluminum foil and make a foil sling if needed.
5. Add 1 ½ cups of water and metal rack to the Instant Pot. Lower the baking dish onto the metal rack.
6. Secure the lid. Choose the "Manual" setting and cook for 9 minutes at High pressure. Once cooking is complete, use a quick pressure release; carefully remove the lid. Bon appétit!

Nutrition Info:
Per Serving: 539 Calories; 1g Fat; 5g Carbs; 2g Protein; 2.6g Sugars

Pork In Mushroom Gravy

Servings: 4
Cooking Time: 35 Mins
Ingredients:
- 4 Pork Chops
- 1 tbsp Olive oil
- 3 cloves Garlic, minced
- Salt and black pepper to taste
- 1 tsp Garlic Powder
- 1 (10 oz) Mushroom Soup
- 8 oz Mushrooms, sliced
- 1 small Onion, chopped
- 1 cup Beef Broth
- 1 sprig Fresh Thyme
- Chopped Parsley to garnish

Directions:
1. Heat oil on Sauté, and add mushrooms, garlic, and onion. Sauté stirring occasionally until translucent, for 3 minutes. Season pork chops with salt, garlic powder, and pepper.
2. Add into the pot followed by the thyme and broth. Seal the lid, select Meat/Stew and cook on High pressure for 15 minutes. Once ready, do a natural pressure release for about 10 minutes, then a quick pressure release to let the remaining steam out.
3. Select Sauté and add mushroom soup. Stir until the mixture thickens. Dish the pork and gravy into a serving bowl and garnish with parsley. Serve with a side of creamy squash mash.

Nutrition Info: Calories 227, Protein 5g, Net Carbs 0g, Fat 5g

Southern Pork Roast

Servings: 4

Cooking Time: 45 Mins
Ingredients:
- 1 stick Butter, sliced
- 1 cup Beef Broth
- ¼ cup Banana Pepper Ring Brine
- 3 pounds Pork Roast
- 1 tbsp Dill
- 1 tbsp Onion Powder
- ½ tbsp Garlic Powder
- 4 tbsp Banana Pepper Rings
- Salt and black pepper to taste

Directions:
1. In the pot, pour the broth, and add pork, brine, garlic, onion, and dill. Stir to combine. Season with salt and pepper. Arrange banana pepper rings on top and cover with butter slices.
2. Seal the lid, select Manual and set the cooking time to 35 minutes. Cook on HIGH pressure. When it goes off, do a quick pressure release. Let the pork sit for 10 minutes before slicing.

Nutrition Info: Calories 411, Protein 32g, Net Carbs 3g, Fat 30g

Beef Pot Roast

Servings: 5
Cooking Time: 40 Minutes
Ingredients:
- 1-pound beef chuck roast, chopped
- 1 teaspoon salt
- 4 tablespoon apple cider vinegar
- ¾ teaspoon xanthan gum
- 1 cup beef broth
- 1 teaspoon olive oil

Directions:
1. Sprinkle the beef with olive oil and salt.
2. Then put it in the instant pot and add beef broth, apple cider vinegar, and xanthan gum. Stir the ingredients gently with the help of the spoon. Close and seal the lid.
3. Cook the meal on manual mode (high pressure) for 40 minutes.
4. Then allow the natural pressure release for 10 minutes.

Nutrition Info:
Per Serving: calories 350, fat 4, fiber 0.7, carbs 1, protein 7

Ground Beef With Veggies

Servings: 4
Cooking Time: 25 Mins
Ingredients:
- 1 lb. lean ground beef

- 2 medium (6 to 8 inches each) zucchinis, diced
- 1 tbsp. coconut oil
- 1-2 cloves garlic, minced
- 2 medium tomatoes, diced
- 2 tbsp. dried oregano
- 1/2 yellow onion, diced

Directions:
1. Rinse and prepare the veggies.
2. Set your instant pot on manual high and melt coconut oil; stir in onions and sauté for about 4 Mins or until translucent.
3. Roll ground beef into small balls and add to the pot along with oregano and garlic; cook for about 5 Mins. Add tomatoes and zucchini and lock lid. Cook on high for 20 Mins and then let pressure come down on its own.
4. Serve and enjoy!

Nutrition Info:
Per Serving: Calories: 287; Total Fat: 9g; Carbs: 6.1g; Protein: 3g

Spicy Soutzoukaika (greek Meatballs)

Servings: 4
Cooking Time: 30 Mins
Ingredients:
- 2 tbsp olive oil
- 1 pound ground beef
- ¼ pound pork rinds, crushed
- ¼ cup feta cheese, grated
- 3 garlic cloves, minced
- 1 onion, chopped
- 1 egg, beaten
- 1 tsp cumin
- 1 tsp oregano
- Salt and black pepper to taste
- ½ tsp cayenne pepper
- 2 cups tomato sauce
- 1 cup chicken broth
- 1 cup mozzarella cheese, shredded
- 10 Kalamata olives, pitted and sliced

Directions:
1. In a bowl, combine ground beef, pork rinds, feta cheese, garlic, onion, egg, cumin, oregano, salt, and pepper. Mix with hands and form into meatballs. Set your IP to Sauté and heat the oil. Fry the meatballs for 5-6 minutes on all sides. Pour in tomato sauce and broth.
2. Seal the lid, select Manual on High, and cook for 10 minutes. When done, perform a quick pressure release. Serve scattered with mozzarella cheese and Kalamata olives.

Nutrition Info: Calories 543, Protein 41g, Net Carbs 4g, Fat 27g

The Best Homemade Sloppy Joes

Servings: 4
Cooking Time: 35 Minutes
Ingredients:

- Sloppy Joes
- 1 tablespoon olive oil
- 1 pound lean ground pork
- 1/2 yellow onion, chopped
- 2 cloves garlic, minced
- 1 tomato, puréed
- 1 teaspoon stone ground mustard
- 1 tablespoon coconut aminos
- 1 cup roasted vegetable broth
- Sea salt and ground black pepper, to taste
- Oopsies:
- 2 eggs, separated yolks and whites
- 1/4 teaspoon sea salt
- 3 ounces cream cheese
- 1/4 teaspoon baking powder

Directions:

1. Press the "Sauté" button to heat up the Instant Pot. Heat the oil until sizzling. Brown the ground pork for 2 to 3 minutes, crumbling with a fork.
2. Add the other ingredients for Sloppy Joes and stir to combine well.
3. Secure the lid. Choose the "Manual" setting and cook for 5 minutes under High pressure. Once cooking is complete, use a quick pressure release; carefully remove the lid.
4. To make your oopsies, beat the egg whites together with salt until very firm peaks form.
5. In another bowl, thoroughly combine the egg yolks with cream cheese. Now, add the baking powder and stir well.
6. Next, fold the egg white mixture into the egg yolk mixture. Divide the mixture into oopsies and transfer them to a silicon sheet.
7. Bake in the preheated oven at 290 degrees F for about 23 minutes. Serve Sloppy Joes between 2 oopsies and enjoy!

Nutrition Info:
Per Serving: 524 Calories; 45g Fat; 5.5g Total Carbs; 8g Protein; 1.9g Sugars

Beef Stroganoff With A Twist

Servings: 6
Cooking Time: 20 Minutes
Ingredients:

- 1 tablespoon lard
- 1 ½ pounds beef stew meat, cubed
- 1 yellow onion, chopped

- 2 garlic cloves, chopped
- 1 red bell pepper, chopped
- Kosher salt and freshly ground black pepper, to taste
- 1/2 teaspoon dried rosemary
- 1/2 teaspoon dried thyme
- 2 cups mushrooms, chopped
- 2 ½ cups broth, preferably homemade
- 1 (10-ounce box frozen chopped spinach, thawed and squeezed dry
- 1 cup sour cream
- 4 slices Muenster cheese

Directions:

1. Press the "Sauté" button to heat up the Instant Pot. Now, melt the lard; once hot, cook the beef for 3 to 4 minutes.
2. Add the onion, garlic, bell pepper, salt, black pepper, rosemary, thyme, mushrooms, and broth.
3. Secure the lid. Choose "Manual" mode and High pressure; cook for 10 minutes. Once cooking is complete, use a quick pressure release; carefully remove the lid.
4. Lastly, stir in the spinach, sour cream and cheese. Let it stand in the residual heat until everything is well incorporated. Ladle into soup bowls and serve warm. Bon appétit!

Nutrition Info:

Per Serving: 347 Calories; 7g Fat; 7.9g Carbs; 5g Protein; 2.2g Sugars

Balsamic Beef Pot Roast

Servings: 8

Cooking Time: 45 Minutes

Ingredients:

- 3 pounds boneless beef chuck roast
- 1 small yellow onion
- 2 cups water
- Salt and pepper
- 1 tablespoon olive oil
- ¼ cup balsamic vinegar
- ¼ teaspoon xanthan gum

Directions:

1. Turn the Instant Pot on to the Sauté setting and let it heat up.
2. Add the oil to the pot and season the beef with salt and pepper.
3. Place the beef in the pot (you may need to cut it into two pieces) and cook for 2 to minutes on each side to brown.
4. Sprinkle in the onions then pour in the water and balsamic vinegar.
5. Close and lock the lid, then press the Manual button and adjust the timer to 40 minutes.
6. When the timer goes off, do a Quick Release by pressing Cancel and switching the steam valve to "venting."
7. When the pot has depressurized, open the lid.

8. Remove the beef to a bowl and break it up into pieces while you simmer the cooking liquid on the Sauté setting.
9. Whisk in the xanthan gum and simmer until thickened.
10. Stir the beef back into the sauce and serve hot.

Nutrition Info: calories 335 fat 5g ,protein 52g ,carbs 1g ,fiber 0.5g ,net carbs 0.5g

Taco Lamb Pepper Bowls

Servings: 4
Cooking Time: 18 Minutes
Ingredients:

- 1 lb. lamb stew meat, sliced
- 1 cup sweet onion, chopped
- ¾ cup green chilies, chopped
- 2 cups mixed bell peppers, chopped
- 1 (15 oz) can tomatoes, chopped
- ½ cup chicken broth
- ¼ cup enchilada sauce
- 3 garlic cloves, minced
- 1 pack taco seasoning
- 1 cup broccoli rice
- For topping:
- ½ cup grated cheddar cheese
- ½ cup pico de gallo
- 3 tbsp fresh parsley leaves
- 1 avocado, halved, pitted and sliced

Directions:

1. Season the lamb with salt and black pepper and add to the inner pot.
2. Top with the onion, green chilies, bell peppers, tomatoes, beef broth, enchilada sauce, garlic, and taco seasoning.
3. Lock the lid in place; select Manual mode on High Pressure and set the timer to 5 minutes.
4. After cooking, perform a natural pressure release for 10 minutes, then a quick pressure release to let out the remaining steam, and open the lid.
5. Stir in broccoli rice and cook in Sauté mode until softened, 3 minutes. Adjust the taste with salt and black pepper.
6. Dish the food and the toppings.
7. Serve warm.

Nutrition Info:
Per Serving: : Calories 442 Fats 85g Carbs 99g Net Carbs 7.79g Protein 47g

No-beans Lamb Chili

Servings: 4
Cooking Time: 16 Minutes
Ingredients:

- 3 tbsp olive oil
- 1 lb. ground lamb
- 1 medium red onion, chopped
- 2 garlic cloves, minced
- 2 tbsp freshly chopped parsley
- 1 ½ cups tomato sauce
- 1 cup chicken stock
- 1 cup chopped green beans
- 1 green chili, deseeded and chopped
- 1 tbsp Mexican seasoning
- Salt and black pepper to taste

Directions:
1. Set the IP in Sauté mode and adjust to Medium heat.
2. Heat 1 tablespoon of olive oil in the inner pot and cook the lamb until brown, 5 minutes. Add the onion, garlic, parsley, and cook until fragrant, 1 minute.
3. Mix in tomato sauce, chicken stock, green beans, green chili, Mexican seasoning, salt, and black pepper.
4. Lock the lid in place; select Manual mode on High Pressure and set the timer to 10 minutes.
5. After cooking, perform a quick pressure release to let out the steam and open the lid.
6. Stir and adjust the taste with salt and black pepper.
7. Dish food and serve warm.

Nutrition Info:
Per Serving: : Calories 426 Fats 73g Carbs 34g Net Carbs 53g Protein 59g

Healthy Pork Chops With Squash Salad

Servings: 6
Cooking Time: 35 Minutes
Ingredients:
- 4 pork chops
- 2 tablespoons grapeseed oil
- 1/2 teaspoon sea salt
- 1/4 teaspoon ground black pepper
- 1/2 teaspoon paprika
- 1/2 teaspoon garlic powder
- 1 teaspoon shallot powder
- 1 teaspoon dried parsley flakes
- 1 cup water
- 1 cup winter squash, diced
- 1 head Iceberg lettuce
- 1 cucumber, sliced
- 3 ounces feta cheese, crumbled

Directions:

1. Press the "Sauté" button to heat up the Instant Pot. Heat tablespoon of the grapeseed oil and brown pork chops for 2 minutes per side.
2. Add the salt, black pepper, paprika, garlic powder, shallot powder, parsley flakes, and water.
3. Secure the lid. Choose the "Manual" setting and cook for 8 minutes under High pressure. Once cooking is complete, use a quick pressure release; carefully remove the lid.
4. Meanwhile, preheat your oven to 390 degrees F. Toss winter squash with remaining 1 tablespoon oil; now, bake for 18 minutes on a lightly greased cookie sheet. Allow it to cool completely.
5. Add cooked squash to a salad bowl; toss with Iceberg lettuce and cucumber.
6. Mound the salad onto each serving plate. Scatter crumbled feta cheese over the top. Top with pork chops and enjoy.

Nutrition Info:
Per Serving: 481 Calories; 29g Fat; 6g Total Carbs; 29g Protein; 5.2g Sugars

Bacon Brussel Sprout Dish

Servings: 2 To 3
Cooking Time: 17 Mins
Ingredients:
- 2 cups Brussel Sprouts, trimmed and halved
- 4 slices Bacon Slices, chopped
- Salt to taste
- 1 tsp Monk Fruit Syrup

Directions:
1. Chop the bacon into small squares. Set the pot on Sauté. Add the bacon and cook until brown and crumbly. Add the brussels sprout and cook for 5 minutes. Add ¼ cup of water and stir.
2. Seal the lid, and cook on High Pressure mode for minutes. Once ready, quickly release the pressure. Remove to a plate, drizzle with the syrup and salt.

Nutrition Info: Calories 83, Protein 3g, Net Carbs 0g, Fat 5.3g

Pork&mushrooms Ragout

Servings: 4
Cooking Time: 28 Minutes
Ingredients:
- 1 cup shiitake mushrooms, sliced
- ½ cup okra, chopped
- 11 oz pork tenderloin
- 1 teaspoon Erythritol
- ½ teaspoon salt
- 1 tablespoon lemon juice
- 1 teaspoon dried rosemary
- 2 tablespoons olive oil
- 1/3 cup water

- 2 tablespoons cream cheese

Directions:

1. Cut the pork tenderloin into the strips and put in the instant pot. Add olive oil and stir well. Set sauté mode and cook the meat for 3 minutes. After this, stir the meat and sprinkle it with salt, lemon juice, and dried rosemary. Stir again. Add Erythritol, okra, cream cheese, and mushrooms. Mix up ingredients well. Add water and close the lid. Cook the ragout with the closed lid on stew mode for 20 minutes.

Nutrition Info: calories 215, fat 7, fiber 1.3, carbs 6.3, protein 6

Pork Shakshuka

Servings: 4
Cooking Time: 22 Minutes
Ingredients:

- 1 tbsp olive oil
- ½ lb. ground pork
- 1 small white onion, chopped
- 1 garlic clove, minced
- 1 small red bell pepper, chopped
- 2 tbsp tomato paste
- 4 cups tomatoes, chopped
- 1 tsp smoked paprika
- 1 tsp chili powder
- Salt and black pepper to taste
- 4 large eggs, cracked into a bowl
- 1 tbsp freshly chopped parsley

Directions:

1. Set the IP in Sauté mode and adjust to Medium heat.
2. Heat the olive oil in the inner pot and cook the pork until brown, 5 minutes.
3. Stir in the onion, garlic, red bell pepper, and cook until softened, minutes.
4. Stir in the tomato paste, tomatoes, paprika, chili powder, salt, and black pepper.
5. Lock the lid in place; select Manual mode on Low and set the timer to 2 minutes.
6. After cooking, perform a natural pressure release for 10 minutes, then a quick pressure release to let out the remaining steam and open the lid.
7. Set the IP in Sauté mode, stir and create four holes in sauce. Pour each egg into each hole and allow setting for 1 to 2 minutes.
8. Spoon the shakshuka into serving bowls, garnish with the parsley and serve warm.

Nutrition Info:
Per Serving: : Calories 319 Fats 48g Carbs 52g Net Carbs 7.42g Protein 01g

Green Bean Beef Soup

Servings: 5
Cooking Time: 45 Mins
Ingredients:

- 2 tsp Olive oil
- 2 lb Ground beef
- 2 Onions, chopped
- 2 tbsp Minced Garlic
- 2 tsp Thyme
- 2 tsp Oregano
- 3 cups Green Beans, cut in short strips
- 2 cups Diced Tomatoes
- 2 cups Beef Broth
- Salt and black pepper to taste
- Parmesan Cheese, grated to garnish

Directions:
1. Heat oil on Sauté, and brown the beef. Stir in tomatoes, broth and green beans. Seal the lid, select Manual and cook on Low Pressure for 30 minutes. Once done, quickly release the pressure. Season with pepper and salt. Dish soup, sprinkle with Parmesan cheese and serve.

Nutrition Info: Calories 186, Protein 14g, Net Carbs 3g, Fat 12g

Beef Short Ribs With Cilantro Cream

Servings: 8
Cooking Time: 25 Minutes
Ingredients:
- 1 tablespoon sesame oil
- 2 ½ pounds beef short ribs
- 1/2 teaspoon red pepper flakes, crushed
- Sea salt and ground black pepper, to taste
- Cilantro Cream:
- 1 cup cream cheese, softened
- 1/3 cup sour cream
- A pinch of celery salt
- A pinch of paprika
- 1 teaspoon garlic powder
- 1 bunch fresh cilantro, chopped
- 1 tablespoon fresh lime juice

Directions:
1. Press the "Sauté" button to heat up the Instant Pot. Now, heat the sesame oil. Sear the ribs until nicely browned on all sides.
2. Season the ribs with red pepper, salt, and black pepper.
3. Secure the lid. Choose "Manual" mode and High pressure; cook for 20 minutes. Once cooking is complete, use a quick pressure release; carefully remove the lid.
4. Meanwhile, mix all ingredients for the cilantro cream. Place in the refrigerator until ready to serve. Serve warm ribs with the chilled cilantro cream on the side. Bon appétit!

Nutrition Info:
Per Serving: 346 Calories; 1g Fat; 2.1g Carbs; 31g Protein; 1.1g Sugars

Sticky Pork Spare Ribs

Servings: 4
Cooking Time: 25 Minutes
Ingredients:

- 1 ½ pounds spare ribs
- 1 thin sliced fresh ginger, peeled
- 4 garlic cloves, halved
- 1 jalapeño pepper, thinly sliced
- 1 bay leaf
- 1/2 teaspoon black peppercorns
- 1 tablespoon tamarind paste
- 1 teaspoon shrimp paste
- Sea salt and ground black pepper, to taste
- 1/2 cup marinara sauce

Directions:

1. Arrange spare ribs on the bottom of your Instant Pot. Add fresh ginger, garlic, jalapeño pepper, bay leaf, and peppercorns.
2. Next, mix the tamarind paste, shrimp paste, salt, black pepper, marinara sauce, and water. Pour this tamarind sauce over the ribs in the Instant Pot.
3. Add enough water to cover the spare ribs.
4. Secure the lid. Choose the "Manual" setting and cook for 20 minutes at High pressure. Once cooking is complete, use a quick pressure release; carefully remove the lid.
5. Serve warm and enjoy!

Nutrition Info:
Per Serving: 266 Calories; 9.7g Fat; 6.2g Total Carbs; 7g Protein; 2.9g Sugars

Five-star Tender Pulled Pork

Servings: 6
Cooking Time: 55 Minutes
Ingredients:

- 2 pounds pork butt
- Celery salt and ground black pepper, to your liking
- 1 tablespoon lard
- 4 cloves garlic, smashed
- 1/2 teaspoon caraway seeds
- 1/2 teaspoon mustard seeds
- 1 bay leaf
- 1 cup beef bone broth
- 1 tablespoon chile powder
- 1 teaspoon cayenne pepper
- 1/2 teaspoon hot Hungarian paprika
- 1/2 teaspoon onion powder

Directions:
1. Season the pork butt with salt and ground black pepper.
2. Press the "Sauté" button to heat up the Instant Pot. Melt the lard and brown the pork on all sides.
3. Add the remaining ingredients.
4. Secure the lid. Choose the "Manual" setting and cook for 50 minutes under High pressure. Once cooking is complete, use a natural pressure release; carefully remove the lid.
5. Shred the meat with two forks and serve with keto bread rolls. Bon appétit!

Nutrition Info:
Per Serving: 434 Calories; 1g Fat; 1.5g Total Carbs; 6g Protein; 0.4g Sugars

Pork In Thyme Creamy Sauce

Servings: 4
Cooking Time: 75 Minutes
Ingredients:
- 1 tbsp olive oil
- 1 tbsp butter
- 1 pork shoulder, cut into 2-inch cubes
- 1 tsp dried thyme
- Salt and black pepper to taste
- ½ tsp dried mustard powder
- 1 small yellow onion, diced
- 3 garlic cloves, minced
- 1 ½ cup chicken broth
- ¾ cup heavy cream
- 1 tbsp arrowroot starch
- 1 tsp dried parsley
- 1 tsp dried basil

Directions:
1. Set the IP in Sauté mode and adjust to Medium heat.
2. Heat the olive oil and butter in the inner pot, season the pork with thyme, salt, black pepper, and mustard. Sear in the oil until golden on the outside, 7 minutes. Transfer to a plate.
3. Sauté the onion until softened, minutes. Stir in the garlic and cook until fragrant, 30 seconds.
4. Pour in the chicken broth and return the meat to the pot.
5. Lock the lid in place; select Manual mode on High Pressure and set the timer to 20 minutes.
6. After cooking, perform a natural pressure release for 10 minutes, then a quick pressure release to let out the remaining steam, and open the lid.
7. Remove the pork onto a plate and set the IP in Sauté mode.
8. Whisk in the heavy cream, arrowroot starch, parsley and basil. Cook for 2 minutes and return the pork to the sauce. Allow warming for 3 minutes.
9. Dish the food and serve warm.

Nutrition Info:
Per Serving: : Calories 459 Fats 73g Carbs 6.02g Net Carbs 5.32g Protein 57g

Mexican Chile Verde

Servings: 6
Cooking Time: 25 Minutes
Ingredients:

- 1 tablespoon olive oil
- 2 pounds Boston butt, trimmed, cut into cubes
- 2 tomatoes, diced
- 1 cup water
- 1/2 cup mild green chilies, roasted, seeded and diced
- 1 red bell pepper, seeded and chopped
- 1/2 cup green onions, chopped
- 3 cloves garlic, peeled and halved
- 1 teaspoon cumin, ground
- 1 teaspoon dried Mexican oregano
- Kosher salt and ground black pepper, to taste
- 1 teaspoon red pepper flakes
- 2 tablespoons fresh cilantro leaves, chopped

Directions:

1. Press the "Sauté" button to heat up the Instant Pot. Heat the oil until sizzling. Then, sear Boston butt for 2 to 4 minutes, stirring frequently.
2. Add the other ingredients, except for cilantro leaves.
3. Secure the lid. Choose the "Meat/Stew" setting and cook for 20 minutes under High pressure. Once cooking is complete, use a natural pressure release; carefully remove the lid; reserve the pork.
4. Add cilantro to the cooking liquid. Blitz the mixture in your food processor until creamy and uniform. Return the pork to the Instant Pot.
5. Ladle into individual bowls and serve immediately. Bon appétit!

Nutrition Info:
Per Serving: 358 Calories; 2g Fat; 4.5g Total Carbs; 7g Protein; 2.1g Sugars

Crispy Pork Loin Sliders

Servings: 6
Cooking Time: 20 Minutes
Ingredients:

- 2 teaspoons canola oil
- 2 pounds pork tenderloins, trimmed
- Sea salt and freshly ground pepper
- 1/2 teaspoon cayenne pepper
- 1/2 cup leek, thinly sliced
- 2 garlic cloves, finely chopped
- 1/2 cup broth, preferably homemade
- 1 cup water

- 2 sprigs thyme
- 1/2 teaspoon ground bay leaf
- 6 Oopsie bread rolls
- 6 leaves Iceberg lettuce
- 4 tablespoons mayonnaise

Directions:

1. Press the "Sauté" button to heat up the Instant Pot; add canola oil.
2. Sear the pork until browned on all sides. Season with salt, black pepper, and cayenne pepper. Add the leeks, garlic, broth, water, thyme, and ground bay leaf.
3. Secure the lid. Choose the "Manual" setting and cook for 12 minutes under High pressure. Once cooking is complete, use a natural pressure release; carefully remove the lid.
4. Serve over oopsie bread rolls, garnished with lettuce and mayo!

Nutrition Info:
Per Serving: 357 Calories; 4g Fat; 2.7g Total Carbs; 7g Protein; 1.1g Sugars

Herbed Crusted Lamb Cutlets

Servings: 4
Cooking Time: 30 Minutes
Ingredients:

- 8 lamb cutlets
- 4 tablespoons mustard
- 3 tablespoons olive oil
- ¼ cup parmesan, grated
- 1 tablespoon parsley, chopped
- 1 tablespoon thyme, chopped
- 1 tablespoon rosemary
- 1 cup tomato passata

Directions:

1. In a bowl, mix the lamb with the rest of the ingredients except the tomato passata. Add the sauce to the instant pot, add the lamb, put the lid on and cook on High for 30 minutes. Release the pressure naturally for minutes, divide the mix between plates and serve.

Nutrition Info: calories 162, fat 14, fiber 3.3, carbs 6.5, protein 4

Best Burgers With Kale And Cheese

Servings: 6
Cooking Time: 15 Minutes
Ingredients:

- 1 pound ground beef
- 1/2 pound beef sausage, crumbled
- 1 ½ cups kale, chopped
- 1/4 cup scallions, chopped
- 2 garlic cloves, minced
- 1/2 Romano cheese, grated

- 1/3 cup blue cheese, crumbled
- Salt and ground black pepper, to taste
- 1 teaspoon crushed dried sage
- 1/2 teaspoon oregano
- 1/2 teaspoon dried basil
- 1 tablespoon olive oil

Directions:
1. Place ½ cups of water and a steamer basket in your Instant Pot.
2. Mix all ingredients until everything is well incorporated.
3. Shape the mixture into 6 equal sized patties. Place the burgers on the steamer basket.
4. Secure the lid. Choose "Manual" mode and High pressure; cook for 6 minutes. Once cooking is complete, use a quick pressure release; carefully remove the lid. Bon appétit!

Nutrition Info:
Per Serving: 323 Calories; 3g Fat; 5.8g Total Carbs; 9g Protein; 0.6g Sugars

Steamed Gingered Pork Salad

Servings: 4
Cooking Time: 23 Minutes
Ingredients:
- 1 tbsp olive oil
- 1 lb. ground pork
- 1 small red chili, minced
- 2 ½ tbsp freshly grated ginger
- 2 garlic cloves, minced
- 2 tbsp coconut aminos
- 2 limes, juiced
- 1 tsp swerve brown sugar
- ½ cup chicken broth
- 1 medium cucumber, thinly sliced
- 2 green onions, thinly sliced
- 1 cup freshly chopped cilantro
- ½ cup freshly chopped mint leaves

Directions:
1. Set the IP in Sauté mode and adjust to Medium heat.
2. Heat the olive oil in the inner pot and cook the pork until brown, 5 minutes.
3. Stir in the red chili, ginger, garlic, and cook until fragrant, minutes.
4. In a medium bowl, mix the coconut aminos, lime juice, swerve brown sugar, and chicken broth. Stir the mixture into the pork.
5. Lock the lid in place; set in Manual mode on High Pressure and set the timer to minutes.
6. After cooking, perform a natural pressure release for 10 minutes, then a quick pressure release to let out the remaining steam, and open the lid.
7. Stir and spoon pork into a serving bowl.
8. Top with the cucumber, green onions, cilantro, and mint leaves.

9. Serve immediately.
Nutrition Info:
Per Serving: : Calories 385 Fats 91g Carbs 4.44g Net Carbs 3.24g Protein 91g

Italian Beef

Servings: 8
Cooking Time: 60 Minutes
Ingredients:
- 4-pound beef chuck, chopped
- 3 tablespoons almond butter
- ½ cup shallot, sliced
- 2 garlic cloves, sliced
- ½ cup pepperoncini peppers
- 1 cup chicken broth
- 1 teaspoon Italian seasonings
- ½ teaspoon chili powder
- 1 teaspoon Erythritol

Directions:
1. Melt almond butter on sauté mode and add sliced shallot and garlic cloves. Cook the vegetables for 5-6 minutes or until they are soft. After this, add chopped beef chuck, pepperoncini, Italian seasonings, and chili powder. Then add Erythritol and chicken broth. Close and seal the lid. Cook the beef on manual mode (high pressure) for 55 minutes. When the cooking time is finished, allow the natural pressure release for minutes. Shred the meat with the help of the fork.

Nutrition Info: calories 474, fat 9, fiber 0.7, carbs 3.5, protein 71

Sub Salad

Servings: 4
Cooking Time: 15 Minutes
Ingredients:
- 1 tomato, chopped
- 1/3 cup black olives, sliced
- 1 cup lettuce, chopped
- 1 tablespoon olive oil
- ½ teaspoon chicken seasonings
- 10 oz pork fillet
- 1/3 cup water, for cooking

Directions:
1. Slice the pork fillet and sprinkle with chicken seasonings.
2. Then place the sliced meat in the instant pot, add olive oil and cook on saute mode for 5 minutes.
3. Stir it from time to time.
4. When the meat is light brown, add water and close the lid.

5. Cook it on meat/stew mode for 10 minutes.
6. Meanwhile, in the salad bowl, mix up tomato, black olives, and lettuce.
7. Top the salad with the cooked pork slices.

Nutrition Info:

Per Serving: calories 213, fat 8, fiber 0.6, carbs 1.7, protein 20

Adobo Pork

Servings: 6

Cooking Time: 30 Minutes

Ingredients:

- 1-pound pork belly, chopped
- 1 bay leaf
- 1 teaspoon salt
- 2 tablespoons apple cider vinegar
- 1 teaspoon cayenne pepper
- 1 garlic clove, peeled
- 2 cups of water

Directions:

1. Put all ingredients in the instant pot.
2. Close and seal the lid.
3. Cook Adobo pork for minutes on manual mode (high pressure).
4. When the cooking time is finished, make a quick pressure release and transfer the pork belly in the bowls.
5. Add 1 ladle of the pork gravy.

Nutrition Info:

Per Serving: calories 352, fat 4, fiber 0.1, carbs 0.5, protein 35

Pork Dumpling Meatballs

Servings: 2

Cooking Time: 19 Minutes

Ingredients:

- 6 oz ground pork
- 1 teaspoon minced garlic
- ½ teaspoon chives, chopped
- 1 teaspoon coconut aminos
- ½ teaspoon cayenne pepper
- 1 tablespoon coconut oil
- 1 teaspoon ginger paste
- ½ cup chicken broth

Directions:

1. In the bowl, mix up ground pork, minced garlic, chives, coconut aminos, cayenne pepper, and ginger paste.
2. Make the small balls (dumplings) from the meat mixture.

3. After this, melt the coconut oil and put the meatballs inside.
4. Roast them on saute mode for 1 minute from each side.
5. Then add chicken broth and close the lid.
6. Saute the meal on saute mode for 15 minutes.

Nutrition Info:

Per Serving: calories 199, fat 3, fiber 0.3, carbs 2.1, protein 7

Zucchini Pork Ragu

Servings: 4

Cooking Time: 41 Minutes

Ingredients:
- 1 tbsp olive oil
- 1 lb. pork shoulder, cubed
- 1 white onion, chopped
- 2 garlic cloves, minced
- 2 tbsp unsweetened tomato paste
- 2 (15 oz) tomatoes with juice, chopped
- 2/3 cup beef broth
- 1 tsp dried oregano
- 1 tsp dried thyme
- Salt and black pepper to taste
- 3 medium zucchinis, sliced into ribbons
- ¼ grated Parmesan cheese for garnishing

Directions:
1. In the inner pot, add all the ingredients except for the zucchinis and Parmesan cheese.
2. Lock the lid in place; select Manual mode on High Pressure and set the timer to 30 minutes.
3. After cooking, perform a natural pressure release for 10 minutes, then a quick pressure release to let out the remaining steam, and open the lid.
4. Stir in zucchinis, adjust the taste with salt, black pepper, and cook in Sauté mode until the zucchinis are tender, 1 minute.
5. Garnish with the Parmesan cheese and serve warm.

Nutrition Info:

Per Serving: : Calories 396 Fats 14g Carbs 93g Net Carbs 8.43g Protein 43g

Traditional Pork Roast

Servings: 6

Cooking Time: 40 Minutes

Ingredients:
- 2 tablespoons unsalted butter
- 2 pounds sirloin pork roast, cubed
- 8 ounces Cremini mushrooms, thinly sliced
- 2 garlic cloves, minced
- 1 heaping tablespoon fresh parsley, chopped

- 1/2 cup roasted vegetable broth
- 2/3 cup water
- 2 tablespoons dry white wine
- 1/2 teaspoon dried sage
- 1/2 teaspoon dried basil
- 1 teaspoon dried oregano
- Sea salt and ground black pepper, to taste
- 1 teaspoon cayenne pepper
- 1/3 cup Castelvetrano olives, pitted and halved

Directions:
1. Press the "Sauté" button to heat up the Instant Pot. Melt the butter and sear the pork about 3 minutes or until delicately browned on all sides; reserve.
2. In pan drippings, cook the mushrooms and garlic until tender and fragrant.
3. Add parsley, broth, water, wine, sage, basil, oregano, salt, black pepper, and cayenne pepper; gently stir to combine.
4. Secure the lid. Choose the "Meat/Stew" setting and cook for 35 minutes at High pressure.
5. Once cooking is complete, use a natural pressure release; carefully remove the lid. Serve garnished with Castelvetrano olives. Bon appétit!

Nutrition Info:
Per Serving: 310 Calories; 4g Fat; 2.1g Total Carbs; 5g Protein; 0.7g Sugars

Beef And Turnips Plate

Servings: 4
Cooking Time: 30 Minutes
Ingredients:
- 2 tbsp olive oil
- 1 lb. ground beef
- 1 small onion, finely chopped
- 1 celery stick, chopped
- ¾ cup chopped cremini mushrooms
- 1 garlic clove, minced
- 2 tbsp unsweetened tomato paste
- 1 tbsp Worcestershire Sauce
- 1 tsp cinnamon powder
- 2 cups chicken stock
- 2 medium turnips, peeled and chopped

Directions:
1. Set the IP in Sauté mode and adjust to Medium heat.
2. Heat the olive oil in the inner pot and cook the beef until brown, 5 minutes. Mix in the onion, celery, mushrooms, garlic, and cook until softened, 5 minutes.
3. Mix in the tomato paste, Worcestershire sauce, and cinnamon powder; continue cooking further for 1 minute. Stir in the beef stock and turnips.
4. Lock the lid in place; select Manual mode on High Pressure and set the timer to 10 minutes.

5. After cooking, perform a natural pressure release for 10 minutes, then a quick pressure release to let out the steam, and open the lid.
6. Stir and adjust taste with salt and black pepper.
7. Dish food and serve warm.

Nutrition Info:
Per Serving: : Calories 859 Fats 39g Carbs 6.08g Net Carbs 4.48g Protein 15g

Beef And Beer Stew

Servings: 4
Cooking Time: 60 Mins
Ingredients:
- 2 lb Beef Stew, cut into pieces
- Salt and black pepper to taste
- ¼ cup Almond flour
- 3 tbsp Butter
- 2 tbsp Worcestershire Sauce
- 2 cloves Garlic, minced
- 1 packet Dry Onion Soup Mix
- 2 cups Beef Broth
- 1 medium bottle Beer, low carb
- 1 tbsp Tomato Paste

Directions:
1. In a zipper bag, add the beef, salt, almond flour, and pepper. Close the bag up and shake to coat the beef well with the mixture. Select Sauté mode and melt the butter.
2. Add the beef and brown them on both sides for 5 minutes. Add the beef to deglaze the bottom of the pot. Add the tomato paste, beer, Worcestershire sauce, and the onion soup mix. Stir.
3. Seal the lid, select Meat/Stew on High for minutes. Once ready, do a natural pressure release for 10 minutes, and then a quick pressure release to let out any remaining steam. Spoon beef stew into bowls and serve with over a bed of vegetable mash.

Nutrition Info: Calories 235, Protein 5g, Net Carbs 0.2g, Fat 2g

Lean Steak With Oregano-orange Chimichurri & Arugula Salad

Servings: 4
Cooking Time: 10 Mins
Ingredients:
- 1 teaspoon finely grated orange zest
- 1 teaspoon dried oregano
- 1 small garlic clove, grated
- 2 teaspoon vinegar (red wine, cider, or white wine)
- 1 tablespoon fresh orange juice

- 1/2 cup chopped fresh flat-leaf parsley leaves
- 1 ½ pound lean steak, cut into 4 pieces
- Sea salt and pepper
- 1/4 cup and 2 teaspoons extra virgin olive oil
- 4 cups arugula
- 2 bulbs fennel, shaved
- 2 tablespoons whole-grain mustard

Directions:
1. Make chimichurri: In a medium bowl, combine orange zest, oregano and garlic. Mix in vinegar, orange juice and parsley and then slowly whisk in ¼ cup of olive oil until emulsified. Season with sea salt and pepper.
2. Sprinkle the steak with salt and pepper; heat the remaining olive oil in an instant pot and set on manual high; cook steak for about 6 Mins per side or until browned. Add water to an instant pot and insert a trivet; place beef over the trivet and lock lid. Cook on high for 10 Mins and then let pressure come down on its own. Let rest and slice.
3. Toss steak, greens, and fennel with mustard in a medium bowl; season with salt and pepper.
4. Serve steak with chimichurri and salad. Enjoy!

Nutrition Info:
Per Serving: Calories: 343; Total Fat: 6 g; Carbs: 2 g; Dietary Fiber: 0.5 g; Sugars: 0.8 g; Protein: 0.6 g; Cholesterol: 99 mg; Sodium: 146 mg

Dairy-free Beef Stew

Servings: 3
Cooking Time: 90 Mins
Ingredients:
- 1 lb Sirloin Tip Roast, cut in 3 large chunks
- Salt and black pepper to taste
- 1 tsp Olive oil
- 1 large Onion, sliced
- 1 Red Bell pepper, sliced
- 1 Yellow Bell pepper, sliced
- 3 cloves Garlic, minced
- 1 tsp dried Oregano
- 1 tsp Cumin Powder
- 1 tsp Smoked Paprika
- ½ tsp Turmeric
- 1/6 cup Dry White Wine
- 1 cup Diced Tomatoes
- 1 Bay Leaf
- 1/6 cup Capers
- 1 Pimiento Pepper, minced
- ½ tbsp Plain Vinegar

Directions:

1. Season the beef with white pepper and salt. Heat oil on Sauté and brown the beef; remove to a plate. Add peppers and onion and cook for 4 minutes. Add garlic, spices, and oregano.
2. Add the wine, cook to reduce it for 3 minutes. Add the tomatoes and bay leaf, stir. Add the beef back. Seal the lid, select Manual and cook on High Pressure for 40 minutes. Once ready, do a natural pressure release for minutes. Shred the meat, add the remaining ingredients, and simmer for 5 minutes on Sauté.

Nutrition Info: Calories 271, Protein 2g, Net Carbs 3.9g, Fat 17g

Lamb Chops, Fennel And Tomatoes

Servings: 4
Cooking Time: 25 Minutes
Ingredients:
- 4 lamb chops
- 1 tablespoon olive oil
- 4 garlic cloves, minced
- A pinch of salt and black pepper
- Zest of 1 lime, grated
- 2 bay leaves
- 1 tablespoon rosemary, chopped
- 1 fennel bulb, cut into 8 wedges
- ½ cup cherry tomatoes, halved
- 1 teaspoon sweet paprika
- 1 cup veggie stock

Directions:
1. Set your instant pot on Sauté mode, add the oil, heat it up, add the meat and the garlic and brown for 5 minutes. Add the rest of the ingredients, put the lid on and cook on High for 20 minutes. Release the pressure naturally for minutes, divide everything between plates and serve.

Nutrition Info: calories 194, fat 7.9, fiber 2.3, carbs 5.3, protein 7.5

Instant Ground Beef With Cabbage

Servings: 5
Cooking Time: 25 Minutes
Ingredients:
- 2 tablespoons olive oil
- 1 ½ lb. ground beef
- ½ teaspoon pepper
- 1 cup beef broth
- 4 cups green cabbage, chopped
- 1 tablespoon soy sauce
- 1 teaspoon dried marjoram
- 2 garlic cloves, pressed
- 1 can tomato puree

- ½ teaspoon salt
- 1 large yellow onion, diced
- 1 teaspoon dried thyme

Directions:

1. Press the "Sauté" button and heat the olive oil. Saute the onion and garlic until aromatic.
2. Stir in the ground beef and cook until brown. Then add the tomato pure, beef broth, green cabbage, soy sauce, dried marjoram, dried thyme, salt, and pepper.
3. Secure the lid. Choose "Manual" mode and High pressure; cook for 20 minutes. When cooking is complete, use a natural pressure release and carefully remove the lid.
4. Serve warm. Bon appétit!

Nutrition Info:
Per Serving: 491 Calories; 7g Fat; 7g Carbs; 5g Protein; 1.8g Sugars

Pork And Mint Zucchinis

Servings: 6
Cooking Time: 25 Minutes
Ingredients:

- 2 pounds pork stew meat, cubed
- A pinch of salt and black pepper
- 1 cup beef stock
- 1 cup zucchinis, sliced
- 1 tablespoon balsamic vinegar
- 1 tablespoon olive oil
- 1 tablespoon garlic, minced
- 1 tablespoon mint, chopped

Directions:

1. Set the instant pot on Sauté mode, add the oil, heat it up, add the pork and the garlic and brown for 5 minutes. Add the rest of the ingredients, put the lid on and cook on High for 20 minutes. Release the pressure naturally for minutes, divide everything between plates and serve.

Nutrition Info: calories 349, fat 1, fiber 0.3, carbs 1.2, protein 2

Sweet Ham

Servings: 6
Cooking Time: 7 Minutes
Ingredients:

- 1-pound ham
- ½ cup butter
- 3 tablespoons Erythritol
- ½ teaspoon cumin seeds
- 1 cup water, for cooking

Directions:

1. Pour water in the instant pot and insert the steamer rack.

2. After this, in the mixing bowl, mix up Erythritol, butter, and cumin seeds.
3. Brush the ham with the sweet mixture well and transfer it in the instant pot.
4. Add the remaining sweet mixture. Close and seal the lid.
5. Cook the ham on manual mode (high pressure) for 7 minutes.
6. Make a quick pressure release and slice the ham.

Nutrition Info:
Per Serving: calories 260, fat 9, fiber 1, carbs 3, protein 7

Italian Pepperoncini Beef

Servings: 3
Cooking Time: 55 Mins
Ingredients:
- 2 lb Beef Roast, cut into cubes
- 14 oz jar Pepperoncini Peppers, with liquid
- 1 pack Brown Gravy Mix
- 1 pack Italian Salad Dressing Mix

Directions:
1. To the pot, add in the beef, pepperoncini peppers, brown gravy mix, Italian salad dressing mix, and ½ cup water. Seal the lid, secure the pressure valve, and select Meat/Stew on High for 55 minutes.
2. Once ready, do a quick pressure release, and open the pot. Dish the ingredients to a bowl and use two forks to shred the beef. Serve the beef sauce in plates with a side of steamed veggies.

Nutrition Info: Calories 161, Protein 27g, Net Carbs 0g, Fat 28g

Beef With Garlic & Broccoli

Servings: 3 To 4
Cooking Time: 35 Mins
Ingredients:
- 2 lb Chuck Roast, Boneless, cut into strips
- 4 cloves Garlic, minced
- 7 cups Broccoli Florets
- 1 tbsp Olive oil
- 1 cup Beef Broth
- 1 tbsp Arrowroot Starch
- ¾ cup sugar-free Soy Sauce
- 3 tbsp Swerve Sugar
- Salt to taste

Directions:
1. Select Sauté mode. Heat the olive oil, and add the beef and minced garlic. Cook the beef until browned. Then, add soy sauce, broth, and swerve sugar. Use a spoon to stir the ingredients well so that the sugar dissolves. Seal the lid, select Meat/Stew on High pressure for minutes.

2. Meanwhile, put the broccoli in a bowl and steam in a microwave for 4 to 5 minutes. After, remove and set aside. Once ready, do a quick pressure release. Use a soup spoon to fetch out a quarter of the liquid into a bowl, add the arrowroot starch, and mix until well dissolved.
3. Pour the starch mixture into the pot and select Sauté. Stir the sauce and allow to thicken. Add in broccoli and let simmer for 4 minutes. Serve with squash spaghetti.

Nutrition Info: Calories 232, Protein 8g, Net Carbs 3g, Fat 8.8g

Herbed Mustard Beef Shanks

Servings: 8
Cooking Time: 35 Minutes
Ingredients:
- 2 teaspoons lard, room temperature
- 2 ½ pounds beef shanks, 1 ½-inch wide
- 1 ½ cups beef broth
- 1 teaspoon Dijon mustard
- 1/2 teaspoon cayenne pepper
- 1/4 teaspoon freshly cracked black pepper
- 1 teaspoon salt
- 1 bay leaf
- 1/2 teaspoon dried marjoram, crushed
- 1/2 teaspoon caraway seeds
- 1 teaspoon dried sage, crushed
- 2 sprigs mint, roughly chopped

Directions:
1. Press the "Sauté" button to heat up the Instant Pot. Melt the lard. Once hot, sear the beef shanks for 2 to 3 minutes per side.
2. Add the remaining ingredients, except for the mint.
3. Secure the lid. Choose "Meat/Stew" mode and High pressure; cook for minutes. Once cooking is complete, use a quick pressure release; carefully remove the lid.
4. Serve garnished with fresh mint and enjoy!

Nutrition Info:
Per Serving: 210 Calories; 6.6g Fat; 4.2g Carbs; 1g Protein; 0g Sugars

Braised Lamb Shanks

Servings: 4
Cooking Time: 71 Minutes
Ingredients:
- 2 tbsp olive oil
- 3 lbs. lamb shanks
- Salt and black pepper to taste
- 6 garlic cloves, minced
- ¾ cup red wine
- 1 cup chicken broth

- 2 cups crushed tomatoes
- 1 tsp dried oregano
- 1 tsp dried basil
- ¼ cup chopped fresh parsley to garnish

Directions:
1. Set the IP in Sauté mode and adjust to Medium heat.
2. Heat the olive oil in the inner pot, season the lamb with salt and black pepper, and sear in the oil until brown outside, 6 minutes. Transfer to a plate.
3. Stir-fry the garlic and sauté until fragrant, seconds.
4. Mix in the red wine and cook for 2 minutes while stirring and scraping the bottom of any stuck bits.
5. Add the tomatoes, oregano, and basil. Stir and cook for 2 minutes.
6. Return the lamb to pot and coat with the sauce.
7. Lock the lid in place; select Manual mode on High Pressure and set the timer to 45 minutes.
8. After cooking, perform a natural pressure release for 15 minutes, then a quick pressure release to let out the remaining steam, and open the lid.
9. Stir in the parsley and adjust taste with salt and black pepper.
10. Dish and serve warm.

Nutrition Info:
Per Serving: : Calories 510 Fats 82g Carbs 6.06g Net Carbs 4.56g Protein 37g

Herbed Pork Tenderloin

Servings: 4
Cooking Time: 18 Minutes
Ingredients:
- ¼ teaspoon ground cumin
- ½ teaspoon ground nutmeg
- ½ teaspoon dried thyme
- ½ teaspoon ground coriander
- 1 tablespoon sesame oil
- 1-pound pork tenderloin
- 2 tablespoons apple cider vinegar
- 1 cup of water

Directions:
1. In the mixing bowl, mix up ground cumin, ground nutmeg, thyme, ground coriander, and apple cider vinegar.
2. Then rub the meat with the spice mixture.
3. Heat up sesame oil on saute mode for 2 minutes.
4. Put the pork tenderloin in the hot oil and cook it for 5 minutes from each side or until meat is light brown.
5. Add water.
6. Close and seal the lid. Cook the meat on manual mode (high pressure) for 5 minutes.
7. When the time is finished, allow the natural pressure release for 15 minutes.

Nutrition Info:

Per Serving: calories 196, fat 7.5, fiber 0.1, carbs 0.4, protein 7

Ground Beef With Peppers

Servings: 3
Cooking Time: 15 Mins
Ingredients:
- 1 tbsp Olive oil
- ½ cup Tomato sauce
- 1 lb Ground Beef
- 2 green Peppers, sliced
- 2 red Peppers, sliced
- 1 Onion, chopped
- ½ tbsp Chili powder
- Salt and black pepper to taste

Directions:
1. Add onion and vegetable oil to the pot. Press Sauté and stir in the meat, tomato sauce, green peppers and red peppers. Season with salt, pepper and chili powder.
2. Pour half cup of water, seal the lid, and cook for 15 minutes on High pressure. When ready, allow for a natural pressure release for 10 minutes, and serve immediately.

Nutrition Info: Calories 515, Protein 3g, Net Carbs 7.5g, Fat 4g

Easy Pulled Pork

Servings: 4
Cooking Time: 45 Minutes
Ingredients:
- 2 tablespoons olive oil
- 1 teaspoon onion powder
- 1/2 teaspoon mustard seeds
- ½ teaspoon salt
- 2 lbs. pork roast, cut into cubes
- ½ teaspoon garlic powder
- ½ teaspoon pepper
- 1 tablespoon cumin
- 1/2 teaspoon paprika
- 1 cup vegetable broth

Directions:
1. Season the pork roast with salt and pepper.
2. Press the "Sauté" button and heat the olive oil. Sear the pork for 3 minutes on all sides.
3. Stir in the onion powder, mustard seeds, cumin, garlic powder, paprika, and vegetable broth.
4. Secure the lid. Choose the "Manual" setting and cook for 35 minutes under High pressure. When cooking is complete, use a natural pressure release and carefully remove the lid.
5. Shred the meat with two forks and serve warm. Enjoy!

Nutrition Info:

Per Serving: 511 Calories; 2g Fat; 2.5g Carbs; 6g Protein; 0.8g Sugars

Mediterranean Youvarlakia

Servings: 4
Cooking Time: 30 Minutes
Ingredients:

- 1 pound ground pork
- 1/2 cup green onions, chopped
- 1 teaspoon garlic paste
- 2 tablespoons parsley, finely chopped
- 1 tablespoon cilantro, finely chopped
- 1 teaspoon basil
- 1 teaspoon dill
- 1 egg white
- Sea salt, to taste
- 1/2 teaspoon ground black pepper
- 1/2 teaspoon cayenne pepper
- 1 tablespoon olive oil
- 4 cups beef bone broth
- 1 tablespoon butter
- 1/2 cup feta cheese, sliced
- Avgolemono Sauce:
- 2 eggs
- 3 tablespoons freshly squeezed lemon juice

Directions:

1. In a mixing bowl, thoroughly combine ground pork, green onions, garlic paste, parsley, cilantro, basil, dill, egg white, salt, black pepper, and cayenne pepper. Roll the mixture into meatballs.
2. Press the "Sauté" button to heat up the Instant Pot. Once hot, add the oil; sear your meatballs until no longer pink in center.
3. Add broth and butter. Secure the lid. Choose the "Soup/Broth" setting and cook for 20 minutes at High pressure. Once cooking is complete, use a quick pressure release; carefully remove the lid.
4. In a small mixing dish, whisk two eggs with lemon juice. Add Avgolemono sauce to the hot soup. Press the "Sauté" button and let it simmer for a couple of minutes more or until heated through.
5. Serve garnished with feta cheese. Enjoy!

Nutrition Info:
Per Serving: 525 Calories; 5g Fat; 3.9g Total Carbs; 40g Protein; 1.8g Sugars

Pork In Vegetable Sauce

Servings: 4
Cooking Time: 40 Mins

Ingredients:
- 2 lb Pork Loin Roast
- Salt and black pepper to taste
- 3 cloves Garlic, minced
- 1 medium Onion, diced
- 2 tbsp Butter
- 3 stalks Celery, chopped
- 3 Carrots, chopped
- 1 cup Chicken Broth
- 2 tbsp sugar-free Worcestershire Sauce
- ½ tbsp Monk Fruit Sugar
- 1 tsp Yellow Mustard
- 2 tsp dried Basil
- 2 tsp dried Thyme
- 1 tbsp Arrowroot Starch
- ¼ cup Water

Directions:
1. Turn on the Instant Pot, open the lid, and select Sauté mode. Pour the oil in and while heats quickly season the pork with salt and pepper. Put the pork to the oil and sear to golden brown on both sides. This is about 4 minutes.
2. Then, include the garlic and onions and cook them until they are soft for 4 minutes too.
3. Top with the celery, carrots, chicken broth, Worcestershire sauce, mustard, thyme, basil, and monk fruit sugar. Use a spoon to stir it. Seal the lid, select Meat/Stew mode on High pressure for 20 minutes. Once ready, do a quick pressure release.
4. Remove the meat from the pot onto a serving platter. Add the arrowroot starch to the water, mix with a spoon, and add to the pot. Select Sauté and cook the sauce to become a slurry with a bit of thickness. Season with salt and pepper and spoon the sauce over the meat in the serving platter.Serve with a side of steamed almond garlicky rapini mix.

Nutrition Info: Calories 326, Protein 7g, Net Carbs 0g, Fat 1g

Grandma's Cheeseburger Soup

Servings: 4
Cooking Time: 20 Minutes
Ingredients:
- 2 slices bacon, chopped
- 1 pound ground chuck
- 1 teaspoon ghee, room temperature
- Salt and ground black pepper, to taste
- 4 cups vegetable stock, preferably homemade
- 2 garlic cloves, minced
- 1/2 cup scallions, chopped
- 1 teaspoon mustard seeds
- 1 teaspoon paprika

- 1 teaspoon chili powder
- 1/2 cup tomato puree
- 1 bay leaf
- 1 ½ cups Monterey-Jack cheese, shredded
- 2 ounces sour cream
- 1 small handful fresh parsley, roughly chopped

Directions:
1. Press the "Sauté" button to heat up the Instant Pot. Once hot, cook the bacon and ground beef for 2 to 3 minutes, crumbling them with a fork.
2. Add the ghee, salt, black pepper, vegetable stock, garlic, scallions, mustard seeds, paprika, chili powder, tomato puree, and bay leaf.
3. Secure the lid. Choose "Manual" mode and High pressure; cook for 8 minutes. Once cooking is complete, use a natural pressure release; carefully remove the lid.
4. After that, add Monterey-Jack cheese and sour cream; seal the lid and let it stand for at least 5 minutes.
5. Serve warm in individual bowls garnished with fresh parsley. Bon appétit!

Nutrition Info:
Per Serving: 571 Calories; 39g Fat; 3.6g Total Carbs; 4g Protein; 1.6g Sugars

Chunky Flank Steak

Servings: 6
Cooking Time: 20 Minutes
Ingredients:
- 1 tablespoon grapeseed oil
- 2 pounds beef flank steak, cubed
- 1 jalapeño pepper, seeded and diced
- 2 shallots, diced
- 1 celery stalk, diced
- 2 Romano tomatoes, puréed
- Coarse sea salt and ground black pepper, to your liking
- 2 tablespoons fresh coriander, coarsely chopped
- 1 tablespoon coconut aminos
- 1 tablespoon Kashmiri chili powder
- 1/2 teaspoon smoked cayenne pepper
- 1/2 teaspoon red pepper flakes, crushed
- 1/3 cup fresh chives, chopped

Directions:
1. Press the "Sauté" button to heat up the Instant Pot. Now, heat the oil. Once hot, cook the beef for 3 minutes per side or until it is delicately browned.
2. Add the other ingredients, except for fresh chives. Add 1 cup of water and stir.
3. Secure the lid. Choose "Manual" mode and High pressure; cook for 15 minutes. Once cooking is complete, use a natural pressure release; carefully remove the lid.
4. Serve in individual bowls garnished with fresh chives. Bon appétit!

Bacon & Onion Jam

Servings: 6
Cooking Time: 6 Hrs 40 Mins
Ingredients:
- 1 lb Bacon strips, cut in ½-inch pieces
- 4 Onions, chopped
- 2 cloves Garlic
- ¼ cup Monk Fruit Powder
- ¼ cup Starfruit Juice
- ¼ cup Plain Vinegar
- 1 tsp fresh Thyme Leaves
- 1/6 tsp Cinnamon Powder
- A pinch Cayenne Pepper

Directions:
1. Add bacon and fry until slightly cooked but not crispy, on Sauté. Remove to a paper-towel-lined plate and refrigerate. Scoop out the grease from the pot leaving a tablespoon of oil.
2. Add the garlic and onion and cook for 5 minutes. Stir in the remaining ingredients, seal the lid, and cook on Slow Cook mode for 6 hours. Once done, quickly release the pressure.
3. Stir in the bacon, and cook on Sauté for 10 minutes. Scoop into an airtight container, refrigerate and use for up to a week.

Nutrition Info: Calories 40, Protein 22g, Net Carbs 0g, Fat 26g

Cauli Beef Burger

Servings: 2
Cooking Time: 15 Minutes
Ingredients:
- ½ cup cauliflower, shredded
- 5 oz ground beef
- 1 teaspoon garlic salt
- ¼ teaspoon ground cumin
- 1 tablespoon scallions, diced
- 1 egg, beaten
- 1 tablespoon coconut oil
- ¼ cup hot water

Directions:
1. In the mixing bowl, mix up shredded cauliflower, ground beef, garlic salt, ground cumin, and diced scallions.
2. When the meat mixture is homogenous, add egg and stir it well.
3. Make the burgers from the cauli-meat mixture.
4. After this, heat up the coconut oil on saute mode.

5. Place the burgers in the hot oil in one layer and cook them for minutes from each side.
6. Then add water and close the lid. Cook the meal on saute mode for 5 minutes more.

Nutrition Info:

Per Serving: calories 235, fat 5, fiber 0.9, carbs 2.9, protein 1

Blackberry Beef

Servings: 2
Cooking Time: 30 Minutes
Ingredients:
- 15 oz beef loin, chopped
- 1 tablespoon blackberries
- 1 cup of water
- ½ teaspoon ground cinnamon
- 1/3 teaspoon ground black pepper
- ½ teaspoon salt
- 1 tablespoon butter

Directions:
1. Pour water in the instant pot bowl.
2. Add chopped beef loin, blackberries, ground cinnamon, salt, and ground black pepper. Add butter.
3. Close the instant pot lid and set the "Meat" mode.
4. Cook the meat for 30 minutes. Then remove the meat from the instant pot. Blend the remaining blackberry mixture.
5. Pour it over the meat.

Nutrition Info:

Per Serving: calories 372, fat 21, fiber 0.6, carbs 3.7, protein 4

Oregano And Thyme Beef

Servings: 4
Cooking Time: 30 Minutes
Ingredients:
- 1 pound beef stew meat, cubed
- 2 garlic cloves, minced
- 1 tablespoon olive oil
- 1 teaspoon thyme, dried
- A pinch of salt and black pepper
- 1 tablespoon oregano, chopped
- 1 and ½ cups beef stock

Directions:
1. Set your instant pot on Sauté mode, add the oil, heat it up, add the garlic, thyme and the meat and brown for 5 minutes. Add the rest of the ingredients, put the lid on and cook on High for 25 minutes. Release the pressure naturally for minutes, divide the mix between plates and serve.

Nutrition Info: calories 247, fat 7, fiber 0.6, carbs 1.4, protein 2

Juicy Steak With Rainbow Noodles

Servings: 6
Cooking Time: 45 Minutes
Ingredients:

- 1 zucchini
- 1 carrot
- 1 yellow onion
- 2 tablespoons ghee
- Sea salt, to taste
- 2 pounds beef steak
- 2 large cloves garlic
- 1/3 teaspoon ground black pepper

Directions:

1. Slice the zucchini, carrot, and yellow onion using a mandolin.
2. Preheat an oven to 390 degrees F. Grease a baking sheet with the ghee; toss the vegetables with salt and bake for 18 to minutes, tossing once or twice.
3. Meanwhile, add the beef, garlic, and black pepper to your Instant Pot.
4. Secure the lid. Choose "Manual" mode and High pressure; cook for 20 minutes. Once cooking is complete, use a quick pressure release; carefully remove the lid. Salt the beef to taste.
5. Serve the prepared beef steak over roasted vegetable noodles and enjoy!

Nutrition Info:
Per Serving: 259 Calories; 2g Fat; 3g Total Carbs; 4g Protein; 1.2g Sugars

Beef With Broccoli Sauce

Servings: 3
Cooking Time: 45 Mins
Ingredients:

- 1 lb Beef Chuck Roast, Boneless and cut in strips
- Salt and black pepper to taste
- 2 tsp Olive oil
- 1 Onion, chopped
- 3 cloves Garlic
- ½ cup Beef Broth
- ¼ cup Soy Sauce
- ¼ cup Swerve Sweetener
- 2 tbsp Sesame OIl
- 1 Red Pepper Flakes
- ½ lb Broccoli Florets
- 2 tbsp Water
- 2 tbsp Arrowroot Flour

- Toasted Sesame Seeds to garnish

Directions:
1. On Sauté, heat the olive oil, season the beef with pepper and salt. and brown on all sides. Remove to a plate and set aside. Add onion to the pot. Stir and cook for 2 minutes.
2. Add the garlic and cook for 1 minute. Add the pepper flakes, soy sauce, broth, sesame oil and sweetener. Mix until fully incorporated. Stir in the beef and resulting juices. Seal the lid, select Manual and cook on HIgh Pressure mode for 1minutes.
3. Meanwhile, place broccoli in a bowl with ¼ cup of water and steam in a microwave for minutes. To the pot, do a quick release. Mix the arrowroot flour with 2 tbsp of water, and stir in the sauce. Stir in the broccoli and serve in bowls with sesame seeds garnishing.

Nutrition Info: Calories 235, Protein 19g, Net Carbs 2g, Fat 17g

Tender Pork Steaks With Pico De Gallo

Servings: 6
Cooking Time: 15 Minutes
Ingredients:
- 1 tablespoon lard
- 2 pounds pork steaks
- 1 bell pepper, seeded and sliced
- 1/2 cup shallots, chopped
- 2 garlic cloves, minced
- 1 cup chicken bone broth, preferably homemade
- 1/4 cup water
- 1/4 cup dry red wine
- Salt, to taste
- 1/4 teaspoon freshly ground black pepper, or more to taste
- Pico de Gallo:
- 1 tomato, chopped
- 1 chili pepper, seeded and minced
- 1/2 cup red onion, chopped
- 2 garlic cloves, minced
- 1 tablespoon fresh cilantro, finely chopped
- Sea salt, to taste

Directions:
1. Press the "Sauté" button to heat up the Instant Pot. Melt the lard and sear the pork steaks about 4 minutes or until delicately browned on both sides.
2. Add bell pepper, shallot, garlic, chicken bone broth, water, wine, salt, and black pepper to the Instant Pot.
3. Secure the lid. Choose the "Manual" setting and cook for 8 minutes at High pressure. Once cooking is complete, use a quick pressure release; carefully remove the lid.
4. Meanwhile, make your Pico de Gallo by mixing all of the above ingredients. Refrigerate until ready to serve.
5. Serve warm pork steaks with well-chilled Pico de Gallo on the side. Bon appétit!

Spinach And Fennel Pork Stew

Servings: 4
Cooking Time: 40 Minutes
Ingredients:

- 2 cups fresh spinach, chopped
- 8 oz fennel, chopped
- 10 oz pork tenderloin, chopped
- 1 teaspoon salt
- 1 teaspoon onion powder
- 1 teaspoon cumin seeds
- 1 cup chicken broth
- 1 teaspoon dried rosemary
- 1 teaspoon butter

Directions:

1. Put butter in the instant pot and melt it on sauté mode. Then add the chopped meat and cook it on sauté mode for 3-4 minutes. Stir it well and sprinkle with salt, onion powder, cumin seeds, and dried rosemary. Add chicken broth and close the lid. Cook the meat on sauté mode for 35 minutes. When the time is finished, stir the meat well and add fennel and fresh spinach. Stir the stew and close the lid. Cook the meal on manual mode (high pressure) for 3 minutes. When the time is finished, make the quick pressure release. Allow the cooked stew cool for 5- minutes before serving.

Nutrition Info: calories 145, fat 4.1, fiber 2.3, carbs 5.8, protein 1

Wine-braised Pulled Beef

Servings: 4
Cooking Time: 45 Mins
Ingredients:

- 2 tbsp olive oil
- 1 pound strip steak, boneless
- ½ cup red wine
- ½ cup vegetable broth
- 1 tbsp coconut aminos
- 1 tbsp Worcestershire sauce
- 1 tsp dried tarragon
- 1 tsp mustard seeds
- 2 garlic cloves, pressed
- 10 shallots, peeled
- 2 tbsp fresh parsley, chopped

Directions:

1. Set your IP to Sauté and heat the olive oil. Place the beef and cook for 3 minutes per side. Add in the remaining ingredients.
2. Seal the lid, select Manual on High, and cook for 40 minutes. When done, perform a natural pressure release. Serve sprinkled with parsley.

Nutrition Info: Calories 320, Protein 33g, Net Carbs 2.5g, Fat 19g

Bbq Pulled Beef

Servings: 2
Cooking Time: 40 Minutes
Ingredients:
- 9 oz beef loin
- 1 cup of water
- ½ cup BBQ sauce (keto-friendly)

Directions:
1. Put all ingredients in the instant pot.
2. Close and seal the lid.
3. Cook the beef on manual (high pressure) for 40 minutes.
4. Then make a quick pressure release and shred the beef with the help of the forks.

Nutrition Info:
Per Serving: calories 267, fat 2, fiber 1, carbs 3, protein 1

Tuscan Pork Chops

Servings: 4
Cooking Time: 52 Minutes
Ingredients:
- 1 tbsp olive oil
- 4 pork chops, fat trimmed
- Salt and black pepper to taste
- 1 large red onion, chopped
- 5 garlic cloves, minced
- 1 ½ chopped tomatoes
- 2 tsp dried oregano
- 1 tsp basil
- 1 tsp dried sage
- ½ cup chicken broth

Directions:
1. Set the IP in Sauté mode and adjust to Medium heat.
2. Heat the olive oil in the inner pot, season the pork with salt, black pepper, and sear in the oil until golden brown on both sides, 6 to 8 minutes.
3. Stir in the onion and garlic until softened and fragrant, 2 minutes. Stir in the remaining ingredients.
4. Lock the lid in place; select Manual mode on High Pressure and set the timer to 15 minutes.

5. After cooking, perform a natural pressure release for 10 minutes, then a quick pressure release to let out the remaining steam, and open the lid.
6. Stir, adjust the taste with salt, black pepper, and serve warm.

Nutrition Info:

Per Serving: : Calories 377 Fats 9g Carbs 4.08g Net Carbs 3.18g Protein 22g

Tandoori Bbq Pork Ribs

Servings: 4 To 6
Cooking Time: 40 Mins
Ingredients:

- 1 ½ lb Pork Ribs
- 1 Bay Leaf
- 1 inch Ginger, grated
- 3 cloves Garlic
- 2 tbsp Tandoori Spice Mix
- 1 cup Water
- Salt to taste
- ¼ cup BBQ Sauce

Directions:

1. Line ribs flat in the Instant Pot, add water, ginger, garlic, bay leaf, one tbsp of Tandoori spice mix and salt. Seal the lid, select Manual and cook on High for 20 minutes. Once done, do a natural pressure release for minutes. Carefully remove the ribs and place on a flat surface.
2. Wrap the bony sides with foil, pat dry the meaty sides and coat with the BBQ sauce. Sear with a torch or broil for 5 minutes per side. Serve immediately.

Nutrition Info: Calories 296, Protein 22g, Net Carbs 0g, Fat 23g

Pork And Tofu Tuscan Soup

Servings: 4
Cooking Time: 40 Mins
Ingredients:

- 2 tbsp Olive oil
- 2 lb Pork Sausage, cut in 2 inch chunks
- 1 Sweet Onion, diced
- 1 tsp dried Oregano
- ½ lb Tofu, pressed
- 8 cups Chicken Broth
- 1 cup chopped Kale Leaves
- 1 ½ cups Heavy Cream
- Salt and black pepper to taste
- ½ cup Parmesan Cheese, grated

Directions:

1. Heat oil on Sauté, add sausage and tofu. Cook until brown for 6 minutes. Stir in garlic, onion, and oregano and cook for 3 minutes. Stir in broth and scrape the bottom of the pot to deglaze.
2. Stir in salt and pepper, seal the lid, select Manual and cook on High Pressure for 5 minutes. Check to make sure the contents don't go over the Max Fill line marked on the inner liner.
3. Once done, do a natural pressure release for 10 minutes and then quickly release the remaining pressure. Stir in kale and cook on Sauté mode for minutes. Stir in heavy cream and serve.

Nutrition Info: Calories 132, Protein 13g, Net Carbs 2.9g, Fat 2.3g

Delicious Provolone-stuffed Meatballs

Servings: 5
Cooking Time: 15 Minutes
Ingredients:
- 1 pound ground pork
- 1/4 cup double cream
- 2 eggs, beaten
- 2 cloves garlic, minced
- 2 tablespoons green onions, minced
- 1 tablespoon fresh parsley, minced
- 1/4 teaspoon dried thyme
- 1/2 teaspoon dried marjoram
- 1/2 teaspoon ground black pepper
- 1 teaspoon kosher salt
- 10 (1-inch cubes of provolone cheese

Directions:
1. Prepare your Instant Pot by adding ½ cups of water and a steamer basket to the bottom of the inner pot.
2. Thoroughly combine all ingredients, except the cubes of provolone cheese, in a mixing bowl.
3. Shape the mixture into 10 patties by using oiled hands. Now, place a cube of provolone cheese in the center of each patty, wrap the meat around the cheese, and roll into a ball.
4. Now, arrange the meatballs in the steamer basket.
5. Secure the lid. Choose the "Manual" setting and cook for 6 minutes at High pressure. Once cooking is complete, use a quick pressure release; carefully remove the lid.
6. Serve immediately, garnished with low-carb salsa. Bon appétit!

Nutrition Info:
Per Serving: 440 Calories; 9g Fat; 2.1g Carbs; 7g Protein; 0.8g Sugars

Ginger Lamb And Basil

Servings: 4
Cooking Time: 30 Minutes
Ingredients:

- 1 and ½ pounds leg of lamb, boneless and cubed
- 1 tablespoon olive oil
- 2 tablespoons basil, chopped
- 1 tablespoon ginger, grated
- A pinch of salt and black pepper
- 1 and ½ cups veggie stock
- 1 cup tomato passata

Directions:

1. Set the instant pot on Sauté mode, add the oil, heat it up, add the meat and brown for 5 minutes. Add the rest of the ingredients, put the lid on and cook on High for 25 minutes. Release the pressure naturally for minutes, divide the mix between plates and serve.

Nutrition Info: calories 320, fat 6, fiber 0.9, carbs 4.4, protein 6

Mexican Chili Con Carne

Servings: 4
Cooking Time: 15 Mins
Ingredients:
- 2 tbsp olive oil
- 1 pound stewed beef meat, cubed
- 1 green bell pepper, chopped
- 2 red chilies, minced
- 1 yellow onion, chopped
- 2 garlic cloves, minced
- 1 tsp ground cumin
- 1 tsp oregano
- 1 tsp crushed red pepper
- 1 tsp smoked paprika
- Salt and black pepper to taste
- 1 (14-oz) can tomatoes, chopped
- 2 cups green beans, chopped

Directions:

1. Set your IP to Sauté and heat the oil. Place the beef and cook for 5-6 minutes, until no longer pink. Add in green bell pepper, onion, and garlic, cook for another 2 minutes. Stir in the remaining ingredients except for the crushed red pepper. Pour in cup of water. Seal the lid, select Manual on High, and cook for 20 minutes. When done, perform a natural pressure release. Serve topped with crushed red pepper warm.

Nutrition Info: Calories 300, Protein 26g, Net Carbs 2.3g, Fat 17g

Za'atar-rubbed Pork Shank

Servings: 6
Cooking Time: 45 Minutes
Ingredients:
- 1 ½ pounds pork shank

- Seasoned salt and ground black pepper, to taste
- 2 tablespoons za'atar
- 1 tablespoon olive oil
- 1 medium-sized leek, sliced
- 2 garlic cloves, smashed
- 1 carrot, chopped
- 1 parsnip, chopped
- 1 celery with leaves, chopped
- 1 tablespoon dark soy sauce
- 1/2 teaspoon mustard powder
- 1 cup beef bone broth
- 1 tablespoon flaxseed meal

Directions:
1. Generously season the pork shank with salt and black pepper. Now, sprinkle with za'atar on all sides.
2. Press the "Sauté" button to heat up the Instant Pot. Heat the olive oil. Once hot, sear the pork shank for to 4 minute per side; reserve.
3. Now, sauté leeks in pan drippings for minutes.
4. After that, add the garlic, carrot parsnip, celery with leaves, soy sauce, mustard powder, and broth.
5. Add the pork shank back to the Instant Pot.
6. Secure the lid. Choose the "Meat/Stew" setting and cook for 35 minutes under High pressure. Once cooking is complete, use a natural pressure release; carefully remove the lid.
7. Mix flaxseed meal with 1 tablespoon of water. Add this slurry to the Instant Pot. Press the "Sauté" button again to thicken the cooking liquid. Serve warm.

Nutrition Info:
Per Serving: 328 Calories; 1g Fat; 9g Carbs; 6g Protein; 2.6g Sugars

Ground Pork Pizza Crust

Servings: 4
Cooking Time: 15 Minutes
Ingredients:
- ½ cup Cheddar cheese, shredded
- 1 cup ground pork
- 1 teaspoon Italian seasonings
- 1 tablespoon Psyllium husk
- 1 teaspoon olive oil
- 1 cup water, for cooking

Directions:
1. In the mixing bowl, mix up shredded cheese, ground pork, Italian seasonings, and Psyllium husk.
2. Line the round instant pot pan with baking paper and brush with olive oil.
3. Then put the ground pork mixture in the pan and flatten it in the shape of the pizza crust.

4. Pour water and insert the steamer rack in the instant pot.
5. Put the pan with pizza crust on the rack. Close and seal the lid.
6. Cook the meal on manual mode (high pressure) for 15 minutes. Make a quick pressure release.

Nutrition Info:

Per Serving: calories 324, fat 5, fiber 7, carbs 8.8, protein 6

Beef Gumbo

Servings: 4
Cooking Time: 15 Minutes
Ingredients:
- 1 tbsp olive oil
- 1 lb. chuck roast, cubed
- Salt and black pepper to taste
- 2 large red bell peppers, deseeded and diced
- 1 large red onion, chopped
- 2 garlic cloves, minced
- 1 tbsp almond flour
- 2 cups beef broth
- 1 cup canned whole tomatoes
- 1 cup sliced okras
- ¼ cup cauliflower rice
- ¼ tsp dried oregano
- 1 bay leaf
- ½ tsp hot sauce
- 2 cups chicken broth

Directions:
1. Set the IP in Sauté mode and adjust to Medium heat.
2. Melt the olive oil in the inner pot, season the beef with salt and black pepper, and brown on both sides in the oil, 5 minutes.
3. Pour in the bell peppers, onion, garlic, almond flour, beef broth, tomatoes, okras, cauliflower rice, oregano, bay leaf, hot sauce, and chicken broth.
4. Lock the lid in place; select Manual mode on High Pressure and set the timer to 10 minutes.
5. Open the lid; adjust the taste with salt and black pepper.
6. Stir, dish the food and serve.

Nutrition Info:

Per Serving: : Calories 293 Fats 91g Carbs 7.85g Net Carbs 5.95g Protein 77g

Green Chile Pork Carnitas

Servings: 4
Cooking Time: 55 Mins
Ingredients:
- 4 lb Pork Shoulder, cut 3 pieces

- 3 tbsp Olive oil
- Salt and black pepper to taste
- 2 Jalapenos, seeded, minced
- 2 Green Bell peppers, seeded, chopped
- 2 Poblano Peppers, seeded, minced
- 1 ½ lb Tomatillos, husked, quartered
- 4 cloves Garlic, peeled
- 2 medium Red Onions, chopped
- 2 tsp Cumin Powder
- 2 tsp Dried Oregano
- 2 ½ cups Pork Broth
- 3 Bay Leaves
- Toppings:
- Red Onion, chopped
- Queso Fresco
- Cilantro, roughly chopped

Directions:

1. Season the pork with pepper and salt. Heat oil on Sauté, and brown pork on all sides for 6 minutes. Add bell pepper, peppers, tomatillo, onion, cumin, garlic, oregano, bay leaves and broth.
2. Stir, close the lid, secure the pressure valve and select Manual mode on High Pressure for 10 minutes. Once done, do a natural pressure release for 15 minutes.
3. Remove the meat from the pot, shred it in a plate; set aside. Puree the remaining ingredients in the pot using a stick blender. Add the pork back. Set on Sauté and simmer for 5 minutes. Stir twice and serve in keto tacos with the toppings.

Nutrition Info: Calories 690, Protein 27g, Net Carbs 1g, Fat 48g

Rosemary Barbecue Pork Chops

Servings: 2

Cooking Time: 18 Minutes

Ingredients:

- 2 pork chops
- 1 teaspoon dried rosemary
- 1 teaspoon avocado oil
- ½ teaspoon salt
- 1 tablespoon BBQ sauce
- 1 tablespoon cream cheese

Directions:

1. Mix up together dried rosemary and avocado oil. Rub the pork chops with rosemary mixture and leave for minutes to marinate. After this, place them in the instant pot and cook on sauté mode for 4 minutes from each side. Then add BBQ sauce, cream cheese, and salt. Close the lid and cook the pork chops for 10 minutes on sauté mode.

Nutrition Info: calories 290, fat 22, fiber 0.4, carbs 3.5, protein 4

Traditional Greek Youvarlakia

Servings: 4
Cooking Time: 30 Minutes
Ingredients:

- 1 pound ground pork
- 1/2 cup green onions, chopped
- 1 teaspoon garlic paste
- 2 tablespoons parsley, finely chopped
- 1 tablespoon cilantro, finely chopped
- 1 teaspoon basil
- 1 teaspoon dill
- 1 egg white
- Sea salt, to taste
- 1/2 teaspoon ground black pepper
- 1/2 teaspoon cayenne pepper
- 1 tablespoon olive oil
- 4 cups beef bone broth
- 1 tablespoon butter
- 1/2 cup feta cheese, sliced
- Avgolemono Sauce:
- 2 eggs
- 3 tablespoons freshly squeezed lemon juice

Directions:

1. In a mixing bowl, thoroughly combine ground pork, green onions, garlic paste, parsley, cilantro, basil, dill, egg white, salt, black pepper, and cayenne pepper. Roll the mixture into meatballs.
2. Press the "Sauté" button to heat up the Instant Pot. Once hot, add the oil; sear your meatballs until no longer pink in center.
3. Add broth and butter. Secure the lid. Choose the "Soup/Broth" setting and cook for 20 minutes at High pressure. Once cooking is complete, use a quick pressure release; carefully remove the lid.
4. In a small mixing dish, whisk two eggs with lemon juice. Add Avgolemono sauce to the hot soup. Press the "Sauté" button and let it simmer for a couple of minutes more or until heated through.
5. Serve garnished with feta cheese. Enjoy!

Nutrition Info:
Per Serving: 525 Calories; 5g Fat; 3.9g Carbs; 40g Protein; 1.8g Sugars

Tunisian Lamb Stew

Servings: 4
Cooking Time: 40 Minutes
Ingredients:

- 2 tbsp olive oil
- 1 lb. lamb shoulder, cubed
- 1 medium red onion, thinly sliced
- 8 garlic cloves, thickly sliced
- 2-3 tsp ras-el-hanout
- 1 tbsp fresh rosemary leaves
- 1/3 cup fresh thyme leaves
- 1 tsp turmeric
- 1 tsp red chili flakes
- 1 cup freshly chopped parsley + a little extra for garnishing
- 2 large tomatoes, roughly chopped
- 2 large red bell peppers, peeled and cut into thick strips
- 2 cups vegetable stock
- Salt to taste

Directions:
1. Set the IP in Sauté mode and adjust to Medium heat.
2. Heat the olive oil in the inner pot and cook the lamb until brown on the outside, 6 to 7 minutes.
3. Stir in the onion, garlic, and cook until softened, minutes.
4. Stir in the ras el hanout, rosemary, thyme, turmeric, red chili flakes, and parsley. Cook until fragrant, 3 minutes.
5. Mix in the tomatoes, bell peppers, vegetable stock, and salt.
6. Lock the lid in place; select Manual mode on High Pressure and set the timer to 20 minutes.
7. After cooking, perform natural pressure release for 10 minutes, then a quick pressure release to let out the remaining steam, and open the lid.
8. Taste the stew and adjust the taste with salt.
9. Spoon the food into serving bowls, garnish with parsley, and serve.

Nutrition Info:
Per Serving: : Calories 817 Fats 89g Carbs 48g Net Carbs 7.78g Protein 81g

Chili Fried Steak With Toasted Cashews & Sautéed Spinach

Servings: 4
Cooking Time: 25 Mins
Ingredients:
- 3 tbsp. extra virgin olive oil or canola oil
- 1 pound sliced lean beef
- 2 tablespoons apple cider vinegar
- 2 teaspoon fish sauce
- 2 teaspoons red curry paste
- 1 cup green capsicum, diced
- 24 toasted cashews

- 1 teaspoon arrowroot
- 1 teaspoon liquid Stevia
- ½ cup water
- 2 cups spinach
- 1 tablespoon butter
- 1 red onion, chopped

Directions:
1. Prepare spinach: melt butter in a skillet and sauté onion until fragrant; stir in kale for 3 Mins or until wilted.
2. Add oil to an instant pot set on manual high; add beef and fry until it is no longer pink inside. Stir in red curry paste and cook for a few more Mins.
3. Stir in Stevia, vinegar, fish sauce, capsicum and water. Lock lid and cook on high for 10 Mins. Naturally release the pressure.
4. Mix cooked arrowroot with water to make a paste; stir the paste into the sauce and cook on manual high until the sauce is thick. Stir in toasted cashews and serve with sautéed spinach.

Nutrition Info:
Per Serving: Calories: 346; Fat: 1g; Carbs: 7.9g; Protein: 4g

Beef Meatloaf With Chives

Servings: 4
Cooking Time: 10 Minutes
Ingredients:
- 10 oz ground beef
- 1 egg, beaten
- ½ teaspoon salt
- 1 teaspoon smoked paprika
- 3 tablespoons water
- 1 tablespoon chives, chopped
- 1 cup water, for cooking

Directions:
1. In the mixing bowl, mix up ground beef, egg, salt, smoked paprika, 3 tablespoons of water, and chives.
2. Take the loaf pan and place the meat mixture there.
3. Flatten it well to make the shape of the meatloaf.
4. Pour 1 cup of water in the instant pot.
5. Insert the trivet in the instant pot and place the meatloaf pan on it.
6. Cook the meal on High pressure (QPR) for 10 minutes.

Nutrition Info:
Per Serving: calories 149, fat 5.6, fiber 0.2, carbs 0.4, protein 23

Spicy Beef Tortillas

Servings: 4
Cooking Time: 38 Minutes

Ingredients:
- 1 tbsp olive oil
- 1 lb. beef stew meat, cut into strips
- Salt and black pepper to taste
- 1 small white onion, chopped
- 3 garlic cloves, minced
- 1 tsp dried basil
- 2 tsp hot sauce
- ¼ cup beef broth
- 1 medium cucumber, thinly sliced
- 1 medium tomato, chopped
- 4 low-carb tortillas, warmed
- 1 cup Greek yogurt
- 1 tsp freshly chopped dill

Directions:
1. Set the IP in Sauté mode and adjust to Medium heat.
2. Heat the olive oil in the inner pot, season the beef with salt, black pepper, and cook until brown on the outside, 5 minutes. Transfer to a plate and set aside.
3. Add the onion, garlic, and sauté until softened and fragrant, minutes.
4. Return the beef to the inner pot, stir in the basil, hot sauce, and beef broth.
5. Lock the lid in place; select Manual mode on High Pressure and set the timer to 20 minutes.
6. After cooking, perform a natural pressure release for 10 minutes, then a quick pressure release to let out the remaining steam, and open the lid.
7. Stir the beef and spoon into a bowl. Mix in the tomatoes, cucumber, and spoon beef mixture onto the tortillas.
8. In a medium bowl, mix the Greek yogurt and dill.
9. Top the food with the yogurt mixture and serve.

Nutrition Info:
Per Serving: : Calories 237 Fats 11g Carbs 9.62g Net Carbs 8.52g Protein 06g

Indian-style Pork Vindaloo

Servings: 6
Cooking Time: 20 Minutes
Ingredients:
- 1 tablespoon olive oil
- 2 pounds pork loin, sliced into strips
- Sea salt, to taste
- 2 garlic cloves, minced
- 2 tablespoons coconut aminos
- 1 teaspoon oyster sauce
- 1 head cauliflower, broken into florets
- 1 teaspoon ground cardamom
- 3 cloves, whole

- 1/2 teaspoon mixed peppercorns
- 1 teaspoon brown mustard seeds
- 1 teaspoon cayenne pepper
- 1 cup water
- 2 tablespoons fresh cilantro, roughly chopped

Directions:
1. Press the "Sauté" button to heat up the Instant Pot. Heat the oil and sear the pork loin for 3 to 4 minutes, stirring periodically.
2. Add the remaining ingredients, except for fresh cilantro.
3. Secure the lid. Choose the "Meat/Stew" setting and cook for 12 minutes at High pressure.
4. Once cooking is complete, use a natural pressure release; carefully remove the lid. Serve topped with fresh cilantro. Bon appétit!

Nutrition Info:
Per Serving: 354 Calories; 3g Fat; 3.3g Total Carbs; 8g Protein; 1.1g Sugars

Mexican Style Pork Steaks

Servings: 6
Cooking Time: 15 Minutes
Ingredients:
- 1 tablespoon lard
- 2 pounds pork steaks
- 1 bell pepper, seeded and sliced
- 1/2 cup shallots, chopped
- 2 garlic cloves, minced
- 1 cup chicken bone broth, preferably homemade
- 1/4 cup water
- 1/4 cup dry red wine
- Salt, to taste
- 1/4 teaspoon freshly ground black pepper, or more to taste
- Pico de Gallo:
- 1 tomato, chopped
- 1 chili pepper, seeded and minced
- 1/2 cup red onion, chopped
- 2 garlic cloves, minced
- 1 tablespoon fresh cilantro, finely chopped
- Sea salt, to taste

Directions:
1. Press the "Sauté" button to heat up the Instant Pot. Melt the lard and sear the pork steaks about 4 minutes or until delicately browned on both sides.
2. Add bell pepper, shallot, garlic, chicken bone broth, water, wine, salt, and black pepper to the Instant Pot.
3. Secure the lid. Choose the "Manual" setting and cook for 8 minutes at High pressure. Once cooking is complete, use a quick pressure release; carefully remove the lid.

4. Meanwhile, make your Pico de Gallo by mixing all of the above ingredients. Refrigerate until ready to serve.
5. Serve warm pork steaks with well-chilled Pico de Gallo on the side. Bon appétit!

Nutrition Info:
Per Serving: 448 Calories; 2g Fat; 4.1g Total Carbs; 4g Protein; 1.8g Sugars

Creamy Lamb With Mustard Greens

Servings: 4
Cooking Time: 14 Minutes
Ingredients:
- 1 tbsp olive oil
- 1 lb. ground lamb
- ½ medium brown onion, diced
- 2 garlic cloves, minced
- 1 ½ tsp dried mixed herbs
- 2 tbsp almond flour
- 2 cups chicken stock
- 1 (15-oz) can tomato sauce
- ¾ cup heavy cream
- 1 cup mustard greens, chopped
- 6 oz cheddar cheese, shredded

Directions:
1. Set the IP in Sauté mode and adjust to Medium heat.
2. Heat the olive oil in the inner pot and cook the lamb until brown, 5 minutes.
3. Add the onion and cook until softened, minutes, then top with the garlic, mixed herbs; cook until fragrant, 1 minute.
4. Mix in the almond flour, chicken stock, and tomato sauce.
5. Lock the lid in place; select Manual mode on High Pressure and set the timer to minutes.
6. After cooking, perform a quick pressure release to let out the steam, and open the lid.
7. Set the IP in Sauté mode.
8. Stir in the heavy cream, mustard greens, salt, black pepper, and cheddar cheese. Cook until the cheese melts and greens wilt.
9. Dish the food and serve immediately.

Nutrition Info:
Per Serving: : Calories 964 Fats 09g Carbs 65g Net Carbs 8.75g Protein 185g

Pork And Celery Curry

Servings: 4
Cooking Time: 35 Minutes
Ingredients:
- 10 oz pork loin, chopped
- 1 cup celery stalk, chopped
- 1 teaspoon curry paste

- 1 tablespoon fresh cilantro, chopped
- ½ cup coconut cream
- ½ cup of water
- 1 teaspoon avocado oil
- ½ teaspoon fennel seeds

Directions:

1. Pour avocado oil in the instant pot. Add chopped pork loin and cook it on sauté mode for 6 minutes (for 3 minutes from each side). Then add fennel seeds and water. Cook the ingredients for 4 minutes more. Meanwhile, in the bowl whisk together curry paste with coconut cream. When the mixture is smooth, pour it over the meat. Add celery stalk and close the lid. Cook the meal on meat/stew mode for 20 minutes. Then stir it well and add cilantro. Cook the curry for 5 minutes more.

Nutrition Info: calories 146, fat 3, fiber 0.7, carbs 1.7, protein 6

Chipotle Braised Lamb Shank

Servings: 3
Cooking Time: 90 Mins
Ingredients:

- 3 Lamb Shanks
- Salt and black pepper to taste
- 2 tsp Garlic Powder
- 2 tsp Cumin Powder
- 1 tsp Coriander Powder
- 1 tsp Mustard Powder
- 2 tbsp Olive oil
- 1 cup Diced Tomatoes
- 1 cup Water
- 1 tbsp Chipotle in Adobo Sauce
- 2 cloves Garlic
- ¼ White Onion, sliced
- 3 Carrots, chopped
- Chopped Cilantro to garnish
- 1 Radish, sliced to garnish
- 1 Lime, cut in wedges

Directions:

1. Place the lamb on a flat surface and mix salt, pepper, oil and powders, in a bowl. Season the lamb with the mixture. Let sit for 30 minutes. Heat oil on Sauté, add the lamb and brown on all sides. Remove to a plate. In a blender, puree tomato, chipotle, salt and water, and pour the mixture in the pot.
2. Add garlic, onion, carrots, lamb shanks, and seal the lid, select Manual and cook on High Pressure for 45 minutes. Once ready, do a natural pressure release for 10 minutes. Remove the lamb onto a serving plate and select Sauté. Let the sauce thicken for 10 minutes.

Nutrition Info: Calories 255, Protein 23g, Net Carbs 1g, Fat 10g

Meatloaf With Eggs

Servings: 6
Cooking Time: 25 Minutes
Ingredients:

- 1 ½ cup ground pork
- 1 teaspoon chives
- 1 teaspoon salt
- ½ teaspoon ground black pepper
- 3 eggs, hard-boiled, peeled
- 2 tablespoons coconut flour
- 1 tablespoon avocado oil
- 1 cup water, for cooking

Directions:

1. Brush the loaf mold with avocado oil.
2. After this, in the mixing bowl, mix up ground pork, chives, salt, ground black pepper, and coconut flour.
3. Transfer the mixture in the loaf mold and flatten well.
4. Fill it with hard-boiled eggs.
5. Pour water and insert the steamer rack in the instant pot.
6. Put the meatloaf in the instant pot. Close and seal the lid.
7. Cook the meal on manual (high pressure) for 25 minutes. Allow the natural pressure release for 10 minutes.

Nutrition Info:
Per Serving: calories 277, fat 19, fiber 1.2, carbs 2.1, protein 3

Spicy Pork Carnitas

Servings: 10
Cooking Time: 55 Minutes
Ingredients:

- ¼ teaspoon cayenne
- 5 pounds boneless pork shoulder, cut into large pieces
- 1 cup water
- Salt and pepper
- 2 teaspoons ground cumin
- 1 tablespoon chili powder

Directions:

1. Combine the chili powder, cumin, and cayenne in a small bowl then rub the mixture into the pork.
2. Place the pork in the Instant Pot, then pour in the water.
3. Close and lock the lid, then press the Manual button and adjust the timer to 40 minutes.
4. When the timer goes off, let the pressure vent for 15 minutes then do a Quick Release by pressing Cancel and switching the steam valve to "venting."
5. When the pot has depressurized, open the lid.

6. Shred the pork and season with salt and pepper then serve hot.

Nutrition Info: calories 330 fat 8g ,protein 5g ,carbs 2g ,fiber 0.5g ,net carbs 1.5g

Country-style Pork Loin Ribs

Servings: 6
Cooking Time: 25 Minutes
Ingredients:

- 2 pounds country-style pork loin ribs, bone-in
- Coarse salt and ground black pepper, to taste
- 1 tablespoon lard, at room temperature
- 1 teaspoon chili powder
- 1 teaspoon porcini powder
- 1/3 cup champagne
- 1 cup water
- 1 celery with leaves, diced
- 1 parsnip, quartered
- 1 brown onion, chopped
- 2 garlic cloves, crushed
- 1 teaspoon liquid smoke
- 1 tablespoon coconut aminos

Directions:

1. Generously season the pork ribs with the salt and black pepper.
2. Press the "Sauté" button to heat up the Instant Pot. Melt the lard and sear the pork ribs for to 3 minutes on each side.
3. Add the remaining ingredients. Secure the lid. Choose the "Meat/Stew" setting and cook for 20 minutes at High pressure.
4. Once cooking is complete, use a natural pressure release; carefully remove the lid. Serve with favorite keto sides. Enjoy!

Nutrition Info:
Per Serving: 335 Calories; 1g Fat; 4.7g Carbs; 9g Protein; 2g Sugars

Pork Sausage Cassoulet

Servings: 8)
Cooking Time: 10 Mins
Ingredients:

- 2 tbsp white wine
- 8 pork sausages
- 1 cup green beans, chopped
- 1 red bell pepper, chopped
- 2 garlic cloves, minced
- 1 onion, chopped
- 1 cup canned tomatoes, chopped
- 1 cup vegetable broth

319

- ½ tsp dried oregano

Directions:
1. Set your IP to Sauté and heat the olive oil. Cook the sausages for 8 minutes until golden all over. Add in green beans, bell pepper, onion, tomatoes, and garlic and cook for 3 more minutes. Pour in the remaining ingredients. Seal the lid, select Manual on High, and cook for 8 minutes. When done, perform a quick pressure release. Serve warm.

Nutrition Info: Calories 200, Protein 12g, Net Carbs 6.5g, Fat 12g

Shredded Mexican Beef

Servings: 6
Cooking Time: 23 Mins
Ingredients:
- 2 pounds Chuck Roast
- 1 tsp Chili Powder
- ½ tsp Smoked Paprika
- ½ tsp Cumin
- ¼ cup Butter
- 1 ½ cups canned diced Tomatoes
- 1 cup Beef Broth
- Salt and black pepper to taste
- ½ tsp Garlic Powder

Directions:
1. Melt butter on Sauté, add the beef and sear on all sides. Remove to a plate.
2. Place the tomatoes and all of the spices in the pot and cook for minutes. Pour in broth and stir to combine. Return the beef to the pot. Close the lid on and turn it clockwise to seal.
3. Press Manual and set the cooking time to 20 minutes on High pressure. When ready, press Cancel and release the pressure quickly. Grab two forks and shred the beef inside the pot.

Nutrition Info: Calories 265, Protein 32g, Net Carbs 1g, Fat 15g

Pot Roast

Servings: 4
Cooking Time: 35 Mins
Ingredients:
- 2 lb Beef Chuck Roast
- 3 tbsp Olive oil, divided into 2
- Salt to taste
- 1 cup Beef Broth
- 1 packet Onion Soup Mix
- 1 cup chopped Broccoli
- 2 Red Bell pepper, seeded and quartered
- 1 Yellow Onion, quartered

Directions:

1. Season the chuck roast with salt and set aside. Turn on the Instant Pot, open the lid, and select Sauté mode. Add the olive oil, once heated add the chuck roast and sear for 5 minutes on each side.Then, add the beef broth to pot.
2. In a zipper bag add the broccoli, onions, bell peppers, the remaining olive oil, and onion soup. Close the bag and shake the mixture to coat the vegetables well. Use tongs to remove the vegetables into the pot and stir with a spoon.
3. Seal the lid,select Meat/Stew on High for 25 minutes. Once ready, do a quick pressure release, and open the pot. Remove the Beef onto a cutting board, let cool slightly, and then slice it. Plate and serve with the vegetables and a drizzle of the sauce in the pot.

Nutrition Info: Calories 142, Protein 2g, Net Carbs 0g, Fat 3.8g

Ground Beef With Flax Seeds

Servings: 4
Cooking Time: 30 Mins
Ingredients:
- 1 ½ lb ground Beef
- 1 package Sausage
- 2 tsp dried, chopped Onion
- 1 tsp Garlic powder
- 1 tsp dried Basil
- 1 tsp dried Parsley
- ½ cup Flax seed meal
- ½ tsp Salt
- 1 tsp ground fennel
- 1 cup dried Tomatoes, sliced
- 2 Eggs, beaten
- 1 tsp Coconut oil

Directions:
1. In a deep bowl, mix onion, garlic powder, dried basil, flax seed meal, salt, and fennel.
2. Squeeze the sausage out of any casings and place in the bowl; cut in very small pieces. Place the meat in the same bowl and mix the ingredients with hands. Shape the meat into the form of two loaves. Heat a teaspoon of coconut oil on Sauté.
3. Transfer the meatloaves, brown for a few minutes. Add half cup of water, lower the trivet, and place the meatloaf on top. Seal the lid, press Meat/Stew and cook on High pressure for minutes. When ready, do a quick pressure release.

Nutrition Info: Calories 487, Protein 2g, Net Carbs 3.1g, Fat 4g

Cilantro Pork Shoulder

Servings: 4
Cooking Time: 85 Minutes
Ingredients:
- 1-pound pork shoulder, boneless
- ¼ cup fresh cilantro, chopped

- 1 cup of water
- 1 teaspoon salt
- 1 teaspoon coconut oil
- ½ teaspoon mustard seeds

Directions:
1. Pour water in the instant pot.
2. Add pork shoulder, fresh cilantro, salt, coconut oil, and mustard seeds.
3. Close and seal the lid. Cook the meat on high pressure (manual mode) for 85 minutes.
4. Then make a quick pressure release and open the lid.
5. The cooked meat has to be served with the remaining liquid from the instant pot.

Nutrition Info:
Per Serving: calories 343, fat 5, fiber 0.1, carbs 0.2, protein 5

Low Carb Beef & Sweet Potato Dish

Servings: 6
Cooking Time: 25 Mins
Ingredients:
- 4 tablespoons olive oil
- 2 pounds ground beef
- 3 cups beef stock
- 2 sweet potatoes, peeled and diced
- 1 clove garlic, minced
- 1 onion, diced
- 1 (14-oz) can petite minced tomatoes
- 1 (14-oz) can tomato sauce
- 3-4 tbsp. chili powder
- ¼ tsp. oregano
- 2 tsp. salt
- ½ tsp. black pepper
- Cilantro, optional, for garnish

Directions:
1. Brown the beef in a pan over medium heat; drain excess fat and then transfer it to an instant pot. Stir in the remaining ingredients and lock lid; cook on high for 25 Mins and then release pressure naturally. Garnish with cilantro and serve warm.

Nutrition Info:
Per Serving: Calories: 240; Total Fat: 6 g; Carbs: 12 g; Dietary Fiber: 3.5 g; Sugars: 4.2 g; Protein: 3 g; Cholesterol: 81 mg; Sodium: 1201 mg

Ruby Port-braised Pork

Servings: 4
Cooking Time: 20 Minutes
Ingredients:
- 1 tablespoon grapeseed oil

- 1 ½ pounds pork tenderloins
- Sea salt and ground pepper, to your liking
- 1 teaspoon roasted garlic paste
- 1/2 cup ruby port
- 1 cup vegetable stock
- 1/2 cup scallions, chopped
- 1/4 teaspoon dried dill weed
- 1/2 teaspoon dried basil
- 1/4 teaspoon dried oregano
- 2 cups mustard greens

Directions:
1. Press the "Sauté" button to heat up the Instant Pot. Heat the grapeseed oil until sizzling. Once hot, cook the pork until delicately browned on both sides.
2. Season with the salt and black pepper; add garlic paste, ruby port, vegetable stock, scallions, dill, basil, and oregano.
3. Secure the lid. Choose "Manual" mode and High pressure; cook for 12 minutes. Once cooking is complete, use a quick pressure release; carefully remove the lid.
4. Lastly, add mustard greens; cover your Instant Pot and let it sit until your greens are wilted. Taste, adjust the seasonings, and serve warm. Bon appétit!

Nutrition Info:
Per Serving: 320 Calories; 10g Fat; 3.4g Total Carbs; 9g Protein; 0.9g Sugars

Chili Hot Dog Bake

Servings: 6
Cooking Time: 55 Minutes
Ingredients:
- 1 tablespoon olive oil
- 1 ½ pounds beef chuck, ground for chili
- Salt and ground black pepper, to taste
- 2 ripe tomatoes, chopped
- 1 onion, chopped
- 2 ounces tomato sauce
- 2 garlic cloves, pressed
- 1 chili pepper, minced
- 1 teaspoon smoked paprika
- 1/2 cup lager-style beer
- 1/2 cup water
- 6 beef hot dogs, sliced lengthwise
- 1 ½ cups Mexican cheese blend, shredded

Directions:
1. Press the "Sauté" button to heat up the Instant Pot. Heat the olive oil and cook the beef until no longer pink. Season with salt and black pepper to taste.

2. Transfer the beef to a mixing dish. Then, add tomatoes, onion, tomato sauce, garlic, chili pepper, and smoked paprika to the mixing dish.
3. Lay hot dogs flat on the bottom of a lightly greased baking dish. Cover with the chili mixture. Pour in the beer and water.
4. Wipe down the Instant Pot with a damp cloth. Add 1 ½ cups of water and a metal rack to the Instant Pot.
5. Lower the baking dish onto the metal rack.
6. Secure the lid. Choose "Meat/Stew" mode and High pressure; cook for 35 minutes. Once cooking is complete, use a quick pressure release; carefully remove the lid.
7. Top with the shredded cheese and seal the lid. Let it sit for 5 minutes or until the cheese is completely melted.
8. Let the chili hot dog bake sit for 10 minutes before slicing and serving. Bon appétit!

Nutrition Info:
Per Serving: 452 Calories; 5g Fat; 7.1g Carbs; 6g Protein; 2.9g Sugars

Pork In Cream Of Mushroom Soup

Servings: 4
Cooking Time: 20 Minutes
Ingredients:
- 8 slices bacon, chopped
- 1 medium yellow onion, chopped
- 4 boneless pork chops
- 1 (21 oz) can cream of mushroom soup
- ½ cup almond milk
- Salt and black pepper to taste
- ¾ tsp dried rosemary

Directions:
1. Set the IP in Sauté mode and adjust to Medium heat.
2. Add the bacon to the inner pot and cook until brown and crispy, 5 minutes. Plate and set aside.
3. Combine the remaining ingredients in the inner pot.
4. Lock the lid in place; select Manual mode on High Pressure and set the timer to 5 minutes.
5. Once done cooking, perform natural pressure release for 10 minutes, then a quick pressure release until remaining steam is out; open the lid.
6. Mix in the bacon and dish the soup.
7. Serve warm.

Nutrition Info:
Per Serving: : Calories 675 Fats 76g Carbs 73g Net Carbs 5.93g Protein 59g

Attractive Pork Ribs

Servings: 5
Cooking Time: 3 Hours And 35 Minutes
Ingredients:

- 2 lbs. spare ribs
- 1 teaspoon salt
- 1 teaspoon pepper
- 1 teaspoon garlic powder
- 1 teaspoon onion powder
- 1 teaspoon smoked paprika
- 1 teaspoon dried oregano
- ½ cup tomato puree
- 2 tablespoons olive oil
- 2 tablespoons fresh lemon juice
- 2 tablespoons sesame oil

Directions:

1. In a large dish mix the lemon juice, salt, pepper, garlic powder, onion powder, smoked paprika, olive oil, dried oregano, and tomato puree.
2. Add the spare ribs to the dish and marinate for at least 3 hours.
3. Remove the spare ribs from the marinade. Then press the "Sauté" button and heat the sesame oil. Add the spare ribs and brown them for 2 minutes per side.
4. Secure the lid. Choose the "Meat/Stew" setting and cook for 25 minutes under High pressure. When cooking is complete, use a natural pressure release and carefully remove the lid.
5. Serve warm with your favorite Keto salad. Bon appetite!

Nutrition Info:
Per Serving: 527 Calories; 2g Fat; 5g Carbs; 9g Protein; 1.9g Sugars

Sloppy Joes With Homemade Oopsies

Servings: 4
Cooking Time: 35 Minutes
Ingredients:

- Sloppy Joes
- 1 tablespoon olive oil
- 1 pound lean ground pork
- 1/2 yellow onion, chopped
- 2 cloves garlic, minced
- 1 tomato, puréed
- 1 teaspoon stone ground mustard
- 1 tablespoon coconut aminos
- 1 cup roasted vegetable broth
- Sea salt and ground black pepper, to taste
- Oopsies:
- 2 eggs, separated yolks and whites
- 1/4 teaspoon sea salt
- 3 ounces cream cheese
- 1/4 teaspoon baking powder

Directions:
1. Press the "Sauté" button to heat up the Instant Pot. Heat the oil until sizzling. Brown the ground pork for 2 to 3 minutes, crumbling with a fork.
2. Add the other ingredients for Sloppy Joes and stir to combine well.
3. Secure the lid. Choose the "Manual" setting and cook for 5 minutes under High pressure. Once cooking is complete, use a quick pressure release; carefully remove the lid.
4. To make your oopsies, beat the egg whites together with salt until very firm peaks form.
5. In another bowl, thoroughly combine the egg yolks with cream cheese. Now, add the baking powder and stir well.
6. Next, fold the egg white mixture into the egg yolk mixture. Divide the mixture into oopsies and transfer them to a silicon sheet.
7. Bake in the preheated oven at 290 degrees F for about 23 minutes. Serve Sloppy Joes between 2 oopsies and enjoy!

Nutrition Info:
Per Serving: 524 Calories; 45g Fat; 5.5g Carbs; 8g Protein; 1.9g Sugars

Light Beef Salad

Servings: 5
Cooking Time: 30 Minutes
Ingredients:
- 1 cup vegetable broth
- 1 lb. sirloin steak, cut into small cubes
- 1/2 cup green onions, chopped
- 1 ½ cucumber, thinly sliced
- 1 ½ cup red cabbage, sliced
- 2 tablespoons fresh cilantro, chopped
- 1 ½ cup bok choy cabbage, sliced
- 2 teaspoons sesame seeds
- 2 tablespoons fresh lemon juice
- 2 tablespoon canola oil
- 2 tablespoons extra-virgin olive oil

Directions:
1. Press the "Sauté" button to preheat your Instant Pot. Heat the canola oil and add the beef cubes. Cook for 2 minutes and stir in the vegetable broth.
2. Secure the lid. Choose "Meat/Stew" mode and High pressure; cook for minutes. When cooking is complete, use a natural pressure release and carefully remove the lid.
3. Leave the beef to cool and transfer to a large salad bowl.
4. Then, add the cucumber, green onion, red cabbage, bok choy cabbage, sesame seeds, and fresh cilantro. Drizzle the salad with lemon juice and olive oil.
5. Mix well and serve. Bon appétit!

Nutrition Info:
Per Serving: 236 Calories; 6g Fat; 4.3g Carbs; 4g Protein; 1.9g Sugars

Keto Beef Chili

Servings: 4
Cooking Time: 23 Mins
Ingredients:

- 1 pound ground Beef
- 2 (14-ounce) cans of diced Tomatoes
- 3 cups Cauliflower Rice
- 1 tbsp Chili Powder
- ½ cup Beef Broth
- 1 Onion, diced
- 1 tsp Cumin
- 1 tbsp Worcestershire sauce
- 1 tsp Garlic Powder
- ½ tsp Smoked Paprika
- Salt and black pepper to taste
- 1 tbsp Olive oil

Directions:

1. Set on Sauté and heat the oil. Add the beef and cook for a few minutes, until browned. Dump all remaining ingredients in the pot. Give the mixture a good stir and seal the lid.
2. Select Meat/Stew and cook for 15 minutes on High pressure. When it goes off, press Cancel and allow for a natural pressure release, for 10 minutes. Serve with keto bread and enjoy.

Nutrition Info: Calories 283, Protein 30g, Net Carbs 3.5g, Fat 24g

Hot Shredded Pork

Servings: 4
Cooking Time: 30 Mins
Ingredients:

- 2 Pork fillets, boiled, shredded
- ½ tbsp Garlic paste
- Salt and black pepper to taste
- ½ tbsp Soy sauce
- 2 tbsp Lemon juice
- 2 tbsp Barbecue sauce
- ½ cup Chili Garlic sauce
- 2 tbsp Vinegar
- ½ tbsp Chili powder
- 2 tbsp Olive oil

Directions:

1. Heat oil on Sauté, and cook garlic for minute. Add the pork and brown for 10 minutes per side. Add soy sauce, chili sauce, vinegar, barbecue sauce, salt, and chili powder and cook for another 5 minutes. Transfer to a serving dish and drizzle lemon juice.

Nutrition Info: Calories 351, Protein 1g, Net Carbs 5.1g, Fat 9g

Ground Beef Chili With Kale

Servings: 6
Cooking Time: 15 Minutes
Ingredients:

- 2 tablespoons olive oil
- 1 ½ pounds ground chuck
- 1 green bell pepper, chopped
- 1 red bell pepper, chopped
- 2 red chilies, minced
- 1 red onion
- 2 garlic cloves, smashed
- 1 teaspoon cumin
- 1 teaspoon Mexican oregano
- 1 teaspoon cayenne pepper
- 1 teaspoon smoked paprika
- Salt and freshly ground black pepper, to taste
- 1 ½ cups puréed tomatoes
- 4 cups kale, fresh

Directions:

1. Press the "Sauté" button to heat up the Instant Pot. Then, heat the oil; once hot, cook the ground chuck for 2 minutes, crumbling it with a fork or a wide spatula.
2. Add the pepper, onions, and garlic; cook an additional minutes or until fragrant. Stir in the remaining ingredients, minus kale leaves.
3. Choose the "Manual" setting and cook for 6 minutes at High pressure. Once cooking is complete, use a natural pressure release; carefully remove the lid.
4. Add kale, cover with the lid and allow the kale leaves to wilt completely. Bon appétit!

Nutrition Info:
Per Serving: 238 Calories; 6g Fat; 6g Carbs; 8g Protein; 2.8g Sugars

Beef Endive Stir-fry

Servings: 4
Cooking Time: 12 Minutes
Ingredients:

- 1 tbsp olive oil
- 1 lb. ground beef
- Salt and black pepper to taste
- 1 tbsp freshly grated ginger
- 3 garlic cloves, minced
- 2 medium endives, shredded
- 1 medium red bell pepper, deseeded and chopped
- 2 tbsp coconut aminos
- 1 tbsp hot sauce

- ½ tbsp sugar-free maple syrup
- 2 tbsp cashew nuts
- 1 tsp toasted sesame seeds, for garnishing

Directions:
1. Set the IP in Sauté mode and adjust to Medium heat.
2. Heat the olive oil in the inner pot; add the beef, season with salt, black pepper, ginger, garlic, and cook until brown, 5 minutes.
3. Add the endive, bell pepper, and stir-fry until softened, 5 minutes.
4. Meanwhile, in a medium bowl, combine coconut aminos, hot sauce and maple syrup. Pour over the stir-fry, add the cashew nuts, and cook for 1 to 2 minutes.
5. Dish the food, garnish with sesame seeds and serve warm.

Nutrition Info:

Per Serving: : Calories 352 Fats 84g Carbs 6.03g Net Carbs 4.73g Protein 77g

Instant Pot Bbq Pork Ribs

Servings: 5
Cooking Time: 1 Hour 30 Mins
Ingredients:
- 4 tablespoons olive oil
- 2 ½ pounds pork ribs
- 1 cup barbeque sauce
- 1 tablespoon garlic powder
- 2 tablespoons sea salt
- 1 teaspoon ground black pepper
- 5 cups steamed broccoli

Directions:
1. Add oil to an instant pot and set on sauté mode, but not smoking. Add in the pork ribs and cook until seared on both sides. Add in enough water to cover the pork ribs and season with salt, garlic powder and pepper. Lock lid and cook on meat/stew for 20 Mins and the quick release the pressure.
2. Preheat your oven to 3 degrees.
3. Transfer the ribs to a baking dish and pour over the barbecue sauce. Cover with foil and bake for about 1 hour Mins. Remove and let rest for at least 10 Mins before serving. Serve with steamed broccoli. Enjoy!

Nutrition Info:

Per Serving: Calories: 556; Fat: 9g; Carbs: 6.4g; Protein: 3g

Ground Beef Okra

Servings: 4
Cooking Time: 20 Minutes
Ingredients:
- 1 cup okra, sliced
- 7 oz ground beef

- 1 teaspoon salt
- 1 cup of water
- 1 tablespoon avocado oil
- 1 teaspoon ground black pepper

Directions:
1. Heat up avocado oil in the instant pot and add ground beef.
2. Sprinkle it with salt and ground black pepper and saute for 10 minutes.
3. After this, add sliced okra and stir the mixture well.
4. Cook the meal on saute mode for 10 minutes.

Nutrition Info:
Per Serving: calories 108, fat 3.6, fiber 1.1, carbs 2.4, protein 6

Thai Pork Salad

Servings: 4
Cooking Time: 35 Minutes
Ingredients:
- 1 pound pork loin roast
- 1/2 cup broth, preferably homemade
- 1/2 cup water
- 1/2 head cabbage, shredded
- 2 celery with leaves, chopped
- 4 spring onions, chopped
- 1 cup baby spinach
- 1 cup arugula
- 1 red chili, deseeded and finely chopped
- 2 teaspoons each sesame oil
- 1 teaspoon Thai fish sauce
- 2 teaspoons tamari sauce
- Fresh juice of 1 lemon

Directions:
1. Add pork loin roast, broth and water to the Instant Pot that is previously greased with a nonstick cooking spray.
2. Secure the lid. Choose the "Meat/Stew" setting and cook for 30 minutes at High pressure. Once cooking is complete, use a natural pressure release; carefully remove the lid.
3. Allow the pork loin roast to cool completely. Shred the meat and transfer to a salad bowl.
4. Add the cabbage, celery, green onions, spinach, arugula, and chili.
5. Now, make the dressing by mixing sesame oil with Thai fish sauce, tamari sauce, and lemon juice. Whisk to combine well and dress your salad. Serve well-chilled. Bon appétit!

Nutrition Info:
Per Serving: 279 Calories; 7g Fat; 5.9g Total Carbs; 5g Protein; 2.9g Sugars

Beef And Mushroom Rice

Servings: 4

Cooking Time: 30 Minutes

Ingredients:

- 1 and ½ cups beef stock
- 1 tablespoon olive oil
- 1 and ½ pound beef stew meat, cubed
- 1 cup cauliflower rice
- 1 cup white mushrooms, halved
- 2 spring onions, chopped
- 2 teaspoons sweet paprika
- ¼ cup coconut cream
- 1 tablespoon chives, chopped
- A pinch of salt and black pepper

Directions:

1. Set your instant pot on sauté mode, add the oil, heat it up, add the spring onions, mushrooms and the beef and brown for 5 minutes Add the rest of the ingredients except the chives, put the lid on and cook on High for 25 minutes. Release the pressure naturally for minutes, divide the mix between plates and serve with the chives sprinkled on top.

Nutrition Info: calories 336, fat 4, fiber 0.8, carbs 1.7, protein 2

Traditional Albóndigas Sinaloenses

Servings: 6

Cooking Time: 15 Minutes

Ingredients:

- 1 pound ground pork
- 1/2 pound Italian sausage, crumbled
- 2 tablespoons yellow onion, finely chopped
- 2 garlic cloves, finely minced
- 1/4 teaspoon fresh ginger, grated
- 1/2 teaspoon dried oregano
- 1 sprig fresh mint, finely minced
- 1/2 teaspoon ground cumin
- Seasoned salt and ground black pepper, to taste
- 1 tablespoon olive oil
- 1/2 cup yellow onions, finely chopped
- 2 chipotle chilies in adobo
- 2 tomatoes, pureed
- 2 tablespoons tomato passata
- 1 cup broth, preferably homemade

Directions:

1. In a mixing bowl, thoroughly combine the pork, sausage, 2 tablespoons yellow onion, garlic, ginger, oregano, mint, cumin, salt, and black pepper.
2. Roll the mixture into meatballs and reserve.

3. Press the "Sauté" button to heat up the Instant Pot. Heat the olive oil and cook the meatballs for to 4 minutes, stirring continuously.
4. Stir in 1/2 cup of yellow onions chilies in adobo, tomatoes, passata and broth; afterwards, add reserved meatballs.
5. Secure the lid. Choose the "Manual" setting and cook for 6 minutes at High pressure. Once cooking is complete, use a quick pressure release; carefully remove the lid. Bon appétit!

Nutrition Info:

Per Serving: 408 Calories; 1g Fat; 4.7g Total Carbs; 5g Protein; 2.4g Sugars

Shredded Pork Stew

Servings: 2
Cooking Time: 35 Minutes
Ingredients:

- 16 oz pork chuck roast
- ½ teaspoon coriander
- ½ teaspoon salt
- 1 daikon, chopped
- 1 cup of water

Directions:

1. Put all ingredients in the instant pot. Close and seal the lid.
2. After this, set the "Meat" mode and cook the stew for 35 minutes.
3. When the stew is cooked, carefully shred the meat with the help of the fork.

Nutrition Info:

Per Serving: calories 533, fat 8, fiber 0.5, carbs 1, protein 6

Parmesan Pork Tenderloins

Servings: 4
Cooking Time: 35 Minutes
Ingredients:

- 12 oz pork tenderloin
- ½ white onion, diced
- 1 teaspoon ground black pepper
- ½ teaspoon ground nutmeg
- 1 teaspoon sesame oil
- ½ cup heavy cream
- 2 oz Parmesan, grated
- 1/3 cup water

Directions:

1. Preheat the instant pot on sauté mode for 4 minutes. Meanwhile, rub the pork tenderloin with ground black pepper and nutmeg. Then brush it with sesame oil from each side. Place the meat in the instant pot and cook it on sauté mode for 3 minutes from both sides. After this, add water and bring it to the boil (appx.5 minutes). Then combine together cream with Parmesan. Pour the liquid over the meat and close the lid. Cook the meat on manual mode

(high pressure) for 20 minutes. When the time is over, make the quick pressure release and open the lid. Slice the pork tenderloin and sprinkle it with cheese sauce.

Nutrition Info: calories 237, fat 8, fiber 0.5, carbs 2.7, protein 4

Easy Pork Taco Frittata

Servings: 6

Cooking Time: 35 Minutes

Ingredients:

- 3 ounces Cottage cheese, at room temperature
- 1⁄4 cup double cream
- 2 eggs
- 1 teaspoon taco seasoning
- 6 ounces Cotija cheese, crumbled
- 3/4 pound ground pork
- 1 tablespoon taco seasoning
- 1⁄2 cup tomatoes, puréed
- 3 ounces chopped green chilies
- 6 ounces Queso Manchego cheese, shredded

Directions:

1. Prepare your Instant Pot by adding ½ cups of water and a metal rack to the bottom of the inner pot.
2. In a mixing bowl, thoroughly combine Cottage cheese, double cream, eggs, and taco seasoning.
3. Lightly grease a casserole dish; spread the Cotija cheese over the bottom. Pour in the Cottage/ egg mixture as evenly as possible.
4. Lower the casserole dish onto the rack.
5. Secure the lid. Choose "Manual" mode and High pressure; cook for 20 minutes. Once cooking is complete, use a quick pressure release; carefully remove the lid.
6. In the meantime, heat a cast-iron skillet over a moderately high heat. Now, brown ground pork, crumbling it with a fork.
7. Add taco seasoning, tomato purée and green chilies. Spread this mixture over the prepared cheese crust.
8. Top with shredded Queso Manchego.
9. Secure the lid. Choose "Manual" mode and High pressure; cook for 10 minutes. Once cooking is complete, use a quick pressure release; carefully remove the lid. Serve and enjoy!

Nutrition Info:

Per Serving: 409 Calories; 6g Fat; 4.7g Total Carbs; 7g Protein; 2.7g Sugars

Garbure Gersoise Soup

Servings: 6

Cooking Time: 30 Minutes

Ingredients:

- 1 tablespoon grapeseed oil

- 2 pounds top chuck, trimmed, boneless and cubed
- 3 slices slab bacon, chopped
- 1/2 cup yellow onion, chopped
- 1 celery ribs, sliced
- 1 parsnip, sliced
- 4 teaspoons beef base
- 6 cups water
- 1/4 cup dry white wine
- 7 ounces tomato purée
- 1 head savoy cabbage
- Sea salt, to your liking
- 1 teaspoon dried juniper berries
- 1/2 teaspoon dried sage, crushed
- 1/2 teaspoon dried rosemary, leaves picked
- 1 teaspoon whole mixed peppercorns
- 2 sprigs parsley, roughly chopped

Directions:
1. Press the "Sauté" button to heat up the Instant Pot. Now, heat the oil; once hot, cook the chuck for 2 to 3 minutes on each side.
2. Add the remaining ingredients and stir to combine well.
3. Secure the lid. Choose "Meat/Stew" mode and High pressure; cook for 25 minutes. Once cooking is complete, use a quick pressure release; carefully remove the lid.
4. Serve in individual bowls garnished with some extra fresh parsley if desired. Bon appétit!

Nutrition Info:
Per Serving: 324 Calories; 9g Fat; 6.8g Carbs; 6g Protein; 1.9g Sugars

Parmesan Pork

Servings: 4
Cooking Time: 35 Minutes
Ingredients:
- 4 pork chops
- 1 teaspoon white pepper
- 1 teaspoon sesame oil
- ½ cup heavy cream
- 1 teaspoon dried basil
- 4 oz Parmesan, grated

Directions:
1. Brush the instant pot bowl with sesame oil from inside. Sprinkle pork chops with white pepper and dried basil and put in the instant pot. Then top the meat with Parmesan and heavy cream. Close the lid and cook it on manual mode (high pressure) for 35 minutes. When the time is over, allow the natural pressure release for minutes.

Nutrition Info: calories 410, fat 7, fiber 0.1, carbs 1.8, protein 5

Carnitas Pulled Pork

Servings: 5
Cooking Time: 45 Minutes
Ingredients:
- 1-pound pork shoulder, boneless
- ½ teaspoon minced garlic
- ½ teaspoon ground cumin
- 2 tablespoons butter
- 1 chili pepper, chopped
- ½ teaspoon lime zest, grated
- 1 ½ cup beef broth

Directions:
1. Put all ingredients in the instant pot.
2. Close and seal the lid.
3. Cook the pork for 45 minutes on manual mode (high pressure).
4. Then allow the natural pressure release for 10 minutes and open the lid.
5. Shred the cooked pork with the help of the forks and transfer in the bowl.
6. Add ½ part of all remaining liquid and stir the pulled pork.

Nutrition Info:
Per Serving: calories 319, fat 5, fiber 0.1, carbs 0.6, protein 7

Cheesy Bbq Pulled Pork

Servings: 4
Cooking Time: 40 Minutes
Ingredients:
- 1 tsp onion powder
- 2 tsp garlic powder
- ¼ tsp cayenne powder
- 2 tsp chili powder
- 1 tsp dry mustard
- Salt and freshly ground black pepper
- 1 tbsp swerve brown sugar
- 1 tbsp smoked paprika
- 1 ½ tsp cumin powder
- 2 tbsp olive oil
- 4 lbs. pork shoulder, cut into 2-inch pieces
- 1 cup unsweetened BBQ sauce
- 1 cup ketchup
- 2 tbsp Worcestershire sauce
- ½ cup chicken broth
- ½ cup grated cheddar cheese

Directions:

1. In a medium bowl, mix all the spices up to the olive oil.
2. Set the IP in Sauté mode and adjust to Medium heat.
3. Heat the olive oil in the inner pot, season the pork on all sides with the dry spices, and sear in the oil until golden brown, 10 minutes.
4. Pour in remaining ingredients except for the cheddar cheese.
5. Lock the lid in place; select Manual mode on High Pressure and set the timer to 20 minutes.
6. After cooking, do a natural pressure release for 10 minutes, then a quick pressure release to let out the steam, and open the lid.
7. Using two long forks, shred the pork into strands.
8. Set the IP in Sauté mode, mix in cheddar cheese, and allow melting.
9. Stir the food well and serve warm.

Nutrition Info:

Per Serving: : Calories 773 Fats 25g Carbs 37g Net Carbs 6.37g Protein 25g

Speedy Beef & Turnip Curry

Servings: 4

Cooking Time: 20 Mins

Ingredients:

- 2 tbsp olive oil
- 1 pound roast beef, cubed
- 1 jalapeño pepper, seeded and chopped
- 1 onion, diced
- 1 cup canned tomatoes
- Salt and black pepper to taste
- 2 tbsp fresh cilantro, chopped
- 1 tbsp coconut aminos
- 1 tbsp chili powder
- 2 tsp curry paste
- 2 tbsp fresh cilantro, chopped
- 2 cups turnips, sliced

Directions:

1. Set your IP to Sauté and heat the olive oil. Place the beef and brown for 3 minutes on each side. Add in the remaining ingredients, except the cilantro. Pour cup of water and stir.
2. Seal the lid, select Manual on High, and cook for minutes. Once ready, perform a natural pressure release. Ladle in serving bowls and garnish with cilantro to serve.

Nutrition Info: Calories 276, Protein 27g, Net Carbs 2.3g, Fat 14g

Spicy Tangy Pork Chops

Servings: 4

Cooking Time: 25 Minutes + 30 Minutes Marinating

Ingredients:

- 4 boneless pork chops
- 2 tbsp hot sauce

- 2 tbsp coconut oil
- 1 lemon, juiced
- 1 tbsp coconut aminos
- 1 ½ tsp sriracha sauce
- 2 tbsp olive oil
- 2/3 cup chicken broth

Directions:
1. Put the pork chops in a plastic zipper bag.
2. In a small bowl, mix the remaining ingredients up to the broth and pour over the pork. Massage the marinade onto the pork and sit in the refrigerator for 30 minutes.
3. Set the IP in Sauté mode and adjust to Medium heat.
4. Heat the olive oil in the inner pot, take pork out of fridge and marinade, and sear in oil on both sides until brown, 6 minutes. Pour in chicken broth and season with salt.
5. Lock the lid in place; select Manual mode on High Pressure and set the timer to 20 minutes.
6. After cooking, perform a natural pressure release for 5 minutes, then a quick pressure release to let out the remaining steam, and open the lid.
7. Remove the pork onto serving plates, baste with a little sauce, and serve warm.

Nutrition Info:
Per Serving: : Calories 361 Fats 93g Carbs 1.71g Net Carbs 1.41g Protein 7g

Hunter's Pork Roast

Servings: 6
Cooking Time: 40 Minutes
Ingredients:
- 2 tablespoons unsalted butter
- 2 pounds sirloin pork roast, cubed
- 8 ounces Cremini mushrooms, thinly sliced
- 2 garlic cloves, minced
- 1 heaping tablespoon fresh parsley, chopped
- 1/2 cup roasted vegetable broth
- 2/3 cup water
- 2 tablespoons dry white wine
- 1/2 teaspoon dried sage
- 1/2 teaspoon dried basil
- 1 teaspoon dried oregano
- Sea salt and ground black pepper, to taste
- 1 teaspoon cayenne pepper
- 1/3 cup Castelvetrano olives, pitted and halved

Directions:
1. Press the "Sauté" button to heat up the Instant Pot. Melt the butter and sear the pork about 3 minutes or until delicately browned on all sides; reserve.
2. In pan drippings, cook the mushrooms and garlic until tender and fragrant.

3. Add parsley, broth, water, wine, sage, basil, oregano, salt, black pepper, and cayenne pepper; gently stir to combine.
4. Secure the lid. Choose the "Meat/Stew" setting and cook for 35 minutes at High pressure.
5. Once cooking is complete, use a natural pressure release; carefully remove the lid. Serve garnished with Castelvetrano olives. Bon appétit!

Nutrition Info:
Per Serving: 310 Calories; 4g Fat; 2.1g Carbs; 5g Protein; 0.7g Sugars

Modern Beef Stew

Servings: 6
Cooking Time: 25 Minutes
Ingredients:
- 1 tablespoon tallow, room temperature
- 1 ½ pounds beef stew meat, cubed
- 2 slices bacon, chopped
- 1 parsnip, chopped
- 1 carrot, chopped
- 1 celery with leaves, chopped
- 1/2 cup leeks, chopped
- 2 cloves garlic, chopped
- 1 sprig thyme, chopped
- 1 sprig rosemary, chopped
- 2 bay leaves
- 3 cups water
- 1 teaspoon cayenne pepper
- 1/2 teaspoon Hungarian paprika
- Salt and ground black pepper, to taste
- 2 cups spinach, torn into pieces

Directions:
1. Press the "Sauté" button to heat up the Instant Pot. Now, melt the tallow until hot; cook the beef for 2 to 3 minutes, stirring frequently.
2. Add the remaining ingredients, except for spinach, and stir to combine well.
3. Secure the lid. Choose "Meat/Stew" mode and High pressure; cook for 20 minutes. Once cooking is complete, use a natural pressure release; carefully remove the lid.
4. Add spinach to the Instant Pot; cover it with the lid and let the spinach wilt. Ladle hot stew into individual bowls and serve with a fresh salad of choice. Bon appétit!

Nutrition Info:
Per Serving: 317 Calories; 3g Fat; 5.7g Total Carbs; 40g Protein; 2.1g Sugars

Loaded Flank Steak With Salsa

Servings: 1 Serving
Cooking Time: 24 Mins
Ingredients:

- 150g beef flank steak
- 1 tablespoon softened butter
- 2 tbsp. salad dressing mix
- 3 green onions, chopped
- 1 cooked and crumbled bacon strip
- 1/2 tsp. pepper
- ½ cup broth
- For the salsa
- 1 large tomato, finely chopped
- 1 tablespoon capers, finely chopped
- 1 bird's eye chili, finely chopped
- Juice of 1/4 lemon
- ½ cup parsley, finely chopped

Directions:
1. Make salsa: mix chopped tomato, capers, chili, lemon juice, and parsley in a large bowl.
2. Beat butter, salad dressing mix, onions, bacon strips, and pepper in a small bowl. Horizontally cut a small pocket in the steak and fill with the butter mixture.
3. Set your instant pot on manual high; heat oil and fry the steak for about 7 Mins per side or until well cooked. Add in broth and lock lid. Cook on high setting for 10 Mins and then let pressure come down naturally. Transfer to a chopping board and slice across the grain. Serve with salsa.

Nutrition Info: al Information Per Serving Calories 545; Total Fat: 3 g; Carbs: 9 g; Dietary fiber: 4.9 g; Sugars: 6.1 g; Protein: 7 g; Cholesterol: 185 mg; Sodium: 1289 mg

Provençal Beef Brisket Stew

Servings: 4
Cooking Time: 1 Hr 15 Mins
Ingredients:
- 2 tbsp olive oil
- 1 ½ pounds beef brisket
- 1 red onion, sliced
- Salt and black pepper to taste
- 1 (5-oz) can tomato sauce
- 1 cup beef broth
- 1 tbsp herbes de Provence
- 1 tsp red wine

Directions:
1. Set your IP to Sauté and heat the olive oil. Cook the brisket for 3 minutes on each side. Set aside. Put in the onion and cook until tender, 3 minutes. Add in the remaining ingredients and return the brisket.
2. Seal the lid, select Manual on High, and cook for 60 minutes. Once ready, perform a natural pressure release. Remove the brisket. Let sit for 10 minutes. Slice and serve drizzled with the cooking sauce.

Nutrition Info: Calories 424, Protein 27g, Net Carbs 3.1g, Fat 33g

Creamy Beef Strips

Servings: 3
Cooking Time: 20 Minutes
Ingredients:

- ½ teaspoon salt
- 14 oz beef brisket, cut into the strips
- ½ cup of water
- ½ cup heavy cream
- ½ teaspoon ground black pepper
- 1 tablespoon avocado oil

Directions:

1. Preheat the instant pot on the "Saute" mode.
2. When it is displayed "hot" – pour avocado oil inside and heat it up.
3. Add the meat.
4. Sprinkle the meat with the ground black pepper and salt.
5. Saute it for minutes. Stir it once per cooking time.
6. Add water and heavy cream.
7. Seal the lid and set the "manual" mode.
8. Put the timer on 15 minutes (High Pressure).
9. Make a quick pressure release.

Nutrition Info:
Per Serving: calories 322, fat 2, fiber 0.3, carbs 1.1, protein 6

Fall-apart Pork Butt With Garlic Sauce

Servings: 5
Cooking Time: 55 Mins
Ingredients:

- 2 pounds Pork Butt
- ¼ cup Worcestershire Sauce
- ½ tsp Onion Flakes
- Salt and black pepper to taste
- For garlic sauce
- 2 Garlic cloves, chopped
- 1 tbsp olive oil, plus 2 tsp extra
- 1 onion, minced
- 1 tbsp Lemon juice
- ½ cup Beef stock
- 1 tbsp double cream

Directions:

1. Brush the pork with Worcestershire sauce, and let it sit at room temperature for 90 minutes. Then, transfer to the pot, season with salt and pepper, and pour in the water. Seal the lid, hit the Manual and set the cooking time to 45 minutes on HIGH pressure.
2. Meanwhile, in a bowl, combine the ingredients for the garlic sauce, adjust the seasoning, and set aside. After the beep, do a quick pressure release and open the lid carefully. Pour the garlic mixture over the meat. Select Sauté, and simmer for 10 minutes or until thickened.

Nutrition Info: Calories 680, Protein 25g, Net Carbs 8g, Fat 56g

Lime Pork Chops

Servings: 4
Cooking Time: 25 Minutes
Ingredients:
- 4 pork chops
- 2 tablespoons olive oil
- 2 garlic cloves, minced
- 2 tablespoons lime juice
- ½ cup tomato passata
- ½ cup beef stock
- A pinch of salt and black pepper
- 1 tablespoon cilantro, chopped

Directions:
1. Set your instant pot on Sauté mode, add the oil, heat it up, add the garlic and the pork chops and brown for 5 minutes. Add the rest of the ingredients except the cilantro, put the lid on and cook on High for 20 minutes. Release the pressure fast for 5 minutes, divide everything between plates and serve with the cilantro sprinkled on top.

Nutrition Info: calories 219, fat 18, fiber 0.3, carbs 1.5, protein 4

Spicy Pork Chops

Servings: 3
Cooking Time: 2 Mins
Ingredients:
- 2 lb Pork Chops, Boneless
- Salt to taste
- 1 tbsp Coconut Oil
- 3 tbsp Hot Sauce
- 1 Onion, sliced
- 2 cloves Garlic, minced
- ½ tsp Dried Thyme
- ½ cup Chicken Broth
- 2 Carrots, julienned
- 1 cup String Beans

Directions:

1. Heat oil on Sauté, add the chops, season with salt, and brown them on each side. Remove to a plate. Add the onions, thyme, hot sauce, and garlic. Stir and cook for 3 minutes.
2. Add the pork chops back to the pot with the chicken broth, string beans and carrots. Seal the lid, and cook on High Pressure for 10 minutes. Once ready, quickly release the pressure.

Nutrition Info: Calories 320, Protein 26g, Net Carbs 5g, Fat 19g

Traditional Greek Beef Giros

Servings: 4
Cooking Time: 20 Mins
Ingredients:
- 2 tsp butter
- 1 pound beef chuck roast, sliced
- Salt and black pepper, to taste
- 1 tsp garlic powder
- 1 bay leaf
- ½ tsp Greek seasoning
- 1 cup Greek yogurt
- 2 tbsp extra-virgin olive oil
- ½ lime, juiced
- 1 garlic clove, minced
- 2 tbsp fresh dill, chopped

Directions:
1. Set your IP to Sauté and melt the butter. Sear the beef for 4 minutes. Add in garlic powder, bay leaf, Greek seasoning, salt, pepper, and cup of water.
2. Seal the lid, select Manual on High, and cook for minutes. When done, perform a natural pressure release.Let the beef cool. Mix the Greek yogurt, extra-virgin olive oil, garlic, salt, dill, and lime juice in a bowl. Place the beef in a serving plate and top with yogurt sauce to serve.

Nutrition Info: Calories 343, Protein 33g, Net Carbs 2.5g, Fat 21g

Healthy Zucchini Beef Sauté With Avocado

Servings: 2
Cooking Time: 20 Mins
Ingredients:
- 300g beef, sliced into thin strips
- 1 zucchini, sliced into thin strips
- 1/4 cup cilantro, chopped
- 3 cloves of garlic, diced or minced
- 2 tablespoons gluten-free tamari sauce
- 2 tablespoons avocado oil
- 1 avocado, diced

Directions:

1. Heat oil in an instant pot set on manual high setting; add in beef and sauté for about Mins or until browned. Stir in zucchini and cook for 5 Mins more or until zucchini is tender. Stir in garlic, cilantro and tamari sauce and lock lid. Cook on high for 5 Mins and then serve right away topped with avocado.

Nutrition Info:

Per Serving: Calories: 300; Total Fat: 40g; Carbs: 5g; Dietary Fiber: 1g; Sugars: 2g; Protein: 31g

Bacon & Cheddar Egg Bites

Servings: 3
Cooking Time: 30 Mins
Ingredients:
- 6 Eggs
- 6 Bacon Strips, cooked and chopped
- ½ cup Cheddar Cheese
- ½ cup Cottage Cheese
- 6 tbsp Heavy Cream
- 2 tbsp Chopped Parsley
- 1 cup Water

Directions:
1. Place all ingredients except the bacon and parsley, and puree until smooth. Add the parsley and stir.
2. Grease egg bite molds with cooking spray, add the bacon in each mold and pour the egg mixture in each cup two thirds up way to the top. Cover each mold with a foil.
3. Pour water in the Instant Pot and fit a trivet in it. Place the egg molds on the trivet, seal the lid, secure the pressure valve, and select Steam mode for 8 minutes.
4. Once ready, do a quick release. Remove the egg mold and let sit for 5 minutes.

Nutrition Info: Calories 310, Protein 19g, Net Carbs 5g, Fat 22g

Instant Pot Chipotle Shredded Beef

Servings: 2
Cooking Time: 1 Hour 10 Mins
Ingredients:
- 2 tbsp. olive oil
- 2 pounds beef chuck roast
- 1 tbsp. adobo sauce
- 1 chipotle in adobo, chopped
- ½ tsp. chili powder
- 2 tsp. dried oregano
- 2 tsp. dried cumin
- 1 tsp. black pepper
- 2 tsp. salt
- 1 cup fresh cilantro, chopped

- 1 green bell pepper, diced
- 1 onion, chopped
- 1 cup water

Directions:

1. Generously season the roast with salt and pepper.
2. Add olive oil to your instant pot and press the sauté button; add the roast and brown on both sides; spread adobo sauce and chipotle pepper over the roast and sprinkle with seasoning and cilantro; add bell pepper and onions and pour water around the edges of meat. Lock lid; cook on high for 60 Mins and then release pressure naturally.
3. Shred meat and serve with cooking sauce.

Nutrition Info:

Per Serving: Calories: 665; Total Fat: 1 g; Carbs: 3.8 g; Dietary Fiber: 0.9 g; Sugars: 1.9 g; Protein: 45 g; Cholesterol: 175 mg; Sodium: 756 mg

Keto Lasagna With Zucchini

Servings: 6
Cooking Time: 45 Minutes
Ingredients:

- 1 ½ pounds ground chuck
- 1/3 pound bacon, chopped
- 2 tablespoons yellow onion, chopped
- 2 cloves garlic, minced
- 4 eggs
- 8 ounces puréed tomatoes
- 1/2 cup double cream
- 1/2 cup ricotta cheese
- Sea salt and ground pepper, to your liking
- 1 teaspoon cayenne pepper
- 1/2 teaspoon celery seeds
- 1 teaspoon dried parsley flakes
- 10 ounces Monterey-Jack cheese, shredded
- 1 large zucchini, thinly sliced

Directions:

1. Press the "Sauté" button to heat up the Instant Pot. Then, brown the meat and sausage for 2 to 3 minutes, crumbling it with a fork.
2. Add the onion and garlic; continue sautéing for minutes more or until they are fragrant.
3. In a mixing bowl, thoroughly combine the eggs, puréed tomatoes, heavy cream, ricotta, salt, black pepper, cayenne pepper, celery seeds, and dried parsley.
4. Fold in 5 ounces of Monterey-Jack cheese and gently stir to combine.
5. In a casserole dish, place a layer of the ground meat. Then, create 2 layers of the zucchini crisscrossing.
6. Add a layer of the egg/cream mixture. Top with remaining 5 ounces of shredded Monterey-Jack cheese.

7. Secure the lid. Choose "Meat/Stew" mode and High pressure; cook for 35 minutes. Once cooking is complete, use a quick pressure release; carefully remove the lid.
8. Let your lasagna stand for 10 minutes before slicing and serving. Bon appétit!

Nutrition Info:

Per Serving: 533 Calories; 2g Fat; 6.1g Total Carbs; 6g Protein; 2.6g Sugars

Smothered Pork Chops

Servings: 4

Cooking Time: 17 Minutes

Ingredients:
- 4 pork chops
- 1 teaspoon pork seasonings
- ½ teaspoon ground black pepper
- ¼ cup heavy cream
- ½ cup chicken broth
- 1 teaspoon olive oil

Directions:
1. Heat up olive oil on saute mode for minute.
2. Then place the pork chops in the instant pot and cook them for 3 minutes from each side or until they are light brown.
3. Sprinkle the meat with pork seasonings, ground black pepper, chicken broth, and heavy cream.
4. Close and seal the lid.
5. Cook the meal for 10 minutes on manual mode (high pressure).
6. Make a quick pressure release.

Nutrition Info:

Per Serving: calories 298, fat 24, fiber 0.1, carbs 0.6, protein 8

Mb Shank

Servings: 4

Cooking Time: 45 Minutes

Ingredients:
- 1-pound lamb shank
- 2 garlic cloves, diced
- 3 tablespoon apple cider vinegar
- ¼ cup crushed tomatoes
- 1 teaspoon dried parsley
- 1 teaspoon olive oil
- 4 chipotles in adobo
- 1 cup of water
- 1 teaspoon cayenne pepper

Directions:

1. Cut the lamb shank into 4 pieces and sprinkle with dried parsley and apple cider vinegar. Add olive oil and diced garlic. After this, sprinkle the meat with cayenne pepper. Mix it up and leave for -15 minutes to marinate. Then preheat the instant pot on sauté mode for 5 minutes. Add lamb pieces and all liquid from the meat (marinade). Cook the meat for 2 minutes and flip on another side. Cook it for 2 minutes more. After this, add crushed tomatoes, chipotles in adobo, and water. Close the lid and cook the meat on manual mode (high pressure) for 35 minutes. When the time of cooking is over, allow the natural pressure release for 15 minutes.

Nutrition Info: calories 245, fat 6, fiber 2.7, carbs 3.1, protein 4

Winter Beef Chowder

Servings: 6
Cooking Time: 30 Minutes
Ingredients:

- 1 tablespoon grapeseed oil
- 2 pounds top chuck, trimmed, boneless and cubed
- 3 slices slab bacon, chopped
- 1/2 cup yellow onion, chopped
- 1 celery ribs, sliced
- 1 parsnip, sliced
- 4 teaspoons beef base
- 6 cups water
- 1/4 cup dry white wine
- 7 ounces tomato purée
- 1 head savoy cabbage
- Sea salt, to your liking
- 1 teaspoon dried juniper berries
- 1/2 teaspoon dried sage, crushed
- 1/2 teaspoon dried rosemary, leaves picked
- 1 teaspoon whole mixed peppercorns
- 2 sprigs parsley, roughly chopped

Directions:

1. Press the "Sauté" button to heat up the Instant Pot. Now, heat the oil; once hot, cook the chuck for 2 to 3 minutes on each side.
2. Add the remaining ingredients and stir to combine well.
3. Secure the lid. Choose "Meat/Stew" mode and High pressure; cook for 25 minutes. Once cooking is complete, use a quick pressure release; carefully remove the lid.
4. Serve in individual bowls garnished with some extra fresh parsley if desired. Bon appétit!

Nutrition Info:
Per Serving: 324 Calories; 9g Fat; 6.8g Total Carbs; 6g Protein; 1.9g Sugars

Ginger Soy-glazed Pork Tenderloin

Servings: 4

Cooking Time: 15 Minutes
Ingredients:
- ¼ cup water
- 1 (1-pound) boneless pork tenderloin
- 1 tablespoon coconut flour
- Salt and pepper
- 2 tablespoons fresh grated ginger
- ½ cup soy sauce

Directions:
1. Whisk together the soy sauce, water, and ginger in a bowl.
2. Season the pork with salt and pepper then add to the Instant Pot.
3. Close and lock the lid then press the Manual button and adjust the timer to 5 minutes.
4. When the timer goes off, let the pressure vent for 10 minutes then do a Quick Release by pressing Cancel and switching the steam valve to "venting."
5. When the pot has depressurized, open the lid.
6. Remove the pork to a cutting board and cover with foil.
7. Stir the coconut flour into the cooking liquid then press the Sauté button.
8. Cook until thickened then slice the pork and pour the glaze over it to serve.

Nutrition Info: calories 160 fat 4g ,protein 24g ,carbs 7.5g ,fiber 2g ,net carbs 5.5g

Mackerel And Basil Sauce

Servings: 4
Cooking Time: 15 Minutes
Ingredients:
- 1 cup veggie stock
- 2 chili peppers, chopped
- 2 tablespoons olive oil
- 1 pound mackerel, skinless, boneless and cubed
- 2 teaspoons red pepper flakes
- A pinch of salt and black pepper
- ½ cup basil, chopped

Directions:
1. Set your instant pot on Sauté mode, add the oil, heat it up, add the chili peppers and the pepper flakes and cook for 2 minutes. Add the rest of the ingredients, put the lid on and cook on High for minutes. Release the pressure naturally for 10 minutes, divide everything between plates and serve.

Nutrition Info: calories 362, fat 7, fiber 0.4, carbs 0.8, protein 5

Malabar Fish Curry

Servings: 4
Cooking Time: 15 Minutes
Ingredients:
- 1 tablespoon canola oil

- 1/2 cup Cheriya ulli, finely sliced
- 1 red bell pepper, chopped
- 1 serrano pepper, chopped
- 1 teaspoon garlic, pressed
- 1 (1-inch piece fresh ginger root, grated
- 4-5 curry leaves
- 1 pound Ocean perch, cut into bite-size pieces
- 1 teaspoon tamarind paste
- 2 tablespoons curry paste
- 2 ripe tomatoes, chopped
- 1/2 cup unsweetened coconut milk
- 1 ½ cup broth, preferably homemade
- Salt and ground black pepper, to taste

Directions:

1. Press the "Sauté" button to heat up the Instant Pot. Now, heat the oil and sauté Cheriya ulli and peppers until softened and fragrant.
2. Then, stir in the garlic, ginger, and curry leaves. Continue to sauté an additional minute or until they are fragrant.
3. Deglaze the bottom with the broth and add the remaining ingredients.
4. Secure the lid. Choose "Manual" mode and Low pressure; cook for 6 minutes. Once cooking is complete, use a quick pressure release; carefully remove the lid.
5. Taste, adjust the seasonings, and serve right now. Bon appétit!

Nutrition Info:
Per Serving: 235 Calories; 8g Fat; 9g Carbs; 5g Protein; 3.8g Sugars

Spicy Herbed Tuna

Servings: 3
Cooking Time: 15 Mins
Ingredients:

- 4 sprigs each Parsley, Tarragon, Basil and Thyme
- 2 cloves Garlic, crushed
- 1 lb Tuna Steaks
- 1 tbsp Red Chili Flakes
- 1 tbsp Olive oil
- Salt to taste
- 1 tsp Garlic Powder
- ½ tsp dried Thyme, Parsley, Basil and Tarragon
- 5 Lemon Slices
- 3 tbsp Butter
- ½ lb Asparagus, hard ends cut off
- 1 cup Water

Directions:

1. Add the water, crushed garlic and fresh herbs to the Instant Pot. Place in a trivet and arrange tuna on top; season with peppers, salt and garlic powder. Drizzle with olive oil and arrange lemon slices on top. Seal the lid and cook on High Pressure for 4 minutes. Once ready, quickly release the pressure.
2. Remove the tuna to a plate. Remove the inner pot of the Instant Pot and discard the water and herbs. Place it back to the pot and set on Sauté. Melt the butter, add the asparagus and sauté for 3 minutes. Season with salt and add the dried herbs; toss. Serve immediately.

Nutrition Info: Calories 132, Protein 17g, Net Carbs 2g, Fat 4.2g

Spicy Fish Balls

Servings: 3
Cooking Time: 10 Minutes
Ingredients:
- 1 tablespoon butter
- 15 oz cod
- ¼ teaspoon dried oregano
- 1 teaspoon ground nutmeg
- ½ teaspoon dried dill

Directions:
1. Grind the cod and mix it up with all spices.
2. Heat up the butter on saute mode.
3. Make the small balls from the cod mixture and put them in the hot butter.
4. Cook the fish balls for 3 minutes from each side on saute mode.

Nutrition Info:
Per Serving: calories 187, fat 5.4, fiber 0.2, carbs 0.5, protein 5

Spicy Chanterelles And Scampi Boil

Servings: 4
Cooking Time: 10 Minutes
Ingredients:
- 12 ounces lager beer
- 1 tablespoon Creole seasoning
- 1/2 teaspoon paprika
- 1/3 teaspoon dried dill weed
- Sea salt and ground black pepper, to taste
- 1 shallot, chopped
- 2 cloves garlic, crushed
- 1/2 teaspoon Sriracha
- 1/2 pound chanterelles, sliced
- 1 pound scampi, deveined

Directions:
1. Simply throw all of the above ingredients into your Instant Pot.

2. Secure the lid. Choose "Manual" mode and Low pressure; cook for minutes. Once cooking is complete, use a quick pressure release; carefully remove the lid.
3. Serve with fresh cucumbers and radishes on the side.

Nutrition Info:
Per Serving: 281 Calories; 6g Fat; 9.1g Carbs; 6g Protein; 0.9g Sugars

Steamed Alaskan Crab Legs

Servings: 6
Cooking Time: 5 Mins
Ingredients:
- 3 pounds crab legs
- 1 cup water
- 1/2 tbsp. salt
- melted butter

Directions:
1. Place a steamer basket in your instant pot and add a cup of water and salt to the pot; add crab legs to the basket and lock lid; cook on manual high for 5 Mins. Quick release pressure and then serve the steamed crab legs with melted butter.

Nutrition Info:
Per Serving: Calories: 246; Total Fat: 5.4 g; Carbs: 0g; Dietary Fiber: 0 g; sugars: 0g; Protein: 6 g; Cholesterol: 131 mg; Sodium: 3026 mg

Carp Steaks With Aioli

Servings: 4
Cooking Time: 10 Minutes
Ingredients:
- 1 pound carp steaks
- 2 tablespoons ghee
- 1 teaspoon granulated garlic
- 1 teaspoon onion powder
- 1/2 teaspoon dried dill
- Salt, to taste
- 1/4 teaspoon freshly ground black pepper
- 1/2 teaspoon cayenne pepper
- For Aioli:
- 1 egg yolk
- 1 teaspoon garlic, minced
- 1 tablespoon fresh lemon juice
- 1/2 cup extra-virgin olive oil
- 1/3 teaspoon Dijon mustard

Directions:
1. Start by adding ½ cups water and a steamer basket to the Instant Pot. Now, place the fish in the steamer basket.

2. Drizzle the fish with melted ghee; sprinkle granulated garlic, onion powder, dill, salt, black pepper, and cayenne pepper over the fish.
3. Secure the lid. Choose "Manual" mode and High pressure; cook for 4 minutes. Once cooking is complete, use a quick pressure release; carefully remove the lid.
4. Then, make your homemade aioli by mixing the egg yolk, garlic, and lemon juice. Add olive oil and mix with an immersion blender; add mustard and mix again.
5. Serve the prepared carp steaks with the homemade aioli on the side. Bon appétit!

Nutrition Info:
Per Serving: 315 Calories; 8g Fat; 0.6g Total Carbs; 1g Protein; 0.1g Sugars

Hot Oyster Stew With Sour Cream

Servings: 4
Cooking Time: 15 Minutes
Ingredients:
- 1 tablespoon ghee
- 1 medium-sized leek, chopped
- 2 cloves garlic, pressed
- 1 ½ cups double cream
- 1 ½ cups fish stock
- 2 tablespoons sherry
- 1 parsnip, trimmed and sliced
- 1 celery with leaves, diced
- 1 ½ pounds oysters, shucked
- Sea salt and ground black pepper, to taste
- 1 tablespoon paprika
- 1 or 2 dashes Tabasco
- 1/2 cup sour cream

Directions:
1. Press the "Sauté" button to heat up your Instant Pot. Now, melt the ghee and cook the leek and garlic until aromatic.
2. Add coconut milk, fish stock, sherry, parsnip, celery, oysters, salt, pepper, paprika, and Tabasco.
3. Secure the lid. Choose "Manual" mode and Low pressure; cook for 6 minutes. Once cooking is complete, use a quick pressure release; carefully remove the lid.
4. Serve dolloped with chilled sour cream. Bon appétit!

Nutrition Info:
Per Serving: 421 Calories; 6g Fat; 7.2g Carbs; 1g Protein; 2.3g Sugars

Sardines With Lemon Sauce

Servings: 2
Cooking Time: 15 Minutes
Ingredients:
- 8 fresh sardines, gutted and cleaned

- 4 tablespoons olive oil
- ½ teaspoon oregano
- 2 tablespoons lemon juice
- 1 bay leaf
- ½ teaspoon chili flakes
- Salt and pepper, to taste
- lemon wedges, for serving
- 1 cup vegetable broth

Directions:
1. Press the "Sauté" button and preheat the Instant Pot. Add the olive oil and sauté the sardines for 30 seconds. If necessary, work in batches.
2. Then, stir in the oregano, lemon juice, bay leaf, vegetable broth, chili flakes, salt, and pepper.
3. Secure the lid. Choose "Manual" mode and High pressure; cook for 4 minutes. When cooking is complete, use a quick pressure release and carefully remove the lid.
4. Serve warm and garnish with lemon wedges. Bon appétit!

Nutrition Info:
Per Serving: 379 Calories; 8g Fat; 5.6g Carbs; 3g Protein; 2.7g Sugars

Halibut Ceviche

Servings: 2
Cooking Time: 1 Minute
Ingredients:
- 6 oz halibut fillet
- 1 tomato, chopped
- ¼ red onion, diced
- 1 tablespoon fresh cilantro, chopped
- ½ jalapeno pepper, chopped
- ¼ teaspoon minced garlic
- 2 tablespoons lemon juice
- ¼ teaspoon salt
- ¼ teaspoon ground black pepper
- 1 teaspoon avocado oil
- 1 cup water, for cooking

Directions:
1. Pour water and insert the steamer rack in the instant pot. Line it with the baking paper and place the halibut fillet on it. Close the lid and cook fish for minute on manual mode (high pressure). When the time is over, make a quick pressure release and open the lid. Cool the fish well. Meanwhile, in the mixing bowl combine together tomato, onion, cilantro, jalapeno pepper, and minced garlic. Then sprinkle the halibut with lemon juice, avocado oil, and ground black pepper. Massage the fish gently and leave for 10 minutes to marinate. Then chop the halibut roughly and add in the mixing bowl. Shake the cooked meal gently and transfer in the serving glasses.

Sea Bass In Tomato Sauce

Servings: 3 To 4
Cooking Time: 10 Mins
Ingredients:
- 1 cup Coconut Milk
- 1 Lime, juiced
- 1 tbsp Tomato Puree
- 1 tsp Fish Sauce
- 2 cups Tomatoes, chopped
- 1 tsp Hot Sauce
- 3 cloves Garlic, minced
- 1 inch Ginger, grated
- Salt and white pepper to taste
- 1 lb Sea Bass, cut in 2 inch chunks
- ½ cup Cilantro, chopped
- 4 Lime Wedges

Directions:
1. In a bowl, mix all ingredients, except the fish, lime wedges and cilantro. Place fish chunks in the pot and pour tomato mixture over. Seal the lid and cook on High Pressure for 3 minutes. Once ready, quickly release the pressure. Dish the sauce into serving bowls, sprinkle with cilantro and lime wedges.

Nutrition Info: Calories 111, Protein 2g, Net Carbs 1.4g, Fat 2.3g

King Crab With Baby Bellas

Servings: 6
Cooking Time: 10 Minutes
Ingredients:
- 1 ½ pounds king crab legs, halved
- 1/2 stick butter, softened
- 10 ounces baby Bella mushrooms
- 2 garlic cloves, minced
- 1 lemon, sliced

Directions:
1. Start by adding cup water and a steamer basket to your Instant Pot.
2. Now, add the king crab legs to the steamer basket.
3. Secure the lid. Choose "Manual" mode and Low pressure; cook for minutes. Once cooking is complete, use a quick pressure release; carefully remove the lid.
4. Wipe down the Instant Pot with a damp cloth; then, warm the butter. Once hot, cook baby Bella mushrooms with minced garlic for 2 to 3 minutes.
5. Spoon the mushrooms sauce over prepared king crab legs and serve with lemon. Bon appétit!

Nutrition Info:
Per Serving: 176 Calories; 8.5g Fat; 2.4g Carbs; 3g Protein; 1.1g Sugars

Cod And Asparagus

Servings: 4
Cooking Time: 15 Minutes
Ingredients:

- 4 cod fillets, boneless and skinless
- 2 tablespoons lemon juice
- A pinch of salt and black pepper
- 1 tablespoon parsley, chopped
- 2 tablespoons ghee, melted
- ¼ cup chicken stock
- 1 pound asparagus, trimmed
- ½ teaspoon garlic powder
- 2 teaspoons capers, drained

Directions:

1. Set the instant pot on Sauté mode, add the ghee, heat it up, add the asparagus and the rest of the ingredients except the fish, and cook for 5 minutes. Add the fish, put the lid on and cook on High for minutes. Release the pressure naturally for 10 minutes, divide everything between plates and serve.

Nutrition Info: calories 237, fat 1, fiber 2.5, carbs 6.2, protein 6

Hangover Seafood Bowl

Servings: 6
Cooking Time: 15 Minutes
Ingredients:

- 1 ½ pounds shrimp, peeled and deveined
- 1/2 pound calamari, cleaned
- 1/2 pound lobster
- 2 bay leaves
- 2 rosemary sprigs
- 2 thyme sprigs
- 4 garlic cloves, halved
- 1/2 cup fresh lemon juice
- Sea salt and ground black pepper, to taste
- 3 ripe tomatoes, puréed
- 1/2 cup olives, pitted and halved
- 2 tablespoons fresh coriander, chopped
- 2 tablespoons fresh parsley, chopped
- 3 tablespoons extra-virgin olive oil
- 3 chili peppers, deveined and minced
- 1/2 cup red onion, chopped

- 1 avocado, pitted and sliced

Directions:
1. Add shrimp, calamari, lobster, bay leaves, rosemary, thyme, and garlic to your Instant Pot. Pour in cup of water.
2. Secure the lid. Choose "Manual" mode and Low pressure; cook for 3 minutes. Once cooking is complete, use a quick pressure release; carefully remove the lid.
3. Drain the seafood and transfer to a serving bowl.
4. In a mixing bowl, thoroughly combine lemon juice, salt, black pepper, tomatoes, olives, coriander, parsley, olive oil, chili peppers, and red onion.
5. Transfer this mixture to the serving bowl with the seafood. Stir to combine well; serve well-chilled, garnished with avocado. Bon appétit!

Nutrition Info:
Per Serving: 280 Calories; 14g Fat; 9g Carbs; 32g Protein; 2.8g Sugars

Mackerel Packets

Servings: 6
Cooking Time: 25 Mins
Ingredients:
- 3 large Whole Mackerel, cut into 2 pieces
- 6 medium Tomatoes, quartered
- 1 large Brown Onion, sliced thinly
- 1 Orange Bell pepper, seeded and chopped
- Salt and black pepper to taste
- 2 ½ tbsp Pernod
- 3 cloves Garlic, minced
- 2 Lemons, halved
- 1 ½ cups Water

Directions:
1. Cut out 6 pieces of parchment paper a little longer and wider than a piece of fish with kitchen scissors. Then, cut out 6 pieces of foil slightly longer than the parchment papers.
2. Lay the foil wraps on a flat surface and place each parchment paper on each aluminium foil. In a bowl, add the tomatoes, onions, garlic, bell pepper, Pernod, salt, and pepper. Use a spoon to mix them.
3. Place each fish piece on the layer of parchment and foil wraps. Spoon the tomato mixture on each fish. Then, wrap the fish and place the fish packets in the refrigerator to marinate for 2 hours. After 2 hours, remove the fish onto a flat surface.
4. Open the Instant Pot, pour the water into and fit the trivet at the bottom of the pot. Put the packets on the trivet. Close the lid, secure the pressure valve, and select Steam on High pressure for 5 minutes. Once ready, do a quick pressure release. Remove the trivet with the fish packets onto a flat surface.
5. Carefully open the foil and use a spoon to dish the soup with vegetables and sauce onto serving plates. Serve with a side of roasted daikon radish and the lemon wedges.

Nutrition Info: Calories 95, Protein 9g, Net Carbs 0g, Fat 5.3g

Snapper With Tomato Sauce

Servings: 6
Cooking Time: 10 Minutes
Ingredients:

- 2 teaspoons coconut oil, melted
- 1/2 teaspoon cumin seeds
- 1 teaspoon celery seeds
- 1/2 teaspoon fresh ginger, grated
- 1 yellow onion, chopped
- 2 cloves garlic, minced
- 1 ½ pounds snapper fillets
- 3/4 cup vegetable broth
- 1 (14-ounce can fire-roasted diced tomatoes
- 1 bell pepper, sliced
- 1 jalapeño pepper, minced
- Sea salt and ground black pepper, to taste
- 1/4 teaspoon chili flakes
- 1/2 teaspoon turmeric powder

Directions:

1. Press the "Sauté" button to heat up your Instant Pot. Now, heat the oil and cook the cumin seeds, celery seeds, and fresh ginger.
2. Then, add the onion and sauté until it is softened and fragrant.
3. Add minced garlic and continue to sauté an additional seconds. Stir in the remaining ingredients.
4. Secure the lid. Choose "Manual" mode and Low pressure; cook for 3 minutes. Once cooking is complete, use a quick pressure release; carefully remove the lid. Serve warm.

Nutrition Info:
Per Serving: 175 Calories; 5.2g Fat; 5.8g Total Carbs; 5g Protein; 3.2g Sugars

Beer-poached Alaskan Cod

Servings: 4
Cooking Time: 10 Minutes
Ingredients:

- 1 pound Alaskan cod fillets
- 1/2 cup butter
- 1 cup white ale beer
- 1 tablespoon fresh basil, chopped
- 1 teaspoon fresh tarragon, chopped
- 2 garlic cloves, minced
- 1 teaspoon whole black peppercorns
- 1/2 teaspoon coarse sea salt

Directions:

1. Add all of the above ingredients to your Instant Pot.
2. Secure the lid. Choose "Manual" mode and Low pressure; cook for 3 minutes. Once cooking is complete, use a quick pressure release; carefully remove the lid.
3. Serve right away. Bon appétit!

Nutrition Info:

Per Serving: 310 Calories; 5g Fat; 2.7g Carbs; 9g Protein; 0g Sugars

Fish Curry

Servings: 2
Cooking Time: 3 Minutes
Ingredients:
- 8 oz cod fillet, chopped
- 1 teaspoon curry paste
- 1 cup organic almond milk

Directions:
1. Mix up curry paste and almond milk and pour the liquid in the instant pot.
2. Add chopped cod fillet and close the lid.
3. Cook the fish curry on manual mode (high pressure) for minutes.
4. Then make the quick pressure release for 5 minutes.

Nutrition Info:

Per Serving: calories 138, fat 3.7, fiber 0, carbs 4.7, protein 9

Smoked Tuna Bisque

Servings: 4
Cooking Time: 20 Minutes
Ingredients:
- 1 tbsp butter
- 1 small red onion, chopped
- 2 celery stalks, chopped
- 2 garlic cloves, minced
- ½ cup diced tomatoes
- 2 ½ cup chicken broth
- 1 tsp dried dill
- 1 tsp Italian seasoning
- Salt and black pepper to taste
- 3 tsp smoked paprika
- 2 cups chopped smoked tuna
- 1 cup heavy cream
- 1 tbsp freshly chopped parsley

Directions:
1. Set the IP in Sauté mode and adjust to Medium heat.
2. Melt the butter in the inner pot and sauté the onion and celery until softened, 5 minutes. Mix in the garlic and cook until fragrant, 30 seconds.

3. Stir in the tomatoes, chicken broth, dill, Italian seasoning, salt, black pepper, paprika, and tuna.
4. Lock the lid in place; select Manual mode on High Pressure and set the timer to minutes.
5. When the timer reads to the end, do a natural pressure release for 10 minutes, then a quick pressure release to let out the remaining steam and open the lid.
6. Remove the tuna onto a plate and set aside for serving.
7. Using an immersion blender, puree the soup until smooth and stir in the heavy cream.
8. Spoon the soup into serving bowls, top with tuna, and garnish with some parsley.
9. Serve warm.

Nutrition Info:

Per Serving: Calories 376 Fats 87g Carbs 17g Net Carbs 8.57g Protein 28g

Thai Chili Scallops

Servings: 4
Cooking Time: 2 Minutes
Ingredients:

- 3 tbsp coconut oil
- 4 garlic cloves, minced
- ¼ cup fresh Thai basil, chopped
- 1 tsp red chili paste or to taste
- 1 cup coconut milk
- 1 lb. scallops, tendons removed and patted dry
- Salt and black pepper to taste
- 1 lemon, cut into wedges

Directions:

1. Set the IP in Sauté mode and adjust to Medium heat.
2. Melt the coconut oil in the inner pot and stir-fry the garlic, basil, and chili paste until golden, 30 seconds.
3. Pour in the coconut milk, scallops, salt, black pepper, and mix well.
4. Lock the lid in place; select Manual mode on High Pressure and set the timer to 1 minute.
5. After cooking, perform a quick pressure release to let out the steam, and open the lid.
6. Dish the food into serving bowls and serve with the lemon wedges.

Nutrition Info:

Per Serving: Calories 534 Fats 29g Carbs 6.9g Net Carbs 5g Protein 1g

Pressure Steamed Salmon

Servings: 4
Cooking Time: 6 Mins
Ingredients:

- 1 tablespoon extra-virgin olive oil
- 6 ounces wild salmon fillets, skinless
- Fennel fronds
- 1 tablespoon chopped parsley

- 1 tablespoon chopped dill
- 1 tablespoon chopped chives
- 1 tablespoon chopped tarragon
- 1 tablespoon chopped basil
- 1 tablespoon chopped shallot
- 1 tablespoon lemon juice

Directions:
1. Add water to an instant pot and insert a trivet; place salmon and fennel wedges over the trivet and lock lid. Cook on high for 6 Mins. In a bowl, combine the chopped herbs, extra virgin olive oil, and shallot and lemon juice; stir until well combined. Season and spoon over cooked fish.

Nutrition Info:
Per Serving: Calories: 98; Total Fat: 6.3 g; Carbs: 2.5 g; Dietary Fiber: 0.9 g; sugars: trace; Protein: 8.9 g; Cholesterol: 19 mg; Sodium: 33 mg

Simple Steamed Clams

Servings: 3
Cooking Time: 10 Mins
Ingredients:
- ¼ cup White Wine
- ¼ cup Water
- 1 tsp Minced Garlic
- 1 lb Clams

Directions:
1. Pour water and wine in the Instant Pot, add garlic and stir evenly. Fit a steamer basket in the in and arrange the clams in the basket.
2. Seal the lid, select Manual mode on High Pressure mode for 4 minutes. Once ready, quickly release the pressure. Serve clams with steamed veggies.

Nutrition Info: Calories 26, Protein 4.4g, Net Carbs 0.8g, Fat 0.3g

Cajun Cod

Servings: 2
Cooking Time: 4 Minutes
Ingredients:
- 10 oz cod fillet
- 1 tablespoon olive oil
- 1 teaspoon Cajun seasonings
- 2 tablespoons coconut aminos

Directions:
1. Sprinkle the cod fillet with coconut aminos and Cajun seasonings.
2. Then heat up olive oil in the instant pot on saute mode.
3. Add the spiced cod fillet and cook it for 4 minutes from each side.
4. Then cut it into halves and sprinkle with the oily liquid from the instant pot.

Nutrition Info:
Per Serving: calories 189, fat 8.3, fiber 0, carbs 3, protein 3

Fresh Cod Steaks

Servings: 4
Cooking Time: 10 Minutes
Ingredients:

- 4 cod steaks, 1 ½-inch thick
- 2 tablespoons garlic-infused oil
- Sea salt, to taste
- 1/2 teaspoon mixed peppercorns, crushed
- 1 sprig rosemary
- 2 sprigs thyme
- 1 yellow onion, sliced

Directions:

1. Prepare your Instant Pot by adding ½ cups of water and a metal rack to the inner pot.
2. Then, massage the garlic-infused oil into the cod steaks; sprinkle them with salt and crushed peppercorns.
3. Lower the cod steaks onto the rack skin side down; place rosemary, thyme, and onion on the top.
4. Secure the lid. Choose "Manual" mode and High pressure; cook for minutes. Once cooking is complete, use a quick pressure release; carefully remove the lid.
5. Serve immediately with a fresh salad of choice. Bon appétit!

Nutrition Info:
Per Serving: 190 Calories; 7.7g Fat; 2.6g Total Carbs; 2g Protein; 1.1g Sugars

Easy Lemon Pepper Salmon

Servings: 4
Cooking Time: 8 Minutes
Ingredients:

- 3 sprigs fresh herbs (your choice)
- 1 pound boneless salmon fillets
- ½ lemon, sliced thin
- ¾ cup of water
- Salt and pepper
- 1 tablespoon olive oil

Directions:

1. Pour ¾ cup of water in the Instant Pot and add the herbs.
2. Place the steamer rack in the pot and place the salmon on it, skin-side-down.
3. Season with salt and pepper then drizzle with oil and layer with lemon slices.
4. Close and lock the lid.
5. Press the Steam button and adjust the timer to 3 minutes.

6. When the timer goes off, do a Quick Release by pressing Cancel and switching the steam valve to "venting."
7. When the pot has depressurized, open the lid.
8. Remove the salmon to a plate and serve immediately.

Nutrition Info: calories 180 fat 5g ,protein 22g ,carbs 0g ,fiber 0g ,net carbs 0g

Salmon And Dill Sauce

Servings: 6
Cooking Time: 20 Minutes
Ingredients:
- 6 salmon fillets, boneless
- ½ teaspoon lemon pepper
- 1 spring onion, chopped
- Juice of ½ lemon
- A pinch of salt and black pepper
- 1 tablespoon chives, chopped
- ½ cup avocado mayonnaise
- ½ cup heavy cream
- 1 teaspoon dill, chopped

Directions:
1. Set the instant pot on Sauté mode, add the cream, dill and the rest of the ingredients except the salmon and the mayonnaise, whisk and cook for 5 minutes. Add the fish, put the lid on and cook on High for minutes. Release the pressure naturally for 10 minutes, add the avocado mayonnaise, toss gently, divide everything between plates and serve.

Nutrition Info: calories 399, fat 1, fiber 0.2, carbs 1.1, protein 8

Snapper In Aromatic Tomato Sauce

Servings: 6
Cooking Time: 10 Minutes
Ingredients:
- 2 teaspoons coconut oil, melted
- 1/2 teaspoon cumin seeds
- 1 teaspoon celery seeds
- 1/2 teaspoon fresh ginger, grated
- 1 yellow onion, chopped
- 2 cloves garlic, minced
- 1 ½ pounds snapper fillets
- 3/4 cup vegetable broth
- 1 (14-ounce can fire-roasted diced tomatoes
- 1 bell pepper, sliced
- 1 jalapeño pepper, minced
- Sea salt and ground black pepper, to taste
- 1/4 teaspoon chili flakes

- 1/2 teaspoon turmeric powder

Directions:
1. Press the "Sauté" button to heat up your Instant Pot. Now, heat the oil and cook the cumin seeds, celery seeds, and fresh ginger.
2. Then, add the onion and sauté until it is softened and fragrant.
3. Add minced garlic and continue to sauté an additional seconds. Stir in the remaining ingredients.
4. Secure the lid. Choose "Manual" mode and Low pressure; cook for 3 minutes. Once cooking is complete, use a quick pressure release; carefully remove the lid. Serve warm.

Nutrition Info:
Per Serving: 175 Calories; 5.2g Fat; 5.8g Carbs; 5g Protein; 3.2g Sugars

Cod Under The Bagel Spices Crust

Servings: 2
Cooking Time: 10 Minutes
Ingredients:
- 6 oz cod fillet
- 1 tablespoon bagel spices
- 1 teaspoon olive oil
- 1 teaspoon butter

Directions:
1. Cut the cod fillet into 2 servings and sprinkle the bagel spices generously.
2. Then melt the butter in the instant pot. Add olive oil and stir gently.
3. Put the prepared cod fillets in the hot oil mixture and cook for 5 minutes per side on saute mode.
4. After this, close the lid and cook the fish on saute mode for 3 minutes.

Nutrition Info:
Per Serving: calories 133, fat 5, fiber 1.8, carbs 6.3, protein 7

Salmon With Spinach Pesto

Servings: 4
Cooking Time: 3 Minutes
Ingredients:
- 1 cup chicken broth
- 1 lemon, juiced
- Salt and black pepper to taste
- 4 salmon fillets
- 1 ½ cups baby spinach
- ½ cup fresh basil leaves
- 2 garlic cloves, minced
- 2 tbsp toasted pine nuts
- 3 tbsp grated Parmesan cheese
- Salt to taste

- ¼ cup olive oil

Directions:

1. In the inner pot, mix the chicken broth, lemon juice, salt, black pepper, and place the salmon in the liquid.
2. Lock the lid in place; select Steam mode and set the timer to 3 minutes.
3. When the timer is done, perform a quick pressure release to let out the steam, and open the lid.
4. Remove the fish onto serving plates and set aside for serving.
5. In a food processor, combine the remaining ingredients and blend until smooth.
6. Drizzle the mixture (pesto) over the salmon and serve immediately.

Nutrition Info:

Per Serving: Calories 709 Fats 08g Carbs 5.93g Net Carbs 2.93g Protein 24g

Instant Pot Bbq Shrimp

Servings: 2

Cooking Time: 30 Mins

Ingredients:

- 2 tbsp. butter
- ½ pound peeled, deveined shrimp
- 2 tsp minced garlic
- 1/4 cup BBQ sauce
- 2 tbsp. Worcestershire sauce
- Salt & pepper
- Lemon wedges,

Directions:

1. Add shrimp to your instant pot and add the remaining ingredients except lemon wedge; lock lid and cook on high for 30 Mins. Naturally release the pressure. Serve warm, garnished with lemon wedge and a side dish of veggies.

Nutrition Info:

Per Serving: Calories: 247; Total Fat: 7.8 g; Carbs: 7g; Dietary Fiber: 0.3 g; sugars: 9.7g; Protein: 26 g; Cholesterol: 254 mg; Sodium: 750 mg

Red Wine Poached Salmon

Servings: 4

Cooking Time: 6 Minutes

Ingredients:

- 2 cups dry red wine
- 2 tbsp red wine vinegar
- 1 cup water
- 5 thyme sprigs
- 2 celery stalks, chopped
- 1 tbsp stevia
- Salt and black pepper to taste

- 4 salmon fillets
- 2 tbsp freshly chopped parsley to garnish

Directions:

1. In the inner pot, mix all the ingredients except for the fish and parsley until well combined. Lay the fish in the liquid and spoon some liquid on the fish.
2. Lock the lid in place; select Steam mode and set the timer to 3 minutes.
3. After cooking, perform a quick pressure release to let out the steam and open the lid.
4. Remove the salmon onto serving plates.
5. Set the IP in Sauté mode and cook the sauce until reduced by half and syrup while frequently stirring, 2 to 3 minutes.
6. Spoon the sauce all over the salmon, garnish with the parsley and serve warm.

Nutrition Info:

Per Serving: Calories 507 Fats 15g Carbs 2.09g Net Carbs 1.59g Protein 21g

Crab Quiche

Servings: 4 To 6
Cooking Time: 65 Mins
Ingredients:

- 6 Eggs
- 1 ¼ cups Half and Half
- Salt and black pepper to taste
- 2 tsp Smoked Paprika
- 1 ¼ Herbes de Provence
- 1 ½ cups Parmesan Cheese, grated
- 1 cup Scallions, chopped
- 3 cups Crab Meat
- 2 cups Water

Directions:

1. Break eggs into a bowl and add half and half. Beat to incorporate evenly. Add pepper, salt, herbs, smoked paprika and cheese; stir evenly. Add scallions and mix; add crab meat and stir evenly.
2. Cover the bottom part of a spring form pan with aluminum foil. Pour the crab mixture into the pan and level the surface flat. Fit a trivet in the Instant Pot and pour water.
3. Place the pan on the trivet, seal the lid and cook on High Pressure for 40 minutes. Once ready, quickly release the pressure. Remove the pan carefully, run around the edges of the quiche in the pan, and remove the quiche. Cut in slices and serve.

Nutrition Info: Calories 395, Protein 22g, Net Carbs 7g, Fat 25g

Shrimp Salad With Avocado

Servings: 4
Cooking Time: 7 Minutes
Ingredients:

- ½ avocado, chopped

- 7 oz shrimps, peeled
- 1 cup lettuce, chopped
- 2 bacon slices, chopped
- 2 tablespoons heavy cream
- 1 teaspoon peanuts, chopped
- ½ teaspoon ground black pepper
- ¼ teaspoon Pink salt
- 1 cup water, for cooking

Directions:

1. Pour water and insert the steamer rack in the instant pot. Place the shrimps in the rack and close the lid. Cook them on manual mode (high pressure) for minute. Then make quick pressure release and transfer the shrimps in the salad bowl. Remove the steamer rack and clean the instant pot bowl. Place the bacon in the instant pot and cook it on sauté mode for 6 minutes. Stir it every minute to avoid burning. Then transfer the cooked bacon to the shrimps. Add chopped bacon, lettuce, and peanuts. Then in the shallow bowl mix up together heavy cream, peanuts, ground black pepper, and Pink salt. Pour the liquid over the salad and shake it gently.

Nutrition Info: calories 194, fat 9, fiber 1.9, carbs 4, protein 7

Salmon With Broccoli

Servings: 4
Cooking Time: 10 Mins
Ingredients:

- Juice from half lemon
- 1 tbsp Stevia
- 2 tbsp Soy sauce
- 1 tbsp Coconut oil
- 2 Skinned Salmon fillets
- 6 oz Broccoli
- 4 oz green Beans
- 2 peeled, stoned, and sliced Avocados
- 6 halved Cherry Tomatoes
- 6 oz baby Spinach
- 2 oz Walnut halves
- 2 oz Almonds

Directions:

1. Mix the lemon juice, stevia, and soy sauce. Heat the coconut oil in the Instant Pot on Sauté mode. Add the broccoli and stir for 2 minutes. Add the salmon filets and green beans and sauté the mixture for 3 more minutes. Add the rest of the ingredients, seal the lid and cook for 4 minutes on High pressure. Once ready, do a quick release and serve immediately.

Nutrition Info: Calories 576, Protein 2g, Net Carbs 6.1g, Fat 4g

Lime Cod Mix

Servings: 4
Cooking Time: 15 Minutes
Ingredients:
- 4 cod fillets, boneless
- ½ teaspoon cumin, ground
- A pinch of salt and black pepper
- 1 tablespoon olive oil
- ½ cup chicken stock
- 3 tablespoons cilantro, chopped
- 2 tablespoons lime juice
- 2 teaspoons lime zest, grated

Directions:
1. Set the instant pot on Sauté mode, add the oil, heat it up, add the cod and cook for minute on each side. Add the remaining ingredients, put the lid on and cook on High for 13 minutes. Release the pressure naturally for 10 minutes, divide the mix between plates and serve.

Nutrition Info: calories 187, fat 1, fiber 0.2, carbs 1.6, protein 1

Winter Tuna Salad

Servings: 4
Cooking Time: 10 Minutes
Ingredients:
- 1 pound tuna steaks
- 2 Roma tomatoes, sliced
- 1 red bell pepper, sliced
- 1 green bell pepper, sliced
- 1 head lettuce
- 2 tablespoons Kalamata olives, pitted and halved
- 1 red onion, chopped
- 2 tablespoons balsamic vinegar
- 2 tablespoons extra-virgin olive oil
- Sea salt, to taste
- 1/2 teaspoon chili flakes

Directions:
1. Prepare your Instant Pot by adding ½ cups of water and steamer basket to the inner pot.
2. Place the tuna steaks in your steamer basket. Place the tomato slices and bell peppers on top of the fish.
3. Secure the lid. Choose "Manual" mode and High pressure; cook for 4 minutes. Once cooking is complete, use a quick pressure release; carefully remove the lid. Flake the fish with a fork.
4. Divide lettuce leaves among serving plates to make a bad for your salad. Now, add olives and onions. Drizzle balsamic vinegar and olive oil over the salad.

5. Sprinkle salt and chili flakes over your salad. Top with the prepared fish, tomatoes, and bell peppers. Enjoy!

Nutrition Info:
Per Serving: 163 Calories; 4.7g Fat; 5.4g Total Carbs; 5g Protein; 2.1g Sugars

Stuffed Peppers With Haddock And Cheese

Servings: 3
Cooking Time: 15 Minutes
Ingredients:
- 3 bell peppers, stems and seeds removed, halved
- 3/4 pound haddock fillets. Flaked
- 1 cup Romano cheese, grated
- 4 tablespoons scallion, chopped
- 2 garlic cloves, minced
- 4 tablespoons fresh coriander, chopped
- 1 tablespoon ketchup
- Sea salt and ground black pepper, to taste
- 1 teaspoon cayenne pepper
- 1/2 cup tomato sauce
- 1 cup water
- 2 ounces Pepper-Jack cheese, shredded

Directions:
1. In a mixing bowl, thoroughly combine the fish, Romano cheese, scallions, garlic, coriander, ketchup, salt, black pepper, and cayenne pepper; mix to combine well.
2. Now, divide this mixture among pepper halves. Add 1 cup of water and a metal rack to your Instant Pot.
3. Arrange the peppers on the rack. Top each pepper with tomato sauce.
4. Secure the lid. Choose "Manual" mode and High pressure; cook for 10 minutes. Once cooking is complete, use a natural pressure release; carefully remove the lid.
5. Lastly, top with Pepper-Jack cheese, cover and allow the cheese to melt. Serve warm and enjoy!

Nutrition Info:
Per Serving: 352 Calories; 1g Fat; 6.6g Total Carbs; 3g Protein; 2.6g Sugars

Chili Black Mussels

Servings: 4
Cooking Time: 45 Mins
Ingredients:
- 1 ½ lb Black Mussels, cleaned and de-bearded
- 3 tbsp Olive oil
- 3 large Chilies, seeded and chopped
- 3 cloves Garlic, peeled and crushed
- 1 White Onion, chopped finely

- 10 large Tomatoes, skin removed and chopped
- 4 tbsp reduced sugar Tomato Paste
- 1 cup Dry White Wine
- 3 cups Vegetable Broth
- ½ cup fresh Basil Leaves
- 1 cup fresh Parsley Leaves

Directions:
1. Turn on the Instant Pot, open the lid, and select Sauté mode. Add the olive oil, once heated add the onion and cook to soften.
2. Then, add the chilies and garlic, and cook for minutes while stirring frequently. Add the tomatoes and tomato paste, stir and cook for 2 minutes. Then, add the wine and vegetable broth. Let simmer for 5 minutes.
3. Now, add the mussels, close the lid, secure the pressure valve, and select Steam mode on High pressure for 5 minutes. Once ready, do a natural pressure release for 15 minutes, then a quick pressure release. Remove and discard any unopened mussels. Add half of the basil and parsley, and stir.
4. Dish the mussels with sauce in serving bowls and garnish with the remaining basil and parsley. Serve with a side of low carb crusted bread.

Nutrition Info: Calories 120, Protein 10g, Net Carbs 1g, Fat 8g

Favorite Fish Chili

Servings: 4
Cooking Time: 10 Minutes
Ingredients:
- 2 tablespoons olive oil
- 1 red onion, coarsely chopped
- 1 teaspoon ginger-garlic paste
- 1 celery stalk, diced
- 1 carrot, sliced
- 1 bell pepper, deveined and thinly sliced
- 1 jalapeño pepper, deveined and minced
- 2 ripe Roma tomatoes, crushed
- 1/2 pound snapper, sliced
- 1/2 cup water
- 1/2 cup broth, preferably homemade
- 2 tablespoons fresh coriander, minced
- Sea salt and ground black pepper, to taste
- 1/2 teaspoon cayenne pepper
- 1 bay leaf
- 1/4 teaspoon dried dill
- 1/2 cup Cheddar cheese, grated

Directions:

1. Press the "Sauté" button to heat up your Instant Pot. Now, heat the olive oil and cook the onion until translucent and tender.
2. Now, add the remaining ingredients, except for the grated Cheddar cheese.
3. Secure the lid. Choose "Manual" mode and High pressure; cook for 6 minutes. Once cooking is complete, use a quick pressure release; carefully remove the lid.
4. Ladle into individual bowl and serve garnished with grated Cheddar cheese. Bon appétit!

Nutrition Info:
Per Serving: 213 Calories; 7g Fat; 5.9g Total Carbs; 1g Protein; 2.1g Sugars

Fish Nuggets

Servings: 4
Cooking Time: 9 Minutes
Ingredients:
- 1-pound tilapia fillet
- ½ cup almond flour
- 3 eggs, beaten
- ¼ cup avocado oil
- 1 teaspoon salt

Directions:
1. Cut the fish into the small pieces (nuggets) and sprinkle withs alt.
2. Then dip the fish nuggets in the eggs and coat in the almond flour.
3. Heat up avocado oil for minutes on saute mode.
4. Put the prepared fish nuggets in the hot oil and cook them on saute mode for 3 minutes from each side or until they are golden brown.

Nutrition Info:
Per Serving: calories 179, fat 7.8, fiber 1, carbs 1.8, protein 2

Basil Wine Scallops

Servings: 5
Cooking Time: 10 Minutes
Ingredients:
- 1 tablespoon olive oil
- 1 brown onion, chopped
- 2 garlic cloves, minced
- 1/2 cup port wine
- 1 ½ pounds scallops, peeled and deveined
- 1/2 cup fish stock
- 1 ripe tomato, crushed
- Sea salt and ground black pepper, to taste
- 1 teaspoon smoked paprika
- 2 tablespoons fresh lemon juice
- 1/2 cup cream cheese, at room temperature
- 2 tablespoons fresh basil, chopped

Directions:
1. Press the "Sauté" button to heat up your Instant Pot. Now, heat the oil and cook the onion and garlic until fragrant.
2. Add the wine to deglaze the bottom. Add the scallops, fish stock, tomato, salt, black pepper, and paprika.
3. Secure the lid. Choose "Manual" mode and Low pressure; cook for 1 minute. Once cooking is complete, use a quick pressure release; carefully remove the lid.
4. Drizzle fresh lemon juice over the scallops and top them with cream cheese. Cover and let it sit in the residual heat for 3 to 5 minutes. Serve warm garnished with fresh basil leaves, and enjoy!

Nutrition Info:
Per Serving: 209 Calories; 5g Fat; 8.8g Carbs; 2g Protein; 2.6g Sugars

Mackerel And Shrimp Mix

Servings: 6
Cooking Time: 12 Minutes
Ingredients:
- 1 pound shrimp, peeled and deveined
- 1 pound mackerel, skinless, boneless and cubed
- 1 cup radishes, cubed
- ½ cup chicken stock
- 2 garlic cloves, minced
- 1 tablespoon olive oil
- 1 cup tomato passata

Directions:
1. Set instant pot on Sauté mode, add the oil, heat it up, add the radishes and the garlic and sauté for 2 minutes. Add the rest of the ingredients, put the lid on and cook on High for minutes. Release the pressure fast for 5 minutes, divide the mix into bowls and serve.

Nutrition Info: calories 332, fat 4, fiber 0.9, carbs 4.4, protein 4

Lemon Salmon

Servings: 4
Cooking Time: 4 Minutes
Ingredients:
- 1-pound salmon fillet
- 1 tablespoon butter, melted
- 2 tablespoons lemon juice
- 1 teaspoon dried dill
- 1 cup of water

Directions:
1. Cut the salmon fillet on 4 servings.
2. Line the instant pot baking pan with foil and put the salmon fillets inside in one layer.
3. Then sprinkle the fish with dried dill, lemon juice, and butter.

4. Pour water in the instant pot and insert the rack.
5. Place the baking pan with salmon on the rack and close the lid.
6. Cook the meal on manual mode (high pressure) for 4 minutes. Allow the natural pressure release for 5 minutes and remove the fish from the instant pot.

Nutrition Info:

Per Serving: calories 178, fat 10, fiber 0.1, carbs 0.3, protein 1

Fish Sausages With Spinach And Cheese

Servings: 6

Cooking Time: 15 Minutes

Ingredients:

- 1 tablespoon lard, at room temperature
- 2 pounds chipolata sausages
- 1 yellow onion, chopped
- 1/2 cup dry red wine
- 1 cup water
- Freshly ground black pepper, to taste

Directions:

1. Press the "Sauté" button to heat up the Instant Pot. Heat the oil. Once hot, cook the sausage for a couple of minutes, moving them around.
2. Add the remaining ingredients.
3. Secure the lid. Choose "Manual" mode and High pressure; cook for 8 minutes. Once cooking is complete, use a quick pressure release; carefully remove the lid. Serve warm. Bon appétit!

Nutrition Info:

Per Serving: 403 Calories; 33g Fat; 5.5g Total Carbs; 16g Protein; 0.7g Sugars

Grouper With Cremini Mushrooms And Sausage

Servings: 4

Cooking Time: 15 Minutes

Ingredients:

- 2 tablespoons butter
- 1/2 pound smoked turkey sausage, casing removed
- 1 pound Cremini mushrooms, sliced
- 2 garlic cloves, minced
- 4 grouper fillets
- Sea salt, to taste
- 1/2 teaspoon black peppercorns, freshly cracked
- 1/2 cup dry white wine
- 1 tablespoon fresh lime juice
- 2 tablespoons fresh cilantro, chopped

Directions:
1. Press the "Sauté" button to heat up the Instant Pot. Now, melt the butter. Once hot, cook the sausage until nice and browned on all sides; reserve.
2. Then, cook Cremini mushrooms in pan drippings for about 3 minutes or until fragrant.
3. Add the garlic and continue to sauté an additional seconds. Now, add the fish, salt, black peppercorns, and wine. Return the sausage back to the Instant Pot.
4. Secure the lid. Choose "Manual" mode and Low pressure; cook for 3 minutes. Once cooking is complete, use a quick pressure release; carefully remove the lid. Bon appétit!
5. Afterwards, divide your dish among serving plates and drizzle fresh lime juice over each serving. Serve garnished with fresh cilantro. Bon appétit!

Nutrition Info:

Per Serving: 431 Calories; 7g Fat; 5.9g Total Carbs; 4g Protein; 2.3g Sugars

Instant Pot Shrimp & Grits

Servings: 4

Cooking Time: 25 Mins

Ingredients:
- Shrimp Ingredients
- 3 strips smoked bacon, diced
- 1-pound shrimp, peeled and deveined
- 1 tbsp. garlic, minced
- 1/2 cup bell peppers, chopped
- 1/3 cup onion, chopped
- 1 1/2 cups diced tomatoes
- 2 tsp. Old Bay seasoning
- 1/4 tsp hot sauce
- 2 tbsp. lemon juice
- 1/4 cup chicken broth
- 2 tbsp. dry white wine
- 1/2 tsp salt
- 1/4 tsp pepper
- 1/4 cup heavy cream
- 1/4 cup scallions, sliced
- Grits Ingredients
- 1/2 cup grits
- 1 tbsp. butter
- 1 cup milk
- salt & pepper
- 1 cup water

Directions:
1. Season shrimp with Old Bay seasoning and set aside.

2. Set your instant pot on sauté mode and cook bacon for 3 Mins or until crisp; transfer to a plate. Add bell peppers and onions to the pot and cook for about 3 Mins; stir in garlic and cook for 1 minute.

3. Turn off your pot and then stir in white wine to deglaze; stir in hot sauce, broth, lemon juice, tomatoes, salt and pepper and then add in a trivet.

4. In a heat-proof bowl, mix together milk, grits, salt, water and pepper and place it over the trivet; lock lid and cook on manual for 10 Mins; let pressure come down on its own. Remove the grits and trivet and the stir in shrimp; lock lid and let shrimp cook. Fluff grits and add butter. Stir the shrimp and then turn the pot on sauté mode; stir in cream and serve with grits garnished with bacon and scallions.

Nutrition Info:
Per Serving: Calories: 385; Total Fat: 4 g; Carbs: 9g; Dietary Fiber: 2.9 g; sugars: 9.6g; Protein: 6 g; Cholesterol: 201 mg; Sodium: 873 mg

Paprika Salmon Skewers

Servings: 4
Cooking Time: 5 Minutes
Ingredients:
- 1-pound salmon fillet, fresh, cubed
- 1 tablespoon paprika
- ½ teaspoon salt
- ½ teaspoon ground turmeric
- 1 teaspoon avocado oil
- ½ teaspoon lemon juice
- 1 cup water, for cooking

Directions:
1. Make the sauce: mix up together paprika, salt, ground turmeric, avocado oil, and lemon juice. Then coat the salmon cubes in the sauce well and string on the wooden skewers. Pour water and insert trivet in the instant pot. Arrange the salmon skewers on the trivet and close the lid. Cook the meal on manual mode (high pressure) for 5 minutes. Then make a quick pressure release and remove the fish from the instant pot.

Nutrition Info: calories 158, fat 7.4, fiber 0.8, carbs 1.2, protein 3

Simple Garlicky Halibut Steak

Servings: 3
Cooking Time: 10 Minutes
Ingredients:
- 3 halibut steaks
- 4 garlic cloves, crushed
- Coarse sea salt, to taste
- 1/4 teaspoon ground black pepper, to taste

Directions:
1. Prepare your Instant Pot by adding ½ cups of water and steamer basket to the inner pot.

2. Place the halibut steaks in the steamer basket; season them with salt and black pepper.
3. Secure the lid. Choose "Manual" mode and High pressure; cook for 5 minutes. Once cooking is complete, use a quick pressure release; carefully remove the lid.
4. Serve with favorite keto sides. Bon appétit!

Nutrition Info:
Per Serving: 287 Calories; 9g Fat; 1.3g Carbs; 9g Protein; 0g Sugars

Salmon Chili-lime Sauce

Servings: 2
Cooking Time: 5 Mins
Ingredients:
- For steaming salmon:
- 2 salmon fillets
- 1 cup water
- sea salt & pepper
- For chili-lime sauce:
- 1 jalapeno seeds removed and diced
- 2 cloves garlic minced
- 2 tbsp. lime juice
- 1 tbsp. olive oil
- 1 tbsp. chopped parsley
- 1/2 tsp. cumin
- 1/2 tsp. paprika
- 1 tbsp. liquid Stevia
- 1 tbsp. hot water

Directions:
1. In a bowl, mix all sauce ingredients and set aside.
2. Add water to your instant pot and place salmon in a steamer basket inside the pot; sprinkle fish with salt and pepper and then lock lid; cook on high for 5 Mins and then let pressure come down naturally.
3. Transfer fish to a plate and drizzle with sauce to serve.

Nutrition Info:
Per Serving: Calories: 319; Total Fat: 2 g; Carbs: 8g; Dietary Fiber: 3.4 g; sugars: 6.7g; Protein: 8 g; Cholesterol: 13 mg; Sodium: 715 mg

Norwegian Salmon Steaks With Garlic Yogurt

Servings: 4
Cooking Time: 10 Minutes
Ingredients:
- 2 tablespoons olive oil
- 4 salmon steaks

- Coarse sea salt and ground black pepper, to taste
- Garlic Yogurt:
- 1 (8-ounce container full-fat Greek yogurt
- 2 tablespoons mayonnaise
- 1/3 teaspoon Dijon mustard
- 2 cloves garlic, minced

Directions:
1. Start by adding cup of water and a steamer rack to the Instant Pot.
2. Now, massage olive oil into the fish; generously season with salt and black pepper on all sides. Place the fish on the steamer rack.
3. Secure the lid. Choose "Manual" mode and High pressure; cook for 4 minutes. Once cooking is complete, use a quick pressure release; carefully remove the lid.
4. Then, make the garlic yogurt by whisking Greek yogurt, mayonnaise, Dijon mustard, and garlic.
5. Serve salmon steaks with the garlic yogurt on the side. Bon appétit!

Nutrition Info:
Per Serving: 364 Calories; 2g Fat; 4.2g Total Carbs; 2g Protein; 3.3g Sugars

Cheesy Shrimp Salad

Servings: 4
Cooking Time: 10 Minutes
Ingredients:
- 28 ounces shrimp, peeled and deveined
- 1/2 cup apple cider vinegar
- 1/2 cup water
- 1/3 cup mayonnaise
- 1/4 cup cream cheese
- 1 celery with leaves, chopped
- 1 red onion, chopped
- 1 large-sized cucumber, sliced
- 1 tablespoon lime juice
- 2 tablespoons cilantro, roughly chopped

Directions:
1. Toss the shrimp, apple cider vinegar and water in your Instant Pot.
2. Secure the lid. Choose "Manual" mode and Low pressure; cook for minutes. Once cooking is complete, use a quick pressure release; carefully remove the lid.
3. Allow your shrimp to cool completely. Toss the shrimp with the remaining ingredients. Serve this salad well-chilled and enjoy!

Nutrition Info:
Per Serving: 326 Calories; 3g Fat; 4.1g Total Carbs; 9g Protein; 1.9g Sugars

Fennel Alaskan Cod With Turnips

Servings: 4

Cooking Time: 20 Mins

Ingredients:

- 2 (18 oz) Alaskan Cod, cut into 4 pieces each
- 4 tbsp Olive oil
- 2 cloves Garlic, minced
- 2 small Onions, chopped
- ½ cup Olive Brine
- 2 cups Chicken Broth
- Salt and black pepper to taste
- ½ cup sugar-free Tomato Puree
- 1 head Fennel, quartered
- 2 Turnips, peeled and quartered
- 1 cup Green Olives, pitted and crushed
- 1/2 cup Basil Leaves
- Lemon Slices to garnish

Directions:

1. Turn on the Instant Pot, open the pot, and select Sauté mode. Add the olive oil, once heated add the garlic and onion. Stir fry them until the onion has softened. Pour the chicken broth in and tomato puree. Let simmer for about 3 minutes.
2. Add the fennel, olives, turnips, salt, and pepper. Close the lid, secure the pressure valve, and select Steam mode on Low pressure for 8 minutes. Once ready, do a quick pressure release. Transfer the vegetables onto a plate with a slotted spoon.
3. Adjust broth's taste with salt and pepper and add the cod pieces.Close the lid again, secure the pressure valve, and select Steam mode on Low pressure for minutes. Once ready, do a quick pressure release.
4. Remove the cod into soup plates, top with the veggies and basil leaves, and spoon the broth over them. Serve with a side of low carb crusted bread.

Nutrition Info: Calories 64, Protein 8g, Net Carbs 5g, Fat 4.3g

Trout And Eggplant Mix

Servings: 4

Cooking Time: 15 Minutes

Ingredients:

- 4 trout fillets, boneless
- 2 scallions, chopped
- 2 eggplants, cubed
- ½ cup chicken stock
- 2 tablespoons parsley, chopped
- 3 tablespoons olive oil
- A pinch of salt and black pepper
- 2 tablespoons smoked paprika

Directions:

1. Set the instant pot on Sauté mode, add the oil, heat it up, add the scallions and the eggplant and cook for 2 minutes, Add the rest of the ingredients except the parsley, put the lid on and cook on High for minutes. Release the pressure naturally for 10 minutes, divide the mix between plates and serve with the parsley sprinkled on top.

Nutrition Info: calories 291, fat 8, fiber 4.5, carbs 6.4, protein 20

Hot Anchovies

Servings: 4
Cooking Time: 20 Mins
Ingredients:

- 1 Chili, sliced
- 1 tsp Chili Powder
- ½ tsp Red Chili Flakes
- 10 ounces Anchovy
- 4 tbsp Butter
- ½ cup ground Almonds
- 1 tsp Dill
- Salt and black pepper to taste

Directions:

1. Melt butter on Sauté. Combine the chili and all spices in a bowl. Coat the anchovy with the mixture well. When the butter is melted, add the anchovy and cook until browned, for about 4-5 minutes per side. Serve with keto bread and tangy tomato dip.

Nutrition Info: Calories 331, Protein 28g, Net Carbs 3g, Fat 25g

Cod And Basil Tomato Passata

Servings: 4
Cooking Time: 12 Minutes
Ingredients:

- 1 pound cod, skinless, boneless and cubed
- 2 tablespoons avocado oil
- 2 garlic cloves, minced
- 10 ounces canned tomatoes, chopped
- 2 tablespoons basil, chopped
- ½ cup veggie stock

Directions:

1. Set your instant pot on Sauté mode, add the oil, heat it up, add the garlic, stir and brown for 2 minutes. Add the rest of the ingredients, put the lid on and cook on High for minutes. Release the pressure naturally for 10 minutes, divide the mix into bowls and serve.

Nutrition Info: calories 240, fat 7, fiber 1.2, carbs 3.7, protein 1

Chili Haddock And Tomatoes

Servings: 4

Cooking Time: 15 Minutes

Ingredients:

- 4 haddock fillets, boneless
- 1 tablespoon red chili powder
- A pinch of salt and black pepper
- ½ cup chicken stock
- 1 cup tomatoes, cubed
- 4 garlic cloves, minced
- 2 tablespoons avocado oil
- 1 tablespoon chives, chopped

Directions:

1. Set the instant pot on Sauté mode, add the oil, heat it up, add the garlic and the rest of the ingredients except the fish and the chives, whisk and cook for 5 minutes. Add the fish, put the lid on and cook on High for minutes. Release the pressure naturally for 10 minutes, divide the mix into bowls and serve with the chives sprinkled on top.

Nutrition Info: calories 197, fat 2.8, fiber 1.5, carbs 2.2, protein 4

Red Snapper In Hot Veggie Sauce

Servings: 4

Cooking Time: 20 Mins

Ingredients:

- 2-pounds red snapper filets
- ¼ cup canola or extra virgin olive oil
- ½ red bell pepper, chopped
- ½ green bell pepper, chopped
- 4 scallions, thinly sliced
- 2 tomatoes, diced
- 2 cloves garlic
- 2 tablespoon fresh lemon juice
- ½ cup freshly squeezed lime juice
- 1 teaspoon cayenne pepper
- 1 teaspoon pepper
- Cilantro for garnish

Directions:

1. Add extra virgin olive oil to an instant pot set on manual high and sauté garlic for about 4 Mins or until golden brown. Place fish in the oil and drizzle with lemon and lime juice. Sprinkle with black pepper and cayenne pepper and top with green and red bell peppers, scallions, and tomatoes.
2. Lock lid and cook on high for 15 Mins and then quick release the pressure.
3. To serve, garnish with cilantro.

Nutrition Info:

Per Serving: Calories: 431; Total Fat: 9 g; Carbs: 7 g; Dietary Fiber: 1.9 g; Sugars: 3.7 g; Protein: 61 g; Cholesterol: 107 mg; Sodium: 138 mg

Red Curry Perch Fillets

Servings: 4
Cooking Time: 10 Minutes
Ingredients:

- 1 cup water
- 1 large-sized lemon, sliced
- 2 sprigs rosemary
- 1 pound perch fillets
- Sea salt and ground black pepper, to taste
- 1 teaspoon cayenne pepper
- 1 tablespoon red curry paste
- 1 tablespoons butter

Directions:

1. Pour cup of water into the Instant Pot; add the lemon slices and rosemary; place a metal trivet inside.
2. Now, sprinkle the perch fillets with salt, black pepper, and cayenne pepper. Spread red curry paste and butter over the fillets.
3. Lower the fish onto the trivet.
4. Secure the lid. Choose "Manual" mode and Low pressure; cook for 6 minutes. Once cooking is complete, use a quick pressure release; carefully remove the lid.
5. Serve with your favorite keto sides. Bon appétit!

Nutrition Info:
Per Serving: 135 Calories; 4.1g Fat; 1.3g Carbs; 3g Protein; 0.6g Sugars

Classic Jambalaya

Servings: 6
Cooking Time: 25 Minutes
Ingredients:

- 2 teaspoons olive oil
- 1 pound chicken breasts, boneless, skinless and cubed
- 1 cup smoked sausage, chopped
- 3/4 pound prawns
- 1 teaspoon Creole seasoning
- Sea salt and ground black pepper, to taste
- 1/2 cup onion, chopped
- 2 cloves garlic, minced
- 2 bell peppers, chopped
- 1 habanero pepper, chopped
- 1 stalk celery, chopped
- 2 ripe tomatoes, puréed
- 2 cups vegetable stock
- 1 tablespoon freshly squeezed lemon juice

- 1 tablespoon fresh cilantro, chopped

Directions:

1. Press the "Sauté" button to heat up the Instant Pot. Now, heat the olive oil. Now, cook the chicken and sausage until no longer pink.
2. Then, add prawns and cook for minutes more; season the meat with Creole seasoning, salt, and black pepper and reserve.
3. Add the onion, garlic, peppers, celery, tomatoes, and vegetable stock.
4. Secure the lid. Choose "Manual" mode and High pressure; cook for 9 minutes. Once cooking is complete, use a quick pressure release; carefully remove the lid.
5. Now, add the reserved chicken, sausage, and prawns. Seal the lid and allow it to sit for 6 to 7 minutes.
6. Drizzle fresh lemon over each serving and garnish with fresh cilantro. Bon appétit!

Nutrition Info:

Per Serving: 351 Calories; 1g Fat; 3.9g Total Carbs; 49g Protein; 1.9g Sugars

Lobster With Lime Cream

Servings: 4
Cooking Time: 15 Minutes
Ingredients:

- 1 pound lobster tails
- 1 tablespoon Creole seasoning blend
- Lime Cream Sauce:
- 1 stick butter
- 2 tablespoons shallots, finely chopped
- 1/4 teaspoon salt
- 1/4 teaspoon black pepper
- 1/4 teaspoon cayenne pepper
- 2 tablespoons lime juice
- 1/4 cup heavy cream

Directions:

1. Prepare the Instant Pot by adding ½ cups of water and a steamer basket to the bottom of the inner pot.
2. Place lobster tails in the steamer basket. Sprinkle with Creole seasoning blend.
3. Secure the lid. Choose "Manual" mode and Low pressure; cook for minutes. Once cooking is complete, use a quick pressure release; carefully remove the lid.
4. Wipe down the Instant Pot with a damp cloth. Now, press the "Sauté" button and melt the butter.
5. Now, add the shallots, salt, black pepper, and cayenne pepper; cook for 1 minute and add lime juice and heavy cream. Cook until the sauce has reduced.
6. Spoon the sauce over the fish and serve right now. Bon appétit!

Nutrition Info:

Per Serving: 322 Calories; 5g Fat; 1.8g Total Carbs; 3g Protein; 0.7g Sugars

Ginger Steamed Scallion Fish

Servings: 4
Cooking Time: 15 Mins
Ingredients:

- 2 lb Tilapia Fillet
- 4 tbsp Soy Sauce
- 2 inch Ginger, grated
- 2 cloves Garlic, minced
- 2 tbsp Olive oil
- 3 tbsp Ginger, julienned
- ½ cup Scallions, cut in long strips
- ½ cup Cilantro chopped
- 2 cups Water

Directions:

1. Mix the soy sauce, garlic, and minced ginger in a bowl. Place the fish and pour the mixture over it. Marinate for 30 minutes. Pour water in the Instant Pot and fit a steamer basket in.
2. Remove and place the fish in the steamer basket, but reserve the marinade. Seal the lid, select Manual and cook on Low Pressure for minutes.
3. Once ready, quickly release the pressure. Set aside and wipe the pot clean. Heat oil on Sauté and stir-fry the scallions, ginger and cilantro for minutes. Add the reserved marinade. Cook for 2 minutes. Press Cancel. Pour the sauce over the fish and serve warm.

Nutrition Info: Calories 171, Protein 23g, Net Carbs 0g, Fat 5g

King Crabs With Wine Sauce

Servings: 4
Cooking Time: 10 Minutes
Ingredients:

- 3 lbs. frozen king crab legs
- 1/2 cup water
- 1/3 cup lemon juice
- 1/3 cup dry white wine
- Sea salt and pepper, to taste
- 1 tablespoon sesame oil
- 1/2 tablespoon fresh thyme, chopped

Directions:

1. Add the frozen king crab legs, sesame oil, water, dry white wine, fresh thyme, salt, and pepper to the inner pot.
2. Secure the lid. Choose the "Manual" mode and cook for 3 minutes at High pressure. When cooking is complete, use a quick pressure release and carefully remove the lid.
3. Serve the crab legs warm and drizzle with the lemon juice Enjoy!

Nutrition Info:
Per Serving: 351 Calories; 8.9g Fat; 2.7g Carbs; 4g Protein; 1.3g Sugars

Simple Swai With Wine Sauce

Servings: 4
Cooking Time: 15 Minutes
Ingredients:

- 1 tablespoon butter, melted
- 2 garlic cloves, minced
- 2 tablespoon green onions, chopped
- 1 teaspoon fresh ginger, grated
- 1 pound swai fish fillets
- 1/2 cup port wine
- 1/2 tablespoon lemon juice
- 1 teaspoon parsley flakes
- 1/2 teaspoon chili flakes
- Coarse sea salt and ground black pepper, to taste
- 1/2 teaspoon cayenne pepper
- 1/4 teaspoon ground bay leaf
- 1/2 teaspoon fennel seeds

Directions:

1. Press the "Sauté" button to heat up your Instant Pot. Now, melt the butter and cook the garlic, green onions and ginger until softened and aromatic.
2. Add the remaining ingredients and gently stir to combine well.
3. Secure the lid. Choose "Manual" mode and Low pressure; cook for 6 minutes. Once cooking is complete, use a quick pressure release; carefully remove the lid.
4. Serve warm over cauli rice. Bon appétit!

Nutrition Info:
Per Serving: 109 Calories; 3.3g Fat; 1.2g Total Carbs; 6g Protein; 0.5g Sugars

Salmon With Gingery Orange Sauce

Servings: 4
Cooking Time: 5 Mins
Ingredients:

- 1-pound salmon
- 1 tbsp. dark soy sauce
- 2 tbsp. marmalade
- 1 tsp. minced garlic
- 2 tsp. minced ginger
- 1 tsp. salt
- 1 ½ tsp pepper

Directions:

1. Add fish to a Ziplock bag; mix all remaining ingredients and add to the bag; let marinate for at least Mins.

2. Add two cups of water to your instant pot and add in a steamer rack. Place the bag with fish on the rack and lock lid; cook on high for 5 Mins and then let pressure come down on its own.

Nutrition Info:

Per Serving: Calories: 281; Total Fat: 7.9g; Carbs: 1g; Dietary Fiber: 0.4 g; sugars: 7.1g; Protein: 2 g; Cholesterol: 50 mg; Sodium: 653 mg

Tuna And Mustard Greens

Servings: 4

Cooking Time: 10 Minutes

Ingredients:

- 2 cups mustard greens
- 1 tablespoon olive oil
- 1 cup tomato passata
- 1 shallot, chopped
- 1 tablespoon basil, chopped
- A pinch of salt and black pepper
- 14 ounces tuna fillets, boneless, skinless and cubed

Directions:

1. Set your instant pot on Sauté mode, add the oil, heat it up, add the shallot and sauté for 2 minutes. Add rest of the ingredients, put the lid on and cook on High for 8 minutes. Release the pressure naturally for minutes, divide the mix between plates and serve.

Nutrition Info: calories 124, fat 3.7, fiber 1.9, carbs 2.6, protein 1.6

Bluefish In Tarragon-vermouth Sauce

Servings: 4

Cooking Time: 10 Minutes

Ingredients:

- 2 teaspoons butter
- 1/2 yellow onion, chopped
- 1 garlic clove, minced
- 1 pound bluefish fillets
- Sea salt and ground black pepper, to taste
- 1/4 cup vermouth
- 1 tablespoon rice vinegar
- 2 teaspoons tamari
- 1 teaspoon fresh tarragon leaves, chopped

Directions:

1. Press the "Sauté" button to heat up the Instant Pot. Now, melt the butter. Once hot, sauté the onion until softened.
2. Add garlic and sauté for a further minute or until aromatic. Stir in the remaining ingredients.
3. Secure the lid. Choose "Manual" mode and Low pressure; cook for minutes. Once cooking is complete, use a quick pressure release; carefully remove the lid. Bon appétit!

Nutrition Info:
Per Serving: 204 Calories; 7.9g Fat; 4.4g Carbs; 5g Protein; 2.3g Sugars

Warm Tuna Salad

Servings: 4
Cooking Time: 10 Minutes
Ingredients:

- 1 pound tuna steaks
- 2 Roma tomatoes, sliced
- 1 red bell pepper, sliced
- 1 green bell pepper, sliced
- 1 head lettuce
- 2 tablespoons Kalamata olives, pitted and halved
- 1 red onion, chopped
- 2 tablespoons balsamic vinegar
- 2 tablespoons extra-virgin olive oil
- Sea salt, to taste
- 1/2 teaspoon chili flakes

Directions:

1. Prepare your Instant Pot by adding ½ cups of water and steamer basket to the inner pot.
2. Place the tuna steaks in your steamer basket. Place the tomato slices and bell peppers on top of the fish.
3. Secure the lid. Choose "Manual" mode and High pressure; cook for 4 minutes. Once cooking is complete, use a quick pressure release; carefully remove the lid. Flake the fish with a fork.
4. Divide lettuce leaves among serving plates to make a bad for your salad. Now, add olives and onions. Drizzle balsamic vinegar and olive oil over the salad.
5. Sprinkle salt and chili flakes over your salad. Top with the prepared fish, tomatoes, and bell peppers. Enjoy!

Nutrition Info:
Per Serving: 163 Calories; 4.7g Fat; 7.4g Carbs; 5g Protein; 4.1g Sugars

Instant Pot Coconut Fishbowl

Servings: 8
Cooking Time: 15 Mins
Ingredients:

- 1 ½ pounds fish fillets, sliced into bite-size pieces
- 2 cups coconut milk
- 1 tbsp. freshly grated ginger
- 2 garlic cloves, minced
- 2 medium onions, chopped
- 2 green chilies, sliced into strips
- 1 tomato, chopped

- 6 curry leaves
- 3 tbsp. curry powder mix
- 2 tbsp. fresh lemon juice
- 2 tsp. salt

Directions:
1. Set your instant pot on sauté mode and add oil; sauté curry leaves for minute and then add ginger, garlic and onion; cook until tender; stir in curry powder mix and cook for 2 Mins or until fragrant.
2. Add coconut milk and then stir in fish, tomatoes, and green chilies until well combined; lock lid and cook on high for 5 Mins. Let pressure come down naturally and then stir in lemon juice and salt.

Nutrition Info:
Per Serving: Calories: 296; Total Fat: 1 g; Carbs: 4g; Dietary Fiber: 0.2 g; sugars: 6.5g; Protein: 8 g; Cholesterol: 88 mg; Sodium: 1121 mg

Thyme Lobster Tails

Servings: 4
Cooking Time: 4 Minutes
Ingredients:
- 4 lobster tails
- 1 tablespoon butter, softened
- 1 teaspoon dried thyme
- 1 cup of water

Directions:
1. Pour water and insert the steamer rack in the instant pot.
2. Put the lobster tails on the rack and close the lid.
3. Cook the meal on manual mode (high pressure) for 4 minutes. Make a quick pressure release.
4. After this, mix up butter and dried thyme.
5. Peel the lobsters and rub them with thyme butter.

Nutrition Info:
Per Serving: calories 126, fat 2.9, fiber 0.1, carbs 0.2, protein 1

Tuna Fillets With Arugula

Servings: 4
Cooking Time: 10 Minutes
Ingredients:
- 2 lbs. tuna filets
- 2 ½ cup arugula
- 1 cup of water
- 2 tablespoons ghee
- Salt and pepper, to taste
- ½ cup fresh lemon juice

385

Directions:
1. Put the water in the inner pot and place the steamer rack.
2. Place the tuna fillets onto the rack. Brush the tuna fillets with ghee and season with salt and pepper.
3. Secure the lid. Choose the "Steam" mode and cook for 4 minutes at Low pressure. When cooking is complete, use a quick pressure release and carefully remove the lid.
4. Serve warm with the arugula and drizzle with fresh lemon juice. Bon appetite!

Nutrition Info:
Per Serving: 210 Calories; 7.9g Fat; 2.6g Carbs; 6g Protein; 1.8g Sugars

Creamy Cheesy Shrimp Salad

Servings: 4
Cooking Time: 10 Minutes
Ingredients:
- 28 ounces shrimp, peeled and deveined
- 1/2 cup apple cider vinegar
- 1/2 cup water
- 1/3 cup mayonnaise
- 1/4 cup cream cheese
- 1 celery with leaves, chopped
- 1 red onion, chopped
- 1 large-sized cucumber, sliced
- 1 tablespoon lime juice
- 2 tablespoons cilantro, roughly chopped

Directions:
1. Toss the shrimp, apple cider vinegar and water in your Instant Pot.
2. Secure the lid. Choose "Manual" mode and Low pressure; cook for minutes. Once cooking is complete, use a quick pressure release; carefully remove the lid.
3. Allow your shrimp to cool completely. Toss the shrimp with the remaining ingredients. Serve this salad well-chilled and enjoy!

Nutrition Info:
Per Serving: 326 Calories; 3g Fat; 4.1g Carbs; 9g Protein; 1.9g Sugars

Salmon With Bok Choy

Servings: 4
Cooking Time: 15 Minutes
Ingredients:
- 2 tablespoons unsalted butter
- 4 (1-inch thick salmon fillets
- Sea salt and freshly ground pepper, to taste
- 1/2 teaspoon cayenne pepper
- 3 cloves garlic, minced
- 2 cups Bok choy, sliced

- 1 cup broth, preferably homemade
- 1 teaspoon grated lemon zest
- 1/2 teaspoon dried dill weed

Directions:
1. Start by adding ½ cups of water and a metal rack to the bottom of your Instant Pot.
2. Brush the salmon with melted butter; sprinkle the fish with salt, black pepper, and cayenne pepper on all sides.
3. Secure the lid. Choose "Manual" mode and Low pressure; cook for minutes. Once cooking is complete, use a quick pressure release; carefully remove the lid. Reserve your salmon.
4. Now, add the remaining ingredients.
5. Secure the lid. Choose "High" mode and High pressure; cook for minutes. Once cooking is complete, use a quick pressure release; carefully remove the lid.
6. Serve the poached salmon with the vegetables on the side.

Nutrition Info:
Per Serving: 220 Calories; 1g Fat; 1.9g Total Carbs; 6g Protein; 1g Sugars

Lemon-butter Calamari

Servings: 4
Cooking Time: 2 Minutes
Ingredients:
- 1/3 cup butter, divided
- 4 garlic cloves, minced
- 1 lb. prepared squid rings
- Salt and black pepper to taste
- ½ lemon, juiced
- 2 tbsp fish broth
- 2 tbsp freshly chopped parsley, to garnish

Directions:
1. Set the IP in Sauté mode and adjust to Medium heat.
2. Melt tablespoons of butter in the inner pot and sauté the garlic until fragrant, 30 seconds.
3. Mix in the squid, salt and black pepper, lemon juice, and fish broth.
4. Lock the lid in place; select Manual mode on High Pressure and set the timer to 1 minute.
5. After cooking, do a quick pressure release to let out the steam, and open the lid.
6. Stir in the remaining butter until melted.
7. Dish the food, garnish with the parsley and serve warm.

Nutrition Info:
Per Serving: Calories 149 Fats 75g Carbs 9.59g Net Carbs 7.59g Protein 83g

Bluefish In Special Sauce

Servings: 4
Cooking Time: 10 Minutes
Ingredients:
- 2 teaspoons butter

- 1/2 yellow onion, chopped
- 1 garlic clove, minced
- 1 pound bluefish fillets
- Sea salt and ground black pepper, to taste
- 1/4 cup vermouth
- 1 tablespoon rice vinegar
- 2 teaspoons tamari
- 1 teaspoon fresh tarragon leaves, chopped

Directions:
1. Press the "Sauté" button to heat up the Instant Pot. Now, melt the butter. Once hot, sauté the onion until softened.
2. Add garlic and sauté for a further minute or until aromatic. Stir in the remaining ingredients.
3. Secure the lid. Choose "Manual" mode and Low pressure; cook for minutes. Once cooking is complete, use a quick pressure release; carefully remove the lid. Bon appétit!

Nutrition Info:
Per Serving: 204 Calories; 7.9g Fat; 4.4g Total Carbs; 5g Protein; 2.3g Sugars

Cod Lime Pieces

Servings: 2
Cooking Time: 9 Minutes
Ingredients:
- 6 oz cod fillet
- 1 teaspoon lime zest, grated
- 1 tablespoon lime juice
- 1 tablespoon coconut oil
- 1 egg, beaten

Directions:
1. Cut the cod fillet into medium cubes and sprinkle with lime juice and lime zest.
2. Then dip the fish cubes in the egg.
3. Heat up coconut oil on saute mode for minutes.
4. Put the cod cubes in the hot oil in one layer and cook on saute mode for minutes.
5. Then flip the on another side and cook for 2 minutes more.

Nutrition Info:
Per Serving: calories 161, fat 9.8, fiber 0.1, carbs 0.9, protein 18

Carolina Crab Soup

Servings: 4
Cooking Time: 45 Mins
Ingredients:
- 2 lb Crabmeat Lumps
- 6 tbsp Butter
- 6 tbsp Almond flour
- Salt to taste

- 1 White Onion, chopped
- 3 tsp minced Garlic
- 2 Celery Stalk, diced
- 1 ½ cup Chicken Broth
- ¾ cup Heavy Cream
- ½ cup Half and Half Cream
- 2 tsp Hot Sauce
- 3 tsp sugar-free Worcestershire Sauce
- 3 tsp Old Bay Seasoning
- ¾ cup Muscadet
- Lemon Juice to serve
- Chopped Dill to serve

Directions:

1. Turn on the Instant Pot, open the lid, and select Sauté mode. Put the butter in to melt and then add the almond flour and mix in a fast motion to make a rue. Add the celery, onion, and garlic. Stir and cook until the onion softens for 3 minutes.
2. While whisking, gradually adds the half and half cream, heavy cream, and broth. Let simmer for minutes. Then, add the Worcestershire sauce, old bay seasoning, Muscadet, and hot sauce. Stir and let simmer for 15 minutes.
3. Mix the crabmeat into the sauce. Leave the Instant Pot in Sauté mode and let the soup simmer for an additional 15 minutes. Press Cancel. Dish the soup into serving bowls, garnish with dill and drizzle squirts of lemon juice over. Serve with a side of keto garlic crusted bread.

Nutrition Info: Calories 256, Protein 4g, Net Carbs 0g, Fat 5g

Special Scallops With Sour Cream

Servings: 4
Cooking Time: 15 Minutes
Ingredients:
- 1 tablespoon fresh rosemary, chopped
- 1 ½ lb. scallops, peeled and deveined
- 1 tablespoon fresh thyme, chopped
- 2 tablespoons coconut oil, melted
- 1 ½ cup double cream
- 1 celery, chopped
- ½ sour cream
- Sea salt and pepper, to taste
- 1 cup fish broth
- 1 green onion, chopped

Directions:

1. Press the "Sauté" button and heat your Instant Pot. Add the coconut oil, fish broth, scallops, celery, salt, pepper, fresh rosemary, fresh thyme, and green onion

2. Secure the lid. Choose "Manual" mode and Low pressure; cook for 3 minutes. When cooking is complete, use a natural pressure release and carefully remove the lid.
3. Then, stir in the sour cream and double cream. Close the lid and set to "Warm" for 4 minutes.
4. Serve immediately! Bon appetite!

Nutrition Info:
Per Serving: 376 Calories; 5g Fat; 7g Carbs; 7g Protein; 3g Sugars

Fried Salmon

Servings: 4
Cooking Time: 7 Minutes
Ingredients:
- 1 teaspoon Erythritol
- ¼ teaspoon lemongrass
- ¼ teaspoon ground nutmeg
- ½ teaspoon cayenne pepper
- ¼ teaspoon salt
- 1-pound salmon fillet
- 1 tablespoon coconut oil

Directions:
1. Cut the salmon fillet into 4 fillets. In the shallow bowl combine together spices: lemongrass, ground nutmeg, cayenne pepper, and salt. Rub every salmon fillet with spices. Then toss coconut oil in the instant pot and melt it on sauté mode (approximately 2-3 minutes). Place the salmon fillets in one layer and cook them for 2 minutes from each side. Then sprinkle the salmon fillets with Erythritol and flip on another side. Cook the fish for minute more and transfer in the plate.

Nutrition Info: calories 181, fat 5, fiber 0.1, carbs 1.5, protein 22

Cheese Melt

Servings: 2
Cooking Time: 6 Minutes
Ingredients:
- 2 low carb tortillas
- ¼ cup Cheddar cheese, shredded
- 4 oz tuna, canned
- 1 teaspoon cream cheese
- ½ teaspoon Italian seasonings
- 1 teaspoon sesame oil

Directions:
1. Shred the tuna and mix it with Italian seasonings and cream cheese. Then spread the mixture over the tortillas. Top the mixture with Cheddar cheese and fold into the shape of pockets. Pour sesame oil in the instant pot and heat it up on sauté mode for 2 minutes. Then arrange the cheese pockets in the instant pot and cook them for 2 minutes from each side. Transfer

the cooked meal in the serving plates. It is recommended to eat the cheese melts immediately after cooking.

Nutrition Info: calories 272, fat 5, fiber 7, carbs 4, protein 7

Crab Bisque

Servings: 4
Cooking Time: 20 Minutes
Ingredients:

- 1 tbsp butter
- 1 small red onion, chopped
- 2 celery stalks, chopped
- 2 garlic cloves, minced
- 2 ½ cup chicken broth
- ½ cup diced tomatoes
- 1 tsp dried dill
- 1 tsp Old Bay seasoning
- 5 tsp paprika
- Salt and black pepper to taste
- 2 cups chopped crab meat
- 1 cup heavy cream
- 1 tbsp freshly chopped parsley

Directions:

1. Set the IP in Sauté mode and adjust to Medium heat.
2. Melt the butter in the inner pot and sauté the onion and celery until softened, 5 minutes. Mix in the garlic and cook until fragrant, 30 seconds.
3. Stir in the chicken broth, tomatoes, dill, Old Bay seasoning, paprika, salt, black pepper, and crab meat.
4. Lock the lid in place; select Manual mode on High Pressure and set the timer to minutes.
5. After cooking, perform a natural pressure release for 10 minutes, then a quick pressure release to let out the remaining steam and open the lid.
6. Use a slotted spoon to remove the crabmeat onto a plate and set aside.
7. Using an immersion blender, puree the soup until smooth and mix in the heavy cream.
8. Spoon the soup into serving bowls, top with the crabmeat, and garnish with parsley.
9. Serve warm.

Nutrition Info:
Per Serving: Calories 595 Fats 33g Carbs 89g Net Carbs 19g Protein 73g

Steamed Bass With Fennel, Parsley, And Capers

Servings: 2
Cooking Time: 15 Mins
Ingredients:

- 2- 5-ounce portions of striped bass
- 2 tablespoons extra-virgin olive oil
- 1/2 lemon, juiced
- 1 fennel bulb, sliced
- 1/4 medium onion, sliced
- 1/4 cup chopped parsley
- 1 tablespoon capers, rinsed
- 1/2 teaspoon sea salt
- Chopped parsley and olive oil, for garnish

Directions:

1. Add lemon juice, fennel and onion to an instant pot and cover with inch water; bring the mixture to a gentle boil on manual high. Add seasoned fish and sprinkle with parsley and capers; lock lid and cook on high for 10 Mins. Let pressure come down on its own.
2. Transfer to a serving bowl and drizzle with extra virgin olive oil and top with more parsley to serve.

Nutrition Info:

Per Serving: Calories: 325; Total Fat: 6g; Carbs: 5g; Dietary Fiber: 4.3g; Protein: 9g; Cholesterol: 0mg; Sodium: 661mg; sugars: 0.7g

Cod And Broccoli

Servings: 4
Cooking Time: 15 Minutes
Ingredients:

- 4 cod fillets, boneless and skinless
- A pinch of salt and black pepper
- 1 pound broccoli florets
- 2 tablespoon tomato passata
- 1 cup chicken stock
- 1 tablespoon cilantro, chopped

Directions:

1. In your instant pot, combine all the ingredients, put the lid on and cook on High for minutes. Release the pressure fast for 5 minutes, divide the mix between plates and serve.

Nutrition Info: calories 197, fat 10, fiber 3.1, carbs 4.3, protein 4

Crustless Fish Pie

Servings: 6
Cooking Time: 15 Minutes
Ingredients:

- 1 cup cauliflower, boiled, mashed
- 3 eggs, hard-boiled, peeled, chopped
- 10 oz salmon, chopped, boiled
- ½ cup mozzarella cheese, shredded
- ½ cup heavy cream

- ¼ cup chicken broth
- 1 teaspoon salt
- ½ teaspoon ground paprika

Directions:
1. Mix up chopped salmon and eggs and transfer them in the instant pot bowl.
2. Sprinkle the mixture with salt and ground paprika.
3. After this, top it with mashed cauliflower and mozzarella.
4. Add chicken broth and heavy cream.
5. Close and seal the lid.
6. Cook the pie for 15 minutes on manual mode (high pressure). Make a quick pressure release.

Nutrition Info:
Per Serving: calories 141, fat 9.3, fiber 0.5, carbs 1.6, protein 4

Tilapia Fillets With Arugula

Servings: 4
Cooking Time: 10 Minutes
Ingredients:
- 1 lemon, juiced
- 1 pound tilapia fillets
- 2 teaspoons ghee
- Sea salt and ground black pepper, to taste
- 1/2 teaspoon cayenne pepper, or more to taste
- 1/2 teaspoon dried basil
- 2 cups arugula

Directions:
1. Add fresh lemon juice and cup of water to the bottom of your Instant Pot. Add a metal steamer insert.
2. Brush the fish fillets with melted ghee.
3. Season the fish with salt, black pepper, cayenne pepper; arrange the tilapia fillets in the steamer insert; sprinkle dried basil on top of the fish.
4. Secure the lid. Choose "Manual" mode and Low pressure; cook for minutes. Once cooking is complete, use a quick pressure release; carefully remove the lid.
5. Serve with fresh arugula and enjoy!

Nutrition Info:
Per Serving: 145 Calories; 4.9g Fat; 2.4g Carbs; 3g Protein; 1.1g Sugars

Creamy And Lemony Tuna Fillets

Servings: 4
Cooking Time: 10 Minutes
Ingredients:
- 1 cup water
- 1/3 cup lemon juice
- 2 sprigs fresh rosemary

- 2 sprigs fresh thyme
- 2 sprigs fresh parsley
- 1 pound tuna fillets
- 4 cloves garlic, pressed
- Sea salt, to taste
- 1/4 teaspoon black pepper, or more to taste
- 2 tablespoons butter, melted
- 1 lemon, sliced

Directions:
1. Prepare your Instant Pot by adding cup of water, lemon juice, rosemary, thyme, and parsley to the bottom. Add a steamer basket too.
2. Now, place tuna fillets in the steamer basket. Place the garlic on the top of fish fillets; sprinkle with salt and black pepper.
3. Drizzle the melted butter over the fish fillets and top with the sliced lemon.
4. Secure the lid. Choose "Manual" mode and Low pressure; cook for 3 minutes. Once cooking is complete, use a quick pressure release; carefully remove the lid. Serve warm and enjoy!

Nutrition Info:
Per Serving: 175 Calories; 6.9g Fat; 1.9g Total Carbs; 2g Protein; 0.3g Sugars

Tilapia And Zucchini Noodles

Servings: 4
Cooking Time: 15 Minutes
Ingredients:
- 4 tilapia fillets, boneless
- ¼ teaspoon garlic powder
- 2 zucchinis, cut with a spiralizer
- ½ teaspoon cumin, ground
- 2 garlic cloves, minced
- ½ teaspoon smoked paprika
- A pinch of salt and black pepper
- 2 teaspoons olive oil
- ½ cup tomato passata

Directions:
1. Set the instant pot on Sauté mode, add the oil, heat it up, add the garlic, cumin, garlic powder, paprika, salt and pepper, stir and cook for 3 minutes. Add the rest of the ingredients, put the lid on and cook on High for minutes. Release the pressure naturally for 10 minutes, divide the whole mix between plates and serve.

Nutrition Info: calories 259, fat 9, fiber 2.2, carbs 4.9, protein 2

Parmesan Scallops

Servings: 4
Cooking Time: 11 Minutes
Ingredients:

- 11 oz scallops
- 4 oz Parmesan, grated
- 1 tablespoon butter, melted
- ½ teaspoon avocado oil
- 1 teaspoon garlic powder

Directions:
1. Brush scallops with butter and sprinkle with garlic powder. Brush the instant pot bowl with avocado oil and heat it up for 3 minutes on sauté mode. Then place the scallops in the instant pot in one layer and cook them for 3 minutes. Flip the scallops and top with grated Parmesan. Close the lid and sauté the meal for 5 minutes more.

Nutrition Info: calories 188, fat 6.9, fiber 0.1, carbs 3.4, protein 4

Fast Ahi Tuna Salad

Servings: 4
Cooking Time: 10 Minutes + Chilling Time
Ingredients:
- 1 cup water
- 2 sprigs parsley
- 2 sprigs thyme
- 2 sprigs rosemary
- 1 lemon, sliced
- 1 pound ahi tuna
- 1/3 teaspoon ground black pepper
- 1 cup cherry tomatoes, halved
- 1 head lettuce
- 1 red bell pepper julienned
- 1 carrot julienned
- Sea salt, to taste
- 2 tablespoons extra-virgin olive oil
- 1 teaspoon Dijon mustard

Directions:
1. Pour cup of water into the Instant Pot; add the parsley, thyme, rosemary, and lemon; place a metal trivet inside.
2. Lower the fish onto the trivet; sprinkle with ground black pepper.
3. Secure the lid. Choose "Manual" mode and High pressure; cook for 4 minutes. Once cooking is complete, use a quick pressure release; carefully remove the lid.
4. Place the other ingredients in a salad bowl; toss to combine. Add flaked tuna and toss again. Serve well-chilled.

Nutrition Info:
Per Serving: 252 Calories; 8g Fat; 5.8g Total Carbs; 8g Protein; 3g Sugars

Fish Sticks

Servings: 2

Cooking Time: 7 Minutes
Ingredients:
- 8 oz tilapia fillet
- ¼ cup coconut flakes
- 1 egg, beaten
- ¼ teaspoon chili flakes
- ¼ teaspoon ground nutmeg
- 1 tablespoon sesame oil
- 1 cup water, for cooking

Directions:
1. Cut the tilapia fillet into 2 sticks. Then pour water and insert the steamer rack in the instant pot. Line the rack with foil and place the tilapia sticks on it. Close the lid and cook them for 3 minutes on manual mode (high pressure). When the time is over, make a quick pressure release and open the lid. Dip the cooked fish sticks in the egg and then coat in the coconut flakes. Clean the instant pot and remove the steamer rack. Pour sesame oil in the instant pot and place the tilapia sticks. Cook them for minute from each side on sauté mode or until the fish sticks are light brown.

Nutrition Info: calories 222, fat 5, fiber 1, carbs 1.8, protein 2

Prawn Salad In Portobello "buns"

Servings: 4
Cooking Time: 20 Minutes
Ingredients:
- 1 ½ pounds prawns, peeled and deveined
- Juice of one lemon, freshly squeezed
- 2/3 cup water
- 1/2 teaspoon sea salt
- 1/4 teaspoon chili flakes
- 1 red onion, chopped
- 1 celery stalk with leaves, chopped
- 1 bell pepper, chopped
- 1 ½ tablespoons balsamic vinegar
- 1 cup mayonnaise
- 1 teaspoon yellow mustard
- 2 heaping tablespoons fresh cilantro, chopped
- 8 large Portobello mushroom caps, stems removed
- 1 tablespoon olive oil

Directions:
1. Toss the prawns, lemon juice, and water into your Instant Pot.
2. Secure the lid. Choose "Manual" mode and Low pressure; cook for minutes. Once cooking is complete, use a quick pressure release; carefully remove the lid.
3. Allow your prawns to cool completely.

4. Then, toss the prawns with sea salt, chili flakes, onion, celery, bell pepper, vinegar, mayonnaise, and mustard. Gently stir to combine and set aside.
5. Now, drizzle 1 tablespoon of olive oil over Portobello mushroom caps and roast them for 10 to 13 minutes at 4 degrees F.
6. To assemble your sandwiches, divide the prepared shrimp salad among roasted Portobello mushroom caps. Garnish with fresh cilantro and serve right now.

Nutrition Info:
Per Serving: 436 Calories; 2g Fat; 7.5g Carbs; 1g Protein; 4.1g Sugars

Seafood Keto Pasta

Servings: 4
Cooking Time: 10 Minutes
Ingredients:
- 1 tbsp butter
- 1 medium white onion, chopped
- 4 garlic cloves, minced
- ½ tsp red chili flakes
- 2 cups crushed tomatoes
- 3 cups chicken broth
- Salt and black pepper to taste
- ½ cup red wine
- 20 frozen jumbo shrimp
- 4 large zucchinis, spiralized
- ½ cup heavy cream
- 1 cup grated Parmesan cheese

Directions:
1. Set the IP in Sauté mode and adjust to Medium heat.
2. Melt the butter in the inner pot and sauté the onion until softened, 3 minutes. Mix in garlic and cook until fragrant, 30 seconds.
3. Stir in the remaining ingredients except for the heavy cream, Parmesan cheese, and zucchinis.
4. Lock the lid in place; select Manual mode on High Pressure and set the timer to 1 minute.
5. After cooking, perform a quick pressure release to let out the steam and open the lid.
6. Set the IP in Sauté mode and stir in the zucchinis. Allow softening for 2 to 3 minutes.
7. Mix in the heavy cream and half of the Parmesan cheese. Allow melting for 1 minute.
8. Dish the food, top with the remaining Parmesan cheese, and serve warm.

Nutrition Info:
Per Serving: Calories 76 Fats 8.83g Carbs 6.68g Net Carbs 6.28g Protein 1.65g

Chunky Fish Paprikash

Servings: 4
Cooking Time: 15 Minutes
Ingredients:

- 2 teaspoons olive oil
- 1 yellow onion, chopped
- 1 carrot, sliced
- 1 celery, diced
- 1 bell pepper, sliced
- 2 garlic cloves, minced
- 2 ripe tomatoes, crushed
- 3 cups fish stock
- 3/4 pound haddock fillets
- 1 cup shrimp
- 1/2 teaspoon caraway seeds
- 1 tablespoon sweet Hungarian paprika
- 1 teaspoon hot Hungarian paprika

Directions:
1. Press the "Sauté" button to heat up the Instant Pot. Now, heat the oil and sauté the onions until softened and fragrant.
2. Add the carrot, celery, pepper, and garlic; continue sautéing until softened.
3. Add the remaining ingredients. Secure the lid. Choose "Manual" mode and High pressure; cook for 5 minutes. Once cooking is complete, use a quick pressure release; carefully remove the lid.
4. Ladle into individual soup bowls and serve hot. Bon appétit!

Nutrition Info:
Per Serving: 179 Calories; 6.6g Fat; 5.7g Carbs; 9g Protein; 3.2g Sugars

Crab Rangoon Fat Bombs

Servings: 2
Cooking Time: 7 Minutes
Ingredients:
- 2 bacon slices, chopped
- 5 oz crab meat, canned, chopped
- ¼ cup Cheddar cheese, shredded
- ½ teaspoon garlic powder
- ¼ teaspoon onion powder
- ¼ teaspoon ground black pepper

Directions:
1. Put the chopped bacon in the instant pot and cook it on sauté mode until golden brown (appx. 5-7 minutes). Stir the bacon from time to time. Meanwhile, in the mixing bowl combine together crab meat, Cheddar cheese, garlic powder, onion powder, and ground black pepper. Stir the mixture with the help of the spoon until homogenous. Cool the cooked bacon to the room temperature. With the help of the scooper make the small balls from the crab meat mixture. Coat every crab ball in the chopped bacon.

Nutrition Info: calories 227, fat 9, fiber 0.2, carbs 2.6, protein 6

Cinnamon Prawns

Servings: 2
Cooking Time: 6 Minutes
Ingredients:
- 1 teaspoon ground cinnamon
- 12 oz prawns
- 1 teaspoon butter
- ½ cup cream

Directions:
1. Set the "Saute" mode and toss the butter in the instant pot bowl. Melt it.
2. Then add prawns and sprinkle them with the ground cinnamon.
3. Stir well and cook for minutes.
4. After this, add cream and lock the instant pot lid. Cook the meal for 3 minutes (QR).

Nutrition Info:
Per Serving: calories 260, fat 8.1, fiber 0.6, carbs 5.4, protein 3

Simple Steamed Cod

Servings: 4
Cooking Time: 10 Mins
Ingredients:
- 2 large fresh Cod Fillets, cut in 3 pieces each
- 1 cup Cherry Tomatoes
- Salt and black pepper to taste
- 4 tbsp Butter

Directions:
1. In an oven-safe dish to fit in the Instant Pot, make a bed of tomatoes at the bottom of the dish. Season the fish with the pepper and salt and place them on the tomatoes.
2. Add butter on the fish. Pour 1cup water in the Instant Pot and fit in a trivet. Place the dish in the pot, seal the lid, and cook on High Pressure for 5 minutes. Once ready, quickly release the pressure. Serve fish with tomatoes and steamed green veggies.

Nutrition Info: Calories 116, Protein 26g, Net Carbs 2g, Fat 0.9g

Spicy Grilled Cod

Servings: 4
Cooking Time: 20 Mins
Ingredients:
- 1-pound cod filets
- 2 tablespoons extra virgin olive oil
- 2 minced garlic cloves
- 1/8 teaspoon cayenne pepper
- 3 tablespoons fresh lime juice
- 1 ½ teaspoon fresh lemon juice

- ¼ cup freshly squeezed orange juice
- 1/3 cup water
- 1 tablespoon chopped fresh thyme
- 2 tablespoon chopped fresh chives
- Healthy Steamed Vegetables
- 1 head broccoli
- 2 red bell peppers, sliced in bite-sized lengths
- ¼ cup zucchini, sliced into rounds
- 2 baby carrots, sliced into rounds

Directions:
1. Prepare Veggies: Add water to an instant pot, up to ½ inches from the bottom; set the steamer inside the pot and heat over medium high heat or until the water boils. Add the veggies to the steamer and season with salt and garlic powder. Lock lid and cook for 5 Mins on high setting. Let pressure come down naturally
2. In a bowl, mix together lemon juice, lime juice, orange juice, cayenne pepper, extra virgin olive oil, garlic and water. Place fish in a dish and add the marinade, reserving ¼ cup; marinate in the refrigerator for at least 30 Mins. Broil or grill the marinated fish for about 4 Mins per side, basting regularly with the marinade. Serve the grilled fish on a plate with steamed veggies topped with chives, thyme and the reserved marinade.

Nutrition Info:
Per Serving: Calories: 200; Total Fat: 8.1 g; Carbs: 5.5 g; Dietary Fiber: 0.5 g; Sugars: 2 g; Protein: 4 g; Cholesterol: 62 mg; Sodium: 91 mg

Tomato Steamed Trout With Black Olives

Servings: 4
Cooking Time: 11 Minutes
Ingredients:
- 2 tbsp olive oil
- 1 small red onion, chopped
- 2 garlic cloves, minced
- 1 ½ cups chopped tomatoes
- 1 tsp tomato paste
- ½ cup fish broth
- Salt and black pepper to taste
- ¼ tsp red pepper flakes + more to garnish
- ¼ tsp dried basil
- ¼ tsp dried dill
- 4 trout fillets
- ¼ cup black olives, pitted

Directions:
1. Set the IP in Sauté mode and adjust to Medium heat.
2. Heat the olive oil in the inner pot and sauté the onion until softened, 3 minutes. Mix in the garlic and cook until fragrant, 30 seconds.

3. Add the tomatoes, tomato paste, fish broth, salt, black pepper, red pepper flakes, basil and dill. Allow boiling for 2 minutes and lay the trout in the sauce; spoon the sauce all over the fish.
4. Lock the lid in place; select Manual mode on High Pressure and set the timer to 2 minutes.
5. After cooking, perform a quick pressure release to let out the steam and open the lid
6. Carefully remove the fish onto serving plates and stir the black olives into the sauce.
7. Cook in Sauté mode for 2 to 3 minutes and adjust taste with salt and black pepper.
8. Spoon the sauce all over the fish and serve warm.

Nutrition Info:
Per Serving: Calories 349 Fats 39g Carbs 46g Net Carbs 7.56g Protein 4g

Asparagus With Colby Cheese

Servings: 4
Cooking Time: 10 Minutes
Ingredients:
- 1 ½ pounds fresh asparagus
- 2 tablespoons olive oil
- 4 garlic cloves, minced
- Sea salt, to taste
- 1/4 teaspoon ground black pepper
- 1/2 cup Colby cheese, shredded

Directions:
1. Add cup of water and a steamer basket to your Instant Pot.
2. Now, place the asparagus on the steamer basket; drizzle your asparagus with olive oil. Scatter garlic over the top of the asparagus.
3. Season with salt and black pepper.
4. Secure the lid. Choose "Manual" mode and High pressure; cook for 1 minute. Once cooking is complete, use a quick pressure release; carefully remove the lid.
5. Transfer the prepared asparagus to a nice serving platter and scatter shredded cheese over the top. Enjoy!

Nutrition Info:
Per Serving: 164 Calories; 2g Fat; 8.1g Carbs; 7.8g Protein; 3.3g Sugars

Winter Vegetable Soup With Shirataki Rice

Servings: 6
Cooking Time: 30 Mins
Ingredients:
- ½ cup grated Parmesan Cheese
- 6 cups Veggie Broth
- 1 Celery stick, chopped
- 2 Garlic cloves, minced

- 2 cups kale, shredded
- 1 Parsnip, chopped
- 1 leek, (green part removed) finely sliced, rinsed
- 2 Rosemary Sprigs
- 2 tbsp Butter
- 1 package Shirataki rice, cooked
- Salt and black pepper to taste

Directions:
1. Melt butter on Sauté, and add the leek. Cook for 3 minutes, until soft. Add the garlic and cook for another minute. Stir in the kale and cook for 3 minutes, until soft.
2. Pour in broth and add the rosemary, parsnip, and celery. Seal the lid, select Manual cook for minutes on High pressure.
3. When the timer goes off, do a quick pressure release. Discard the rosemary. Stir in the Parmesan cheese and shirataki rice, adjust the seasoning and serve immediately.

Nutrition Info: Calories 181, Protein 11g, Net Carbs 2.5g, Fat 11g

Collard Wraps

Servings: 4
Cooking Time: 6 Minutes
Ingredients:
- 1 cup scallions, chopped
- 3 eggs
- 2 tablespoon cream cheese
- 1/3 teaspoon salt
- 1 teaspoon chili flakes
- 1 cup collard greens, only leaves
- 1 cup water, for cooking

Directions:
1. Cook the eggs: pour water and insert the steamer rack in the instant pot. Place the eggs on the rack and close the lid. Cook them in manual mode (high pressure) for 6 minutes. Then make the quick pressure release. Cool and peel the eggs. After this, chop the eggs and mix them up with the scallions. Add cream cheese, salt, and chili flakes. Trim the collard greens if needed. Spread the mixture over the collard greens leaves and wrap them.

Nutrition Info: calories 76, fat 5.2, fiber 1, carbs 2.9, protein 5.3

Bell Peppers And Brussels Sprouts

Servings: 4
Cooking Time: 15 Minutes
Ingredients:
- 1 pound mixed bell peppers, cut into wedges
- ½ pound Brussels sprouts, halved
- 1 cup veggie stock
- 1 tablespoon ghee, melted

- 1 teaspoon smoked paprika
- 1 teaspoon cumin, ground
- 1 tablespoon chives, chopped

Directions:

1. Set the instant pot on Sauté mode, add the ghee, heat it up, add the peppers and the sprouts and cook for 3 minutes. Put the lid on, cook on High for minutes, release the pressure fast for 5 minutes, divide the mix between plates and serve.

Nutrition Info: calories 68, fat 4.2, fiber 2.3, carbs 3.4, protein 2.4

Spectacular Fennel With Goat Cheese

Servings: 3
Cooking Time: 10 Minutes
Ingredients:

- 1 lb. fennel bulbs, cut into wedges
- 2 tablespoons butter, melted
- 1 cup goat cheese, crumbled
- ½ teaspoon dried dill weed
- 2 tablespoons dry white wine
- 1/2 cup vegetable broth
- 1/4 cup of water
- ½ teaspoon salt
- ½ teaspoon pepper

Directions:

1. Press the "Sauté" button and preheat your Instant Pot. Add the melted butter and saute fennel for minute.
2. Then, stir in water, salt, pepper, vegetable broth, dry white wine, and dried dill.
3. Secure the lid. Choose "Manual" mode and Low pressure; cook for 2 minutes. When cooking is complete, use a quick pressure release and carefully remove the lid.
4. Serve and top with goat cheese. Bon appétit!

Nutrition Info:
Per Serving: 313 Calories; 4g Fat; 7g Carbs; 5g Protein; 3.8g Sugars

Feta-stuffed Mushrooms With Walnuts

Servings: 2
Cooking Time: 30 Mins
Ingredients:

- 4 Portobello Mushrooms
- 1 Garlic Clove, minced
- 1 cup crumbled Feta Cheese
- 1 Onion, chopped
- ¼ cup Walnuts, roughly chopped
- 2 tap fresh Dill, chopped
- 1 egg, beaten

- Salt and black pepper to taste
- 1 tbsp Olive oil
- 1 ½ cups Water

Directions:

1. Pour in the water and lower the trivet. Grease a baking dish with cooking spray and set aside.
2. Prepare the mushrooms by removing the stems and washing them well. In a bowl, combine garlic, feta, onion, walnuts, and dill well. Fill the mushrooms with the feta mixture and then drizzle with the oil; season to taste. Arrange the stuffed portobellos in the baking dish.
3. Place the dish on top of the trivet and seal the lid. Cook on High pressure for 20 minutes. When the timer goes off, do a quick pressure release and open the lid carefully.

Nutrition Info: Calories 326, Protein 15g, Net Carbs 5g, Fat 29g

Spicy Asian-style Soup

Servings: 4
Cooking Time: 10 Minutes
Ingredients:

- 2 tablespoons butter, softened
- 1 shallot, diced
- 2 cloves garlic, diced
- 2 cups Crimini mushrooms
- 4 cups water
- 2 chicken bouillon cubes
- 1/2 cup soy milk
- 1 cup celery, diced
- 1/2 pound asparagus, diced
- 1 tablespoon coconut aminos
- Sea salt and black pepper, to taste
- 1 teaspoon Taco seasoning
- 1/4 teaspoon freshly ground black pepper
- 1 bay leaf

Directions:

1. Press the "Sauté" button to heat up your Instant Pot. Once hot, melt the butter; then, sweat the shallot until softened.
2. Stir in garlic; cook an additional 40 seconds, stirring frequently.
3. Add the remaining ingredients.
4. Secure the lid. Choose "Manual" mode and High pressure; cook for 7 minutes. Once cooking is complete, use a quick pressure release; carefully remove the lid.
5. Ladle into individual bowls and serve warm. Bon appétit!

Nutrition Info:
Per Serving: 104 Calories; 7g Fat; 6.6g Total Carbs; 3.9g Protein; 3.5g Sugars

Faux-tatoes

Servings: 4
Cooking Time: 18 Minutes
Ingredients:
- 1 daikon radish, sliced
- 3 oz scallions, diced
- 1 tablespoon coconut oil
- 1 teaspoon salt

Directions:
1. Mix up daikon radish and scallions in the bowl and sprinkle with salt.
2. Then toss the coconut oil in the instant pot and melt it on saute mode.
3. Add daikon radish mixture and close the lid.
4. Saute the vegetables for 5 minutes and turn into another side.
5. Cook the vegetables for 10 minutes more. Stir them from time to time.

Nutrition Info:
Per Serving: calories 39, fat 3.4, fiber 0.8, carbs 2.1, protein 0.6

Chili Cauliflower Rice

Servings: 4
Cooking Time: 20 Minutes
Ingredients:
- A pinch of salt and black pepper
- ½ teaspoon cayenne pepper
- 1 teaspoon chili powder
- 2 tablespoons green onions, chopped
- 1 cup chicken stock
- 2 cups cauliflower rice

Directions:
1. In your instant pot, mix the cauliflower rice with the stock and the rest of the ingredients, put the lid on and cook on Low for 20 minutes. Release the pressure naturally for minutes, divide the mix between plates and serve.

Nutrition Info: calories 52, fat 1.5, fiber 0.2, carbs 0.3, protein 0.7

Celery Soup With Salsiccia

Servings: 4
Cooking Time: 30 Minutes
Ingredients:
- 3 cups celery, chopped
- 1 carrot, chopped
- 1/2 cup brown onion, chopped
- 1 garlic clove, pressed
- 1/2 pound with Salsiccia links, casing removed and sliced

- 1/2 cup full-fat milk
- 3 cups roasted vegetable broth
- Kosher salt, to taste
- 1/2 teaspoon ground black pepper
- 1/2 teaspoon dried chili flakes
- 2 teaspoon coconut oil

Directions:
1. Simply throw all of the above ingredients into your Instant Pot; gently stir to combine.
2. Secure the lid. Choose "Soup/Broth" mode and High pressure; cook for minutes. Once cooking is complete, use a quick pressure release; carefully remove the lid.
3. Ladle into four soup bowls and serve hot. Enjoy!

Nutrition Info:
Per Serving: 150 Calories; 5.9g Fat; 7.9g Carbs; 4g Protein; 4.7g Sugars

Aromatic Eggplant Mix

Servings: 2
Cooking Time: 30 Minutes
Ingredients:
- 8 oz eggplant, chopped
- 3 oz asparagus, chopped
- 1 teaspoon salt
- 1 teaspoon ground cumin
- 1 cup chicken broth
- 1 bell pepper, chopped

Directions:
1. Put all vegetables in the instant pot.
2. Close the lid and cook the meal on saute mode for 30 minutes.
3. When the time is finished and the meal is cooked, stir it well with the help of the spoon.

Nutrition Info:
Per Serving: calories 186, fat 1, fiber 4.9, carbs 2, protein 8

Garlic Green Beans

Servings: 4
Cooking Time: 10 Minutes
Ingredients:
- 1 pound green beans, sliced
- 1 cup water
- Salt and pepper
- 3 cloves minced garlic
- 2 tablespoons butter

Directions:
1. Place the green beans in the Instant Pot.
2. Add the water, butter, and garlic then stir well.

3. Close and lock the lid, then press the Manual button and cook on Low Pressure for 5 minutes.
4. When the timer goes off, do a Quick Release by pressing Cancel and switching the steam valve to "venting."
5. When the pot has depressurized, open the lid.
6. Season the beans with salt and pepper and serve hot.

Nutrition Info: calories 90 fat 6g ,protein 2g ,carbs 8.5g ,fiber 4g ,net carbs 4.5g

Fake Mac And Cheese

Servings: 4
Cooking Time: 11 Mins
Ingredients:
- 1 Cauliflower Head, finely chopped
- ½ cup shredded Cheddar Cheese
- ¼ cup shredded Mozzarella Cheese
- 2 tbsp grated Parmesan Cheese
- ½ cup Heavy Cream
- Salt and black pepper to taste

Directions:
1. Combine the heavy cream, cauliflower, cheddar, and mozzarella, in the Instant Pot. Season with salt and pepper. Seal the lid on and cook on High pressure for 6 minutes. Do a quick pressure release and open the lid carefully. Sprinkle with the Parmesan cheese and serve.

Nutrition Info: Calories 230, Protein 7g, Net Carbs 2.5g, Fat 12g

Spinach With Cheese

Servings: 4
Cooking Time: 10 Minutes
Ingredients:
- 2 tablespoons butter, melted
- 1/2 cup scallions, chopped
- 2 cloves garlic, smashed
- 1 ½ pounds fresh spinach
- 1 cup vegetable broth, preferably homemade
- 1 cup cream cheese, cubed
- Seasoned salt and ground black pepper, to taste
- 1/2 teaspoon dried dill weed

Directions:
1. Press the "Sauté" button to heat up the Instant Pot. Then, melt the butter; cook the scallions and garlic until tender and aromatic.
2. Add the remaining ingredients and stir to combine well.
3. Secure the lid. Choose "Manual" mode and High pressure; cook for 2 minutes. Once cooking is complete, use a quick pressure release; carefully remove the lid.
4. Ladle into individual bowls and serve warm. Bon appétit!

Nutrition Info:
Per Serving: 283 Calories; 9g Fat; 6.4g Total Carbs; 7g Protein; 2.2g Sugars

Flax And Swiss Chard Patties

Servings: 4
Cooking Time: 22 Mins
Ingredients:

- 1 cup shredded Mozzarella Cheese
- 1 tbsp Flaxseed Meal
- 2 Green Onions, chopped
- ½ Cauliflower Head
- 1 cup chopped Swiss Chard
- 1 tbsp Olive oil
- 1 tsp chopped Thyme
- 2 Eggs
- ½ cup grated Parmesan Cheese
- 2 tbsp Butter
- Salt and black pepper to taste

Directions:

1. Place cauliflower in a food processor and blend it until rice-like consistency forms. Stir in thyme, Swiss chard, and green onions. Process until smooth and transfer to a bowl. Mix in the remaining ingredients.
2. Melt half of the butter on Sauté. Place ¼ of the batter in the pot and cook for a few minutes on both sides, until golden and crispy. Repeat the process one more time. Then, melt the remaining batter and do the same with the remaining batch. Serve with garlic yogurt sauce.

Nutrition Info: Calories 281, Protein 16g, Net Carbs 3.5g, Fat 20g

Cilantro Red Cabbage And Artichokes

Servings: 4
Cooking Time: 20 Minutes
Ingredients:

- ½ cup canned artichoke hearts, drained and chopped
- 3 garlic cloves, minced
- 2 small red cabbage heads, shredded
- A pinch of salt and black pepper
- 1 cup chicken stock
- ½ cup tomato passata
- 1 tablespoon cilantro, chopped

Directions:

1. In your instant pot, combine the artichokes with the garlic and the rest of the ingredients except the cilantro, put the lid on and cook on High for 20 minutes. Release the pressure naturally for minutes, divide the mix between plates and serve with the cilantro sprinkled on top.

Nutrition Info: calories 141, fat 1.5, fiber 0.2, carbs 1.2, protein 7.3

Sesame Bok Choy

Servings: 2
Cooking Time: 7 Minutes
Ingredients:

- 2 cups bok choy, sliced
- 1 teaspoon sesame seeds
- 1 tablespoon apple cider vinegar
- 1 teaspoon sesame oil
- ¾ teaspoon salt
- 1 cup water, for cooking

Directions:

1. Pour water and insert the steamer rack in the instant pot.
2. Put the bok choy in the steamer rack and close the lid.
3. Cook the vegetables on the "Steam" mode for minutes.
4. Make a quick pressure release and transfer the bok choy on the plate.
5. Sprinkle the meal with salt, sesame oil, apple cider vinegar, and sesame seeds.
6. Shake the bok choy gently.
7. Serve the bok choy warm!

Nutrition Info:
Per Serving: calories 35, fat 2.9, fiber 0.7, carbs 1.8, protein 1.3

Spiced Radishes

Servings: 4
Cooking Time: 18 Mins
Ingredients:

- 16 Radishes, halved
- 2 tsp minced Garlic
- ¼ cup Olive oil
- 1 tsp chopped Rosemary
- ½ tsp Red Pepper Flakes
- Salt and black pepper to taste

Directions:

1. Set to Sauté and dump all ingredients inside, and stir well to combine. Cook until the radishes are roasted, slightly brown color and caramelized.

Nutrition Info: Calories 105, Protein 1g, Net Carbs 1g, Fat 14g

Tuscan Mushrooms Sauce

Servings: 3
Cooking Time: 10 Minutes
Ingredients:

- 1 teaspoon almond butter
- ½ cup fresh spinach, chopped
- ½ cup white mushrooms, sliced
- 2 tablespoons flax meal
- 1 oz Parmesan, grated
- 1 cup coconut cream
- 1 teaspoon Tuscan seasonings
- ½ cup cherry tomatoes, chopped

Directions:
1. Heat up the almond butter in the instant pot on sauté mode. Put mushrooms in the hot almond butter and cook them for 3 minutes. After this, stir them and add spinach. Stir well. Sprinkle the vegetables with Tuscan seasonings and flax meal. After this, add coconut cream and cherry tomatoes. Close the lid and cook the sauce on manual (high pressure) for 5 minutes. Allow the natural pressure release for minutes. Open the lid and add Parmesan. With the help of the spatula, mix up the meal until cheese is melted.

Nutrition Info: calories 279, fat 9, fiber 4.2, carbs 9.2, protein 8.1

Swiss Chard With Ham Hock

Servings: 4
Cooking Time: 45 Minutes
Ingredients:
- 2 tablespoons olive oil
- 1 cup leeks, chopped
- 2 garlic cloves, minced
- Sea salt and ground black pepper, to taste
- 1/2 teaspoon cayenne pepper
- 3 cups beef bone broth
- 1 (1-pound ham hock
- 1 pound Swiss chard, torn into pieces

Directions:
1. Press the "Sauté" button to heat up your Instant Pot; now, heat the olive oil. Cook the leeks for about 2 minutes or until softened.
2. Stir in the garlic and cook an additional 40 seconds or until aromatic.
3. Add the salt, black pepper, cayenne pepper, broth, and ham hock.
4. Secure the lid. Choose "Meat/Stew" mode and High pressure; cook for 35 minutes. Once cooking is complete, use a natural pressure release; carefully remove the lid.
5. Then, add Swiss chard and choose "Manual" mode; cook for minutes. Once cooking is complete, use a quick pressure release; carefully remove the lid. Bon appétit!

Nutrition Info:
Per Serving: 268 Calories; 3g Fat; 8.1g Carbs; 9g Protein; 2.2g Sugars

Zucchini With Green Peppercorn Sauce

Servings: 4

Cooking Time: 10 Minutes

Ingredients:

- 1 cup water
- 2 zucchini, sliced
- Sea salt, to taste
- Green Peppercorn Sauce:
- 2 tablespoons butter
- 1/2 cup green onions, minced
- 2 tablespoons Cognac
- 1 ½ cups chicken broth
- 1 cup whipping cream
- 1 ½ tablespoons green peppercorns in brine, drained and crushed slightly

Directions:

1. Add water and a steamer basket to the Instant Pot. Arrange your zucchini on the steamer basket.
2. Secure the lid. Choose "Manual" mode and Low pressure; cook for 3 minutes. Once cooking is complete, use a quick pressure release; carefully remove the lid.
3. Season zucchini with salt and set aside.
4. Wipe down the Instant Pot with a damp cloth. Press the "Sauté" button to heat up your Instant Pot.
5. Melt the butter and then, sauté green onions until tender. Add Cognac and cook for 2 minutes longer. Then, pour in chicken broth and let it boil another 4 minutes.
6. Lastly, stir in the cream and peppercorns. Continue to simmer until the sauce is thickened and thoroughly warmed.
7. Serve your zucchini with the sauce on the side. Bon appétit!

Nutrition Info:

Per Serving: 251 Calories; 3g Fat; 3.2g Carbs; 2g Protein; 1.5g Sugars

Family Cauliflower Soup

Servings: 4

Cooking Time: 10 Minutes

Ingredients:

- 4 tablespoons butter, softened
- 1/2 cup leeks, thinly sliced
- 2 cloves garlic, minced
- 3/4 pound cauliflower, broken into florets
- 1 cup water
- 2 cups chicken stock
- 1 cup full-fat milk
- Kosher salt, to taste
- 1/3 teaspoon ground black pepper

Directions:

1. Press the "Sauté" button to heat up your Instant Pot. Then, melt the butter; sauté the leeks until softened.
2. Then, sauté the garlic until fragrant, about 30 seconds. Add the remaining ingredients and gently stir to combine.
3. Secure the lid. Choose "Manual" mode and Low pressure; cook for 5 minutes. Once cooking is complete, use a quick pressure release; carefully remove the lid.
4. Ladle into individual bowls and serve warm. Bon appétit!

Nutrition Info:
Per Serving: 167 Calories; 7g Fat; 8.7g Carbs; 3.8g Protein; 5.1g Sugars

Sichuan Style Green Beans

Servings: 4
Cooking Time: 7 Minutes
Ingredients:
- 1 tablespoon apple cider vinegar
- ½ teaspoon chili flakes
- ½ teaspoon minced garlic
- 1 tablespoon sesame oil
- ½ teaspoon minced ginger
- 12 oz green beans, trimmed
- 1 cup water, for cooking

Directions:
1. Pour water and insert the steamer rack in the instant pot. Put the green beans in the rack and close the lid. Cook the vegetables for 7 minutes on steam mode. Then make a quick pressure release. Put the cooked green beans in the bowl. Sprinkle them with chili flakes, minced garlic, minced ginger, sesame oil, and apple cider vinegar. Mix up the green beans and leave for minutes to marinate.

Nutrition Info: calories 59, fat 3.5, fiber 2.9, carbs 6.4, protein 1.6

Tomato And Dill Sauté

Servings: 4
Cooking Time: 15 Minutes
Ingredients:
- 1 pound tomatoes, cubed
- 1 tablespoon dill, chopped
- 1 teaspoon garlic, minced
- A pinch of salt and black pepper
- ½ cup chicken stock
- 1 tablespoon parsley, chopped

Directions:
1. In your instant pot, mix the tomatoes with the dill and the rest of the ingredients, put the lid on and cook on High for minutes. Release the pressure naturally for 10 minutes, divide the mix between plates and serve.

Nutrition Info: calories 25, fat 1.9, fiber 0.5, carbs 1.4, protein 1.4

Nutmeg Zucchini Rice

Servings: 4
Cooking Time: 15 Minutes
Ingredients:

- 2 tablespoons avocado oil
- 1 shallot, chopped
- 2 garlic cloves, minced
- 2 cups cauliflower rice
- 1 and ½ cups chicken stock
- 1 big zucchini, grated
- ½ teaspoon allspice, ground
- 1 tablespoon parsley, chopped

Directions:

1. Set your instant pot on Sauté mode, add the oil, heat it up, add the shallot and the garlic and sauté for 2 minutes. Add the rest of the ingredients, toss, put the lid on and cook on High for minutes. Release the pressure naturally for 10 minutes, divide the mix between plates and serve as a side dish.

Nutrition Info: calories 62, fat 1.7, fiber 1, carbs 1.4, protein 1.2

Superpower Broccoli Salad Bowl

Servings: 4
Cooking Time: 10 Minutes
Ingredients:

- 1 pound broccoli, broken into florets
- 2 tablespoons balsamic vinegar
- 2 garlic cloves, minced
- 1 teaspoon mustard seeds
- 1 teaspoon cumin seeds
- Salt and pepper, to taste
- 1 cup Cottage cheese, crumbled

Directions:

1. Place cup of water and a steamer basket in your Instant Pot.
2. Place the broccoli in the steamer basket.
3. Secure the lid. Choose "Manual" mode and High pressure; cook for 5 minutes. Once cooking is complete, use a quick pressure release; carefully remove the lid.
4. Then, toss your broccoli with the other ingredients. Serve and enjoy!

Nutrition Info:
Per Serving: 95 Calories; 3.1g Fat; 5.6g Total Carbs; 9.9g Protein; 2.8g Sugars

Cauliflower Cheese

Servings: 2
Cooking Time: 15 Minutes
Ingredients:

- ½ cup cauliflower, cut into florets
- ½ teaspoon dried dill
- ¼ teaspoon dried cilantro
- ¼ teaspoon dried sage
- 3 oz Parmesan, grated
- ¼ cup of organic almond milk

Directions:

1. Put cauliflower in the instant pot bowl. Sprinkle it with dried dill, cilantro, and sage. In the separated bowl mix up together almond milk and Parmesan. Pour the liquid over the cauliflower and close the lid. Cook the meal on sauté mode for minutes. Stir the cauliflower every 5 minutes to avoid burning.

Nutrition Info: calories 164, fat 7, fiber 1.2, carbs 4, protein 7

Cheesy Green Beans

Servings: 4
Cooking Time: 22 Mins
Ingredients:

- 12 ounces Green Beans
- 2 cups Water
- ½ cup grated Parmesan Cheese
- 1 Egg
- ¼ tsp Garlic Powder
- 2 tbsp Olive oil
- ¼ tsp Onion Powder
- Salt and black pepper to taste

Directions:

1. Pour the water into the Instant Pot. Place the green beans inside the steamer basket and lower the basket into the water. Seal the lid and cook on High pressure for 3 minutes.
2. When it goes off, release the pressure quickly. Remove the steamer basket using mittens. Discard the water and wipe the pot clean. Prepare an ice bath and add in the green beans.
3. Meanwhile, beat the egg and heat half of the olive oil on Sauté. Place all remaining ingredients in a bowl and stir to combine. Dip half of the green beans in egg first, then coat in Parmesan mixture. Place in the pot and cook for a minute per side. Cook in batches.

Nutrition Info: Calories 151, Protein 11g, Net Carbs 3g, Fat 8g

Braised Sauerkraut With Bacon

Servings: 6
Cooking Time: 15 Minutes

Ingredients:
- 6 ounces meaty bacon, roughly chopped
- 1 yellow onion, chopped
- 2 garlic cloves, minced
- 1/4 cup dry white wine
- 1 carrot, grated
- 1 bell pepper, chopped
- 2 anchos, minced
- 3 cups sauerkraut, rinsed and drained
- 1 teaspoon cayenne pepper
- 1 bay leaf
- 1 teaspoon mixed peppercorns
- 4 cups beef bone broth

Directions:
1. Press the "Sauté" button to heat up your Instant Pot. Once hot, cook the bacon until crisp; reserve.
2. Now, cook the onion and garlic in pan drippings. Add a splash of wine to deglaze the bottom of the Instant Pot.
3. Then, stir in the remaining ingredients.
4. Secure the lid. Choose "Manual" mode and High pressure; cook for 10 minutes. Once cooking is complete, use a natural pressure release; carefully remove the lid.
5. Divide your sauerkraut among serving bowls and top with the reserved bacon. Bon appétit!

Nutrition Info:
Per Serving: 184 Calories; 5g Fat; 7.1g Carbs; 7.1g Protein; 3.2g Sugars

Hash Brown Casserole

Servings: 4
Cooking Time: 20 Minutes
Ingredients:
- ½ cup cauliflower stalk, shredded
- 2 oz turnip, grated
- ½ cup Cheddar cheese, shredded
- ½ teaspoon onion powder
- ¼ teaspoon ground black pepper
- ¼ teaspoon white pepper
- ¼ teaspoon salt
- 1 teaspoon coconut oil
- 1 cup of coconut milk

Directions:
1. Place the coconut oil in the instant pot. Heat it up on sauté mode until the oil is melted. Add shredded cauliflower and turnip. Sprinkle the vegetables with onion powder, ground black pepper, and white pepper. Add salt and stir the vegetables. Cook them on sauté mode for 5

minutes. After this, add coconut milk and shredded Cheddar cheese. Close the lid and cook the casserole on meat/stew mode for minutes.

Nutrition Info: calories 213, fat 1, fiber 1.9, carbs 5.4, protein 5.3

Lemon Peppers And Bok Choy

Servings: 4
Cooking Time: 20 Minutes
Ingredients:

- 1 pound mixed bell peppers, cut into wedges
- 1 cup bok choy, chopped
- 2 tablespoons sweet paprika
- A pinch of salt and black pepper
- ½ cup chicken stock
- ¼ cup lemon juice
- 1 tablespoon cilantro, chopped

Directions:

1. In your instant pot, mix the bell peppers with the bok choy and the rest of the ingredients except the cilantro, put the lid on and cook on High for 20 minutes. Release the pressure naturally for minutes, divide the mix between plates, sprinkle the cilantro on top and serve.

Nutrition Info: calories 34, fat 1, fiber 0.2, carbs 0.5, protein 1.3

Vegetables à La Grecque

Servings: 4
Cooking Time: 10 Minutes
Ingredients:

- 2 tablespoons olive oil
- 2 garlic cloves, minced
- 1 red onion, chopped
- 10 ounces button mushrooms, thinly sliced
- 1 (1-pound eggplant, sliced
- 1/2 teaspoon dried basil
- 1 teaspoon dried oregano
- 1 thyme sprig, leaves picked
- 2 rosemary sprigs, leaves picked
- 1/2 cup tomato sauce
- 1/4 cup dry Greek wine
- 1/4 cup water
- 8 ounces Halloumi cheese, cubed
- 4 tablespoons Kalamata olives, pitted and halved

Directions:

1. Press the "Sauté" button to heat up your Instant Pot; now, heat the olive oil. Cook the garlic and red onions for to 2 minutes, stirring periodically.
2. Stir in the mushrooms and continue to sauté an additional to 3 minutes.

3. Add the eggplant, basil, oregano, thyme, rosemary, tomato sauce, Greek wine, and water.
4. Secure the lid. Choose "Manual" mode and Low pressure; cook for 3 minutes. Once cooking is complete, use a quick pressure release; carefully remove the lid.
5. Top with cheese and olives. Bon appétit!

Nutrition Info:

Per Serving: 326 Calories; 1g Fat; 8.4g Carbs; 7g Protein; 4.3g Sugars

Italian Style Kale

Servings: 3

Cooking Time: 3 Minutes

Ingredients:

- 10 oz kale, Italian dark-leaf
- 1 tablespoon Italian seasonings
- 1 cup water, for cooking

Directions:

1. Chop the kale roughly and put it in the steamer pan. Sprinkle the greens with seasonings and stir well.
2. Then pour water and insert the steamer rack in the instant pot.
3. Put the pan with kale in the instant pot.
4. Cook the meal on the "Steam" mode for 3 minutes.

Nutrition Info:

Per Serving: calories 61, fat 1.4, fiber 1.4, carbs 4, protein 2.8

Parmesan Onion Rings

Servings: 4

Cooking Time: 5 Minutes

Ingredients:

- 1 big white onion
- 1 egg, beaten
- 1 teaspoon cream cheese
- 2 oz Parmesan, grated
- 2 tablespoons almond meal
- 1 tablespoon butter

Directions:

1. Trim and peel the onion. Then slice it roughly and separate every onion slice into the rings. In the mixing bowl combine together Parmesan and almond meal. Then take a separated bowl and mix up cream cheese and egg in it. Dip the onion rings in the egg mixture and then coat well in cheese mixture. Toss butter in the instant pot and melt it on sauté mode. Then arrange the onion rings in the melted butter in one layer. Cook the onion rings for 2 minutes from each side on sauté mode.

Nutrition Info: calories 122, fat 8.8, fiber 1.2, carbs 4.8, protein 7.1

Bok Choy Salad

Servings: 4
Cooking Time: 20 Minutes
Ingredients:
- 10 oz baby bok choy, trimmed
- ¼ teaspoon of sea salt
- 1 tablespoon peanut oil
- ½ teaspoon chili flakes
- ½ cup chicken broth
- 1 teaspoon olive oil
- 4 oz prosciutto, chopped

Directions:
1. Pour peanut oil in the instant pot and preheat it on sauté mode. When the oil is hot, add baby bok choy, sea salt, and chili flakes. Cook the vegetables for 3-4 minutes or until they are light brown. Add chicken broth and close the lid. Cook the bok choy on manual (high pressure) for 4 minutes. Then make the quick pressure release. Transfer the bok choy in the salad bowl. Add prosciutto and olive oil. Mix the salad.

Nutrition Info: calories 95, fat 6.4, fiber 0.7, carbs 2.1, protein 7.6

New Asparagus With Cheddar Cheese

Servings: 4
Cooking Time: 10 Minutes
Ingredients:
- 2 tablespoons canola oil
- ½ teaspoon salt
- 2 lbs. fresh asparagus
- 1 cup Cheddar cheese, shredded
- ½ teaspoon pepper
- 3 garlic cloves, minced
- 1 cup of water

Directions:
1. Add to your Instant Pot cup of water and a steamer basket
2. Place the asparagus on the steamer basket. Then drizzle with canola oil and season with minced garlic, salt, and pepper.
3. Secure the lid. Choose "Manual" mode and High pressure; cook for 1 minute. When cooking is complete, use a quick pressure release and carefully remove the lid.
4. Serve warm and top with cheddar cheese. Enjoy!

Nutrition Info:
Per Serving: 247 Calories; 4g Fat; 7g Carbs; 1g Protein; 4.3g Sugars

Sauteed Green Mix

Servings: 2

Cooking Time: 10 Minutes
Ingredients:
- 2 cups spinach, chopped
- 1 cup kale, chopped
- ½ cup chicken stock
- 1 teaspoon cream cheese
- ½ teaspoon salt
- ½ cup broccoli raab, chopped

Directions:
1. Pour the chicken stock in the instant pot bowl.
2. Add cream cheese, salt, spinach, kale, and broccoli raab.
3. Cook the meal on the "Saute" mode for 5 minutes. Stir well.
4. Discard the greens from the chicken stock gravy and transfer on the plates.

Nutrition Info:
Per Serving: calories 37, fat 0.8, fiber 1.2, carbs 5.6, protein 2.7

Tomato Soup With Goat Cheese Topping

Servings: 6
Cooking Time: 16 Mins
Ingredients:
- 1 cup Olive oil
- 2 tbsp Lemon Juice
- 2 tbsp Apple Cider Vinegar
- 1 Cucumber, chopped
- 2 Red Peppers, roasted and chopped
- 1 Small Red Onion, chopped
- 2 Green Peppers, chopped
- 4 Tomatoes, chopped
- 2 Spring Onions, chopped
- 2 Garlic Cloves
- 7 ounces Goat Cheese, crumbled
- 2 Avocados, flesh scooped out
- 6 cups water

Directions:
1. Dump all the ingredients, except the cheese, in a food processor and pulse until smooth. Pour the mixture into your Instant Pot and seal the lid. Cook for minutes on High pressure. When the timer goes off, do a quick pressure release and ladle into 6 serving bowls. Top with goat cheese, to serve.

Nutrition Info: Calories 532, Protein 18g, Net Carbs 6.5g, Fat 50g

Asparagus And Tomatoes

Servings: 4
Cooking Time: 15 Minutes

Ingredients:
- 1 pound asparagus, trimmed
- 1 cup chicken stock
- A pinch of salt and black pepper
- 2 cups cherry tomatoes, halved
- 1 tablespoon basil, chopped
- 1 tablespoon chives, chopped

Directions:
1. In your instant pot, mix the asparagus with the stock and the rest of the ingredients, put the lid on and cook on High for minutes. Release the pressure fast for 5 minutes, divide mix between plates and serve.

Nutrition Info: calories 42, fat 1.2, fiber 0.7, carbs 1, protein 3.5

Green Beans And Kale

Servings: 4
Cooking Time: 8 Minutes
Ingredients:
- 2 cups kale, torn
- 1 tablespoon avocado oil
- 1 garlic clove, minced
- 1 pound green beans, trimmed
- 1 tablespoon chives, chopped
- 1 tablespoon oregano, chopped
- ¼ cup chicken stock
- 1 teaspoon chili powder

Directions:
1. Set your instant pot on Sauté mode, add the oil, heat it up, add the garlic and cook for minute. Add the rest of the ingredients, put the lid on and cook on High for 7 minutes. Release the pressure naturally for 10 minutes, divide the mix between plates and serve.

Nutrition Info: calories 64, fat 1.9, fiber 0.5, carbs 1.4, protein 3.4

Cheesy Artichokes On The Go

Servings: 3
Cooking Time: 10 Minutes
Ingredients:
- 3 medium-sized artichokes, cleaned and trimmed
- 3 cloves garlic, smashed
- 3 tablespoons butter, melted
- Sea salt, to taste
- 1/2 teaspoon cayenne pepper
- 1/4 teaspoon ground black pepper, or more to taste
- 1 lemon, freshly squeezed
- 1 cup Monterey-Jack cheese, shredded

- 1 tablespoon fresh parsley, roughly chopped

Directions:

1. Start by adding cup of water and a steamer basket to the Instant Pot. Place the artichokes in the steamer basket; add garlic and butter.
2. Secure the lid. Choose "Manual" mode and High pressure; cook for 8 minutes. Once cooking is complete, use a quick pressure release; carefully remove the lid.
3. Season your artichokes with salt, cayenne pepper, and black pepper. Now, drizzle them with lemon juice.
4. Top with cheese and parsley and serve immediately. Bon appétit!

Nutrition Info:

Per Serving: 173 Calories; 5g Fat; 6g Total Carbs; 8.1g Protein; 0.9g Sugars

Traditional Caramelized Onion Soup

Servings: 4

Cooking Time: 15 Minutes

Ingredients:

- 1/2 stick butter, softened
- 3/4 pound yellow onions, sliced
- 4 cups chicken stock
- 1/2 teaspoon dried basil
- Kosher salt and ground black pepper, to taste
- 1/2 cup Swiss cheese, freshly grated

Directions:

1. Press the "Sauté" button to heat up your Instant Pot. Once hot, melt the butter and sauté the onions until caramelized and tender.
2. Add chicken stock, basil, salt, and black pepper.
3. Secure the lid. Choose "Manual" mode and High pressure; cook for 10 minutes. Once cooking is complete, use a quick pressure release; carefully remove the lid.
4. Ladle the soup into individual bowls and top with grated cheese. Enjoy!

Nutrition Info:

Per Serving: 228 Calories; 18g Fat; 7.3g Carbs; 5g Protein; 4.5g Sugars

Sweet Smokies

Servings: 3

Cooking Time: 15 Minutes

Ingredients:

- 1 teaspoon Erythritol
- ½ teaspoon sesame seeds
- 2 tablespoons keto BBQ sauce
- 8 oz cocktail sausages
- 1/3 cup chicken broth

Directions:

1. Put Erythritol, sesame seeds, BBQ sauce, and chicken broth in the instant pot.

2. Preheat the mixture on saute mode for minutes.
3. Then add cocktail sausages and stir the mixture well.
4. Cook the meal for 10 minutes on saute mode. Stir the sausages every 2 minutes.

Nutrition Info:
Per Serving: calories 49, fat 2.5, fiber 5.7, carbs 0.1, protein 2.3

Bok Choy And Parmesan Mix

Servings: 4
Cooking Time: 10 Minutes
Ingredients:
- 2 cups bok choy, torn
- ½ cup chicken stock
- 2 tablespoons dill, chopped
- 1 tablespoon tomato passata
- 3 tablespoons parmesan cheese, grated

Directions:
1. In your instant pot, combine the bok choy with the stock and the other ingredients except the parmesan, put the lid on and cook on High for minutes. Release the pressure fast for 5 minutes, divide the mix between plates, sprinkle the parmesan on top and serve.

Nutrition Info: calories 24, fat 1.6, fiber 0.6, carbs 1, protein 2.5

Wrapped Bacon Carrot

Servings: 3
Cooking Time: 4 Minutes
Ingredients:
- 2 large carrots, peeled
- 3 bacon slices
- ¾ teaspoon salt
- ¼ teaspoon ground turmeric
- 1 teaspoon avocado oil
- 1 cup water, for cooking

Directions:
1. Sprinkle the bacon slices with salt and ground turmeric. Pour avocado oil in the instant pot and heat it up on sauté mode for 2 minutes. Meanwhile, cut the carrots into 6 pieces. Cut the bacon into 6 pieces too. Wrap every carrot piece in the bacon and put in the hot oil in one layer. Cook the vegetables on sauté mode for minute and then flip on another side. Cook the carrot for 1 minute more. Then transfer in the plate. Clean the instant pot and add water. Insert the trivet and put a carrot on it. Close and seal the lid. Cook the wrapped bacon carrot for 2 minutes. Then make the quick pressure release.

Nutrition Info: calories 102, fat 7.2, fiber 1.3, carbs 4.9, protein 5.4

The Best Italian Zuppa Ever

Servings: 4
Cooking Time: 10 Minutes
Ingredients:

- 2 tablespoons olive oil
- 1 onion, chopped
- 16 ounces Cotechino di Modena, sliced
- 2 cups tomatoes, purée
- 3 cups roasted vegetable broth
- 1 cup water
- Sea salt and ground black pepper, to taste
- 1/2 teaspoon crushed chili
- 1 tablespoon Italian seasonings
- 1/2 cup Parmigiano-Reggiano cheese, shaved

Directions:

1. Press the "Sauté" button to heat up your Instant Pot. Once hot, heat the oil and sauté the onions until tender and translucent.
2. Now, add the sausage and cook an additional 3 minutes,
3. Stir in tomatoes, broth, water, sea salt, black pepper, crushed chili, and Italian seasonings.
4. Secure the lid. Choose "Manual" mode and High pressure; cook for 5 minutes. Once cooking is complete, use a quick pressure release; carefully remove the lid.
5. Top with shaved Parmigiano-Reggiano cheese and serve warm.

Nutrition Info:
Per Serving: 340 Calories; 9g Fat; 8g Carbs; 1g Protein; 3.6g Sugars

Tomato & Celery Okra

Servings: 4
Cooking Time: 20 Mins
Ingredients:

- 1 pound Okra
- 14 ounces canned diced Tomatoes
- 2 Celery Stalks, diced
- ½ tsp Italian Seasoning
- ½ small Onion, diced
- ½ tsp Garlic Powder
- 1 tbsp Butter
- 1 ½ cups Water

Directions:

1. Pour the water inside the Instant Pot. Place the okra inside the steamer basket and lower the basket into the pot. Seal the lid and, pres Steam and cook on High pressure for 4 minutes.
2. After the beep, do a quick pressure release and remove okra to a cutting board. Slice thinly.

3. Discard the water from the pot and wipe clean. Set to Sauté and melt the butter. Add the onions and celery; cook for minutes. Stir in tomatoes and spices; cook for 2 minutes. Stir in the okra and cook for 2 more minutes.

Nutrition Info: Calories 95, Protein 5g, Net Carbs 6g, Fat 5g

Tuscan Style Soup

Servings: 4
Cooking Time: 8 Minutes
Ingredients:
- 2 tablespoons butter, melted
- 1/2 cup leeks, sliced
- 2 garlic cloves, minced
- 4 cups broccoli rabe, broken into pieces
- 2 cups water
- 2 cups broth, preferably homemade
- 1 zucchini, shredded
- 1 carrot, trimmed and grated
- Sea salt, to taste
- 1/4 teaspoon ground black pepper

Directions:
1. Press the "Sauté" button to heat up your Instant Pot; now, melt the butter. Cook the leeks for about 2 minutes or until softened.
2. Add minced garlic and cook an additional 40 seconds.
3. Add the remaining ingredients. Secure the lid.
4. Choose "Manual" mode and Low pressure; cook for 3 minutes. Once cooking is complete, use a quick pressure release; carefully remove the lid. Bon appétit!

Nutrition Info:
Per Serving: 95 Calories; 6.7g Fat; 5.2g Total Carbs; 4.2g Protein; 1.4g Sugars

Tomatoes And Olives

Servings: 4
Cooking Time: 15 Minutes
Ingredients:
- 1 pound cherry tomatoes, halved
- 1 cup kalamata olives, pitted and halved
- 2 tablespoons goat cheese, crumbled
- 1 tablespoon balsamic vinegar
- ¼ cup veggie stock
- 1 tablespoon chives, chopped
- A pinch of salt and black pepper

Directions:
1. In your instant pot, mix the tomatoes with the olives and the rest of the ingredients except the cheese and the stock, put the lid on and cook o High for minutes. Release the pressure

424

naturally for 10 minutes, divide the mix between plates, sprinkle the cheese and the chives on top and serve.

Nutrition Info: calories 60, fat 3.8, fiber 2.1, carbs 3.5, protein 1.3

Eggplant Parm

Servings: 2
Cooking Time: 10 Minutes
Ingredients:

- 1 eggplant, sliced
- 1 teaspoon dried basil
- 1/3 cup keto marinara sauce
- ¼ cup Mozzarella, shredded
- 1 tablespoon butter
- ½ cup beef broth

Directions:

1. Grease the instant pot bowl with butter.
2. Then place the layer of the sliced eggplants in the instant pot and sprinkle it with shredded cheese and dried basil.
3. Repeat the step one more time.
4. Add beef broth and keto marinara sauce.
5. Close and seal the lid and cook the eggplant parm for 10 minutes.
6. Make a quick pressure release and cool the meal for 5 minutes before serving.

Nutrition Info:
Per Serving: calories 140, fat 7.7, fiber 8.4, carbs 5, protein 4.5

Radish Hash Browns

Servings: 4
Cooking Time: 15 Mins
Ingredients:

- 4 Eggs
- 1 pound Radishes, shredded
- ½ cup grated Parmesan Cheese
- ¼ tsp Garlic Powder
- Salt and black pepper to taste
- 1 ½ cups Water

Directions:

1. Pour the water in and lower the trivet. Grease a baking dish with cooking spray and set aside.
2. In a bowl, beat the eggs along with garlic powder, salt, and pepper. Stir in radishes and the Parmesan cheese. Pour the mixture into the greased baking dish and place the dish on top of the trivet.
3. Seal the lid and cook for 20 minutes on High pressure. When it goes off, release the pressure quickly. Open the lid carefully. Cut the hash browns into 4 squares, and serve with aioli.

Nutrition Info: Calories 80, Protein 7g, Net Carbs 5g, Fat 5g

Minty Green Beans

Servings: 4
Cooking Time: 15 Minutes
Ingredients:
- 1 pound green beans, trimmed
- 1 green onion, sliced
- 1 tablespoon mint, chopped
- 1 cup chicken stock
- A pinch of salt and black pepper
- 1 tablespoon cilantro, chopped

Directions:
1. In your instant pot, combine the green beans with the green onion and the rest of the ingredients, put the lid on and cook on High for minutes. Release the pressure naturally for 10 minutes, divide the mix between plates and serve.

Nutrition Info: calories 40, fat 1.2, fiber 0.4, carbs 0.6, protein 2.4

Reuben Pickles

Servings: 6
Cooking Time: 2 Hours
Ingredients:
- 1-pound corned beef brisket
- 2 cups of water
- 1 cup pickled cucumbers
- 2 oz provolone cheese, sliced

Directions:
1. Put corned beef brisket and water in the instant pot.
2. Cook the meat on manual mode (high pressure) for hours. Allow the natural pressure release for 10 minutes.
3. Then remove the meat from water and slice it.
4. Make the Reuben pickles: pin the meat piece, pickled cucumber, and provolone cheese together to get the small bites.

Nutrition Info:
Per Serving: calories 164, fat 12, fiber 0.1, carbs 0.8, protein 7

Marjoram Cauliflower Florets

Servings: 2
Cooking Time: 1 Minute
Ingredients:
- 1 teaspoon butter
- ½ teaspoon salt

- 1 teaspoon dried marjoram
- ½ cup beef broth
- 10 oz cauliflower

Directions:
1. Cut the cauliflower into the florets and sprinkle with the dried marjoram and salt.
2. Transfer the vegetables in the instant pot.
3. Add butter and beef broth.
4. Close the lid and set "Manual" mode (High pressure); cook the meal for 1 minute.
5. Then make quick pressure release and open the lid.
6. Add the butter in the cauliflower.

Nutrition Info:
Per Serving: calories 63, fat 2.4, fiber 3.7, carbs 7.9, protein 4.1

Vegetable Fritters

Servings: 4
Cooking Time: 6 Minutes
Ingredients:
- ½ cup turnip, boiled
- ½ cup cauliflower, boiled
- 1 egg, beaten
- 1 teaspoon dried parsley
- 3 tablespoons coconut flour
- 1 teaspoon avocado oil
- 1/3 teaspoon salt
- 1 teaspoon ground turmeric

Directions:
1. Mash turnip and cauliflower with the help of the potato masher. Then add egg, dried parsley, coconut flour, salt, and ground turmeric in the mashed mixture and stir well. Make the medium side fritters and place them in the instant pot. Add avocado oil. Cook the fritters on sauté mode for 3 minutes from each side.

Nutrition Info: calories 50, fat 1.9, fiber 3, carbs 6, protein 2.6

Lemon Artichokes

Servings: 4
Cooking Time: 12 Minutes
Ingredients:
- 4 artichokes, trimmed
- 1 tablespoon olive oil
- 1 tablespoon lemon juice
- 1 tablespoon chives, chopped
- 1 tablespoon sweet paprika
- 1 tablespoon parsley, chopped
- 2 cups water

Directions:

1. In a bowl, mix the artichokes with the oil and the other ingredients except the water and toss. Put the water in your instant pot, add the steamer basket, put the artichokes inside, put the lid on and cook on High for minutes. Release the pressure naturally for 10 minutes, divide the artichokes between plates and serve.

Nutrition Info: calories 113, fat 4, fiber 2.4, carbs 3.5, protein 5.6

Aromatic Tomato Soup

Servings: 2
Cooking Time: 10 Minutes
Ingredients:

- 1 tablespoon avocado oil
- 2 cloves garlic, minced
- 2 ripe tomatoes, puréed
- 1/2 cup double cream
- 1/3 cup water
- 1/2 teaspoon basil
- 1 teaspoon dried sage
- Salt, to taste
- 1/4 teaspoon ground black pepper
- 1/2 teaspoon cayenne pepper
- 1/2 cup Colby cheese, shredded

Directions:

1. Press the "Sauté" button to heat up the Instant Pot; heat the oil. Once hot, cook the garlic until aromatic.
2. Add the remaining ingredients and stir to combine.
3. Secure the lid. Choose "Manual" mode and Low pressure; cook for minutes. Once cooking is complete, use a quick pressure release; carefully remove the lid.
4. Ladle into individual bowls and serve immediately. Bon appétit!

Nutrition Info:
Per Serving: 339 Calories; 5g Fat; 9.1g Carbs; 8g Protein; 5.6g Sugars

Mediterranean Pasta With Avocado

Servings: 2
Cooking Time: 13 Mins
Ingredients:

- 1 tbsp chopped Oregano
- 1 cup Baby Spinach
- ¼ cup grated Parmesan Cheese
- 2 tbsp chopped Capers
- ¼ cup chopped Sun-Dried Tomatoes
- 1 tsp minced Garlic
- 1 tsp fresh rosemary, chopped

- 1 tbsp fresh parsley, roughly chopped
- ½ cup chopped Kalamata Olives
- 1 avocado, pitted and sliced
- 2 Zucchinis, spiralized
- 2 tbsp Butter

Directions:

1. Melt butter on Sauté. When sizzling, add the garlic and cook for 30 seconds, until fragrant. Stir in the spinach and zucchini, and cook for about 5 minutes. Add the rest of the ingredients except Parmesan cheese and avocado, stir well to combine, and cook for 2 more minutes.
2. Finally, sprinkle with Parmesan cheese and avocado slices, and enjoy!

Nutrition Info: Calories 315, Protein 15g, Net Carbs 6.5g, Fat 28g

Chili Mushroom-cauliflower Plate

Servings: 4
Cooking Time: 7 Minutes
Ingredients:

- 1 large head cauliflower, cut into bite-size pieces
- 2 tbsp olive oil
- 1 cup chopped mixed mushrooms
- 2 tsp hot sauce
- Salt and black pepper to taste
- 2 tbsp chopped pecans

Directions:

1. Pour cup of water into the inner pot, fit in a steamer basket, and put in the cauliflower.
2. Lock the lid in place; select manual mode on high pressure and set the timer to minutes.
3. After cooking, do a quick pressure release to let out the steam, and open the lid.
4. Transfer the cauliflower to a medium bowl, empty the inner pot, clean, and return to the base.
5. Set the IP in Sauté mode.
6. Heat the olive oil in the inner pot and sauté the mushrooms until softened 5 minutes.
7. Mix in the cauliflower, hot sauce, salt, and black pepper. Sauté until well coated in the sauce.
8. Turn the IP off and mix in the pecans.
9. Serve.

Nutrition Info:
Per Serving: Calories 111 Fats 9.64g Carbs 2.77g Net Carbs 1.67g Protein 2.6g

Thyme Cauliflower Head

Servings: 3
Cooking Time: 3 Minutes
Ingredients:

- 1-pound cauliflower head, trimmed

- 1 teaspoon thyme
- 2 tablespoons avocado oil
- ¼ teaspoon minced garlic
- 1 cup water, for cooking

Directions:
1. Pour water in the instant pot and insert the steamer rack. Place the cauliflower head in the steamer rack and close the lid. Cook it on manual mode (high pressure) for 3 minutes. Then allow the natural pressure release for 5 minutes and transfer the cauliflower in the serving plate. In the shallow bowl whisk together avocado oil, minced garlic, and thyme. Brush the cooked cauliflower head with the thyme-oil mixture.

Nutrition Info: calories 51, fat 1.4, fiber 4.3, carbs 8.8, protein 3.2

Spinach Dip

Servings: 4
Cooking Time: 6 Hours
Ingredients:
- 2 cups spinach, chopped
- 1 cup Mozzarella, shredded
- 2 artichoke hearts, chopped
- 1 teaspoon ground ginger
- 1 teaspoon butter
- ½ teaspoon white pepper
- ½ cup heavy cream

Directions:
1. Put the spinach, artichoke hearts, and butter in the instant pot bowl.
2. Add Mozzarella, ground ginger, white pepper, and heavy cream. Stir the mixture gently.
3. Cook it in manual mode (Low pressure) for 6 hours. Then stir well and transfer in the serving bowl.

Nutrition Info:
Per Serving: calories 124, fat 8, fiber 4.8, carbs 2, protein 5.5

Cream Cheese Puree

Servings: 2
Cooking Time: 5 Minutes
Ingredients:
- 1 cup of water
- ½ teaspoon salt
- 2 tablespoons cream cheese
- 10 oz cauliflower, chopped

Directions:
1. Place the chopped cauliflower in the instant pot.
2. Add salt and water.
3. Set the "Manual" mode (High pressure) on the instant pot.

4. Set the timer for 5 minutes.
5. When the time is over – use the quick pressure release method.
6. Transfer the cauliflower (without liquid) in the blender. Blend it until smooth.
7. After this, transfer the cauliflower mash in the bowl. Add cream cheese and stir the puree until homogenous.

Nutrition Info:

Per Serving: calories 70, fat 3.6, fiber 3.5, carbs 7.8, protein 3.6

Medley With Broccoli And Bacon

Servings: 4

Cooking Time: 15 Minutes

Ingredients:
- 4 slices bacon, chopped
- 1 teaspoon ginger-garlic paste
- 1 cup broccoli, broken into florets
- 1 celery with leaves, chopped
- 2 cups water
- 2 beef bouillon cubes
- Salt and ground black pepper, to your liking
- 1/2 teaspoon red pepper flakes, crushed
- 1 cup double cream
- 1/2 cup Colby cheese, shredded
- 2 tablespoons fresh chives, sliced

Directions:
1. Press the "Sauté" button to heat up your Instant Pot. Once hot, cook the bacon until nice and crisp; set aside.
2. Add ginger-garlic paste and cook an additional 30 seconds. Add the broccoli, celery, water, beef bouillon cubes, salt, black pepper, red pepper, and double cream.
3. Secure the lid. Choose "Manual" mode and High pressure; cook for 6 minutes. Once cooking is complete, use a natural pressure release; carefully remove the lid.
4. Top with Colby cheese and press the "Sauté" button. Let it simmer an additional minutes or until the cheese is melted.
5. Garnish with fresh chives and the reserved bacon; serve immediately and enjoy!

Nutrition Info:

Per Serving: 303 Calories; 2g Fat; 5.8g Total Carbs; 9.8g Protein; 3.6g Sugars

Baked Green Beans

Servings: 1

Cooking Time: 6 Minutes

Ingredients:
- 4 oz green beans, chopped
- ½ teaspoon butter
- 1 tablespoon almond meal

- 1 oz Provolone cheese, grated
- 1 cup water, for cooking

Directions:
1. Pour water and insert the steamer rack in the instant pot. Place the green beans on the rack and cook them on manual mode (high pressure) for minute. After this, make a quick pressure release and open the lid. Place the cooked green beans in the bowl. Add almond meal and grated Provolone cheese. Then clean the instant pot and remove the rack. Put the green beans mixture in the instant pot bowl. Add butter and close the lid. Cook the baked green beans for 5 minutes.

Nutrition Info: calories 186, fat 6, fiber 4.6, carbs 10, protein 6

Walnuts Green Beans And Avocado

Servings: 6
Cooking Time: 15 Minutes
Ingredients:
- 2 cups green beans, halved
- ½ cup chicken stock
- ½ cup walnuts, chopped
- 1 avocado, peeled, pitted and cubed
- ¼ teaspoon sweet paprika
- A pinch of salt and black pepper
- 2 teaspoons balsamic vinegar

Directions:
1. In your instant pot, mix the green beans with the stock and the rest of the ingredients, put the lid on and cook on High for minutes. Release the pressure naturally for 10 minutes, divide the mix between plates and serve.

Nutrition Info: calories 146, fat 8, fiber 2.5, carbs 6.7, protein 3.9

Vegetable Medley With Pork Sausage

Servings: 4
Cooking Time: 15 Minutes
Ingredients:
- 2 tablespoons olive oil
- 2 garlic cloves, minced
- 1/2 cup scallions
- 2 pork sausages, casing removed, sliced
- 2 cups cauliflower, chopped into small florets
- 1/2 pound button mushrooms, sliced
- 2 bell peppers, chopped
- 1 red chili pepper, chopped
- 2 cups turnip greens
- Sea salt and freshly ground black pepper, to taste
- 1 teaspoon cayenne pepper

- 2 bay leaves
- 1 cup water

Directions:

1. Press the "Sauté" button to heat up your Instant Pot. Heat the oil and sauté the garlic and scallions until aromatic, about 2 minutes.
2. Add sausage and cook an additional 3 minutes or until it is no longer pink. Now, stir in the remaining ingredients.
3. Secure the lid. Choose "Manual" mode and High pressure; cook for 5 minutes. Once cooking is complete, use a quick pressure release; carefully remove the lid. Bon appétit!

Nutrition Info:

Per Serving: 248 Calories; 5g Fat; 8.5g Carbs; 9.1g Protein; 2.9g Sugars

Mushrooms And Endives Mix

Servings: 4
Cooking Time: 15 Minutes
Ingredients:

- 1 pound white mushrooms, sliced
- 2 spring onions, chopped
- 1 garlic clove, minced
- 2 endives, trimmed and halved
- 1 tablespoon balsamic vinegar
- 1 tablespoon chives, chopped
- 1 cup chicken stock

Directions:

1. In your instant pot, mix the mushrooms with the rest of the ingredients, put the lid on and cook on High for minutes. Release the pressure naturally for 10 minutes, divide the mix between plates and serve.

Nutrition Info: calories 31, fat 3.1, fiber 1.3, carbs 2.3, protein 3.9

Rosemary Cauliflower

Servings: 4
Cooking Time: 12 Minutes
Ingredients:

- 1 pound cauliflower florets
- 1 cup chicken stock
- 2 garlic cloves, minced
- A pinch of salt and black pepper
- 1 tablespoon rosemary, chopped
- 1 teaspoon hot chili sauce

Directions:

1. In your instant pot, combine the cauliflower with the stock and the rest of the ingredients, put the lid on and cook on High for minutes. Release the pressure naturally for 10 minutes, divide the mix between plates and serve.

Nutrition Info: calories 36, fat 2.4, fiber 1.5, carbs 2.3, protein 3.6

Ginger Cabbage

Servings: 2
Cooking Time: 15 Minutes
Ingredients:

- ½ tablespoon ginger paste
- 10 oz white cabbage, shredded
- 1 teaspoon butter
- ½ cup heavy cream
- ½ teaspoon salt

Directions:

1. Place the cabbage in the big mixing bowl.
2. Sprinkle the cabbage with the ginger paste and salt.
3. Melt the butter on the "Saute" mode in the instant pot.
4. Then add all the shredded cabbage and heavy cream.
5. Set the "steam" mode and cook the cabbage for 10 minutes.
6. Transfer the cooked meal on the serving plates and enjoy!

Nutrition Info:
Per Serving: calories 160, fat 2, fiber 3.7, carbs 10, protein 2.6

Curried Eggplant

Servings: 4
Cooking Time: 25 Mins
Ingredients:

- 12 ounces Eggplants, sliced
- 1 tsp minced Garlic
- 1 tsp minced Ginger
- 1 Onion, diced
- 1 tsp Curry Powder
- ½ cup Tomato Sauce
- 1 cup Chicken Broth
- 2 tbsp Butter

Directions:

1. Melt half of the butter on Sauté. Add eggplants and brown on both sides. Remove to a plate. Melt the remaining butter, add the onions and cook for 3 minutes. Stir in garlic and ginger, and cook for another minute. Stir in the remaining ingredients and return the eggplant slices to the pot. Seal the lid and cook on High for 7 minutes. Do a quick pressure release.

Nutrition Info: Calories 145, Protein 2g, Net Carbs 8g, Fat 14g

Creamy Spinach

Servings: 4

Cooking Time: 15 Mins
Ingredients:
- 1 pound Baby Spinach
- ¾ cup Heavy Cream
- 1 Tomato, diced
- 1 tsp Onion Powder
- 2 Garlic Cloves, minced
- 1 tbsp Butter
- ¼ cup Water
- Salt and black pepper to taste

Directions:
1. Melt butter on Sauté. Add garlic and cook for a minute. Stir in the tomato and cook for 2 more minutes. Pour the remaining ingredients and give the mixture a good stir to combine. Seal the lid and cook on High pressure for 2 minutes. When ready, do a quick release.

Nutrition Info: Calories 95, Protein 5g, Net Carbs 3g, Fat 8g

Instant Zucchini With Green Peppercorn Sauce

Servings: 4
Cooking Time: 10 Minutes
Ingredients:
- 1 cup water
- 2 zucchini, sliced
- Sea salt, to taste
- Green Peppercorn Sauce:
- 2 tablespoons butter
- 1/2 cup green onions, minced
- 2 tablespoons Cognac
- 1 ½ cups chicken broth
- 1 cup whipping cream
- 1 ½ tablespoons green peppercorns in brine, drained and crushed slightly

Directions:
1. Add water and a steamer basket to the Instant Pot. Arrange your zucchini on the steamer basket.
2. Secure the lid. Choose "Manual" mode and Low pressure; cook for 3 minutes. Once cooking is complete, use a quick pressure release; carefully remove the lid.
3. Season zucchini with salt and set aside.
4. Wipe down the Instant Pot with a damp cloth. Press the "Sauté" button to heat up your Instant Pot.
5. Melt the butter and then, sauté green onions until tender. Add Cognac and cook for 2 minutes longer. Then, pour in chicken broth and let it boil another 4 minutes.

6. Lastly, stir in the cream and peppercorns. Continue to simmer until the sauce is thickened and thoroughly warmed.
7. Serve your zucchini with the sauce on the side. Bon appétit!

Nutrition Info:
Per Serving: 251 Calories; 3g Fat; 3.2g Total Carbs; 2g Protein; 1.5g Sugars

Ginger Cabbage And Radish Mix

Servings: 4
Cooking Time: 15 Minutes
Ingredients:
- 1 red cabbage head, shredded
- 2 tablespoons veggie stock
- 1 cup radish, sliced
- 3 garlic cloves, minced
- 1 tablespoon coconut aminos
- 1 tablespoon olive oil
- ½ inch ginger, grated

Directions:
1. Set the instant pot on Sauté mode, add the oil, heat it up, add the garlic and the ginger and sauté for 3 minutes. Add the rest of the ingredients, put the lid on and cook on High for minutes. Release the pressure naturally for 10 minutes, divide the mix between plates and serve as a side dish.

Nutrition Info: calories 83, fat 4.4, fiber 2.1, carbs 3.3, protein 2.6

White Cabbage In Cream

Servings: 4
Cooking Time: 7 Hours
Ingredients:
- 12 oz white cabbage, roughly chopped
- 1 cup cream
- 1 tablespoon cream cheese
- 1 teaspoon salt
- 1 teaspoon chili powder

Directions:
1. Put all ingredients in the instant pot bowl and close the lid. Cook the vegetables for 7 minutes on manual mode (high pressure). When the time is over, make a quick pressure release. Open the instant pot lid and stir the cooked side dish well.

Nutrition Info: calories 71, fat 4.4, fiber 2.4, carbs 7.2, protein 1.8

Broccoli And Watercress Mix

Servings: 4
Cooking Time: 15 Minutes

Ingredients:
- 1 pound broccoli florets
- 1 tablespoon olive oil
- 2 shallots, chopped
- 1 bunch watercress
- 1 tablespoon sweet paprika
- ½ cup tomato passata

Directions:
1. Set the instant pot on Sauté mode, add the oil, heat it up, add the shallots and cook for 2 minutes Add the rest of the ingredients, put the lid on and cook on High for minutes. Release the pressure naturally for 10 minutes, divide the mix into bowls and serve.

Nutrition Info: calories 81, fat 4.2, fiber 2.3, carbs 3.5, protein 3.8

Low Carb Fall Vegetables

Servings: 5
Cooking Time: 8 Minutes
Ingredients:
- 1 cup mushrooms, chopped
- 1 cup zucchini, chopped
- 1/2 cup bell pepper, chopped
- 1 eggplant, chopped
- 3 tablespoons butter
- ½ teaspoon salt
- 1 teaspoon dried basil
- 1 teaspoon dried thyme
- ½ teaspoon ground black pepper
- ½ teaspoon cayenne pepper
- 1 cup water, for cooking

Directions:
1. Pour water and insert the trivet in the instant pot. Put all vegetables in the instant pot baking pan. Sprinkle them with salt, dried basil, thyme, ground black pepper, and cayenne pepper. Mix up the vegetables and top with butter. Arrange the baking pan with vegetables in the instant pot. Close the lid and cook the side dish for 8 minutes on Manual mode (high pressure). Make a quick pressure release.

Nutrition Info: calories 96, fat 7.2, fiber 4, carbs 7.9, protein 1.9

Braised Garlicky Endive

Servings: 3
Cooking Time: 6 Minutes
Ingredients:
- 1 tablespoon extra-virgin olive oil
- 2 garlic cloves, minced
- 2 large-sized Belgian endive, halved lengthwise

- 1/2 cup apple cider vinegar
- 1/2 cup broth, preferably homemade
- Sea salt and freshly ground black pepper, to taste
- 1 teaspoon cayenne pepper

Directions:
1. Press the "Sauté" button to heat up the Instant Pot; heat the oil. Once hot, cook the garlic for 30 seconds or until aromatic and browned.
2. Add Belgian endive, vinegar, broth, salt, black pepper, and cayenne pepper.
3. Secure the lid. Choose "Manual" mode and Low pressure; cook for 2 minutes or until tender when pierced with the tip of a knife.
4. Once cooking is complete, use a quick pressure release; carefully remove the lid. Bon appétit!

Nutrition Info:
Per Serving: 91 Calories; 5.3g Fat; 9.1g Carbs; 3.6g Protein; 1.8g Sugars

Beet And Pecan Bowl

Servings: 4
Cooking Time: 25 Mins
Ingredients:
- 4 Large Beets, chopped
- ½ Shallot, minced
- 2 Garlic Cloves, minced
- ½ cup chopped Walnuts
- 1 cup Veggie Broth
- 1 tbsp Olive oil
- ½ cup grated Parmesan Cheese

Directions:
1. Place the beets in a food processor and pulse until a rice-like consistency is formed. Heat olive oil on Sauté. When sizzling, add the shallots and cook for 2 minutes.
2. Stir in the garlic and cook for an additional minute. Pour the broth over and stir in the beet rice. Seal the lid and cook on High pressure for 1minutes.
3. When it goes off, do a quick release. If the liquid hasn't been absorbed fully, drain the beets a bit. Stir in the Parmesan cheese. Divide among 4 bowls and top with walnuts, to serve.

Nutrition Info: Calories 273, Protein 9g, Net Carbs 8.5g, Fat 22g

Cabbage With Bacon

Servings: 4
Cooking Time: 10 Minutes
Ingredients:
- 2 teaspoons olive oil
- 4 slices bacon, chopped
- 1 head green cabbage, cored and cut into wedges
- 1 cups vegetable stock

- Sea salt, to taste
- 1/2 teaspoon whole black peppercorns
- 1 teaspoon cayenne pepper
- 1 bay leaf

Directions:
1. Press the "Sauté" button to heat up the Instant Pot. Then, heat olive oil and cook the bacon until it is nice and delicately browned.
2. Then, add the remaining ingredients; gently stir to combine.
3. Secure the lid. Choose "Manual" mode and High pressure; cook for minutes. Once cooking is complete, use a quick pressure release; carefully remove the lid.
4. Serve warm and enjoy!

Nutrition Info:
Per Serving: 166 Calories; 13g Fat; 5.8g Total Carbs; 6.8g Protein; 2.7g Sugars

Cilantro Cauliflower Rice Mix

Servings: 4
Cooking Time: 15 Minutes
Ingredients:
- 1 shallot, chopped
- 1 teaspoon garlic, minced
- 1 tablespoon avocado oil
- 1 and ½ cups cauliflower rice
- 1 and ½ cups chicken stock
- A pinch of salt and black pepper
- 2 tablespoons chives, chopped

Directions:
1. Set your instant pot on Sauté mode, add the oil, heat it up, add the shallot and the garlic and sauté for 2 minutes Add the rest of the ingredients except the chives, put the lid on and cook on High for minutes Release the pressure naturally for 10 minutes, divide the mix between plates and serve as a side dish.

Nutrition Info: calories 55, fat 2.3, fiber 0.2, carbs 0.3, protein 0.1

Buttery Eggplants

Servings: 4
Cooking Time: 12 Minutes
Ingredients:
- 1 pound eggplants, sliced
- A pinch of salt and black pepper
- 2 shallots, chopped
- 1 cup chicken stock
- 1 tablespoon ghee, melted
- 2 tablespoons parsley, chopped

Directions:

1. Set your instant pot on Sauté mode, add the ghee, heat it up, add the shallots and cook for 2 minutes. Add the eggplants and the rest of the ingredients, put the lid on and cook on High for minutes. Release the pressure fast for 5 minutes, divide the mix between plates and serve.

Nutrition Info: calories 60, fat 3.5, fiber 1.8, carbs 3, protein 1.4

Kale And Cauliflower Stew

Servings: 4
Cooking Time: 17 Mins
Ingredients:
- 2 Celery Stalks, diced
- 3 cups Cauliflower Rice
- 2 tbsp Olive oil
- 2 Garlic Cloves, minced
- 2 Carrots, sliced
- 2 cups Kale, chopped
- 1 Onion, diced
- 4 cups Veggie Broth
- 14 ounces canned diced Tomatoes
- 2 tsp Cumin
- Salt and black pepper to taste

Directions:
1. Heat the olive oil on Sauté. Add the celery, onions, and carrots, and cook for a few minutes, until softened. Then, stir in the garlic and cook for 45 seconds more.
2. Add the rest of the ingredients to the pot and stir to combine. Seal the lid and cook on High pressure for 8 minutes. When the timer goes off, let the pressure valve drop on its own for a natural pressure release. Open the lid gently and ladle into serving bowls.

Nutrition Info: Calories 320, Protein 12g, Net Carbs 4g, Fat 14g

Cranberries Cauliflower Rice

Servings: 4
Cooking Time: 15 Minutes
Ingredients:
- 2 tablespoons avocado oil
- 2 shallots, chopped
- ½ cup cranberries
- 1 and ½ cups cauliflower rice
- 1 cup veggie stock
- A pinch of salt and black pepper
- ½ cup cilantro, chopped

Directions:
1. Set your instant pot on Sauté mode, add the oil, heat it up, add the shallots and sauté for 2 minutes Add the rest of the ingredients, stir, put the lid on and cook on High for minutes.

Release the pressure naturally for 10 minutes, divide the mix between plates and serve as a side dish.

Nutrition Info: calories 34, fat 2, fiber 0.2, carbs 1.7, protein 1

Mozzarella Broccoli

Servings: 4
Cooking Time: 10 Minutes
Ingredients:

- 1 pound broccoli florets
- ½ cup veggie stock
- 2 shallots, chopped
- A pinch of salt and black pepper
- 1 cup mozzarella, shredded
- 1 tablespoon cilantro, chopped
- 3 tablespoons olive oil

Directions:

1. Set the instant pot on Sauté mode, add the oil, heat it up, add the shallots and sauté for 2 minutes. Add the rest of the ingredients except the mozzarella and toss. Sprinkle the mozzarella on top, put the lid on and cook on High for 8 minutes. Release the pressure naturally for minutes, divide the mix between plates and serve.

Nutrition Info: calories 149, fat 1, fiber 3, carbs 7.8, protein 5.2

Chili Green Beans With Coconut

Servings: 4
Cooking Time: 20 Mins
Ingredients:

- ¾ pound Green Beans, sliced crosswise
- ¾ cup shredded unsweetened Coconut
- 2 Chilies, seeded and diced
- 2 tsp minced Garlic
- 2 tbsp Butter
- ¼ tsp Cumin
- ½ tsp minced Ginger
- ½ cup Chicken Broth
- Salt and black pepper to taste

Directions:

1. Melt butter on Sauté. Add ginger, chilies, and garlic, and cook for a minute. Then, stir in the green beans and cumin, and cook for 2 minutes. Pour in broth and coconut; give it a stir.
2. Seal the lid and cook on High pressure for 3 minutes. When ready, do a quick pressure release. For 'drier' beans, set to Sauté and cook for 3 minutes until the liquid evaporates.

Nutrition Info: Calories 153, Protein 3g, Net Carbs 4g, Fat 15g

Tasty Vegetables à La Grecque

Servings: 4
Cooking Time: 10 Minutes
Ingredients:

- 2 tablespoons olive oil
- 2 garlic cloves, minced
- 1 red onion, chopped
- 10 ounces button mushrooms, thinly sliced
- 1 (1-pound eggplant, sliced
- 1/2 teaspoon dried basil
- 1 teaspoon dried oregano
- 1 thyme sprig, leaves picked
- 2 rosemary sprigs, leaves picked
- 1/2 cup tomato sauce
- 1/4 cup dry Greek wine
- 1/4 cup water
- 8 ounces Halloumi cheese, cubed
- 4 tablespoons Kalamata olives, pitted and halved

Directions:

1. Press the "Sauté" button to heat up your Instant Pot; now, heat the olive oil. Cook the garlic and red onions for to 2 minutes, stirring periodically.
2. Stir in the mushrooms and continue to sauté an additional to 3 minutes.
3. Add the eggplant, basil, oregano, thyme, rosemary, tomato sauce, Greek wine, and water.
4. Secure the lid. Choose "Manual" mode and Low pressure; cook for 3 minutes. Once cooking is complete, use a quick pressure release; carefully remove the lid.
5. Top with cheese and olives. Bon appétit!

Nutrition Info:
Per Serving: 326 Calories; 1g Fat; 6.4g Total Carbs; 7g Protein; 2.3g Sugars

Asian Bok Choy

Servings: 4
Cooking Time: 10 Minutes
Ingredients:

- 2 tablespoons butter, melted
- 2 cloves garlic, minced
- 1 (1/2-inch slice fresh ginger root, grated
- 1 ½ pounds Bok choy, trimmed
- 1 cup vegetable stock
- Celery salt and ground black pepper to taste
- 1 teaspoon Five-spice powder
- 2 tablespoons soy sauce

Directions:

1. Press the "Sauté" button to heat up the Instant Pot. Now, warm the butter and sauté the garlic until tender and fragrant.
2. Now, add grated ginger and cook for a further 40 seconds.
3. Add Bok choy, stock, salt, black pepper, and Five-spice powder.
4. Secure the lid. Choose "Manual" mode and High pressure; cook for 6 minutes. Once cooking is complete, use a quick pressure release; carefully remove the lid.
5. Drizzle soy sauce over your Bok choy and serve immediately. Bon appétit!

Nutrition Info:
Per Serving: 83 Calories; 6.1g Fat; 5.7g Total Carbs; 3.2g Protein; 2.4g Sugars

Cheese Sandwich With Chimichurri

Servings: 1
Cooking Time: 15 Mins
Ingredients:
- 2 tbsp Almond flour
- 2 Eggs
- 3 tbsp Butter
- ½ tsp Baking Powder
- 1 ½ tbsp Psyllium Husk Powder
- 2 slices Swiss Cheese
- 1 tsp Lime juice
- 1 tbsp fresh chives, finely chopped
- ½ tsp garlic powder
- 1 tsp Avocado oil
- Crushed red pepper, to taste
- 1 tsp fresh Cilantro, chopped
- Salt and black pepper to taste

Directions:
1. In a bowl, mix avocado oil, chives, garlic powder, cilantro, salt, and red pepper; set aside.
2. Add the flour, tbsp of the butter, eggs, baking powder, psyllium husk powder, and salt and pepper, in a microwave-safe bowl with a square shape. Beat until smooth and fully combined.
3. Place in the microwave and microwave for about 90 seconds. Invert the 'bun' onto a cutting board and cut it in half.
4. Melt a tbsp of butter on Sauté. Lay in one 'bread' slice, cover with the cheese and top with the other slice. Press with a spatula and cook for about 2-3 minutes. Flip over and cook for a couple of minutes until the cheese melts and sandwich is golden. Drizzle with the chimichurri.

Nutrition Info: Calories 621, Protein 32g, Net Carbs 6g, Fat 65g

Celery Soup

Servings: 4
Cooking Time: 30 Minutes

Ingredients:
- 3 cups celery, chopped
- 1 carrot, chopped
- 1/2 cup brown onion, chopped
- 1 garlic clove, pressed
- 1/2 pound with Salsiccia links, casing removed and sliced
- 1/2 cup full-fat milk
- 3 cups roasted vegetable broth
- Kosher salt, to taste
- 1/2 teaspoon ground black pepper
- 1/2 teaspoon dried chili flakes
- 2 teaspoon coconut oil

Directions:
1. Simply throw all of the above ingredients into your Instant Pot; gently stir to combine.
2. Secure the lid. Choose "Soup/Broth" mode and High pressure; cook for minutes. Once cooking is complete, use a quick pressure release; carefully remove the lid.
3. Ladle into four soup bowls and serve hot. Enjoy!

Nutrition Info:
Per Serving: 150 Calories; 5.9g Fat; 5.9g Total Carbs; 4g Protein; 4.1g Sugars

Turnip Cubes

Servings: 6
Cooking Time: 3 Minutes
Ingredients:
- 1-pound turnip, cubed
- 1 teaspoon salt
- ½ teaspoon ground black pepper
- 1 teaspoon avocado oil
- 1 cup water, for cooking

Directions:
1. Pour water and insert the steamer rack in the instant pot. In the mixing bowl mix up together turnip cubes, salt, and ground black pepper. Sprinkle the vegetables with avocado oil and place them in the steamer rack. Close and seal the lid. Cook the turnip on Manual mode (high pressure) for 3 minutes. Then allow the natural pressure release for 5 minutes.

Nutrition Info: calories 23, fat 0.2, fiber 1.4, carbs 5, protein 0.7

Cocktail Sausages Asian-style

Servings: 8
Cooking Time: 10 Minutes
Ingredients:
- 1 teaspoon sesame oil
- 20 mini cocktail sausages
- 1/2 cup tomato puree

- 1/2 cup chicken stock
- 1 tablespoon dark soy sauce
- 1/3 teaspoon ground black pepper
- 1/2 teaspoon paprika
- Himalayan salt, to taste
- 1/2 teaspoon mustard seeds
- 1/2 teaspoon fennel seeds
- 1/4 teaspoon fresh ginger root, peeled and grated
- 1 teaspoon garlic paste

Directions:
1. Simply throw all ingredients into your Instant Pot.
2. Secure the lid. Choose "Manual" mode and High pressure; cook for 4 minutes. Once cooking is complete, use a quick pressure release; carefully remove the lid.
3. Serve with cocktail sticks and enjoy!

Nutrition Info:
Per Serving: 330 Calories; 8g Fat; 2.7g Total Carbs; 7g Protein; 1.2g Sugars

Bacon Cheeseburger Dip

Servings: 6
Cooking Time: 10 Mins
Ingredients:
- ½ cup chopped Tomatoes
- 10 oz shredded Cheddar-Monterey Jack Cheese
- 10 oz Cream Cheese
- 10 Bacon Slices, chopped roughly
- 4 tbsp Water

Directions:
1. Select Sauté on your instant Pot. Add the bacon pieces and cook for 5 minutes. Use a spoon to fetch out the grease and add the water, cream cheese, and tomatoes. Do Not Stir.
2. Close the lid, secure the pressure valve, and select Steam mode on High pressure for 4 minutes. Once ready, do a quick pressure release. Add the cheddar cheese and stir until is well combined. Serve the dip with a side of low carb chips.

Nutrition Info: Calories 53, Protein 3.9g, Net Carbs 0.5g, Fat 5.3g

Bbq Lil Smokies

Servings: 8
Cooking Time: 10 Minutes
Ingredients:
- 1 ½ pounds beef cocktail wieners
- 1 cup water
- 1/4 cup apple cider vinegar
- 1/2 tablespoon onion powder
- 1/2 teaspoon ground black pepper

- 1 teaspoon ground mustard
- 2 ounces ale

Directions:
1. Simply throw all ingredients into your Instant Pot.
2. Secure the lid. Choose "Manual" mode and High pressure; cook for minutes. Once cooking is complete, use a natural pressure release; carefully remove the lid.
3. Serve with cocktail sticks and enjoy!

Nutrition Info:
Per Serving: 120 Calories; 4.9g Fat; 1.2g Total Carbs; 5g Protein; 0.6g Sugars

Eggs In Sausage

Servings: 4
Cooking Time: 30 Mins
Ingredients:
- 4 Eggs
- 2 cups Water
- 1 lb ground Sausage
- 4 tbsp Olive oil

Directions:
1. Put the trivet at the bottom of the Instant Pot. Place the eggs on top of the trivet. Add the water and seal the lid. Set to Manual mode and cook for 6 minutes on High pressure.
2. When boiled, allow 5 minutes of natural pressure release. Take the eggs out and place in an ice bath for 5 minutes. Then, peel off the skin. Take each egg, cover with the ground sausage, and shape it into a ball. Lightly brush the egg ball with olive oil. Place inside the pot. Repeat with all eggs. Seal the lid and cook for 10 minutes on High pressure. When it beeps, do a quick release.

Nutrition Info: Calories 512, Protein 46g, Net Carbs 1.7g, Fat 37g

Crunchy Mushrooms

Servings: 4
Cooking Time: 10 Minutes
Ingredients:
- 2 tablespoons butter, melted
- 20 ounces button mushrooms, brushed clean
- 2 cloves garlic, minced
- 1 teaspoon dried basil
- 1 teaspoon dried rosemary
- 1 teaspoon dried sage
- 1 bay leaf
- Sea salt, to taste
- 1/2 teaspoon freshly ground black pepper
- 1/2 cup water
- 1/2 cup broth, preferably homemade

- 1 tablespoon soy sauce
- 1 tablespoon fresh parsley leaves, roughly chopped

Directions:
1. Press the "Sauté" button to heat up your Instant Pot. Once hot, melt the butter and sauté the mushrooms and garlic until aromatic.
2. Add seasonings, water, and broth. Add garlic, oregano, mushrooms, thyme, basil, bay leaves, veggie broth, and salt and pepper to your instant pot.
3. Secure the lid. Choose "Manual" mode and High pressure; cook for 5 minutes. Once cooking is complete, use a quick pressure release; carefully remove the lid.
4. Arrange your mushrooms on a serving platter and serve with cocktail sticks. Bon appétit!

Nutrition Info:
Per Serving: 91 Calories; 6.4g Fat; 5.5g Total Carbs; 5.2g Protein; 2.8g Sugars

Easy Party Mushrooms

Servings: 6
Cooking Time: 10 Minutes
Ingredients:
- 3 tablespoons sesame oil
- 3/4 pound small button mushrooms
- 1 teaspoon garlic, minced
- 1/2 teaspoon cayenne pepper
- 1/2 teaspoon smoked paprika
- Salt and ground black pepper, to taste

Directions:
1. Press the "Sauté" button and heat the oil. Once hot, cook your mushrooms for 4 to 5 minutes.
2. Add the other ingredients.
3. Secure the lid. Choose "Manual" mode and High pressure; cook for 5 minutes. Once cooking is complete, use a quick pressure release; carefully remove the lid.
4. Serve with toothpicks and enjoy!

Nutrition Info:
Per Serving: 73 Calories; 7g Fat; 2g Carbs; 1.7g Protein; 1.1g Sugars

Watercress And Zucchini Salsa

Servings: 4
Cooking Time: 12 Minutes
Ingredients:
- 1 bunch watercress, trimmed
- Juice of 1 lime
- ¼ cup chicken stock
- 2 teaspoons thyme, dried
- 2 tablespoons avocado oil
- 1 cup tomato, cubed

- 1 avocado, peeled, pitted and cubed
- 2 zucchinis, cubed
- 2 spring onions, chopped
- 3 garlic cloves, minced
- ¼ cup cilantro, chopped
- 1 tablespoon balsamic vinegar

Directions:

1. Set the instant pot on Sauté mode, add the oil, heat it up, add the garlic and sauté for 2 minutes. Add the rest of the ingredients, put the lid on and cook on High for minutes. Release the pressure fast for 5 minutes, divide the salsa into cups and serve as an appetizer.

Nutrition Info: calories 144, fat 1, fiber 4.4, carbs 5.3, protein 3

Thyme Eggplants And Celery Spread

Servings: 4

Cooking Time: 12 Minutes

Ingredients:

- 2 pounds eggplant, roughly chopped
- A pinch of salt and black pepper
- 2 celery stalks, chopped
- 2 tablespoons olive oil
- 4 garlic cloves, minced
- ½ cup veggie stock
- 2 tablespoons lime juice
- 1 bunch thyme, chopped

Directions:

1. Set your instant pot on sauté mode, add the oil, heat it up, add the celery stalks and the garlic and sauté for 2 minutes. Add the rest of the ingredients, put the lid on and cook on High for minutes. Release the pressure naturally for 10 minutes, blend the mix using an immersion blender, divide into cups and serve as a spread.

Nutrition Info: calories 123, fat 7.4, fiber 1.8, carbs 3.7, protein 2.5

Egg Fat Balls

Servings: 6

Cooking Time: 25 Minutes

Ingredients:

- 6 eggs
- 1 teaspoon Creole seasonings
- 1/4 cup mayonnaise
- 1/4 cup cream cheese
- 1/3 cup Cheddar cheese, grated
- Sea salt and ground black pepper, to taste
- 4 slices pancetta, chopped

Directions:

1. Place cup of water and a steamer basket in your Instant Pot. Now, arrange the eggs on the steamer basket.
2. Secure the lid. Choose "Manual" mode and Low pressure; cook for 5 minutes. Once cooking is complete, use a quick pressure release; carefully remove the lid.
3. Allow the eggs to cool for 15 minutes; then, chop the eggs and add the remaining ingredients; mix to combine well.
4. Shape the mixture into balls. Serve well-chilled. Keep in the refrigerator up to days.

Nutrition Info:

Per Serving: 236 Calories; 6g Fat; 3.1g Total Carbs; 4g Protein; 1.7g Sugars

Asparagus With Chervil Dip

Servings: 6

Cooking Time: 5 Minutes

Ingredients:

- 1 ½ pounds asparagus spears, trimmed
- 1/2 cup sour cream
- 1/2 cup mayonnaise
- 2 tablespoons fresh chervil
- 2 tablespoons scallions, chopped
- 1 teaspoon garlic, minced
- Salt, to taste

Directions:

1. Add cup of water and a steamer basket to you Instant Pot.
2. Secure the lid. Choose "Manual" mode and High pressure; cook for 1 minute. Once cooking is complete, use a quick pressure release; carefully remove the lid.
3. Then, thoroughly combine the remaining ingredients to make your dipping sauce. Serve your asparagus with the dipping sauce on the side. Bon appétit!

Nutrition Info:

Per Serving: 116 Calories; 8.5g Fat; 6.9g Carbs; 4.5g Protein; 2.4g Sugars

Spring Deviled Eggs With Bacon

Servings: 4

Cooking Time: 25 Minutes

Ingredients:

- 1 tablespoon green onions, finely chopped
- 1 teaspoon Dijon mustard
- 5 eggs
- 1/3 cup cheddar cheese, shredded
- 2 tablespoons bacon, finely chopped
- 1/2 teaspoon dried dill
- 1/3 cup mayonnaise
- 1 teaspoon red pepper
- ½ teaspoon pepper

- ½ teaspoon salt

Directions:
1. Add cup of water and a steamer basket in your Instant Pot. Arrange the eggs on the steamer basket.
2. Secure the lid. Choose "Manual" mode and Low pressure; cook for 4 minutes. When cooking is complete, use a quick pressure release and carefully remove the lid.
3. Leave the eggs to cool for 10 minutes. Then, peel the eggs and slice them into halves.
4. Place the egg yolks in a bowl along with mayonnaise, Dijon mustard, green onions, cheddar cheese, bacon, dried dill, red pepper, salt, and pepper. Combine well.
5. Stuff the egg whites with mayo mixture. Serve and enjoy!

Nutrition Info:
Per Serving: 282 Calories; 6g Fat; 3.1g Carbs; 3g Protein; 1.4g Sugars

Classic Sausage Dip

Servings: 12
Cooking Time: 45 Minutes
Ingredients:
- 1 tablespoon ghee
- 3/4 pound spicy breakfast sausage, casings removed and crumbled
- 16 ounces Velveeta cheese
- 8 ounces Cotija cheese shredded
- 2 (10-ounce cans diced tomatoes with green chilies
- 1 cup chicken broth
- 1 package taco seasoning

Directions:
1. Press the "Sauté" button and melt the ghee. Once hot, cook the sausage until it is no longer pink.
2. Add the remaining ingredients.
3. Secure the lid. Choose "Slow Cook" mode and Low pressure; cook for 40 minutes. Once cooking is complete, use a quick pressure release; carefully remove the lid.
4. Serve with your favorite keto dippers. Bon appétit!

Nutrition Info:
Per Serving: 251 Calories; 3g Fat; 5.2g Total Carbs; 5g Protein; 2.3g Sugars

Warm Kale And Spinach Dip

Servings: 4
Cooking Time: 3 Minutes
Ingredients:
- 1 cup chopped frozen spinach, thawed
- 1 cup chopped frozen kale, thawed
- 3 garlic cloves, minced
- ¼ tsp smoked paprika
- Salt and black pepper to taste

- ¼ cup water
- 1 cup mayonnaise
- 8 oz cream cheese, softened
- 1 cup grated Monterey Jack cheese
- ¼ cup grated Parmesan cheese

Directions:

1. Combine the spinach, kale, garlic, paprika, salt, black pepper, and water in the inner pot.
2. Lock the lid in place; select Manual mode on High Pressure and set the timer to 1 minute.
3. After cooking, perform a quick pressure release to let out all the steam, and open the lid.
4. Set the IP in Sauté mode and mix in the remaining ingredients until the cheeses melt, 2 minutes.
5. Spoon the dip into serving bowls and enjoy!

Nutrition Info:

Per Serving: Calories 539 Fats 46g Carbs 15g Net Carbs 7.45g Protein 18g

Colby Cheese Dip With Peppers

Servings: 8
Cooking Time: 10 Minutes
Ingredients:

- 1 tablespoon butter
- 2 red bell peppers, sliced
- 1 teaspoon red Aleppo pepper flakes
- 1 cup cream cheese, room temperature
- 2 cups Colby cheese, shredded
- 1 teaspoon sumac
- 2 garlic cloves, minced
- 1 cup chicken broth
- Salt and ground black pepper, to taste

Directions:

1. Press the "Sauté" button to heat up your Instant Pot. Once hot, melt the butter. Sauté the peppers until just tender.
2. Add the remaining ingredients; gently stir to combine.
3. Secure the lid. Choose "Manual" mode and High pressure; cook for minutes. Once cooking is complete, use a quick pressure release; carefully remove the lid.
4. Serve with your favorite keto dippers. Bon appétit!

Nutrition Info:

Per Serving: 237 Calories; 6g Fat; 3.1g Carbs; 2g Protein; 1.8g Sugars

Stuffed Mushrooms With Pancetta And Cheddar

Servings: 3
Cooking Time: 10 Minutes

Ingredients:
- 9 large white mushrooms, stems removed
- 1/2 teaspoon dried rosemary
- 1 ½ cup pancetta, chopped
- 2 tablespoons fresh parsley, finely chopped
- 1 ½ tablespoon olive oil
- 1 ½ cup cheddar cheese, shredded
- 2 cloves garlic, minced
- 1/2 teaspoon dried oregano
- ½ teaspoon salt
- 1 shallot, chopped
- ½ teaspoon pepper
- 1 cup of water

Directions:
1. Press the "Sauté" button and preheat your Instant Pot. Add the olive oil and sauté the shallots until tender.
2. Stir in the garlic and cook until aromatic. Now, add the pancetta, fresh parsley, cheddar cheese, dried oregano, dried rosemary, salt, and pepper.
3. Then, fill the mushroom caps with this mixture.
4. Add 1 cup of water and a steamer basket to you Instant Pot. Place the stuffed mushrooms in the steamer basket.
5. Secure the lid. Choose "Manual" mode and High pressure; cook for 6 minutes. When cooking is complete, use a quick pressure release and carefully remove the lid.
6. Serve warm. Bon appetite!

Nutrition Info:
Per Serving: 372 Calories; 2g Fat; 5.3g Carbs; 9g Protein; 2.3g Sugars

Lime Spinach And Leeks Dip

Servings: 4
Cooking Time: 20 Minutes
Ingredients:
- 1 shallot, chopped
- 2 tablespoons avocado oil
- 2 leeks, chopped
- 2 garlic cloves, minced
- 4 cups spinach, torn
- ¼ cup veggie stock
- ¼ cup lime juice
- 1 bunch basil, chopped
- A pinch of salt and black pepper

Directions:
1. Set your instant pot on Sauté mode, add the oil, heat it up, add the shallot, leeks and garlic and sauté for 5 minutes. Add the rest of the ingredients, put the lid on and cook on High for

minutes. Release the pressure naturally for 10 minutes, blend the mix using an immersion blender, transfer to bowls and serve as a snack.

Nutrition Info: calories 56, fat 1.8, fiber 0.5, carbs 1.6, protein 1.7

Bacon Avocado Bombs

Servings: 8
Cooking Time: 10 Minutes
Ingredients:

- 1 avocado, pitted, peeled
- 3 eggs
- 2 bacon slices, chopped
- 4 tablespoons cream cheese
- ½ teaspoon green onion, minced
- 1 cup water, for cooking

Directions:

1. Pour water and insert the steamer rack in the instant pot. Place the egg on the rack and close the lid. Cook them for 5 minutes on steam mode. When the time is over, allow the natural pressure release for 5 minutes more. Then cool the eggs in ice water and peel. Clean the instant pot and remove the steamer rack. Put the chopped bacon slices in the instant pot and cook them on sauté mode for minutes or until crunchy. Stir the bacon every minute. Meanwhile, chop the avocado and eggs into tiny pieces and place the ingredients in the big bowl. Add minced green onion and cream cheese. With the help of the fork mix up the mixture and smash it gently (we don't need smooth texture).Then add cooked bacon and stir until homogenous. With the help of the scopper make the balls and refrigerate them for -15 minutes. Store the bacon avocado bombs in the fridge in the closed vessel for up to 8 days.

Nutrition Info: calories 118, fat 3, fiber 1.7, carbs 2.5, protein 4.7

Zucchini Loaded Meatballs

Servings: 8
Cooking Time: 15 Minutes
Ingredients:

- 1 pound ground turkey
- 1/2 cup Romano cheese, grated
- 1 teaspoon dried basil
- 1/2 teaspoon dried oregano
- 1/2 teaspoon dried dill
- 1 teaspoon dried chives
- 2 tablespoons shallots, chopped
- 1 garlic clove, minced
- 1 egg, beaten
- 1 cup zucchini, grated
- 1 tablespoon olive oil
- 1/2 cup chili sauce

- 1/2 cup broth, preferably homemade

Directions:
1. In a mixing bowl, thoroughly combine ground turkey, grated cheese, basil, oregano, dill, chives, shallots, garlic, egg, and zucchini.
2. Shape the mixture into meatballs.
3. Press the "Sauté" button and heat the oil. Once hot, brown your meatballs for 2 to minutes, turning them occasionally.
4. Add chili sauce and broth to your Instant Pot. Place the meatballs in the liquid.
5. Secure the lid. Choose "Manual" mode and High pressure; cook for 8 minutes. Once cooking is complete, use a quick pressure release; carefully remove the lid.
6. Serve with toothpicks. Bon appétit!

Nutrition Info:
Per Serving: 161 Calories; 9.2g Fat; 4.2g Carbs; 7g Protein; 2.1g Sugars

Shrimp Scampi Dip

Servings: 4
Cooking Time: 3 Minutes
Ingredients:
- 3 tbsp unsalted butter
- 1 lb. medium shrimp, cleaned and chopped
- 1 tsp red chili flakes
- 4 garlic cloves, minced
- 1/3 cup white wine
- 3 tbsp freshly squeezed lemon juice
- Salt and black pepper
- 5 tbsp mayonnaise
- 6 oz cream cheese, softened
- ½ cup sour cream
- 1 cup grated mozzarella cheese, divided
- 3 tbsp grated parmesan cheese
- 2 tbsp chopped fresh parsley + extra for garnishing

Directions:
1. Add the butter, shrimp, red chili flakes, garlic, white wine, lemon juice, salt, and black pepper to inner pot.
2. Lock the lid in place; select Manual mode on High Pressure, and set the timer to 1 minute.
3. After cooking, perform a quick pressure release to let out the steam, and open the lid.
4. Set the IP in Sauté mode and mix in the remaining ingredients except for the parsley until the cheeses melt, 2 minutes.
5. Spoon the dip into serving bowls and garnish with the parsley. Enjoy!

Nutrition Info:
Per Serving: Calories 484 Fats 24g Carbs 9.92g Net Carbs 8.82g Protein 5g

Stuffed Mushrooms With Cheese

Servings: 5
Cooking Time: 10 Minutes
Ingredients:

- 1 tablespoon butter, softened
- 1 shallot, chopped
- 2 cloves garlic, minced
- 1 ½ cups Cottage cheese, at room temperature
- 1/2 cup Romano cheese, grated
- 1 red bell pepper, chopped
- 1 green bell pepper, chopped
- 1 jalapeno pepper, minced
- 1/2 teaspoon dried basil
- 1/2 teaspoon dried oregano
- 1/2 teaspoon dried rosemary
- 10 medium-sized button mushrooms, stems removed

Directions:

1. Press the "Sauté" button to heat up your Instant Pot. Once hot, melt the butter and sauté the shallots until tender and translucent.
2. Stir in the garlic and cook an additional 30 seconds or until aromatic. Now, add the remaining ingredients, except for the mushroom caps, and stir to combine well.
3. Then, fill the mushroom caps with this mixture.
4. Add 1 cup of water and a steamer basket to you Instant Pot. Arrange the stuffed mushrooms in the steamer basket.
5. Secure the lid. Choose "Manual" mode and High pressure; cook for minutes. Once cooking is complete, use a quick pressure release; carefully remove the lid.
6. Arrange the stuffed mushroom on a serving platter and serve. Enjoy!

Nutrition Info:
Per Serving: 151 Calories; 9.2g Fat; 6g Total Carbs; 9g Protein; 3.6g Sugars

Nuts With Smoky Brussels Sprouts

Servings: 4
Cooking Time: 4 Minutes
Ingredients:

- 1 tsp liquid smoke
- ½ cup water
- 1 cup baby Brussels sprouts
- 1 tbsp butter
- ½ cup mixed pecans and almonds
- 2 tbsp sugar-free maple syrup
- Salt to taste

Directions:

1. Mix the liquid smoke and water in the inner pot and insert a steamer basket; pour in the Brussels
2. Lock the lid in place; select Steam mode and set the timer for minutes.
3. After cooking, perform a quick pressure release to let out the steam and open the lid.
4. Remove the steamer basket with the Brussels sprouts, empty and clean the inner pot, and return to the base.
5. Select Sauté mode on the pot, adjust to Medium heat and melt the butter.
6. Stir in the Brussels sprouts, pecans, almonds and maple syrup, and cook until the nuts are tender, 2 minutes. Season with salt.
7. Spoon the snack into serving bowls and enjoy warm.

Nutrition Info:

Per Serving: : Calories 120 Fats 85g Carbs 3.69g Net Carbs 1.69g Protein 2.91g

Spinach Jalapeno Dip

Servings: 4
Cooking Time: 2 Minutes
Ingredients:

- 2 cups chopped frozen spinach, thawed and squeezed dry
- 2 medium white onion, chopped
- 1 cup heavy cream
- 1 cup grated Parmesan cheese
- 2 jalapeno peppers, deseeded and chopped
- 2 tsp hot sauce
- 2 tsp Worcestershire sauce
- 1 tsp garlic powder
- 16 oz cream cheese, softened

Directions:

1. In the inner pot, add the spinach, onion, heavy cream, jalapeno peppers, hot sauce, Worcestershire sauce, and garlic powder.
2. Lock the lid in place; select Manual mode on High Pressure, and set the timer to 1 minute.
3. After cooking, perform a quick pressure release to let out the steam, and open the lid.
4. Set the IP in Sauté mode and add the cream cheese. As the cheese melts, occasionally stir until well combined, 2 minutes.
5. Spoon the dip into serving bowls and enjoy with zucchini chips.

Nutrition Info:

Per Serving: : Calories 587 Fats 03g Carbs 46g Net Carbs 7.96g Protein 44g

Asian Chicken Wings

Servings: 6
Cooking Time: 15 Minutes
Ingredients:

- 2 teaspoons butter, melted
- 1 ½ pounds chicken wings

- 1/2 cup chicken broth
- 1/2 cup barbecue sauce
- 1 tablespoon fish sauce
- 1/4 cup rice vinegar
- 1 teaspoon grated fresh ginger
- Sea salt ground black pepper, to your liking
- 1/2 teaspoon cumin
- 1/2 teaspoon caraway seeds
- 1/2 teaspoon celery seeds
- 1/2 teaspoon garlic powder
- 1/2 teaspoon red pepper, crushed
- 2 tablespoons Thai basil

Directions:
1. Add butter, chicken wings, broth, barbecue sauce, fish sauce, vinegar, ginger, and spices to your Instant Pot.
2. Secure the lid. Choose "Poultry" mode and High pressure. Cook the chicken wings for 10 minutes. Once cooking is complete, use a natural pressure release; carefully remove the lid.
3. Serve garnished with Thai basil. Bon appétit!

Nutrition Info:
Per Serving: 200 Calories; 5.5g Fat; 6g Total Carbs; 6g Protein; 3g Sugars

Keto Broccoli Balls

Servings: 8
Cooking Time: 25 Minutes
Ingredients:
- 1 head broccoli, broken into florets
- 1/2 cup Añejo cheese, shredded
- 1 ½ cups Cotija cheese, crumbled
- 3 ounces Ricotta cheese, cut into small chunks
- 1 teaspoon chili pepper flakes

Directions:
1. Add cup of water and a steamer basket to the Instant Pot.
2. Place broccoli florets in the steamer basket.
3. Secure the lid. Choose "Manual" mode and Low pressure; cook for 5 minutes. Once cooking is complete, use a quick pressure release; carefully remove the lid.
4. Add the broccoli florets along with the remaining ingredients to your food processor. Process until everything is well incorporated.
5. Shape the mixture into balls and place your balls on a parchment-lined baking sheet. Bake in the preheated oven at 390 degrees F for 1minutes. Bon appétit!

Nutrition Info:
Per Serving: 137 Calories; 9.5g Fat; 4.8g Total Carbs; 8.9g Protein; 1.5g Sugars

Mushrooms Salsa

Servings: 4
Cooking Time: 10 Minutes
Ingredients:

- 1 pound white mushrooms, halved
- A pinch of salt and black pepper
- 1 tablespoon ghee, melted
- ¼ cup chicken stock
- 1 tablespoon rosemary, chopped
- 1 tablespoon basil, chopped
- 1 tablespoon oregano, chopped
- 2 tomatoes, cubed
- 1 avocado, peeled, pitted and cubed

Directions:

1. In your instant pot, combine the mushrooms with salt, pepper and the rest of the ingredients, put the lid on and cook on High for minutes. Release the pressure naturally for 10 minutes, divide the salsa into bowls and serve as an appetizer.

Nutrition Info: calories 173, fat 7, fiber 6.2, carbs 7.7, protein 5.3

Eggplant Spread

Servings: 3 To 5
Cooking Time: 30 Mins
Ingredients:

- 3 tbsp Olive oil
- 1 ½ Eggplants, head removed, halved
- 2 cloves Garlic, skin on
- 1 clove Garlic, peeled
- Salt to taste
- 1 cup Water
- ½ Lemon, juiced
- 2 tsp Tahini
- To Garnish:
- 3 sprigs Fresh Thyme
- Extra Virgin Olive oil
- ¼ cup Black Olives, pitted and unpitted

Directions:

1. Peel skins off the eggplants and set the cooker to Sauté. Heat the olive oil; add half of the eggplants face down and 2 unskinned garlic cloves. Caramelize for 5 minutes and turn eggplants over. Add the remaining eggplant, water, and salt; stir. Seal the lid, select Manual and cook on High for 3 minutes.
2. Once ready, quickly release the pressure, and strain the eggplants. Reserve a little of the brown liquid and remove the garlic's skin. Put the eggplant and garlic in the pot. Add tahini,

fresh garlic, lemon juice and some pitted black olives. Puree with a stick blender. Dish into serving bowls, drizzle extra virgin olive oil and garnish with thyme leaves and the remaining black olives.

Nutrition Info: Calories 157, Protein 6.6g, Net Carbs 3.8g, Fat 9 g

Mini Margharita Pizzas In Mushroom Caps

Servings: 4
Cooking Time: 10 Minutes
Ingredients:
- 4 Portobello mushroom caps
- 1/3 cup Mozzarella, shredded
- 1 teaspoon fresh basil, chopped
- 1 teaspoon cream cheese
- ¼ teaspoon dried oregano
- 1 teaspoon tomato sauce
- 1 cup water, for cooking

Directions:
1. Pour water and insert the trivet in the instant pot. Then mix up together shredded Mozzarella, basil, cream cheese, and dried oregano. Fill the mushroom caps with the Mozzarella mixture. Top every Portobello cap with tomato sauce and transfer in the trivet. Close the lid and cook pizzas for minutes on manual mode (high pressure). When the time is over, make a quick pressure release and transfer the cooked Margharita pizzas on the plate.

Nutrition Info: calories 10, fat 0.7, fiber 0.1, carbs 0.3, protein 0.8

Tender Jicama Fritters

Servings: 4
Cooking Time: 18 Minutes
Ingredients:
- 4 oz jicama, peeled, grated
- 1 egg, beaten
- 2 tablespoons Cheddar cheese, shredded
- ½ teaspoon ground coriander
- 1 teaspoon almond butter
- 2 tablespoons coconut flakes
- 1 tablespoon almond flour
- ½ teaspoon baking powder
- ½ teaspoon apple cider vinegar

Directions:
1. Mix up together jicama, egg, cheese, ground coriander, coconut flakes, baking powder, apple cider vinegar, and almond flour. Stir the mixture with the help of the spoon until homogenous. Then heat up the instant pot on sauté mode for 4 minutes or until it is hot. Add

almond butter and melt it. Separate the jicama mixture into 4 parts. With the help of the spoon arrange the fritters in the instant pot (2 fritters per one cooking). Cook them for 3 minutes from each side. The cooked fritters should be golden brown. Dry the fritters with the help of the paper towel if needed.

Nutrition Info: calories 85, fat 6.2, fiber 2.2, carbs 4.5, protein 3.8

Lemon Berry Pudding

Servings: 4
Cooking Time: 30 Minutes + 4 Hours Chilling
Ingredients:
- 1 tsp melted butter, for greasing
- 3 ½ tbsp butter, room temperature
- 2/3 cup swerve confectioner's sugar
- 1/3 cup almond flour
- ¼ tsp salt
- 2/3 cup unsweetened almond milk
- 1 lemon, zested and juiced
- 2 eggs, beaten
- 1 ½ cups strawberries and raspberries, mashed

Directions:
1. Grease 4 medium ramekins with melted butter and set aside.
2. Whisk the remaining butter in a medium bowl and using an electric hand mixer, whisk until creamy. Add swerve confectioner's sugar, almond flour, salt, and continue whisking until smooth.
3. Top with the almond milk, lemon zest, lemon juice, eggs, and combine well. Fold in the berries until adequately incorporated. Divide the mixture into the ramekins and cover with foil.
4. Pour 2 cups of water in the inner pot, set in a trivet, and place the ramekins on top.
5. Lock the lid in place; select Steam mode and set the timer to 30 minutes.
6. After cooking, perform a quick pressure release to let out the steam, and open the lid.
7. Carefully remove the ramekins, allow complete cooling, and chill in the refrigerator for at least 4 hours.
8. Serve afterwards.

Nutrition Info:
Per Serving: Calories 292 Fats 13g Carbs 7.7g Net Carbs 6.2g Protein 8.5g

Queso Fundido Dip

Servings: 10
Cooking Time: 15 Minutes
Ingredients:
- 1 pound chorizo sausage, chopped
- 1/2 cup water
- 1/2 cup tomato salsa

- 1 cup cream cheese
- 1 red onion, chopped
- 1/4 teaspoon ground black pepper
- 1/2 teaspoon cayenne pepper
- 1 teaspoon Mexican oregano
- 1 teaspoon coriander
- 1 cup Cotija cheese

Directions:

1. Stir sausage, water, tomato salsa, cream cheese, red onion, black pepper, cayenne pepper, oregano, and coriander into your Instant Pot.
2. Secure the lid. Choose "Manual" mode and High pressure; cook for 6 minutes. Once cooking is complete, use a natural pressure release; carefully remove the lid.
3. Add Cotija cheese and press the "Sauté" button. Stir until everything is heated through. Enjoy!

Nutrition Info:
Per Serving: 232 Calories; 1g Fat; 2.9g Carbs; 1g Protein; 1.5g Sugars

Basil Stuffed Bell Peppers

Servings: 4
Cooking Time: 15 Minutes
Ingredients:

- 4 red bell peppers, tops cut off and deseeded
- 2 tablespoons parsley, chopped
- 2 cups basil, chopped
- ¼ cup mozzarella, shredded
- 1 tablespoon garlic, minced
- 2 teaspoons lemon juice
- 1 cup baby spinach, torn
- 2 cups water

Directions:

1. In a bowl, mix all the ingredients except the water and the peppers, stir well and stuff the peppers with this mix. Add the water to your instant pot, add the trivet inside, arrange the bell peppers in the pot, put the lid on and cook on High for minutes. Release the pressure naturally for 10 minutes, arrange the peppers on a platter and serve as an appetizer.

Nutrition Info: calories 52, fat 4.8, fiber 2.4, carbs 3.6, protein 2.5

Artichoke Dip With Cheese

Servings: 10
Cooking Time: 15 Minutes
Ingredients:

- 2 medium-sized artichokes, trimmed and cleaned
- 1 cup Ricotta cheese, softened
- 2 cups Monterey-jack cheese, shredded

- 1/2 cup mayonnaise
- 1/2 cup Greek yogurt
- 1 garlic clove, minced
- 2 tablespoons coriander
- 1/4 cup scallions
- 1/4 teaspoon ground black pepper, or more to taste
- 1 teaspoon dried rosemary

Directions:

1. Start by adding cup of water and a steamer basket to the Instant Pot. Place the artichokes in the steamer basket.
2. Secure the lid. Choose "Manual" mode and High pressure; cook for 8 minutes. Once cooking is complete, use a quick pressure release; carefully remove the lid.
3. Coarsely chop your artichokes and add the remaining ingredients.
4. Press the "Sauté" button and let it simmer until everything is heated through. Bon appétit!

Nutrition Info:
Per Serving: 204 Calories; 4g Fat; 5.6g Total Carbs; 5g Protein; 1.3g Sugars

Pao De Queijo

Servings: 4
Cooking Time: 35 Mins
Ingredients:

- 2 cups Almond flour
- 1 cup Full Fat Milk
- A pinch to taste
- 2 Eggs, cracked into a bowl
- 2 cups grated Parmesan Cheese
- ½ cup Olive oil

Directions:

1. Grease the steamer basket with cooking spray and set aside. Put a pot on medium heat on a stovetop. Add the milk, oil, and salt; let them boil. Add the almond flour and mix vigorously with a spoon.
2. Turn off the heat and let the mixture cool. Once it has cooled, use the hand mixer to mix the dough very well and then add the Eggs and cheese while still mixing. The dough will be thick and sticky after. Use your hands to make 14 balls out of the mixture and put them in the steamer basket and cover the basket with foil.
3. Open the Instant Pot, pour the water in, and place the steamer basket in and cover. Seal the lid, select Steam on High Pressure for 20 minutes. Once ready, do a quick pressure release, and open the pot. Put the balls in a baking tray and brown them in a broiler for minutes.

Nutrition Info: Calories 225, Protein 6g, Net Carbs 2.6g, Fat 14g

Asparagus With Mayo Dip

Servings: 6
Cooking Time: 5 Minutes

Ingredients:

- 1 ½ pounds asparagus spears, trimmed
- 1/2 cup sour cream
- 1/2 cup mayonnaise
- 2 tablespoons fresh chervil
- 2 tablespoons scallions, chopped
- 1 teaspoon garlic, minced
- Salt, to taste

Directions:

1. Add cup of water and a steamer basket to you Instant Pot.
2. Secure the lid. Choose "Manual" mode and High pressure; cook for 1 minute. Once cooking is complete, use a quick pressure release; carefully remove the lid.
3. Then, thoroughly combine the remaining ingredients to make your dipping sauce. Serve your asparagus with the dipping sauce on the side. Bon appétit!

Nutrition Info:
Per Serving: 116 Calories; 8.5g Fat; 6.9g Total Carbs; 4.5g Protein; 2.4g Sugars

Creamy Pumpkin Puree Soup

Servings: 3
Cooking Time: 55 Mins
Ingredients:

- 1 cup Pumpkin puree
- 2 cups Chicken broth
- 4-5 Garlic cloves
- Salt and black pepper to taste
- 1 cup Heavy Cream
- 2 tbsp Olive oil

Directions:

1. In the Instant Pot, add all ingredients. Seal the lid and cook for 40 minutes on Meat/Stew mode on High. When ready, press Cancel and do a quick pressure release. Transfer to a blender and blend well. Pour into serving bowls to serve.

Nutrition Info: Calories 465, Protein 4g, Net Carbs 6.2g, Fat 5g

Zucchini-avocado Fritters

Servings: 4
Cooking Time: 15 Minutes
Ingredients:

- 2 ½ cups grated zucchinis
- 1 small avocado, pitted and peeled
- 3 garlic cloves, crushed
- 2 tbsp ginger powder
- Salt and black pepper to taste
- 2 tbsp chopped parsley

- 1 fresh red chili, deseeded and minced
- ½ cup freshly chopped oregano
- ¼ cup water
- 2 tbsp olive oil

Directions:
1. Mix all the ingredients in a food processor except for the olive oil. Form 2-inch patties from the mixture, place on cookie sheet and refrigerate for 20 minutes to firm up.
2. Set the IP in Sauté mode and adjust to medium heat.
3. Heat the olive oil in the inner pot and working in batches, fry the patties on both sides until golden brown, 12 to 15 minutes.
4. Transfer to a paper towel-lined plate to drain grease and serve warm with avocado dip.

Nutrition Info:
Per Serving: Calories 148 Fats 22g Carbs 4.96g Net Carbs 3.16g Protein 6.67g

Asparagus Chowder

Servings: 5
Cooking Time: 45 Mins
Ingredients:
- 1 tbsp Olive oil
- 2 cups chopped Onion
- 2 tbsp grated Lemon rind
- 1 cup Cauliflower rice
- 3 cans fat-free, Chicken broth
- 2 cups sliced Asparagus
- 2 cups chopped Spinach
- ¼ tbsp ground Nutmeg
- ½ cup grated Parmesan cheese
- Salt and black pepper to taste

Directions:
1. Heat oil on Sauté mode. Add onion and cook for 5 minutes until transparent. Add the cauli rice, lemon rind, asparagus, spinach, broth, and salt. Seal the lid, press Manual and cook for minutes on High pressure. When ready, do a quick pressure release. Top with Parmesan and ground nutmeg.

Nutrition Info: Calories 109, Protein 6g, Net Carbs 6.1g, Fat 8g

Oregano Green Beans Salsa

Servings: 4
Cooking Time: 10 Minutes
Ingredients:
- 1 pound green beans, trimmed and halved
- ¼ cup veggie stock
- 1 tablespoon olive oil
- 2 garlic cloves, minced

- A pinch of salt and black pepper
- 2 tomatoes, cubed
- 2 cucumbers, cubed
- 1 avocado, peeled, pitted and cubed
- 2 tablespoons balsamic vinegar
- 1 tablespoon oregano, chopped

Directions:
1. In your instant pot mix the green beans with the stock, garlic, salt and pepper, put the lid on and cook on High for minutes. Release the pressure naturally for 10 minutes, transfer the green beans to a bowl, add the rest of the ingredients, toss, divide the salsa into cups and serve.

Nutrition Info: calories 209, fat 2, fiber 3, carbs 4.4, protein 4.8

Nutmeg Endives

Servings: 4
Cooking Time: 10 Minutes
Ingredients:
- 4 endives, trimmed and halved
- 1 cup water
- Salt and black pepper to the taste
- 2 tablespoons olive oil
- 1 teaspoon nutmeg, ground
- 1 tablespoon chives, chopped

Directions:
1. Add the water to your instant pot, add steamer basket, add the endives inside, put the lid on and cook on High for minutes. Release the pressure naturally for 10 minutes, arrange the endives on a platter, drizzle the oil, season with salt, pepper and nutmeg, sprinkle the chives at the end and serve as an appetizer.

Nutrition Info: calories 63, fat 7.2, fiber 0.1, carbs 0.3, protein 0.1

Yummy Baby Carrots

Servings: 8
Cooking Time: 10 Minutes
Ingredients:
- 28 ounces baby carrots
- 1 cup chicken broth
- 1/2 cup water
- 1/2 stick butter
- 2 tablespoons balsamic vinegar
- Coarse sea salt, to taste
- 1/2 teaspoon red pepper flakes, crushed
- 1/2 teaspoon dried dill weed

Directions:

1. Simply add all of the above ingredients to your Instant Pot.
2. Secure the lid. Choose "Manual" mode and High pressure; cook for 3 minutes. Once cooking is complete, use a quick pressure release; carefully remove the lid.
3. Transfer to a nice serving bowl and serve. Enjoy!

Nutrition Info:
Per Serving: 94 Calories; 6.1g Fat; 5.9g Total Carbs; 1.4g Protein; 3.1g Sugars

Bacon Sushi

Servings: 6
Cooking Time: 4 Minutes
Ingredients:
- 6 bacon slices
- 1 cucumber
- 3 teaspoons cream cheese
- ¼ teaspoon ground black pepper
- ¼ teaspoon salt
- ¼ teaspoon dried thyme
- ½ teaspoon coconut oil

Directions:
1. Sprinkle the bacon slices with dried thyme, salt, and ground black pepper. Put coconut oil in the instant pot. Melt it on sauté mode. Then arrange the bacon in one layer. Cook it for minute and flip on another side. Cook the bacon for 1 minute more. Then transfer the bacon on the paper towel and dry well. Place the dried bacon on the sushi mat in the shape of the net. Then spread the bacon net with cream cheese. Cut the cucumber into the sticks. Place the cucumber sticks over the cream cheese. Roll the bacon in the shape of sushi and cut into 6 servings.

Nutrition Info: calories 120, fat 9, fiber 0.3, carbs 2.2, protein 7.5

Chicken Celery Boats

Servings: 2
Cooking Time: 10 Minutes
Ingredients:
- 2 celery stalks
- 3 oz chicken fillet
- ¼ teaspoon minced garlic
- ¼ teaspoon salt
- 1 teaspoon cream cheese
- 1 cup water, for cooking

Directions:
1. Pour water and insert the steamer rack in the instant pot. Put the chicken on the rack and close the lid. Cook it on manual mode (high pressure) for minutes. Then make a quick pressure release and remove the chicken from the instant pot. Shred the chicken and mix it up with minced garlic, salt, and cream cheese. Fill the celery stalks with chicken mixture.

Nutrition Info: calories 90, fat 3.8, fiber 0.3, carbs 0.7, protein 6

Green Beans, Mint, And Chili Dip

Servings: 4
Cooking Time: 3 Minutes
Ingredients:

- 1 cup chopped green beans
- ¼ cup chopped mint leaves
- 1 tsp cumin powder
- 1 lemon, juiced
- ¼ cup vegetable broth
- 1 small red chili, deseeded and chopped
- ¼ cup Greek yogurt
- Salt and black pepper to taste

Directions:

1. In the inner pot, combine all the ingredients except for the heavy cream.
2. Lock the lid in place; select Manual mode on High Pressure, and set the timer to 3 minutes.
3. After cooking, perform a quick pressure release to let out the steam, and open the lid.
4. Using an immersion blender, puree the ingredients until smooth and mix in the yogurt.
5. Adjust the taste with salt and black pepper, and dish into serving bowls.
6. Serve the dip with julienned celery.

Nutrition Info:
Per Serving: Calories 190 Fats 36g Carbs 4.07g Net Carbs 3.07g Protein 0.91g

Hawaiian Meatballs

Servings: 4
Cooking Time: 15 Minutes
Ingredients:

- 2 cups Italian meatballs
- 1 cup unsweetened cranberry juice
- 1 small red bell pepper, deseeded and chopped
- 1 tbsp coconut aminos
- ¼ cup finely chopped red onion
- 1/3 cup water

Directions:

1. Combine all the ingredients in the inner pot.
2. Lock the lid in place; select Manual mode on High Pressure and set the timer to 10 minutes.
3. After cooking, perform a natural pressure release for 5 minutes, then a quick pressure release to let out all the steam, and open the lid.
4. Stir and remove the meatballs onto a serving plate. Insert toothpicks into the meatballs.
5. Serve warm.

Nutrition Info:
Per Serving: Calories 255 Fats 59g Carbs 04g Net Carbs 5.94g Protein 52g

Beef, Arugula And Olives Salad

Servings: 4
Cooking Time: 20 Minutes
Ingredients:

- 1 and ½ pounds beef, cut into strips
- 2 tomatoes, cubed
- ¼ cup beef stock
- ½ cup black olives, pitted and sliced
- 1 tablespoon avocado oil
- 2 spring onions, chopped
- ½ cup cilantro chopped
- 2 cups tomatoes, chopped
- 1 tablespoon basil, chopped
- A pinch of salt and black pepper
- 1 cup baby arugula

Directions:

1. Set your instant pot on Sauté mode, add the oil, heat it up, add the onions and the meat and brown for 5 minutes. Add the rest of the ingredients except the arugula, put the lid on and cook on High for minutes. Release the pressure naturally for 10 minutes, transfer the mix to a bowl, add the arugula, toss and serve as an appetizer.

Nutrition Info: calories 378, fat 7, fiber 2.8, carbs 7.8, protein 3

Spanish Fat Bombs

Servings: 8
Cooking Time: 10 Minutes
Ingredients:

- 1 tablespoon tallow, melted
- 1 yellow onion, chopped
- 1 pound Chorizo sausage
- 1 garlic clove, minced
- 1 red bell pepper, chopped
- 1 cup chicken broth
- 1/2 teaspoon deli mustard
- 1 plum tomato, puréed
- 10 ounces Halloumi cheese, crumbled
- 1/3 cup mayonnaise

Directions:

1. Press the "Sauté" button and melt the tallow. Once hot, cook the onion until tender and translucent.
2. Add Chorizo and garlic to your Instant Pot; cook until the sausage is no longer pink; crumble the sausage with a fork.
3. Now, stir in bell pepper, broth, mustard, and tomato.

4. Secure the lid. Choose "Manual" mode and High pressure; cook for minutes. Once cooking is complete, use a quick pressure release; carefully remove the lid.
5. Add the cheese and mayo. Shape the mixture into 2-inch balls and serve. Bon appétit!

Nutrition Info:

Per Serving: 307 Calories; 8g Fat; 5.1g Total Carbs; 9g Protein; 2.9g Sugars

Basil Shallots And Peppers Dip

Servings: 2
Cooking Time: 15 Minutes
Ingredients:

- ½ cup lemon juice
- 3 shallots, minced
- ½ teaspoon hot sauce
- 1 tablespoon balsamic vinegar
- 1 and ½ pounds mixed peppers, roughly chopped
- ¼ cup chicken stock
- 1 tablespoon olive oil
- 2 tablespoons basil, chopped

Directions:

1. Set the instant pot on Sauté mode, add the oil, heat it up, add the shallots and sauté for 2 minutes. Add the rest of the ingredients, put the lid on and cook on High for minutes. Release the pressure fast for 5 minutes, blend the mix using an immersion blender, divide into bowls and serve.

Nutrition Info: calories 78, fat 7.6, fiber 0.3, carbs 1.5, protein 0.7

Mini Haddock Bites

Servings: 8
Cooking Time: 15 Mins
Ingredients:

- 1 pound Haddock, chopped
- 3 Eggs
- Juice of 1 Lemon
- ½ cup Half and Half
- 3 tbsp Olive oil
- 1 tsp Coriander
- 2 tbsp ground Almonds
- 1 tsp Lemon Zest
- A pinch of Pepper

Directions:

1. In a bowl, whisk together the eggs, flour, zest, and spices. Set the pot on Sauté and add the oil. Dip the haddock pieces in egg mixture and then fry in the Instant Pot for a minute per side. Pour the half and half and lemon juice over and stir to combine. Seal the lid and cook on High pressure for 2 minutes. After the beep, do a quick pressure release. Serve chilled.

Easy Cheesy Taco Dip

Servings: 12
Cooking Time: 10 Minutes
Ingredients:

- 2 teaspoons sesame oil
- 1/2 cup yellow onion, chopped
- 1 pound ground turkey
- 1 teaspoon roasted garlic paste
- 1 teaspoon ancho chili powder
- 1/2 teaspoon dried basil
- 1/2 teaspoon dried Mexican oregano
- 1/4 teaspoon freshly ground black pepper, or more to taste
- Sea salt, to taste
- 10 ounces Ricotta cheese, at room temperature
- 1 cup Mexican cheese, shredded
- 1 cup broth, preferably homemade
- 2 ripe tomatoes, chopped
- 1/3 cup salsa verde

Directions:

1. Press the "Sauté" button to heat up your Instant Pot. Once hot, heat the sesame oil; now, sauté the onion until translucent.
2. Stir in ground turkey and continue to sauté until it is no longer pink. Add the remaining ingredients and stir until everything is combined well.
3. Secure the lid. Choose "Manual" mode and High pressure; cook for 6 minutes. Once cooking is complete, use a natural pressure release; carefully remove the lid. Bon appétit!

Nutrition Info:
Per Serving: 275 Calories; 7g Fat; 2.6g Carbs; 4g Protein; 1.2g Sugars

Two-cheese And Caramelized Onion Dip

Servings: 12
Cooking Time: 15 Minutes
Ingredients:

- 3 tablespoons butter
- 2 pounds white onions, chopped
- Sea salt and freshly ground black pepper, to taste
- 1/4 teaspoon dill
- 1 tablespoon coconut aminos
- 1 cup broth, preferably homemade
- 10 ounces Ricotta cheese
- 6 ounces Swiss cheese

Directions:

1. Press the "Sauté" button and melt the butter. Once hot, cook the onions until they are caramelized.
2. Add the salt, pepper, dill, coconut aminos, and broth.
3. Secure the lid. Choose "Manual" mode and High pressure; cook for 10 minutes. Once cooking is complete, use a natural pressure release; carefully remove the lid.
4. Fold in the cheese and stir until everything is well combined. Serve with your favorite dippers. Bon appétit!

Nutrition Info:
Per Serving: 148 Calories; 10g Fat; 7.2g Carbs; 7.5g Protein; 4.1g Sugars

Chili Tomato And Zucchini Dip

Servings: 4
Cooking Time: 15 Minutes
Ingredients:
- 2 cups tomatoes, cubed
- 2 cups zucchinis, cubed
- 1 tablespoon hot paprika
- 2 red chilies, chopped
- ¼ cup veggie stock
- 1 tablespoon basil, chopped
- A pinch of salt and black pepper
- 2 scallions, chopped
- 1 tablespoon olive oil

Directions:
1. Set the instant pot on Sauté mode, add the oil, heat it up, add the chilies and the scallions and sauté for 2 minutes. Add the tomatoes and the rest of the ingredients except the basil, put the lid on and cook on High for minutes. Release the pressure naturally for 10 minutes, blend the mix with an immersion blender, divide into bowls, sprinkle the basil on top and serve.

Nutrition Info: calories 58, fat 3.5, fiber 1.9, carbs 2.3, protein 1.6

Caulicheese Mini Bowls

Servings: 4
Cooking Time: 15 Mins
Ingredients:
- ½ cup Half & Half
- 2 cups Cauliflower Rice
- 2 tbsp Cream Cheese
- ½ cup shredded Cheddar Cheese
- Salt and black pepper to taste
- 1 ½ cups Water

Directions:

1. Pour water in and lower the trivet. Place all ingredients in a baking dish. Stir to combine well and season with salt and pepper. Place the dish on top and seal the lid. Select Manual and set the cooking time to 5 minutes. Cook on High pressure. After the sound, allow for a natural pressure release, for 5 minutes. Divide between 4 bowls and serve.
2. Place the dish on top of the trivet and seal the lid. Cook on High pressure for minutes. When it goes off, do a quick pressure release. Arrange the peppers on a platter and drizzle with the olive oil and balsamic vinegar.

Nutrition Info: Calories 134, Protein 5g, Net Carbs 4g, Fat 10g

Pesto Wings

Servings: 6
Cooking Time: 15 Minutes
Ingredients:
- 6 chicken wings
- 1 teaspoon ground paprika
- 1 teaspoon butter
- 4 teaspoons pesto sauce
- 2 tablespoons cream cheese

Directions:
1. Rub the chicken wings with ground paprika. Toss butter in the instant pot and heat it up on sauté mode. When the butter is melted, place the chicken wings inside (in one layer) and cook them for 3 minutes from each side or until you get light brown color. Then add pesto sauce and cream cheese. Coat the chicken wings in the mixture well, bring to boil, and close the lid. Saute the wings for 4 minutes.

Nutrition Info: calories 127, fat 9.6, fiber 0.3, carbs 3.7, protein 6.4

Simple Herbed Shrimp

Servings: 4
Cooking Time: 10 Minutes
Ingredients:
- 2 tablespoons olive oil
- 3/4 pound shrimp, peeled and deveined
- 1 teaspoon paprika
- 1/2 teaspoon dried oregano
- 1/2 teaspoon dried thyme
- 1/2 teaspoon dried rosemary
- 1/2 teaspoon dried basil
- 1/4 teaspoon red pepper flakes
- 1 teaspoon dried parsley flakes
- 1 teaspoon onion powder
- 1 teaspoon garlic powder
- Coarse sea salt and ground black pepper, to taste
- 1 cup chicken broth, preferably homemade

Directions:
1. Press the "Sauté" button and heat the olive oil. Once hot, cook your shrimp for 2 to 3 minutes.
2. Sprinkle all seasoning over your shrimp, pour the chicken broth into your Instant Pot, and secure the lid.
3. Choose "Manual" mode and Low pressure; cook for 2 minutes. Once cooking is complete, use a quick pressure release; carefully remove the lid.
4. Arrange shrimp on a serving platter and serve with toothpicks. Bon appétit!

Nutrition Info:
Per Serving: 142 Calories; 7.5g Fat; 0.2g Total Carbs; 3g Protein; 0g Sugars

Umami Party Chicken Wings

Servings: 6
Cooking Time: 15 Minutes
Ingredients:
- 2 teaspoons butter, melted
- 1 ½ pounds chicken wings
- 1/2 cup chicken broth
- 1/2 cup barbecue sauce
- 1 tablespoon fish sauce
- 1/4 cup rice vinegar
- 1 teaspoon grated fresh ginger
- Sea salt ground black pepper, to your liking
- 1/2 teaspoon cumin
- 1/2 teaspoon caraway seeds
- 1/2 teaspoon celery seeds
- 1/2 teaspoon garlic powder
- 1/2 teaspoon red pepper, crushed
- 2 tablespoons Thai basil

Directions:
1. Add butter, chicken wings, broth, barbecue sauce, fish sauce, vinegar, ginger, and spices to your Instant Pot.
2. Secure the lid. Choose "Poultry" mode and High pressure. Cook the chicken wings for 10 minutes. Once cooking is complete, use a natural pressure release; carefully remove the lid.
3. Serve garnished with Thai basil. Bon appétit!

Nutrition Info:
Per Serving: 200 Calories; 5.5g Fat; 9g Carbs; 6g Protein; 8g Sugars

Prawns With Garlic And Lime

Servings: 6
Cooking Time: 10 Minutes
Ingredients:
- 2 tablespoons olive oil

- 1 pound prawns, cleaned and deveined
- 2 garlic cloves, minced
- Sea salt and ground black pepper, to taste
- 1 teaspoon cayenne pepper
- 1/2 teaspoon dried dill
- 2 tablespoons fresh lime juice
- 1 cup roasted vegetable broth, preferably homemade

Directions:

1. Press the "Sauté" button and heat the olive oil. Once hot, cook your prawns for 2 to 3 minutes.
2. Add garlic and cook an additional 40 seconds.
3. Stir in the remaining ingredients.
4. Secure the lid. Choose "Manual" mode and Low pressure; cook for 2 minutes. Once cooking is complete, use a quick pressure release; carefully remove the lid.
5. Arrange prawns on a serving platter and serve with toothpicks. Bon appétit!

Nutrition Info:
Per Serving: 122 Calories; 5.8g Fat; 2.7g Total Carbs; 2g Protein; 0.5g Sugars

Ginger Cauliflower Spread

Servings: 4
Cooking Time: 15 Minutes
Ingredients:

- 1 shallot, chopped
- 1 tablespoon avocado oil
- 2 tablespoons ginger, minced
- 1 pound cauliflower florets
- ¼ cup chicken stock
- 2 red hot chilies, chopped
- 1 and ¼ tablespoon balsamic vinegar

Directions:

1. Set your instant pot on Sauté mode, add the oil, heat it up, add the ginger and the shallot and sauté for 2 minutes. Add the rest of the ingredients, put the lid on and cook on High for minutes. Release the pressure naturally for 10 minutes, blend the mix a bit with an immersion blender, divide into bowls and serve as a party spread.

Nutrition Info: calories 45, fat 2.5, fiber 1.3, carbs 2 , protein 2.6

Marinated Shrimp

Servings: 4
Cooking Time: 6 Minutes
Ingredients:

- 1 and ½ pounds shrimp, peeled and deveined
- ¼ cup chicken stock
- 1 tablespoon avocado oil

- Juice of ½ lemon
- 4 garlic cloves, minced
- 2 thyme springs, chopped
- 1 tablespoon rosemary, chopped
- Salt and black pepper to the taste

Directions:

1. In your instant pot, combine the shrimp with the stock and the rest of the ingredients, put the lid on and cook on High for 6 minutes. Release the pressure naturally for minutes, arrange the shrimp on a platter and serve as an appetizer.

Nutrition Info: calories 282, fat 4.5, fiber 0.6, carbs 2.3, protein 4

Party Garlic Prawns

Servings: 6
Cooking Time: 10 Minutes
Ingredients:

- 2 tablespoons olive oil
- 1 pound prawns, cleaned and deveined
- 2 garlic cloves, minced
- Sea salt and ground black pepper, to taste
- 1 teaspoon cayenne pepper
- 1/2 teaspoon dried dill
- 2 tablespoons fresh lime juice
- 1 cup roasted vegetable broth, preferably homemade

Directions:

1. Press the "Sauté" button and heat the olive oil. Once hot, cook your prawns for 2 to 3 minutes.
2. Add garlic and cook an additional 40 seconds.
3. Stir in the remaining ingredients.
4. Secure the lid. Choose "Manual" mode and Low pressure; cook for 2 minutes. Once cooking is complete, use a quick pressure release; carefully remove the lid.
5. Arrange prawns on a serving platter and serve with toothpicks. Bon appétit!

Nutrition Info:
Per Serving: 122 Calories; 5.8g Fat; 2.7g Carbs; 2g Protein; 0.5g Sugars

Cheesy Chicken Dip

Servings: 4
Cooking Time: 1 Hour 20 Mins
Ingredients:

- 1 lb Chicken Breast
- ½ cup pork rinds, crushed
- 10 oz Cheddar Cheese
- ½ cup Sour Cream
- 10 oz Cream Cheese

- ½ cup Water

Directions:

1. Add chicken, water, and cream cheese to your Instant Pot. Seal the lid, select Manual on High, and cook for minutes. Once ready, do a quick pressure release, and open the pot.
2. Add the cheddar cheese and shred the chicken with two forks. Spoon into a baking dish, sprinkle pork rinds on top and place in a broiler to brown for 3 minutes. Serve warm with veggie bites or crunchies.

Nutrition Info: Calories 287, Protein 17g, Net Carbs 2g, Fat 20g

Veggie Tomato Dip

Servings: 8
Cooking Time: 20 Mins
Ingredients:

- 1 cup chopped Broccoli
- 1 cup chopped Cauliflower
- ¼ Onion, diced
- 1 cup diced canned Tomatoes
- 1 tbsp Butter
- ¼ cup shredded Cheddar Cheese
- ¼ tsp Garlic Powder
- Salt and black pepper to taste

Directions:

1. Pour cup water into your Instant Pot. Place cauliflower and broccoli in a steamer basket and lower into the pot. Seal the lid, and cook on High pressure for 4 minutes. Do a quick pressure release and transfer the veggies to a bowl. Mash finely with a potato masher. Discard the water from the pot and wipe clean. Melt the butter on Sauté. Add onions and cook for 3 minutes. Pour in tomatoes and spices; cook for 2 minutes. Stir in the mashed veggies and cheese.

Nutrition Info: Calories 120, Protein 4g, Net Carbs 4g, Fat 5g

Strawberry Protein Bars

Servings: 4
Cooking Time: 5 Minutes + 20 Minutes Chilling
Ingredients:

- 1 ½ cups cashew nut butter
- 4 tbsp butter
- ¼ cup unsweetened coconut flakes
- 3 scoops vanilla collagen powder
- 1 ½ tsp maple (sugar-free) syrup or to taste
- ½ tsp salt or to taste
- 4 tbsp dried strawberries, chopped

Directions:

1. Pour cup of water in the inner pot and fit in a trivet.

2. In a medium heatproof bowl, mix all the ingredients, cover with foil, and place the bowl on the trivet.
3. Lock the lid in place; select Manual mode on High Pressure and set the timer to 5 minutes.
4. After cooking, perform a quick pressure release to let out the steam, and open the lid.
5. Spread the mixture on a baking paper-lined cookie sheet and chill in the refrigerator for at least 20 minutes.
6. Break the mixture into bars and enjoy.

Nutrition Info:

Per Serving: Calories 201 Fats 89g Carbs 6.71g Net Carbs 5.61g Protein 9.31g

Oregano Cheesy Nuts

Servings: 4

Cooking Time: 5 Minutes

Ingredients:
- 1 egg white
- 1 ½ cups mixed nuts
- ½ cup mixed seeds
- 4 tsp yeast extract
- 1 tsp swerve brown sugar
- Salt and black pepper to season
- 3 tbsp grated Parmesan cheese
- ½ tsp dried oregano

Directions:
1. Pour cup of water in the inner pot and fit in a trivet.
2. In a medium heatproof bowl, mix all the ingredients, cover with foil, and place the bowl on the trivet.
3. Lock the lid in place; select Manual mode on High Pressure and set the timer to 5 minutes.
4. After cooking, perform a quick pressure release to let out the steam, and open the lid.
5. Spread the mixture on a baking paper-lined cookie sheet, allow complete cooling, and separate the mixture into nut-size pieces.
6. Enjoy after.

Nutrition Info:

Per Serving: Calories 494 Fats 2g Carbs 34g Net Carbs 6.04g Protein 02g

Parmesan Cauliflower Tots

Servings: 2

Cooking Time: 5 Minutes

Ingredients:
- 1 oz Parmesan, grated
- ¼ cup cauliflower, shredded
- 1 egg white
- ¼ teaspoon ground paprika
- 1 tablespoon almond flour

- 1 teaspoon butter
- ¼ teaspoon ground black pepper

Directions:
1. Whisk the egg white little and combine it with Parmesan and shredded cauliflower. Then add ground paprika and ground black pepper. Stir the mixture. Add almond flour and stir the mixture until it is homogenous and non-sticky. Make the small tots with the help of the fingertips. Melt butter in the instant pot on sauté mode. Place the cauliflower tots in the instant pot and cook them for 2 minutes from each side. If you prefer crunchy crust – increase the time of cooking to 3 minutes per one side.

Nutrition Info: calories 97, fat 6.7, fiber 0.9, carbs 2.4, protein 7.4

Hot Lager Chicken Wings

Servings: 6
Cooking Time: 15 Minutes
Ingredients:
- 2 tablespoons butter, melted
- 1 pound chicken thighs
- Coarse sea salt and ground black pepper, to taste
- 1 teaspoon cayenne pepper
- 1 teaspoon shallot powder
- 1 teaspoon garlic powder
- 1 teaspoon hot sauce
- 1/2 cup lager
- 1/2 cup water

Directions:
1. Press the "Sauté" button and melt the butter. Once hot, brown the chicken thighs for 2 minutes per side.
2. Add the remaining ingredients to your Instant Pot.
3. Secure the lid. Choose "Poultry" mode and High pressure; cook for 6 minutes. Once cooking is complete, use a quick pressure release; carefully remove the lid.
4. Serve at room temperature and enjoy!

Nutrition Info:
Per Serving: 216 Calories; 4g Fat; 2.2g Carbs; 9g Protein; 0.5g Sugars

Roasted Pepper Dip With Feta Cheese

Servings: 4
Cooking Time: 3 Minutes
Ingredients:
- ½ cup heavy cream
- 1 (12 oz) jar roasted red bell pepper, finely chopped
- 1 garlic clove, minced
- ½ lb. feta cheese, crumbled
- ½ tsp red chili flakes

- 4 oz cream cheese, softened

Directions:

1. Combine the heavy cream and roasted pepper in the inner pot.
2. Lock the lid in place; select Manual mode on High Pressure and set the timer to 1 minute.
3. After cooking, perform a quick pressure release to let out all the steam, and open the lid.
4. Set the IP in Sauté mode and mix in the remaining ingredients until the cream cheese melts, 2 minutes.
5. Spoon the dip into serving bowls and serve.

Nutrition Info:

Per Serving: Calories 292 Fats 8g Carbs 5.22g Net Carbs 4.92g Protein 7g

Pizza Dip

Servings: 4
Cooking Time: 8 Minutes
Ingredients:

- 1 tbsp olive oil
- 2/3 cup Italian sausage, chopped
- 2 pepperonis, sliced thinly
- 1/3 cup chopped cremini mushrooms
- 1 tsp garlic powder
- 2 ½ tsp mixed herb seasoning
- 3 cups shredded Italian cheese blend
- 2/3 cup red pizza sauce
- ¼ cup chicken broth
- 1 small green bell pepper, chopped
- 2 tbsp chopped fresh oregano
- 12 oz cream cheese, softened

Directions:

1. Set the IP in Sauté mode and adjust to Medium heat.
2. Heat the olive oil in the inner pot and cook the sausage, pepperoni, and mushrooms until brown, 5 minutes.
3. Stir in the rest of the ingredients except for the cream cheese.
4. Lock the lid in place; select Manual mode on High Pressure, and set the timer to 1 minute.
5. After cooking, perform a quick pressure release to let out the steam, and open the lid.
6. Set the IP in Sauté mode and mix in the cream cheese until melted, 2 minutes.
7. Spoon the dip into serving bowls and enjoy.

Nutrition Info:

Per Serving: Calories 656 Fats 89g Carbs 25g Net Carbs 55g Protein 96g

Spicy Pork Bites

Servings: 3
Cooking Time: 25 Minutes
Ingredients:

- 1 lb. pork steak, cut into cubes
- ½ teaspoon dried rosemary
- 1/2 teaspoon red pepper flakes
- 3 tablespoons dry white wine
- 1 teaspoon chili powder
- ½ teaspoon salt
- 1/2 teaspoon dried marjoram
- 1 tablespoon canola oil
- 1/2 teaspoon pepper
- 1 cup vegetable broth
- 1/3 cup parmesan cheese, shredded

Directions:
1. Press the "Sauté" button and heat the canola oil. Cook the pork for 2 minutes.
2. Then stir in the pepper, salt, red pepper flakes, chili powder, marjoram, vegetable broth, rosemary, and white wine. Combine well.
3. Secure the lid. Choose "Manual" mode and High pressure; cook for 15 minutes. When cooking is complete, use a natural pressure release and carefully remove the lid.
4. Serve immediately and sprinkle with parmesan cheese. Bon appétit!

Nutrition Info:
Per Serving: 297 Calories; 9g Fat; 3.8g Carbs; 4g Protein; 1.1g Sugars

Chicken Salad Skewers

Servings: 4
Cooking Time: 10 Minutes
Ingredients:
- 1 pound chicken breast halves, boneless and skinless
- Celery salt and ground black pepper, to taste
- 1/2 teaspoon Sriracha
- 1 red onion, cut into wedges
- 1 cup cherry tomatoes, halved
- 1 zucchini, cut into thick slices
- 1/4 cup olives, pitted
- 2 tablespoons olive oil
- 1 tablespoon lemon juice, freshly squeezed

Directions:
1. Add cup of water and a metal trivet to the Instant Pot.
2. Arrange the chicken on the metal trivet.
3. Secure the lid. Choose "Poultry" mode and High pressure. Cook the chicken for 5 minutes. Once cooking is complete, use a natural pressure release; carefully remove the lid.
4. Slice the chicken into cubes. Sprinkle chicken cubes with salt, pepper, and Sriracha.
5. Thread chicken cubes, onion, cherry tomatoes, zucchini, and olives onto bamboo skewers. Drizzle olive oil and lemon juice over skewers and serve.

Nutrition Info:

Per Serving: 287 Calories; 2g Fat; 5.6g Carbs; 6g Protein; 2.8g Sugars

Prosciutto Wrapped Asparagus

Servings: 6
Cooking Time: 10 Mins
Ingredients:
- 1 lb Asparagus, stalks trimmed
- 10 oz Prosciutto, thinly sliced
- 1 cup Water

Directions:
1. Wrap each asparagus with a slice of prosciutto from the top of the asparagus to the bottom of it. Open the Instant Pot, pour the water into and fit the steamer basket in it. Put in the wrapped asparagus and then close the lid, secure the pressure valve, and select Steam mode on High Pressure for 4 minutes.
2. Once ready, do a quick pressure release, and open the pot. Remove the wrapped asparagus onto a plate and serve them with cheese dip.

Nutrition Info: Calories 24, Protein 2.4g, Net Carbs 0g, Fat 2.4g

Easy Buttery Brussels Sprouts

Servings: 4
Cooking Time: 10 Minutes
Ingredients:
- 1 tablespoon butter
- 1/2 cup shallots, chopped
- 3/4 pound whole Brussels sprouts
- Sea salt, to taste
- 1/4 teaspoon ground black pepper
- 1/2 cup water
- 1/2 cup chicken stock

Directions:
1. Press the "Sauté" button to heat up your Instant Pot. Once hot, melt the butter and sauté the shallots until tender and translucent.
2. Add the remaining ingredients to the Instant Pot.
3. Secure the lid. Choose "Manual" mode and High pressure; cook for 4 minutes. Once cooking is complete, use a quick pressure release; carefully remove the lid.
4. Transfer Brussels sprouts to a serving platter. Serve with cocktail sticks and enjoy!

Nutrition Info:
Per Serving: 68 Calories; 3.3g Fat; 7.8g Carbs; 3.5g Protein; 1.9g Sugars

Coconut Shrimp Platter

Servings: 4
Cooking Time: 4 Minutes

Ingredients:
- 2 pounds shrimp, peeled and deveined
- 2 tablespoons coconut aminos
- 3 tablespoons balsamic vinegar
- ¾ cup veggie stock
- 1 tablespoon chives, chopped
- 1 tablespoon basil, chopped
- 1 tablespoon chervil, chopped

Directions:
1. In your instant pot, combine the shrimp with the aminos and the rest of the ingredients, put the lid on and cook on High for 5 minutes. Release the pressure naturally for minutes, arrange the shrimp on a platter and serve.

Nutrition Info: calories 273, fat 3.9, fiber 0.1, carbs 3.8, protein 8

Cheesy Cauliflower Bites

Servings: 6
Cooking Time: 10 Minutes
Ingredients:
- 1 pound cauliflower, broken into florets
- Sea salt and ground black pepper, to taste
- 2 tablespoons lemon juice
- 2 tablespoons extra-virgin olive oil
- 1 cup Cheddar cheese, preferably freshly grated

Directions:
1. Add cup of water and a steamer basket to your Instant Pot.
2. Now, arrange cauliflower florets on the steamer basket.
3. Secure the lid. Choose "Manual" mode and Low pressure; cook for minutes. Once cooking is complete, use a quick pressure release; carefully remove the lid.
4. Sprinkle salt and pepper over your cauliflower; drizzle with lemon juice and olive oil. Scatter grated cheese over the cauliflower florets.
5. Press the "Sauté" button to heat up your Instant Pot. Let it cook until the cheese is melted or about minutes. Bon appétit!

Nutrition Info:
Per Serving: 130 Calories; 9.6g Fat; 5.1g Carbs; 6.9g Protein; 2g Sugars

Colorful Stuffed Mushrooms

Servings: 5
Cooking Time: 10 Minutes
Ingredients:
- 1 tablespoon butter, softened
- 1 shallot, chopped
- 2 cloves garlic, minced
- 1 ½ cups Cottage cheese, at room temperature

- 1/2 cup Romano cheese, grated
- 1 red bell pepper, chopped
- 1 green bell pepper, chopped
- 1 jalapeno pepper, minced
- 1/2 teaspoon dried basil
- 1/2 teaspoon dried oregano
- 1/2 teaspoon dried rosemary
- 10 medium-sized button mushrooms, stems removed

Directions:

1. Press the "Sauté" button to heat up your Instant Pot. Once hot, melt the butter and sauté the shallots until tender and translucent.
2. Stir in the garlic and cook an additional 30 seconds or until aromatic. Now, add the remaining ingredients, except for the mushroom caps, and stir to combine well.
3. Then, fill the mushroom caps with this mixture.
4. Add 1 cup of water and a steamer basket to you Instant Pot. Arrange the stuffed mushrooms in the steamer basket.
5. Secure the lid. Choose "Manual" mode and High pressure; cook for minutes. Once cooking is complete, use a quick pressure release; carefully remove the lid.
6. Arrange the stuffed mushroom on a serving platter and serve. Enjoy!

Nutrition Info:
Per Serving: 151 Calories; 9.2g Fat; 6g Carbs; 9g Protein; 3.6g Sugars

Cream Cheese & Salami Snack

Servings: 6
Cooking Time: 15 Mins
Ingredients:
- 4 ounces Cream Cheese
- ¼ cup chopped Parsley
- 7 ounces dried Salami
- 1 cup Water

Directions:

1. Pour water in and lower the trivet. Grab a baking sheet and arrange the salami slices in it. Place the baking sheet on top of the trivet and seal the lid.
2. Select Manual and cook on High pressure for 3 minutes. When ready, do a quick pressure release. Remove the salami to a platter, top with cream cheese and sprinkle with parsley.

Nutrition Info: Calories 176, Protein 9g, Net Carbs 1g, Fat 15g

Cauliflower Fat Bombs

Servings: 6
Cooking Time: 10 Minutes
Ingredients:
- 1 pound cauliflower, broken into florets
- Sea salt and ground black pepper, to taste

- 2 tablespoons lemon juice
- 2 tablespoons extra-virgin olive oil
- 1 cup Cheddar cheese, preferably freshly grated

Directions:
1. Add cup of water and a steamer basket to your Instant Pot.
2. Now, arrange cauliflower florets on the steamer basket.
3. Secure the lid. Choose "Manual" mode and Low pressure; cook for minutes. Once cooking is complete, use a quick pressure release; carefully remove the lid.
4. Sprinkle salt and pepper over your cauliflower; drizzle with lemon juice and olive oil. Scatter grated cheese over the cauliflower florets.
5. Press the "Sauté" button to heat up your Instant Pot. Let it cook until the cheese is melted or about minutes. Bon appétit!

Nutrition Info:
Per Serving: 130 Calories; 9.6g Fat; 5.1g Total Carbs; 6.9g Protein; 2g Sugars

Easy Cauliflower Hummus

Servings: 4
Cooking Time: 50 Mins
Ingredients:
- 2 cups Cauliflower, chunks
- 1 pinch Salt
- ¼ tbsp Chili powder
- 3 cups Water
- 2 tbsp Olive oil
- 1 Onion, chopped
- 2 Garlic cloves, minced

Directions:
1. Place water, cauliflower, salt, onion and garlic in the Instant Pot. Seal the lid and cook for minutes on High pressure. When done, allow for a naturally release for 5 minutes.
2. Let it cool a little then transfer into a blender and pulse to a puree. Add olive oil gradually and blend. Put to a serving dish and sprinkle chili powder on top.

Nutrition Info: Calories 98, Protein 2g, Net Carbs 3.5g, Fat 8g

Cheesy Cauliflower Balls

Servings: 8
Cooking Time: 25 Minutes
Ingredients:
- 1 head of cauliflower, broken into florets
- 2 tablespoons butter
- Coarse sea salt and white pepper, to taste
- 1/2 teaspoon cayenne pepper
- 1 garlic clove, minced
- 1/2 cup Parmesan cheese, grated

- 1 cup Asiago cheese, shredded
- 2 tablespoons fresh chopped chives, minced
- 2 eggs, beaten

Directions:
1. Add cup of water and a steamer basket to the Instant Pot. Now, add cauliflower to the steamer basket.
2. Secure the lid. Choose "Manual" mode and High pressure; cook for 3 minutes. Once cooking is complete, use a quick pressure release; carefully remove the lid.
3. Transfer the cauliflower to a food processor. Add the remaining ingredients; process until everything is well incorporated.
4. Shape the mixture into balls. Bake in the preheated oven at 0 degrees F for 18 minutes. Bon appétit!

Nutrition Info:
Per Serving: 157 Calories; 1g Fat; 3.6g Carbs; 8.9g Protein; 1.2g Sugars

Party Turkey Skewers

Servings: 4
Cooking Time: 15 Minutes
Ingredients:
- 1 yellow onion, cut into wedges
- 1/3 cup olives, pitted
- 2 red bell peppers, cut into slices
- ½ cup pickles, cut into circles
- 1 ½ lb. turkey breasts
- 2 tablespoons avocado oil
- 1 tablespoon lemon juice, freshly squeezed
- Salt and pepper, to taste

Directions:
1. Add cup of water and a metal trivet to the Instant Pot. Then arrange the turkey on the metal trivet.
2. Secure the lid. Choose the "Poultry" mode and High pressure. Cook the chicken for 9 minutes. Once cooking is complete, use a natural pressure release and carefully remove the lid.
3. Slice the turkey breasts into cubes and season with salt and pepper.
4. Thread the turkey cubes, yellow onion, olives, pickles, red bell peppers onto bamboo skewers. Drizzle with lemon juice and avocado oil and serve. Enjoy!

Nutrition Info:
Per Serving: 362 Calories; 8g Fat; 4.7g Carbs; 1g Protein; 2.6g Sugars

Dog Nuggets

Servings: 6
Cooking Time: 20 Minutes
Ingredients:

- 5 oz Piza keto dough
- 3 pork sausages
- 1 cup water, for cooking

Directions:
1. Roll up the dough and cut it into 6 strips. Then cut every pork sausage into halves. Roll every sausage half in the doughs trip. Pour water in the instant pot and insert the steamer rack. Line the rack with baking paper. Place the dog nuggets on the baking paper and close the lid. Cook the snack for 20 minutes on manual mode (high pressure). Then make a quick pressure release and transfer the meal in the serving plate.

Nutrition Info: calories 199, fat 2, fiber 3.2, carbs 6.7, protein 1

Edamame Hummus

Servings: 8
Cooking Time: 5 Minutes
Ingredients:
- 1 ½ cup edamame beans, shelled
- 1 teaspoon salt
- ½ teaspoon harissa
- 1 garlic clove, peeled
- 4 tablespoons olive oil
- 1 tablespoon lemon juice
- 1 avocado, pitted, peeled, chopped
- 1 cup water, for cooking

Directions:
1. Pour water in the instant pot. Add edamame beans and garlic, and close the lid. Cook the beans on manual mode (high pressure) for 2 minutes. Then make a quick pressure release and open the lid. Transfer the edamame beans and garlic in the blender. Add 3 cup of water from the instant pot. Then add harissa, salt, lemon juice, and avocado. Blend the mixture until it is smooth and soft. Add more water if the texture of the hummus is very thick. Then add olive oil and pulse the hummus for 10 seconds. Transfer the cooked edamame hummus in the serving bowl.

Nutrition Info: calories 99, fat 9, fiber 2.2, carbs 3.5, protein 2.5

Spicy Queso Dip

Servings: 4
Cooking Time: 10 Mins
Ingredients:
- 16 oz American Cheese
- 1 cup Cotija
- 1 ½ cups Full Milk
- 3 Jalapenos, minced
- 3 cloves Garlic, minced
- 3 tsp Paprika

- 2 tsp Cayenne Pepper
- 1 tsp Salt
- Chopped Cilantro

Directions:
1. Place all ingredients, except the cilantro, in the Instant Pot. Seal the lid, and cook on High Pressure for 5 minutes. Once ready, quickly release the pressure and stir in cilantro, to serve.

Nutrition Info: Calories 235, Protein 12g, Net Carbs 4g, Fat 5g

Green Beans And Cod Salad

Servings: 4
Cooking Time: 15 Minutes
Ingredients:
- 1 pound cod fillets, skinless, boneless and cubed
- 2 tablespoons parsley, chopped
- 2 teaspoons lime juice
- 2 cups green beans, trimmed and halved
- A pinch of salt and black pepper
- 1 cup coconut cream
- 1 tablespoon oregano, chopped
- 1 tablespoon chives, chopped

Directions:
1. In your instant pot, combine the cod with the green beans and the rest of the ingredients except the oregano and chives, put the lid on and cook o High for minutes. Release the pressure naturally for 10 minutes, divide the mix into small bowls, sprinkle the oregano and the chives on top and serve as an appetizer.

Nutrition Info: calories 160, fat 5, fiber 3.8, carbs 8.1, protein 2.6

Creamy Cauliflower Bites

Servings: 8
Cooking Time: 25 Minutes
Ingredients:
- 1 head of cauliflower, broken into florets
- 2 tablespoons butter
- Coarse sea salt and white pepper, to taste
- 1/2 teaspoon cayenne pepper
- 1 garlic clove, minced
- 1/2 cup Parmesan cheese, grated
- 1 cup Asiago cheese, shredded
- 2 tablespoons fresh chopped chives, minced
- 2 eggs, beaten

Directions:
1. Add cup of water and a steamer basket to the Instant Pot. Now, add cauliflower to the steamer basket.

2. Secure the lid. Choose "Manual" mode and High pressure; cook for 3 minutes. Once cooking is complete, use a quick pressure release; carefully remove the lid.
3. Transfer the cauliflower to a food processor. Add the remaining ingredients; process until everything is well incorporated.
4. Shape the mixture into balls. Bake in the preheated oven at 0 degrees F for 18 minutes. Bon appétit!

Nutrition Info:

Per Serving: 157 Calories; 1g Fat; 3.6g Total Carbs; 8.9g Protein; 1.2g Sugars

Middle-eastern Eggplant Dip

Servings: 10
Cooking Time: 10 Minutes
Ingredients:
- 1/4 cup sesame oil
- 2 bell peppers, seeded and sliced
- 1 serrano pepper, seeded and sliced
- 1 eggplant, peeled and sliced
- 3 cloves garlic, minced
- 1 cup broth, preferably homemade
- Kosher salt and ground black pepper, to taste
- 1/2 teaspoon cayenne pepper
- 1/2 teaspoon chili flakes
- A few drops of liquid smoke
- 2 tablespoons coriander, chopped
- 2 teaspoons extra-virgin olive oil

Directions:
1. Press the "Sauté" button to heat up your Instant Pot. Now, heat the oil and sauté the peppers and eggplant until softened.
2. Add the garlic, broth, salt, black pepper, cayenne pepper, chili flakes, liquid smoke, and coriander.
3. Secure the lid. Choose "Manual" mode and Low pressure; cook for minutes. Once cooking is complete, use a quick pressure release; carefully remove the lid.
4. Transfer the mixture to a serving bowl; drizzle olive oil over the top and serve well-chilled. Enjoy!

Nutrition Info:

Per Serving: 81 Calories; 6.6g Fat; 5g Carbs; 1.4g Protein; 2.7g Sugars

Crab Rangoon Dip

Servings: 4
Cooking Time: 3 Minutes
Ingredients:
- 1 tsp garlic powder
- 1 tbsp lemon juice

- 1 tsp Worcestershire sauce
- ¼ tsp red chili flakes + extra for garnishing
- ½ tsp chopped parsley
- ½ tsp black pepper
- ¼ cup almond milk
- 2 (8 oz) cans crabmeat, drained
- ½ cup sour cream
- ¼ cup mayonnaise
- 8 oz cream cheese, softened
- 1 ¼ cup grated mozzarella cheese, divided
- 2 tbsp chopped green onions, green part only

Directions:

1. Combine all the ingredients up to the sour cream in the inner pot. Mix well.
2. Lock the lid in place; select Manual mode on High Pressure, and set the timer to 1 minute.
3. After cooking, perform a quick pressure release to let out the steam, and open the lid.
4. Set the IP in Sauté mode and add the sour cream, mayonnaise, and cheese. As the cheese melts, occasionally stir until well combined, 2 minutes.
5. Spoon the dip into serving bowls and garnish with the green onions. Enjoy!

Nutrition Info:
Per Serving: Calories 365 Fats 87g Carbs 9.03g Net Carbs 7.03g Protein 3g

Spinach And Artichokes Spread

Servings: 6
Cooking Time: 15 Minutes
Ingredients:

- 14 ounces canned artichoke hearts, drained
- 8 ounces mozzarella cheese, shredded
- 1 pound spinach, torn
- 1 teaspoon garlic powder
- ½ cup chicken stock
- ½ cup coconut cream
- A pinch of salt and black pepper

Directions:

1. In your instant pot, mix the artichokes with the rest of the ingredients, put the lid on and cook on High for minutes. Release the pressure naturally for 10 minutes, blend the mix using an immersion blender, stir well, transfer to a bowl and serve as a snack.

Nutrition Info: calories 204, fat 5, fiber 3.1, carbs 4.2, protein 5.9

Mediterranean Asparagus

Servings: 6
Cooking Time: 10 Minutes
Ingredients:

- 1 pound asparagus spears

- Sea salt and ground black pepper, to taste
- Homemade Aioli Sauce:
- 1 teaspoon garlic, minced
- 1 egg yolk
- 1/2 cup olive oil
- Sea salt and ground black pepper, to your liking
- 1/4 cup Greek yogurt
- 2 teaspoons freshly squeezed lemon juice

Directions:
1. Start by adding cup of water and a steamer basket to the Instant Pot. Place the asparagus in the steamer basket.
2. Secure the lid. Choose "Manual" mode and High pressure; cook for 1 minute. Once cooking is complete, use a quick pressure release; carefully remove the lid.
3. Season your asparagus with salt and pepper; reserve.
4. In a blender or a food processor, mix garlic, egg yolk, and oil until well incorporated.
5. Now, add the salt, ground black pepper, and Greek yogurt. Afterwards, add the lemon juice and mix until your aioli is thickened and emulsified.
6. Serve the reserved asparagus spears with this homemade aioli on the side. Enjoy!

Nutrition Info:
Per Serving: 194 Calories; 2g Fat; 4.5g Total Carbs; 2.6g Protein; 2.4g Sugars

Stuffed Baby Bell Peppers

Servings: 5
Cooking Time: 10 Minutes
Ingredients:
- 10 baby bell peppers, seeded and sliced lengthwise
- 1 tablespoon olive oil
- 4 ounces cream cheese
- 4 ounces Monterey-Jack cheese, shredded
- 1 teaspoon garlic, minced
- 2 tablespoons scallions, chopped
- 1/4 teaspoon ground black pepper, or more to taste
- 1/2 teaspoon cayenne pepper

Directions:
1. Start by adding cup of water and a steamer basket to the Instant Pot.
2. In a mixing bowl, thoroughly combine all ingredients, except for bell peppers. Then, stuff the peppers with cheese mixture.
3. Place the stuffed peppers in the steamer basket.
4. Secure the lid. Choose "Manual" mode and High pressure; cook for 5 minutes. Once cooking is complete, use a quick pressure release; carefully remove the lid.
5. Serve at room temperature and enjoy!

Nutrition Info:
Per Serving: 224 Calories; 5g Fat; 9g Carbs; 8.7g Protein; 5.5g Sugars

Soul Bread

Servings: 10
Cooking Time: 35 Minutes
Ingredients:

- 1 cup of protein powder
- ¼ teaspoon salt
- ½ teaspoon baking powder
- ½ teaspoon xanthan gum
- 2 tablespoons cream cheese
- 2 eggs, beaten
- 2 tablespoons sesame oil
- 4 tablespoons whipped cream
- 1 tablespoon butter, melted
- 3 tablespoons coconut flour
- 1 cup water, for cooking

Directions:

1. In the big mixing bowl combine together protein powder, salt, baking powder, xanthan gum, and coconut flour. Then add cream cheese, eggs, sesame oil, whipped cream, and melted butter. With the help of the hand blender whisk the mixture until you get a smooth batter. Then pour water and insert the rack in the instant pot. Pour the bread batter in the instant pot baking pan and transfer it in the instant pot. Close the lid and cook the soul bread on manual (high pressure) for 35 minutes. When the time is over, make a quick pressure release and open the lid. Cook the cooked bread to the room temperature and remove it from the baking pan. Slice the soul bread into the servings.

Nutrition Info: calories 117, fat 7.7, fiber 3.5, carbs 6.8, protein 7

Keto Taquitos

Servings: 6
Cooking Time: 20 Minutes
Ingredients:

- 3 low carb tortillas
- ¼ teaspoon onion powder
- ¼ cup Cheddar cheese, shredded
- 5 oz chicken breast, skinless, boneless
- ½ teaspoon ground black pepper
- ¼ teaspoon salt
- ½ teaspoon cayenne pepper
- 1 teaspoon butter
- 1 cup water, for cooking

Directions:

1. Rub the chicken breast with salt, cayenne pepper, and ground black pepper. Pour water and insert the steamer rack in the instant pot. Arrange the chicken in the steamer rack and close

the lid. Cook it on manual mode (high pressure) for minutes. Then make a quick pressure release and transfer the chicken on the chopping board. Shred the chicken. Place the shredded chicken in the mixing bowl. Add onion powder and shredded Cheddar cheese. Mix up the mixture well. Then spread tortillas with chicken mixture and roll. Clean the instant pot and remove the rack. Toss the butter in the instant pot, melt it on sauté mode. Arrange the rolled tortillas in the instant pot in one layer. Cook them for 2 minutes from each side. When taquitos are cooked, remove them from the instant pot and cut into 6 servings.

Nutrition Info: calories 93, fat 3.8, fiber 3.6, carbs 6.3, protein 7.7

Simple Almond-buttered Walnuts

Servings: 8
Cooking Time: 15 Mins
Ingredients:
- 1 ½ cups Walnut Halves
- 4 tbsp Sugar-Free Almond Butter

Directions:
1. Add cup of water into the Instant Pot and lower the trivet. Place the walnuts in a baking dish and pour the almond butter over. Toss them a few times until the walnuts are well coated.
2. Seal the lid and select Manual. Set the cooking time to 4 minutes and cook on High pressure.Do a quick pressure release. Stir once again, and allow for the butter to set before serving.

Nutrition Info: Calories 90, Protein 1g, Net Carbs 3g, Fat 12g

Tropic Sweet Potato Gravy

Servings: 4
Cooking Time: 25 Mins
Ingredients:
- 2 sweet potatoes, boiled, peeled, cut into cubes
- 1 Onion, chopped
- 1 tbsp Cumin seeds
- 1 tbsp Chili powder
- ½ tbsp Cumin powder
- 1 cup Tomato puree
- ½ tbsp Cinnamon powder
- ½ tbsp Garlic paste
- ½ tbsp Thyme
- ¼ tbsp Turmeric powder
- 2 tbsp Olive oil
- ½ cup Chicken broth

Directions:
1. Heat oil in the Instant Pot on Sauté mode and cook the onion, cumin seeds and garlic for 2 minutes. Add the tomato puree, salt, chili powder, turmeric powder, and garlic paste and cook for another 5-6 minutes. Add the potatoes and mix thoroughly. Stir in the chicken broth

and cook for minutes on medium heat. Sprinkle cinnamon powder, thyme and cumin powder on top.

Nutrition Info: Calories 216, Protein 4.1g, Net Carbs 8.1g, Fat 8.4g

Parmigiano Chicken Wings

Servings: 12
Cooking Time: 20 Minutes
Ingredients:

- 4 pounds chicken wings cut into sections
- 1/2 cup butter, melted
- 1 tablespoon Italian seasoning mix
- 1/2 teaspoon onion powder
- 1/2 teaspoon garlic powder
- 1 teaspoon paprika
- 1/2 teaspoon coarse sea salt
- 1/2 teaspoon ground black pepper
- 1 cup Parmigiano-Reggiano cheese, shaved
- 2 eggs, lightly whisked

Directions:

1. Add chicken wings, butter, Italian seasoning mix, onion powder, garlic powder, paprika, salt, and black pepper to your Instant Pot.
2. Secure the lid. Choose "Poultry" mode and High pressure. Cook the chicken wings for 10 minutes. Once cooking is complete, use a natural pressure release; carefully remove the lid.
3. Mix Parmigiano-Reggiano cheese with eggs. Spoon this mixture over the wings.
4. Secure the lid. Choose "Manual" mode and High pressure; cook for minutes longer. Once cooking is complete, use a quick pressure release; carefully remove the lid. Bon appétit!

Nutrition Info:
Per Serving: 443 Calories; 8g Fat; 6.2g Total Carbs; 2g Protein; 3.5g Sugars

Beef Enchilada Dip With Olives

Servings: 4
Cooking Time: 8 Minutes
Ingredients:

- 2 tbsp olive oil
- 2 lb. ground beef
- 3 green chilies, chopped
- 2 cups enchilada sauce (see sauce recipes)
- ¼ cup chicken broth
- Salt and black pepper to taste
- 1 cup shredded cheddar cheese
- 1 cup Monterey Jack cheese
- ¼ cup sliced Kalamata olives
- 2 tbsp chopped parsley

Directions:
1. Set the IP in Sauté mode and adjust to Medium heat.
2. Heat the olive oil in the inner pot and cook the beef until brown, 5 minutes.
3. Stir in the green chilies, enchilada sauce, chicken broth, salt, and black pepper.
4. Lock the lid in place; select Manual mode on High Pressure, and set the timer to 1 minute.
5. After cooking, perform a quick pressure release to let out the steam, and open the lid.
6. Set the IP in Sauté mode and mix in the cheeses until melted, 2 minutes. Stir in the olives until well distributed.
7. Spoon the dip into serving bowls, garnish with the parsley and enjoy.

Nutrition Info:
Per Serving: Calories 855 Fats 2g Carbs 11g Net Carbs 8.31g Protein 74g

Simple Zucchini Bites

Servings: 6
Cooking Time: 10 Minutes
Ingredients:
- 2 tablespoons olive oil
- 1 red chili pepper, chopped
- 1 pound zucchini, cut into thick slices
- 1 teaspoon garlic powder
- 1 cup chicken broth
- Coarse sea salt and ground black pepper, to taste
- 1/2 teaspoon paprika
- 1/2 teaspoon ground coriander

Directions:
1. Press the "Sauté" button and heat the olive oil. Once hot, cook chili pepper for minute.
2. Add the remaining ingredients.
3. Secure the lid. Choose "Manual" mode and Low pressure; cook for minutes. Once cooking is complete, use a quick pressure release; carefully remove the lid. Bon appétit!

Nutrition Info:
Per Serving: 70 Calories; 5.1g Fat; 4.4g Total Carbs; 3.2g Protein; 0.9g Sugars

Chocolate Chip Cookies In Jars

Servings: 4
Cooking Time: 7 Minutes
Ingredients:
- ½ cup butter, melted
- 1 cup swerve brown sugar
- 1 tsp vanilla extract
- 1 cup almond flour
- 1 tsp baking soda
- ¼ tsp salt
- 1 tbsp almond milk

- 3 ½ oz unsweetened dark chocolate, chopped + extra for topping

Directions:

1. Mix all the ingredients in a medium bowl, divide into 4 medium mason jars, and cover the jars with foil.
2. Pour cups into the inner pot, fit in a trivet and place the jars on top.
3. Lock the lid in place; select Manual mode on High Pressure, and set the timer for 7 minutes.
4. When ready, perform a quick pressure release until all the steam has escaped, and open the lid.
5. Remove the jars, take off the foil and top with some more chocolate chips.
6. Allow cooling for a few minutes and enjoy.

Nutrition Info:

Per Serving: Calories 333 Fats 93g Carbs 2.02g Net Carbs 0.2g Protein 2.72g

Beef Bites With A Twist

Servings: 6
Cooking Time: 25 Minutes
Ingredients:

- 2 tablespoons olive oil
- 1 pound beef steak, cut into cubes
- Sea salt and ground black pepper, to taste
- 1 teaspoon cayenne pepper
- 1/2 teaspoon dried marjoram
- 1 cup beef bone broth
- 1/4 cup dry white wine

Directions:

1. Press the "Sauté" button and heat the olive oil. Once hot, cook the beef for 2 to 3 minutes, stirring periodically.
2. Add the remaining ingredients to the Instant Pot.
3. Secure the lid. Choose "Manual" mode and High pressure; cook for 20 minutes. Once cooking is complete, use a natural pressure release; carefully remove the lid.
4. Arrange beef cubes on a nice serving platter and serve with sticks. Bon appétit!

Nutrition Info:

Per Serving: 169 Calories; 9.9g Fat; 1.1g Total Carbs; 9g Protein; 0.5g Sugars

Au Jus Dip

Servings: 2
Cooking Time: 20 Mins
Ingredients:

- ¼ cup Soy Sauce
- 1 tbsp Worcestershire sauce
- ½ tsp Monk Fruit Powder
- 1 cup Keto Beef Broth
- 1 Shallot, minced

- ½ tsp dry Oregano
- ½ tsp dried Thyme
- ½ bay Leaf
- 1 clove Garlic, minced

Directions:
1. Select Saute mode. Add the liquid ingredients with the shallot and garlic. Sauté for 5 minutes. Stir in the remaining ingredients and let simmer for minutes. Strain the sauce through a strainer.

Nutrition Info: Calories 30, Protein 1g, Net Carbs 1g, Fat 1g

Shrimp Souvlaki Salad

Servings: 6
Cooking Time: 10 Minutes
Ingredients:
- 1 pound shrimp, peeled and deveined
- 1/4 cup rice wine vinegar
- 3/4 cup water
- 1 celery stalk, diced
- 2 bell peppers, sliced
- 4 ounces blue cheese, cubed
- 1/2 cup olives, pitted
- 1 cup cherry tomatoes
- 1 tablespoon olive oil
- Sea salt and ground black pepper, to taste
- 1/2 teaspoon cayenne pepper
- 1/2 teaspoon paprika

Directions:
1. Place shrimp, rice wine vinegar, and water in your Instant Pot.
2. Secure the lid. Choose "Manual" mode and High pressure; cook for 1 minute. Once cooking is complete, use a quick pressure release; carefully remove the lid.
3. Thread shrimp, celery, peppers, blue cheese, olives and cherry tomatoes onto cocktail sticks.
4. Drizzle olive oil over them; sprinkle with salt, black pepper, cayenne pepper, and paprika. Arrange these skewers on a serving platter and serve. Bon appétit!

Nutrition Info:
Per Serving: 187 Calories; 9.3g Fat; 6.3g Total Carbs; 9g Protein; 3.9g Sugars

Lemon-blackberry Tarte Tatin

Servings: 4
Cooking Time: 50 Minutes
Ingredients:
- For the crust:
- ¼ cup almond flour + extra for dusting
- 3 tbsp coconut flour

- ½ tsp salt
- ¼ cup butter, cold and crumbled
- 3 tbsp erythritol
- 1 ½ tsp vanilla extract
- 4 whole eggs
- For the filling:
- 4 tbsp melted butter
- 3 tsp swerve brown sugar
- 1 cup fresh blackberries
- 1 tsp vanilla extract
- 1 lemon, juiced
- 1 cup cottage cheese
- 3 to 4 fresh basil leaves

Directions:

1. Mix all the crust's ingredients in a medium bowl and spoon into a pie pan. Use the back of the spoon to press the mixture to fit onto the bottom of the pan. Chill in the refrigerator while you prepare the filling.
2. Flatten the dough a clean flat surface, cover in plastic wrap, and refrigerate for 1 hour.
3. After, lightly dust a clean flat surface with almond flour, unwrap the dough, and roll out the dough into a 1-inch diameter circle. Set aside.
4. In a food processor, combine all the filling's ingredients and blend until smooth. Pour the mixture into a pie pan and cover with the flattened dough. Press the sides to fit the edge of the pan.
5. Pour 2 cups of water into the inner pot, fit in a trivet, and place the pie pan on top.
6. Lock the lid in place; select Manual mode on High Pressure and set the timer to 40 minutes.
7. After cooking, perform a natural pressure release for 10 minutes, then a quick pressure release to let out the remaining steam, and open the lid.
8. Carefully remove the pan, allow cooling for 10 minutes.
9. Slice and serve.

Nutrition Info:
Per Serving: Calories 382 Fats 34g Carbs 5.62g Net Carbs 4.32g Protein 64g

Keto Sugar Cookie Mix

Servings: 4
Cooking Time: 35 Minutes
Ingredients:

- 1 ½ cups unsweetened chocolate chips
- 2 cups almond milk
- 2 tbsp sugar-free maple syrup
- 1 cup almond flour
- ¼ cup swerve brown sugar

Directions:

1. Line a 7-inch springform pan with parchment paper and set aside.

2. Combine all the ingredients in a medium bowl until smooth and pour into the cake pan; cover with foil.
3. Pour 1 cup of water into the inner pot, fit in a trivet, and place the cake pan on top.
4. Lock the lid in place; select Manual mode on High Pressure and set the timer to 20 minutes.
5. After cooking, perform a natural pressure release for minutes, then a quick pressure release to let out the remaining steam, and open the lid.
6. Remove the cake pan, take off the foil, allow cooling for 10 minutes and chill in the refrigerator for at least 1 hour.
7. Take out the pan, release the dessert, and cut into square shapes.
8. Enjoy!

Nutrition Info:
Per Serving: Calories 611 Fats 55g Carbs 11g Net Carbs 9.71g Protein 68g

Watermelon Cream

Servings: 4
Cooking Time: 10 Minutes
Ingredients:
- 2 cups watermelon, peeled and cubed
- 1 cup heavy cream
- 1 tablespoon vanilla extract
- ½ cup swerve
- 1 cup water

Directions:
1. In a bowl, mix the watermelon and the cream and the other ingredients except the water, whisk and divide into 4 ramekins. Add the water to the instant pot, add the steamer basket, put the ramekins inside, put the lid on and cook on High for minutes. Release the pressure naturally for 10 minutes and serve the mix cold.

Nutrition Info: calories 136, fat 2, fiber 0.2, carbs 7, protein 1.1

Raspberry And Chocolate Lava Muffins

Servings: 6
Cooking Time: 15 Minutes
Ingredients:
- 1 cup chocolate, sugar-free
- 1 stick butter
- 3 eggs
- 1 cup Swerve
- 1 cup almond flour
- A pinch of salt
- 1/2 teaspoon vanilla extract
- 1/2 teaspoon ground star anise
- 1/2 teaspoon ground cinnamon
- 1 ½ cups raspberries, mashed with a fork

- 1/4 cup confectioner's Swerve

Directions:

1. Start by adding ½ cups of water and a metal rack to your Instant Pot. Now, spritz muffin cups with a nonstick cooking spray.
2. Melt the chocolate in a microwave. Add butter and whip with an electric mixer. Fold in the eggs and mix with the machine running.
3. Gradually mix in Swerve and flour. Then, add the salt, vanilla, star anise, and cinnamon. Lastly, fold in raspberries and gently stir to combine well.
4. Divide the mixture among muffin cups.
5. Secure the lid. Choose "Manual" mode and High pressure; cook for 6 minutes. Once cooking is complete, use a natural pressure release; carefully remove the lid.
6. Dust your muffins with confectioner's Swerve. Serve warm and enjoy!

Nutrition Info:
Per Serving: 180 Calories; 6g Fat; 7.4g Carbs; 3.2g Protein; 1.2g Sugars

Mini Cakes With Cherries

Servings: 6
Cooking Time: 25 Minutes
Ingredients:

- 4 eggs, beaten
- 1/3 cup granulated Swerve
- 2 tablespoons coconut oil, melted
- 1/2 cup cream cheese
- 1/2 cup Greek-style yogurt
- 1 teaspoon vanilla extract
- 1/2 cup almond flour
- 1/2 cup coconut flour
- A pinch of grated nutmeg
- A pinch of salt
- 1 teaspoon baking powder
- 1/2 teaspoon baking soda
- 1/2 cup cherries, pitted

Directions:

1. Start by adding ½ cups of water and a metal rack to your Instant Pot. Now, spritz 6 ramekins with a nonstick cooking spray.
2. Whip the eggs and Swerve until uniform and smooth. Add the coconut oil, cheese, yogurt, and vanilla; mix until everything is well incorporated.
3. In another bowl, thoroughly combine the flour, nutmeg, salt, baking powder, and baking soda. Add this mixture to the egg/cheese mixture.
4. Fold in the cherries and gently stir to combine. Pour the batter into the prepared ramekins.
5. Secure the lid. Choose "Manual" mode and High pressure; cook for 20 minutes. Once cooking is complete, use a natural pressure release; carefully remove the lid.
6. Transfer your ramekins to a cooling rack. Loosen the sides of your cakes from the ramekins and turn them over onto plates. Serve well-chilled.

Nutrition Info:
Per Serving: 255 Calories; 6g Fat; 6.1g Total Carbs; 9.7g Protein; 2.8g Sugars

Cinnamon Flan

Servings: 6
Cooking Time: 15 Minutes
Ingredients:

- 6 eggs
- 1 cup Swerve
- 1 ½ cups double cream
- 1/2 cup water
- 3 tablespoons dark rum
- A pinch of salt
- A pinch of freshly grated nutmeg
- 1/4 teaspoon ground cinnamon
- 1 teaspoon vanilla extract

Directions:

1. Start by adding ½ cups of water and a metal rack to your Instant Pot.
2. In a mixing bowl, thoroughly combine eggs and Swerve. Add double cream, water, rum, salt, nutmeg, cinnamon, and vanilla extract.
3. Pour mixture into a baking dish. Lower the dish onto the rack.
4. Secure the lid. Choose "Manual" mode and High pressure; cook for 10 minutes. Once cooking is complete, use a natural pressure release; carefully remove the lid.
5. Serve well chilled and enjoy!

Nutrition Info:
Per Serving: 263 Calories; 2g Fat; 3.2g Total Carbs; 5g Protein; 2.8g Sugars

Blackberry Espresso Brownies

Servings: 8
Cooking Time: 30 Minutes
Ingredients:

- 4 eggs
- 1 ¼ cups coconut cream
- 1 teaspoon Stevia liquid concentrate
- 1/3 cup cocoa powder, unsweetened
- 1/2 teaspoon grated nutmeg
- 1/2 teaspoon cinnamon powder
- 1 teaspoon espresso coffee
- 1 teaspoon pure almond extract
- 1 teaspoon pure vanilla extract
- 1 teaspoon baking powder
- A pinch of kosher salt
- 1 cup blackberries, fresh or frozen (thawed

Directions:

1. Start by adding ½ cups of water and a metal rack to your Instant Pot. Now, spritz a baking pan with a nonstick cooking spray.
2. Now, mix eggs, coconut cream, Stevia, cocoa powder, nutmeg, cinnamon, coffee, pure almond extract vanilla, baking powder, and salt with an electric mixer.
3. Crush the blackberries with a fork. After that, fold in your blackberries into the prepared mixture.
4. Pour the batter into the prepared pan.
5. Secure the lid. Choose "Bean/Chili" mode and High pressure; cook for 2minutes. Once cooking is complete, use a natural pressure release; carefully remove the lid. Bon appétit!

Nutrition Info:

Per Serving: 151 Calories; 6g Fat; 6.7g Total Carbs; 4.1g Protein; 1.1g Sugars

Extraordinary Chocolate Cheesecake

Servings: 10
Cooking Time: 25 Minutes + Chilling Time
Ingredients:

- Crust:
- 1/3 cup coconut flour
- 1/3 cup almond flour
- 2 tablespoons arrowroot flour
- 2 tablespoons cocoa powder, unsweetened
- 2 tablespoons monk fruit powder
- 1/4 cup coconut oil, melted
- Filling:
- 10 ounces cream cheese, softened
- 8 ounces heavy cream, softened
- 1 teaspoon monk fruit powder
- 1/2 cup cocoa powder, unsweetened
- 3 eggs yolks, at room temperature
- 1/3 cup sour cream
- 4 ounces butter, melted
- 1/2 teaspoon vanilla essence

Directions:

1. Prepare your Instant Pot by adding ½ cups of water and a metal rack to its bottom.
2. Coat a bottom of a baking pan with a piece of parchment paper.
3. In mixing bowl, combine coconut flour, almond flour, arrowroot powder, 2 tablespoons of cocoa powder, and 2 tablespoons of monk fruit powder; now, stir in melted coconut oil.
4. Press the crust mixture into the bottom of the prepared baking pan.
5. To make the filling, mix the cream cheese, heavy cream, monk fruit powder, and cocoa powder.
6. Now, fold in the eggs, sour cream, butter, and vanilla; continue to blend until everything is well incorporated,
7. Lower the baking pan onto the rack. Cover with a sheet of foil, making a foil sling.

8. Secure the lid. Choose "Manual" mode and High pressure; cook for 1minutes. Once cooking is complete, use a natural pressure release; carefully remove the lid.
9. Place this cheesecake in your refrigerator for 3 to 4 hours. Bon appétit!

Nutrition Info:
Per Serving: 351 Calories; 6g Fat; 4.8g Total Carbs; 4.3g Protein; 1.7g Sugars

Chocolate-coconut Milk Bites

Servings: 4
Cooking Time: 12 Minutes
Ingredients:
- 1 (36 oz) unsweetened chocolate chips, melted
- 2 tbsp sugar-free maple syrup
- ½ cup coconut milk
- 1 ½ cups of water

Directions:
1. Lightly grease a silicone egg-bite tray with cooking spray and set aside.
2. In a medium bowl, mix the chocolate, maple syrup, and coconut milk. Pour the mixture into the silicone tray, two third way up and cover with foil.
3. Pour 1 ½ cups of water in the inner pot, fit in a trivet, and place the egg bite tray on top.
4. Lock the lid in place; select Manual mode on High Pressure and set the timer to 12 minutes.
5. After cooking, perform a quick pressure release to let out the steam, and open the lid.
6. Carefully remove the tray, take off the foil, allow cooling for 5 minutes, and pop out the dessert bites onto plates.
7. Enjoy the dessert.

Nutrition Info:
Per Serving: Calories 69 Fats 7.15g Carbs 1.66g Net Carbs 0.96g Protein 0.69g

Keto Chocolate Brownies

Servings: 6
Cooking Time: 30 Minutes
Ingredients:
- 4 ounces chocolate, sugar-free
- 1/2 cup coconut oil
- 2 cups Swerve
- 4 eggs, whisked
- 1 teaspoon vanilla paste
- 1/4 teaspoon sea salt
- 1/4 teaspoon grated nutmeg
- 1/2 teaspoon dried lavender flowers
- 1/4 cup almond flour
- 1/2 cup whipped cream

Directions:

1. Start by adding ½ cups of water and a metal trivet to your Instant Pot. Now, spritz a baking pan with a nonstick cooking spray.
2. Thoroughly combine the chocolate, coconut oil, and Swerve. Gradually, whisk in the eggs. Add the vanilla paste, salt, nutmeg, lavender flowers and almond flour; mix until everything is well incorporated.
3. Secure the lid. Choose "Bean/Chili" mode and High pressure; cook for 25 minutes. Once cooking is complete, use a natural pressure release; carefully remove the lid.
4. Top with whipped cream and serve well chilled. Bon appétit!

Nutrition Info:
Per Serving: 384 Calories; 6g Fat; 5.2g Total Carbs; 7.7g Protein; 1.3g Sugars

Blueberry-strawberry Pie

Servings: 4
Cooking Time: 50 Minutes + 2 Hours Chilling
Ingredients:
- For the crust:
- 1/3 cup ground almonds
- ½ tsp salt
- ¼ cup butter, cold and crumbled
- 3 tbsp erythritol
- 1 ½ tsp vanilla extract
- For the filling:
- 2 ¼ cup blueberries and strawberries, mashed
- 1 cup erythritol + extra for sprinkling
- 1 vanilla bean, caviar extracted
- 1 egg, beaten

Directions:
1. Mix all the crust's ingredients in a medium bowl and spoon into a pie pan. Use the back of the spoon to press the mixture to fit onto the bottom of the pan. Chill in the refrigerator while you prepare the filling.
2. In a large bowl, using an electric hand mixer, whisk the filling's ingredients one after another until smooth.
3. Remove the pie pan from the fridge, pour in the filling, and cover with foil.
4. Pour 2 cups of water into the inner pot, fit in a trivet, and place the pie pan on top.
5. Lock the lid in place; select Manual mode on High Pressure and set the timer to 40 minutes.
6. After cooking, perform a natural pressure release for 10 minutes, then a quick pressure release to let out the remaining steam, and open the lid.
7. Carefully, remove the pan and take off the foil.
8. Allow cooling for 10 minutes and chill in the fridge for 2 hours or more.
9. Remove, top the pie with whipped cream, slice and serve.

Nutrition Info:
Per Serving: Calories 220 Fats 6 g Carbs 6.95 g Net Carbs 5.25g Protein 8.33g

Pistachio Cake

Servings: 4
Cooking Time: 50 Mins
Ingredients:

- 2 tbsp Pistachio powder
- 4-5 tbsp Mint leaves, finely chopped
- ½ cup Stevia
- 1 cup Almond flour
- 1 tbsp Vanilla extract
- 1 tbsp Cocoa powder
- 2 Eggs
- ½ cup Butter

Directions:

1. In a bowl, beat the eggs until fluffy. In a separate bowl, mix butter, stevia, add vanilla extract and beat for 2 minutes. Add it to the eggs mixture and flour, mint, and pistachio.

Nutrition Info: Calories 191, Protein 4.4g, Net Carbs 0.5g, Fat 4g

Cheesecake Fat Bombs

Servings: 2
Cooking Time: 30 Minutes
Ingredients:

- 1 egg yolk
- 2 tablespoons cream cheese
- 1 teaspoon swerve
- ¼ teaspoon vanilla extract
- 3 tablespoons heavy cream
- 1 teaspoon coconut flakes

Directions:

1. Whisk the egg yolk with swerve until smooth. Then add heavy cream and pour the liquid in the instant pot. Stir it until homogenous and cook on manual mode (low pressure) for 30 minutes. Meanwhile, mix up together cream cheese with vanilla extract, and coconut flakes. When the time is over and the egg yolk mixture is cooked, open the instant pot lid. Combine together cream cheese mixture with egg yolk mixture and stir until homogenous. Place the mixture in the silicone muffin molds and transfer in the freezer for 20 minutes. The cooked cheesecake fat bombs should be tender but not liquid.

Nutrition Info: calories 146, fat 4, fiber 0.1, carbs 2.4, protein 2.6

Coconut And Chocolate Fudge

Servings: 6
Cooking Time: 10 Minutes + Chilling Time
Ingredients:

- 1/2 cup melted coconut oil

- 1/2 cup coconut milk
- 1/2 cup coconut flour
- 1/2 cup cocoa powder
- 1/2 cup Swerve
- 1/4 teaspoon ground cinnamon
- 1/4 teaspoon ground cloves
- 1 teaspoon vanilla paste
- 1 teaspoon coconut extract
- A pinch sea salt
- A pinch of grated nutmeg

Directions:
1. Place coconut oil, milk, flour, cocoa powder, and Swerve in the Instant Pot.
2. Add the remaining ingredients and mix until everything is well incorporated.
3. Press the "Sauté" button and let it simmer stir until thoroughly heated.
4. Now, spoon the mixture into a baking sheet lined with a piece of foil. Transfer to your refrigerator for 2 to 3 hours.
5. Cut into squares and serve. Bon appétit!

Nutrition Info:
Per Serving: 189 Calories; 8g Fat; 5.8g Carbs; 2.1g Protein; 1.6g Sugars

Pecan Bites

Servings: 4
Cooking Time: 8 Minutes
Ingredients:
- 2 pecans, crushed
- 1 tablespoon coconut oil, softened
- 1 egg, whisked
- ½ cup almond flour
- 1 tablespoon Erythritol
- ½ teaspoon vanilla extract
- ¼ cup of coconut milk
- ¾ teaspoon ground cinnamon
- ½ teaspoon sesame oil

Directions:
1. Spread the non-sticky springform mold with the sesame oil.
2. Then combine together the softened coconut oil, whisked egg, almond flour, vanilla extract, coconut milk, Erythritol, and ground cinnamon. Add pecans.
3. Check if all the ingredients are added and mix up the mixture until smooth.
4. Transfer the mixture in the prepared springform pan and flatten it well.
5. Place the pan in the instant pot and cover with the foil.
6. Close the lid and cook the dessert on the "Manual" mode for 8 minutes (follow the directions of your instant pot). NPR for 15 minutes.
7. Cut the meal into bites.

Spiced Pudding

Servings: 2
Cooking Time: 30 Minutes
Ingredients:

- 1 egg, beaten
- ¼ cup heavy cream
- 1 tablespoon Erythritol
- ¼ teaspoon pumpkin pie spices
- 1 teaspoon coconut oil
- 1 cup of water (for instant pot)

Directions:

1. Whisk the egg and mix it up with the heavy cream.
2. Add Erythritol and pumpkin pie spices. Stir the mixture.
3. Grease the cake pan with the coconut oil and transfer the pudding mixture inside.
4. Pour 1 cup of water in the instant pot.
5. Put the pudding on the steamer rack in the instant pot.
6. Cover the pudding with the foil and secure edges.
7. Put the "Manual" mode (High pressure) for 20 minutes.
8. Make the natural pressure release for 10 minutes.
9. Chill the pudding for 10 hours before serving.

Nutrition Info:
Per Serving: calories 101, fat 10, fiber 0, carbs 8.2, protein 3.1

Cocoa Walnut Cake

Servings: 6
Cooking Time: 30 Mins
Ingredients:

- 1 cup Almond or Coconut Flour
- 3 Eggs
- ¼ cup chopped Walnuts
- ¼ cup Coconut Oil
- ¼ cup Cocoa Powder, unsweetened
- ½ cup Sweetener
- ½ cup Heavy Whipping Cream
- 1 tsp Baking Powder

Directions:

1. Pour ½ cups water into your Instant Pot and lower the trivet. Place all ingredients in a large bowl, and mix with an electric mixer until well-combined and fluffy. Grease a cake pan with cooking spray and pour the batter in. Place the pan on top of the trivet. Seal the lid and cook on High pressure for 20 minutes. After the beep, release the pressure quickly.

Nutrition Info: Calories 313, Protein 8g, Net Carbs 7g, Fat 28g

Sweet Zucchini Crisps

Servings: 2
Cooking Time: 8 Minutes
Ingredients:

- 1 tablespoon Erythritol
- 1 zucchini
- 1 tablespoon butter

Directions:

1. Slice the zucchini into thin rounds.
2. The heat up butter on saute mode. When the butter is hot, add zucchini slices and cook them for 4 minutes from each side or until they become light crispy.
3. Then sprinkle the cooked crisps with Erythritol and put on the paper towel for 10 minutes to cool.

Nutrition Info:
Per Serving: calories 67, fat 5.9, fiber 1.1, carbs 3.3, protein 1.3

Mini Vanilla Custards

Servings: 4
Cooking Time: 29 Minutes
Ingredients:

- 2 tablespoons water
- 1 cup unsweetened almond milk
- 3 large eggs
- Pinch salt
- 1 cup heavy cream
- ¾ cup powdered erythritol, divided
- 1 tablespoon vanilla extract

Directions:

1. Whisk together ½ cup of the powdered erythritol and water in a saucepan over medium heat until the erythritol melts.
2. Divide the mixture among four small ramekins and set aside to cool.
3. Combine the almond milk and cream in a saucepan and cook over medium heat until it starts to steam, then whisk in the rest of the erythritol, vanilla extract and salt.
4. Beat the eggs in a mixing bowl.
5. Whisk a few tablespoons of the milk mixture into the eggs, then whisk in the rest in a steady stream.
6. Cover the ramekins with foil and place them in the steamer insert in your Instant Pot.
7. Pour in ½ cup water, then close and lock the lid.
8. Press the Manual button and adjust the timer for 9 minutes.
9. When the timer goes off, let the pressure vent naturally, then press Cancel.
10. When the pot has depressurized, open the lid.

11. Remove the ramekins and let the custards cool for 10 minutes then serve warm.
Nutrition Info: calories 175 fat 16g ,protein 5.5g ,carbs 2g ,fiber 0.5g ,net carbs 1.5g

Almond Tart

Servings: 6
Cooking Time: 20 Minutes
Ingredients:

- ½ cup almond flour
- 2 tablespoons almond butter
- ¼ teaspoon baking powder
- 1 egg, beaten
- ½ teaspoon ground cinnamon
- 1 tablespoon almond flakes
- ½ cup of organic almond milk
- 3 tablespoons coconut flour
- 2 tablespoons Erythritol
- 1 cup water, for cooking

Directions:

1. Make the tart crust: mix up together almond flour with almond butter, baking powder, and egg. Knead the dough. Then place the dough in the instant pot tart mold. Flatten it with the help of the fingertips in the shape of the tart crust. Pour water and insert the steamer rack in the instant pot. Place the tart mold on the rack and close the lid. Cook it on manual mode (high pressure) for 8 minutes. Then make a quick pressure release and remove the tart crust from it. Cool it well. After this, clean the instant pot and remove the steamer rack. Pour almond milk in the instant pot. Add coconut flour, Erythritol, and ground cinnamon. Bring the liquid to boil on sauté mode. Stir it constantly. Then switch off the instant pot. Pour the almond milk thick liquid over the pie crust and flatten well. Top the tart with almond flakes and refrigerate for at least hour in the fridge.

Nutrition Info: calories 122, fat 4, fiber 2.8, carbs 5.2, protein 3.8

Coconut Flan

Servings: 6
Cooking Time: 29 Minutes
Ingredients:

- 2 tablespoons water
- 1 cup unsweetened coconut milk
- 3 large eggs
- Pinch salt
- 1 cup heavy cream
- ¾ cup powdered erythritol, divided
- 2 teaspoons vanilla extract

Directions:

1. Whisk together ½ cup of the powdered erythritol and water in a saucepan over medium heat until it starts to darken. Divide the mixture among six small ramekins and set aside to cool.
2. Combine the coconut milk and cream in a saucepan and cook over medium heat until it starts to steam, then whisk in the rest of the erythritol, vanilla extract and salt. Beat the eggs in a mixing bowl then pour a few tablespoons of the warmed milk into it while whisking.
3. Pour the egg mixture into the milk mixture and whisk smooth, then pour into the ramekins.
4. Cover the ramekins with foil and place them in the steamer insert in your Instant Pot. Pour in ½ cup water, then close and lock the lid.
5. Press the Manual button and adjust the timer for 9 minutes.
6. When the timer goes off, let the pressure vent naturally, then press Cancel.
7. When the pot has depressurized, open the lid.
8. Remove the ramekins and let the flan cool to room temperature then chill until ready to serve.

Nutrition Info: calories 205 fat 5g ,protein 4.5g ,carbs 3g ,fiber 1g ,net carbs 2g

Great Strawberry Curd

Servings: 2
Cooking Time: 20 Minutes + Chilling Time
Ingredients:
- 1/3 cup unsalted butter
- ½ cup Swerve
- 4 egg yolks, beaten
- 1 teaspoon grated lemon zest
- 1/2 teaspoon vanilla extract
- 1 cup fresh strawberry, pureed

Directions:
1. Blend the unsalted butter and Swerve in a food processor. Stir in the eggs and blend for minute longer.
2. Then, add the strawberries, lemon zest, and vanilla. Divide the mixture among four Mason jars and cover them with lids.
3. Add 2 cups of water and a metal rack to the Instant Pot. Lower your jars onto the rack.
4. Secure the lid. Choose "Manual" mode and High pressure; cook for 13 minutes. When cooking is complete, use a natural pressure release and carefully remove the lid.
5. Leave to cool in your refrigerator and serve. Bon appétit!

Nutrition Info:
Per Serving: 320 Calories; 6g Fat; 1.4g Carbs; 8.9g Protein; 3.9g Sugars

Special Coconut Fudge

Servings: 6
Cooking Time: 10 Minutes + Chilling Time
Ingredients:
- 1/2 cup melted coconut oil
- 1/2 cup coconut milk

- 1/2 cup coconut flour
- 1/2 cup cocoa powder
- 1/2 cup Swerve
- 1/4 teaspoon ground cinnamon
- 1/4 teaspoon ground cloves
- 1 teaspoon vanilla paste
- 1 teaspoon coconut extract
- A pinch sea salt
- A pinch of grated nutmeg

Directions:
1. Place coconut oil, milk, flour, cocoa powder, and Swerve in the Instant Pot.
2. Add the remaining ingredients and mix until everything is well incorporated.
3. Press the "Sauté" button and let it simmer stir until thoroughly heated.
4. Now, spoon the mixture into a baking sheet lined with a piece of foil. Transfer to your refrigerator for 2 to 3 hours.
5. Cut into squares and serve. Bon appétit!

Nutrition Info:
Per Serving: 189 Calories; 8g Fat; 5.8g Total Carbs; 2.1g Protein; 1.6g Sugars

Cinnamon Mini Rolls

Servings: 10
Cooking Time: 21 Minutes
Ingredients:
- 1 cup almond flour
- ¼ cup coconut flour
- 1 teaspoon baking powder
- 1 teaspoon apple cider vinegar
- 3 tablespoons butter, melted
- 1 tablespoon cream cheese
- ¼ cup Erythritol
- 1 tablespoon cinnamon
- 1 egg, beaten
- 1 teaspoon vanilla extract
- 1 cup water, for cooking

Directions:
1. In the bowl mix up almond flour, coconut flour, baking powder, and apple cider vinegar. Then add melted butter, cream cheese, egg, and vanilla extract. Knead the soft and non-sticky dough. Roll it up in the shape of a square. In the shallow bowl combine together Erythritol and ground cinnamon. Sprinkle the surface of dough square with ground cinnamon mixture and roll it into the log. Then cut the dough log on pieces. Press ever cinnamon dough piece with the help of the hand palm. Pour water and insert the trivet in the instant pot. Line the trivet with baking paper and place the cinnamon rolls on it. Close the lid and cook the dessert for 21 minutes on manual mode (high pressure). When the time is

finished, make a quick pressure release and open the lid. Cool the cooked cinnamon rolls for 5 minutes and remove from the instant pot

Nutrition Info: calories 72, fat 6, fiber 1.9, carbs 9.5, protein 1.7

Pandan Custard

Servings: 3
Cooking Time: 25 Minutes
Ingredients:

- 1 teaspoon pandan extract
- 1 egg, beaten
- 4 tablespoons Truvia
- ½ cup of coconut milk
- 1 cup water, for cooking

Directions:

1. In the mixing bowl blend together pandan extract, egg, Truvia, and coconut milk. When the mixture is smooth, pour it in the ramekins. Then pour water in the instant pot and insert the rack. Place the ramekins on the rack and close the lid. Cook the custard on manual mode (high pressure) for 25 minutes. When the time is over, make a quick pressure release.

Nutrition Info: calories 113, fat 11, fiber 0.9, carbs 8.6, protein 2.8

Chocolate Fudge With White Peanut Butter

Servings: 6
Cooking Time: 10 Minutes + Chilling Time
Ingredients:

- 1 stick butter, melted
- 1/2 cup coconut milk
- 1/2 cup Swerve
- 1/2 cup white chocolate chips, unsweetened
- 1/3 cup melted peanut butter
- 1/4 teaspoon ground cloves
- 1/4 teaspoon ground cinnamon
- 1 teaspoon vanilla extract
- 1/8 teaspoon kosher salt
- 1/8 teaspoon grated nutmeg

Directions:

1. Place the butter, milk, and Swerve in your Instant Pot.
2. Press the "Sauté" button and let it simmer until thoroughly heated.
3. Stir in the chocolate chips; stir until the chocolate is completely melted. Add the other ingredients and continue to stir until everything is well incorporated.
4. Now, spoon the mixture into a square cookie sheet lined with a piece of foil. Transfer to your refrigerator for 2 to 3 hours.

5. Cut into squares and serve. Bon appétit!
Nutrition Info:
Per Serving: 259 Calories; 2g Fat; 6.6g Total Carbs; 3.3g Protein; 2.8g Sugars

Espresso Souffle

Servings: 5
Cooking Time: 35 Minutes
Ingredients:
- 1/2 cup double cream
- ½ cup whipping cream
- 1/3 cup butter, melted
- 1 teaspoon ground cinnamon
- 1 teaspoon vanilla extract
- 3 tablespoons cocoa powder, unsweetened
- 1 tablespoon instant coffee granules
- 1/4 cup coconut flour
- ½ teaspoon salt
- ½ teaspoon nutmeg, grated
- 3 eggs plus 2 egg yolks
- 1/2 cup Swerve
- 2 cups of water

Directions:
1. Add 2 cups of water and a metal rack to your Instant Pot. Spritz a soufflé dish with a nonstick cooking spray.
2. In a large bowl mix the coconut flour, salt, cocoa powder, and cinnamon.
3. Then, in another bowl add the eggs, Swerve, nutmeg, melted butter, double cream and whipping cream. Mix.
4. Gradually add the egg mixture to the dry mixture. Combine well.
5. Pour the batter into the prepared soufflé dish.
6. Secure the lid. Choose "Manual" mode and Low pressure; cook for 22 minutes. When cooking is complete, use a natural pressure release and carefully remove the lid.
7. Leave to cool and serve. Bon appétit!

Nutrition Info:
Per Serving: 319 Calories; 3g Fat; 5.1g Carbs; 8.9g Protein; 1.9g Sugars

Grandma's Zucchini Cake

Servings: 6
Cooking Time: 35 Minutes
Ingredients:
- 1 cup almond flour
- A pinch of table salt
- 1 ½ teaspoons baking powder
- 1 teaspoon pumpkin pie spice

- 2/3 cup Swerve, powdered
- 2 eggs, beaten
- 3 tablespoons coconut oil
- 1/2 cup double cream
- 1/2 pound zucchini, shredded, drained and squeezed dry
- 1 teaspoon vanilla paste
- 1/4 cup walnuts, chopped
- Frosting:
- 4 ounces mascarpone cheese, room temperature
- 1/4 cup coconut oil, softened
- 1 ½ cups Swerve powdered

Directions:
1. Start by adding ½ cups of water and a metal rack to the Instant Pot. Now, lightly grease a cake pan with a nonstick cooking spray.
2. In a mixing bowl, thoroughly combine almond flour, salt, baking powder, and pumpkin pie spice.
3. Then, thoroughly combine Swerve, eggs, coconut oil, cream, zucchini and vanilla using an electric mixer
4. With the machine running on low, gradually add the prepared dry mixture; mix until everything is well combined.
5. Fold in the chopped walnuts. Spoon the batter into the prepared cake pan. Cover the pan with paper towels; then, top with a piece of aluminum foil making a foil sling.
6. Lower the pan onto the rack.
7. Secure the lid. Choose "Manual" mode and Low pressure; cook for 30 minutes. Once cooking is complete, use a natural pressure release; carefully remove the lid.
8. In the meantime, beat the cheese, 1/4 cup of coconut oil, and Swerve until well combined. Frost the cake and serve well chilled. Enjoy!

Nutrition Info:
Per Serving: 359 Calories; 1g Fat; 6.6g Carbs; 8g Protein; 1.9g Sugars

Easy Chocolate Cheesecake

Servings: 6
Cooking Time: 40 Minutes
Ingredients:
- 1/3 cup whole-milk ricotta cheese
- 2 large eggs
- 1 (8-ounce) package cream cheese, softened
- ¼ cup powdered erythritol
- 1 teaspoon vanilla extract
- ¼ cup unsweetened cocoa powder

Directions:
1. Combine all of the ingredients except the eggs in a mixing bowl.
2. Beat until the mixture is smooth then adjust erythritol to taste.

3. Lower the mixer speed and blend in the eggs until they are fully incorporated, being careful not to overmix.
4. Grease a 6-inch springform pan and pour in the cheesecake mixture.
5. Cover the pan with foil and place it in the Instant Pot on top of the trivet.
6. Pour in 2 cups of water, then close and lock the lid.
7. Press the Manual button and adjust the timer for 30 minutes on High Pressure.
8. When the timer goes off, let the pressure vent naturally.
9. When the pot has depressurized, open the lid.
10. Let the cheesecake cool a little then chill for at least 6 hours before serving.

Nutrition Info: calories 180 fat 16g ,protein 6.5g ,carbs 3.5g .fiber 1g ,net carbs 2.5g

Summer Strawberry Yogurt

Servings: 10
Cooking Time: 24 Hours + Chilling Time
Ingredients:
- 3 teaspoons probiotic yogurt starter
- 1 ½ cup fresh strawberries, sliced
- 1 teaspoon stevia powder
- 2 quarts raw milk

Directions:
1. Add the raw milk to the Instant Pot.
2. Secure the lid. Choose the "Yogurt" mode. Press the "Adjust" button until you see the word "Boil". Turn off the Instant Pot.
3. Use a food thermometer to read the temperature; 110 degrees is good and then stir in the probiotic starter.
4. Press the "Yogurt" button again and then, press the "Adjust" button to reach 2hours.
5. Place in your refrigerator for a few hours. Serve with fresh strawberries and stevia. Bon appétit!

Nutrition Info:
Per Serving: 128 Calories; 7.6g Fat; 3.8g Carbs; 8.9g Protein; 4g Sugars

Red Velvet Muffins

Servings: 2
Cooking Time: 15 Minutes
Ingredients:
- ¼ teaspoon red food coloring
- 2 teaspoons butter
- ¼ teaspoon baking powder
- 1 teaspoon apple cider vinegar
- 4 tablespoons coconut flour
- 1 teaspoon vanilla extract
- 3 tablespoons heavy cream
- 1 cup water, for cooking

Directions:
1. In the mixing bowl, mix up red food coloring, butter, baking powder, apple cider vinegar, coconut flour, vanilla extract, and heavy cream.
2. Stir the mixture until it is smooth.
3. After this, pour the mixture in the muffin molds.
4. Pour water and insert the steamer rack in the instant pot.
5. Place the muffin molds on the rack. Close and seal the lid.
6. Cook the muffins on manual (high pressure) for 15 minutes. Make a quick pressure release.

Nutrition Info:
Per Serving: calories 179, fat 6, fiber 6, carbs 2, protein 2.5

Rose Water Cauliflower Pudding

Servings: 4
Cooking Time: 12 Minutes
Ingredients:
- 1 ½ cups cauliflower rice
- ½ cup coconut milk
- ½ cup sugar-free maple syrup
- ½ tsp rose water
- ½ tsp pink food coloring
- A pinch salt
- ¼ cup dried cranberries
- ¼ cup chopped mixed nuts
- Pumpkin seeds for topping

Directions:
1. In the inner pot, mix all the ingredients except for the nuts and pumpkin seeds.
2. Lock the lid in place; set in Manual mode on High Pressure and set the timer to minutes.
3. After cooking, perform a natural pressure release for 10 minutes, then a quick pressure release to let out the remaining steam, and open the lid.
4. Stir and adjust the taste with maple syrup.
5. Spoon into serving bowls, top with the nuts, pumpkin seeds, and serve warm or chilled.

Nutrition Info:
Per Serving: Calories 286 Fats 74g Carbs 7.9 g Net Carbs 4.9g Protein 4 g

Vanilla Pudding

Servings: 4
Cooking Time: 35 Mins
Ingredients:
- 1 cup Heavy Cream
- 4 Egg Yolks
- ½ cup Almond Milk
- 1 tsp Vanilla
- ½ cup Swerve Sugar

- 8 Strawberries, sliced

Directions:
1. Fit the trivet in Instant Pot and pour in cup water. Set a pan over low heat, add 4 tablespoons water and swerve sugar. Stir constantly until dissolves. Turn off the heat. Add almond milk, heavy cream, and vanilla. Stir with a whisk until evenly combined.
2. Crack eggs into a bowl and add a tablespoon of the cream mixture. Whisk and then very slowly add the remaining cream mixture while whisking. Pour the mixture into the ramekins and place them on the trivet in the Instant Pot. Seal the lid select Manual on High and cook for 4 minutes. Once ready, do a quick pressure release. Remove the ramekins onto a flat surface. Let them cool. Remove from Garnish with strawberry slices and serve.

Nutrition Info: Calories 83, Protein 4g, Net Carbs 8g, Fat 9g

Simple Chocolate Mousse

Servings: 6
Cooking Time: 20 Minutes + Chilling Time
Ingredients:
- 1 cup full-fat milk
- 1 cup heavy cream
- 4 egg yolks, beaten
- 1/3 cup sugar
- 1/4 teaspoon grated nutmeg
- 1/4 teaspoon ground cinnamon
- 1/4 cup unsweetened cocoa powder

Directions:
1. In a small pan, bring the milk and cream to a simmer.
2. In a mixing dish, thoroughly combine the remaining ingredients. Add this egg mixture to the warm milk mixture.
3. Pour the mixture into ramekins.
4. Add 1 ½ cups of water and a metal rack to the Instant Pot. Now, lower your ramekins onto the rack.
5. Secure the lid. Choose "Manual" mode and High pressure; cook for 10 minutes. Once cooking is complete, use a natural pressure release; carefully remove the lid. Serve
6. Serve well chilled and enjoy!

Nutrition Info:
Per Serving: 205 Calories; 3g Fat; 5.2g Total Carbs; 3.2g Protein; 2.6g Sugars

Frozen Strawberry Cheesecake

Servings: 2
Cooking Time: 10 Minutes
Ingredients:
- 1 tablespoon gelatin
- 4 tablespoon water (for gelatin)
- 4 tablespoon cream cheese

- 1 strawberry, chopped
- ¼ cup of coconut milk
- 1 tablespoon swerve

Directions:
1. Mix up gelatin and water and leave the mixture for minutes.
2. Meanwhile, pour coconut milk in the instant pot.
3. Bring it to boil on saute mode (appx. For 10 minutes).
4. Meanwhile, mash the strawberry and mix it up with cream cheese.
5. Add the mixture in the hot coconut milk and stir until smooth.
6. Cool the liquid for 10 minutes and add gelatin. Whisk it until gelatin is melted.
7. Then pour the cheesecake in the mold and freeze in the freezer for 3 hours.

Nutrition Info:
Per Serving: calories 155, fat 1, fiber 0.8, carbs 3.7, protein 5.2

Macadamia Blackberry Stew

Servings: 4
Cooking Time: 20 Minutes
Ingredients:
- 12 ounces blackberries
- 2 tablespoons lime juice
- 2 tablespoons stevia
- 1 and ½ cups coconut nectar
- 1 tablespoon macadamia nuts, chopped
- 1 teaspoon vanilla extract

Directions:
1. In your instant pot, mix the blackberries with the rest of the ingredients, put the lid on and cook on High for minutes. Release the pressure fast for 5 minutes, divide the mix into bowls and serve.

Nutrition Info: calories 78, fat 2, fiber 1.2, carbs 1.5, protein 1.4

Lime Coconut Vanilla Cream

Servings: 4
Cooking Time: 20 Minutes
Ingredients:
- 2 cups coconut cream
- 1 tablespoon lime zest
- 1 tablespoon lime juice
- 4 eggs, whisked
- 2 teaspoon vanilla extract
- 1 cup water

Directions:
1. In a bowl, combine the coconut cream with the rest of the ingredients except the water, whisk well and divide into 4 ramekins. Put the water in the instant pot, add the steamer

basket, put the ramekins inside, put the lid on and cook on High for 20 minutes. Release the pressure naturally for minutes and serve.
Nutrition Info: calories 342, fat 7, fiber 2.7, carbs 7.4, protein 8.3

Berries And Nuts Pudding

Servings: 4
Cooking Time: 20 Minutes
Ingredients:
- 1 cup blackberries
- ½ cup blueberries
- 1 egg, whisked
- 1 teaspoon baking soda
- 2 cups coconut milk
- 1 tablespoon macadamia nuts, chopped
- 1 tablespoon pecans, chopped
- 3 tablespoons swerve
- 1 cup coconut cream
- 1 cup water

Directions:
1. In a bowl, mix the berries with the egg and the rest of the ingredients except the water, whisk well and pour into a pudding pan. Put the water in the instant pot, add the steamer basket, put the pudding pan inside, put the lid on and cook on High for 20 minutes. Release the pressure naturally for minutes and serve the pudding cold.

Nutrition Info: calories 342, fat 8, fiber 3.4, carbs 6.4, protein 6.2

Coconut Balls

Servings: 2
Cooking Time: 8 Minutes
Ingredients:
- 2 tablespoon coconut flakes
- 1 egg, whisked
- 2 tablespoons coconut flour
- ¾ teaspoon vanilla extract
- 1 teaspoon Erythritol
- 1 tablespoon coconut oil
- 1 cup of water (for instant pot)

Directions:
1. Combine together the whisked egg, coconut flour, coconut flakes, and vanilla extract. Add coconut oil.
2. Add baking powder and Erythritol.
3. Make the balls from the coconut flour mixture.
4. Pour 1 cup of water in the instant pot.
5. Insert the steamer rack inside and place the ramekin on it. Add coconut balls.

6. Close and lock the instant pot lid.
7. Set the "Manual" mode for 8 minutes – high pressure. QPR
8. Chill the dessert for 5-10 minutes or until they are warm.

Nutrition Info:
Per Serving: calories 142, fat 4, fiber 3.5, carbs 6.8, protein 3.9

Classic Carrot Cake

Servings: 8
Cooking Time: 35 Minutes
Ingredients:
- Carrot Cake:
- 2 cups carrots, grated
- 1 cup almond flour
- 1/2 cup coconut, shredded
- 1/4 cup hazelnuts, chopped
- 1/4 teaspoon ground cloves
- 1/4 teaspoon grated nutmeg
- 1/2 teaspoon ground cinnamon
- 1/2 teaspoon baking soda
- 1 teaspoon baking powder
- 4 tablespoons Swerve
- 1 teaspoon pure vanilla extract
- 4 eggs, beaten
- 1 stick butter, melted
- Cream Cheese Frosting:
- 1 cup cream cheese
- 2 tablespoons Swerve
- 1/2 teaspoon pure vanilla extract

Directions:
1. Start by adding ½ cups of water and a metal rack to your Instant Pot. Now, spritz a cheesecake pan with a nonstick cooking spray.
2. In a mixing bowl, thoroughly combine dry ingredients for the cake. Then, mix the wet ingredients until everything is well combined.
3. Pour the wet mixture into the dry mixture and stir to combine well. Spoon the batter into the cheesecake pan.
4. Cover with a sheet of foil. Lower the pan onto the rack.
5. Secure the lid. Choose "Bean/Chili" mode and High pressure; cook for 30 minutes. Once cooking is complete, use a quick pressure release; carefully remove the lid.
6. Meanwhile, mix the frosting ingredients. Frost the carrot cake and serve chilled. Enjoy!

Nutrition Info:
Per Serving: 381 Calories; 1g Fat; 4.4g Total Carbs; 3g Protein; 1.7g Sugars

Daikon Cake

Servings: 12
Cooking Time: 45 Minutes
Ingredients:

- 5 eggs, beaten
- ½ cup heavy cream
- 1 cup almond flour
- 1 daikon, diced
- 1 teaspoon ground cinnamon
- 2 tablespoon Erythritol
- 1 tablespoon butter, melted
- 1 cup water, for cooking

Directions:

1. In the mixing bowl, mix up eggs, heavy cream, almond flour, ground cinnamon, and Erythritol.
2. When the mixture is smooth, add daikon and stir it carefully with the help of the spatula.
3. Pour the mixture in the cake pan.
4. Then pour water and insert the steamer rack in the instant pot.
5. Place the cake in the instant pot.
6. Close and seal the lid.
7. Cook the cake in manual mode (high pressure) for 45 minutes. Make a quick pressure release.

Nutrition Info:
Per Serving: calories 67, fat 5.8, fiber 0.4, carbs 3.6, protein 3

Grandma's Orange Cheesecake

Servings: 10
Cooking Time: 35 Minutes + Chilling Time
Ingredients:

- Crust:
- 1/2 cup almond flour
- 1/2 cup coconut flour
- 1 ½ tablespoons powdered erythritol
- 1/4 teaspoon kosher salt
- 3 tablespoons butter, melted
- Filling:
- 8 ounces sour cream, at room temperature
- 8 ounces cream cheese, at room temperature
- 1/2 cup powdered erythritol
- 3 tablespoons orange juice
- 1/2 teaspoon ginger powder
- 1 teaspoon vanilla extract

- 3 eggs, at room temperature

Directions:
1. Line a round baking pan with a piece of parchment paper.
2. In a mixing bowl, thoroughly combine all crust ingredients in the order listed above.
3. Press the crust mixture into the bottom of the pan.
4. Then, make the filling by mixing the sour cream and cream cheese until uniform and smooth; add the remaining ingredients and continue to beat until everything is well combined.
5. Pour the cream cheese mixture over the crust. Cover with aluminum foil, making a foil sling.
6. Place 1 ½ cups of water and a metal trivet in your Instant Pot. Then, place the pan on the metal rack.
7. Secure the lid. Choose "Manual" mode and High pressure; cook for 30 minutes. Once cooking is complete, use a natural pressure release; carefully remove the lid. Serve well chilled and enjoy!

Nutrition Info:
Per Serving: 188 Calories; 2g Fat; 4.5g Carbs; 5.5g Protein; 1.3g Sugars

Party Blueberry Cobbler

Servings: 6
Cooking Time: 20 Minutes
Ingredients:
- 1 cup almond flour
- 3 tablespoons sunflower seed flour
- 1/2 cup Swerve
- 1/2 teaspoon baking soda
- 1 teaspoon baking powder
- 1/4 cup coconut cream
- 1/4 cup water
- 1/4 cup coconut oil, softened
- 2 tablespoons dark rum
- 1/2 teaspoon vanilla
- 1/2 cup blueberries

Directions:
1. Start by adding ½ cups of water and a metal trivet to your Instant Pot.
2. Mix all ingredients, except blueberries, until everything is well incorporated. Spoon the mixture into a lightly greased baking pan.
3. Fold in blueberries and gently stir to combine. Lower the baking dish onto the trivet.
4. Secure the lid. Choose "Bean/Chili" mode and High pressure; cook for 15 minutes. Once cooking is complete, use a natural pressure release; carefully remove the lid.
5. Allow the cobbler to cool slightly before serving. Bon appétit!

Nutrition Info:
Per Serving: 240 Calories; 5g Fat; 9.4g Carbs; 4.8g Protein; 5.1g Sugars

Chocolate-blueberries Cake Bites

Servings: 4
Cooking Time: 13 Minutes
Ingredients:

- 1 cup melted unsweetened chocolate
- 3 tbsp sugar-free maple syrup
- 2 large eggs
- ¼ cup almond flour
- 14 fresh blueberries
- 1 ½ cups of water

Directions:

1. Lightly grease a silicone egg-bite tray with cooking spray and set aside.
2. In a medium bowl, mix the chocolate, maple syrup, eggs, and almond flour until well combined, and fold in the blueberries. Spoon the mixture into the silicone tray with at least 1 blueberry in each mold and cover the tray with foil.
3. Pour 1 ½ cups of water into the inner pot, fit in a trivet, and place the egg bite tray on top.
4. Lock the lid in place; select Manual mode on High Pressure and set the timer to 13 minutes.
5. After cooking, perform a quick pressure release to let out the steam, and open the lid.
6. Carefully remove the tray, take off the foil, allow cooling for 5 minutes, and pop out the dessert bites onto plates.
7. Enjoy the dessert.

Nutrition Info:
Per Serving: Calories 29 Fats 15g Carbs 0.88g Net Carbs 0.78g Protein 3.19g

Muffins With Blueberry And Lime

Servings: 6
Cooking Time: 30 Minutes
Ingredients:

- 3/4 cup almond flour
- 1/4 cup coconut flour
- 1/2 teaspoon baking powder
- A pinch of salt
- A pinch of grated nutmeg
- 1 ½ teaspoons cinnamon, ground
- 3 whole eggs, beaten
- 1/4 cup coconut oil
- 1/4 cup granulated Swerve
- A few drops vanilla butternut flavor
- 1/2 teaspoon grated lemon peel
- Topping:
- 1 cup blueberries
- 4 tablespoons water

- 1/2 tablespoon freshly squeezed lime juice
- 1/2 cup Swerve
- 1 teaspoon arrowroot, mixed with 1 teaspoon water

Directions:

1. Start by adding ½ cups of water and a rack to your Instant Pot.
2. In a mixing dish, thoroughly combine all ingredients for the muffins. Divide the batter between silicone cupcake liners. Cover with a piece of foil.
3. Place the cupcakes on the rack.
4. Secure the lid. Choose "Manual" mode and High pressure; cook for 25 minutes. Once cooking is complete, use a natural pressure release; carefully remove the lid.
5. In the meantime, place the blueberries, water, lime juice and Swerve into a saucepan over moderate heat; let it simmer until thoroughly heated.
6. Now, stir in the arrowroot slurry and simmer until the sauce is reduced. Place this topping over your muffins and serve at room temperature.

Nutrition Info:
Per Serving: 209 Calories; 3g Fat; 5.1g Total Carbs; 5.6g Protein; 2.3g Sugars

Pancake Bites

Servings: 4
Cooking Time: 10 Minutes
Ingredients:

- 1 teaspoon apple cider vinegar
- 1 teaspoon vanilla extract
- 1 cup of coconut milk
- 1/3 cup coconut flour
- 1 tablespoon Erythritol
- ½ teaspoon baking powder
- 1 tablespoon coconut oil

Directions:

1. Melt the almond butter on saute mode.
2. Then mix up all the remaining ingredients in the mixing bowl.
3. Pour the small amount of pancake batter in the instant pot to get the small rounds.
4. Cook the pancake bites on saute mode for 1.5 minutes from each side.

Nutrition Info:
Per Serving: calories 211, fat 7, fiber 5.3, carbs 2, protein 2.7

Luscious Tropical Dream Dessert

Servings: 4
Cooking Time: 15 Minutes + Chilling Time
Ingredients:

- 3 egg yolks, well whisked
- 1/3 cup Swerve
- 1/4 cup water

- 3 tablespoons cacao powder, unsweetened
- 3/4 cup whipping cream
- 1/3 cup coconut milk
- 1/4 cup shredded coconut
- 1 teaspoon vanilla essence
- A pinch of grated nutmeg
- A pinch of salt

Directions:
1. Place the egg in a mixing bowl.
2. In a pan, heat the Swerve, water and cacao powder and whisk well to combine.
3. Now, stir in the whipping cream and milk; cook until heated through. Add shredded coconut, vanilla, nutmeg, and salt.
4. Now, slowly and gradually pour the chocolate mixture into the bowl with egg yolks. Stir to combine well and pour into ramekins.
5. Add 1 ½ cups of water and a metal rack to the Instant Pot. Now, lower your ramekins onto the rack.
6. Secure the lid. Choose "Manual" mode and High pressure; cook for 8 minutes. Once cooking is complete, use a quick pressure release; carefully remove the lid.
7. Place in your refrigerator until ready to serve. Bon appétit!

Nutrition Info:
Per Serving: 118 Calories; 8.2g Fat; 7.6g Carbs; 3.7g Protein; 2.6g Sugars

Creamy Lemon Sponge Cake

Servings: 4
Cooking Time: 1 Hour 20 Minutes + 2 Hour Chilling
Ingredients:
- For the lemon puree:
- 4 large lemons
- ¼ cup sugar-free maple syrup
- ¼ tsp salt
- For the cake:
- ½ cup unsalted butter, softened
- ½ cup swerve sugar
- 1 tsp vanilla extract
- 3 large eggs, lightly beaten
- ½ cup almond flour, sifted

Directions:
1. Mix the lemon juice, maple syrup, and salt in a medium pot and cook over low heat until syrupy, 30 minutes.
2. Pour the mixture into a blender and process until smooth. Pour into a jar and set aside.
3. Grease a 7-inch springform pan with cooking spray and set aside.
4. In a large mixing bowl, whisk the butter, swerve sugar, and vanilla extract until light and fluffy. Beat in the eggs one after another and then mix in the almond flour until smooth. Pour the batter into the cake pan and cover with foil.

5. Pour 2 cups of water into the inner pot, fit in a trivet, and place the cake pan on top.
6. Lock the lid in place; select Manual mode on High Pressure and set the timer to 40 minutes.
7. After cooking, perform a natural pressure release for 10 minutes, then a quick pressure release to let out the remaining steam, and open the lid.
8. Carefully remove the pan, allow cooling for 10 minutes and chill in the fridge for 2 hours or more.
9. Remove and release the cake after, slice and serve.

Nutrition Info:
Per Serving: Calories 195 Fats 19g Carbs 3.93g Net Carbs 3.73 g Protein 6.15g

Mug Muffins

Servings: 3
Cooking Time: 8 Minutes
Ingredients:
- 1 teaspoon avocado oil
- 2 tablespoons coconut flour
- 1 tablespoon Erythritol
- ½ teaspoon vanilla extract
- ¼ teaspoon baking powder
- 1 tablespoon almond butter
- 1 cup of water (for instant pot)

Directions:
1. Brush the mugs with avocado oil
2. Mix up together all remaining the liquid ingredients and almond butter.
3. Add all the dry ingredients and stir the mixture with the help of the spoon.
4. When you get a smooth batter – transfer it into the prepared mugs.
5. Pour 1 cup of water in the instant pot and insert the steamer rack.
6. Put the mugs on the rack and close the lid.
7. Cook the meal on "Manual" (High pressure) for 8 minutes. QPR for 5 minutes.

Nutrition Info:
Per Serving: calories 58, fat 3.7, fiber 2.6, carbs 9.4, protein 2.3

Pecans And Plums Bread

Servings: 4
Cooking Time: 30 Minutes
Ingredients:
- 1 cup coconut flour
- 3 eggs, whisked
- 1 tablespoon vanilla extract
- 1 and ½ cups swerve
- 2 cups plums, pitted and chopped
- 2 cups coconut milk
- 2 tablespoons pecans, chopped

- ¼ teaspoon baking powder
- 2 cups water
- Cooking spray

Directions:

1. In a bowl, combine the coconut flour with the eggs and the rest of the ingredients except the cooking spray and the water and whisk well. Grease a loaf pan with the cooking spray and pour the bread mix inside. Add the water to the instant pot, add the steamer basket, put the loaf pan inside, put the lid on and cook on High for 30 minutes. Release the pressure naturally for minutes, cool the bread down, slice and serve.

Nutrition Info: calories 348, fat 5, fiber 3.1, carbs 6.6, protein 7.2

Pumpkin Cake

Servings: 10
Cooking Time: 10 Mins
Ingredients:

- 3 cups Almond flour
- 1 tbsp Baking powder
- 2 tsp Baking soda
- 2 tsp ground Cinnamon
- 1 tsp ground Nutmeg
- ½ tsp ground Cloves
- 1 tsp ground Ginger
- 1 tsp Salt
- 4 beaten Eggs
- 2 cup Stevia
- 1 can Pumpkin
- 1 cup Coconut oil

Directions:

1. Pour up water and lower a trivet in the pot. Sift flour, baking powder, soda, salt, and spices in a bowl. In a separate bowl, beat the eggs with stevia until thick. Add the pumpkin and oil; beat until smooth. Blend the dry ingredients into the pumpkin mixture. Pour the batter into a greased pan, lower the pan on top of the trivet. Seal the lid and cook on High pressure for 10 minutes. When the timer beeps, naturally release the pressure, for 10 minutes, and serve warm.

Nutrition Info: Calories 250, Protein 3.8g, Net Carbs 1.3g, Fat 26g

Orange-white Chocolate Mini Lava Cakes

Servings: 4
Cooking Time: 10 Minutes
Ingredients:

- Nonstick cooking spray
- 4 ounces white chocolate morsels, sugar-free
- 4 tablespoons coconut oil

- 4 eggs
- 1/8 teaspoon coarse salt
- 1/2 teaspoon ground cinnamon
- 1/4 teaspoon ground cloves
- 1/4 teaspoon freshly grated nutmeg
- 1/2 teaspoon vanilla paste
- 2 drops orange essential oil
- 1/3 cup confectioners' Swerve
- 2/3 cup almond flour

Directions:

1. Start by adding ½ cups of water and a metal rack to your Instant Pot. Now, spritz 4 ramekins with a nonstick cooking spray.
2. Melt the chocolate and coconut oil in a microwave.
3. Then, whip the eggs with an electric mixer, adding the salt, cinnamon, cloves, cloves nutmeg, vanilla, orange essential oil and confectioners' Swerve.
4. Add the melted chocolate mixture and mix again until everything is well incorporated. Lastly, stir in almond flour and mix again.
5. Spoon the batter into the prepared ramekins. Secure the lid. Choose "Manual" mode and High pressure; cook for 6 minutes.
6. Once cooking is complete, use a natural pressure release; carefully remove the lid. Invert cakes onto the serving plates and serve warm. Enjoy!

Nutrition Info:
Per Serving: 409 Calories; 8g Fat; 9.2g Carbs; 9g Protein; 1.1g Sugars

Keto Fudge

Servings: 5
Cooking Time: 6 Minutes
Ingredients:

- ¾ cup of cocoa powder
- 1 oz dark chocolate
- 4 tablespoons butter
- 1 tablespoon ricotta cheese
- ¼ teaspoon vanilla extract

Directions:

1. Preheat the instant pot on sauté mode for 3 minutes. Place chocolate in the instant pot. Add butter and ricotta cheese. Then add vanilla extract and cook the ingredients until you get liquid mixture. Then add cocoa powder and whisk it to avoid the lumps. Line the glass mold with baking paper and pour the hot liquid mixture inside. Flatten it gently. Refrigerate it until solid. Then cut/crack the cooked fudge into the serving pieces.

Nutrition Info: calories 155, fat 8, fiber 4.6, carbs 7, protein 3.3

Almond And Chocolate Crème

Servings: 4

Cooking Time: 15 Minutes
Ingredients:
- 2 cups heavy whipping cream
- 1/2 cup water
- 4 eggs
- 1/3 cup Swerve
- 1 teaspoon almond extract
- 1 teaspoon vanilla extract
- 1/3 cup almonds, ground
- 2 tablespoons coconut oil, room temperature
- 4 tablespoons cacao powder
- 2 tablespoons gelatin

Directions:
1. Start by adding ½ cups of water and a metal rack to your Instant Pot.
2. Blend the cream, water, eggs, Swerve, almond extract, vanilla extract and almonds in your food processor.
3. Add the remaining ingredients and process for a minute longer.
4. Divide the mixture between four Mason jars; cover your jars with lids. Lower the jars onto the rack.
5. Secure the lid. Choose "Manual" mode and High pressure; cook for 7 minutes. Once cooking is complete, use a natural pressure release; carefully remove the lid. Bon appétit!

Nutrition Info:
Per Serving: 401 Calories; 1g Fat; 9.2g Carbs; 9.1g Protein; 2.7g Sugars

Coconut Cupcakes

Servings: 6
Cooking Time: 10 Minutes
Ingredients:
- 4 eggs, beaten
- 4 tablespoons coconut milk
- 4 tablespoons coconut flour
- ½ teaspoon vanilla extract
- 2 tablespoons Erythritol
- 1 teaspoon baking powder
- 1 cup water, for cooking

Directions:
1. In the mixing bowl, mix up eggs, coconut milk, coconut flour, vanilla extract, Erythritol, and baking powder.
2. Then pour the batter in the cupcake molds.
3. Pour water and insert the steamer rack in the instant pot.
4. Place the cupcakes on the rack. Close and seal the lid.
5. Cook the cupcakes for 10 minutes on manual mode (high pressure).
6. Then allow the natural pressure release for 5 minutes.

Nutrition Info:

Per Serving: calories 86, fat 5.8, fiber 2.2, carbs 9.2, protein 4.6

Yummy And Easy Chocolate Mousse

Servings: 6
Cooking Time: 20 Minutes + Chilling Time
Ingredients:
- 1 cup full-fat milk
- 1 cup heavy cream
- 4 egg yolks, beaten
- 1/3 cup sugar
- 1/4 teaspoon grated nutmeg
- 1/4 teaspoon ground cinnamon
- 1/4 cup unsweetened cocoa powder

Directions:
1. In a small pan, bring the milk and cream to a simmer.
2. In a mixing dish, thoroughly combine the remaining ingredients. Add this egg mixture to the warm milk mixture.
3. Pour the mixture into ramekins.
4. Add 1 ½ cups of water and a metal rack to the Instant Pot. Now, lower your ramekins onto the rack.
5. Secure the lid. Choose "Manual" mode and High pressure; cook for 10 minutes. Once cooking is complete, use a natural pressure release; carefully remove the lid. Serve
6. Serve well chilled and enjoy!

Nutrition Info:
Per Serving: 205 Calories; 3g Fat; 9.2g Carbs; 3.2g Protein; 6.6g Sugars

Lime Bars

Servings: 6
Cooking Time: 10 Minutes
Ingredients:
- ½ cup coconut flour
- 2 teaspoons coconut oil
- ¼ teaspoon baking powder
- ½ tablespoon cream cheese
- 1/3 cup coconut cream
- 2 tablespoons lime juice
- 1 teaspoon lime zest, grated
- 2 tablespoons Erythritol
- 1 cup water, for cooking

Directions:
1. Knead the dough from coconut flour, coconut oil, baking powder, and cream cheese. When the mixture is soft and non-sticky, it is prepared. Then line the instant pot bowl with baking paper. Place the dough inside and flatten it in the shape of the pie crust (make the edges).

Close the lid and cook it on sauté mode for 5 minutes. After this, switch off the instant pot. Make the filling: mix up coconut cream, lime juice, lime zest, and Erythritol. Then pour the liquid over the cooked pie crust and cook it on sauté mode for 5 minutes more. When the time is over, transfer the cooked meal in the freezer for minutes. Cut the dessert into bars.

Nutrition Info: calories 88, fat 6, fiber 4.3, carbs 7.9, protein 1.7

Special Pots De Crème

Servings: 4
Cooking Time: 15 Minutes
Ingredients:
- 3/4 cup double cream
- 1 cup Swerve, powdered
- 1/3 cup espresso strong coffee, at room temperature
- 2 eggs, beaten
- 1 (8-ounce container Camembert cheese, at room temperature
- 1/2 teaspoon vanilla extract
- 1/4 teaspoon cinnamon, ground
- 4 ounces chocolate chunks, sugar-free

Directions:
1. In a small saucepan, bring the cream and Swerve to a simmer.
2. In a mixing dish, thoroughly combine the remaining ingredients. Add this egg mixture to the warm cream mixture.
3. Pour the mixture into ramekins.
4. Add 1 ½ cups of water and a metal rack to the Instant Pot. Now, lower your ramekins onto the rack.
5. Secure the lid. Choose "Manual" mode and High pressure; cook for 10 minutes. Once cooking is complete, use a natural pressure release; carefully remove the lid. Serve
6. Serve well chilled. Bon appétit!

Nutrition Info:
Per Serving: 233 Calories; 3g Fat; 5.1g Total Carbs; 2g Protein; 0.2g Sugars

Sweet Strawberry And Nuts Bowls

Servings: 4
Cooking Time: 3 Minutes
Ingredients:
- 2 tbsp swerve brown sugar
- 1/3 cup toasted pecans, chopped
- 1/3 cup dried strawberries
- 1/3 cup dates, cranberries
- 1 tbsp. cinnamon powder
- 4 tbsp butter
- 1 cup Greek yogurt for topping
- 4 tbsp unsweetened chocolate sauce for topping

Directions:

1. In the bowl, mix the swerve brown sugar, pecans, strawberries, cranberries, cinnamon powder, butter, and 3 cup of water.
2. Lock the lid in place; select Manual mode on Low Pressure and set the timer to 3 minutes.
3. After cooking, perform a natural pressure release for 10 minutes, then, a quick pressure release to let out the remaining steam, and open the lid.
4. Stir and spoon the mixture onto serving plates. Top with the yogurt and then the chocolate sauce.
5. Serve immediately.

Nutrition Info:

Per Serving: Calories 205 Fats 45g Carbs 3.44g Net Carbs 4.74g Protein 3.13g

Coconut And Cocoa Doughnuts

Servings: 4
Cooking Time: 20 Minutes
Ingredients:

- ¼ cup swerve
- ¼ cup flaxseed meal
- ¾ cup coconut flour
- 1 teaspoon baking powder
- 1 teaspoon vanilla extract
- 2 eggs, whisked
- 3 tablespoons ghee, melted
- ¼ cup coconut milk
- 1 tablespoon cocoa powder
- Cooking spray
- 1 cup water

Directions:

1. In a bowl, mix the swerve with the flaxmeal and the rest of the ingredients except the cooking spray and the water and stir well. Grease a doughnut pan with the cooking spray and divide the mix. Add the water to the instant pot, add the steamer basket, put the pan inside, put the lid on and cook on High for 20 minutes. Release the pressure naturally for minutes, cool the doughnuts down and serve.

Nutrition Info: calories 196, fat 3, fiber 2.7, carbs 4.5, protein 4.7

Ricotta Lemon Cheesecake

Servings: 6
Cooking Time: 40 Minutes
Ingredients:

- 1/3 cup whole-milk ricotta cheese
- 2 large eggs
- 2 cups of water
- 1 (8-ounce) package cream cheese, softened

- ¼ cup powdered erythritol
- Juice and zest of 1 lemon
- ½ teaspoon lemon extract

Directions:
1. Combine all of the ingredients except the eggs in a mixing bowl.
2. Beat until the mixture is smooth then adjust erythritol to taste.
3. Lower the mixer speed and blend in the eggs until they are fully incorporated, being careful not to overmix.
4. Grease a 6-inch springform pan and pour in the cheesecake mixture.
5. Cover the pan with foil and place it in the Instant Pot on top of the trivet.
6. Pour in 2 cups of water, then close and lock the lid.
7. Press the Manual button and adjust the timer for 30 minutes on High Pressure.
8. When the timer goes off, let the pressure vent naturally.
9. When the pot has depressurized, open the lid.
10. Let the cheesecake cool a little then chill for at least 8 hours before serving.

Nutrition Info: calories 180 fat 16g ,protein 6.5g ,carbs 2g ,fiber 0g ,net carbs 2g

Spice Pie

Servings: 8
Cooking Time: 45 Minutes
Ingredients:
- 1 cup coconut flour
- 2 tablespoons butter
- 2 tablespoons cream cheese
- ½ teaspoon ground cinnamon
- ¼ teaspoon ground turmeric
- ½ teaspoon ground cardamom
- ¼ teaspoon ground nutmeg
- 1 teaspoon vanilla extract
- 1 tablespoon peanuts, chopped
- 3 eggs, beaten
- 1 teaspoon pumpkin spices
- 3 tablespoons Splenda
- 1 cup water, for cooking

Directions:
1. Make the pie batter: whisk together coconut flour, butter, cream cheese, ground cinnamon, ground turmeric, cardamom, nutmeg, vanilla extract, peanuts, eggs, pumpkin spices, and Splenda. When the batter is prepared, pour it in the instant pot pie mold. Flatten the surface of the pie well. Pour water and insert the steamer rack in the instant pot. Place the pie on the steamer rack and close the lid. Cook the pie on manual mode (high pressure) for 45 minutes. When the time is over, make the quick pressure release and open the lid. Cool the pie to the room temperature and cut into the servings.

Nutrition Info: calories 98, fat 6.3, fiber 0.9, carbs 6.4, protein 2.9

Mini Cheesecakes With Berries

Servings: 6
Cooking Time: 25 Minutes
Ingredients:

- 1/4 cup sesame seed flour
- 1/4 cup hazelnut flour
- 1/2 cup coconut flour
- 1 ½ teaspoons baking powder
- A pinch of kosher salt
- A pinch of freshly grated nutmeg
- 1/2 teaspoon ground star anise
- 1/2 teaspoon ground cinnamon
- 1/2 stick butter
- 1 cup Swerve
- 2 eggs, beaten
- 1/2 cup cream cheese
- 1/3 cup fresh mixed berries
- 1/2 vanilla paste

Directions:

1. Start by adding ½ cups of water and a rack to your Instant Pot.
2. In a mixing dish, thoroughly combine all of the above ingredients. Divide the batter between lightly greased ramekins. Cover with a piece of foil.
3. Place the ramekins on the rack.
4. Secure the lid. Choose "Manual" mode and High pressure; cook for 20 minutes. Once cooking is complete, use a natural pressure release; carefully remove the lid.

Nutrition Info:
Per Serving: 232 Calories; 1g Fat; 4.8g Total Carbs; 5.7g Protein; 1.9g Sugars

Star Anise Raspberry Curd

Servings: 4
Cooking Time: 20 Minutes + Chilling Time
Ingredients:

- 4 ounces coconut oil, softened
- 3/4 cup Swerve
- 4 egg yolks, beaten
- 1/2 cup blueberries
- 1 teaspoon grated lemon zest
- 1/2 teaspoon vanilla extract
- 1/2 teaspoon star anise, ground

Directions:

1. Blend the coconut oil and Swerve in a food processor.
2. Gradually mix in the eggs; continue to blend for 1 minute longer.

3. Now, add blueberries, lemon zest, vanilla, and star anise. Divide the mixture among four Mason jars and cover them with lids.
4. Add 1 ½ cups of water and a metal rack to the Instant Pot. Now, lower your jars onto the rack.
5. Secure the lid. Choose "Manual" mode and High pressure; cook for 1minutes. Once cooking is complete, use a natural pressure release; carefully remove the lid. Serve
6. Place in your refrigerator until ready to serve. Bon appétit!

Nutrition Info:
Per Serving: 334 Calories; 9g Fat; 7.6g Carbs; 2.9g Protein; 6.6g Sugars

Avocado Brownies

Servings: 12
Cooking Time: 14 Minutes
Ingredients:
- 1 avocado, peeled, pitted
- 1 tablespoon cocoa powder
- 1 tablespoon almond butter
- 1 teaspoon vanilla extract
- 1 egg, beaten
- 4 tablespoons almond flour
- ½ teaspoon baking powder
- 3 tablespoons Erythritol
- ½ teaspoon apple cider vinegar
- 1 cup water, for cooking

Directions:
1. Churn the avocado till the creamy texture. Add cocoa powder, almond butter, vanilla extract, and egg. Mix up the mixture until it is smooth. Then add almond flour, baking powder, Erythritol, and apple cider vinegar. Stir the mass well and pour in the instant pot baking mold. Flatten the surface and cover it with the foil. Pierce the foil with the help of the toothpick. Pour water and insert the trivet in the instant pot. Place the baking mold with a brownie on the trivet and close the lid. Cook the dessert for minutes on manual mode (high pressure). When the time is finished, make a quick pressure release and remove the brownie. Discard the foil and cut the brownie into bars.

Nutrition Info: calories 103, fat 9.1, fiber 3, carbs 2.4, protein 3.1

Almond Pie

Servings: 8
Cooking Time: 41 Minutes
Ingredients:
- 1 cup almond flour
- ½ cup of coconut milk
- 1 teaspoon vanilla extract
- 2 tablespoons butter, softened

- 1 tablespoon Truvia
- ¼ cup coconut, shredded
- 1 cup water, for cooking

Directions:
1. In the mixing bowl, mix up almond flour, coconut milk, vanilla extract, butter, Truvia, and shredded coconut.
2. When the mixture is smooth, transfer it in the baking pan and flatten.
3. Pour water and insert the steamer rack in the instant pot.
4. Put the baking pan with cake on the rack. Close and seal the lid.
5. Cook the dessert on manual mode (high pressure) for 41 minutes. Allow the natural pressure release for 10 minutes.

Nutrition Info:
Per Serving: calories 90, fat 9.1, fiber 0.9, carbs 2.6, protein 1.2

Lemon Strawberries Stew

Servings: 4
Cooking Time: 20 Minutes
Ingredients:
- 3 cups strawberries
- 1 tablespoon lemon zest, grated
- 1 tablespoon lemon juice
- 1 cup swerve
- 1 teaspoon vanilla extract
- 1 cup water

Directions:
1. In your instant pot, combine the strawberries with the lemon zest and the rest of the ingredients, put the lid on and cook on High for 20 minutes. Release the pressure naturally for minutes, divide the mix into bowls and serve right away.

Nutrition Info: calories 82, fat 1.4, fiber 0.5, carbs 1, protein 0.8

Plums And Rice Pudding

Servings: 4
Cooking Time: 20 Minutes
Ingredients:
- 2 cups coconut milk
- 1 cup cauliflower rice
- ½ cup plums, pitted and chopped
- ¼ cup heavy cream
- 2 eggs, whisked
- ½ cup swerve
- ½ teaspoon vanilla extract

Directions:

1. In your instant pot, mix the cauliflower rice with the plums and the rest of the ingredients, put the lid on and cook on High for 20 minutes. Release the pressure fast for 6 minutes, divide the pudding into bowls and serve cold.

Nutrition Info: calories 339, fat 7, fiber 2.7, carbs 6.5, protein 5.7

Blueberry And Cinnamon Muffins

Servings: 6
Cooking Time: 30 Minutes
Ingredients:
- 3/4 cup almond flour
- 1/4 cup coconut flour
- 1/2 teaspoon baking powder
- A pinch of salt
- A pinch of grated nutmeg
- 1 ½ teaspoons cinnamon, ground
- 3 whole eggs, beaten
- 1/4 cup coconut oil
- 1/4 cup granulated Swerve
- A few drops vanilla butternut flavor
- 1/2 teaspoon grated lemon peel
- Topping:
- 1 cup blueberries
- 4 tablespoons water
- 1/2 tablespoon freshly squeezed lime juice
- 1/2 cup Swerve
- 1 teaspoon arrowroot, mixed with 1 teaspoon water

Directions:
1. Start by adding ½ cups of water and a rack to your Instant Pot.
2. In a mixing dish, thoroughly combine all ingredients for the muffins. Divide the batter between silicone cupcake liners. Cover with a piece of foil.
3. Place the cupcakes on the rack.
4. Secure the lid. Choose "Manual" mode and High pressure; cook for 25 minutes. Once cooking is complete, use a natural pressure release; carefully remove the lid.
5. In the meantime, place the blueberries, water, lime juice and Swerve into a saucepan over moderate heat; let it simmer until thoroughly heated.
6. Now, stir in the arrowroot slurry and simmer until the sauce is reduced. Place this topping over your muffins and serve at room temperature.

Nutrition Info:
Per Serving: 209 Calories; 3g Fat; 8.1g Carbs; 5.6g Protein; 3.3g Sugars

Coconut Zucchini Cake

Servings: 4
Cooking Time: 40 Minutes

Ingredients:
- 2 egg, whisked
- ½ cup swerve
- 2 tablespoons ghee, melted
- 1 cup coconut milk
- ¼ cup coconut flour
- 2 zucchinis, grated
- ½ teaspoon baking soda
- Cooking spray
- 2 cups water

Directions:
1. In a bowl, mix the eggs with the zucchinis and the rest of the ingredients except the water and the cooking spray and whisk well. Grease a cake pan with the cooking spray and pour the zucchini mix inside. Add the water to the pot, add steamer basket, add the cake pan inside, put the lid on and cook on High for 40 minutes. Release the pressure naturally for minutes, cool the cake, slice and serve.

Nutrition Info: calories 242, fat 2, fiber 2.4, carbs 6.8, protein 5.4

Raspberry Chocolate Mousse

Servings: 4
Cooking Time: 15 Minutes + Overnight Refrigeration
Ingredients:
- For the chocolate mousse:
- 12 oz unsweetened dark chocolate, melted
- 8 eggs, separated into yolks and whites
- ¾ cup swerve sugar, divided
- A pinch salt
- ½ cup melted butter
- 3 tbsp brewed coffee, room temperature
- For the stewed raspberries:
- ½ cup swerve sugar
- ½ stick cinnamon
- ½ cup water
- ½ lemon, juiced
- ½ cup fresh raspberries

Directions:
1. In a medium bowl, whisk the egg yolks and half of the swerve sugar until pale yellow color forms. Mix in the salt, butter, coffee and then stir in the melted chocolate until smooth.
2. In another bowl, using an electric hand mixer, whisk the egg whites until a stiff peak form. Sprinkle the remaining swerve sugar over and gently fold in.
3. Fetch a tablespoon of the chocolate mixture and fold into the egg whites mix. Pour in the remaining chocolate mixture and combine until smooth.
4. Pour the mousse into medium ramekins, cover with plastic wrap, and refrigerate overnight.

5. For the raspberry stew:
6. Set the IP in Saute mode and adjust to Medium heat.
7. Add all the stew's ingredients to the inner pot.
8. Lock the lid in place; select Manual mode on High Pressure and set the timer to 5 minutes.
9. After cooking, perform a natural pressure release for 10 minutes, then a quick pressure release to let out the remaining steam, and open the lid.
10. Stir the stew and allow complete cooling.
11. Top the chocolate mousse with the raspberry stew and serve.

Nutrition Info:
Per Serving: Calories 242 Fats 13g Carbs 2.6g Net Carbs 1.4g Protein 4.82g

Cardamom Cauliflower Rice Pudding

Servings: 4
Cooking Time: 12 Minutes
Ingredients:
- 1 ½ cups cauliflower rice
- 1 tsp cardamom powder
- ½ tsp nutmeg powder
- 1 tsp vanilla extract
- 1 tbsp unsalted butter
- ½ cup almond milk
- A pinch of salt
- 3 tbsp swerve sugar

Directions:
1. In the inner pot, mix all the ingredients.
2. Lock the lid in place; set in Manual mode on High Pressure and set the timer to minutes.
3. After cooking, perform a natural pressure release for 10 minutes, then a quick pressure release to let out the remaining steam, and open the lid.
4. Stir and adjust the taste with sugar.
5. Spoon into serving bowls and serve warm or chilled.

Nutrition Info:
Per Serving: Calories 267 Fats 21 g Carbs 45 g Net Carbs 75g Protein 9.87g

Easy Crème Brulee

Servings: 4
Cooking Time: 30 Mins
Ingredients:
- 3 cups Heavy Whipping Cream
- 6 tbsp Swerve Sugar
- 7 large Egg Yolks
- 2 tbsp Vanilla Extract

Directions:

1. In a mixing bowl, add yolks, vanilla, whipping cream, and half of the swerve sugar. Mix until well combined. Pour the mixture into ramekins. Fit trivet into the pot, and pour in cup of water. Place ramekins on the trivet.
2. Seal the lid, select Manual on High and cook for 8 minutes. Once ready, do a natural pressure release for 15 minutes, then a quick release to let out the remaining pressure.
3. Remove the ramekins onto a flat surface and then into a refrigerator to chill. Sprinkle the remaining sugar on and use a hand torch to brown the top of the crème brulee.

Nutrition Info: Calories 404, Protein 4.1g, Net Carbs 3.2g, Fat 1g

Zucchini Bundt Cake With Cream Cheese Frosting

Servings: 6
Cooking Time: 40 Minutes
Ingredients:
- Bundt Cake:
- 1 cup almond flour
- 1 cup Swerve
- 2 ounces cacao powder
- 1 teaspoon baking soda
- 1 teaspoon baking powder
- 1/4 teaspoon ground cinnamon
- 1/8 teaspoon grated nutmeg
- A pinch of salt
- 4 eggs plus 1 egg yolk
- 1 stick butter, softened
- 1/2 pound zucchini, puréed
- 1 teaspoon vanilla extract
- Frosting:
- 3 ounces cream cheese, softened
- 1/2 stick butter, softened
- 1 tablespoon milk
- 1 ½ teaspoons liquid stevia
- 1 ounce walnuts, chopped

Directions:
1. Start by adding ½ cups of water and a metal trivet to your Instant Pot. Spritz a 6-cup bundt pan with a nonstick cooking spray (butter-flavored.
2. Beat all ingredients for the cake using an electric mixer; beat on low speed for 40 seconds. Then, mix on medium speed for to 3 minutes longer.
3. Spoon the mixture into the prepared pan. Cover tightly with a piece of foil. Lower the pan onto the trivet.
4. Secure the lid. Choose "Manual" mode and High pressure; cook for 25 minutes. Once cooking is complete, use a natural pressure release; carefully remove the lid.

5. Allow your cake to cool for to 10 minutes before inverting onto a platter.
6. In a mixing bowl, combine cream cheese, butter, milk, and stevia using an electric mixer. Frost the cake, sprinkle with chopped walnuts, and serve well chilled. Enjoy!

Nutrition Info:
Per Serving: 352 Calories; 1g Fat; 9.1g Carbs; 9.2g Protein; 3.7g Sugars

Pumpkin Spice Cake

Servings: 4
Cooking Time: 50 Minutes
Ingredients:

- 5 eggs
- 1 ¼ cup almond flour
- ½ cup swerve sweetener
- 1 tsp baking powder
- 1 ½ tsp pumpkin pie spice
- ⅓ cup melted butter
- ½ cup heavy cream
- 1 cup pumpkin puree
- ⅓ cup walnuts, chopped

Directions:
1. Grease a 7-inch springform pan with cooking spray and set aside.
2. Mix all the ingredients in a medium bowl and pour the mixture into the cake pan; cover with foil.
3. Pour 2 cups of water into the inner pot, fit in a trivet, and place the cake pan on top.
4. Lock the lid in place; select Cake mode and set the timer for minutes.
5. Once done cooking, do a natural pressure release for 10 minutes, then a quick pressure release to let out the remaining steam, and open the lid.
6. Remove the pan, allow complete cooling, release the cake pan, and slice the cake.
7. Serve warm.

Nutrition Info:
Per Serving: Calories 604 Fats 95g Carbs 14 g Net Carbs 8.14g Protein 51g

Keto Choc Mousse

Servings: 6
Cooking Time: 15 Mins
Ingredients:

- ½ cup Cacao
- 1 cup Almond Milk
- 6 Egg Yolks
- ½ tsp Sea Salt
- 1 tsp Vanilla Extract
- 1 ½ cup Whipping Cream
- ½ cup Water

- ½ cup Erythritol Sweetener

Directions:
1. In a bowl, add the egg yolks and beat it. In a pan, add sweetener, cacao, and water. Whisk until the sweetener has fully melted. Add almond milk, and cream and whisk until fully combined. Transfer to the pot and set to Sauté. Heat up but do not boil. Mix in vanilla and salt. Add a tbsp of the chocolate mixture to the yolk, and slowly mix in the remaining chocolate mixture. Pour the mixture into ramekins.
2. Wipe the pot clean, place a trivet inside and pour in the water. Arrange the ramekins on top and seal the lid. Select Manual and cook on High Pressure for 6 minutes. Once ready, quickly release the pressure and remove ramekins using a napkin. Let to cool and refrigerate for 5h.

Nutrition Info: Calories 231, Protein 7.1g, Net Carbs 4.4g, Fat 12g

Sweet Porridge With A Twist

Servings: 2
Cooking Time: 10 Minutes
Ingredients:
- 1/2 cup coconut shreds
- 1 tablespoon sunflower seeds
- 2 tablespoons flax seeds
- 2 cardamom pods, crushed slightly
- 1 teaspoon ground cinnamon
- 1 teaspoon Stevia powdered extract
- 1 teaspoon rosewater
- 1/2 cup water
- 1 cup coconut milk

Directions:
1. Add all ingredients to the Instant Pot.
2. Secure the lid. Choose "Manual" mode and High pressure; cook for 5 minutes. Once cooking is complete, use a quick pressure release; carefully remove the lid.
3. Ladle into two serving bowls and serve warm. Enjoy!

Nutrition Info:
Per Serving: 363 Calories; 4g Fat; 6.2g Total Carbs; 4.9g Protein; 3.8g Sugars

Cream Cheese And Blackberries Mousse

Servings: 4
Cooking Time: 4 Minutes
Ingredients:
- 8 ounces cream cheese
- 1 teaspoon serve
- 1 cup heavy cream
- 1 tablespoon blackberries
- 1 cup water

Directions:

1. In a bowl, mix the cream with the other ingredients except the water, whisk well and divide into 2 ramekins. Put the water in the instant pot, add the steamer basket, put the ramekins inside, put the lid on and cook on High for 4 minutes. Release the pressure fast for 4 minutes and serve the mousse really cold.

Nutrition Info: calories 202, fat 5, fiber 0.1, carbs 1.7, protein 3.3

Lemon Curd

Servings: 3
Cooking Time: 30 Mins
Ingredients:

- 3 ounces Butter, at room temperature
- 1 ½ tsp Lime Zest
- ½ cup Lime Juice
- 1 cup Sweetener
- 2 Eggs plus 2 Egg Yolks
- 1 ½ cups Water

Directions:

1. Place sweetener and butter in a food processor; pulse for 2 minutes. Add in eggs and egg yolks, and mix for minute. Stir in zest and juice until the mixture is combined. Divide mixture between 3 mason jars. Pour the water in your Instant Pot and lower a trivet. Arrange the jars on the trivet and seal the lid. Select Manual and cook on High for 10 minutes. After the beep, allow for a natural pressure release.

Nutrition Info: Calories 223, Protein 8g, Net Carbs 5g, Fat 4g, Fiber 1.5g

Peanut Cheesecake

Servings: 4
Cooking Time: 8 Hours
Ingredients:

- 1 cup cream cheese
- 4 eggs, beaten
- 1 teaspoon vanilla extract
- ¼ cup of coconut milk
- 1 teaspoon coconut oil
- 1 tablespoon erythritol
- 2 oz peanuts, chopped
- 1 cup water, for cooking

Directions:

1. Mix up together cream cheese, eggs, vanilla extract, coconut milk, coconut oil, Erythritol, and peanuts.
2. Then pour the liquid in the instant pot baking pan. Flatten the surface of the cheesecake if desired.
3. Then pour water in the instant pot and insert the mold with cheesecake.

4. Close the lid and cook the dessert on "low" mode for 8 hours.

Nutrition Info:

Per Serving: calories 393, fat 6.3, fiber 1.5, carbs 8.9, protein 9

Special Peanut Cookies

Servings: 6

Cooking Time: 20 Minutes

Ingredients:

- 1/2 cup almond flour
- 1/2 cup coconut flour
- 1 ½ teaspoons baking powder
- A pinch of salt
- 1/2 cup Swerve
- 1 stick butter, melted
- 2 eggs, beaten
- 4 tablespoons full-fat milk
- 1/2 teaspoon ground cinnamon
- 1/4 teaspoon ground cardamom
- 1/2 teaspoon vanilla essence
- 1/3 cup white chocolate chunks, sugar-free
- 1/4 cup peanuts, chopped

Directions:

1. Start by adding ½ cups of water and a metal rack to the Instant Pot. Line a cake pan with a piece of parchment paper.
2. Mix almond flour, coconut flour, baking powder, salt, and Swerve until well combined.
3. Mix in the melted butter, eggs, milk, and spices; fold in the chocolate and peanuts and mix until everything is well incorporated.
4. Now, grab your dough, smoothen a little bit and roll it to 1/2-inch thickness. Then, cut down the cookies with a cookie cutter.
5. Arrange the cookies on the prepared cake pan and lower it onto the rack in your Instant Pot.
6. Secure the lid. Choose "Manual" mode and Low pressure; cook for 15 minutes. Once cooking is complete, use a natural pressure release; carefully remove the lid. Bon appétit!

Nutrition Info:

Per Serving: 295 Calories; 3g Fat; 4.6g Total Carbs; 7.7g Protein; 2.5g Sugars

Lime Muffins

Servings: 6

Cooking Time: 15 Minutes

Ingredients:

- 1 teaspoon lime zest
- 1 tablespoon lemon juice
- 1 teaspoon baking powder
- 1 cup almond flour

- 2 eggs, beaten
- 1 tablespoon swerve
- ¼ cup heavy cream
- 1 cup water, for cooking

Directions:
1. In the mixing bowl, mix up lemon juice, baking powder, almond flour, eggs, swerve, and heavy cream.
2. When the muffin batter is smooth, add lime zest and mix it up.
3. Fill the muffin molds with batter.
4. Then pour water and insert the rack in the instant pot.
5. Place the muffins on the rack. Close and seal the lid.
6. Cook the muffins on manual (high pressure) for 15 minutes.
7. Then allow the natural pressure release.

Nutrition Info:
Per Serving: calories 153, fat 2, fiber 2.1, carbs 5.1, protein 6

Lemony Ricotta Cake

Servings: 6
Cooking Time: 40 Mins
Ingredients:
- 8 ounces Cream Cheese
- ½ cup Ricotta Cheese
- ¼ cup Sweetener (Xylitol)
- 1 tsp Lemon Zest
- Juice of 1 Lemon
- 2 Eggs
- Topping:
- 1 tsp Sweetener
- 2 tbsp Sour Cream

Directions:
1. Pour in ½ cups water and lower trivet. Add cream cheese, ricotta, sweetener, zest, and juice in a bowl, and mix with an electric mixer until well-combined. Mix in eggs. Pour the batter into a greased springform. Place the pan on the trivet and seal the lid.
2. Select Manual and cook for 30 minutes on High. Do a quick pressure release. Whisk sour cream and sweetener, and spread over the cake.

Nutrition Info: Calories 183, Protein 5g, Net Carbs 2 g, Fat 16g

Chocolate Balls

Servings: 10
Cooking Time: 10 Minutes
Ingredients:
- 1 cup ghee, melted
- 3 tablespoons macadamia nuts, chopped

- ¼ cup stevia
- 5 tablespoons unsweetened coconut powder
- 2 tablespoons cocoa powder
- 1 cup water

Directions:

1. In a bowl, combine the ghee with the macadamia nuts and the rest of the ingredients except the water, whisk really well and shape medium balls out of this mix. Add the water to the instant pot, add the steamer basket, arrange the balls inside, put the lid on and cook on High for minutes. Release the pressure fast for 5 minutes and serve the balls cold.

Nutrition Info: calories 200, fat 4, fiber 0.5, carbs 0.9, protein 0.5

Orange-flavored Cake

Servings: 3
Cooking Time: 23 Mins
Ingredients:

- 2 Eggs
- 2 tsp Stevia
- 2 tbsp Orange zest
- 2 cups Heavy Cream
- 1 tbsp Vanilla extract
- 2 cups Almond flour

Directions:

1. Beat eggs and stevia in a bowl. Mix in orange zest, heavy cream, vanilla extract and flour. Pour the batter into a greased baking tray.
2. To your pot, add the trivet and pour in 1 cup of water. Place the baking dish inside, seal the lid and cook on High pressure for minutes. Once ready, allow the pressure to release naturally for 10 minutes. Remove the cake and let cool slightly, before slicing.

Nutrition Info: Calories 328, Protein 6.1g, Net Carbs 3.1g, Fat 8g

Keto Caramel Cheesecake

Servings: 4
Cooking Time: 50 Minutes + 1 Hour 20 Minutes Chilling
Ingredients:

- For the crust:
- 2 cups toasted almond flour
- 8 tbsp butter, melted
- 2 tbsp sugar-free maple syrup
- 2 tsp cinnamon powder
- 1 tsp vanilla extract
- 2 cups of water
- For the filling:
- 16 oz cream cheese, softened
- ½ cup stevia

- 2 tbsp almond flour
- 1 tsp vanilla extract
- 3 eggs
- 1 cup sugar-free caramel sauce

Directions:
1. Mix all the crust's ingredients in a medium bowl and spoon into a springform pan. Use the back of the spoon to press the mixture to fit onto the bottom of the pan. Chill in the refrigerator while you prepare the filling.
2. In a large bowl, using an electric hand mixer, whisk the cream cheese and stevia until smooth.
3. Add the almond flour gradually while mixing and then the vanilla until well combined. Beat in the eggs on low speed until adequately mixed.
4. Remove the cake pan from the fridge, pour in the filling, and cover with foil.
5. Pour 2 cups of water into the inner pot, fit in a trivet, and place the cake pan on top.
6. Lock the lid in place; select Manual mode on High Pressure and set the timer to 40 minutes.
7. After cooking, perform a natural pressure release for 10 minutes, then a quick pressure release to let out the remaining steam, and open the lid.
8. Carefully, remove the cake pan and take off the foil.
9. Allow cooling for 10 minutes, drizzle the caramel sauce on top and chill in the fridge for at least 1 hour.
10. Remove and release the cake pan, slice the cake, and serve.

Nutrition Info:
Per Serving: Calories 602 Fats 22g Carbs 5.8g Net Carbs 5g Protein 74g

Cinnamon Berries Custard

Servings: 4
Cooking Time: 15 Minutes
Ingredients:
- 3 eggs, whisked
- 2 cups coconut milk
- 1/3 cup swerve
- 1 tablespoon ghee, melted
- ½ cup heavy cream
- 1 tablespoon cinnamon powder
- ½ cup raspberries
- 1 teaspoon vanilla extract
- 1 and ½ cups water

Directions:
1. In a bowl, combine the eggs with the milk and the rest of the ingredients except the water, whisk well and transfer to a pan that fits the instant pot. Add the water to the instant pot, add the steamer basket, put the pan inside, put the lid on and cook on High for minutes. Release the pressure naturally for 10 minutes, divide the mix in bowls and serve really cold.

Nutrition Info: calories 1276, fat 7, fiber 2.4, carbs 6.2, protein 4.9

Peppermint Cookies

Servings: 2
Cooking Time: 5 Minutes
Ingredients:

- ¼ teaspoon peppermint extract
- 2 tablespoons almond flour
- 1 teaspoon heavy cream
- ½ teaspoon butter, softened
- ¼ oz dark chocolate

Directions:

1. Preheat the instant pot on sauté mode for 3 minutes. Then add almond flour, butter, and heavy cream. Add peppermint extract and dark chocolate. Saute the mixture for 2 minutes. Stir well. Then line the tray with baking paper. With the help of the spoon make the cookies from the peppermint mixture and transfer on the prepared baking paper. Refrigerate the cookies for 20 minutes.

Nutrition Info: calories 199, fat 1, fiber 3.3, carbs 8.1, protein 6.2

Romantic Rosewater Dessert Porridge

Servings: 2
Cooking Time: 10 Minutes
Ingredients:

- 1/2 cup coconut shreds
- 1 tablespoon sunflower seeds
- 2 tablespoons flax seeds
- 2 cardamom pods, crushed slightly
- 1 teaspoon ground cinnamon
- 1 teaspoon Stevia powdered extract
- 1 teaspoon rosewater
- 1/2 cup water
- 1 cup coconut milk

Directions:

1. Add all ingredients to the Instant Pot.
2. Secure the lid. Choose "Manual" mode and High pressure; cook for 5 minutes. Once cooking is complete, use a quick pressure release; carefully remove the lid.
3. Ladle into two serving bowls and serve warm. Enjoy!

Nutrition Info:
Per Serving: 363 Calories; 4g Fat; 9.2g Carbs; 4.9g Protein; 4.8g Sugars

Vanilla Blackberries Bowls

Servings: 4
Cooking Time: 10 Minutes
Ingredients:

- 2 teaspoons vanilla extract
- 3 cups blackberries
- 1 tablespoon swerve
- ½ cup coconut nectar

Directions:

1. In your instant pot, mix the blackberries with the vanilla and the rest of the ingredients, put the lid on and cook on High for minutes. Release the pressure naturally for 10 minutes, divide the mix into bowls and serve.

Nutrition Info: calories 70, fat 1, fiber 0.4, carbs 0.9, protein 1.6

Chocolate Squares With Chia Seeds

Servings: 4
Cooking Time: 10 Mins
Ingredients:

- 4 oz dark Chocolate, chopped
- 1 ½ tsp Stevia
- ½ tsp Vanilla Extract
- 4 tsp dried, diced Mango
- 2 tsp chopped Almonds
- ¼ tsp Chia seeds
- ¼ tsp Sea Salt
- Melted Butter to grease muffin cups

Directions:

1. Pour cup water and put steaming basket in the pot. Grease 4 ramekins with butter. Add the chocolate, stevia, and vanilla in a bowl; then pour in the ramekins and sprinkle the rest of the ingredients. Line the ramekins in the steaming basket. Seal the lid and cook on High pressure on Manual for 10 minutes. When the timer beeps, quick release the pressure and serve chilled.

Nutrition Info: Calories 215, Protein 1g, Net Carbs 9.1g, Fat 14g

Coconut Clouds

Servings: 2
Cooking Time: 6 Minutes
Ingredients:

- 2 egg whites
- 4 tablespoons coconut flakes
- 1 tablespoon almond meal
- ¼ teaspoon ghee
- 1 teaspoon Erythritol

Directions:

1. Whisk the egg whites until strong peaks. Then slowly add the almond meal and coconut flakes. Add Erythritol and stir the mixture until homogenous with the help of the silicone spatula. Toss ghee in the instant pot and preheat it on sauté mode for 2 minutes. Then with

the help of the spoon, make the clouds from egg white mixture and put them in the hot ghee. Close the lid and cook the dessert on sauté mode for 4 minutes.

Nutrition Info: calories 74, fat 5.4, fiber 1.3, carbs 2.4, protein 4.6

Vanilla And Cocoa Cream

Servings: 4
Cooking Time: 5 Minutes
Ingredients:

- 1 and ½ cups heavy cream
- 3 tablespoons swerve
- 2 tablespoons cocoa powder
- 1 teaspoon vanilla extract
- 1 and ½ cups water

Directions:

1. In a bowl, combine the heavy cream with the rest of the ingredients except the water, whisk well and divide into 4 ramekins. Put the water in the instant pot, add the steamer basket, put the ramekins inside, put the lid on and cook on High for 5 minutes. Release the pressure fast for 5 minutes and serve the cream cold.

Nutrition Info: calories 216, fat 6, fiber 0.8, carbs 3.3, protein 1.7

Fluffy Brulee

Servings: 3
Cooking Time: 9 Minutes
Ingredients:

- 1 cup coconut cream
- 4 egg yolks
- 2 teaspoons Erythritol
- 1 cup of water (for instant pot)

Directions:

1. Whisk the egg yolk until you get the yellow color.
2. Then add coconut cream and keep whisking the egg yolk mixture until smooth.
3. Add 1 teaspoon of Erythritol. Stir it well and transfer into the ramekins.
4. Pour 1 cup of water in the instant pot bowl. Place the steamer rack inside the instant pot.
5. Transfer the ramekins on the rack and wrap the top of ramekins with the foil.
6. Set the "Manual" mode (High pressure) and cook the dessert for 9 minutes.
7. Allow the natural pressure release for 15 minutes.
8. Chill the dessert for 2 hours.

Nutrition Info:
Per Serving: calories 256, fat 1, fiber 1.8, carbs 8.6, protein 5.4

Creamy Rice Pudding

Servings: 4

Cooking Time: 20 Minutes
Ingredients:
- 2 cups cream cheese, soft
- 2 cups heavy cream
- 3 tablespoons swerve
- 2 cups cauliflower rice
- 1 teaspoon lemon zest, grated
- 1 cup water

Directions:
1. In a bowl, whisk the cream with the cream cheese and the rest of the ingredients except the water, whisk really well and divide into 4 ramekins. Put the water in your instant pot, add the steamer basket, put the ramekins inside, put the lid on and cook on High for 20 minutes. Release the pressure naturally for minutes and serve the puddings warm.

Nutrition Info: calories 306, fat 4, fiber 0, carbs 2.4, protein 5

Coconut Crack Bars

Servings: 4
Cooking Time: 8 Minutes
Ingredients:
- 1 cup unsweetened coconut flakes
- 4 tablespoons coconut oil
- 1 egg, beaten
- 2 tablespoons coconut flour
- 2 tablespoons monk fruit

Directions:
1. In the mixing bowl combine together 3 tablespoons of coconut oil, coconut flour, egg, and coconut flakes. Then add monk fruit and stir the mixture well with the help of the spoon. The prepared mixture should be homogenous. After this, toss the remaining coconut oil in the instant pot and heat it up on sauté mode. Meanwhile, make the small bars from the coconut mixture. Place them in the hot coconut oil in one layer and cook for minute from each side. Dry the cooked coconut bars with a paper towel if needed.

Nutrition Info: calories 218, fat 2, fiber 3.3, carbs 6.1, protein 2.9

Mint And Coconut Mousse

Servings: 4
Cooking Time: 30 Minutes + Chilling Time
Ingredients:
- 1 ¼ cups coconut milk, unsweetened
- 4 eggs
- 1/2 cup Swerve, powdered
- 4 tablespoons coconut, shredded
- 4 drops mint extract

Directions:

1. Start by adding ½ cups of water and a metal rack to your Instant Pot.
2. In a mixing bowl, thoroughly combine all of the above ingredients. Pour the mixture into four Mason jars. Cover with their lids.
3. Secure the lid. Choose "Manual" mode and High pressure; cook for 25 minutes. Once cooking is complete, use a natural pressure release; carefully remove the lid.
4. Serve well chilled and enjoy!

Nutrition Info:
Per Serving: 271 Calories; 4g Fat; 5.9g Carbs; 7.5g Protein; 3.2g Sugars

Strawberries And Pecans Cream

Servings: 4
Cooking Time: 10 Minutes
Ingredients:
- 4 ounces strawberries
- 4 ounces coconut cream
- 1 cup stevia
- 1 teaspoon vanilla extract
- 2 tablespoons pecans, chopped
- 1 and ½ cups water

Directions:
1. In a bowl, mix the strawberries with the cream and the other ingredients except the water, whisk well and divide into 4 ramekins. Add the water to your instant pot, add the steamer basket, add the ramekins inside, put the lid on and cook on High for minutes. Release the pressure naturally for 10 minutes, and serve cold.

Nutrition Info: calories 129, fat 8, fiber 2.3, carbs 5.1, protein 1.6

Macadamia Cookies

Servings: 4
Cooking Time: 13 Minutes
Ingredients:
- 1 oz macadamia nuts, chopped
- ½ cup coconut flour
- 2 tablespoons butter
- 1 tablespoon Erythritol
- 1 egg, beaten
- 2 tablespoons flax meal
- 1 cup water, for cooking

Directions:
1. In the mixing bowl mix up macadamia nuts, coconut flour, butter, Erythritol, egg, and flax meal. Knead the non-sticky dough. Then cut the dough into the pieces and make balls from them. Pour water and insert the trivet in the instant pot. Line the trivet with baking paper and put the dough balls on it. Cook the cookies for minutes on manual mode (high pressure). When the time is over, make a quick pressure release and transfer the cookies on the plate.

Nutrition Info: calories 193, fat 5, fiber 6.6, carbs 1, protein 4.8

Berry Chocolate Cream

Servings: 4
Cooking Time: 10 Minutes
Ingredients:

- 2 cups heavy cream
- 4 ounces chocolate, cut into chunks and melted
- 1 teaspoon stevia
- 1 cup blackberries
- 2 cups water

Directions:

1. In a bowl, mix the heavy cream with the chocolate and the rest of the ingredients except the water, whisk well and divide into ramekins. Put the water in your instant pot, add the steamer basket, add the ramekins inside, put the lid on and cook on High for minutes. Release the pressure fast for 5 minutes, and serve the cream cold.

Nutrition Info: calories 360, fat 2, fiber 2.9, carbs 6.4, protein 3.9

Exotic Coconut Idli

Servings: 6
Cooking Time: 20 Minutes
Ingredients:

- 1/2 cup almond flour
- 1/2 cup coconut flour
- 1 teaspoon baking powder
- 1/2 cup powdered Swerve
- A pinch of kosher salt
- 1/4 teaspoon ginger powder
- 1/2 teaspoon cardamom powder
- 1 teaspoon vanilla essence
- 2 tablespoons coconut oil
- 1 cup cream cheese, room temperature
- 1/4 cup lukewarm water
- 1/4 cup coconut flakes

Directions:

1. Start by adding ½ cups of water to the Instant Pot.
2. Mix almond flour, coconut flour, baking powder, Swerve, salt, ginger powder, and cardamom powder, and vanilla until well combined.
3. Mix in the coconut oil, cream cheese, and water; mix until everything is well incorporated.
4. Now, spread your batter onto the prepared idli molds; lower it onto the bottom of your Instant Pot.
5. Secure the lid. Choose "Manual" mode and Low pressure; cook for 12 minutes. Once cooking is complete, use a natural pressure release; carefully remove the lid.

6. Allow your idlis to cool completely. Sprinkle with coconut flakes and enjoy!

Nutrition Info:

Per Serving: 257 Calories; 9g Fat; 6.1g Carbs; 4.3g Protein; 3.3g Sugars

Yummy Keto Flan

Servings: 5

Cooking Time: 20 Minutes

Ingredients:

- 5 large eggs
- 1 cup Swerve
- 1 cup heavy cream
- 1/2 cup water
- ½ teaspoon salt
- 1/4 teaspoon ground cinnamon
- 1 teaspoon vanilla extract

Directions:

1. Add 2 cups of water and a metal rack to your Instant Pot.
2. In a large bowl combine eggs and Swerve. Stir in salt, vanilla, water, cinnamon, and double cream.
3. Pour mixture into a baking dish and lower the dish onto the rack.
4. Secure the lid. Choose "Manual" mode and High pressure; cook for 11 minutes. When cooking is complete, use a natural pressure release and carefully remove the lid.
5. Leave to cool and serve. Enjoy!

Nutrition Info:

Per Serving: 140 Calories; 4g Fat; 1.3g Carbs; 4.6g Protein; 0.8g Sugars

Cinnamon Muffins

Servings: 4

Cooking Time: 18 Minutes

Ingredients:

- 4 teaspoons cream cheese
- 1 teaspoon ground cinnamon
- 1 tablespoon butter, softened
- 1 egg, beaten
- 4 teaspoons almond flour
- ½ teaspoon baking powder
- 1 teaspoon lemon juice
- 2 scoops stevia
- ¼ teaspoon vanilla extract
- 1 cup of water, for cooking

Directions:

1. In the big bowl make the muffins batter: mix up together cream cheese, ground cinnamon, butter, egg, almond flour, baking powder, lemon juice, stevia, and vanilla extract. When the

mixture is smooth and thick, pour it into the 4 muffin molds. Then pour the water in the instant pot and insert the trivet. Place the muffins on the trivet and close the lid. Cook them for minutes on Manual mode (high pressure). When the time is over, make a quick pressure release and cool the cooked muffins well.

Nutrition Info: calories 216, fat 2, fiber 3.3, carbs 7, protein 7.7

Cocoa Cookie

Servings: 4
Cooking Time: 25 Minutes
Ingredients:
- ½ cup coconut flour
- 3 tablespoons cream cheese
- 1 teaspoon of cocoa powder
- 1 tablespoon Erythritol
- ¼ teaspoon baking powder
- 1 teaspoon apple cider vinegar
- 1 tablespoon butter
- 1 cup water, for cooking

Directions:
1. Make the dough: mix up coconut flour, cream cheese, cocoa powder, Erythritol, baking powder, apple cider vinegar, and butter. Knead the dough,
2. Then transfer the dough in the baking pan and flatten it in the shape of a cookie.
3. Pour water and insert the steamer rack in the instant pot.
4. Put the pan with a cookie in the instant pot. Close and seal the lid.
5. Cook the cookie on manual (high pressure) for 2minutes. Make a quick pressure release. Cool the cookie well.

Nutrition Info:
Per Serving: calories 113, fat 7.1, fiber 6.1, carbs 4, protein 2.7

Old-school Zucchini Cake

Servings: 6
Cooking Time: 35 Minutes
Ingredients:
- 1 cup almond flour
- A pinch of table salt
- 1 ½ teaspoons baking powder
- 1 teaspoon pumpkin pie spice
- 2/3 cup Swerve, powdered
- 2 eggs, beaten
- 3 tablespoons coconut oil
- 1/2 cup double cream
- 1/2 pound zucchini, shredded, drained and squeezed dry
- 1 teaspoon vanilla paste

- 1/4 cup walnuts, chopped
- Frosting:
- 4 ounces mascarpone cheese, room temperature
- 1/4 cup coconut oil, softened
- 1 ½ cups Swerve powdered

Directions:
1. Start by adding ½ cups of water and a metal rack to the Instant Pot. Now, lightly grease a cake pan with a nonstick cooking spray.
2. In a mixing bowl, thoroughly combine almond flour, salt, baking powder, and pumpkin pie spice.
3. Then, thoroughly combine Swerve, eggs, coconut oil, cream, zucchini and vanilla using an electric mixer
4. With the machine running on low, gradually add the prepared dry mixture; mix until everything is well combined.
5. Fold in the chopped walnuts. Spoon the batter into the prepared cake pan. Cover the pan with paper towels; then, top with a piece of aluminum foil making a foil sling.
6. Lower the pan onto the rack.
7. Secure the lid. Choose "Manual" mode and Low pressure; cook for 30 minutes. Once cooking is complete, use a natural pressure release; carefully remove the lid.
8. In the meantime, beat the cheese, 1/4 cup of coconut oil, and Swerve until well combined. Frost the cake and serve well chilled. Enjoy!

Nutrition Info:
Per Serving: 359 Calories; 1g Fat; 3.6g Total Carbs; 8g Protein; 1.9g Sugars

Cashew Nut Sauce

Servings:4
Cooking Time: 15 Minutes
Ingredients:
- ¼ cup swerve brown sugar
- 3 tbsp water
- 3 tbsp unsalted butter
- 1 ½ cups coconut cream
- 1 tbsp white wine
- 1 cup finely chopped cashew nuts

Directions:
1. Set the IP in Sauté mode and adjust to Medium heat.
2. Combine the swerve brown sugar and water in the inner pot and cook until the sugar dissolves while continuously stirring, 3 minutes.
3. Mix in the butter, coconut cream, and white wine.
4. Lock the lid in place; select Manual mode on High Pressure and set the timer to 2 minutes.
5. After cooking, perform a quick pressure release for 10 minutes, and open the lid.
6. Mix in the cashews and spoon the sauce into serving cups.
7. You may puree the sauce for smoother consistency

Nutrition Info:

Per Serving: Calories 511 Fats 99g Carbs 24g Net Carbs 04g Protein 35g

Healthy Breakfast Wraps

Servings: 4
Cooking Time: 10 Minutes
Ingredients:

- 4 eggs, whisked
- 1/3 cup double cream
- 2 ounces Mozzarella cheese, crumbled
- 1/3 teaspoon red pepper flakes, crushed
- Salt, to taste
- 8 leaves of Looseleaf lettuce

Directions:

1. Begin by adding cup of water and a metal rack to your Instant Pot. Spritz a baking dish with a nonstick cooking spray.
2. Then, thoroughly combine the eggs, double cream, cheese, red pepper, and salt. Spoon this combination into the baking dish.
3. Secure the lid. Choose "Manual" mode and High pressure; cook for minutes. Once cooking is complete, use a natural pressure release; carefully remove the lid.
4. Divide the egg mixture among lettuce leaves, wrap each leaf, and serve immediately. Bon appétit!

Nutrition Info:
Per Serving: 202 Calories; 7g Fat; 4.7g Total Carbs; 4g Protein; 2.6g Sugars

Indian Style Egg Muffins

Servings: 5
Cooking Time: 10 Minutes
Ingredients:

- 5 eggs
- Seasoned salt and ground black pepper, to taste
- 2 green chilies, minced
- 5 tablespoons feta cheese, crumbled
- 1/2 tablespoon Chaat masala powder
- 1 tablespoon fresh cilantro, finely chopped

Directions:

1. Begin by adding cup of water and a steamer basket to your Instant Pot.
2. Mix all ingredients together; then, spoon the egg/cheese mixture into silicone muffin cups.
3. Next, lower your muffin cups onto the steamer basket.
4. Secure the lid. Choose "Manual" mode and High pressure; cook for 7 minutes. Once cooking is complete, use a quick pressure release; carefully remove the lid.
5. Let your muffins sit for a few minutes before removing from the cups; serve warm. Bon appétit!

Nutrition Info:

Per Serving: 202 Calories; 7g Fat; 4.7g Total Carbs; 4g Protein; 2.6g Sugars

Enchilada Sauce

Servings:4
Cooking Time: 2 Minutes
Ingredients:

- 3 tbsp olive oil
- 3 tbsp almond flour
- Salt and black pepper to taste
- 2 tbsp unsweetened tomato paste
- 2 tsp chili powder
- 1 tsp cumin powder
- ¼ tsp dried oregano
- ½ tsp garlic powder
- 2 cups vegetable broth
- 1 tsp white vinegar

Directions:

1. Set the IP in Sauté mode and adjust to Medium heat.
2. Heat the olive oil in the inner pot and cook in almond flour until golden, 1 minute.
3. Stir in the remaining ingredients until smooth.
4. Lock the lid in place; select Manual mode on High Pressure and set the timer to 1 minute.
5. After cooking, perform a quick pressure release to let out the steam and open the lid.
6. Spoon the sauce into preservation jars and use immediately.
7. Preserve extras in the refrigerator for later use.

Nutrition Info:
Per Serving: Calories 303 Fats 42g Carbs 5.57g Net Carbs 3.42g Protein 63g

Creamy Cheddar Muffins

Servings: 4
Cooking Time: 10 Minutes
Ingredients:

- 6 eggs
- 4 tablespoons double cream
- Sea salt and ground black pepper, to taste
- 1 cup Swiss chard, chopped
- 1 red bell pepper, chopped
- 1/2 cup white onion, chopped
- 1/2 cup Cheddar cheese, grated

Directions:

1. Begin by adding cup of water and a metal rack to the Instant Pot.
2. Mix all of the above ingredients. Then, fill silicone muffin cups about 3 full.
3. Then, place muffin cups on the rack.

4. Secure the lid. Choose "Manual" mode and High pressure; cook for 7 minutes. Once cooking is complete, use a natural pressure release; carefully remove the lid. Enjoy!

Nutrition Info:

Per Serving: 207 Calories; 8g Fat; 4.9g Total Carbs; 4g Protein; 2.7g Sugars

Classic Bbq Sauce

Servings: 4

Cooking Time: 14 Minutes

Ingredients:

- 3 tbsp olive oil
- 1 medium brown onion, finely chopped
- 6 garlic cloves, minced
- 2 cups unsweetened tomato ketchup
- ½ cup swerve brown sugar
- 2 tbsp chili powder
- ½ cup apple cider vinegar
- 4 tbsp Worcestershire sauce
- Salt and black pepper to taste

Directions:

1. Set the IP in Sauté mode and adjust to Medium heat.
2. Heat the olive oil in the inner pot and stir-fry the onion until softened, 3 minutes. Stir in the garlic and cook until fragrant, 30 seconds.
3. Mix in the remaining ingredients.
4. Lock the lid in place; select Manual mode on High Pressure and set the timer to 5 minutes.
5. After cooking, perform a natural pressure release for minutes, then a quick pressure release to let out the remaining steam, and open the lid.
6. Stir the sauce, turn the IP off, and allow cooling.
7. Spoon the sauce into jars, cover, and refrigerate for later use.
8. Use for up to a month.

Nutrition Info:

Per Serving: Calories 392 Fats 52g Carbs 8.62g Net Carbs 8.12g Protein 94g

Breakfast Eggs De Provence

Servings: 4

Cooking Time: 10 Mins

Ingredients:

- 1 ½ cups cream cheese
- 3 large eggs
- ½-pound cooked ham, diced
- 1 red onion, chopped
- 1 cup cheddar cheese
- 1 ½ cup chopped kale leaves
- 1 tsp Herbes de Provence

- 1/8 tsp. sea salt
- 1/8 tsp. pepper

Directions:
1. In a bowl, beat cream cheese and eggs until well blended; stir in the remaining ingredients and pour the mixture into an instant pot. Lock lid and set it to manual high setting. Cook for Mins and then release the pressure naturally.
2. Serve hot with a glass of fresh orange juice.

Nutrition Info:
Per Serving: Calories: 585; Total Fat: 6g; Carbs: 7.5g; Protein: 5g

Coconut Porridge With Berries

Servings: 2
Cooking Time: 10 Minutes
Ingredients:
- 4 tablespoons coconut flour
- 1 tablespoon sunflower seeds
- 3 tablespoons flax meal
- 1 ¼ cups water
- 1/4 teaspoon coarse salt
- 1/4 teaspoon grated nutmeg
- 1/2 teaspoon ground cardamom
- 2 eggs, beaten
- 2 tablespoons coconut oil, softened
- 2 tablespoons Swerve
- 1/2 cup mixed berries, fresh or frozen (thawed

Directions:
1. Add all ingredients, except for mixed berries, to the Instant Pot.
2. Secure the lid. Choose "Manual" mode and High pressure; cook for 5 minutes. Once cooking is complete, use a quick pressure release; carefully remove the lid.
3. Divide between two bowls, top with berries, and serve hot. Bon appétit!

Nutrition Info:
Per Serving: 242 Calories; 7g Fat; 7.9g Carbs; 7.6g Protein; 2.8g Sugars

Bake With Pork And Green Bean

Servings: 6
Cooking Time: 30 Minutes
Ingredients:
- 1 pound ground pork
- 1 yellow onion, thinly sliced
- 2 garlic cloves, smashed
- 1 green bell pepper, thinly sliced
- 1 red bell pepper, thinly sliced
- 1 habanero chili pepper, thinly sliced

- 1 cup green beans
- 3 ripe tomatoes, chopped
- 1/2 teaspoon cumin, ground
- Salt and ground black pepper, to taste
- 1/2 teaspoon cayenne pepper
- 1 cup Colby cheese, shredded
- 2 tablespoons fresh chives, chopped

Directions:

1. Start by adding ½ cups of water and a metal rack to the bottom of your Instant Pot.
2. Mix the pork, onion, garlic, pepper, green beans, tomatoes, cumin, salt, black pepper, and cayenne pepper until well combined.
3. Pour the mixture into a lightly greased casserole dish that will fit in your Instant Pot. Then, lower the dish onto the rack.
4. Secure the lid. Choose "Manual" mode and Low pressure; cook for 20 minutes. Once cooking is complete, use a quick pressure release; carefully remove the lid.
5. Top with Colby cheese and cover with the lid. Let it sit in a residual heat an additional 7 to 10 minutes.
6. Serve garnished with fresh chives. Bon appétit!

Nutrition Info:
Per Serving: 348 Calories; 1g Fat; 6.6g Total Carbs; 3g Protein; 3.4g Sugars

Broccoli With Asiago Cheese

Servings: 4
Cooking Time: 12 Minutes
Ingredients:

- 1 tablespoon olive oil
- 2 tablespoons green onion, chopped
- 4 cloves garlic, pressed
- 1 pound broccoli, broken into florets
- 1 cup water
- 2 chicken bouillon cubes
- Sea salt and ground black pepper, to taste
- 3/4 cup Asiago cheese, shredded

Directions:

1. Press the "Sauté" button to heat up your Instant Pot. Now, heat the oil and sweat green onions for 2 minutes.
2. Stir in the garlic and continue to sauté an additional 30 seconds. Add broccoli, water, bouillon cubes, salt, and black pepper.
3. Secure the lid. Choose "Manual" mode and High pressure; cook for 7 minutes. Once cooking is complete, use a natural pressure release; carefully remove the lid.
4. Top with shredded cheese and serve immediately. Bon appétit!

Nutrition Info:
Per Serving: 160 Calories; 7g Fat; 5.3g Carbs; 1g Protein; 0.9g Sugars

Keto Muffins

Servings: 6
Cooking Time: 10 Minutes
Ingredients:

- 6 eggs
- 1/4 cup almond milk, unsweetened
- 1/2 teaspoon salt
- A pinch of ground allspice
- 1/2 teaspoon Mexican oregano
- 1/4 cup green onions, chopped
- 1 tomato, chopped
- 1 ½ cups bell peppers, chopped
- 1 jalapeño pepper, seeded and minced
- 1/2 cup Cotija cheese, crumbled

Directions:

1. Prepare your Instant Pot by adding ½ cups of water to the inner pot.
2. Spritz six ovenproof custard cups with a nonstick cooking spray.
3. In a mixing dish, thoroughly combine the eggs, milk, salt, allspice, and Mexican oregano; mix to combine well.
4. Add green onions, tomato, bell peppers, and jalapeño pepper to the custard cups. Pour the egg mixture over them. Top with cheese.
5. Lower 3 custard cups onto a metal trivet; then, place the second trivet on top. Lower the remaining 3 cups onto it.
6. Secure the lid. Choose "Manual" mode and High pressure; cook for 7 minutes. Once cooking is complete, use a quick pressure release; carefully remove the lid. Serve at room temperature.

Nutrition Info:
Per Serving: 189 Calories; 4g Fat; 4.3g Total Carbs; 5g Protein; 2.8g Sugars

Chocolate Fudge Sauce

Servings: 4
Cooking Time: 4 Minutes
Ingredients:

- 2 cups heavy cream
- 3 tbsp swerve sugar
- 4 tbsp unsalted butter
- ¼ cup unsweetened white chocolate, chopped
- 2 tbsp dry white wine

Directions:

1. In the inner pot, add all the ingredients.
2. Lock the lid in place, select Manual mode on High Pressure and set the timer to 4 minutes.
3. After cooking, perform a quick pressure release to let out the steam, and open the lid.
4. Whisk the white wine into the mixture and pour into a serving jar.

5. Use immediately.

Nutrition Info:

Per Serving: Calories 354 Fats 77g Carbs 1.39g Net Carbs 0.99g Protein 64g

Tender Pork Steaks With Sausages And Sauerkraut

Servings: 6
Cooking Time: 35 Minutes
Ingredients:

- 2 pounds blade pork steaks
- Sea salt and ground black pepper, to taste
- 1/2 teaspoon cayenne pepper
- 1/2 teaspoon dried parsley flakes
- 1 tablespoon lard
- 1 ½ cups water
- 2 cloves garlic, thinly sliced
- 2 pork sausages, casing removed and sliced
- 4 cups sauerkraut

Directions:

1. Season the blade pork steaks with salt, black pepper, cayenne pepper, and dried parsley.
2. Press the "Sauté" button to heat up the Instant Pot. Melt the lard and sear blade pork steaks until delicately browned on all sides.
3. Wipe down the Instant Pot with a damp cloth; add water and metal rack to the bottom of your Instant Pot.
4. Place your blade pork steaks on the rack. Make small slits over entire pork with a tip of sharp knife. Now, insert garlic pieces into each slit.
5. Secure the lid. Choose the "Soup/Broth" setting and cook for 30 minutes under High pressure. Once cooking is complete, use a natural pressure release; carefully remove the lid.
6. Then, add the sausage and sauerkraut. Press the "Sauté" button and cook for a couple of minutes more or until heated through. Enjoy!

Nutrition Info:

Per Serving: 471 Calories; 3g Fat; 6.4g Total Carbs; 7g Protein; 2g Sugars

Eggs, Cheese, And Mortadella Roll-ups

Servings: 4
Cooking Time: 10 Minutes
Ingredients:

- 2 teaspoons butter, at room temperature
- 4 eggs
- Salt and red pepper, to taste
- 1/2 cup Cheddar cheese, shredded
- 8 slices mortadella

- 1/4 cup mayonnaise
- 1 tablespoon Dijon mustard
- 8 leaves of Romaine lettuce

Directions:

1. Press the "Sauté" button to heat up your Instant Pot. Now, warm the butter.
2. Add the eggs and stir them with a wooden spoon until the eggs are softly set. Add the salt, red pepper, and cheese.
3. Continue to cook an additional 40 seconds or until the cheese is melted. Turn off the Instant Pot.
4. Now, divide the egg/cheese mixture among mortadella slices; add mayo and mustard. Add one leaf of lettuce to each roll.
5. Create roll-ups and use toothpicks to secure them. Serve immediately and enjoy!

Nutrition Info:

Per Serving: 298 Calories; 2g Fat; 3.6g Carbs; 7g Protein; 1.3g Sugars

Egg Salad "sandwich"

Servings: 4
Cooking Time: 25 Minutes
Ingredients:

- 6 eggs
- 1/2 cup tablespoons mayonnaise
- 1 teaspoon Dijon mustard
- 1/2 cup cream cheese
- 1 cup baby spinach
- Salt and ground black pepper, to taste
- 2 red bell peppers, sliced into halves
- 2 green bell pepper, sliced into halves

Directions:

1. Place cup of water and a steamer basket in your Instant Pot. Next, place the eggs in the steamer basket.
2. Secure the lid. Choose "Manual" mode and Low pressure; cook for 5 minutes. Once cooking is complete, use a quick pressure release; carefully remove the lid.
3. Allow the eggs to cool for 15 minutes. Chop the eggs and combine them with mayonnaise, Dijon mustard, cheese, and baby spinach.
4. Season with salt and pepper. Divide the mixture between four bell pepper "sandwiches". Serve well chilled and enjoy!

Nutrition Info:

Per Serving: 406 Calories; 37g Fat; 7.3g Carbs; 6g Protein; 4.2g Sugars

Gouda Cheesy Vegan Sauce

Servings: 2 Cups
Cooking Time:45 Mins
Ingredients:

- 2 cups Yellow Onion, diced
- 2 small Zucchinis, chopped
- ½ cup Daikon, chopped
- 1 small Cauliflower, cut into florets
- 4 clove Garlic, peeled
- 2 ½ cups Water, shared in 2
- 1 cup raw Cashews, soaked for 10 minutes in Water
- 1 cup Nutritional Yeast
- Salt to taste
- 2 tbsp Smoked Paprika
- 3 tbsp Plain Vinegar

Directions:
1. Add all ingredients to the Instant Pot, seal the lid, select Manual and cook on High Pressure for 4 minutes. When ready, quickly release the pressure. Allow to cool for minutes; then puree using a stick blender. Scoop into an airtight container.

Nutrition Info: Calories 90, Protein 2g, Net Carbs 1g, Fat 8 g

Shirred Eggs With Peppers And Scallions

Servings: 4
Cooking Time: 10 Minutes
Ingredients:
- 4 tablespoons butter, melted
- 4 tablespoons double cream
- 4 eggs
- 4 scallions, chopped
- 2 red peppers, seeded and chopped
- 1/2 teaspoon granulated garlic
- 1/4 teaspoon dill weed
- 1/4 teaspoon sea salt
- 1/4 teaspoon freshly ground pepper

Directions:
1. Start by adding cup of water and a metal rack to the Instant Pot.
2. Grease the bottom and sides of each ramekin with melted butter. Divide the ingredients among the prepared four ramekins.
3. Lower the ramekins onto the metal rack.
4. Secure the lid. Choose "Manual" mode and High pressure; cook for 5 minutes. Once cooking is complete, use a natural pressure release; carefully remove the lid. Bon appétit!

Nutrition Info:
Per Serving: 208 Calories; 7g Fat; 3.9g Carbs; 6.7g Protein; 2.3g Sugars

Holiday Bacon And Leek Quiche

Servings: 6
Cooking Time: 35 Minutes

Ingredients:
- 4 slices Canadian bacon, chopped
- 1 cup leeks, chopped
- 1 garlic clove, minced
- 8 eggs
- 1/2 cup half-and-half
- 1/2 cup cream cheese, room temperature
- Seasoned salt and ground black pepper, to taste
- 1 tablespoon dried sage, crushed
- 1/2 teaspoon marjoram
- 1/2 cup Swiss cheese, freshly grated

Directions:
1. Press the "Sauté" button to heat up your Instant Pot. Once hot, cook the bacon until crisp and browned.
2. Add the leeks and garlic and cook 1 minute more. Add the eggs, half-and-half, cream cheese, salt, black pepper, sage and marjoram.
3. Grease a baking pan with a nonstick cooking spray. Spoon the bacon/egg mixture into the prepared baking pan.
4. Now, add 1 cup of water and a metal trivet to the Instant Pot; lower the baking pan onto the trivet.
5. Secure the lid. Choose "Meat/Stew" mode and High pressure; cook for 2minutes. Once cooking is complete, use a quick pressure release; carefully remove the lid.
6. Add Swiss cheese and cover with the lid; let it sit in the residual heat for 5 minutes. Serve with Dijon mustard.

Nutrition Info:
Per Serving: 231 Calories; 2g Fat; 6.9g Total Carbs; 5g Protein; 3.1g Sugars

Simple Pork Steak With Curry

Servings: 6
Cooking Time: 15 Minutes
Ingredients:
- 1/2 teaspoon mustard seeds
- 1 teaspoon fennel seeds
- 1 teaspoon cumin seeds
- 2 chili peppers, seeded and minced
- 1/2 teaspoon ground bay leaf
- 1 teaspoon mixed peppercorns
- 1 tablespoon sesame oil
- 1 ½ pounds pork steak, sliced
- 1 cup chicken broth
- 2 tablespoons scallions, chopped
- 2 cloves garlic, finely minced
- 1 teaspoon fresh ginger, grated

- 1 teaspoon curry powder
- 2 tablespoons balsamic vinegar
- 3 tablespoons coconut cream
- 1/4 teaspoon ground black pepper
- 1/4 teaspoon red pepper flakes, crushed
- Sea salt, to taste

Directions:
1. Heat a cast-iron skillet over medium-high heat. Once hot, roast mustard seeds, fennel seeds, cumin, peppers, ground bay leaf and peppercorns until aromatic.
2. Press the "Sauté" button to heat up the Instant Pot. Heat the sesame oil until sizzling. Then, sear pork steak until delicately browned.
3. Add the remaining ingredients, including roasted seasonings; stir well.
4. Add vegetable broth and secure the lid. Choose the "Manual" setting and cook for 8 minutes under High pressure.
5. Once cooking is complete, use a quick pressure release; carefully remove the lid. Ladle into individual serving bowls and enjoy!

Nutrition Info:
Per Serving: 362 Calories; 2g Fat; 2.2g Total Carbs; 6g Protein; 0.9g Sugars

Green Beans With Feta And Eggs

Servings: 4
Cooking Time: 10 Minutes
Ingredients:
- 2 tablespoons olive oil
- 2 garlic cloves, pressed
- 1 pound green beans, sliced
- 4 eggs, slightly whisked
- Salt and freshly ground black pepper, to taste
- 1 cup stock, preferably homemade
- 1 cup feta cheese, crumbled

Directions:
1. Press the "Sauté" button to heat up your Instant Pot. Now, heat the olive oil until sizzling.
2. Once hot, stir in garlic and cook for 40 seconds or until fragrant. Add green beans, eggs, salt, pepper, and stock.
3. Secure the lid. Choose "Manual" mode and Low pressure; cook for minutes. Once cooking is complete, use a quick pressure release; carefully remove the lid.
4. Afterwards, add feta cheese and serve immediately.

Nutrition Info:
Per Serving: 249 Calories; 4g Fat; 6.2g Total Carbs; 2g Protein; 2.6g Sugars

Red Wine & Onion Sauce

Servings:4
Cooking Time: 14 Minutes

Ingredients:
- 2 tbsp butter
- 1 small shallot, finely chopped
- 1 tsp almond flour
- 2 cups red wine
- 1 tbsp red wine vinegar
- 1 cup thinly sliced red onion
- 1 cup chicken stock
- 1 tsp dried basil
- 1 tbsp Dijon mustard

Directions:
1. Set the IP in Sauté mode and adjust to Medium heat.
2. Melt half of the butter in the inner pot, sauté the shallots until softened, minutes, and stir in almond flour until sand-like consistency forms.
3. Mix in red wine and vinegar until a thick paste forms while scraping the bottom of the pot of any stuck bits.
4. Stir in the onion, chicken stock, basil, and mustard.
5. Lock the lid in place; select Manual mode on High Pressure and set the timer to 2 minutes.
6. After cooking, perform a natural pressure release for 10 minutes, then a quick pressure release to let out the remaining steam, and open the lid.
7. Mix in remaining butter until melted.
8. Spoon the sauce into serving cups and use immediately.

Nutrition Info:
Per Serving: Calories 550 Fats 47g Carbs 8.47g Net Carbs 6.67g Protein 65g

Tender Beef Shoulder Roast

Servings: 6
Cooking Time: 50 Minutes
Ingredients:
- 2 tablespoons peanut oil
- 2 pounds shoulder roast
- 1/4 cup dark soy sauce
- 1 cup beef broth
- 2 cloves garlic, minced
- 2 tablespoons champagne vinegar
- 1/2 teaspoon hot sauce
- 1 teaspoon porcini powder
- 1 teaspoon garlic powder
- 1 teaspoon celery seeds
- 1 cup purple onions, cut into wedges
- 1 tablespoon flaxseed meal, plus 2 tablespoons water

Directions:

1. Press the "Sauté" button to heat up the Instant Pot. Then, heat the peanut oil and cook the beef shoulder roast for 2 to 3 minutes on each side.
2. In a mixing dish, thoroughly combine dark soy sauce, broth, garlic, vinegar, hot sauce, porcini powder, garlic powder, and celery seeds.
3. Pour the broth mixture into the Instant Pot. Add the onions to the top.
4. Secure the lid. Choose "Meat/Stew" mode and High pressure; cook for minutes. Once cooking is complete, use a natural pressure release; carefully remove the lid.
5. Now, make the slurry by mixing flaxseed meal with 2 tablespoons of water. Add the slurry to the Instant Pot.
6. Press the "Sauté" button and allow it to cook until the cooking liquid is reduced and thickened slightly. Serve warm. Bon appétit!

Nutrition Info:
Per Serving: 313 Calories; 1g Fat; 6.5g Total Carbs; 5g Protein; 3.1g Sugars

Favorite Lettuce Wraps

Servings: 6
Cooking Time: 15 Minutes
Ingredients:
- 2 chicken breasts
- 1 cup chicken stock
- 2 garlic cloves, minced
- 1/2 teaspoon black pepper
- 1 cup green onions, chopped
- 1 bell pepper, seeded and chopped
- 1 red chili pepper, seeded and chopped
- 1 cup cream cheese
- 1/2 cup mayonnaise
- 1 teaspoon yellow mustard
- Sea salt, to taste
- 1 head of lettuce

Directions:
1. Add chicken breasts, stock, garlic, and black pepper to your Instant Pot.
2. Secure the lid. Choose "Poultry" mode and High pressure; cook for 10 minutes. Once cooking is complete, use a quick pressure release; carefully remove the lid.
3. Then, shred the chicken and divide it between lettuce leaves. Divide the remaining ingredients between lettuce leaves and serve immediately. Bon appétit!

Nutrition Info:
Per Serving: 301 Calories; 1g Fat; 6.2g Carbs; 5g Protein; 2.5g Sugars

Egg Drop Soup With Gorgonzola

Servings: 4
Cooking Time: 20 Minutes
Ingredients:

- 1 tablespoon olive oil
- 1 carrot, chopped
- 1 clove garlic, minced
- 3 cups beef bone broth
- 1/2 cup water
- 2 eggs, slightly whisked
- Sea salt and ground black pepper, to your liking
- 1 teaspoon celery seeds
- 1/2 teaspoon paprika
- 1/2 cup Gorgonzola cheese, crumbled
- 1 heaping tablespoon fresh chives, minced

Directions:
1. Press the "Sauté" button to heat up the Instant Pot. Now, heat the olive oil and cook the carrot and garlic until fragrant.
2. Add broth and water.
3. Secure the lid. Choose "Manual" mode and High pressure; cook for 10 minutes. Once cooking is complete, use a quick pressure release; carefully remove the lid.
4. Then, mix the eggs, salt, black pepper, celery seeds, paprika, and cheese until well blended.
5. Stir this mixture into the Instant Pot and press the "Sauté" button. Whisk until heated through.
6. Serve in individual bowls, garnished with fresh chives. Enjoy!

Nutrition Info:
Per Serving: 163 Calories; 7g Fat; 3.1g Carbs; 8g Protein; 1.1g Sugars

Arrabbiata Sauce

Servings:4
Cooking Time: 14 Minutes
Ingredients:
- 2 tbsp olive oil
- 1 long red chili pepper, minced
- 2 garlic cloves, minced
- 1 lb. ripe tomatoes, peeled and chopped
- 1 tbsp unsweetened tomato paste
- 2 cups diced tomatoes
- 1 tbsp fresh lemon zest
- ¼ cup water
- A pinch erythritol
- 1 tbsp balsamic vinegar
- 1 tsp dried marjoram

Directions:
1. Set the IP in Sauté mode and adjust to Medium heat.
2. Heat the olive oil in the inner pot and sauté the chili and garlic until fragrant, 1 minute.
3. Stir in the remaining ingredients except for the vinegar and herb.

4. Lock the lid in place; select Manual mode on High Pressure and set the timer to 3 minutes.
5. After cooking, perform a natural pressure release for 10 minutes, then a quick pressure release to let out the remaining steam, and open the lid.
6. Using an immersion blender, puree the ingredients until fairly smooth.
7. Stir in balsamic vinegar and marjoram, and adjust the taste with salt or sugar.
8. Spoon the sauce into serving bowls and use immediately.
9. Preserve extras in the fridge and use for up to 1 week.

Nutrition Info:
Per Serving: Calories 643 Fats 99g Carbs 1g Net Carbs 4g Protein 8.2g

Blue-mascarpone Cheese Sauce

Servings:4
Cooking Time: 4 Minutes
Ingredients:
- 1 cup coconut cream
- 2/3 cup crumbled blue cheese
- 1 ½ cups mascarpone cheese
- 2 tbsp butter
- 1 tsp dried oregano
- Salt and black pepper to taste

Directions:
1. Add the coconut cream to the inner pot.
2. Lock the lid in place; select Manual mode on High Pressure and set the timer to minutes.
3. After cooking, do a quick pressure release to let out the steam and open the lid.
4. Set the IP in Sauté mode and keep boiling the coconut cream until thickened while occasionally stirring.
5. Whisk in blue cheese, mascarpone cheese, and butter until melted, 2 minutes.
6. Stir in the oregano, salt, and black pepper.
7. Spoon the sauce into serving cups and use immediately.

Nutrition Info:
Per Serving: Calories 242 Fats 15 Carbs 6.96g Net Carbs 6.76g Protein 5.4g

Grandma's Cherry Jam

Servings: 8
Cooking Time: 10 Minutes
Ingredients:
- 2 cups cherries, pitted
- 1/2 cup Swerve, granulated
- 1 tablespoon vanilla extract
- 1 teaspoon rum extract
- 1/2 teaspoon ground cardamom
- 2 teaspoons arrowroot powder
- 1 cup water

Directions:

1. Add cherries to your Instant Pot.
2. Sprinkle with Swerve, vanilla, rum extract, and cardamom. Now, add arrowroot powder and water.
3. Secure the lid. Choose "Manual" mode and High pressure; cook for 2 minutes. Once cooking is complete, use a natural pressure release; carefully remove the lid.
4. Process the mixture with an immersion blender. Store in a mason jar or serve immediately. Bon appétit!

Nutrition Info:

Per Serving: 33 Calories; 0.1g Fat; 6.8g Total Carbs; 0.4g Protein; 3.6g Sugars

Bacon Frittata Muffins

Servings: 6
Cooking Time: 15 Minutes
Ingredients:

- 6 thin meaty bacon slices
- 1 large-sized zucchini, grated
- 1 red bell pepper, chopped
- 1 green bell pepper, chopped
- 4 teaspoons butter, melted
- 1/2 cup Colby cheese, shredded
- 3 egg, beaten
- 2 tablespoons cream cheese, room temperature
- 1 teaspoon shallot powder
- 1/2 teaspoon dried dill weed
- 1/2 teaspoon cayenne pepper
- Salt and black pepper, to taste

Directions:

1. Start by adding ½ cups of water and a metal trivet to the bottom of your Instant Pot.
2. Place bacon slices in 6 silicone cupcake liners. Add zucchini and bell peppers.
3. Now, mix the butter, Colby cheese, eggs, cream cheese, shallot powder, dried dill weed, cayenne pepper, salt, and black pepper. Spoon this mixture into the liners.
4. Put the liners into an oven-safe bowl. Cover with a piece of foil. Lower the bowl onto the trivet.
5. Secure the lid. Choose "Manual" mode and High pressure; cook for 10 minutes. Once cooking is complete, use a natural pressure release; carefully remove the lid. Bon appétit!

Nutrition Info:

Per Serving: 226 Calories; 1g Fat; 2.3g Carbs; 9.3g Protein; 1.3g Sugars

Goat Cheese And Cauliflower Pancake

Servings: 4
Cooking Time: 35 Minutes
Ingredients:

- 3/4 pound cauliflower, riced
- 4 eggs, beaten
- 1/2 cup goat cheese, crumbled
- 1/2 teaspoon onion powder
- 1 teaspoon garlic powder
- Sea salt and white pepper, to taste
- 2 tablespoons butter, melted

Directions:
1. Simply combine all ingredients in a mixing bowl.
2. Now, spritz the bottom and sides of your Instant Pot with a nonstick cooking spray. Pour the batter into the Instant Pot.
3. Secure the lid. Choose "Bean/Chili" mode and Low pressure; cook for minutes. Once cooking is complete, use a natural pressure release; carefully remove the lid.
4. Serve with some extra butter or cream cheese if desired. Bon appétit!

Nutrition Info:
Per Serving: 198 Calories; 2g Fat; 4.9g Carbs; 2g Protein; 1.9g Sugars

Mediterranean-style Savory Tart

Servings: 6
Cooking Time: 35 Minutes
Ingredients:
- 10 ounces cream cheese
- 4 eggs, whisked
- 1 cup almond flour
- 1 tablespoon flaxseed meal
- 1 teaspoon baking powder
- Coarse sea salt and ground black pepper, to taste
- 1/2 stick butter, melted
- 1 ½ cups zucchini, grated
- 1 clove garlic, pressed
- 1/4 teaspoon dried rosemary
- 1/4 teaspoon dried basil
- 1/2 cup Cheddar cheese, shredded

Directions:
1. Begin by adding cup of water and a metal rack to your Instant Pot. Then, spritz a heatproof bowl with a nonstick cooking spray and set aside.
2. In a mixing dish, thoroughly combine the cream and eggs. Gradually stir in the flour. Add the remaining ingredients, except for Cheddar cheese.
3. Spoon the mixture into the prepared heatproof bowl; cover with a piece of aluminum foil, making a foil sling.
4. Secure the lid. Choose "Manual" mode and High pressure; cook for 25 minutes. Once cooking is complete, use a quick pressure release; carefully remove the lid.

5. Add Cheddar cheese to the top of your tart and cover with the lid. Let it sit in a residual heat an additional 7 to 10 minutes. Bon appétit!

Nutrition Info:

Per Serving: 353 Calories; 1g Fat; 4g Carbs; 6g Protein; 2.5g Sugars

Fluffy Berry Cupcakes

Servings: 6

Cooking Time: 30 Minutes

Ingredients:

- 1/4 cup coconut oil, softened
- 3 ounces cream cheese, softened
- 1/4 cup double cream
- 4 eggs
- 1/4 cup coconut flour
- 1/4 cup almond flour
- A pinch of salt
- 1/3 cup Swerve, granulated
- 1 teaspoon baking powder
- 1/4 teaspoon cardamom powder
- 1/2 teaspoon star anise, ground
- 1/2 cup fresh mixed berries

Directions:

1. Start by adding ½ cups of water and a metal rack to your Instant Pot.
2. Mix coconut oil, cream cheese, and double cream in a bowl. Fold in the eggs, one at a time, and continue to mix until everything is well incorporated.
3. In another bowl, thoroughly combine the flour, salt, Swerve, baking powder, cardamom, and anise.
4. Add the cream/egg mixture to this dry mixture. Afterwards, fold in fresh berries and gently stir to combine.
5. Divide the batter between silicone cupcake liners. Cover with a piece of foil. Place the cupcakes on the rack.
6. Secure the lid. Choose "Manual" mode and High pressure; cook for 25 minutes. Once cooking is complete, use a natural pressure release; carefully remove the lid. Enjoy!

Nutrition Info:

Per Serving: 238 Calories; 6g Fat; 4.1g Carbs; 7.5g Protein; 2.2g Sugars

Spinach And Cheese Muffins

Servings: 6

Cooking Time: 15 Minutes

Ingredients:

- 6 eggs
- 1/3 cup double cream
- 1/4 cup cream cheese

- Sea salt and freshly ground black pepper, to taste
- 1/2 teaspoon cayenne pepper
- 1 ½ cups spinach, chopped
- 1/4 cup green onions, chopped
- 1 ripe tomato, chopped
- 1/2 cup cheddar cheese, grated

Directions:

1. Start by adding cup of water and a metal rack to the Instant Pot. Now, spritz a muffin tin with a nonstick cooking spray.
2. In a mixing dish, thoroughly combine the eggs, double cream, cream cheese, salt, black pepper, and cayenne pepper.
3. Then, divide the spinach, green onions, tomato, and scallions among the cups. Pour the egg mixture over the vegetables. Top with cheddar cheese.
4. Lower the cups onto the rack.
5. Secure the lid. Choose "Manual" mode and High pressure; cook for 10 minutes. Once cooking is complete, use a natural pressure release; carefully remove the lid. Serve immediately.

Nutrition Info:

Per Serving: 236 Calories; 8g Fat; 3.3g Carbs; 2g Protein; 2.2g Sugars

Instant Pot Avocado Shrimp Omelet

Servings: 2
Cooking Time: 30 Mins
Ingredients:

- 150g shrimp, peeled and deveined
- 4 large free-range eggs, beaten
- 1 medium avocado, diced
- 1 large tomato, diced
- 2 tablespoons coconut oil
- 1/8 tsp. freshly ground black pepper
- 1/4 tsp. sea salt
- 1 tbsp. freshly chopped cilantro

Directions:

1. Set your instant pot to manual high; cook shrimp until it turns pink; chop the cooked shrimp and set aside.
2. In a small bowl, toss together avocado, tomato, and cilantro; season with sea salt and pepper and set aside.
3. In a separate bowl, beat the eggs and set aside.
4. Melt coconut oil in the pot and then add in the egg mixture. Arrange the shrimp on top of the egg and lock lid; cook for 5 Mins and then let pressure come down on its own.

Nutrition Info:

Per Serving: Calories: 475; Total Fat: 3g; Carbs: 8g; Protein: 2g

Cauliflower "mac And Cheese"

Servings: 6
Cooking Time: 20 Minutes
Ingredients:
- 1 medium head of cauliflower, broken into florets
- 2 tablespoons butter, melted
- 2/3 cup cream cheese
- 1/2 cup milk
- 1/2 teaspoon cumin powder
- 1/2 teaspoon mustard seeds
- 1/2 teaspoon fennel seeds
- Salt and black pepper, to taste
- 2 cups Monterey-Jack cheese, shredded

Directions:
1. Add cup of water and a metal rack to the bottom of your Instant Pot.
2. Then, place cauliflower in a casserole dish that is previously greased with melted butter.
3. In a mixing bowl, thoroughly combine cream cheese, milk, cumin powder, mustard seeds, fennel seeds, salt, and black pepper.
4. Pour this mixture over the cauliflower.
5. Secure the lid. Choose "Manual" mode and High pressure; cook for 7 minutes. Once cooking is complete, use a quick pressure release; carefully remove the lid.
6. Top with shredded Monterey-Jack cheese. Return to the Instant Pot, cover with the lid, and let it sit in a residual heat for 10 minutes. Bon appétit!

Nutrition Info:
Per Serving: 306 Calories; 7g Fat; 5.4g Carbs; 4g Protein; 3.5g Sugars

Buffalo Sauce

Servings: 4
Cooking Time: 1 Minute
Ingredients:
- 2/3 cup hot sauce
- ½ cup unsalted butter
- ¼ tsp Worcestershire sauce
- 1 ½ tbsp white vinegar

Directions:
1. Set the IP in Sauté mode and adjust to Medium heat.
2. In the inner pot, mix all the ingredients.
3. Lock the lid in place; select Manual mode on High Pressure and set the timer to 1 minute.
4. After cooking, perform a quick pressure release to let out the steam, and open the lid.
5. Spoon the sauce into preservation jars and serve.

Nutrition Info:
Per Serving: Calories 57 Fats 3.25g Carbs 7.19g Net Carbs 5.09g Protein 0.19g

Mom's Cheesy Soup

Servings: 4
Cooking Time: 25 Minutes
Ingredients:

- 2 tablespoons butter, melted
- 1/2 cup leeks, chopped
- 2 chicken breasts, trimmed and cut into bite-sized chunks
- 1 carrot, chopped
- 1 celery stalk, chopped
- 1/2 teaspoon granulated garlic
- 1 teaspoon basil
- 1/2 teaspoon oregano
- 1/2 teaspoon dill weed
- 4 ½ cups vegetable stock
- 3 ounces heavy cream
- 3/4 cup Cheddar cheese, shredded
- 1 heaping tablespoon fresh parsley, roughly chopped

Directions:

1. Press the "Sauté" button to heat up your Instant Pot. Now, melt the butter and cook the leeks until tender and fragrant.
2. Add the chicken, carrot, celery, garlic, basil, oregano, dill, and stock.
3. Secure the lid. Choose "Manual" mode and High pressure; cook for 17 minutes. Once cooking is complete, use a natural pressure release; carefully remove the lid.
4. Add cream and cheese, stir, and press the "Sauté" button one more time. Now, cook the soup for a couple of minutes longer or until thoroughly heated.
5. Serve in individual bowls, garnished with fresh parsley. Bon appétit!

Nutrition Info:
Per Serving: 530 Calories; 6g Fat; 4.2g Carbs; 1g Protein; 1.9g Sugars

Special Beef Salad

Servings: 6
Cooking Time: 1 Hour 35 Minutes
Ingredients:

- 1 tablespoon champagne vinegar
- 1/3 cup dry white wine
- 2 tablespoons Shoyu sauce
- 1 cup broth, preferably homemade
- 1 teaspoon finely grated fresh ginger
- 1 tablespoon stone-ground mustard
- 1 teaspoon celery seeds
- 1 ½ pounds beef rump steak
- 1 cup green onions, chopped

- 1 cup cherry tomatoes, halved
- 2 cucumbers, thinly sliced
- 1 bunch fresh coriander, leaves picked
- 1 bunch fresh mint, leaves picked
- 2 tablespoons fresh chives, chopped
- 2 tablespoons fresh lemon juice
- 2 tablespoons extra-virgin olive oil

Directions:

1. In a mixing dish, thoroughly combine the vinegar, white wine, Shoyu sauce, broth, fresh ginger, mustard, and celery seeds.
2. Add the beef steak and allow it to marinate for 40 minutes to 1 hour in your refrigerator.
3. Add beef steak, along with its marinade to the Instant Pot. Add enough water to cover the beef.
4. Secure the lid. Choose "Meat/Stew" mode and High pressure; cook for 35 minutes. Once cooking is complete, use a natural pressure release; carefully remove the lid.
5. Allow the beef to cool completely. Now, slice it into strips and transfer to a nice salad bowl.
6. Now, add the vegetables, coriander, mint, and fresh chives; toss to combine. Afterwards, drizzle the salad with lemon juice and olive oil. Toss to combine and serve well-chilled. Bon appétit!

Nutrition Info:
Per Serving: 346 Calories; 8g Fat; 5.7g Total Carbs; 2g Protein; 2.1g Sugars

Delicious Cheese Soup

Servings: 4
Cooking Time: 25 Minutes
Ingredients:

- 1 carrot, chopped
- ½ teaspoon onion powder
- 1 teaspoon basil
- 1/2 cup cheddar cheese, shredded
- 1/2 cup leeks, chopped
- 5 cups vegetable stock
- ½ cup heavy cream
- 2 celery stalks, chopped
- ½ teaspoon salt
- ½ teaspoon pepper
- 11/2 tablespoon fresh parsley, chopped
- 2 tablespoons avocado oil
- 1/2 teaspoon oregano
- ½ teaspoon garlic powder
- 3/4 cup Monetary Jack cheese, shredded

Directions:

1. Press the "Sauté" button and preheat your Instant Pot. Add the avocado oil and saute the leeks until fragrant.
2. Stir in the celery, oregano, garlic powder, salt, carrot, vegetable broth, basil, pepper, and onion powder.
3. Secure the lid. Choose "Manual" mode and High pressure; cook for 15 minutes. When cooking is complete, use a natural pressure release and carefully remove the lid.
4. Add the cheddar cheese, heavy cream, and Monetary Jack cheese. Stir, and press the "Sauté" button one more time. Then, cook the soup for a couple of minutes longer or until thoroughly heated.
5. Serve warm and top with fresh parsley! Bon appetite!

Nutrition Info:
Per Serving: 298 Calories; 6g Fat; 6.g Carbs; 1g Protein; 2.9g Sugars

Mushroom And Cream Cheese Pâté

Servings: 8
Cooking Time: 10 Minutes
Ingredients:
- 3 tablespoons olive oil
- 1 pound brown mushrooms, chopped
- 1/2 yellow onion, chopped
- 2 garlic cloves, minced
- 2 tablespoons cognac
- Sea salt, to taste
- 1/3 teaspoon black pepper
- 1/2 teaspoon cayenne pepper
- 1 cup cream cheese, at room temperature

Directions:
1. Press the "Sauté" button to heat up the Instant Pot. Now, heat the oil and cook the mushrooms with onions until softened and fragrant.
2. Stir in the garlic, cognac, salt, black pepper, and cayenne pepper.
3. Secure the lid. Choose "Manual" mode and High pressure; cook for 5 minutes. Once cooking is complete, use a quick pressure release; carefully remove the lid.
4. Transfer the mixture to a food processor. Add cream cheese and continue to mix until everything is well incorporated. Serve with veggie sticks. Bon appétit!

Nutrition Info:
Per Serving: 162 Calories; 4g Fat; 3.6g Carbs; 3.9g Protein; 2.4g Sugars

1Egg Salad

Servings: 4
Cooking Time: 30 Minutes
Ingredients:
- 6 eggs
- 1/2 pound green beans, trimmed

- 1 cup of water
- 3 slices prosciutto, chopped
- 1/2 cup green onions, chopped
- 1 carrot, shredded
- 1/2 cup mayonnaise
- 1 tablespoon apple cider vinegar
- 1 teaspoon yellow mustard
- 4 tablespoons Gorgonzola cheese, crumbled

Directions:

1. Pour the water into the Instant Pot; add a steamer basket to the bottom. Arrange the eggs in a steamer basket.
2. Secure the lid. Choose "Manual" mode and High pressure; cook for 5 minutes. Once cooking is complete, use a natural pressure release; carefully remove the lid.
3. Allow the eggs to cool for 15 minutes. Peel the eggs and cut them into slices.
4. Then, add green beans and 1 cup of water to your Instant Pot.
5. Secure the lid. Choose "Manual" mode and Low pressure; cook for minutes. Once cooking is complete, use a quick pressure release; carefully remove the lid.
6. Transfer green beans to a salad bowl. Add prosciutto, green onions, carrot, mayonnaise, vinegar, and mustard. Top with Gorgonzola cheese and sliced eggs. Enjoy!

Nutrition Info:

Per Serving: 342 Calories; 2g Fat; 3.2g Total Carbs; 7g Protein; 1.6g Sugars

1Golden Cheddar Muffins With Chard

Servings: 4
Cooking Time: 10 Minutes
Ingredients:

- 6 eggs
- 4 tablespoons double cream
- Sea salt and ground black pepper, to taste
- 1 cup Swiss chard, chopped
- 1 red bell pepper, chopped
- 1/2 cup white onion, chopped
- 1/2 cup Cheddar cheese, grated

Directions:

1. Begin by adding cup of water and a metal rack to the Instant Pot.
2. Mix all of the above ingredients. Then, fill silicone muffin cups about 3 full.
3. Then, place muffin cups on the rack.
4. Secure the lid. Choose "Manual" mode and High pressure; cook for 7 minutes. Once cooking is complete, use a natural pressure release; carefully remove the lid. Enjoy!

Nutrition Info:

Per Serving: 207 Calories; 8g Fat; 4.9g Carbs; 4g Protein; 2.7g Sugars

Dinner: 1 Shredded Chicken Salad

Printed in Poland
by Amazon Fulfillment
Poland Sp. z o.o., Wrocław

65962188R00325